AF714802

Intellectual Property for the 21st Century

Intellectual Property for the 21st Century:

Interdisciplinary Approaches

B COURTNEY DOAGOO, MISTRALE GOUDREAU,
MADELAINE SAGINUR, AND TERESA SCASSA

IRWIN LAW

Intellectual Property Law for the 21st Century: Interdisciplinary Approaches

Published in 2014 by
Irwin Law Inc
Suite 206, 14 Duncan Street
Toronto, ON M5H 3G8
www.irwinlaw.com

ISBN: 978-1-55221-353-7 e-book ISBN: 978-1-55221-354-4

Cataloguing in Publication available from Library and Archives Canada

The publisher acknowledges the financial support of the Government of Canada through the Canada Book Fund for its publishing activities.

We acknowledge the assistance of the OMDC Book Fund, an initiative of the Ontario Media Development Corporation.

Printed and bound by CPI Group (UK) Ltd, Croydon, CR0 4YY

1 2 3 4 5 17 16 15 14 13

Contents

Foreword

The practice of law has long been interdisciplinary. Rumpole of the Old Bailey knew all about typewriters and bloodstains, and was no doubt the one to brief if "The Case of the Bloodstained Typewriter" ever came along. Lawyers who, on starting, know nothing of medicine or forensics have to become instant experts when they get their first big personal injury or criminal case. They can only hope and pray that, if it comes to court, they will get a judge whose abilities to absorb science transcend that explosion in the school lab.

Interdisciplinarity — a commendable concept but an ugly word — can occur only where there is a discipline to be "inter-" with. Intellectual property is a relative newcomer in these stakes compared with, say, torts or criminal law or contracts or land law. Yet IP has always been interdisciplinary because the fields it deals with involve technology and the arts, and the interests in them that need nurturing, managing, and reconciling as their products go public.

As a field in its own right, however, IP for long remained underdeveloped. Since law curricula tend to track the subjects that practising lawyers believe are important, the fact there seemed to be few IP lawyers around misled scholars to conclude that nothing fertile lay out there for them to work on. Economists and other social scientists woke up earlier.

It has taken the last couple of generations of legal scholars to catch on to the fact that there is a *there* there. IP's importance to society and the economy has become a commonplace, and patents, copyrights, trademarks, designs, and information and image rights have become vibrant individual academic disciplines, and not just in law. Still, academic practice has been slow to realize the full potential of what interdisciplinarity can mean for IP law. The solitudes of science and the arts are mirrored by the solitudes of IP law and the territories it affects. Polymaths may conduct their own interdisciplinary soliloquies, while more focused scholars may swap shoptalk with their soulmates in other university departments. But crosstalk occurs less frequently than it could and joint work, while growing, is still the exception rather than the norm.

That is why this volume assembled by Professors Teresa Scassa and Mistrale Goudreau, together with Courtney Doagoo and Madelaine Saginur, from the papers at a 2012 University of Ottawa workshop on interdisciplinary approaches to intellectual property law is so important. The editors did not get distracted by defining interdisciplinarity too closely. Instead, acting as facilitators, they assembled a group of scholars and practitioners in law and the humanities, told them to get interdisciplinary with IP — whatever that meant to each of them — and hoped for the best.

And, as this volume demonstrates, the best can be very good indeed.

While the authors are mainly Canadian and the subjects they touch on are often focused on Canada, the themes are universal and international, as old as music and Aboriginal art, as new as the Internet, social media, and genetics (yes, what Crick, Watson, and Franklin did still seems to feel "new" to some lawyers). Basic issues such as what it means to create, recreate, appropriate, invent, discover, copy, free-ride, own, share, and research are raised and examined in a variety of contexts — from academic labs and recording studios to courts, continents, competitive sports, and, of course, online — and questions are asked why this or that activity should occur or be privileged over another.

There is discussion of IP law's engagement with other branches of law such as jurisprudence, criminology, and human rights. More often the crossover is broader, refreshingly not just with economics or political theory but with semiotics, environmentalism, anthropology, communications theory, media studies, and more specialized fields such as music theory and film adaptation studies. The "other" discipline is typically used to illuminate some aspect of IP law — e.g., the thing protected or the scope and terms of protection; access, overlap, incentives, or deterrence — to suggest how it might be better studied, conceptualized, reordered, or even banished.

Some papers focus on reform: who does or should do it, why and how, with a view to furthering the public interests that IP laws are ostensibly designed to foster. Other times the spotlight is on custom, how and why practice diverges from formal law, whether convergence matters, and if so in which direction movement should occur. The usual suspects naturally pop up: Locke, Kant, Marx, Hegel, Jhering, Gramsci, Radzinowicz, Rawls, and a bunch of "Bs": Beethoven, Barthes, Bataille, Bourdieu, Benjamin, Bram, and Britney (Stoker and Spears, of course). But there are others too like Jungen, Castells, Kurosawa, and Godard — even Prometheus and Minerva. And, of course, Innis and McLuhan.

This is an intellectual feast worth savouring and digesting. Anyone with even a passing interest in how society and intellectual property interact will enjoy sampling these delights. The editors deserve congratulation for their enterprise (and their introductory chapter), the contributors one and all for their imagination and sometimes even daring.

Is it too much to hope for a repeat, and soon?

David Vaver
Oxford
MMXIII

Acknowledgments

This project has its origins in a workshop hosted by the Centre for Law, Technology and Society at the University of Ottawa in May 2012. From the workshop through to the final completion of the manuscript, there have been many people involved in many different ways in bringing this collection of papers into being.

We gratefully acknowledge the active and engaged participation of all those who attended our workshop. Many good ideas were sparked and much feedback was shared with all participants over the course of the workshop. While not every participant was able to submit a paper for the book, all played an active role in the intensive discussions that we had. Many thanks as well to our rapporteurs Dara Jospe and Sébastien Cusson, who kept a careful transcript of the lively discussions sparked by the different presentations.

In order to offer double-blind peer review of all of the manuscripts we received, we needed the engaged participation of many reviewers from around the world and from a range of different disciplines. We are very grateful to all those who volunteered their time to read and give constructive feedback on our papers.

We are very appreciative of the support we received both to fund the workshop and to fund the research assistance needed for the preparation of the manuscript. We gratefully acknowledge the support of the Social Sciences and Humanities Research Council of Canada through its Aid to Scholarly Conferences and Workshops program. We also greatly appreciate the support of the University of Ottawa's Fund for the Development of Interdisciplinary Initiatives, as well as the University of Ottawa's support for conferences and workshops on campus. Our thanks to the Law Foundation of Ontario for support for research assistance related to the book project, and to the Canada Research

Chairs programme. We acknowledge as well the support and encouragement we received from Dean Sébastien Grammond of the Civil Law Section and Dean Bruce Feldthusen of the Common Law Section of uOttawa's Faculty of Law. We are grateful as well for the administrative support and physical infrastructure provided by the Centre for Law, Technology and Society.

Many student RAs were hired to assist in the painstaking task of preparing the manuscript for publication. We thank Nir Harrel, Dara Jospe, Mathangi Kumaresan, and Luc André Vincent for their hard work in this regard. We want to particularly acknowledge the efforts of Marie-Sophie Gauthier whose diligence and attention to detail were very much appreciated. We are grateful as well to Valérie Leclerc, the Law Faculty's legal translator, and to Marie-Sophie Gauthier, for their work in translating the paper abstracts. We extend warm thanks to our colleague Alain-François Bisson, who gave very generously of his time and advice.

We would like to particularly acknowledge the support of Jeffrey Miller and Irwin Law for this project. Not only is Irwin Law open to publishing works that go beyond the conventional boundaries of law book publishing, it has also shown itself willing to take risks on open access publishing of works like this one. We are delighted to have been able to work with Irwin Law in producing this book. We extend our thanks to Alisa Posesorski, Gillian Buckley, Janis Rose, and Heather Raven for their attention to detail in working with our manuscript.

Many thanks as well to David Vaver, who very kindly agreed to read our manuscript and to write the foreword to this book. Canadian IP scholars are already indebted to Professor Vaver's leadership in this field; his willingness to read and offer his thoughtful comments on this collection is much appreciated.

Last, but of course by no means least, we would like to acknowledge both Margaret Ann Wilkinson and Mark Perry of the University of Western Ontario. Over the course of many years, these two have nurtured and developed a community of IP scholars in Canada through their workshops held at the UWO. Our own workshop built upon their success in creating an engaged and collaborative group of IP scholars.

B Courtney Doagoo
Mistrale Goudreau
Madelaine Saginur
Teresa Scassa
Ottawa, 2013

Intellectual Property for the 21st Century: Interdisciplinary Approaches

TERESA SCASSA, MISTRALE GOUDREAU,
B COURTNEY DOAGOO, & MADELAINE SAGINUR

A. INTRODUCTION

Over the past two decades, globalization, digitization, and the rise of the Internet have each contributed to a new prominence for intellectual property law in public policy debates around the world. Once the preserve of a cadre of highly specialized lawyers in large firms concentrated in major urban centres, intellectual property law has become a subject of heated policy debate in legislatures, a matter of almost daily news reporting, and the topic of wide-ranging popular discourse. In recent years, we have seen corporations attempt to lock up digital content, bolstered by new international treaties aimed at providing legal protection for anti-circumvention measures. Terms of protection have grown longer, and individual users have become the targets of large scale enforcement activity that was previously aimed only at organized or corporate malefactors. Debate has blossomed over the extent to which IP laws limit both creativity and innovation. Intellectual property law has garnered headlines for its role in limiting access to life-saving medicines in developing countries and is increasingly linked to issues of democracy and human rights. Intellectual property law and policy have become the stuff of our daily lives as well: we are creators, consumers, users, and sometimes infringers. Intellectual property policy reaches into our lives through culture and its output, through the branding activities of major corporations, and through the impact of patent laws on the price and accessibility of a wide range of products, from electronics to pharmaceuticals. Questions about how intellectual property is controlled, licensed, used, and reused are all part of a growing public discourse that now engages far more than an elite cadre of lawyers.

In this environment, it is not surprising to find that there has been a corresponding growth in the teaching and research of intellectual property subjects by academics who specialize in this area. While twenty-five years ago there were almost no Canadian academics teaching or writing about intellectual property law, today, most law faculties in Canada boast at least one intellectual property specialist, and many have concentrations of scholars who work in this field. The growth of a Canadian intellectual property academy has been important in developing critical analyses and insights into the changing laws and policies around intellectual property both in Canada and internationally.

Because intellectual property law now trenches so deeply on issues of economics, culture, health, commerce, creativity, and intellectual freedom, it is no surprise that there is also a burgeoning literature on intellectual property issues that comes, not just from legal academics or lawyers, but from those trained in other disciplines.[1] Such authors observe and reflect upon the impact of intellectual property law and policy for society and culture more broadly. No longer an arcane and technical area of the law best left to legal specialists, intellectual property law has evolved into a site of contention over what it means to think, to create, and to participate in culture and in society.

Yet although academics from many disciplines have turned their attention to intellectual property issues, they have, with some notable exceptions, tended to do so within the confines of their own disciplinary silos. In the spring of 2012, the Centre for Law, Technology, and Society at the University of Ottawa hosted a workshop that sought to bring together academics from different disciplines interested in intellectual property law in order to stimulate discussion across disciplines, to encourage the development of collaborative efforts, and to produce a body of research that explores intellectual property law issues from explicitly interdisciplinary perspectives. The collection of papers in this book is the product of this workshop.

---

1 Jerry A Jacobs & Scott Frickel, "Interdisciplinarity: A Critical Assessment" (2009) 35 Annual Review of Sociology 43 (note that Jacobs & Frickel suggest that social change may be a factor driving the development of "interdisciplines" — areas of study that span disciplinary categories. They suggest that "new knowledge fields are fundamentally political outcomes, the result of struggles for resources, identities, and status" at 57).

B. DEFINING INTERDISCIPLINARITY

Universities tend to be structured administratively around specific academic disciplines, which are in turn grouped under broader headings of "humanities," "social sciences," "sciences," and the professions. Each academic discipline reflects a shared set of theories and methodologies, and over time develops its own body of knowledge and literature. These disciplines are reinforced by the administrative structures of universities. Nissani defines a discipline as "any comparatively self-contained and isolated domain of human experience which possesses its own community of experts."[2] Balkin argues that disciplinarity "is the product of a set of social forces of normalization and education, reward and punishment, through which the academic's head gets constructed, and the academic becomes the kind of academic that he or she is."[3] However they are regarded, the established and defined disciplines have played a key role both in generating and communicating knowledge in our society.[4]

The last century has seen the evolution of challenges to disciplinary approaches to research and teaching.[5] It has been argued that strictly disciplinary inquiries may not always yield optimal results, particularly in a world in which problems have become increasingly complex and multi-faceted. A goal of interdisciplinary research has been to "reduce segregation of knowledge by building workable bridges between otherwise compartmentalised knowledges."[6] Moran describes the aspirations of interdisciplinarity as providing "a democratic, dynamic and co-operative alternative to the old-fash-

---

2 Moti Nissani, "Ten Cheers for Interdisciplinarity: The Case for Interdisciplinary Knowledge and Research" (1997) 34:2 The Social Science Journal 201 at 203; see also Joe Moran, *Interdisciplinarity: The New Critical Idiom*, 2d ed (New York: Routledge, 2010) at 13.

3 Jack M Balkin, "Interdisciplinarity as Colonization" (1996) 53:3 Wash & Lee L Rev 949 at 954 (he argues that this is ultimately a good thing because disciplines give structure to thought, and "involve not only shared subject matters and shared problems, but shared ways of thinking and talking" at 955); Moran, above note 2 at 2 suggests that a discipline is at once a body of knowledge and a set of rules regarding how new knowledge should be produced and structured.

4 Moran, *ibid*, is of the view that the term *discipline* evokes "the relationship between knowledge and power" at 2; the concept of discipline is also closely related to the notion of paradigm, as used by Thomas Samuel Kuhn to describe the progress of scientific knowledge: see Thomas S Kuhn, *The Structure of Scientific Revolutions* (Chicago: University of Chicago Press, 1962).

5 Julie Thompson Klein, *Humanities, Culture, and Interdisciplinarity: The Changing American Academy* (Albany: State University of New York Press, 2005) at 2.

6 Lisa Lau & Margaret Pasquini, "'Jack of All Trades'? The Negotiation of Interdisciplinarity Within Geography" (2008) 39:2 Geoforum 552 at 554.

ioned, inward-looking and cliquish nature of disciplines."[7] On this model, disciplinary inquiry is seen as rigid and tightly controlled. Interdisciplinarity explores and exploits the space between disciplines, searching for new knowledge and understanding via the adoption of multiple lenses through which to examine research questions.

Yet, while interdisciplinarity is offered as an antidote to the limitations of disciplinary inquiry, it remains a term that is difficult to define. In very simple terms, Jacobs and Frickel define it as "communication and collaboration across academic disciplines."[8] This description does little to explain what interdisciplinarity actually is in practice. Others discuss interdisciplinarity in terms of its methods.[9] For Lau and Pasquini, it is the "combination and synthesis of methodologies and techniques"[10] across disciplinary boundaries that are at the heart of interdisciplinarity.[11] Still, others focus on its goals or results. For example, according to Nissani, "[i]nterdisciplinary research combines components of two or more disciplines in the search or creation of new knowledge, operations, or artistic expressions."[12] Brewer is even more pragmatically focused on results; he defines interdisciplinarity as "the appropriate combination of knowledge from many different specialities — especially as a means to shed new light on an actual problem."[13]

There is sometimes confusion between the term *interdisciplinary* and the related term *multidisciplinary*. Indeed, Choi and Pak complain that the terms are "ambiguously defined and often used interchangeably."[14] Yet an attempt to define each term separately can give insight into the meaning of interdisciplinarity. Choi and Pak suggest that multidisciplinarity "is a process for providing a juxtaposition of disciplines that is additive, not integrative; the

---

7 Moran, above note 2 at 3.

8 Jacobs & Frickel, above note 1 at 44.

9 To identify a discipline, Freides emphasizes the distinctive method recognized in each discipline rather than the subject matter. Thelma K Freides, *Literature and Bibliography of the Social Sciences* (Los Angeles: Melville Publishing, 1973) at 13–18.

10 Lau & Pasquini, above note 6 at 554 [footnote omitted].

11 Youngblood writes that interdisciplinarity "is a relatively new form of problem-oriented critical thinking focusing on *process* rather than *domain*" [emphasis in original]. Dawn Youngblood, "Interdisciplinary Studies and the Bridging Disciplines: A Matter of Process" (2007) 3:2 Journal of Research Practice 1 at 2.

12 Nissani, above note 2 at 203.

13 Garry D Brewer, "The Challenges of Interdisciplinarity" (1999) 32:4 Policy Sciences 327 at 328.

14 Bernard CK Choi & Anita WP Pak, "Multidisciplinarity, Interdisciplinarity and Transdisciplinarity in Health Research, Services, Education and Policy: 1. Definitions, Objectives, and Evidence of Effectiveness" (2006) 29:6 Clinical & Investigative Medicine 351 at 352.

disciplinary perspectives are not changed, only contrasted."[15] They define interdisciplinarity as "a synthesis of two or more disciplines, establishing a new level of discourse and integration of knowledge."[16] Thus, while both interdisciplinarity and multidisciplinarity draw on the knowledge and methods of different disciplines, the former is integrative while the latter reflects a multi-pronged approach to solving an identified problem. For Youngblood, "[m]*ultidisciplinary* is what happens when members of two or more disciplines cooperate, using the tools and knowledge of their disciplines in new ways to consider multifaceted problems that have at least one tentacle in another area of study."[17] By contrast, interdisciplinarity "is what happens when researchers go beyond establishing a common meeting place to developing new method and theory crafted to transcend the disciplines in order to solve problems."[18] Some have suggested that "interdisciplinary" and "multidisciplinary" simply represent points on a spectrum of interdisciplinarity with "interdisciplinary" reflecting a greater integration of the different disciplines involved and "multidisciplinary" reflecting more separation between disciplinary perspectives brought to bear on a common problem.[19]

C. THE MERITS OF INTERDISCIPLINARY APPROACHES

Advocates of interdisciplinary research argue that it can offer original and important insights that might not otherwise be obtained by purely disciplinary efforts. This is in part because the premises and methodologies of established disciplines may condition how problems are both identified and approached by researchers, resulting in gaps in either knowledge or understanding.[20] A report by the National Academy of Sciences in the United States posited that barriers to interdisciplinarity "diminish our ability to

---

15 *Ibid* at 355 [footnote omitted].

16 *Ibid* [footnote omitted]; Moran, above note 2 at 14 also defines multidisciplinarity as bringing disciplines in proximity to one another, without any attempt at integration.

17 Youngblood, above note 11 at 2 [emphasis in original]; Barbara Von Eckardt, "Multidisciplinarity and Cognitive Science" (2001) 25:3 Cognitive Science 453. Von Eckardt suggests that multidisciplinarity is most often realized in tackling problems that have multiple dimensions such as cognitive science or environmental science.

18 Youngblood, above note 11 at 2 [endnote omitted].

19 Mathias M Siems, "The Taxonomy of Interdisciplinary Legal Research: Finding the Way Out of the Desert" (2009) 7:1 J Commonwealth L & Legal Educ 5 at 6.

20 Nissani, above note 2 at 208. Nissani writes "if we mistake disciplinary knowledge for wisdom; if we forget how much we don't know" at 210; Brewer, above note 13 at 329 (Brewer talks about the importance of defining a problem in conditioning how solutions

address the great questions of science."[21] Most advocates of interdisciplinary research acknowledge the substantial challenges it presents, but take the view that the potential benefits outweigh the particular difficulties.[22]

Detractors of interdisciplinary research raise concerns that its practitioners are merely dabbling in other bodies of knowledge without the appropriate training or background to make proper sense of it.[23] In truth, though, there remain relatively few open detractors of interdisciplinary research; interdisciplinarity seems to have become a favourite university and granting agency buzzword.[24] Jacobs and Frickel, skeptics of interdisciplinarity, lament that there is little or no research that examines "how disciplinary and interdisciplinary relationships develop and whether the consequences of those collaborative outcomes are meaningfully different."[25] They question as well whether the challenges and fruits of collaboration might not be roughly equivalent whether the collaboration is intra- or interdisciplinary.[26] Further, they suggest that there is nothing fundamentally wrong with the disciplinary model of research, noting that established disciplines "remain dynamic centers of knowledge production that are open to external developments even while insisting on internal standards."[27] Yet while the

---

are arrived at — different disciplinary perspectives will result in different definitions of the same problem).

21 Committee on Facilitating Interdisciplinary Research et al, *Facilitating Interdisciplinary Research* (Washington DC: National Academies Press, 2004), online: www.nap.edu/openbook.php?record_id=11153 at 25. Many argue that problem-solving is a primary objective of interdisciplinarity; see, for example, Jacobs & Frickel, above note 1 at 47.

22 Siems, above note 19 at 12 acknowledges the potential drawbacks of insufficient skills or knowledge, but is more optimistic about being able to overcome them; see also Ken Foster & Guy Osborn, "Dancing on the Edge of Disciplines: Law and the Interdisciplinary Turn" (2010) 8:1 Ent & Sports Law Journal xiii. The authors identify the challenges and the critiques of interdisciplinarity, but argue that it permits the development of new areas of study, in their case, sports studies, that permit new theoretical and methodological approaches to complex questions.

23 The words *dilettantism* or *charlatanism* are sometimes associated with interdisciplinary endeavour. See Nissani, above note 2 at 203; see also Jack M Balkin & Sanford Levinson, "Law and the Humanities: An Uneasy Relationship" (2006) 18:2 Yale JL & Human 155 at 178; see Frank H Easterbrook, "Cyberspace and the Law of the Horse" (1996) U Chi Legal F 207; Easterbrook refers to this as the "cross-sterilization of ideas" at 207.

24 Jacobs & Frickel, above note 1 at 44–45, note that interdisciplinarity has received "widespread attention" from university administrators and granting agencies in recent years.

25 *Ibid* at 48; Klein, above note 5 at 7 is also critical of "exaggerated claims" about the merits of interdisciplinary inquiry, although she is nonetheless convinced of its ultimate value.

26 Jacobs & Frickel, above note 1 at 48.

27 *Ibid* at 60.

practice of interdisciplinarity and the claims about its merits deserve critical inquiry, enthusiasm rather than skepticism remains the norm.

D. LAW AND INTERDISCIPLINARITY

Within the actual practice of law, disciplinarity is the rule. True, from time to time one does see the work of those from other disciplines cited in court decisions (usually only those of the Supreme Court),[28] and in some disputes the evidence of experts from other fields is relied upon in order to assist in determining facts or in applying legal principles to those facts.[29] However, there is clearly a general reluctance to rely on some scientific methods or theories or to ask for a scientific precision. In civil liability cases, scientific causation is not required.[30] The Supreme Court has even stressed that expert testimony should be excluded if the danger is too great:

> [t]here is a danger that expert evidence will be misused and will distort the fact-finding process. Dressed up in scientific language which the jury does not easily understand and submitted through a witness of impressive antecedents, this evidence is apt to be accepted by the jury as being virtually infallible and as having more weight than it deserves.[31]

Courts have thus set rules to determine when and how scientific evidence will be admitted. Expert evidence is allowed only if it is necessary, that is, only if it provides information "which is likely to be outside the experience and knowledge of a judge or jury"[32] or if the "subject-matter of the inquiry [is] such that ordinary people are unlikely to form a correct judgment about it, if

---

28 See, for example, *Willick v Willick*, [1994] 3 SCR 670; *Moge v Moge*, [1992] 3 SCR 813; *Carter v Canada (Attorney General)*, 2012 BCSC 886.

29 Expert evidence is, in fact, routinely used in litigation of all kinds. The use of expert evidence from other disciplines is specifically addressed in Chapters 2 and 21 in this collection. Further, in trademark litigation, for example, a kind of social science empirical evidence — survey evidence — is frequently tendered in order to address questions such as the likelihood of consumer confusion. For an examination of survey evidence, see Ruth M Corbin & A Kelly Gill, *Survey Evidence and the Law Worldwide* (Toronto: LexisNexis, 2008); however, see the warnings expressed by the Supreme Court in *Masterpiece Inc v Alavida Lifestyles Inc*, 2011 SCC 27 [*Masterpiece*].

30 *Laferrière v Lawson*, [1991] 1 SCR 541; *Snell v Farrell*, [1990] 2 SCR 311; *Clements v Clements*, 2012 SCC 32.

31 *R v Mohan*, [1994] 2 SCR 9 at 21 [*Mohan*].

32 *R v Abbey*, [1982] 2 SCR 24 at 42 [citation omitted]; see also *Mohan*, above note 31 at 23; *Masterpiece*, above note 29 at para 75.

unassisted by persons with special knowledge."[33] More specifically, experts should not be permitted to usurp the functions of the judge or the finder of fact.[34] Courts have determined that, to be admissible, the expert must be qualified and the evidence must be relevant and reliable.[35] Although judges have not required as a precondition that the scientific theory put forward be "generally accepted" by the scientific community,[36] they have asked that the theory meet a basic threshold of reliability.[37] As for Parliament, in enacting new legislation they have no obligation to consult social scientists and they are clearly not accustomed to providing evidence of the likely effectiveness of their proposed measures.[38] In all these instances, it is clear that knowledge from those other disciplines is invoked to serve the purposes of the discipline of law; there is take, but no give.

There has been some discussion of the idea of multidisciplinarity in legal practice.[39] The concept of multidisciplinary legal practice involves groups of related professionals — lawyers, accountants, actuaries, and consultants — who join together to offer a holistic package of professional services to clients with multi-faceted problems. Interestingly, while there has been some interest in the potential for this type of practice to better meet the

---

33 *R v J-LJ*, 2000 SCC 51 at para 30 [citation omitted] [*J-LJ*].

34 *Mohan*, above note 31 at 24; *J-LJ*, above note 33 at paras 25 and 37; thus, in criminal cases, polygraph evidence adduced to determine the credibility of the accused or of a witness, is not admissible since credibility issues are within the experience of judges and juries: see *R v Béland*, [1987] 2 SCR 398 at 412.

35 *Mohan*, above note 31 at 20; *R v Trochym*, 2007 SCC 6 at para 36 [*Trochym*].

36 *J-LJ*, above note 33 at paras 33–34. The general acceptance of the theory is only one of the factors to be considered by the court: *Trochym*, above note 35 at para 36; as to whether such criteria are appropriate, see Nicole Duval Hesler, "L'admissibilité des nouvelles théories scientifiques" (2002) 62 R du B 359.

37 In *J-LJ*, above note 33 at para 33, and *Trochym*, above note 35, the Court identified four factors to determine if a novel science has a reliable foundation: "(1) whether the . . . technique can be and has been tested . . . [;] (2) whether the . . . technique has been subjected to peer review and publication . . . [;] (3) the known or potential rate of error . . . [;] and, (4) whether the theory or technique used has been generally accepted . . . ." at para 36; for an illustration of the difficulties of relying on social science evidence in litigation, see E Richard Gold & Robert Carbone, "(Mis)reliance on Social Science Evidence in Intellectual Property Litigation: A Case Study" (2012) 28 CIPR 179.

38 Even when the legislation infringes constitutional rights, imposing on Parliament the onus to demonstrate that its legislation is a proportional measure to fulfill a pressing and substantial goal, the courts have not required scientific proof based on concrete evidence: see *R v Sharpe*, 2001 SCC 2 at para 85.

39 Balkin & Levinson, above note 23 at 168, argue that traditional approaches to law began to prove insufficient within an increasingly complex legal environment facing increasingly difficult social and public policy questions.

needs of *clients*, there has been a mixed response from practising lawyers. Initial resistance to such practices as being a form of either unlicensed legal practice or unethical fee-sharing[40] has been criticized as attempts by lawyers to restrict competition in the domain of legal services.[41] Although the debates around the multidisciplinary practice of law are interesting from the point of view of defining legal services and exploring new modes of delivery, this area is less about developing new interdisciplinary knowledge than it is about creating a new model for the competitive delivery of legal services.

For some time now the message from the IP bar to law students is that a background in science or technology (preferably with graduate-level qualifications) is required for the practice of IP law. This is chiefly true of patent law, where those without some scientific expertise would struggle to decipher the nature of inventions for which patents are sought. This would seem to reflect an acceptance that certain aspects of IP practice not only benefit from, but require, an interdisciplinary skill set. Indeed, since granted patents constitute regulations,[42] they perhaps represent a form of "law" explicitly created through an application of interdisciplinary knowledge.

Some areas of interdisciplinary research in law have gained currency in the legal academy.[43] Law and economics, for example, particularly in the United States, is an established movement that brings the methodologies and theories of economics to bear on law and policy questions.[44] It might be fair to say that law and economics reflects one of the most sustained and most successful areas of legal interdisciplinarity. Legal theory is another area where philosophical methods of inquiry are integrated with legal thought to the extent that we speak of "legal theory" rather than "law and philosophy." Similarly, we now recognize a domain of "legal history." Beyond this, there are a number of "law and" courses that find their way onto the curricula of North American law faculties. These include "law and literature" or "law and geography." More recently, the "law ands" have expanded

40 Daniel R Fischel, "Multidisciplinary Practice" (2000) 55:3 Bus Law 951 at 954.

41 *Ibid* at 959–60; John B Attanasio, "The Brave New World of Multidisciplinary Practice: Foreword" (2000) 50:4 J Legal Educ 469 at 469.

42 *Whirlpool Corp v Camco Inc*, 2000 SCC 67 at para 49.

43 To describe this new trend, McConville & Chui refer to empirical and legal scholarship or socio-legal studies as opposed to the traditional doctrinal legal research: see Mike McConville & Wing Hong Chui, eds, *Research Methods for Law* (Edinburgh: Edinburgh University Press, 2007) at 4–7.

44 Balkin, above note 3 at 951, identifies law and economics as an example of a very successful interdisciplinary approach to law.

beyond the social sciences and humanities to include "law and technology" or "law and science."

Within the legal academy, interdisciplinarity is formally encouraged, but the informal constraints can be significant. Indeed, Balkin and Levinson suggest that legal inquiry ultimately returns to questions that define the discipline of law, such as: "how the law should be modified or interpreted or how legal decision makers should do their jobs."[45] They note that "[t]he demand that legal scholarship be cashed out in policy prescriptions deeply circumscribes the legal imagination and the permissible boundaries of legal scholarship, while simultaneously reorienting legal scholarship towards legal practice and policy science."[46]

Balkin and Levinson offer a rather jaded picture of interdisciplinarity in legal scholarship. In their view the fact that law is taught in professional faculties where students are trained for professional practice creates a significant barrier to the "colonization"[47] of law by other disciplines.[48] In addition, they note that legal academics themselves are products of these institutions with their overtly professional goals. These concerns are not new; others have also observed that the particular realities of schools charged with preparing professionals for practice pose a challenge when it comes to innovative curricular design or pedagogical approaches.[49]

In this context it is interesting to contemplate the ongoing tension that exists between law schools in Canada and the professional bar. Frequently, the complaint of law societies about legal education is that it strays too far from the mandate of educating lawyers.[50] These fears are perhaps at the root of attempts to impose compulsory courses on law students, thus

45 Balkin & Levinson, above note 23 at 175.

46 *Ibid.*

47 Balkin, above note 3, characterizes interdisciplinarity as an attempt at colonization of one discipline by another — "colonization of legal scholarship can never be entirely successful because law is at heart a professional, and not an academic, discipline" at 952 [footnote omitted].

48 Vick tends to agree. In a paper on interdisciplinarity in law, he concludes that "[t]he core identity of the discipline has not been, and likely will not be, fundamentally altered by interdisciplinary study." See Douglas W Vick, "Interdisciplinarity and the Discipline of Law" (2004) 31:2 JL & Soc'y 163 at 191.

49 See, for example, Foster & Osborn, above note 22.

50 Balkin, above note 3, writes of "social forces outside of the academy — including, in particular, the bench and the bar — demand that people who go to law schools be trained to be lawyers, whether they end up being lawyers or not" at 952.

inevitably shaping law school curricula.[51] Even where courses are not formally obligatory, implicit and explicit messages from practising lawyers to prospective job candidates, bolstered of late by a sagging economy and fears of unemployment, create unwritten lists of mandatory courses. Without these courses on a student's transcript, so the belief goes, there is little hope of securing an articling position or a well-paid job after graduation. It is perhaps not surprising that it is the "law and" courses that are typically characterized as the ones extraneous to a proper legal education.[52]

Within this environment, legal scholars are often placed in a difficult situation. They may find themselves within a university and grant funding culture which actively encourages interdisciplinarity, and they may also have discovered for themselves the rich potential of collaborations across academic disciplines. At the same time, these forays may be treated with distrust and suspicion by practicing lawyers, some students, and even some colleagues, who see this type of scholarship as extraneous to the general mission of legal education, or legal practice.

At the same time, legal academics are losing their monopoly on legal education. It is no longer the case that law is taught only within professional law faculties whose graduates are qualified to apply to provincial bars for admission to the practice of law. In Canada we have seen the creation and maturation of undergraduate degrees in legal studies at universities such as Carleton University and the University of Waterloo, and there are an increasing number of undergraduate programs across the country that offer

---

51 In the fall of 2012, the Federation of Law Societies of Canada announced a new "competency profile" for those entering the profession of law: see Federation of Law Societies of Canada, *National Admissions Standards Project: National Entry to Practice Competency Profile for Lawyers and Quebec Notaries* (September 2012), online: www.flsc.ca/_documents/NASCompetenciesSept2012.pdf. The impact of this profile on Canadian legal education will be profound. It is expected that it will result in additional obligatory courses in law programs across the country, and will also push students more aggressively towards so-called "core" and "practice-oriented" courses, to the detriment of other electives.

52 In a recent speech, Justice Scalia of the United States Supreme Court said: "The only time you're going to have an opportunity to study a whole area of the law systematically is in law school . . . . You should not waste that opportunity. Take the bread-and-butter courses. Do not take, 'law and women,' do not take 'law and poverty,' do not take 'law and anything.'" See Debra Cassens Weiss, "Scalia's Advice to Law Students: Take Bread-and-Butter Classes, Not 'Law and Women'" *ABA Journal* (26 October 2012), online: American Bar Association Journal www.abajournal.com/news/article/scalias_advice_to_law_students_take_bread-and-butter_classes_not_law_and_po.

majors or minors in law or legal studies.[53] Further, there is growing pressure to admit those without law degrees into graduate programs in law, and some interdisciplinary graduate degree programs have been created with law as a component. Technological development is also having an impact. Materials for law courses can be found online, as can podcasts, and the potential for some law content to be delivered in massively open online courses (MOOCS) is being debated.[54] The secrets of the discipline are no longer as tightly held as they once were.

It is important to note as well that in some respects law is both inherently interdisciplinary and inherently disciplinary. It is inherently *disciplinary* because law schools are professional faculties that are both administratively separate from the rest of the university and distinct in terms of their pedagogical objectives and their curricula which focus on the teaching of the normative legal framework, i.e., the legal norms upon which the courts rely. Unlike other disciplines, graduate and undergraduate students from other disciplines are generally not permitted to enrol in law courses, and law students are very limited in terms of their ability to take elective courses in another faculty or department. At the same time, however, law is inherently *interdisciplinary* because, at least in common law Canada, it is a second degree program: students are expected to come to law school with an undergraduate degree in another field — and an increasing number come to law with graduate training in other disciplines. Faculty members have a similar background, and a growing number hold graduate degrees from disciplines other than law. Further, many legal academics have integrated approaches from other disciplines, notably philosophy, economics, and history.[55] Some emerging areas of legal study are also quite interdisciplinary — or at the

53 For instance, the Civil Law Section of the University of Ottawa started offering a minor in law in French in 2008 and in English in 2011.

54 See for example David Thomson, "Of MOOCS and Legal Education" *Law School 2.0* (16 September 2012) online: Law School 2.0 www.lawschool2.org/ls2/2012/09/of-moocs-and-legal-education.html; see "International Law, Emotional Intelligence Featured in Case Western Reserve's First MOOCs" *The Daily* (21 February 2013) online: The Daily http://cwru-daily.com/news/international-law-emotional-intelligence-featured-in-case-western-reserves-first-moocs. This course in international law was one of the first MOOCS launched by Case Western Reserve University.

55 Balkin & Levinson, above note 23, note that with respect to these disciplines, "the skills, techniques, and knowledges they provide are most easily adapted to the forms of legal argument and legal scholarship that already existed prior to their entry" at 181.

very least are multidisciplinary.[56] These include environmental and health law, and, to some extent human rights.

E. INTERDISCIPLINARY LEGAL SCHOLARSHIP

So what does interdisciplinary scholarship look like when it involves law? Sullivan speaks of two kinds of interdisciplinary legal work—positive research and interpretive research. In this paradigm, positive research is that which looks at "how law actually works in practice"[57] and generally draws upon the social sciences disciplines. Interpretive research draws on the humanities and seeks "to articulate the function, including the expressive function or social meaning, implicit in legal materials."[58] In her view, the specific training received by legal academics allows them to bring specialist skills to this interdisciplinary work that enhance the research output, at least from the perspective of law.[59] In essence, the things legal academics know about how legal institutions and actors operate are invaluable to understanding, contextualizing, or analyzing the results of social sciences- or humanities-based research.

Siems offers a useful taxonomy of interdisciplinarity in law. He identifies four categories of interdisciplinary legal research. The first category, which he defines as "basic," involves addressing a specific legal question, but looking for insights into the question from other disciplines.[60] He then identifies three categories of "advanced" interdisciplinary legal research. In the first of these categories, the research question is not directly about the law. Law may be a factor that feeds into the particular social or economic problem, but the focus of inquiry is on the broader problem and not the specific legal aspect. A second advanced approach involves a research question that focuses on law, but also uses empirical methods to examine the problem. The third advanced approach involves a research question that is not specifically about law; it too is addressed using empirical methods.[61] Siems notes that these advanced approaches can pose significant challenges to the legal academic who will either need advanced training in a relevant

56 Balkin, above note 3, notes that the "most interesting feature of legal interdisciplinarity" is that it is "actively subsidized and supported by the institutions of law and legal education" at 950.

57 Kathleen M Sullivan, "Foreword: Interdisciplinarity" (2002) 100:6 Mich L Rev 1217 at 1221.

58 *Ibid* at 1222.

59 *Ibid* at 1223.

60 Siems, above note 19 at 6–7.

61 *Ibid* at 10–11.

discipline other than law, or will need to develop effective and appropriate collaborative relationships.

This taxonomy is useful in helping to understand the potential scope and variation in what many people refer to as interdisciplinary approaches to law-related research. Indeed, Moran argues that the difficulty in defining *interdisciplinarity* reveals its strengths. In his view interdisciplinary inquiry is valuable because of "its flexibility and indeterminacy, and that there are potentially as many forms of interdisciplinarity as there are disciplines."[62] This breadth of meaning of *interdisciplinary* is reflected in this collection of papers, which reveal a variety of different approaches and methods. Useful questions in exploring this collection are: What approach to interdisciplinarity is adopted by the author(s) of each chapter? What is their source of expertise in related disciplines? How successful are their chosen methods of inquiry in illuminating questions about IP law? In what way do the authors' approaches transform or create new knowledge about IP? Are the questions they ask legal questions or are they broader social, economic or political questions?

F. CHALLENGES OF INTERDISCIPLINARITY

True interdisciplinarity is more than simply reading work from other disciplines and citing it at key points in a book or article. In reality, few in the academy are really trained to do interdisciplinary work. While many (although not all) lawyers and academics have an undergraduate degree in another discipline, it is usually only through wider professional experience and in graduate school that one develops a strong theoretical and methodological grasp of the discipline. It is increasingly the case that legal academics hold PhDs in disciplines other than law, and this will certainly aid in the development of legal literature that is informed by the knowledge, debates, and preoccupations of other fields.[63] It is still rare that academics in disciplines other than law have formal training in law. The result is largely an environment in which academics and researchers have great depth in their own specialized field within their discipline, but little training or experience outside that field.

62 Moran, above note 2 at 14.

63 Balkin & Levinson, above note 23 at 165, observe that those in law have often demonstrated an overconfidence in their abilities such that they either dismiss as irrelevant the contributions of other disciplines, or they assume they can master other disciplines with a bit of reading here and there. They observe that the number of young legal academics with PhDs is something that may have a positive effect in encouraging greater intellectual engagement with other disciplines.

Truly interdisciplinary work is also difficult to do for reasons that are both intrinsic and extrinsic. Extrinsic factors relate to the structures of disciplines and their reward systems. For example, Jacobs and Frickel note:

> Epistemic barriers involve incompatible styles of thought, research traditions, techniques, and language that are difficult to translate across disciplinary domains. Disciplinary structures reinforce these inefficiencies through specialized journals, conferences, and departments that route communication inward. Administrative barriers reinforce this intellectual balkanization.[64]

To make matters worse, there is little incentive to move beyond one's field of specialization. Although universities have for years embraced interdisciplinary research in theory, the institutional rewards for what often amounts to high-risk career behaviour are sometimes sparse. Balkin, writing with the particular perspective of a legal academic, states that:

> Academic disciplines . . . are about authority, and in particular, about authority within particular groups of persons who think alike through training and discipline. As such, this authority must be enforced by punishments and rewards to ensure that the lessons of the discipline become as second nature.[65]

Tenure and promotion committees struggle to recognize the value of publications in journals outside their disciplines, or the merits of pieces that speak to those in another field entirely.[66] Some even mention that interdisci-

---

64 Jacobs & Frickel, above note 1 at 47; the differences in use of terminology between disciplines, power hierarchy between disciplines, and practices concerning authorship are also identified as barriers to the effectiveness of interdisciplinary work: see Christine Haugaard Jakobsen, Tove Hels, & William J McLaughlin, "Barriers and Facilitators to Integration among Scientist in Transdisciplinary Landscape Analyses: a Cross-Country Comparison" (2004) 6:1 Forest Policy and Economics 15.

65 Balkin, above note 3 at 954; see also Vanesa Castán Broto, Maya Gislason, & Melf-Hinrich Ehlers, "Practising Interdisciplinarity in the Interplay Between Disciplines: Experiences of Established Researchers" (2009) 12:7 Environmental Science & Policy 922 for a discussion of the practice of interdisciplinarity and its relationship with institutionalized disciplines.

66 Balkin & Levinson, above note 23 at 166, also note that institutional resistance is a factor in discouraging genuine interdisciplinary approaches to law; see also Lau & Pasquini, above note 6 at 553; Nissani, above note 2 at 213, speaks also about the barriers to interdisciplinary work. He speaks of difficulties that interdisciplinary researchers might face in terms of securing grant funding, and publishing in suitable journals. These challenges, of course, translate into further difficulties in tenure and promotion processes; see also Brewer, above note 13 at 335.

plinary journals are often not considered to be as prestigious as established disciplinary journals.[67] In law, sole authored papers are highly valued and co-authored papers may be regarded with suspicion for tenure or promotion purposes, making interdisciplinary collaboration something perhaps best saved for later in one's career.[68] Publication of interdisciplinary research may also be challenging, as it may be difficult to find a home for research that does not fit easily within one disciplinary framework.[69] Lau and Pasquini suggest that one of the problems facing academics who engage in interdisciplinary research is that "there exists no common understanding of what constitutes interdisciplinary research."[70] Thus, such scholars risk that their work will fall outside not just the parameters of their own discipline, but also outside the parameters of what constitutes interdisciplinary research in the minds of those who evaluate them.[71] Further, the reality is that interdisciplinary research is more demanding — it takes more time to develop the necessary knowledge base, and more time to build collaborative relationships.[72]

---

67 Jakobsen, Hels, & McLaughlin, above note 64 at 23. Some even found that those factors (tenure and promotion criteria, peer-review evaluation) may have an influence on the kind of research undertaken and on the type of researchers likely to engage in interdisciplinary work. Full-time researchers at the top of the promotion scale focusing on problem-solving approaches tend to undertake more interdisciplinary research: see Nicolas Carayol & Thuc Uyen Nguyen Thi, "Why Do Academic Scientists Engage in Interdisciplinary Research" (2005) 14:1 Research Evaluation 70.

68 Jakobsen, Hels, & McLaughlin, above note 64 at 23, also address problems of interdisciplinary work in university environment. Brewer, above note 13, notes that universities tend to reward individual achievement, and are themselves structured around multiple separate disciplines; see also Teresa Scassa et al, "Working at the Intersection of Law and Science: Reflections on a Fruitful Geospatial Data Collaboration" in Nicholas Chrisman & Monica Wachowicz, eds, *The Added Value of Scientific Networking: Perspectives from the GEOIDE Network Members, 1998-2012* (Québec: GEOIDE Network, 2012) at 58; Carayol & Nguyen Thi, above note 67 at 77, who note that the promotion system also tends to favour research on narrow topics with goals to be reached within short periods, not necessarily easily achievable in interdisciplinary projects.

69 Lau & Pasquini, above note 6 at 556; Scassa et al, above note 68 at 60.

70 Lau & Pasquini, *ibid* at 553.

71 See also Jacobs & Frickel, above note 1 at 53. That happens until the interdisciplinary field has reached maturity: see, in the context of collection evaluation in academic libraries, this analysis in Cynthia Dobson, Jeffrey D Kushkowski, & Kristin H Gerhard, "Collection Evaluation for Interdisciplinary Fields: A Comprehensive Approach" (1996) 22:4 Journal of Academic Librarianship 279.

72 Lau & Pasquini, above note 6, write of "a struggle to find a common currency of language in which to communicate and trade ideas, and to find common intellectual ground on which to meet." They also insist that interdisciplinary work requires "huge amounts of goodwill, openness and effort" at 558; see also Scassa et al, above note 68 at 65; Jakobsen, Hels, & McLaughlin, above note 64 at 22–23.

In putting together both the workshop and this collection of papers we experienced a number of these challenges to engaging in interdisciplinary work, as, no doubt, did some of our authors. These challenges were also a factor in the decision of at least one scholar not to participate in our project. While some of these challenges were ones that we had anticipated, others surprised us either in terms of their frequency or intensity.

G. OUR PROJECT

Our workshop grew out of a tradition of bringing together Canadian IP academics every two or three years to meet and share ideas. For the most part, these meetings had been largely composed of legal academics. Although ranks were never closed to those from other disciplines, it was a relatively intimate group and there was no open invitation beyond the field of law. Thus, when we decided to invite those from other disciplines to our workshop, the first challenge was to locate and invite scholars from other disciplines in Canada who were actively working on IP issues. We began by inviting those of whom we were already aware, and then extended further invitations based on the suggestions of others. We quickly reached the maximum number of participants for our workshop. It is clear to us that there are many more academics in other disciplines who are working on IP issues, and we hope that there will be more opportunities in the future to engage with them.

At the workshop itself we had scholars from the disciplines of law, political science, English, music, library and information science, criminology, and sports management. The mixture of perspectives led to many interesting and stimulating discussions; indeed, the workshop was structured so as to maximize the space available for interaction. As is evident from the papers in this collection, different approaches to interdisciplinarity were adopted. Some papers are authored by pairs or teams of authors from different disciplines, others are authored by individuals with high-level experience in more than one discipline, and still others are authored by individuals seeking to draw upon the knowledge of disciplines outside their own in order to enrich their own research. Although many of our contributors are located within a single department (or faculty in the case of law), a number of them are cross-appointed to other faculties or departments within their universities.

Participants were made aware of the interdisciplinary objectives of the workshop at the time they were invited to participate. Specifically, we asked participants to consider the contributions of other disciplines to the issues they considered by actively collaborating with colleagues from other disciplines, and/or by engaging critically with bodies of work from other disciplines. One of the challenges we faced when the papers began to flow in, was deciding whether we were going to establish a threshold for determining whether a paper was sufficiently interdisciplinary to be included in this work. It did raise the issue of what is "interdisciplinary" and we concluded that any definition of interdisciplinarity or any criteria used to assess might not be shared by all of our participants. In the end, we decided to publish all of the papers, without trying to quantify their degree of interdisciplinarity.

Another challenge we faced — in some ways a self-imposed challenge — related to the page limit for contributions. Because of the large number of contributors, we asked our authors to keep their contributions to a fixed word limit. Many of our contributors struggled with this word limit, given that they had to bring different disciplinary perspectives to bear in a manner that would be accessible to readers from different disciplines. We soon realized that it was unrealistic to apply a rigid word limit and decided to approach the issue on a case-by-case basis.

The peer review process itself also presented a challenge. We are very grateful to our peer reviewers for agreeing to undertake the task of reading papers that often fell outside their disciplinary comfort zones. Their support of this project and their willingness to engage with the texts is very much appreciated. We note that one of the challenges in finding peer reviewers for our papers was that some who were approached declined to review papers on the basis that they were not within their area of specialization. This was frustrating, given the particular nature of our project and the fact that many of our authors were breaking new ground. We generally sought one peer reviewer with a background in law and one with expertise in a relevant other discipline; in some cases this produced conflicting reviews.[73] Lau and Pasquini write of their own struggles with interdisciplinarity, that "[a]ll too often, reviewers assess a paper's strength in relation to their specialisms (even if they are not fully aware of this mind-set), and its integrative strength is rarely taken on board."[74] While our reviewers were sensitive to our interdisciplinary objectives, we nevertheless accept that disciplinary training may have a strong impact on how papers are assessed.

---

73 A similar problem is noted by Lau & Pasquini, above note 6 at 557.

74 *Ibid.*

Some authors had to deal with reviews that came from entirely different directions. On the whole, however, our authors received such divergent comments positively since these provided them with insight into the potential reactions of readers to their arguments.

A final challenge we faced with this book is one which is still unresolved. Identifying an audience for this book is not always easy; we are cognizant of this and very appreciative of the support of Irwin Law, a legal publisher that is not afraid to innovate or to take chances. One of the challenges in publishing interdisciplinary works — especially those on the borders of law and other disciplines — is that there is still a substantial amount of segregation between the distribution networks for publications. It is replicated in the academy as well: law books and law journals go into law libraries; those of other disciplines are in more central university collections. In this regard, Irwin Law's willingness to publish the individual chapters of this book online under an open licence not only highlights this publisher's willingness to innovate, but also gives more room for this book to find its audience.

In our view, this collection of papers should be of general interest to all within the legal profession: lawyers, judges, academics, and students, who are interested in the potential of interdisciplinarity for offering fresh perspectives on intellectual property related subjects. We are hopeful that the book will also stimulate fresh interest in, and appreciation of, the merits of interdisciplinary approaches to IP subjects. Indeed, readers will find a broad range of disciplinary approaches and a broad range of subject matter spanning not only the "traditional" categories of IP — patents, copyright, and trademarks — but also emerging areas such as ambush marketing, and the amorphous "right" to sue for the use of one's likeness in fiction or film. We hope as well that readers from outside the discipline of law who have an interest in intellectual property law (and their numbers are growing both within and outside of the academy) will find in this collection papers that are engaging, accessible, and thought-provoking.

The chapters of this book are organized into four themes, the second of which has two sub-themes. We have called the first theme New Windows on Intellectual Property Law. In the papers in this theme, the authors examine aspects of intellectual property law through a different disciplinary lens with a view to advocating for changes in how a particular problem or issue is approached. Cameron Hutchison draws on different disciplinary insights to assess how rights to adapt literary works into film are addressed in copyright law, and how the test for infringement might be influenced as a result. In a similar vein, Carys J Craig and Guillaume Laroche consider how a music theory approach to the infringement of copyright in musical works should — or should not — affect how courts address such cases. Margaret Ann Wilkinson argues that an information-sciences based analysis would help to resolve legal disputes relating to confidential information, particularly in an increasingly complex information environment. Drawing on different disciplinary perspectives, Pierre-Emmanuel Moyse argues that we need to step back from instrumentalist approaches to law to consider how the spirit of law can be realized by incorporating a theory of abuse of rights in intellectual property law. Graham Reynolds examines the precautionary principle developed at the heart of the environmental movement, and suggests how this principle might be incorporated in the intellectual property context with a view to preserving the public domain. In the final piece in this section, Bita Amani argues for a socio-cultural approach to law that might provide new insights into how jurists should approach issues around the patenting of biomedia.

In the second part of our book, the authors look at intellectual property law through a different disciplinary lens in order to better understand some aspect of the intellectual property system or to explain why it functions in a particular way. We call this section New Windows — New Insights. In their work, our contributors focus either on the social structure or forces that have had an impact on the development of intellectual property law or on the discourses, paradigms, and intellectual structures that helped shape the intellectual property regime. In the first sub-theme — A Different Disciplinary Lens — contributors examine intellectual property issues from a variety of different perspectives. These include political science, sociology, anthropology, criminology, information, and media studies. For example, Blayne Haggart uses the lens of historical institutionalism to understand how intellectual property law has developed and how it may continue to do so in the future. B Courtney Doagoo looks at the feminist approaches in anthropology to show how women's creative output is treated in intellectual property law. Matt Stahl focuses on the impact of the employment power structures of the cultural industries on the development of intellectual property. Louis D'Alton, using a Marxist frame, shows how the birth and growth of the public performance right in musical works can be seen as a concrete application of Antonio Gramsci's theory of hegemony. Daniel Downes studies the practice of branding and presents the extension of copyright, trademark, and rights of publicity to fictional characters and authors as a phenomenon of "transpropertization." Mistrale Goudreau and Joao Velloso demonstrate how the statutory damages regime in copyright legislation is a form of punishment, private style and question its coherence and effectiveness based on social sciences scholarship.

In the second sub-theme, which we call Discourses and Paradigms, contributors focus on the discourses, paradigms, and intellectual structures that have influenced the intellectual property regime. Michael McNally explores how information society discourse has paved the way to stronger intellectual property protection while failing to address the issues of agency and power relations that affect intellectual property production. Meera Nair uses a law and communications analysis to explore the dynamic of legislative interpretation and borrows from Harold Adams Innis's thoughts on empires and margins, to provide a better understanding of copyright exceptions. Chidi Oguamanam explores the intersection between human rights and intellectual property, and argues for a critical approach to human rights discourse in intellectual property law. Gregory Hagen, venturing into the realm of political philosophy, asks whether Robert Merges was right to argue that intellectual property rights should be considered basic rights within Rawls's theory of justice. Laura J Murray and Kirsty Robertson examine the rhetoric around appropriation art, and argue that the United States free speech discourse in this area risks occluding the particular Canadian historical and political context in which appropriation art takes place. Andrea Slane, using the controversy surrounding the bestselling 2009 novel and subsequent film *The Help*, takes a literary studies approach to the litigation which ensued, and the attendant legal claims about the wrongful appropriation of one's self as a character. She questions whether a binary distinction between fiction and literary realism can appropriately address the ethics of fictionalization. Marcus Boon examines the politics and ideology behind "copying" on the practices of appropriation or depropriation. Using the work of French filmmaker Jean-Luc Godard as an illustration, he argues that we need to consider broader political economy issues in contemporary intellectual property law.

In the third theme, Interdisciplinarity in Practice, the authors focus on discipline-specific knowledge and insights to address practical contentions within the field of intellectual property. Drawing on his experience with a major international and multidisciplinary research project, Jeremy deBeer explores the lessons to be learned from large-scale collaborative projects such as the African Copyright and Access to Knowledge Project. Norman

Siebrasse argues that empirical evidence regarding whether business method patents promote or hinder innovation enters judicial discourse through academic articles in a manner that does not allow for proper testing of this evidence. He argues that institutional competence to evaluate empirical social science evidence should be taken into account in determining the extent to which it should influence judicial decision-making.

In the fourth and final theme — Impact *of* Law or Impact *on* Law? — the authors consider how law has the ability to impact behaviour in other disciplines while at the same time other disciplines equally have the ability to impact law. Matthew Herder investigates the need for increased empirical evidence to determine the influences that emerging scientists face when making decisions to commercialize their knowledge and what impact the push for commercialization may have on academic research. Jonathon W Penney interrogates the lack of methodology in copyright scholarship pertaining to the ever-expanding online digital sphere, and analyzes the issues that may arise when applying legal doctrines such as the "chilling effects doctrine" to forms of media. Benoit Seguin and Teresa Scassa examine the impact of anti-ambush marketing legislation in a case study of sponsorship at the 2010 Vancouver Olympics, and suggest that this form of protection for brands may have negative and unanticipated consequences. Samuel Trosow reflects on the cultural significance of creativity in the digital landscape, with an emphasis on user-generated content. He warns of the threat posed by restrictive copyright policies on this emerging and valuable form of communication.

Together, this collection of diverse, exciting, and ambitious papers offers a glimpse into the rich potential of interdisciplinary research on intellectual property law questions. We hope that readers will find the authors' insights both stimulating and useful. We also hope that readers will be inspired to reflect upon the broader questions around disciplinarity and interdisciplinarity in law.

THEME ONE

New Windows on Intellectual Property Law

ONE

Adapting Novel into Film

CAMERON HUTCHISON

ABSTRACT (EN): This chapter explores, from an interdisciplinary perspective, the right of copyright holders to adapt literary works into film media. From debates in other fields of study, certain theories emerge which help to better understand the possibility of cinematic adaptation from literary sources. The author begins with the counterintuitive idea that there is no essence to any given work that is available to be adapted to another medium (constructivism). A second school of thought argues that the differences between literature and cinema—the written word and the visual image—are too great for there to be anything approaching equivalency between the two media (adaptation skepticism). Next the author considers the argument that what is adapted from book into film is a narrative structure that in only some respects is amenable to transfer to the film medium (structuralism). The author concludes with a brief look at the argument that reading and visualizing are inverse cognitive processes that suggest the differences between the two media are overstated (cognitive equivalency). After a brief exploration of the adaptation right in law, each of these perspectives is addressed. The author ultimately sides with the structuralist position and concludes that the legal test for infringement has much to gain from this analytical framework.

RÉSUMÉ (FR): Ce chapitre explore, dans une perspective interdisciplinaire, le droit des titulaires de droit d'auteur d'adapter leur œuvre littéraire au cinéma. Certaines théories, issues de débats provenant d'autres domaines d'étude, aident à mieux comprendre les avenues d'adaptation cinématographique des œuvres littéraires. L'auteur débute en explorant l'idée, qui va à l'encontre de l'intuition, qu'il n'y a pas, dans une oeuvre donnée, une essence prête à être adaptée à un autre medium (constructivisme). Une deuxième école de pensée soutient que la différence entre la littérature et le cinéma — le mot écrit et l'image visuelle — est bien trop grande pour qu'il y ait une quelconque équivalence entre les deux médias (scepticisme vis-à-vis de l'adaptation). Ensuite, l'auteur considère l'argument selon lequel ce qui est adapté du livre au film est la structure narrative, qui est susceptible à certains égards seulement d'être transférée au médium du film (structuralisme). L'auteur conclut en abordant brièvement l'argument selon lequel lire et voir sont deux processus cognitifs inverses, ce qui peut suggérer que les différences entre les deux médias sont exagérées (équivalence cognitive). Après un bref survol du droit concernant l'adaptation, chacune de ces quatre perspectives est envisagée. L'auteur finalement se rallie à la thèse structuraliste et conclut que le test juridique servant à déterminer la contrefaçon gagnerait à emprunter de ce cadre analytique.

A. INTRODUCTION

The history of cinema is replete with adaptations of novels into film. Indeed, it seems that almost every movie made these days is based on a book. Beyond mere commercial opportunism,[1] there is at least something about the film medium that lends itself to borrowing from literary sources. The significance of this topic for copyright scholars is that the cinematographic or movie right vests with the author of a book (what I will call the *adaptation right*). Where that right has been at issue, courts have struggled with developing a methodology for determining infringement. The enormously complex topic of assessing whether there has been a substantial taking from a textual medium for adaptation into a visual medium has been oversimplified both by legal tests for infringement and the manner in which they are applied.

The purpose of this short chapter is to explore the topic from extra-legal disciplinary perspectives in an effort to highlight some of the shortcomings of the law in this area, but also to embark on new ways of thinking about the adaptation right. This chapter draws on a field known as adaptation studies, which itself borrows liberally from literary criticism, film studies, art

1 Douglas Y'Barbo, "Aesthetic Ambition Versus Commercial Appeal: Adapting Novels to Film and the Copyright Law" (1998) 10 St Thomas L Rev 299 at 310 argues that best-selling or even popular novels can have a trademark value that can easily translate into commercial success for a movie version; Hollywood underwriters of big budget movies can be assured of a certain amount of commercial success for the movie version of the latest novel from John Grisham or Tom Clancy.

philosophy, and media studies. From debates within and across these fields, certain theories emerge which help to better understand the possibility of cinematic adaptation from literary sources (if indeed it is possible at all).[2] We will begin with the counterintuitive idea that there is no essence to any given work that is available to be adapted to another medium (constructivism). A second school of thought argues that the differences between literature and cinema — the written word and the visual image — are too great for there to be anything approaching equivalency between the two media (adaptation skepticism). Next we consider the argument that what is adapted from book into film is a narrative structure that, in some respects but not others, is amenable to transfer to the film medium (structuralism). We will conclude with a brief look at the argument that reading and visualizing are inverse cognitive processes that might suggest the differences between the two media are overstated (cognitive equivalency). After a brief exploration of the law of the adaptation right, each of these four perspectives will be addressed. I ultimately side with the structuralist position and conclude that the legal test for infringement has much to gain from this analytical framework.

B. LEGAL PERSPECTIVES

Copyright offers exclusive rights to an author who creates an original artistic, literary, musical, or dramatic work.[3] The term *original* has been interpreted by the Supreme Court of Canada to mean that the work must demonstrate the author's "skill and judgment."[4] A work created in one medium can be afforded copyright protection when adapted into another medium. Thus, section 3 of the *Copyright Act*[5] gives the owner of a copyright "the sole right

---

2 Constructivism and structuralism are well known schools of thought, whereas adaptation skepticism and cognitive equivalency are names I have created. Moreover, these theories are presented in stark terms and do not reflect the many variants thereof. Finally, the authors I cite in this paper sometimes belong to more than one school of thought. Bluestone and McFarlane, for example, are both adaptation skeptics and structuralists; however, because the latter elaborated a structuralist methodology while the former emphasized the problems of adaptation, they were categorized accordingly.

3 *Copyright Act*, RSC 1985, c C-42, s 2 (the scope of covered works is broad) [definitions]; see *CCH Canadian Ltd v Law Society of Upper Canada*, 2004 SCC 13 at para 8 [*CCH*]. Furthermore, for copyright to subsist, the work must be fixated in a tangible form.

4 *CCH, ibid* at para 16; see Cameron Hutchison "Insights from Psychology for Copyright's Originality Doctrine" (2012) 52 IDEA 101 for a discussion of the skill and judgment standard from a psychological perspective.

5 *Copyright Act*, above note 3, s 3.

to produce or reproduce the work or any substantial part thereof in any material form whatever . . . ." For our purposes this includes paragraph 3(1)(d), the sole right "in the case of a literary, dramatic or musical work, to make any . . . cinematograph film . . . ."[6] Thus, the author of a novel has the exclusive right to "make" the book, or a substantial part thereof, into a film.

Copyright does not subsist in respect of the ideas or facts that underlie a work, as opposed to its expression. American courts have struggled with whether the borrowed parts of a work at issue are mere ideas (as opposed to their expression) and thus not copyrightable. In this regard, courts often reference *Nichols v Universal Pictures Corp*[7] in which the copyright holder of one play sued the producers of a second play for infringement. In that case, Judge Hand determined on the facts that "[t]he only matter in common to the two [works] is a quarrel between a Jewish and an Irish father, the marriage of their children, the birth of grandchildren and a reconciliation."[8] As such, the borrowing here was in the realm of idea and not expression. The case is famous for the pronouncement of an abstraction test:

> Upon any work, and especially upon a play, a great number of patterns of increasing generality will fit equally well, as more and more of the incident is left out. The last may perhaps be no more than the most general statement of what the play is about, and at times might consist only of its title; but there is a point in this series of abstractions where they are no longer protected, since otherwise the playwright could prevent the use of his "ideas," to which, apart from their expression, his property is never extended.[9]

Separating the idea from the expression is a notoriously difficult exercise. For example, how much more borrowed incident was needed in *Nichols* for the defendant to have been found to have copied expression? As well, courts have historically wrestled with the distinctions, if any, between an "idea," a "plot," and a "theme."[10]

---

6 *Ibid*, s 3(1)(d); the film adaptation right has not been judicially considered in Canada, which stands in contrast to a robust US caselaw on the subject.

7 *Nichols v Universal Pictures Corp*, 45 F 2d 119 (2d Cir 1930) [*Nichols*].

8 *Ibid* at 122.

9 *Ibid* at 121.

10 Melville B Nimmer, "Inroads on Copyright Protection" (1951) 64 Harv L Rev 1125. "At least one court has said that all these terms are synonymous, and another court has maintained that 'plot' and 'theme' are identical . . . . [S]ome courts have indicated that a theme may be protected, and others have held that a plot may be protected" at 1130–31; Robert Fuller Fleming, "Substantial Similarity: Where Plots Really Thicken" (1971) 19

Once into the realm of expression, copyright infringement is found where a defendant appropriates a qualitatively substantial portion of a work without permission of the copyright owner. Copyright infringement analysis compares the two works in question; in our scenario the movie (and not the script) will be reviewed and compared with the book.[11] Infringement analysis has two prongs. The first inquiry is whether there was access to the work (i.e., the second work *derived* from the first and was not the result of independent creation), and may be aided by expert evidence.[12] If access is proven, the question then becomes whether the second work infringed the first as viewed by an "ordinary observer" (and notably *without* the assistance of expert evidence).[13] On this second prong, courts considering the adaptation right generally begin their analysis by discounting elements which are not protected by copyright such as ideas,[14] stock themes,[15] and *scenes a faire*.[16] Then, distilling the two works to their essential elements, a comparative analysis is considered through the following prisms: total concept and feel, theme and plot, mood, characters, pace, setting, sequence of events, and structure.[17] Surprisingly, these terms are not defined in the caselaw.

There is a long legal history, both in caselaw and legal commentary, on the subject of adaptation. Much of the early commentary on the subject takes issue with the "ordinary observer" test or "audience test" for determining substantial appropriation. Nimmer, for example, argued that "[t]here are numerous instances when the ordinary observer is simply not capable of detecting substantial appropriation."[18] He advocated that the dif-

---

Copyright L Symp 252. Moreover, some courts have defined plot as "bare plot" while others refer to it as "the entire sequence of events which lead the story situation from cause to effect" at 261.

11 *Beal v Paramount Pictures Corp*, 20 F 3d 454 at 456 (11th Cir 1994) [*Beal*].

12 Y'Barbo, above note 1 at 307.

13 *Ibid*; see for example *Arden v Columbia Pictures Industries*, 908 F Supp 1248 (SDNY 1995) [*Arden*]. "Courts are asked 'whether an average lay observer would recognize the alleged copy as having been appropriated from the copyrighted work'" at 1248.

14 *Ibid*. Thus in *Arden*, the idea found in the novel *One Fine Day* of a man who is "trapped in a day that repeats itself over and over" was a permissible taking for the producers of the film *Groundhog Day* since the idea was expressed in "very different ways" as between novel and film, at 1249.

15 *Ibid*. "[T]he 'familiar figure of the Irish cop' is a stock theme of police fiction" at 1259.

16 *Ibid* at 1259, meaning those elements that are indispensible, or at least standard, in the expression of a topic.

17 Y'Barbo, above note 1 at 356 ff; *Beal*, above note 11 at 462–64.

18 Nimmer, above note 10 at 1137; Fleming, above note 10; Robert C Sorenson & Theodore C Sorenson, "Re-Examining the Traditional Legal Test of Literal Similarity: A Proposal for

ferences between novel and film, for example, can hide a substantial similarity between two works.[19] He thus called for a measure of literary analysis as a criterion in determining substantial similarity, and a shift away from an "ordinary observer" approach.[20]

In a more recent treatment, Douglas Y'Barbo argues that copyright fails to protect those elements of a novel that are most commonly used for a film adaptation, specifically the story line or plot structure of the book.[21] Copyright infringement is improbable in other ways as well:

> First, the majority of the elements comprising a work of fiction are not protectable. They are either too general, or they are unoriginal to that author . . . . Second, even if a film maker borrows some protectable elements from the novel, those elements may be so trivial, either in quantity or quality, that the film does not resemble the novel. Third, the film maker may take some elements from the novel that comprise its aesthetic appeal—the work's essence. Hence, the film and novel *may be* very similar, even though what was taken was not quantitatively significant. Fourth, the film maker may take the same elements from the novel, yet, once transplanted into the film, they are no longer recognizable as having originated with the novel.[22]

A corollary of his argument is that many literary aspects are inassimilable into film media.[23]

Y'Barbo demonstrates his thesis by critically examining the criteria used by courts to assess infringement. Thus, the "total concept and feel" of a book may lie in its prose and literary devices such as internal monologue whereas filmmakers rely on visual stimuli, actors, linear juxtaposition of

---

Content Analysis" (1951–52) 37 Cornell LQ 638. The authors offer critiques of the ordinary observer test; Robert H Rotstein, "Beyond Metaphor: Copyright Infringement and the Fiction of the Work" (1993) 68 Chicago-Kent L Rev 725 at 785, advocating that a better way to judge infringement would be an "audience competent in the particular genre" test.

19 Nimmer, above note 10 at 1138. "A novel will often be composed of largely introspective thoughts and emotions which of necessity will be expressed in a quite different manner when dramatized" at 1138.

20 *Ibid* at 1140.

21 Y'Barbo, above note 1 at 316–17. Moreover, the "overwhelming majority of any novel is unprotectable, because it consists of ideas, scenes a faire, merged expression, historical fact, and other material in the public domain" at 315; he supports this position by concluding that "[e]very contemporary film-adaptation dispute has been decided on summary judgment for the defendant" at 320.

22 *Ibid* at 321 [emphasis in original][footnotes omitted].

23 *Ibid* at 354.

images, and editing to achieve a pleasing effect.[24] Moreover, the time constraints (and thus editing) of film means that the "pace" of a movie will usually differ from the literary text.[25] While a movie adaptation may follow the story line or "plot" of a book, this is generally not protectable *per se*; often, as well, a "theme" or meaning will change as the filmmaker alters the novel to a happy ending.[26] Filmmakers often simplify the story line and present a linear "sequence of events" (and perhaps even present material in a familiar genre quite different from the book) in an effort not to confuse audiences and to meet the two-hour or less time frame.[27] The portrayal and development of "character" are often simplified due to time limits and the general inability to rely on devices such as internal monologue, and depend heavily on actor portrayal.[28] As we will see shortly, Y'Barbo's analysis echoes many of the arguments advanced by the adaptation skeptics.

C. OTHER DISCIPLINARY PERSPECTIVES

At the most general level, extra legal disciplinary perspectives on book-to-film adaptation separate into four general streams of theory, which I have termed: (1) constructivism, (2) adaptation skepticism, (3) structuralism, and (4) cognitive equivalency. Not surprisingly, the first two theories are highly skeptical of the possibility of adapting book to film (but for very different reasons), while structuralists are guardedly optimistic about the ability to adapt certain aspects of narrative structure. The fourth perspective is still too speculative to be of any analytical assistance.

The notion that a copyrighted work has protectable elements that may survive the transfer into another medium implies that a work possesses certain static and unchanging properties in the first instance. A central question in art philosophy is "what is a work of art?" Are there properties to a work or art — a static essence in other words — that can be objectively identified?[29] Similarly in copyright law, we might ask "are there identifiable, static properties to a work which are capable of being adapted to another medium?" The answer seems to be "yes" in that copyright treats a work as

24 *Ibid* at 356–59.

25 *Ibid* at 360.

26 *Ibid* at 362.

27 *Ibid* at 362–63.

28 *Ibid* at 364.

29 Robert Stecker, *Aesthetics and the Philosophy of Art: An Introduction* (Lanham: Rowman & Littlefield Publishers, 2005) at 9.

"an object with fixed characteristics existing independently of context and audience."[30] When we compare two works for infringement analysis, we are distilling two works to their essential properties before comparing them.[31]

A *constructivist* perspective seriously challenges copyright's essentialist thesis. Constructivists maintain that every time we interpret a work of art, "we are imputing properties to something which either alters that very thing or creates something new. [Thus these] objects of interpretation have a degree of dependence on the interpretation people give [them] . . . are identified in terms of the properties they are conceived as having . . . [and] lack an essence or fixed nature."[32] From this perspective, Rotstein contends that works are not fixed but have changing identities, which depend on audience response to the work in the context in which it appears.[33] These changing identities, or interpretations, may apply to even the most foundational doctrines of copyright's essentialism. For example, the distinction between an idea and its expression is itself an act of interpretation.[34] Noting Nimmer's famous description of a shared fourteen-point plot line between *Romeo and Juliet*[35] on the one hand, and *West Side Story*[36] on the other, Rotstein provides alternative interpretations of these plots lines which show that, even at this most basic level, there is not similarity but rather substantial divergence.[37] For example, the first point, that "[t]he boy and girl are members of a hostile group" seems hardly worthy when the alternative

30 Rotstein, above note 18 at 741.

31 *Ibid*. In this regard, Rotstein quite rightly notes "[i]ronically, for copyright the essence of the work lies, not at some deep core, but at the surface of the work, i.e., the words on the page. Abstract characterizations of the work, though some may still qualify for protection as 'expression,' move further and further away from the surface" at 760, n 154.

32 Stecker, above note 29 at 112.

33 Rotstein, above note 18 at 726–27. "The reader in effect creates the text by virtue of the broader context in which he or she exists. For this reason, the text does not . . . have a fixed identity" at 736–37. "The text is a speech event involving interaction among a producer (the 'author'), a textual artifact (book, movie, song, computer program), and a recipient (reader, viewer, listener).Texts *occur* only upon the dynamic interaction of all three" at 739–40.

34 *Ibid* at 760.

35 William Shakespeare, *Romeo and Juliet. A Tragedy* (Edinburgh: Marin & Wotherspoon, 1768).

36 *West Side Story*, DVD, directed by Robert Wise & Jerome Robbins (1961; Los Angeles, CA: United Artists, 1998).

37 Rotstein, above note 18. "[E]ven an interpretation that seems straightforward and merely descriptive of a plot line is subject to challenge . . . ." at 764, citing Melville B Nimmer & David Nimmer, Nimmer on Copyright (New York: Matthew Bender & Co, 1985) at 13.42–13.42.1.

interpretation is presented: "Maria in *West Side Story* is not a member of a hostile group (the gang) and is indeed unaware of the hostility. The boy in *West Side Story* has withdrawn from the hostile group (the gang). Romeo and Juliet at first both carry the ancient grudge between their families."[38] Constructivists, therefore, are skeptical of the possibility of adaptation since they believe that there is no objective essence of a work, which exists independently of interpretation and context.

The *adaptation skeptics* uphold the unity of form and content, believing that the semiotic systems of text and film are incommensurable. A main proponent here would be the founding father of adaptation studies, George Bluestone, who viewed film and literature as radically different primarily due to the fact that one medium is linguistic while the other is visual.[39] As Bluestone claimed, "changes are *inevitable* the moment one abandons the linguistic for the visual medium."[40] For example, the internal content of thought including "memory, dreams, imagination" — so much a part of literature — cannot adequately be translated into the film form.[41] At most, film can infer thoughts but it cannot directly show them to us.[42] Moreover, whereas literature focuses on internal thought, character, and the psychological, film is about external action, plot, and the social.[43] Even the transfer of characters from novel to film is lacking since the visual medium is not commensurate with the power of language.[44] What is transferable between these two media, according to Bluestone, is the narrative form. Yet even here film directs our visual perception of that narrative.[45] Moreover, the production, business model, and audience demands of each medium are very different which "condition and shape artistic content"; the film is produced collaboratively and needs mass appeal to offset high production costs whereas the writings of the single author need not be geared toward such large-scale commercial success.[46] In sum, Bluestone concludes:

38 Rotstein, above note 18 at 762 [emphasis in original].

39 George Bluestone, *Novels into Film* (Berkeley: University of California Press, 1968) at viii.

40 *Ibid* at 5 [emphasis in original].

41 *Ibid* at viii–ix, 23 and 47.

42 *Ibid* at 48.

43 *Ibid*.

44 *Ibid* at 23.

45 *Ibid* at 31 and 58.

46 *Ibid* at ix, 31 and 34.

> What happens, therefore, when the filmist undertakes the adaptation of a novel, given the inevitable mutation, is that he does not convert the novel at all. What he adapts is a kind of paraphrase of the novel — the novel viewed as raw material. He looks not to the organic novel, whose language is inseparable from its theme, but to characters and incidents which have somehow detached themselves from language and, like the heroes of folk legends, have achieved a mythic life of their own.[47]

One of the adaptations Bluestone examines is *The Grapes of Wrath*,[48] in which both film and novel follow a similar plot line but with major differences in theme and social commentary. The movie, for example, omits the centrality of natural and zoological motifs of the book which act as metaphors for, among other things, the tribulations of the Joad family, i.e., the harsh natural order of things.[49] Moreover, a dominant theme — the political implications of the book — is muted and deradicalized.[50] Some changes, such as the interchapters which present the author's point of view are deleted while others, such as the dialogue are either abridged or sanitized.[51] These reflect both the time constraints of the film medium but also the packaging of movies for mass appeal. Perhaps most important of all is the changed ending which Bluestone claims as "one of the most remarkable narrative switches in film history":

> Instead of ending with the strike-breaking episodes in which Tom is clubbed, Casy killed, and the strikers routed, the film ends with the Govern-

47 *Ibid*. Thus, "the filmist becomes not a translator for an established author, but a new author in his own right." He continues, quoting Balazs, "while 'the subject, or story, of both works is identical, their content is nevertheless different. It is this different *content* that is adequately expressed in the changed form resulting from the adaptation.' It follows that the raw material of reality can be fashioned in many different forms, but a *content* which determines the form is no longer such raw material" at 62 [emphasis in original].

48 John Steinbeck, *The Grapes of Wrath* (New York: The Viking Press, 1939); *The Grapes of Wrath*, DVD, directed by John Ford (1940; Los Angeles, CA: 20th Century Fox Home Entertainment, 2004).

49 Bluestone, above note 39. "The persistence of this imagery reveals at least part of its service. In the first place, even in our random selections, biology supports and comments upon sociology. Sexual activity, the primacy of the family clan, the threat and utility of industrial machinery, the alienation and hostility of the law, the growing anger at economic oppression, the arguments for human dignity, are all accompanied by, or expressed in terms of, zoological images. In the second place, the presence of literal and figurative animals is more frequent when the oppression of the Joads is most severe" at 150–51.

50 *Ibid* at 158–59.

51 *Ibid* at 162–64.

> ment Camp interlude. This reversal . . . accomplishes, in its metamorphic power, an entirely new structure which has far-reaching consequences. Combined with the deletion of the last dismal episode, and the pruning, alterations, and selections we have already traced, the new order changes the parabolic structure to a straight line that continually ascends.[52]

What is perhaps interesting about this comparison is that it reveals profound underlying differences between the two works, which superficially may not have been obvious to an ordinary observer. In other words, while the characterizations and many of the incidents were followed in the movie, important elements from the book were absent either because they were not adaptable to the new media or were consciously altered to change the meaning and presentation of the work.

The third perspective, firmly rooted in the *structuralist* school of thought, argues that elements of the narrative structure of a book can be successfully transferred to the screen. In adaptation studies, the most prominent advocate of this view is Brian McFarlane who rails against the subjectivity of impressionistic responses in favour of a more objective and systematic means of evaluating the similarities and differences between book and film.[53] To be sure, McFarlane is a disciple of Bluestone in the way he conceives of the profound differences between book and film as media in terms of portrayal,[54] form,[55] and semiotics.[56]

However, unlike Bluestone, he is systematic in identifying those elements of narrative structure capable of being adapted. He defines narrative as "a series of events, causally linked, involving a continuing set of char-

---

52 *Ibid*. "Thus, the book, which is an exhortation to action, becomes a film which offers reassurance that no action is required to insure the desired resolution of the issue" at 166–67.

53 Brian McFarlane, *Novel Into Film: An Introduction to the Theory of Adaptation* (Oxford: Clarendon Press, 1996) at 195.

54 *Ibid*. The narrating voice of a book and its "privileged position of knowledge about characters, periods, places . . ." is replaced by a visual presentation of action unfolding at 18; film is agile in presenting visual perspectives but seems largely incapable of portraying a psychological viewpoint of a character. And while film can adequately portray the appearance of a character and setting, we must evaluate character motivations, and thoughts though *mise-en-scène* as, for example, the way an actor looks and gestures at 16–17.

55 *Ibid* at 27. The linear, prodding accretion of knowledge of events and characters of the book is replaced by the immediacy and visual richness of the screen.

56 *Ibid* at 28. Language as a semiotic system is much richer, and more pervasively known, than the codes of cinema.

acters which influence and are influenced by the course of events . . . ."[57] McFarlane argues that certain elements of a novel's narrative structure are *transferable* or "amenable to display in film" while others are *adaptable* in the sense that an element "must find quite different equivalences in the film medium, when such equivalences are sought or are available at all."[58] Whether an element of a narrative structure is transferable or adaptable depends, in a general sense, on the function that element serves.

Here he borrows directly from Roland Barthes who argued that narrative is comprised solely of functions. The main function—*functions proper*—consists of the actions and events, which are presented horizontally throughout the story.[59] These functions are further divided into *cardinal functions* or *hinge points* of narrative where "the actions they refer to open up alternatives of consequence to the development of the story."[60] The "linking together of cardinal functions provides the irreducible bare bones of the narrative" and, furthermore, they are usually transferable from book to novel.[61] An example of altering a cardinal function would be to change a sad ending to a happy ending. Another category is the *catalyzer function*, which are small actions that are complementary to a cardinal function, e.g., the setting of a table for a meal gives occasion for an action of cardinal importance to the story.[62] To the extent that functions proper are actions and events which do not depend on language for their expression, they are transferable from one medium to another.[63] The *integrational functions*, vertical in nature, are *indices proper* and *informants*. The latter consist of pure data and "'ready-made knowledge' such as the names, ages, and professions of characters," and are amenable to transfer.[64] However, *indices proper*

---

57 *Ibid* at 12.

58 *Ibid* at 13.

59 *Ibid*.

60 *Ibid*; Roland Barthes "Introduction to the Structural Analysis of Narratives" in Susana Onega & Jose Angel Garcia Landa, eds, *Narratology: An Introduction* (London: Longman, 1996). To use Barthes's own expression, "[f]or a function to be cardinal, it is enough that the action to which it refers open (or continue, or close) an alternative that is of direct consequence for the subsequent development of the story, in short that it inaugurate or conclude an uncertainty" at 51.

61 McFarlane, above note 53 at 14.

62 *Ibid*; Barthes, above note 60. As Barthes puts it, these are the "trivial incidents or descriptions" at 51.

63 McFarlane, above note 53 at 14.

64 *Ibid*.

relate to diffuse aspects such as "character and atmosphere" and at best can be adapted to the screen.[65]

McFarlane applies Barthes structural analysis to the movie *Cape Fear*[66] as sourced from the novel *The Executioners*.[67] He lists twenty-two cardinal functions found in the book. All but one of these functions is preserved in the movie though almost half of them are elaborated or expressed somewhat differently than in the book.[68] Still, McFarlane maintains:

> Overall, then, there is a close parallel between the cardinal functions which carry the action in the novel and those in the film. Sometimes, as indicated, these appear in different orders in the two texts, and sometimes the motivations for the actions vary from one text to the other. However, in terms of the pattern of narrative development which shapes the film as a whole, as distinct from the cardinal functions of varying degrees of importance within individual segments, there is considerable correspondence. The social and affective discrepancies between the two texts will generally be located at other levels of the texts, sometimes at the level of the catalysers which surround the cardinal functions . . . but more significantly at the level of enunciation, through the exercise of those strategies peculiar to the medium in question.[69]

McFarlane thus adopts Bluestone's criticisms of adaptation yet, relying on Barthes, is systematic in identifying elements of a book that are more and less capable of being expressed in film.

Kamilla Elliott seems perhaps the most sanguine about the adaptation process.[70] Her thesis is that both film and novel possess complete signs that are both approximate and analogous to each other, thus obviating the need to split form from content or morph words into images.[71] Two kinds of analogy help accomplish this task. The more intuitive structural analogy "upholds categorizations of novels as words and films as images and the inviolable bond of signifier and signified" and locates "visual equivalents for

---

65 *Ibid*.

66 *Cape Fear*, DVD, directed by J Lee Thompson (1962; Universal City, CA: Universal Pictures, 2001).

67 John D MacDonald, *The Executioners* (New York: Simon and Shuster, 1957).

68 McFarlane, above note 53 at 175–76.

69 *Ibid* at 178.

70 Kamilla Elliott, *Rethinking the Film/Novel Debate* (Cambridge: Cambridge University Press, 2003).

71 *Ibid* at 4.

verbal expression without admitting any inherence between words and images or any separation of form and content."[72] Secondly, and less intuitively, her looking glass model of analogy takes the possibility of transfer even further. Here, she argues an inverse cognitive process between the visualizing of verbal images and the verbalization of perceptual images:

> Verbalizing and visualizing thus prove to be connected rather than opposed cognitive processes. But they are not simply "connected": rather, they inhere looking glass fashion. The cognition of mental images and of perceptual images has been shown to be a directly inverse process: "the [mental] image is first represented as *sensationless qualities* and later represented as *sensory qualities*, whereas the percept is first represented as *sensory qualities* and later represented as *sensationless qualities*."[73]

The cognitive distinctions between the imagery of the written word and visual perceptions are thus minimized. While this may or may not be so, we know too little about how such processes work to derive much analytical clarity from exploring this approach further.

D. DISCUSSION

In this final section I would like to revisit the key elements of the legal test for infringement of the adaptation right (i.e., plot, theme, and characters) as these are illuminated by the above perspectives.[74] In so doing, I reject the constructivist thesis, i.e., that there is no essence or fixed nature to a work. I do not disagree that interpretations of a work can differ at an abstract level. However, this does not mean that it is impossible to find consensus as to what is basically happening in a plot line or how we may understand a character. Inaccurate descriptions of a plot line, such as between *Romeo and Ju-*

---

72 *Ibid* at 195. "However, given the cliched and monosyllabic nature of most visual symbols, this model of adaptation feeds perceptions that film and television are crude and reductive modes of representation far inferior to verbal representation" at 195.

73 *Ibid* at 222 [emphasis in original][footnote omitted].

74 The other elements of the test must be relatively insignificant to copyright infringement analysis as they are too basic to have much analytical weight: the feel, mood, or pace of a work is too non-specific, while setting must be viewed as incidental to the plot and characters. Sequence of events and structure will be subsumed in the discussion on plot and characterization; see also Y'Barbo, above note 1 at 356–59, in particular see his discussion of "total concept and feel," and "pace"; one might also add that the *concept* of work likely resides in the realm of idea rather than expression and should not be subject to copyright protection.

liet and *West Side Story*, should not be mistaken for interpretative ambiguity. Constructivism assists more in helping us understand that instability may lie in more abstract levels of the work. There may be contested interpretations as to a meaning or message of a work or that cultural or temporal contexts may radically alter an appreciation of a work. For example, the stereotyped portrayal of Jewish characters in *Nichols* may be viewed by a contemporary audience as "highly offensive" rather than "humorous and benign" as they would be to a 1920s audience.[75] At the level of meaning, theme, and aesthetic appeal, works are much less stable than at the more basic level of description.

Having cleared the constructivist hurdle, we now confront the possibility of an essence that may lend itself to adaptation. Bluestone's thesis on adaptation seems as strong today as it was when he wrote his book in the late 1950s. The semiotic systems of literature and film are profoundly different. It is an overly broad claim to argue that while these fundamental differences exist, they can be accommodated through analogical devices. What analogical device exists in film to adapt a long, nuanced internal monologue of a character? Is it possible to communicate this in any way other than by literary text? In addition to the inherent problems of representing or communicating the verbal into the visual, film versions are often intentional mutations of the book whether as an abridged or changed plot line, through omitted and simplified characterizations, or otherwise. The combined impact of intentional modifications and untransferable expression means that the film cannot remain truly faithful to the book. However, we all know from experience that something familiar carries forward from book to film. That something must be the element of the narrative.

McFarlane's approach brings greater analytical clarity to this process by which a book's narrative finds expression in film. We are able to identify that which may be more or less successfully transferred (i.e., for which there are visual equivalents) from that which cannot. Characterization is identified, quite rightly, as less amenable to transfer. To be sure, the raw data of a character, e.g., her age or occupation, are easily transferable to film as is the dialogue of the book. Appearances, and audience reception, of the character are less transferable as actor portrayal and costumes may convey quite a different image and impression than that conjured up in a book. But it is difficult if not impossible, for example, to convey the depth of a character,

75 Rotstein, above note 18 at 793.

or that character's development, in a novel when it relies heavily on internal monologues and other devices as conveyed from the privileged position of the author. Voice-overs, visual stimuli, and/or dialogue can attempt to convey these aspects of character but it will always fall far short of the detailed and nuanced development of the literary portrayal. Apart from dialogue, then, we might have reason to suspect that it would be very difficult to copy a character from book to film.

McFarlane's analytical framework is particularly helpful in dissecting plot. Rather than gauging infringement from impressionistically assessing similarities in plot as a whole, a bifurcated analysis is offered. The main points in the progression of a plot, or *cardinal functions*, are distinguished from the incidents of expression, or *catalyzer functions*. As such, it is possible that cardinal functions may be substantially replicated in film yet adorned with wholly original incidents. The American adaptations of Akira Kurosawa's works are examples of this. Thus, *The Magnificent Seven*[76] shared many (though certainly not all) of the cardinal functions of the *Seven Samurai*.[77] However, this structural similarity may not be apparent to an ordinary observer who might see these as distinct genres of film with little in common. More typically, we can imagine that many of the incidents of a novel may stay the same but in service to crucial changes in cardinal functions. Such portrayals may give the audience a superficial experience of seeing a faithful adaptation though the underlying narrative hinge points have been substantially altered. The changes to *The Grapes of Wrath*, discussed earlier, are an example of this. Of course, not all changes to a plot line are equally important: the changed ending to Steinbeck's classic is much more serious a change than the omission of the novel's natural imagery. Nor should it necessarily matter, as McFarlane's example of *Cape Fear* illustrates, whether the film version alters the sequence of events.

Sometimes the deliberate changing of a plot line — e.g., a different ending or deletion of scenes — can substantially alter a theme notwithstanding a surface fidelity to much of the plot line. A theme or message of the book must, at least for authors and audiences of high literature, be considered of great importance to the integrity and appreciation of a work. Changes in cardinal functions, like the changing of an ending can be a fatal attack on a

---

76 *The Magnificent Seven*, DVD, directed by John Sturges (1960; Los Angeles, CA: United Artists Corp, 2001).

77 *Seven Samurai*, DVD, directed by Akira Kurosawa (1956; Los Angeles, CA: Columbia Pictures USA, 2002).

main theme not to mention a story's main character. The cold war version of *The Quiet American*[78] is a vivid example of this.

Graham Greene's classic story portrays a 1950s English correspondent Thomas Fowler stationed in Saigon who, amid the burgeoning civil war, is too cynical to choose sides. His friendship with an American, Pyle, who earlier in the book saves his life, becomes strained when Pyle wins the affections of Fowler's mistress, to whom Fowler is very strongly attached. Pyle is in fact a CIA agent who is in Vietnam to assist General Thé's third force in their bloody effort to seize power. When Fowler discovers Pyle's true identity and his orchestration in a bombing by the third force, which kills and maims many people, he realizes he must choose sides and intervene to save innocent lives. Fowler's decision to help set up Pyle's assassination is a morally complex one as his motives are at least partly selfish — i.e., the winning back of his mistress. Joseph L Mankiewicz's 1956 adaptation of this book[79] makes the following changes:

- The motive for Fowler's conspiracy with the Communists to kill Pyle is made explicitly personal, i.e., to win back his mistress;[80]
- A changed ending which makes clear that Pyle was not a CIA agent but an innocent and that Fowler was duped by the Communists;[81]
- A favourable portrayal of General Thé and the third force;[82] and
- The omission of the human consequences of war.[83]

With just these few changes, we have a substantial deviation from novel to film in the most important aspects. An anti-war, anti-imperialist theme is replaced with an optimistic view of the third force in Vietnam. The moral complexity of Fowler's decision (i.e., whether to be complicit in the assassination of a man who has saved his own life but threatens the lives of many others and who competes for his mistress) and the development of his character from a man who does not take sides to one who does for a noble reason, is eviscerated by a simplistic portrayal of a man who is both selfish in

78 Graham Greene, *The Quiet American* (London: William Heinemann, 1955).

79 *The Quiet American*, DVD, directed by Joseph L Mankiewicz (1958; Los Angeles, CA: United Artists Corp, 2005).

80 Brian Neve, "Adaptation and the Cold War: Mankiewicz's *The Quiet American*" in James M Welsh & Peter Lev, eds, *The Literature/Film Reader: Issues of Adaptation* (Lanham: Scarecrow Press, 2007) 235 at 238 and 241 [Welsh & Lev, *Adaptation*].

81 *Ibid* at 240–41.

82 *Ibid* at 239.

83 *Ibid* at 240.

his motives, and gullible at the hands of the bad Communists. So jarring are changes in this characterization that one scholar comments: "If one is going to throw away Greene's justly achieved moral ambivalence, then one would do better to choose another source to transform or write one's own script from scratch."[84] Thus, the changing of an important cardinal function or two can have an enormous impact on the themes of, and characterization within, a book.

E. CONCLUSION

The ordinary observer test for copyright infringement sacrifices analytical clarity for the ease of impressionistic comparisons. The tools for a more sophisticated analysis are available when we look outward from law to other disciplines of study. Drawing on these other disciplines, the purpose of this paper has been to (1) highlight the difficulties, and in some aspects impossibilities, of adapting book to film; and (2) provide insights that might contribute to an improved analytical framework for copyright infringement in this context. Importantly, it remains to be seen the manner in which the particular analytical framework advanced in this paper fits with the idea/expression dichotomy. In a recent copyright infringement case, the Quebec Court of Appeal admitted an expert opinion which assessed a work in terms of "its structure and composition and the way its elements are arranged . . . . things that are not perceived directly . . . ."[85] The court believed that the expert opinion assisted in making comparisons that were not perceived directly, i.e., the deeper structure or "'intelligible' form."[86] We can only hope that this represents the beginning of a trend where courts look to extra-legal disciplinary perspectives to assist in their analysis of copyright infringement.

84 Kenneth C Pellow, "All the Quiet Americans" in Welsh & Lev, *Adaptation*, above note 80 at 247.

85 *France Animation sa c Robinson*, 2011 QCCA 1361 at 80, leave to appeal to SCC granted, *Cinar Corporation et al v Claude Robinson et al*, 2012 SCC 25; my thanks to Professor Pierre-Emmanuel Moyse for drawing this case to my attention.

86 *Ibid* at 80.

TWO

Out of Tune: Why Copyright Law Needs Music Lessons

CARYS CRAIG & GUILLAUME LAROCHE

ABSTRACT (EN): This chapter offers a critical analysis of copyright law that integrates insights from music. The authors argue that the unique qualities of musical works magnify the mismatch between creative practices and copyright doctrine, and suggest that an interdisciplinary analysis can shine a revealing light on both the problem and potential paths to improvement. Beginning with an overview of copyright doctrine in Canada in respect of musical works and music infringement claims, the authors then borrow analytical concepts from the discipline of music theory to problematize copyright's "reasonable listener" test for determining substantial copying. Using a specially-designed musical composition, the authors illustrate how and why this test may fail to perform its necessary role in the infringement analysis. The authors conclude by identifying some ways in which the legal analysis could be improved, including a more extensive use of both expert and survey evidence, and greater consideration of the accepted norms and practices of the relevant creative community. The overarching aim of this chapter is to demonstrate the importance of bringing the insights from musical and other creative disciplines to bear on the law of copyright, so that it might more accurately reflect the very practices it is meant to encourage.

RÉSUMÉ (FR) : Ce chapitre présente une analyse critique du droit d'auteur qui intègre des perspectives de la musique. Les auteurs soutiennent que les qualités uniques des œuvres musicales amplifient la dissonance entre les pratiques créatives et la doctrine du droit d'auteur, et estiment qu'une analyse interdisciplinaire peut jeter de la lumière tant sur le problème que sur des pistes potentielles d'amélioration. Commençant d'abord par une vue d'ensemble de la doctrine du droit d'auteur sur les œuvres musicales et des actions en contrefaçon de la musique au Canada, les auteurs empruntent ensuite des concepts analytiques de la théorie musicale pour problématiser le test de « l'auditeur raisonnable » du droit d'auteur comme déterminant du copiage substantiel. En utilisant une composition musicale spécialement créée pour l'article, les auteurs illustrent comment et pourquoi ce test peut échouer dans son rôle lors d'une analyse de contrefaçon. Les auteurs concluent en identifiant certains moyens par lesquels l'analyse juridique pourrait être améliorée, notamment par l'utilisation plus extensive de preuves provenant d'experts et de survols académiques, et avec une plus grande prise en considération des normes et pratiques acceptées par la communauté créative touchée. Le but principal de ce chapitre est donc de démontrer l'apport important de la musique et d'autres disciplines créatives au droit d'auteur, de sorte qu'il puisse mieux refléter les pratiques que ce droit vise justement à encourager.

A. INTRODUCTION

It has been written that "somewhere along the line, the law of music copyright forgot to check in with the world of music."[1] Our aim, in this chapter, is to demonstrate the importance and potential significance of "checking in" with the world of music when considering the application of copyright doctrine to musical works. While this assertion applies with equal force to every aspect of the copyright inquiry — from definitions of originality to adjudications of fair dealing — our focus will be on the determination of substantial similarity in music copyright infringement cases, and in particular, on the so-called "recognizability" test.

We argue that the test for copyright infringement of musical works reveals a disconnect between the nature and processes of musical creation on one hand, and on the other hand, the vision of music and composition that informs the law. By highlighting this disconnect, we make a broader claim that the law does not, therefore, adequately account for the unique nature of music as a subject matter of copyright. This failure may produce regrettable results, both in terms of the practical application of the law in

1 J Michael Keyes, "Musical Musings: The Case for Rethinking Music Copyright Protection" (2004) 10:4 Mich Telecomm & Tech L Rev 407 at 430.

copyright cases, and in the way it is experienced by those in the musical arena. Our suspicion is that musical expression suffers more acutely than other forms of intellectual expression in the face of copyright's conceptual constraints. In a normative sense, common creative activities may be devalued and delegitimized as a result of the gap between cultural and legal norms. In a practical sense, creative processes may be stymied or chilled by the operation, or merely the spectre, of the law.

From a copyright policy perspective, moreover, the law's failure to account for the inherent qualities of music potentially undermines its capacity to advance the purposes of the copyright system — rewarding authors encouraging the creation and dissemination of "works of the arts and intellect"[2] — by upsetting the copyright balance. The problems we identify here may illustrate a more pervasive failure of our copyright system to adequately reflect and encourage creative processes as they occur in specific social and cultural contexts. These broader themes deserve more expansive consideration. For now, our modest goal is to problematize the application of copyright's infringement test in the musical sphere, to illustrate the importance of bringing music theory into the realm of copyright theory, and perhaps to hint at the greater discord that accompanies the legal concepts at play.

We begin, in Section B, with an overview of copyright doctrine in Canada, and its application to musical works and music infringement claims. In Section C we explain some basics of musical structure and composition to critically analyze this legal formula, and use a specially modelled composition to demonstrate some of the problems with its application. We conclude, in Section D, by identifying practical and policy lessons that can be drawn from the musical analysis, as well as offering general observations about the importance of bringing insights from musical disciplines to bear on the law of copyright.

B. THE LAW OF MUSIC COPYRIGHT INFRINGEMENT

1) Why Music Is Special

Musical works, while different in nature from other categories of copyrightable works, are subject to the same legal principles. Copyright's one-size-fits-all model means that, notwithstanding the unique characteristics of any particular form of intellectual expression, the legal rules are applied

2 *Théberge v Galerie d'Art du Petit Champlain Inc*, 2002 SCC 34 at para 30.

across the board. The test for originality — whether a work involved the exercise of non-trivial skill and judgment[3] — applies equally to works of visual art and television listings. The distinction between general ideas and more specific authorial expression remains the same for a dramatic play or computer software code. Significantly, the determination of what constitutes a substantial part of a work involves the same considerations when applied to a cartoon character brooch and the film of a marching band.[4] In one sense, the broad applicability of copyright principles is the law's greatest strength. It has allowed copyright to adapt to vast changes in our cultural and technological environment, evolving from a limited right to copy books into a global system that defines legal rights over intellectual expression in the digital age. In another sense, however, general copyright principles overlook the specific dimensions of particular kinds of expressive activities and their cultural context. To the extent that the nature of music and the realities of its creation and enjoyment raise unique considerations, the copyright system should, we suggest, offer a more tailored legal approach consistent with its broader policy goals.

The claim that music is in some way unique amongst the categories of works that copyright protects seems at once obvious and in need of some justification. We see broadly four ways in which music differs, at least in degree if not in form, from most other types of copyrighted works. The first is that perhaps more than any other art form, music is engaged with and realized through its performance.[5] Music does not develop on paper, nor is it interacted with via visual or tactile means. Rather, the most basic medium of music involves sound waves sent through the air into the ears of an audience and experienced over time. The work does not simply exist as a painting might, it must be brought to life every time it is to be experienced. "[I]n no other type of art does time form so much the basis of, and is so strongly interwoven in, any aspect of artistic manifestation than in music."[6] Few people are just as satisfied to quietly read a musical score, in the way that

3 *CCH Canadian v Law Society of Upper Canada*, 2004 SCC 13 at para 16 [*CCH*].

4 *King Features Syndicate Inc v O and M Kleeman Ltd*, [1941] AC 417 HL; *Hawkes & Son (London) Ltd v Paramount Film Service Ltd*, [1934] 1 Ch 593 [*Hawkes & Son*].

5 We note in passing that choreography is similarly a performance-based media, realized through dance, typically to music. It would not be surprising to find that it shares with music some of the copyright problems that we identify.

6 Andreas Rahmatian, "Music and Creativity as Perceived by Copyright Law" (2005) 3 Intellectual Property Quarterly 267 at 272–73 [footnote omitted].

they would a book, as they are to attend a performance of the work or listen to a recording; performances in music are just better.

Second, music affords biological benefits that elude common understanding. It is not especially surprising that music helps refine the brain's processing of sounds,[7] but musicians' accrued abilities in the learning of foreign languages[8] and in mathematical thinking[9] are somewhat more astounding. While engagement with any art will refine the senses used to interact with the art,[10] music is special insofar as it trains the brain in areas seemingly unrelated to music itself. The neurological, physiological, and psychological responses that hearing music can generate are also well documented and remarkable.[11] Such studies support what we might intuitively know to be true: "More so than any other artistic endeavours, music possesses ethereal qualities that infiltrates and permeates multiple facets of our existence in a complex manner."[12]

Third, music is a language in its own right. The field of music theory seeks to illuminate how this language works, but one need not be a music theorist to grasp the field's basic truths; after all, even people with little musical education can tell when young children learning to play their instruments have accidentally hit the "wrong" note. There is something about the sound that we know does not belong, even though the vast majority of us could not explain why that note is incorrect whereas the one next to it on the keyboard sounds "right." If the sounds of the language of music are familiar, its mechanics are not.

Fourth, and most importantly for copyright, borrowing and copying among musicians is commonplace in the music world and an accepted part of musical practice. For the most part, taking someone else's musical idea and developing it in a new way is largely understood as part of musical culture and thus entirely consistent with cultural norms.[13] In fact, the relatedness of

---

7 Alexandra Parbery-Clark et al, "Musician Enhancement for Speech-In-Noise" (2009) 30:6 Ear & Hearing 653.

8 Patrick CM Wong et al, "Musical Experience Shapes Human Brainstem Encoding of Linguistic Pitch Patterns" (2007) 10:4 Nature Neuroscience 420.

9 Kathryn Vaughn, "Music and Mathematics: Modest Support for the Oft-Claimed Relationship" (2000) 34:3/4 Journal of Aesthetic Education 149.

10 Reading novels or poetry improves one's reading skills, cooking refines one's palette, etc.

11 See Keyes, above note 1 at 420–23; see generally Daniel J Levitin, *This is Your Brain on Music: The Science of a Human Obsession* (New York: Penguin Group, 2006).

12 Keyes, above note 1 at 420–21 [footnote omitted].

13 *Ibid* at 427 (offering numerous examples).

musical ideas is a core theme of the study of music composition. Contemporary classical composers study concepts such as musical unity and variation in the works of the great masters. In jazz, studying "standards" and their re-composition according to performers' unique musical tastes drives much musical education and innovation. "Covers" in popular music fulfill the same goals, albeit in a different style. Sampling and digital manipulation in hip-hop music also exemplify transformative re-use and its centrality in modern music-making.[14] In some sense, music creation *depends* on the borrowing and adaptation of material passed from one musician to another. This is not to suggest, of course, that musicians are the only artists who borrow from one another, and that only music is therefore worthy of special consideration in copyright; copyright law generally assumes a romantic vision of independent origination that sits uneasily with the realities of human creativity and culture at large.[15] Yet, the combination of a clear and established culture of musical borrowing, together with the special characteristics of musical expression (the importance of genres, performance techniques, and aural perception in particular), magnifies the mismatch between creative practice and the structures (and strictures) of copyright law.

Taken as a whole, these features suggest that we do not engage with music in the same way that we engage with the visual or literary arts, nor does music engender only musical appreciation. There is something more fundamental in the nature of musical expression and the human response that it generates. The features of musical culture and the ubiquity of musical borrowing reveal a dramatic divergence between the shared norms and practices of music culture and a doctrinal copyright approach.[16] Hence, there is something to be said about music as a unique category within copyright, both deserving and in need of special consideration.

---

14 Use of prior recordings as the musical object for transformation presents another layer of copyright issues relating to the "neighbouring rights" of performers and sound recording makers (see *Copyright Act*, RSC 1985, c C-42, ss 15–21 [*Copyright Act*]). In order to focus on prima facie infringement of copyright in musical works, we exclude neighbouring rights issues from our analysis. Note that the potential for the assertion of neighbouring rights to prevent *de minimis* uses and fair dealing with recorded music is another highly problematic feature of copyright law in the realm of music: see, for example, *Bridgeport Music Inc v Dimension Films*, 410 F 3d 792 (6th Cir 2005).

15 For a critique of copyright law's vision of the author, originality, and cultural practices, see Carys J Craig, *Copyright, Communication and Culture: Towards a Relational Theory of Copyright Law* (Northamption, MA: Edward Elgar Press, 2011).

16 See Keyes, above note 1 at 426–30; see also Olufunmilayo B Arewa, "From JC Bach to Hip Hop: Musical Borrowing, Copyright and Cultural Context" (2006) 84:2 NC L Rev 547.

2) Copyright's Original Musical Work

Copyright law protects "every original literary, dramatic, musical and artistic work."[17] A musical work is defined, tautologically, as "any work of music or musical composition, with or without words . . . ."[18] Of course, music (like art) has no intrinsic definition, and which sounds count as "music" is inherently contestable.[19] As a cultural category, music is whatever we, in our shared culture, designate as such; as a legal category, the same is now true. Prior to a 1993 amendment, the statutory definition included only "any combination of melody and harmony, or either of them, printed, reduced to writing or otherwise graphically produced or reproduced."[20] By departing from the requirement of melody or harmony, the amended definition opened the door to more experimental, less traditional forms of auditory expression. It also dislodged the assumption that musical works must be fixed as graphical reproductions or sheet music for copyright to vest.[21] As with all copyrightable expression, some form of physical embodiment or "fixation" is required, but this can be achieved through virtually any means of recording. Importantly, the work is not reducible to its fixed form; as a legal category, the musical work refers to the composition *per se*, and not to any particular interpretation or performance thereof.[22]

Although a musical work may be protected by copyright, not every element of that work will belong to the copyright owner. As with any kind of work, critical aspects may belong to the public domain. Thus, non-original

---

17 *Copyright Act*, above note 14, s 5(1).

18 *Ibid*, s 2.

19 See Michael W Carroll, "Whose Music is it Anyway? How We Came to View Musical Expression as a Form of Property" (2004) 72:4 U Cin L Rev 1405. "Music has no intrinsic definition. It is a cultural category consisting of any sounds that those in a society or culture designate as 'music' instead of 'noise,' along with any notation, recording, or other means of capturing or representing such sounds" at 1417.

20 *Copyright Act*, above note 14, s 2, as amended by SC 1993, c 23, s 1.

21 See *Composers, Authors & Publishers Association of Canada Ltd v CTV Television Network Ltd*, [1968] SCR 676 at 680. Justice Pigeon held that transmission of a television signal did not infringe the copyright in a musical work, since musical works, as defined by the Act, consisted of only graphical reproductions of melody and harmony; broadcasting a television signal communicated a "performance of the works," not the "works" themselves.

22 A performer's performance and its sound recording are protected by a "neighbouring rights" regime. The relationship between the performance and the musical work is less clear than this distinction implies: see Keyes, above note 1 at 428–29; *Newton v Diamond*, 204 F Supp (2d) 1244 (2002); Olufunmilayo B Arewa, "Writing Rights: Copyright's Visual Bias and African American Music" (2012) UC Irvine School of Law, Legal Studies Research Paper Series No. 2012-9, online: http://papers.ssrn.com/sol3/papers.cfm?abstract_id=2010024.

elements of a musical work, whether borrowed from another work or from the "common stock" of musical compositions, are not within the scope of the owner's right. The use of arpeggios in major or minor keys, for example, cannot give rise to a copyright interest in the arpeggio, which has been a building block of classical Western music for hundreds of years. The process of selecting or arranging common elements using more than trivial skill and judgment will produce a copyrightable work;[23] the copyright owner cannot, however, lay claim to those elements of the work that are not her original contribution.

Perhaps most fundamentally, the ideas contained in the work are not protected by copyright, but only the expression of these ideas. The critical legal line between ideas and expression is never easy to draw, but in the case of musical works the distinction is particularly elusive. The exclusion of abstract ideas from copyright's scope means that no one can claim an exclusive right to produce songs about, say, falling in love. It also precludes the monopolization of any genre of music, compositional methodology, or general pattern or structure (verse-chorus-verse-chorus-bridge-verse, for example). Copyright's *scènes à faire* doctrine excludes from protection any elements of a work that are mandatory or customary to the work's genre. In the musical context, the doctrine ensures that customary refrains, common chord progressions, scales, and musical metres remain in the public domain. Copyright's "merger" doctrine further ensures that, where a musical expression merges with the idea (because the idea can be expressed in only a limited number of ways), the expression will not be protected.[24] Admittedly, the "considerable difficulty" with the application of the merger doctrine that Justice Reed described in *Apple Computers Inc v Mackintosh Computers Ltd* resonates in the musical context: it might be said that musical works, like poems and paintings, necessarily "exhibit a merger of the idea they convey and the expression thereof . . . ." unless the idea communicated "is described in highly abstract, remote and general terms . . . ."[25] There is no clear answer to the question of when, in music, idea and expression can be said to have merged.

Also unclear is the practical significance of the claim that the idea-expression dichotomy leaves others free to express anew the same musical ideas. Whereas in dealings with literary expression, it is a common and sim-

---

23 *CCH*, above note 3 at para 16.

24 See, for example, *Morrisey v Procter & Gamble*, 379 F 2d 675 (1st Cir 1967); *Delrina Corp v Triolet Systems Inc*, [1993] OJ No 319 (Gen Div), aff'd (2002), 58 OR (3d) 339 (CA) [*Delrina Corp*].

25 *Apple Computers Inc v Mackintosh Computers Ltd*, [1987] 1 FC 173 at 187.

ple practice to abstract and reformulate ideas into non-infringing expression (what we might typically think of as paraphrasing), the reformulation of musical ideas into non-infringing musical expression (wherein the original musical expression is not substantially recognizable) is more challenging. A written statement can readily be expressed in different words but retain the original meaning or idea; it is hard to conceptualize how different musical works could communicate a musical idea that is substantially the same without sounding substantially similar. Said otherwise, a sufficiently different musical expression will almost necessarily express a different idea.

Notwithstanding the difficulties inherent in the application of copyright doctrine to musical works, the principles that limit the reach of an owner's rights are fundamental to the copyright system as a whole, and the balance it must strike. In light of the unique characteristics of music already identified, it is tempting to claim that the limits of copyright and the free accessibility of public domain material are of particular importance in the context of musical works. Copyright infringement claims in this context must be carefully examined to ensure that the law does not, in substance or effect, unduly restrict creative musical practices.

3) Copyright Infringement in Canada

It is an infringement of copyright for any person to do, without the consent of the copyright owner, any act that is within the owner's exclusive rights.[26] There are two necessary components to copyright infringement: first, there must in fact have been copying of the plaintiff's work; second, the amount copied must be of all or a substantial part of the plaintiff's work. In the United States' jurisprudence, these two components have been helpfully labelled as (1) actual copying, and (2) illicit (or unlawful) copying.[27] The bifurcated test underscores two essential propositions: the act of copying is not inherently unlawful, but will infringe copyright only when it amounts to a substantial taking; and a substantially similar work is not necessarily infringing, but will infringe copyright only where the similarity is the result of copying.

---

26 The owner has the exclusive right to reproduce the work or any substantial part thereof in any material form whatever; to perform the work or any substantial part thereof in public; and, if the work is unpublished, to publish the work or any substantial part thereof: see *Copyright Act*, above note 14, ss 3(1) and 27(1).

27 *Arnstein v Porter*, 154 F 2d 464 (2d Cir 1946), aff'd on rehearing 158 F 2d 795 (2d Cir 1946) [*Porter*]; for a more detailed analysis of the two-step test, see Mark A Lemley, "Our Bizarre System for Proving Copyright Infringement" (2010) 57:4 J Copyright Soc'y USA 719 at 719.

a) Proof of Copying

With regard to the requirement of actual copying, there is rarely direct evidence that the defendant composed her music with the plaintiff's work before her or playing in her ears. Rather, to establish copying on the balance of probabilities requires proof that the defendant had access to the plaintiff's work together with a sufficient objective similarity between the two works.[28] The similarities between the works must be the result of a causal connection such that the original is the source of the copy.[29]

Access to the original could be shown by presenting evidence that the defendant attended a performance or received a copy of the plaintiff's work. A causal connection could also be demonstrated through evidence of the popularity or broad dissemination of the work.[30] Arguably, the greater the degree of similarity between the two works at issue, the less is required of the plaintiff to prove that the defendant had access to the original work. Some American cases have gone so far as to find that, where the similarity is so "striking" as to preclude the possibility of independent creation, access may be inferred.[31] However, it should be stressed that, without a causal connection, there is no copying, and any similarities must be the result of coincidence and should not give rise to liability.[32] In the Internet age, even this stricter evidentiary requirement to prove access may have lost some of its significance; any work available online is a work to which access would be at least possible, and certainly difficult to disprove.[33] This new reality raises the specter of findings of copying based almost entirely on the high degree of similarity between musical works. Once sufficient objective similarity and causal connection are established, it is no defence for the defendant to

---

28 *Francis Day & Hunter Ltd v Bron*, [1963] Ch 587 [*Francis Day*]; *Gondos v Hardy et al*, *Gondos v Toth* (1982), 64 CPR (2d) 145 [*Hardy*].

29 See generally *Boutin v Distributions CLB Inc*, [1992] 46 CPR (3d) 395 (QCA); appeal allowed (1994), 54 CPR (3d) 160 (SCC).

30 For example, *Bright Tunes Music v Harrisongs Music*, 420 F Supp 177 (SDNY 1976) [*Harrisongs*].

31 *Heim v Universal Pictures Co*, 154 F 2d 480 (2d Cir 1946); *Jones v Supreme Music Corp*, 101 F Supp 989 (SDNY 1951) at 990. This approach can be contrasted with the famous dicta of Lord Diplock in *Francis Day*, above note 28, and was explicitly rejected by the Ontario court in *Hardy*, above note 28.

32 *Hardy*, *ibid* at para 34, citing Lord Diplock in *Francis Day*, above note 28 at 624.

33 See Ann Bartow, "Copyrights and Creative Copying" (2003–2004) 1 U Ottawa L & Tech J 75 at 83–84, quoting Karen Bevill, "Note: Copyright Infringement and Access: Has the Access Requirement Lost Its Probative Value?" (1999) 52:1 Rutgers L Rev 311 at 311–12; although the defendant does not bear the legal burden of disproving infringement, in the face of substantial similarity, the tactical burden may shift to the defendant to provide some other explanation for objective similarities.

claim that she did not know she was copying. Because neither knowledge nor intent is a requirement for infringement liability, it has been held that even unconscious copying may result in a finding of infringement.[34]

The assessment of objective similarity in this part of the infringement test is conducted with a view to determining the probability of copying. It is appropriate to have regard not only to a note-to-note comparison of the works, but also to the "effect on the ear" of the works.[35] A court may be prepared to infer copying where the degree of similarity between two works "is such that an ordinary reasonably experienced listener might think that perhaps one had come from the other."[36] It is widely accepted that there is also an important role here for expert evidence.[37] The appropriate conclusion to be drawn from apparent similarities between two musical works is a highly technical determination. It may be shown with the use of expert testimony that a striking similarity produced by the repetition of a particular note sequence, for example, is not probative of copying, but rather indicative of a common source or reliance on a compositional trope.[38] By the same token, an expert musicologist may convince the court that an apparently minor similarity is good evidence of copying in light of the uniqueness or idiosyncrasy of the portion reproduced.

b) Proof of Copying a "Substantial Part"

It is a fundamental principle of copyright that there is no inherent legal wrong in copying *per se*, but only in the copying of a whole work or a substantial part thereof. Where copying is established, then, the next question is how much and what has been copied.

The determination of substantial copying involves an assessment of both the quality and quantity of the portion copied in relation to the plaintiff's work as a whole. The addition of significant original content or the relative insignificance of the copied portion in the defendant's work are not,

---

34 See, for example, *Francis Day*, above note 28 at 600; *Hardy*, above note 28; *Harrisongs* above note 30; *Fred Fisher Inc v Dillingham*, 298 F 145 at 147 (SDNY 1924).

35 *Francis Day*, above note 28 at 608, Willmer J, citing in support *Austin v Columbia Gramophone Co Ltd* (1923), Macg CC (1917–1923) 398 at 409 and 415, Justice Astbury stating that infringement is to be determined "by the ear as well as by the eye".

36 *Francis Day*, above note 28 at 596.

37 See *Porter*, above note 27 at 468.

38 See, for example, *Arnstein v Edward B Marks Music Corp*, 82 F 2d 275 (2d Cir 1936); see also *Darrell v Joe Morris Music*, 113 F 2d 80 (2d Cir 1940).

strictly speaking, grounds for refusing to find prima facie infringement.[39] Creative borrowing does not make borrowing lawful.

Perhaps the muddiest part of copyright's infringement doctrine, in application at least, is the integrated analysis of the substantiality of the taking in quantitative and qualitative terms. In *Hawkes & Son*[40] the court found infringement of copyright in "Colonel Bogey's March" when a quantitatively small portion of the musical work was reproduced in a newsreel. The Court of Appeal overturned the ruling of Eve J, who had rejected the plaintiff's claim on grounds that the part copied was merely twenty seconds of the whole work, which would run for about four minutes. On appeal, Slesser LJ found that "other matters beyond mere quantity may and have to be looked at . . . ."[41] No matter how brief, part of a musical work is substantial if it is "a vital, and an essential part . . . ."[42] Justice Romer agreed that a substantial portion of the work was copied when "the principle air" was reproduced; "the air which every one who heard the march played through would recognize as being the essential air . . . ."[43] Following the reasoning of the court in *Hawkes & Son*, the Ontario High Court of Justice in *Canadian Performing Right Society Ltd v Canadian National Exhibition Association*[44] confirmed that, in Canada, "it is not merely by comparing the respective lengths of the whole work and of the part played that one is to reach a decision as to whether the part played is a substantial part . . . ."[45] The court was satisfied that a substantial part of the work was performed on the basis that "the part played was recognizable and in fact recognized . . . ."[46]

According to this so-called "recognizability test," if a part taken would be recognized by an ordinary, reasonable person familiar with the work, then that taking is substantial and may infringe copyright. In the United States, under the *Porter* two-part test, the key to determining whether copying amounted to an illicit appropriation is "whether defendant took from plaintiff's works so much of what is pleasing to the ears of lay listeners, who

39 The extent to which the plaintiff's work has been recontextualized or transformed may be of legal significance in the determining the availability of a fair dealing defence. See *Copyright Act*, above note 14, s 29.1; *Society of Composers, Authors and Music Publishers of Canada v Bell*, 2012 SCC 36 at para 24 [*Bell*].

40 *Hawkes & Son*, above note 4.

41 *Ibid* at 606.

42 *Ibid*.

43 *Ibid* at 609.

44 [1934] OR 610.

45 *Ibid* at 614.

46 *Ibid*.

comprise the audience for whom such popular music is composed, that defendant wrongfully appropriated something which belongs to the plaintiff."[47] Similarly, in the Canadian case of *Preston v 20th Century Fox Canada Ltd*,[48] which concerned the alleged copying of a movie script, the Federal Court described the test of substantial similarity as involving an assessment of "ultimately whether the average lay observer, at least one for whom the work is intended, would recognize the alleged copy as having been appropriated from the copyrighted work."[49]

The "average lay observer" test for determining copying of a "substantial part" is effectively copyright's equivalent to tort law's "reasonable person" test. Keyes suggests that this is a curious cameo by the reasonable person, whose historical and philosophical underpinnings "illustrate that this construct is a fish out of the common law waters that has been blindly cast into the music copyright infringement sea."[50] Whereas the legal function of the reasonable person is to represent social norms and minimum standards of behaviour in a community, copyright's reasonable listener does not gauge the conduct of the litigating parties; he merely determines how two works are likely to be perceived by an ordinary member of the intended audience. As Keyes cautions, "there is no accepted 'social norm' that would provide any meaningful standard on how a piece of music would be perceived by a 'reasonable listener.'"[51] This is because "music perception is an inherently subjective process that differs from individual to individual."[52]

Irina Manta further warns that the reasonable listener test in music infringement cases is vulnerable to all of the vagaries, biases, and misperceptions to which the reasonable person test is demonstrably prone.[53] Specifically, she argues, the substantiality determination lends itself to hindsight bias, such that a finding of copying, for example, will influence a decision maker to find substantial similarity.[54] Furthermore, the copyright inquiry can be distorted by an "anchoring bias" (whereby the plaintiff's original work becomes the "anchor" against which the defendant's work is

47 *Porter*, above note 27 at 473.
48 [1990] FCJ No 1011, 33 CPR (3d) 242 (TD), aff'd (1994), 53 CPR (3d) 407 (FCA) [*Preston*].
49 *Ibid* at 274 (TD cited to CPR).
50 Keyes, above note 1 at 431.
51 *Ibid* at 432.
52 *Ibid*.
53 Irina D Manta, "Reasonable Copyright" (2012) 53:4 BC L Rev 1303.
54 *Ibid* at 1339, citing Shyamkrishna Balganesh, "Foreseeability and Copyright Incentives" (2009) 122:6 Harv L Rev 1569 at 1631.

measured[55]), and "confirmation bias" (which leads a decision maker to favour a finding that confirms "existing beliefs, expectations or the hypothesis at hand"[56]). Each of these potential biases in the application of the lay listener infringement test tends towards favouring the plaintiff who alleges unlawful copying over the defendant tasked with refuting the claim.[57]

In addition to such principled and practical objections to the "average lay listener" test, considered in greater detail below, the test raises challenging questions about the role and relevance of expert testimony in music infringement cases. Applying the reasoning in *Porter*, at this second stage of the infringement determination, expert evidence is inappropriate. To the extent that it has been admitted by some courts, its (somewhat counter-intuitive) role has been restricted to supporting a conclusion about the likely response of the reasonable listener.[58] Mark Lemley convincingly argues that the availability of expert evidence in determinations of copying and its effective exclusion in respect to unlawful appropriation "has the analysis of proof exactly backwards . . . ."[59] The ordinary, lay listener may be well equipped to decide whether copying is likely in light of the degree of objective similarity between two works; the question of what has been copied and the legal significance of that copying, however, requires careful dissection of the plaintiff's work to separate protectable from non-protectable elements. Whereas the reasonable listener might discern copying from the similarities in the "aural appeal" of works taken as a whole, the lay listener will not — and likely cannot — parse musical ideas from expression, distinguish between original and borrowed musical elements, separate musical composition from performance techniques, or disregard commonplace compositional features. In short, the degree of legal complexity inherent in the substantiality determination makes it ill-suited to a reasonable person inquiry.[60]

This problem is compounded by the question that the average lay observer is notionally answering: is the plaintiff's work recognizable in the defendant's work? The mere recognizability of a work does not adequately

---

55 *Ibid* at 1341.

56 *Ibid* at 1342, quoting Raymond S Nickerson, "Confirmation Bias: A Ubiquitous Phenomenon in Many Guises" (1998) 2 Review of General Psychology 175 at 175.

57 *Ibid*.

58 *Porter*, above note 27 at 473; for a critique of this use of expert testimony, see Keyes, above note 1 at 435–36.

59 Lemley, above note 27 at 719.

60 Amy B Cohen, "Masking Copyright Decisionmaking: The Meaninglessness of Substantial Similarity" (1987) 20:4 UC Davis L Rev 719 at 740.

address the critical question of whether the part taken is a part that copyright protects. Musical ideas, non-original melodies, famous riffs, commonplace rhythms, generic chord progressions — all of these may be recognizable to the average listener, but none is legally relevant to the infringement determination. By focusing on whether the part taken can or cannot be recognized, the test fails to distinguish the protected from the public domain. The difficulty with the test is not merely one of potential overprotection of the plaintiff; by the same token, substantial original musical expression may in fact be copied without being recognizable to the average untrained ear.

Simply put, there are grounds for concern that copyright's test for determining infringement of musical works bears little relationship either to the appropriate legal inquiry or to the specificities of the subject matter at issue. In the following section, we turn to the world of music to highlight the nature and extent of these gaps in the law's approach to finding musical infringement.

C. SECOND GUESSING SUBSTANTIAL SIMILARITY

It is our argument that judicial assessments of musical similarity and recognizability at best distort, and in some cases radically depart from, the standards of music communities. By examining aspects of music theory[61] — alongside research into musical psychology[62] — we identify below some serious flaws that, in combination, suggest that current methods of evaluating claims of music copyright infringement are deeply problematic. A specially designed composition illustrates many of these problems.

1) Determining Similarity

As noted by Keyes, there is no such thing as an accepted social norm on how musical similarities should be perceived for copyright purposes.[63] This is

---

61 Don Michael Randel, ed, *The New Harvard Dictionary of Music* (Cambridge, MA: Belknap Press of Harvard University Press, 1986). Matthew Brown defines music theory as "the abstract principles embodied in music and the sounds of which it consists" *sub verbo* "theory" at 844; see also Patrick McCreless, "Contemporary Music Theory and the New Musicology: An Introduction" (1997) 15:3 Journal of Musicology 291.

62 Diana Deutsch et al, "Psychology of Music" Grove Music Online, Oxford Music Online (Oxford University Press), that is, "the discipline that studies individual human musical thought and behaviour from a scientific perspective" at introduction.

63 Keyes, above note 1 at 432.

far from the only challenge faced by the lay listener test in its determination of objective similarity. We focus on two particular problems: how aural determinations of similarity are easily manipulable; and how straightforward assessments of similarity fail to address the significance of the similarity in musical terms, with the result that they fail to distinguish the musical *scène à faire* from the protected musical expression.

It may seem to be stating the obvious to say that the lay listener test privileges an aural appreciation of music. But it bears emphasis that an uncritical acceptance of hearing-based evaluations of music may undermine the validity of such tests by conflating musical expression with what is aurally apparent. Jamie Lund suggests that the aural appreciation of music can be deeply flawed, and is more directed by similarity of timbre[64] than the similarity or prominence of musical events.[65] Simply put, two melodies sound more similar when they are played by the same instrument. Music psychologists back Lund's findings, with Carterette and Kendall agreeing that "[h]armonically related spectra [i.e., timbre] reinforce the sense of musical pitch . . . ."[66] This means that aural similarity is not necessarily the same thing as musical similarity, counterintuitive as this may seem. Our ears are biologically hardwired to believe two violin melodies are more alike than two melodies for two different instruments. This is not an absolute standard; timbre is only one part of the determination. Still, the fact that timbral similarities affect judgments of pitch-based similarity is important information for a court tasked by copyright law with determining whether two pitch-based melodies (or even harmonies, rhythms, etc.) sound the same — not whether they feature the same instrument. Musical laypersons are more likely to conflate the two because of their unspecialized understanding of music. This matters because the overwhelming majority of music copyright litigation features popular music, which rarely strays from its basic instrumental setup of a vocalist, an electric guitar, a bass guitar, and a drum kit. The influence of timbre on judgments of pitch-based music-

64 Timbre is the quality of a sound that makes a trumpet sound like a trumpet, and a piano sound like a piano (and not like a trumpet). Both the trumpet and piano can be playing the same note, but their respective timbres allow us to differentiate one instrument from the other.

65 See, generally, Jamie Lund, "An Empirical Examination of the Lay Listener Test in Music Composition Copyright Infringement" (2011) 11:1 Va Sports & Ent LJ 137 at 171.

66 Edward C Carterette & Roger A Kendall, "Comparative Music Perception and Cognition" in Diana Deutsch, ed, *The Psychology of Music*, 2d ed (San Diego: Academic Press, 1999) at 762.

al similarity, and the fallibility of the human ear that it reveals, suggests that the lay listener test should, at the very least, be supplemented by additional, non-aural kinds of musical analysis.

This is not to say, of course, that the lay ear is incapable of good musical observations. *Bright Tunes Music Corp v Harrisongs*[67] is an excellent case study in this regard. In comparing George Harrison's "My Sweet Lord" to The Chiffons' "He's So Fine," Owen J correctly noted:

> "He's So Fine," recorded in 1962, is a catchy tune consisting essentially of four repetitions of a very short basic musical phrase, "sol-mi-re," (hereinafter motif A), altered as necessary to fit the words, followed by four repetitions of another short basic musical phrase, "sol-la-do-la-do," (hereinafter motif B).[68]

In this particular instance, Owen J discovered musical form through listening (that is, he perceived by ear the sequencing of musical events in time). He later remarked that "My Sweet Lord" uses a similar form. What Owen J did next is of critical importance: he assessed the musical significance of the similarity he identified, relying on experts' testimony to conclude that such a form represents "a highly unique pattern."[69] Regrettably, few judges include this step in the lay listener test; after all, as previously noted, the lay listener test is supposed to represent a non-expert view of the music. But Owen J correctly appreciates that, without assessing the musical significance of a similarity, he has no way to tell if it is common stock or "a highly unique pattern." Said otherwise, he has no basis on which to determine if the similarity is probative of unlawful copying. A survey of copyright infringement cases, as well as descriptions of the lay listener test, confirm that Owen J's vital extra step is often lost in music copyright actions.[70]

This point leads to the second core problem: the significance of identified similarities. Some aspects of musical composition, regardless of genre, are inherently alike. Probably the best example of this is the notion of "con-

---

67 *Harrisongs*, above note 30.

68 *Ibid* at 178 [footnotes omitted].

69 *Ibid*. We disagree with this assessment in musical terms, but for our purposes it is more important that Owen J assessed the importance in and of itself than it is that he drew what we view as the correct conclusion.

70 A small sampling includes: *Hawkes & Son*, above note 4; *Redwood Music Ltd v Chappell & Co Ltd*, [1982] RPC 109; *Godfrey v Lees*, [1995] EMLR 307 (Ch); *Hadley v Kemp*, [1999] EMLR 589; *Herald Square Music v Living Music*, 205 USPQ 1241 (SDNY 1978).

cluding functions."[71] Concluding functions in music fulfill the same role as the period in written language: they mark the end of a complete musical thought. Instead of doing so through symbolic means as does language, or a lowering of vocal intonation and short pause when speaking, concluding functions in music are harmonically constructed around a limited number of chord sequences, the appearance of which marks the end of a musical phrase. While the harmonies of concluding functions may vary from style to style—Mozart's concluding functions are unlike Led Zeppelin's—the notion of the concluding function remains constant. A common concluding function in rock music sees the chord of IV move to the chord of I in a certain metric disposition (that is, the relationship of strongly and weakly stressed beats). Many rock phrases end with this "cadence." To an astute but context-ignorant layperson in court, two rock phrases in two contested works may thus appear similar because both phrases end with the same harmonic pattern; harmonies necessarily affect the selection of consonant pitches that can be used in the melody, meaning phrase endings often feature the same notes in a particular style of music. Additionally, rhythmic activity in the music slows at phrase endings. Hence, a layperson might conclude that similar phrase endings in two contested melodies represent strong evidence of copying. It would be a reasonable conclusion for the average listener to draw, given her knowledge, but it would be dreadfully wrong in music — as wrong as concluding that one fairy tale is copied from another because both end with "happily ever after."

Many of the similarities in "aural appeal" that might give rise to a finding of copying simply cannot support it. Without sufficient appreciation of the musical significance of apparent similarities, the fundamental distinction between independent creation and unlawful copying cannot be satisfactorily drawn. The understanding that music theory brings to copyright cases is not merely "interesting but extraneous" information; it is vital to upholding some of copyright's most foundational norms. The lay listener test circumvents music theory, thus bypassing critical steps in the infringement inquiry—steps that are of recognized importance in respect of other expressive forms.[72]

71 We borrow the terms of music theorist William Caplin here, from his study of phrase-functional forms in classical music. The same principles — musical phrases have a beginning, middle, and end — are present in all styles of music: see William Caplin, *Classical Form: A Theory of Formal Functions for the Instrumental Music of Haydn, Mozart, and Beethoven* (Oxford: Oxford University Press, 1998) at 254.

72 See, for example, *Preston*, above note 48; *Delrina Corp*, above note 24; Lemley, above note 27 at 719 similarly compares the infringement test in music copyright cases unfavourably to the more careful dissection undertaken in computer software cases.

2) Determining Recognizability

It is with regard to determinations of "recognizability" that the lay listener test takes on its primary importance; after all, if recognizability is the key to establishing substantial copying, then it does not matter how great the similarities between two works are unless they can be recognized aurally by the average lay listener. Two scenarios require special consideration of the ramifications of this test: first, a situation where copying has occurred but goes unrecognized; and second, when copying has not occurred, but some similarities between two works are nonetheless recognizable. To help illustrate the problems that emerge from each scenario, consider this model composition, which we have specially prepared for this purpose:

Figure 2.1

A recording of the work is available for readers' benefit,[73] and we encourage readers to listen to the composition a few times. The first few times one listens to the work, there is nothing particularly special about it. It sounds like something your talented nephew might play. Almost certainly, no copyright issues are immediately apparent.

Yet, that initial impression is mistaken. The composition is replete with instances of potential infringement. Key phrases from four extremely well-known musical works were copied and inserted into the work — not all of them currently protected by copyright, but for our purposes, let us suppose that they are. We openly admit that we copied musical expression from other sources, and that, were the purposes of the work not to make an academic point but rather to reap riches of our creative genius, then we might be found liable for copyright infringement. Such admissions, however, have no bearing on the recognizability of the copied melodies. Their timbres are different, heard on a piano instead of their original performing forces; the musical segments fulfill different musical functions, where a melody is transformed into a bass line, or an initiating function (similar to a concluding function, except marking the beginning of a musical phrase) is shifted into a different syntactical role; or the metric alignment of a well-known fragment is displaced, emphasizing different notes than in the original. The musical context of the copied expression is different, and, even though the musical expressions are note-for-note the same, they manage to express something different than they did in their original context. All of this means that the lay listener — presumably, you — has difficulty pinpointing from which works we have borrowed. It is similarity without recognizability. In copyright terms, it is literal copying of an essential and vital part of a protected work without substantial similarity (and so, it would seem to follow, without infringing copyright).

Such a failure of the lay listener test on copyright's own terms ought handily to illustrate why a simple listening standard for music copyright infringement is an unsuitable arbiter of unlawful copying. Copied material gets by the ear where it would not get by the letter of the law. While it would be easy to dismiss all of this as merely academic, musical culture suggests otherwise. As other copyright scholars have noted,[74] in pop musical culture, the taking and adapting of others' musical ideas is what drives innova-

---

73 Guillaume Laroche, "Sinfonietta in C Minor" (2012), online: IP Osgoode www.iposgoode.ca/?attachment_id=21753.

74 See generally Anne Barron, "Introduction: Harmony or Dissonance? Copyright Concepts and Musical Practice" (2006) 15:1 Soc & Leg Stud 25; see also Lionel Bently, "Authorship of Popular Music in UK Copyright Law" (2009) 12:2 Information, Communication & Society 179.

tion; copyright, by imposing liability for adaptations of existing works, sits askew of this culture. On its face, the protection afforded to the exclusive rights of the copyright owner would seem to demand that such substantial reproduction constitute prima facie infringement — a conclusion that the "recognizability test," as currently understood, apparently fails to produce in the case of our model composition. The test, then, runs counter to some central claims of copyright. We cannot resist suggesting, in passing, that this failure of copyright law is a victory for musical culture, but for now, our intention is merely to identify this internal inconsistency.

The second scenario, where copying is questionable but some degree of recognizability is easily perceived, demands that we reveal which works we borrowed from in our earlier model composition. Here they are:

Figure 2.2

For the purposes of this second scenario, let us suppose that we did not copy the above works, but rather, by extraordinary coincidence, we composed a work with such similarities to those of Nirvana, Beethoven, Wagner, and Britney Spears.[75] The question now becomes how familiarity affects recognizability. Listen to the work a few more times with these musical referential markers on which to focus. Eventually, the infringing melodies reveal themselves to the ear, and, increasingly, they stand out from the rest of the music; the piece becomes a series of quotations. In short, recognizing a well-known melodic theme in a new musical context is possible, given a sufficient number of listenings, and perhaps even easy when one knows what to listen for.

A musical psychology study by Lucy Pollard-Gott showed the same process as that described above, albeit in a more complex musical environment.[76] Pollard-Gott based her study around Franz Liszt's Sonata in B minor, a tricky work in which three main musical ideas (named Theme A, Theme B, and the Transfer Theme in the study) continuously reinvent themselves in a twenty-five-minute solo piano piece. Theme A is heard as a melody, later as a bass line, later again as a countermelody to another theme, and so on, never quite the same but always similar. The other themes follow the same pattern. The question Pollard-Gott asked was to what extent familiarity with a theme (say, Theme B) affects its recognizability in some modified form (say, the sixth appearance of Theme B). She tested both musicians and non-musicians. She found that, as listeners became more familiar with a given theme and listened to varied versions of that theme, both musicians and non-musicians were more able to identify elements of "theme structure"[77] in variations. In plain language, the better someone knows a musical theme, and in a context where she is asked to compare that theme to another, the more likely it is she will draw a link between the two themes and deem them to be related, even when the two themes are somewhat dissimilar yet loosely share some common musical features.

This finding has tremendous implications for the lay listener test. First, it suggests that the recognition of similarity is an acquired skill, not a stable

75 We trust the Beethoven and Wagner excerpts are sufficiently well known. In the original recording of Nirvana's "Smells Like Teen Spirit," our excerpt is lifted from the beginning of the chorus at ~1:06. In Britney Spears' "Oops! . . . I Did It Again" (composed by Max Martin and Rami Yacoub), our excerpt comes from the beginning of the chorus at about ~0:50.

76 Lucy Pollard-Gott, "Emergence of Thematic Concepts in Repeated Listening to Music" (1983) 15:1 Cognitive Psychology 66 at 85–92 (see Experiment 2).

77 *Ibid* at 80.

binary *yes/no* response. Rather, *no* can become *yes* over time and repeated listenings, to a point where the two themes need not be particularly alike in order for connections to be drawn between them. Second, it suggests this process is unidirectional; while *no* can become *yes* over time, *yes* cannot become *no*. Once points of similarity are drawn, a listener cannot go back to a state of mind in which those connections do not exist. Our model composition is useful here again. Once you hear Beethoven's Fifth Symphony in the melody, there is no way to go back to not hearing that connection. One's attention is turned to comparing the melody around measure 7 of our piece to Beethoven's most famous theme simply by having the connection suggested, and then encouraging repeated listenings. This is an example of the "anchoring bias" described earlier. It is all too simple to create the conditions that favour a finding of recognizable similarity.

Thus, the question of "recognizability" of one work in another is not as objective as the lay listener test purports to be; quite the contrary, one can train people to hear connections between melodies, given sufficient time. This does not bode well for composers falsely accused of infringement where there is merely coincidental similarity, even where there are notable differences in the musical themes or expressive details that the composer might point to as evidence of independent creation. One might object that this assessment pays insufficient heed to the significance of the differences between the works. Perhaps so, but this only underscores the weakness of the recognizability inquiry: greater recognition of similarity minimizes appreciation of differences. Put otherwise, if a plaintiff wishes to win an infringement case through the application of a lay listener test, the best thing she can do is to play the two musical excerpts over and over again, building irreversible similarity connections between the two melodies over time. Eventually, everyone hears the "Smells Like Teen Spirit" chorus in our bass line, even if it takes a while to get to that point. The differences correspondingly fade to insignificance.

D. CONCLUDING THOUGHTS

1) Music's Lessons

Anyone who works with the law is used to dealing with the complexities that necessarily arise when applying general legal rules to real-world situations. It is unremarkable to encounter legal uncertainties ("is this infringing?") and normative indeterminacy ("should it be?"). Perhaps this explains why copyright scholars, practitioners, and judges feel reasonably confident examining music through the lens of law, notwithstanding the complexity of the endeavour; but when we look back at law through the lens of music, we see that our nicely articulated legal doctrine suffers from more than typical legal uncertainty. The compositional example offered in Section C presents fundamental practical and policy questions that merit greater consideration.

On the practical side, it provokes us to ask how substantial similarity can be fairly assessed when the human perception of similarities is so subjective, context-specific, and vulnerable to suggestion. Musical experts may detect substantial copying and technical similarities where the lay ear cannot. Moreover, the capacity to detect copying depends on many factors including the music's phraseology, complexity, and structure, and the listener's knowledge, sophistication, and expectations. We have argued that this challenges copyright's "ordinary lay listener" test for determining unlawful copying. Not only is the test ill-suited to the legal task at hand, but it is also virtually impossible to apply in light of its inevitable manipulability, which is only exacerbated in a litigation context.

From a policy perspective, our illustration suggests, first, that extensive copying may produce works that sound very different, and secondly, that works may sound very similar even in the absence of copying. The first point hints at a copyright policy conundrum: if substantial copying evades detection by the ordinary lay listener, but is otherwise evident, should infringement be found? If a composer borrows another's musical melody and writes it backwards, for example, an ordinary listener is unlikely to hear it, while an educated musician will likely discern the copying upon examining the score.[78] Doctrinally speaking, it might seem that the first composer should be entitled to claim infringement, but he is unlikely to succeed. Which result is correct? A proprietary understanding of the copyright interest might lead us to conclude that substantial copying should attract liability even where undetectable to the intended audience or the reasonable listener.[79] A

78 This example is examined by E Scott Fruehwald in "Copyright Infringement of Musical Compositions: A Systematic Approach" (1992) 26:1 Akron L Rev 15 at 27–28.

79 See Jeffrey G Sherman, "Musical Copyright Infringement: The Requirement of Substantial Similarity" (1975) 22 Copyright L Symp 81, quoting Melville Nimmer, *Nimmer on Copyright* (1970) s 143.52: "[the] *Copyright Act* is intended to protect writers from the theft of the fruits of their labor, not to protect against the general public's 'spontaneous

more consequentialist vision of copyright as an economic incentive to spur creativity might inform a different response: where copying is not noticeable to the intended audience of the original work, then the copying will not produce any harm to the market for the original. As such, there may be no reason to prevent it.

These are, we think, interesting arguments deserving of more attention than we can give them here.[80] For now, we note that the proprietary approach sits uneasily with the Supreme Court of Canada's "move away from an earlier, author-centric view which focused on the exclusive right of authors . . ." to control their works in the marketplace.[81] The Court's recent focus on the public interest, the dissemination of artistic works, and the development of "a robustly cultured and intellectual public domain"[82] points in favour of finding no infringement where musical borrowing is unrecognizable. In the absence of harm to the original author, the copyright balance is not furthered by restricting the creative expression of a derivative author and thereby depriving the public of the benefits of her creativity. This suggests an interesting possibility: the lay listener test may be unsatisfactory as a basis for *finding* infringement; however, the lack of substantial similarity to a layperson's ear might be a sound basis on which to *rule out* infringement on policy grounds.

The second scenario, where readily perceived similarities between two works do not reflect unlawful copying, identifies a very real policy concern for copyright law. It demonstrates that reliance on the reasonable listener standard risks capturing within copyright's domain independent creations or public domain uses that ought to be unrestricted. It is critical that courts are alive to this possibility and the threat that it represents both to the copyright system and to creative practices. The limits of copyright are as important to the proper functioning of the copyright system as the rights that it protects. If we fail to draw the appropriate limits to copyright, we upset the copyright balance by overcompensating owners while establishing un-

---

and immediate' *impression* that the fruits have been stolen" at 94 [emphasis in original]. Sherman counters, "but what are 'the fruits' of a composer's labor? . . . If the lay ear can detect no similarities, is it not arguable that the 'fruits' of plaintiff's work have not in fact been stolen, even though experts might be able to detect technical similarities of the most 'striking' kind?" at 95.

80 For a critical analysis of the property-based vision of copyright, see Craig, above note 15 at ch 4.

81 *Bell*, above note 39 at para 9.

82 *Ibid* at para 10.

necessary obstacles to creativity. For musicians whose creative activities take shape under the shadow of potential legal liability — and often under the watchful eye of risk-averse music publishers — the perceived need to avoid any detectable similarity to pre-existing works can be stultifying. If our legal standards do not accommodate the realities of musical creativity, there is a very real risk that musical creativity will adapt and constrict in the shadow of the law.

While our modest aim here has been to shine a light on the problems with substantial similarity determinations in music infringement cases, our critique illuminates some possible avenues towards improvement. Our general plea is that copyright law must take into account the nature of the creative musical practices that it purports to encourage. Jessica Litman famously pointed to "the gulf between what authors really do and the way the law perceives them,"[83] and warned that "we must guard against protecting authors at the expense of the enterprise of authorship."[84] This warning is extremely pertinent in the context of musical composition, which "has historically enjoyed a healthy diet of musical borrowings" and "has developed its own informal rules for borrowing."[85]

Given the technical nature and complexity of musical expression, one key to improving the alignment between what composers do and the law of copyright would be to more fully engage musical expertise in the substantiality determination.[86] We agree with Lemley's assertion that expert evidence would be most usefully and appropriately employed in determining unlawful copying (analytically weeding out unprotected from protected elements of a plaintiff's work) rather than in assessing the probability of copying as a matter of fact, for which a lay listener's ear may be sufficient.[87] Lemley compares the proposed role of the music expert to that of the soft-

83 Jessica Litman "The Public Domain" (1990) 39:4 Emory LJ 965 at 968.

84 *Ibid* at 969.

85 Keyes, above note 1 at 426 [footnote omitted].

86 Some scholars charge that judges rely too heavily on expert testimony; see, for example, Bently, above note 74 at 193. Some judges believe themselves ideal reasonable persons for testing musical similarity. See, for example, Denault J in *Grignon v Roussel*, [1991] FCJ No 557, 38 CPR (3d) 4 (TD). However, since 1991, substantial advances in mathematical models for analyzing musical similarity have yielded more meaningful data sets, strengthening claims that these models should be given some consideration in infringement actions; see, for example, Guillaume Laroche, "Striking Similarities: Toward a Quantitative Measure of Melodic Copyright Infringement" (2011) 25 Intégral 39 at 47–57.

87 Lemley, above note 27 at 728–29.

ware expert in the United States' software cases, namely, assisting the court with separating ideas from expression, filtering out other unprotectable elements of the work, and then comparing the defendant's work with the plaintiff's protected expression.[88] Whether or not Canadian law embraces the "abstraction-filtration-comparison" approach to software claims that Lemley invokes, our courts have accepted that "some method must be found to weed out or remove from copyright protection those portions which . . . cannot be protected by copyright."[89]

We also agree with Lemley that a better solution would be to employ expert testimony and analytic dissection of the work in both prongs of the substantial similarity test. Assessing the probative significance of discernible similarities could be greatly aided by expert evidence. And if the ordinary reasonable listener has any role to play in the second prong of the analysis, we would restrict it, as already mentioned, to supporting a finding in favour of the defendant where the copied portion is recognizable *only* to expert eyes or ears, and not to the intended audience. After all, as Manta notes, "the potential harm that infringement causes to copyright owners, both financial and non-financial, results from the perceptions of those members of the public who will encounter the works . . . ."[90]

Where reliance continues to be placed on the lay listener, there are ways to alleviate some of the biases to which the test is prone. In particular, we see some potential in Manta's proposal that courts assessing similarity allow the use of survey evidence in copyright cases, similar to that used in trademark litigation. Conducted correctly, and subject to the usual rules of admissibility, a survey could offer a court more objective, scientific evidence of the extent of similarities perceived by the intended audience.[91] Surveys would assist the decision maker to separate her own perception of the material from the question of fact at hand, and would minimize the impact of cognitive biases, such as hindsight or anchoring bias, on the infringement inquiry.

---

88 *Computer Associates Intern Inc v Altai Inc*, 982 F 2d 693 (2d Cir 1992); see Lemley, above note 27 at 729.

89 *Delrina Corp*, above note 24 at para 43 [citation omitted]; see also *Preston*, above note 48.

90 Manta, above note 53 at 1347 [footnote omitted].

91 *Ibid* at 1346; this is also consistent with the Supreme Court of Canada's acknowledgement of the value of surveys in *Masterpiece v Alavida Lifestyle*, 2011 SCC 27, namely, "to provide empirical evidence which demonstrates consumer reactions in the marketplace — exactly the question that the trial judge is addressing . . . ." at para 93.

Perhaps above all, what is needed is an attitudinal shift away from the law's idea of ownership and exclusive control and towards a more nuanced understanding of the creative works at issue, and the creative process from which they emerge. The law must afford sufficient space for musical inspiration, influence, and transformation; this space should not be confined only to the zone of fair dealing (wherein the defendant must defend her actions on limited statutory grounds or be held liable[92]), but should also inform the law's approach to determining prima facie infringement.[93] We must resist the idea that every recognizable similarity is both legally probative of copying and legally relevant to establishing infringement. Moreover, it should be accepted that what constitutes "substantial similarity" may vary across different expressive forms in accordance with the norms and conventions of the relevant creative community. Formulating a more fine-tuned approach to infringement is thus an important piece of a much larger puzzle.

2) The Value of an Interdisciplinary Approach to Music Copyright

This volume is intended to demonstrate the importance and critical value of interdisciplinary approaches to copyright scholarship. With this in mind, we conclude with some final thoughts about the complementarity of music and law as areas of intellectual inquiry. Music theory can help correct some common misunderstandings and sharpen general perceptions. By cutting through musical illusions, it might help to identify copying where it is hidden. More importantly, it tempers the possibility of false infringement findings and the overreach of copyright in cases where common musical devices are employed to similar aural effect. In a world where people learn to separate general ideas from specific expressions in everyday language

92 The space opened up for downstream users by the fair dealing defence has been dramatically expanded by recent developments in Canada. In *Bell*, above note 39, the Supreme Court of Canada identified as an important goal of fair dealing "to allow users to employ copyrighted works in a way that helps them engage in their own acts of authorship and creativity" at para 21. The defence remains available only for dealings for purposes expressly enumerated in the Act. As such, many creative uses of musical works will not benefit from the extended reach of fair dealing.

93 David Vaver, *Intellectual Property Law*, 2d ed (Toronto: Irwin Law, 2011), describing the "overall goal" of the substantial part determination in terms of a balance between encouraging the production and dissemination of creative work and allowing "public access to and use of a work for socially desirable ends" at 188.

but not in the language of music, music theorists can restore this core copyright concept to the judicial treatment of musical works. Additionally, the insights offered by musical psychology reveal how inexact and manipulable are laypersons' hearing senses, and how overconfident we tend to be in our own musical interpretations and conclusions. These revelations suggest the possibility of improved models for gauging similarities built upon the knowledge of how musical listening really works. Finally, a greater appreciation of the actual practice of musical composition promises a more informed discussion about the appropriate role and limits of copyright protection in the musical realm.

While these music lessons may leave the reader with more questions than answers, the fact that music theory turns our attention to such questions, shining a revealing light on the assumptions at play, surely speaks to its value and potential importance for copyright law. If nothing else, we hope to have demonstrated that a critical analysis of copyright's recognizability test is enriched by a technical analysis of musical structures and compositional practices, combined with an appreciation of the complex nature of music perception. Attention to musical disciplines and the lessons they afford holds the promise of a better copyright system than the one we have today — a system that more carefully calibrates copyright's norms and processes with the norms of musical communities and the processes of musical creativity.

THREE

The Confidentiality of Seclusion: Studying Information Flows to Test Intellectual Property Paradigms

MARGARET ANN WILKINSON[1]

ABSTRACT (EN): In the information age, law is challenged by the nature of information: expandable, diffusive, and shareable. This chapter illustrates the efficacy of an information science-based analysis, focusing on the flow of information and its effect upon the participants (from producers to users), for determining legal disputes involving information, including intellectual property matters. *Jones v Tsige* (Ontario Court of Appeal, 2012), declaring a new tort of intrusion upon seclusion (which the court termed an aspect of privacy protection), is critiqued. From the critique two observations flow: first, the matter at issue in that case, analyzed in terms of the information flow involved, would have been more properly decided under the federal *Personal Information Protection and Electronic Documents Act* (*PIPEDA*) as it involved protection of confidential information and not privacy issues; second, protection of confidential information, now in a business context considered an aspect of intellectual property in the international trade environment (e.g., in the World Trade Organization's *Agreement on Trade-Related Aspects of Intellectual Property Rights* [*TRIPS*]), completely contradicts the effect of traditional intellectual property devices on information flow and therefore should be exclusively considered in the context of legal regimes governing secrecy, personal data protection and access, and not intellectual property.

1 Author wishes to acknowledge the assistance of law student Devin Fulop in preparing this chapter and the comments of her peers in its final editing.

RÉSUMÉ (FR): Dans notre ère informationnelle, le droit est mis au défi par la nature de l'information : extensible, diffuse et partageable. Ce chapitre illustre l'efficacité de l'analyse basée sur les sciences de l'information, qui mettent l'accent sur la circulation des renseignements et leur effet sur les participants (des producteurs aux usagers de l'information), pour régler les différents juridiques portant sur cette information, dont les litiges de propriété intellectuelle. La décision *Jones c Tsige* (de la Cour d'appel de l'Ontario, 2012), créant un nouveau délit d'intrusion dans l'intimité (que la Cour qualifie de protection de la vie privée), est critiquée. Deux points ressortent de cette critique : premièrement, la question en litige dans cette décision, analysée sur la base de la circulation de l'information concernée, aurait dû être réglée en vertu de la Loi fédérale sur la protection des renseignements personnels et les documents électroniques (*LPRPDE*), puisqu'elle portait sur la protection de renseignements confidentiels et non sur la protection de la vie privée; deuxièmement, la protection des renseignements confidentiels, maintenant considérée dans le milieu des affaires comme une partie de la propriété intellectuelle dans le contexte du commerce international (par exemple, dans l'Accord de l'Organisation mondiale du commerce sur les Aspects des droits de propriété intellectuelle qui touchent au commerce [ADPIC]), contredit complètement l'effet des mécanismes de circulation de l'information mis en place par la propriété intellectuelle et devrait être examinée exclusivement dans le cadre des régimes juridiques applicables au secret, à l'accès à l'information et à la protection des données personnelles, et non dans le contexte de la propriété intellectuelle.

A. INTRODUCTION

This chapter demonstrates the central role that information flow model-based analysis should play in intellectual property (IP) and information-related legal analyses. Two landmark copyright judgments from the Supreme Court of Canada (SCC) can be viewed as examples of the information flow model (a model most prevalent in library and information science [LIS] theory):[2]

2 By contrast, in a number of recent decisions, courts, including the SCC, have failed to adopt analytic strategies parallelling communications or LIS approaches. The decisions appear to be the weaker for that failure: for example, the SCC was split in both *Théberge v Galerie d'Art du Petit Champlain*, 2002 SCC 34 [*Théberge*] and *Robertson v Thomson*, 2006 SCC 43. In *Robertson v Thomson*, the majority (LeBel J and Fish J for themselves and Rothstein J, Bastarache J, and Deschamps J) said "process" was not important — just the "context" of the presentation of the works at issue, distinguishing the Court's approach

LSUC[3] and *Tariff 22*.[4] In the original decision of the Copyright Board in the latter case, the analysis closely followed an LIS model, using language such as:

> Generally speaking, information transmitted over the Internet is delivered in a unicast pull mode: pull, because the user requests or "pulls" the information when desired, and unicast, because packets go to only one recipient. Alternative delivery modes associated with audio files involve multicasting and the use of streaming software.[5]

In its turn, the SCC approved much of the Board's decision and entirely approved its analytic approach, at one point quoting directly from the Board:

> [T]he Copyright Board provided a succinct description of an Internet transmission:
>
> > First, the file is incorporated to an Internet-accessible server. Second, upon request and at a time chosen by the recipient, the file is broken down into packets and transmitted from the host server to the recipient's server, via one or more routers. Third, the recipient, usually using a computer, can reconstitute and open the file upon reception or save it to open it later . . . .[6]

---

in *SOCAN v Canadian Association of Internet Providers*, 2004 SCC 45 [*Tariff 22*]. The minority (Abella J for herself and Charron J, McLachlin CJ, the latter author of the unanimous judgment in *CCH Canadian Ltd v Law Society of Upper Canada*, [2004] 1 SCR 339 [*LSUC*], and Binnie J (author of the majority judgments in *Théberge* (a 4:3 split) and *Tariff 22*)) endorsed the "process" approach.

3 *Ibid*.

4 *Ibid*. Justice Binnie for himself and Iacobucci J, Major J, Bastarache J, Arbour J, Deschamps J, Fish J, and McLachlin CJ in the majority. Justice LeBel wrote a judgment concurring for the most part but dissenting on other grounds. The case is referred to as the "Tariff 22" case because it arose from consideration by the Copyright Board of "Tariff 22," filed by the Society of Composers, Authors and Music Publishers of Canada (SOCAN) to target Internet Service Providers (ISPs).

5 *Society of Composers, Authors & Music Publishers of Canada v Canadian Assn of Internet Providers*, (1999) 1 CPR (4th) 417 at para 54 (Copyright Board of Canada) [*Copyright Board*].

6 *Tariff 22*, above note 2 at para 10, citing *Copyright Board* above note 5 at para 82.

More recently, the Copyright Board initiated an analysis of information use in schools[7] later accepted by the Federal Court of Appeal (FCA)[8] and, ultimately, by the SCC.[9]

In this chapter, the utility of an information science-based analysis in the wider context of all intellectual property and information law cases[10] will be demonstrated through a re-examination of the scenario with which the Ontario Court of Appeal (ONCA) dealt in the recent case of *Jones v Tsige*.[11] Based on this analysis of *Tsige*, it will be demonstrated that the decision of the ONCA in the *Tsige* case is flawed. Moreover, the analysis will lead, in turn, to the chapter's conclusion casting doubt on the appropriateness of including the law of confidential information (or privacy or personal data protection [PDP]) within the rubric of IP.

B. THE LIS PERSPECTIVE

Historically, the relationship in written communication was one of a single sender to a serial set of receivers as a single manuscript was passed around amongst readers. Only oral communication was able to achieve the relationship of one sender to many simultaneous receivers (with the exception of public monuments which, where the population was literate, could reach a mass audience through writing). Of course, a choir would be an oral/aural instance of many senders to many simultaneous receivers and, in written communication, a manuscript authored by a number of writers would be an early example of "many to many (serial)" communication.

Librarianship, based in these information distribution realities over the millennia, has understood concepts of communication, including those recently modelled by communications theorists focusing on the relationship between the sender of a communication and the receiver of that

7 "Reprographic Reproductions (2005–2009): Statement of Royalties to be Collected by Access Copyright for the Reprographic Reproduction, in Canada, of Works in its Repertoire" *Copyright Board of Canada* (26 June 2009), online: Copyright Board of Canada www.cb-cda.gc.ca/decisions/2009/Access-Copyright-2005-2009-Schools.pdf; see also Margaret Ann Wilkinson, "Copyright, Collectives, and Contracts: New Math for Educational Institutions and Libraries" in Michael Geist, ed, *From "Radical Extremism" to "Balanced Copyright": Canadian Copyright and the Digital Agenda* (Toronto: Irwin Law, 2010) at 503.

8 *Alberta (Minister of Education) et al v Canadian Copyright Licensing Agency*, 2010 FCA 198.

9 *Alberta (Minister of Education) et al v Canadian Copyright Licensing Agency*, 2012 SCC 37.

10 See *Crookes v Newton*, 2011 SCC 47, where the SCC draws a direct analogy between hyperlinks and footnotes, the latter information resources long embraced by LIS.

11 2012 ONCA 32 [*Tsige* CA], allowing the appeal from Whitaker J, 2011 ONSC 1475 [*Tsige* SC].

communication and on the mediation between sender and receiver of both the content and the channel for that content[12] (see Figure 3.1). There are many variations on this basic model—recently transmission of information from many to many has become common—but the analytic focus of this model is on the flow of information *from* the sender(s) *to* the receiver(s).

Figure 3.1

Basic Communications Model

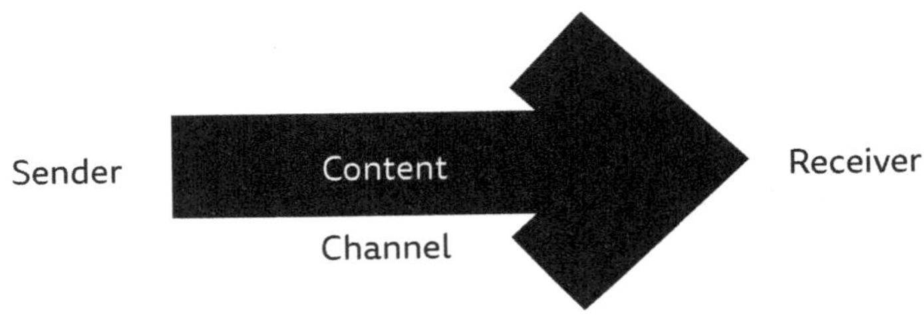

While LIS can embrace communications analyses, with its roots in librarianship,[13] LIS is always firmly focused on the user perspective and the insight that information will be neither sought nor received unless the user wishes it. Users seek information and evaluate it to fit their needs based both on availability (access) *and* on the perceived authority of the source of the information.[14] Information is absorbed by users hierarchically, involving both objective and subjective experience specific to each user: a user must source data useful to meeting an information need and combine it with her or his own cognitive framework to acquire knowledge and, ultim-

12 The seminal work is Claude E Shannon & Warren Weaver, *The Mathematical Theory of Communication* (Illinois: University of Illinois Press, 1949); later, but key, is Marshall McLuhan, *Understanding Media: The Extensions of Man* (Toronto: McGraw-Hill, 1964).

13 Boyd P Holmes, *An Enquiry into the Domain of Information Science, with an Emphasis on Contributing Disciplines: 1973–1998* (PhD dissertation, Western University, 2002).

14 Margaret Ann Wilkinson, "The Public Interest in Moral Rights Protection" (2006) 1 Mich St L Rev 193 [Wilkinson, "The Public Interest"]; see also Margaret Ann Wilkinson & Natasha Gerolami, "The Author as Agent of Information Policy: the Relationship between Economic and Moral Rights in Copyright" (2009) 26:2 Government Information Quarterly 321.

ately, gain wisdom[15] (see Figure 3.2). In LIS theory, both information producers (or senders) *and* information users (or receivers) control information during its lifecycle, not just "senders."[16]

Figure 3.2

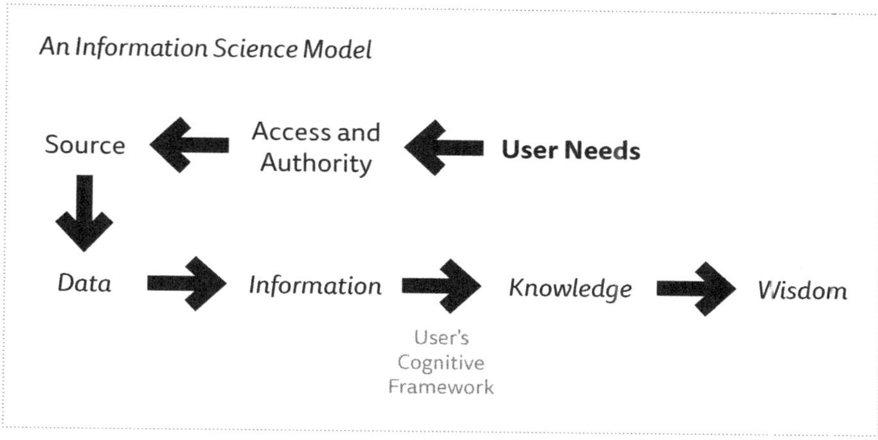

Sources of LIS-inspired insight on IP and information law-related questions are slowly accumulating in the scholarly literature.[17] Margaret Stieg has documented the reaction of law to the information changes emerging from industrialization in her canvas of nineteenth-century British law.[18] Catherine Maskell has drawn attention to the unequal treatment of information producers and users under the Canadian *Copyright Act*[19] in that cartels of information producers have been encouraged since 1988 in Part VII of the *Act* (which exempts them, as collectives under the purview of the

---

15 (1) Data, (2) Information — into which data is converted once someone is looking for it, (3) Knowledge — information absorbed by the user, and (4) Wisdom — knowledge combined into the user's already extant cognitive framework.

16 The author does not claim LIS offers the only lens through which emerging legal problems in IP and information law should be analyzed; from the humanities, see, for example, Marilyn Randal, *Pragmatic Plagiarism: Authorship, Profit and Power* (Toronto: University of Toronto Press, 2001). The author does assert that LIS offers a unique and important framework for decision makers and policy makers that will prove extremely valuable to law reform.

17 See, for example, Margaret Ann Wilkinson & Lynne EF McKechnie, "Implementing the Information Rights of Canadian Children" (2002) 20:1 CFLQ 429.

18 Margaret F Stieg, "The Nineteenth-Century Information Revolution" (1980) 15:1 Journal of Library History 22.

19 RSC 1985, c C-42.

Copyright Board, from the *Competition Act*[20]) while cartels of information users or their agents are not so exempted.[21] Charles Maina asks whether the voice of indigenous peoples as represented in international negotiations over indigenous knowledge is authentic, not only surveying the formal international and regional instruments, but also interviewing elders from First Nations, establishing that they believe theirs is the authentic voice and that it has been missing.[22] Maina has also commented on patents as knowledge-bearing artifacts.[23] As ownership of research data becomes an increasingly contested area of IP law development, Carole Perry offers an empirical study of attempts by the Social Science and Humanities Research Council of Canada to require the researchers it funds to deposit data in open repositories.[24]

C. REGULATING THE FLOW OF INFORMATION

Laws related to ordering the flow of information in society, such as censorship, defamation, and criminal prohibitions on blackmail, have arisen at many times in many places. Emerging separately in law, the publication of expressions (copyright), the spread of innovation (patent), and protection of consumers from confusion about products (trademark) developed to protect and encourage certain aspects of information flow. By the second half of the twentieth century, the three had become more commonly viewed together as part and parcel of the same theoretical construct: *intellectual property*. At the same time, societies and economies began to undergo changes which observers identified as so profound as to require a new moniker: *the information age*. Now, when information, rather than industry, is the lynchpin, it is not surprising that law designed to meet the information needs of a society based on industry is being severely tried by the needs of a society

20 RSC 1985, c C-34.

21 Catherine Maskell, *Consortia Activity in Public Libraries: Anti-Competitive or in the Public Good?* (PhD dissertation, Western University, 2006); Catherine A Maskell, "Consortia: Anti-Competitive or in the Public Good?" (2008) 26:2 Library Hi-Tech 164.

22 Charles K Maina, *Traditional Knowledge Protection Debate: Protecting Traditional Knowledge Against Versus Through Intellectual Property Mechanisms* (PhD dissertation, Western University, 2009).

23 Charles K Maina, "What Patents Tell: Limitations of Patent-Based Indicators of Innovation" (2007) 1:1 Journal of Law, Ethics, and Intellectual Property, online: Scientific Journals International www.scientificjournals.org/journals2007/articles/1254.pdf.

24 Carole Marie Perry, "Archiving of Publicly Funded Research Data: A Survey of Canadian Researchers" (2008) 25:1 Government Information Quarterly 133.

whose information needs are its raison d'être. By the final quarter of the twentieth century, the emerging changes had spawned a new global concern about the effect of telecommunications and computerization of data on the handling of data about individuals.[25] Inevitably, such new law-making and the pressures of technological change on the old laws become challenges that will reverberate particularly in IP laws: laws that were specifically designed to order the flow of information as it was transformed by the previous industrial age.

D. BACKGROUND TO *JONES v TSIGE*

In approaching the analysis of *Tsige*, it is useful to note that the FCA, in the reasons for decision in the earlier *BMG v John Doe*,[26] had already considered relationships between the areas of law to be explored in this chapter. In *BMG v John Doe*, music publishers[27] had launched a lawsuit against a group of individuals who, it claimed, were infringing copyrights in music by each downloading large numbers of songs from the Internet. However, since the plaintiffs only had evidence of the *behaviour* of these Internet users and did not have any knowledge of the "real world" individuals behind these Internet identities, the plaintiffs had to launch the lawsuit against unknowns (hence "John Doe"). [28] The plaintiffs then brought a motion against certain Internet Service Providers (ISPs)[29] seeking to have the Federal Court force the ISPs to reveal actual identities for these certain subscribers so they could become the named targets of the lawsuit. On appeal when the motion

---

25 Organisation for Economic Cooperation and Development, *Guidelines on the Protection of Privacy and Transborder Flows of Personal Data* (adopted 23 September 1980), online: OECD www.oecd.org/internet/interneteconomy/oecdguidelinesontheprotectionofprivacyandtransborderflowsofpersonaldata.htm [OECD, *Guidelines*]

26 2005 FCA 19 [*BMG* FCA], aff'g 2004 FC 488 [*BMG* FC].

27 *Ibid*. The style of cause included: BMG Canada Inc, EMI Music Canada, Sony Music Entertainment [Canada], Universal Music Canada, Warner Music Canada, BMG Music, Arista Records Inc, Zomba Recording Corporation, EMI Music Sweden AB, Capitol Records Inc, Chrysalis Records Limited, Virgin Records Limited, Sony Music Entertainment Inc, Sony Music Entertainment [UK] Inc, UMG Recordings Inc, Mercury Records Limited, and WEA International Inc.

28 *Ibid*. The style of cause cited "John Doe, Jane Doe and All Those Persons Who are Infringing Copyright in the Plaintiffs' Sound Recordings."

29 Identified as Shaw Communications Inc, Roger Cable Communications Inc, Bell Canada, Telus Inc, and Videotron Ltée.

was dismissed, Sexton J, for the FCA, framed the problem as a contrast between privacy rights and IP:

> [I]n my view, in cases where plaintiffs show that they have a *bona fide* claim that unknown persons are infringing their copyright, they have a right to have the identity revealed for the purpose of bringing action.[30]

An LIS-inspired analysis, however, establishes that the real question before the courts in *BMG* was the appropriate application of PDP legislation.[31]

Unfortunately, in part due to an overlap between the vocabulary of PDP and that of privacy, the role of PDP has been much misunderstood, both by the public, but also, more unfortunately, in the courts.[32] In the FCA in *BMG*, for example, Sexton J's analysis concerning the federal *Personal Information Protection and Electronic Documents Act* (*PIPEDA*) became completely circular. After stating that if there is a court order, *PIPEDA* permits disclosure of information otherwise not to be disseminated, he used *PIPEDA* to determine whether there ought to *be* an order — which inevitably led him to the conclusion that, indeed, there ought to be one.[33] His key question should have been whether there was a public interest in favour of disclosure to the plaintiffs in the copyright infringement action before him that outweighed the legitimate privacy concerns of the potential defendants. If there was not, then PDP would prevail because the court had no jurisdiction to compel production of the identities of ISP customers in the face of *PIPEDA* (which dictated the terms of the confidential relationship between the ISPs and their customers and required the ISPs to keep the information confidential).

---

30 *BMG* FCA, above note 26 at para 42.

31 In that case, the *Personal Information Protection and Electronic Documents Act*, SC 2000, c 5 [*PIPEDA*]; see Margaret Ann Wilkinson, "Battleground between New and Old Orders: Control Conflicts between Copyright and Personal Data Protection" in Ysolde Gendreau, ed, *Emerging Intellectual Property Paradigm — Perspectives from Canada* (Cheltenham, UK: Edward Elgar, 2008) at 227 [Wilkinson, "Battleground"].

32 Confusingly, Canada's PDP legislation governing federal private sector institutions was re-enacted in 1982 as the *Privacy Act*, SC 1982, c 111 (now RSC 1985, c P-21). It is entirely distinct from the four provincial statutes entitled "Privacy Act" in Saskatchewan (RSS 1978, c P-24), Manitoba (RSM 1987, c P-125), Newfoundland and Labrador (RSNL 1990, c P-22), and British Columbia (RSBC 1996, c 373). The latter are directed primarily at prohibiting surveillance.

33 *BMG* FCA, above note 26 at para 42. Ultimately, the court dismissed the appeal because time had passed and the holders of these ISP accounts might have changed — but without prejudice to a right to commence a fresh application.

The only possible public interest in disclosure in *BMG* would have been an interest which would make *all* litigants able to compel defendants' identities from third parties — a position clearly not taken by the legislators and not consistent with any prior law.[34] If, as this author believes, *PIPEDA* should have governed the outcome in *BMG*, the FCA would have left it to plaintiffs to find some way, other than court orders compelling third party businesses to identify their customers, to identify those they allege infringed.

PIPEDA is one of a web of PDP statutes created by legislatures across Canada, stemming from an international initiative to protect the privacy of individuals while enabling the flow of information in a digital society.[35] While privacy concerns the "state of being let alone," PDP comes into play only once an individual has not been "left alone" and has had information about herself or himself come into the hands of an organization governed by PDP legislation.[36] PDP legislation is *not* designed to regulate the flow of information between individuals in society — relationships that *would* be regulated as part of law protecting privacy — but rather is designed to regulate organizations that obtain information about individuals from various sources.

Over the same period during which many legislatures in Canada and other countries have been developing the balance between data transfer and the right of individuals to protection of data about themselves into comprehensive schemes of PDP, there has also been an accretion of the concept of legal protection for confidential information into the domain of IP.

Concepts of confidentiality historically played no part in the development of the classic IP devices: no part in copyright *per se*;[37] no part in trade-

---

34 Wilkinson, "Battleground," above note 31 at 259.

35 See OECD, *Guidelines*, above note 25; see also Colin J Bennett, *Regulating Privacy: Data Protection and Public Policy in Europe and the United States* (Ithaca: Cornell University Press, 1992) at 136–40.

36 There are two important distinctions in this characterization. First, the definition of privacy has recently become virtually crystallized as "the *right* to be let alone" (the emphasis is added here by this author), a formulation which presupposes a legal consequence — whereas it is best characterized analytically as "the state of being let alone": see Wilkinson, "Battleground," above note 31 at 244–45. Second, privacy concerns an individual and PDP concerns organizations: see Wilkinson, "Battleground," above note 31 at 252–58; see also Margaret Ann Wilkinson, "Confidential Information and Privacy-Related Law in Canada and in International Instruments" in Chios Carmody, ed, *Is Our House in Order? Canada's Implementation of International Law* (Montreal: McGill-Queen's University Press, 2010) at 275 [Wilkinson, "Confidential"].

37 Anonymity has become linked with the framing of moral rights in copyright but it should be considered as privacy and not moral rights: see Wilkinson, "The Public Interest," above note 14.

mark (because confidentiality is the antithesis of trademark, which is based on consumer identification of information signals about products); and no part in the theory of patent protection, with its bargain of publication of the invention in return for a limited term monopoly on manufacture, use, distribution, and sale. Nonetheless, in the landmark *Agreement on Trade-Related Aspects of Intellectual Property Rights*,[38] Article 39, paragraph 2 provides that

> 2. Natural . . . persons shall have the possibility of preventing information lawfully within their control from being disclosed to, acquired by, or used by others without their consent in a manner contrary to honest commercial practices* so long as such information:
> (a) is secret in the sense that it is not . . . generally known among or readily accessible to persons within the circles that normally deal with the information in question;
> (b) has commercial value because it is secret; and
> (c) has been subject to reasonable steps under the circumstances, by the person lawfully in control of the information, to keep it secret.[39]

The note to the text of *TRIPS* denoted by the asterisk reproduced above is to the effect that "contrary to honest commercial practices"

> mean[s] at least . . . breach of contract, breach of confidence . . . and includes the acquisition of undisclosed information by third parties who knew, or were grossly negligent in failing to know, that such practices were involved in the acquisition.[40]

Although it declares confidential information to be part of IP, *TRIPS* is a product of trade negotiations and not necessarily theoretically sound. While it is true, as a practical matter, that confidentiality has long played a practical role in patent practice because preserving the secret, non-public status of an invention so that its novelty can be established when application is made for a patent is important, at a theoretical level, despite the inclusion of confidentiality in *TRIPS*, it nonetheless remains an open question whether the legal protection of confidentiality belongs as a part of IP law or is more appropriate to another area of law.

---

38 15 April 1994, 1869 UNTS 299, 33 ILM 1197 [*TRIPS*].

39 *Ibid* at Article 39(2).

40 *Ibid* at Part II, note 10.

While an international consensus on providing legal protection for confidences may be appropriate, it is equally important to be analytically clear about what the information flow consequences of such a development will be. It is premature to identify such a development with IP not least because there is no public aspect to the protection of confidentiality like there is in patent, trademark, and copyright.[41]

E. *JONES v TSIGE*

Within the past year, the ONCA self-consciously saw itself as creating a watershed moment not in IP law but in the law of privacy:

> [I]t is appropriate for this court to confirm the existence of a right of action for intrusion upon seclusion. Recognition of such a cause of action would amount to an incremental step that is consistent with the role of this court to develop the common law in a manner consistent with the changing needs of society.[42]

In developing the argument for the new tort, certain facts in *Tsige* were identified by the ONCA as key:

1) Tsige was an employee of the Bank of Montreal [BMO].
2) Tsige used her employee access at BMO to access the customer accounts held by Jones multiple times: "As a bank employee, Tsige had full access to Jones' banking information and, contrary to the bank's policy, locked into Jones' banking records at least 174 times over a period of four years."[43]
3) Jones was a customer of BMO: "Jones maintains her primary bank account there."[44]

These three facts alone can be used to construct an information flow diagram of the circumstances relevant to determination of this dispute (see Figure 3.3).

---

41 See Wilkinson, "Confidential" above note 36.

42 *Tsige* CA, above note 11 at para 65, Sharpe J, also speaking for Winkler CJO, and Cunningham ACJ.

43 *Ibid* at para 2.

44 *Ibid* at para 4. Justice Whitaker on the original motion stated: "Ms. Jones is a Project Manager employed by BMO. She is also a customer of BMO and maintains her primary banking accounts there. Ms. Jones' pay is deposited to these accounts and all of her personal financial transactions are managed in these accounts" *Tsige* SC, above note 11 at para 12.

Figure 3.3

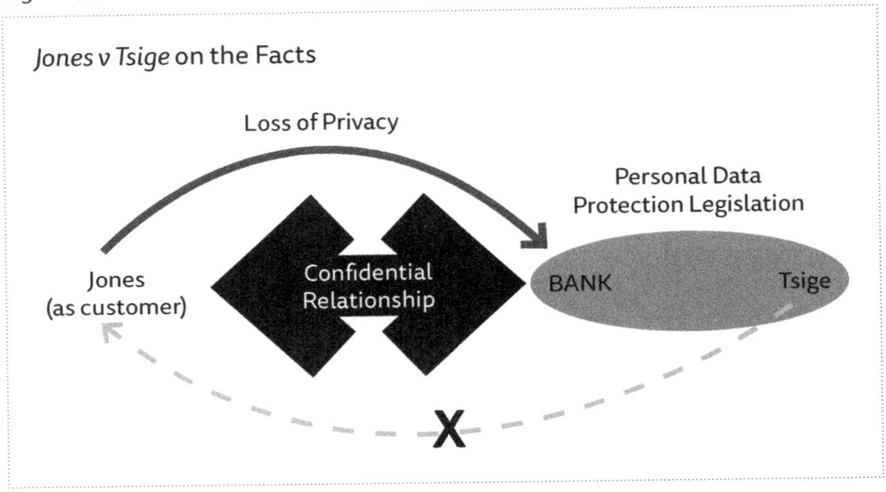

Certain additional implications, which the ONCA did not identify, become clear from the relationships evident in the representation of the known facts diagrammed in Figure 3.3:

1) The bank must comply with *PIPEDA* with respect to its treatment of customer data.
2) Jones would have a customer account agreement with the bank.[45]

Notably, Whitaker J, the judge of first instance in *Tsige*, was absolutely clear that

> there is no doubt that *PIPEDA* applies to the banking sector and Ms. Jones had the right to initiate a complaint to the Commissioner under that statute with eventual recourse to the Federal Court. For this reason I do not accept the suggestion that Ms. Jones would be without any remedy for a wrong, if I were to determine that there is no tort for the invasion of privacy.[46]

The role of *PIPEDA* in *Tsige* led Whitaker J to hold that "[i]n Ontario, it cannot be said that there is a legal vacuum that permits wrongs to go unrighted — requiring judicial intervention"[47] and was a principal reason behind his judgment denying Jones' claim to a common law right of privacy

45 Tsige and Jones would both be in an employment contract with BMO or covered by a collective agreement.

46 *Tsige* SC, above note 11 at para 54.

47 *Ibid* at para 53.

in the situation. However, when the matter was appealed to the ONCA, although acknowledging briefly that all the action involved in the dispute took place within BMO,[48] Sharpe J did not characterize the bank as a participant in the information flow involved in the case — treating BMO rather as the setting of the action, not a participating actor.[49]

The analysis Sharpe J used to arrive at the declaration of a new privacy-related tort of "intrusion upon seclusion" focused upon the person of "Ms. Jones" — not on the flow of information. Information flow inevitably involves more than one player — the information must flow from a source to a user. Seeing the bank as a player, at least in the role of repository for the information about Jones, which Tsige accessed, might have changed the way the ONCA perceived the issue.

If the flow of information in the situation had been traced, the ONCA would have realized that Jones had given up her privacy in the information held by the bank.[50] As a consequence of doing her banking, Jones had no privacy since the bank was privy to all transactions. In order to bank, Jones had chosen to rely on a relationship of confidence with this bank. This, in turn, leads to the analytic consequence that, when Tsige accessed Jones' information, it was the bank that held it, and not Jones herself. By focusing in on Jones as the one player important to the situation, Sharpe J mischaracterized her, ignored the other participants and obscured the analysis.[51] Justice Sharpe highlighted facts that should have been considered completely irrelevant to the resolution of the matter:

---

48 *Tsige* CA, above note 11. BMO is identified as the workplace of both parties at para 4; also again in connection with the women's roles at paras 5 and 6; BMO is only mentioned in the "Analysis" where Sharpe J disposes of the arguments concerning *PIPEDA* at para 50.

49 Justice Sharpe never mentions the regulatory environment within which banks in Canada operate: for example, the *Bank Act*, SC 1991, c 46 and the *Office of the Superintendent of Financial Institutions Act*, RSC 1985, c 18 (3rd Supp).

50 Note that Sharpe J accepts the concept of privacy as involving "the right to be let alone" not the "state . . ." (see *Tsige* CA, above note 11 at para 17).

51 In *Tsige* SC, above note 11, Justice Whitaker saw the matter as governed by *PIPEDA* — which applied to the bank — and his findings about the two individual litigants did not dominate although he provided details: "Ms. Jones is a Project Manager employed by BMO" at para 12; "[Ms. Tsige] was involved in a financial dispute with Mr. Moodie (at the time Ms. Tsige's common-law spouse and former husband of Ms. Jones) and wished to confirm whether he was paying child support to Ms. Jones" at para 21; "Ms. Tsige has been employed by BMO for twenty years. She has worked as a licensed Financial Planner for the last ten years. Prior to that she was a financial services manager for eight years and before that a customer service representative for two years" at para 13; "Ms. Tsige has completed the Canadian Securities Course and has received extensive training in privacy and ethical issues as they arise in the financial services sector" at para 14.

1) Jones was an employee of the bank.[52]
2) Although they had never met each other or communicated, Jones and Tsige had a connection in their personal lives: "Tsige and Jones did not know each other despite the fact that they both worked for the same bank and Tsige had formed a common-law relationship with Jones' former husband."[53]

Figure 3.3 is analytically correct in identifying only Tsige as a BMO employee. While Sharpe J was factually correct when he identified both Tsige and Jones as employees of the bank,[54] the accounts held by Jones and accessed by Tsige were personal accounts held by Jones as a *customer* of BMO, not as an employee of the bank. In analyzing the legal implications of the information flow that occurred in this situation, Jones' identity as a BMO employee is irrelevant. In contradistinction to Jones' situation in the dispute, it *is* Tsige's identity as an employee of BMO that is the aspect of her identity relevant to this situation. While Jones' work identity as a bank employee is irrelevant and her private identity as a customer of the bank is paramount, Tsige's identity as a bank employee is key and her private identity as a participant in a domestic contretemps also involving Jones is irrelevant. These analytic distinctions become clear under the information flow analysis presented in Figure 3.3 but were obscured and lost in the FCA's analysis.

Identifying Tsige's employee role as the material one then points to the bank as *the* key player in the information transaction at issue in *Tsige*: it is only by virtue of her employment that Tsige had access to the accounts of Jones, a customer of BMO. *PIPEDA* is therefore clearly the applicable law and a legal solution should not have been sought by the ONCA in the common law of privacy.

In the *BMG* case, discussed above, the FCA, like the ONCA in *Tsige*, turned to privacy law when appeal to *PIPEDA* alone should have resolved the matter — but, in *BMG*, *PIPEDA* was brand new.[55] The *Tsige* case was heard re-

---

52 *Tsige* CA, above note 11 at para 2.

53 *Ibid*.

54 *Ibid* at paras 2 and 4.

55 *BMG* FC, above note 26. Justice von Finckenstein's judgment was released 31 March 2004, just after *PIPEDA* came into force on 1 January 2004, in respect of businesses including ISPs. All parties agreed on two points, recited at para 9: "[1] ISP account holders have an expectation that their identity will be kept private and confidential. This expectation of privacy is based on both the terms of their account agreements with the ISPs and sections 3 and 5 of . . . [PIPEDA] [2] The exceptions contained in PIPEDA apply in

cently and *PIPEDA* is now over a decade old in its application to the banking sector. Indeed, in *Tsige*, Sharpe J acknowledged that "[t]he federal and Ontario governments have enacted a complex legislative framework addressing the issue of privacy. These include: [*PIPEDA*]; *Personal Health Information Protection Act*; *Freedom of Information and Protection of Privacy Act*; *Municipal Freedom of Information and Protection of Privacy Act*; *Consumer Reporting Act*."[56] Unfortunately, much of what Sharpe J then said about *PIPEDA* is incorrect.

Justice Sharpe stated categorically that "the remedies available under *PIPEDA* do not include damages and it is difficult to see what Jones would gain from such a complaint."[57] In fact, this is one of the key differences between the private sector *PIPEDA* and the public sector PDP regimes passed by the various Canadian jurisdictions, including the federal government's *Privacy Act*.[58] Section 16 of *PIPEDA* provides the possibility of a court-ordered remedy in damages for Jones:

> The Court may, in addition to any other remedies . . .
>
> (c) award damages to the complainant, including damages for any humiliation that the complainant has suffered.[59]

Indeed, in the recent case *Landry v Royal Bank*,[60] involving another Canadian bank, the Federal Court awarded damages (from the bank) to a customer in the amount of $4,500 (with interest and costs).

Further, Sharpe J introduced a complete red herring when, after holding "Tsige acted as a rogue employee contrary to BMO's policy,"[61] he thought

---

this case and an ISP by virtue of s. 7(3)(c) of PIPEDA may disclose personal information without consent pursuant to a court order."

56 *Tsige* CA, above note 11 at para 47.

57 *Ibid* at para 50.

58 *Privacy Act*, RSC 1985, c P-21.

59 *PIPEDA*, above note 31 at s 16.

60 2011 FC 687 [*Landry*].

61 See *Tsige* CA, above note 11 at para 50. Characterizing Tsige as a "rogue employee" originated in the ONCA, not with Whitaker J, who found "[o]ver the course of four years and on 174 occasions, Ms. Tsige accessed and reviewed on her computer screen at work, Ms. Jones' private banking records" (*Tsige* SC, above note 11 at para 4); second, "[a]fter being caught doing this by BMO, Ms. Tsige acknowledged that she had no legitimate purpose in reviewing Ms. Jones' records. Ms. Tsige claims to have done it for personal reasons" (*Tsige* SC, above note 11 at para 5); and, finally, "[w]hen confronted by BMO, Ms. Tsige acknowledged that she had no legitimate need or interest to explain her conduct. She also confirmed that she understood that this was contrary to her professional training and contrary to BMO policies" (*Tsige* SC, above note 11 at para 20).

"that may provide BMO with a complete answer to the complaint."[62] Canadian PDP legislation specifically places the onus for protecting data about identifiable individuals on institutions: there is no suggestion in the drafting that institutions may escape responsibility if their employees behave in a "rogue" manner. In *PIPEDA*, specifically, Schedule 1 provides the following:

> **4.1 Principle 1 — Accountability**
>
> An organization is responsible for personal information under its control . . . [and for]compliance with the following principles.
>
> . . . .
>
> **4.7 Principle 7 — Safeguards**
>
> Personal information shall be protected by security safeguards appropriate to the sensitivity of the information.
>
> **4.7.1**
>
> The security safeguards shall protect personal information against . . . unauthorized access . . . .

The Royal Bank clerk in *Landry* appears to have behaved in at least as "roguish" a manner as Tsige and yet in *Landry* the bank was held to account: "[T]he fax cover page . . . clearly establishes that the [bank's] clerk, Ms. Bouchard, had sent the information to Ms. Arsenault [the husband's lawyer], thereby directly breaching Bank policy and procedures."[63] The personal account information was sent, without the customer's consent, to counsel for the customer's husband in divorce proceedings and the Royal Bank was ordered to pay the customer, Landry, $4,500 plus interest and costs. The bank was ordered to do so even though Scott J acknowledged that

> the respondent [bank] did not benefit commercially from the error made by one of its clerks and . . . there is no evidence that the respondent acted in bad faith, except for Ms. Bouchard denying any knowledge of the file even though she herself was responsible for the wrongful disclosure. The disclosure of personal information in the present case is not trivial; it is a major error, especially as the Bank's employee tried to cover up her wrongful conduct.[64]

---

62 See *Tsige CA*, above note 11 at para 50.
63 *Landry*, above note 60 at para 5.
64 *Ibid* at para 28.

The third instance of Sharpe J's confusion about *PIPEDA* in *Tsige* not only reveals his misunderstanding but also highlights the analytic fallacy of Sharpe J's focus on Jones. Justice Sharpe wrote "[f]irst, Jones would be forced to lodge a complaint against her own employer rather than against Tsige, the wrongdoer."[65] Justice Sharpe's concern is surprising since he himself recites that Jones did not hesitate to complain to the bank about her suspicions of Tsige initially:[66] "Jones became suspicious that Tsige was accessing her account and complained to BMO."[67] Analytically, Sharpe J's concern is misplaced in that Jones would not be lodging this complaint against her *employer* but against her *banker* (who also happens to be her employer).[68] It is not uncommon for individuals to have multiple relationships with organizations or institutions. Where a given relationship is governed by statute, the common law cannot be invoked to create new causes of action because one individual in that statute-governed relationship also happens to have a different relationship with the institution or organization which the individual would rather not jeopardize in seeking legal redress connected to the statute-governed relationship.

Clearly Jones had a remedy in this situation under *PIPEDA*, albeit directed against the bank, BMO, rather than its employee, Jones. While it is axiomatic at common law that "the categories of tort are never closed,"[69] they are closed where a legislature has spoken. Justice Sharpe acknowledges this in *Tsige*:

> Tsige argues that it is not open to this court to adapt the common law to deal with the invasion of privacy on the ground that privacy is already the subject of legislation in Ontario and Canada that reflects carefully considered economic and policy choices. It is submitted that expanding the reach of the common law in this area would interfere with these carefully

65 *Tsige* CA, above note 11 at para 50.

66 *Tsige* SC, above note 11. Justice Whitaker states that "Ms. Tsige was only stopped from continuing this behaviour [accessing Ms. Jones' accounts] when BMO detected her activity" at para 19.

67 *Tsige* CA, above note 11 at paras 5 & 6.

68 Presumably Sharpe J would not create a new cause of action at common law for daycare employees of a municipal government who also lived in the municipality if that municipality failed to provide garbage pick up services: he would not create a new cause of action for the daycare workers against the garbage workers.

69 Lord MacMillan in *Donaghue v Stevenson*, [1932] UKHL 100.

> crafted regimes and that any expansion of the law relating to the protection of privacy should be left to Parliament and the legislature.[70]

Nevertheless, Sharpe J wrote:

> I am not persuaded that the existing legislation provides a sound basis for this court to refuse to recognize the emerging tort of intrusion upon seclusion and deny Jones a remedy. In my view, it would take a strained interpretation to infer from these statutes a legislative intent to supplant or halt the development of the common law in this area . . . .[71]

This is because, unfortunately, he misapprehended the scope of *PIPEDA*, saying "*PIPEDA* is federal legislation dealing with 'organizations' subject to federal jurisdiction and does not speak to the existence of a civil cause of action in the province."[72] This understates *PIPEDA*'s ambit in two ways. First, while it is true that *PIPEDA* is federal legislation and speaks to "organizations" subject to federal jurisdiction, the application of *PIPEDA* is much wider than that: it is directed to all organizations which carry on commercial activities in Canada, except organizations carrying on activities exclusively within provinces or territories which have passed legislation which the federal cabinet deems to be "substantially similar" to *PIPEDA*. Second, as *PIPEDA does* provide for a civil cause of action, it indeed "speak[s] to the existence of a civil cause of action in the province."[73]

On this information flow-based analysis, the federal government in *PIPEDA*, when combined with the equivalent legislation passed by provincial or territorial governments, has occupied this arena. *PIPEDA* gives Jones lawful control over her information while in the hands of the bank — and the *Tsige* case was solely about Jones' control over her customer information held at the bank.

This aspect of *Tsige* mirrors the question that came years earlier before the same court in *Seneca College v Bhadauria*.[74] When that ONCA decision was appealed to the SCC, Laskin, then CJ, reversed the ONCA, concluding Ms Bhadauria had no cause of action at common law:

70 *Tsige* CA, above note 11 at para 48.
71 *Ibid* at para 49 [citation omitted].
72 *Ibid* at para 50.
73 *Ibid*.
74 (1979), 27 OR (2d) 142, rev'd [1981] 2 SCR 181 [*Bhadauria*].

> The view taken by the Ontario Court of Appeal is a bold one and may be commended as an attempt to advance the common law. In my opinion, however, this is foreclosed by the legislative initiative which overtook the existing common law in Ontario and established a different regime which does not exclude the courts but rather makes them part of the enforcement machinery under the Code . . . . I would hold that not only does the Code foreclose any civil action based directly upon a breach thereof but it also excludes any common law action based on an invocation of the public policy expressed in the Code. The Code itself has laid out the procedures for vindication of that public policy, procedures which the plaintiff respondent did not see fit to use.[75]

The legislation at issue in *Bhadauria* was the then newly minted Ontario *Human Rights Code*.[76] The SCC found that Code contained some gaps in enforcement:

> The comprehensiveness of the Code is obvious from this recital of its substantive and enforcement provisions. There is a possibility of a breakdown in full enforcement if the Minister refuses to appoint a board of inquiry where a complaint cannot be settled . . . . I do not, however, regard this as supporting . . . the contention that the Code itself gives or envisages a civil cause of action . . . .[77]

Given the relatively stronger enforcement provisions in *PIPEDA*, it would appear that the same decision, excluding other civil causes of action except as provided in *PIPEDA*, should have been made by the ONCA in *Tsige*.[78]

F. CONCLUSION

Tsige did not present a factual situation supporting the introduction of a new tort of "intrusion upon seclusion." Not taking an information flow analytic approach to the facts, Sharpe J persuaded the ONCA that

> [f]inally, and most importantly, we are presented in this case with facts that cry out for a remedy. While Tsige is apologetic and contrite, her actions were deliberate, prolonged and shocking. Any person in Jones' position

75 *Ibid* at 195.

76 Now RSO 1990, c H-19.

77 *Bhadauria*, above note 74 at 188.

78 No further appeal of *Tsige* was taken.

> would be profoundly disturbed by the significant intrusion into her highly personal information. The discipline administered by Tsige's employer was governed by the principles of employment law and the interests of the employer and did not respond directly to the wrong that had been done to Jones. In my view, the law of this province would be sadly deficient if we were required to send Jones away without a legal remedy.[79]

But, under existing legislation, *PIPEDA*, Jones *was* entitled to a remedy — a remedy created by Parliament exactly for the wrong that Jones experienced. Analytically, the question is not one of Jones' privacy but rather of Jones' entitlement to a confidential relationship with her bank. An LIS-inspired analysis of the facts in *Tsige*, based on the flow of information, would have led the ONCA to a focus on Jones, her confidential relationship with her bank as a *customer* of that bank, and her entitlement to protection under *PIPEDA*. In turn, this analysis should have led to a recognition that Parliament has already created law to assist Jones in this situation, crafting a careful balance between individual's privacy interests and encouraging the flow of information in society, and there was neither need nor room for a new judicially-created common law remedy based on a purported cause of action for intrusion upon seclusion.

The consequence of finding that Jones was entitled to confidentiality (as enacted under *PIPEDA*, in this case), rather than a direct remedy to protect her privacy interests (including the purported right of seclusion), brings this discussion full circle to a consideration of the theoretical underpinnings of confidential information as a facet of IP.

Protection of commercial confidences has been brought within *TRIPS*, which purports to focus on IP, and from this development, it might be argued, it is axiomatic that protection of confidentiality has become part of IP. But, while it is true that, in the service industry of banking, the confidence between customers and the bank is essential to the commerce of the institution, it is demonstrable from this analysis of the *Tsige* situation that, where PDP is legislated, such provisions override any other law concerning such confidences. And, while PDP has been shown here to be quite different from privacy law, it *is* related to confidential information protection. Privacy

---

79 *Tsige* CA, above note 11 at para 69. The ONCA allowed the appeal, set aside the summary judgment below dismissing the action, and substituted an order granting summary judgment of $10,000 damages, leaving the parties to bear their own costs throughout, at paras 92 & 93.

is only one of the impulses behind PDP, regimes which themselves legislate certain relationships of confidence. Further, nothing in the analysis of privacy interests, confidentiality, or PDP suggests any of the three share characteristics normally associated with IP devices.

None of privacy, confidentiality, or PDP speaks to the public aspect that has been a hallmark of the development of IP. The recent case of *Girao v Zarek Taylor Grossman Hanrahan LLP*[80] illustrates the non-public and censoring nature of PDP. A law firm posted to the web the decision it had received from the federal Privacy Commissioner's Office holding a complaint against its client unfounded. Girao, the complainant, then launched a further complaint about the posting, this time against the law firm, which was, in turn, found to be "well-founded" but "resolved" by the Commissioner's Office.[81] Girao applied to the Federal Court for review and for remedies against the law firm (not the insurance company which had been the target of the original complaint), including $5 million for public humiliation and emotional damage.[82] The original Commissioner's decision was held to have been placed in the public domain by the law firm contrary to *PIPEDA* and the law firm was ordered to pay $1,500 damages and $500 costs to Girao.

Nothing in the legal protection of personal data or privacy or confidentiality encourages the spread of ideas in ways consistent with the basic tenets of IP; analytically, the essence of all three (privacy, PDP, and confidentiality) is to exclude others completely from access. Intellectual property, on the other hand, encourages public dissemination of ideas. The tensions between exploitation of confidential information in a business context, providing appropriate PDP for individuals in the context of those same businesses, and balancing privacy with demands for access are becoming real social, economic, and political issues.[83] Recognizing that these concepts — and the IP devices — are all facets of information flow and focusing analysis of situations on that perspective, as has been demonstrated here, will help the law respond to the emerging demands of a changing society, one increasingly challenged by new claims asserted in respect of informa-

---

80 2011 FC 1070.

81 *Ibid* at para 13.

82 *Ibid* at para 1.

83 See Mark Perry & Margaret Ann Wilkinson, "The Creation of University Intellectual Property: Confidential Information, Data Protection, and Research Ethics" (2010) 26 CIPR 93.

tion and flows of information and yet increasingly universally dependent upon information and information flow.

FOUR

The Precautionary Principle and Its Application in the Intellectual Property Context: Towards a Public Domain Impact Assessment

GRAHAM J REYNOLDS[1]

ABSTRACT (EN): This chapter considers whether the precautionary principle—a central element of contemporary environmental law and policy—can be usefully applied in the intellectual property context as a means through which the public domain can be protected. Assuming the importance of the public domain, and arguing that expansions in intellectual property protection risk harming the public domain, this chapter contends that it is appropriate to apply the precautionary principle in the intellectual property context in order to guard against harm to the public domain; suggests several ways in which a precautionary principle (or a precautionary approach) could be applied in the intellectual property context; and considers one possible instantiation of the precautionary principle in the context of intellectual property reform, namely in the form of a Public Domain Impact Assessment (PDIA). Modelled on the *Canadian Environmental Assessment Act*, the PDIA is envisioned as a process through which proposals for intellectual property reform, prior to their enactment, are evaluated by an in-

1 The author is grateful to Scott Campbell, Meinhard Doelle, Matthew Herder, Jennifer Llewellyn, Meghan Murtha, Justine Pila, David VanderZwaag, and two anonymous reviewers, for their valuable comments on an earlier draft of this chapter. He would also like to thank participants at the Multidisciplinary Approaches to Intellectual Property Law workshop in Ottawa, Ontario, for their valuable feedback on a presentation of an earlier version of this chapter. Any errors or omissions are solely the responsibility of the author.

dependent review panel in order to determine their potential impact on the public domain.

RÉSUMÉ (FR): Dans ce chapitre, on examine dans quelle mesure le principe de précaution — un élément central du droit et des politiques en environnement — peut être appliqué à bon escient dans le contexte de la propriété intellectuelle, en tant qu'outil servant à protéger le domaine public. En tenant compte de l'importance du domaine public, et en affirmant que l'extension de la protection de la propriété intellectuelle risque de porter préjudice au domaine public, on soutient dans ce chapitre qu'il convient d'appliquer le principe de précaution au contexte de la propriété intellectuelle dans le but d'éviter de nuire au domaine public. L'auteur propose différentes manières d'appliquer le principe de précaution (ou, à tout le moins, une approche de précaution) au contexte de la propriété intellectuelle; il examine en outre une éventuelle mise en application du principe de précaution dans le contexte de la réforme de la propriété intellectuelle, notamment sous la forme d'un Processus d'évaluation de l'impact sur le domaine public (PÉIDP). Façonné suivant le modèle de la *Loi canadienne sur l'évaluation environnementale*, le PÉIDP est conçu comme un processus au moyen duquel des propositions de réforme de la propriété intellectuelle seraient, avant leur adoption, évaluées par un comité d'examen indépendant, chargé de se prononcer sur leur incidence éventuelle sur le domaine public.

A. INTELLECTUAL PROPERTY LAW, THE ENVIRONMENTAL MOVEMENT, AND THE PUBLIC DOMAIN

In 1997, James Boyle, seeking to protect the public domain through the construction of a politics of intellectual property, drew inspiration from the environmental movement.[2] Pointing to the ways in which the environmental movement "piggybacked on existing sources of conservationist sentiment, including the aesthetic and recreational values held by hikers, campers, and birdwatchers" in order to "buil[d] coalitions between those who might be affected by environmental changes,"[3] Boyle argued that "[i]n one very real sense, the environmental movement *invented* the environment so that

2 James Boyle, "A Politics of Intellectual Property: Environmentalism for the Net?" (1997) 47 Duke LJ 87.

3 *Ibid* at 112.

farmers, consumers, hunters and birdwatchers could all discover themselves as environmentalists."[4] Boyle concluded that "[p]erhaps we need to *invent* the public domain in order to call into being the coalition that might protect it."[5]

Just as Boyle drew inspiration from the environmental movement in order to "invent" the public domain, techniques developed by the environmental movement or drawn from environmental law and policy can be employed to help safeguard it. Molly Shaffer Van Houweling states that since Boyle issued his call to action to "invent" the public domain, "advocates for the value of open access to cultural raw materials [have borrowed] not just the politics of the environmental movement, but also specific techniques that environmentalists have used to protect important natural resources."[6] Van Houweling herself, for instance, has discussed the ways in which "lessons that emerge from the conservation easement movement . . . might inform copyright policy."[7]

In this chapter, I will consider whether the precautionary principle — a central element of contemporary environmental law and policy — can be usefully applied in the intellectual property context as a means through which the public domain can be protected. This chapter is part of a broader project in which, building on the work of Boyle, Van Houweling, and others,[8] I examine whether and to what extent concepts, tools, and techniques developed by the environmental movement or drawn from environmental law or policy can assist in protecting the public domain.

---

4 *Ibid* at 113.

5 *Ibid*. This is not to suggest that Boyle was the first to discuss the public domain. See, for instance, David Lange, "Recognizing the Public Domain" (1981) 44 Law & Contemp Probs 147. In the years since Boyle's call to action to "invent" the public domain, many developments have occurred with respect to the public domain. Among other developments, numerous works exploring the topic of the public domain have been published: see, for instance Carys J Craig, "The Canadian Public Domain: What, Where, and to What End?" (2010) 7 CJLT 221. Courts have commented on the nature and importance of the public domain. In Canada, for instance, see *Society of Composers, Authors and Music Publishers of Canada v Bell Canada*, 2012 SCC 36 at para 10; and institutions devoted to the study of the public domain have been founded: see, for instance, online: Center for the Study of the Public Domain at Duke University http://web.law.duke.edu/cspd.

6 Molly Shaffer Van Houweling, "Cultural Environmentalism and the Constructed Commons" (2007) 70 Law & Contemp Probs 23 at 24.

7 *Ibid* at 49.

8 See, for instance, James Boyle & Lawrence Lessig, eds, Symposium, *Cultural Environmentalism @10* (2007) 70 Law & Contemp Probs.

Boyle defines the public domain as "material that is not covered by intellectual property rights."[9] For the purposes of this chapter, I will use Boyle's definition as a starting point and expand upon it by suggesting that the public domain encompasses material that has never been covered by intellectual property rights; material formerly covered by intellectual property rights in which the grant of rights has expired (or has been declared invalid); uses of material that are deemed not to be covered by intellectual property rights through the application of defences/exceptions to intellectual property infringement (or that can be considered to be user's rights[10]); and uses of material that are not covered by intellectual property rights by virtue of the application, by intellectual property owners, of flexible licences through which certain rights are disclaimed.[11]

This chapter assumes the importance of the public domain. It accepts that the public domain fosters creativity, facilitates innovation, enables self-expression, and that it is instrumental in both the development of individual identity and in the construction of communities.[12] If these assumptions are correct, and the public domain is important, then it is necessary to develop mechanisms through which it can be protected. Among other potential threats, expansions in intellectual property protection (for instance by increasing the term of copyright) risk harming the public domain by placing more material under the control of rights-holders for longer periods of time.[13]

Although recognizing that the risk of harm to the public domain that may flow from the expansion of intellectual property rights differs from the risk of harm to the environment that may flow from persons engaging in polluting or environmentally destructive activities, I suggest that it is appropriate to apply the precautionary principle in the intellectual property context. Both the environment and the public domain provide significant benefits to society. These benefits may be overlooked in favour of other benefits that might flow from development or enhanced intellectual prop-

---

9 James Boyle, *The Public Domain: Enclosing the Commons of the Mind* (New Haven: Yale University Press, 2008) at 38.

10 *CCH Canadian Ltd v Law Society of Upper Canada*, 2004 SCC 13.

11 Creative Commons licences, for instance. See Ronan Deazley, *Rethinking Copyright: History, Theory, Language* (Northampton: Edward Elgar, 2006) at 107 for a similar definition.

12 For an in depth discussion of the importance of the public domain, see, for example, Craig, above note 5; and Boyle, above note 9.

13 It can also be argued that the intellectual property regime does not sufficiently consider the impact of the exercise of rights on the public domain.

erty protection, respectively (such as economic benefits for certain industries or political benefits). As well, in the case of both the environment and the public domain, the impact of harm caused by polluting/environmentally destructive activities and intellectual property expansion, respectively, is both uncertain and difficult to establish.

There are several ways through which a precautionary principle or a precautionary approach[14] could be implemented in the intellectual property context. For example, a precautionary principle/approach could be applied in determining whether intellectual property rights such as patents and trademarks ought to be granted, as an interpretive tool in determining whether rights have been infringed, or at the point at which proposals are submitted to ministers or Cabinet for approval.

In this chapter, I will discuss another way in which the precautionary principle could be applied in the intellectual property context. Specifically, I will suggest that the precautionary principle could be applied at the point at which proposals for reform of intellectual property legislation are formally introduced as part of the legislative process. In the final section of this chapter, I will propose the creation of a Public Domain Impact Assessment (PDIA), a process through which proposals for intellectual property reform, prior to their enactment, are evaluated by an independent review panel in order to determine their potential impact on the public domain.

B. OVERVIEW OF THE PRECAUTIONARY PRINCIPLE

The roots of the precautionary principle can be traced back to Swedish and German domestic environmental law and policy. Joakim Zander states that "something resembling a modern precautionary principle guiding all environmental and health regulation has been in effect" in Sweden "[s]ince the late 1960s."[15] At approximately the same time as the concept underlying the precautionary principle emerged in Sweden, the principle of *Vorsorgeprinzip* began to appear in German environmental policy.[16] Mike Feintuck,

14 In this paper, I refer both to a precautionary approach and the precautionary principle. I employ both terms in order to acknowledge that there are several ways through which precautionary measures may be implemented.

15 Joakim Zander, *The Application of the Precautionary Principle in Practice: Comparative Dimensions* (Cambridge: Cambridge University Press, 2010) at 152.

16 Mike Feintuck, "Precautionary Maybe, but What's the Principle? The Precautionary Principle, the Regulation of Risk, and the Public Domain" (2005) 32 JL & Soc'y 371 at 374; Scott LaFranchi, "Surveying the Precautionary Principle's Ongoing Global Development:

quoting Sonja Boehmer-Christiansen, states that "[i]mplying both 'foresight' and 'preparedness,' *Vorsorge* requires that 'if wisdom and science combine to warn that current actions may lead to harm, government has the duty to change society by persuasion and regulation.'"[17]

In the 1980s, a precautionary approach began to be incorporated into international environmental declarations. For example, in 1987, the Declaration of the Second International North Sea Conference on the Protection of the North Sea (Second Declaration) "gave explicit reference to a precautionary approach."[18] In 1992, the precautionary principle was enshrined in the Rio Declaration on Environment and Development (Rio Declaration). Principle 15 of the Rio Declaration states that "[i]n order to protect the environment, the precautionary approach shall be widely applied by States according to their capabilities. Where there are threats of serious or irreversible damage, lack of full scientific certainty shall not be used as a reason for postponing cost-effective measures to prevent environmental degradation."[19]

Nicolas de Sadeleer notes that since its incorporation in the Rio Declaration, the precautionary principle has been included in the "majority of bilateral and multilateral international treaties relating to environmental protection."[20] While the question of whether the precautionary principle has reached the status of customary international law has not yet been definitively resolved,[21] Charmian Barton concludes that "its widespread use

---

The Development of an Emergent Environmental Management Tool" (2005) 32 BC Envtl Aff L Rev 679 at 681; Ronnie Harding & Elizabeth Fisher, "Introducing the Precautionary Principle" in Ronnie Harding & Elizabeth Fishers, eds, *Perspectives on the Precautionary Principle* (Sydney: The Federation Press, 1999) at 4.

17 Feintuck, above note 16, quoting Sonja Boehmer-Christiansen, "The Precautionary Principle in Germany — Enabling Government" in Tim O'Riordan & James Cameron, eds, *Interpreting the Precautionary Principle* (London: Cameron May, 1994) at 39.

18 LaFranchi, above note 16 at 682.

19 United Nations Conference on Environment and Development, "Rio Declaration on Environment and Development" (1992) 31 ILM 874 at 879 (Principle 15).

20 Nicolas de Sadeleer, "The Effect of Uncertainty on the Threshold Levels to which the Precautionary Principle Appears to be Subject" in John S Applegate, ed, *Environmental Risk, Volume II* (Dartmouth: Ashgate, 2004) 453 at 457.

21 Harding & Fisher, above note 16 at 5. In "The Precautionary Approach and the International Control of Toxic Chemicals: Beacon of Hope, Sea of Confusion and Dilution" (2011) 33 Hous J Int'l L 605 at 629, David L VanderZwaag notes that the Seabed Disputes Chamber of the International Tribunal for the Law of the Sea, in an Advisory Opinion, stated that "the Rio Declaration has initiated a trend towards making the precautionary approach part of customary international law": See *Responsibilities and Obligations of States Sponsoring Persons and Entities with Respect to Activities in the Area* (2011), Advisory Opinion, Seabed Disputes Chamber of the International Tribunal for the Law of the Sea No 135.

indicates that it is recognized as a legitimate approach to environmental protection."[22]

There is no single, universally accepted definition of the precautionary principle. Rather, multiple versions of the precautionary principle have been proposed and implemented in different contexts. One way of classifying differing conceptions of the precautionary principle is by characterizing some as "weak" versions of the principle, and others as "strong" versions of the principle.[23] As Noah Sachs states, "[w]hereas weak versions of the Precautionary Principle *permit* the government to regulate risks under conditions of scientific uncertainty, the Strong Precautionary Principle suggests that some precautionary regulation should be a *default response* to serious risks under conditions of scientific uncertainty."[24] Sachs notes that "strong" versions of the precautionary principle also "explicitly [place] the burden on the private proponent of the risk-creating activity to . . . [prove] that risks are acceptable or reasonable."[25] Both "weak" and "strong" versions of the precautionary principle, though they differ in certain ways, also share some common characteristics. Recognizing that not all harms can be remedied after the fact, both versions emphasize anticipating future harm.[26] Both versions also emphasize that, in the face of uncertainty with respect to harm, preventative measures should be taken.[27]

Despite its widespread use and application,[28] the precautionary principle has been subject to criticism from numerous commentators.[29] Cass Sunstein, one of the most prominent critics of the precautionary principle, while suggesting that "weak" versions of the precautionary principle are "sensible,"[30] "unobjectionable and important,"[31] has advocated for the rejec-

---

22 Charmian Barton, "The Status of the Precautionary Principle in Australia: Its Emergence in Legislation and as a Common Law Doctrine" (1998) 22 Harv Envtl L Rev 509 at 518.

23 See Julian Morris, "Defining the Precautionary Principle" in Julian Morris, ed, *Rethinking Risk and the Precautionary Principle* (Woburn: Butterworth-Heinemann, 2000) 1.

24 Noah M Sachs, "Rescuing the Strong Precautionary Principle from its Critics" (2011) U Ill L Rev 1285 at 1295.

25 *Ibid.*

26 *Ibid.*

27 *Ibid.*

28 In addition to the field of environmental law and policy, the precautionary principle is also influential in the field of health policy and practice.

29 See, for instance, Morris, above note 23; Frank B Cross, "Paradoxical Perils of the Precautionary Principle" (1996) 53 Wash & Lee L Rev 851.

30 Cass R Sunstein, "Beyond the Precautionary Principle" (2003) 151 U Pa L Rev 1003 at 1018.

31 *Ibid* at 1016.

tion of "strong" versions of the precautionary principle. Stating that "every step, including inaction, creates a risk,"[32] Sunstein argues that "strong" versions of the precautionary principle, by requiring parties to "[a]void steps that will create a risk of harm," have the effect of "forbidding inaction, stringent regulation, and everything in between."[33] Rather than assisting policy-makers in determining which route to pursue when faced with the risk of harm, Sunstein states that strong versions of the precautionary principle "[offer] no guidance"[34] and "[lead] in no direction at all."[35]

Notwithstanding this criticism, some commentators, such as Sachs, argue that the precautionary principle, in both its "weak" and "strong" formulations, remains a valuable tool in seeking to assess and regulate risk in environmental and other contexts.[36]

C. APPLYING THE PRECAUTIONARY PRINCIPLE IN THE INTELLECTUAL PROPERTY CONTEXT

In considering the application of the precautionary principle in the intellectual property context, three preliminary questions must be addressed. First, is it appropriate to apply the precautionary principle in the intellectual property context in order to guard against harm to the public domain? Second, in what types of situations (if any) might the precautionary principle be usefully applied in the intellectual property context? Third, how might the precautionary principle be instantiated in the intellectual property context?

1) Is it Appropriate to Apply the Precautionary Principle in Order to Guard Against Harm to the Public Domain?

As noted above, the precautionary principle emphasizes both anticipating future harm (recognizing that not all harm can be remedied *ex post facto*),[37] and taking preventative measures in the face of uncertainty with respect to

32 *Ibid* at 1003.
33 *Ibid*.
34 *Ibid* at 1020.
35 *Ibid* at 1003.
36 Sachs, above note 24. See also LaFranchi, above note 16; Feintuck, above note 16; David Dana, "The Contextual Rationality of the Precautionary Principle" (2009) 35 Queen's LJ 67.
37 Sachs, above note 24 at 1295.

harm.[38] As is the case with harm to the environment, not all harms done to the public domain can be remedied *ex post facto*. For instance, it has been argued that copyright laws may prevent individuals and institutions from taking steps to preserve, for the benefit of society, existing expression in which they do not hold copyright, such as by transferring old movies from film prints to digital files.[39] The loss of this expression through the passage of time, or by an unfortunate event such as a fire or a flood, is irreversible and would have a negative impact on the public domain.[40]

However, it cannot be assumed that the risk of harm to the public domain caused by expanding intellectual property protection is the same as the risk of harm to the environment caused by pollution or development. For instance, it is generally not argued that permitting the release of a noxious substance into a waterway would benefit the environment. In contrast, if we accept that intellectual property acts as an incentive for individuals to invest in the creation and dissemination of expression, and that this incentive leads to the creation and dissemination of expression that would not otherwise have been created or disseminated, then increasing intellectual property protection may benefit the public domain, as opposed to harming or impoverishing it. Expression, once created, immediately becomes part of the public domain with respect to certain uses (fair dealing, for instance, in the context of copyright), and, at a later date (after the expiration of the term of intellectual property protection) for all other uses.

This is not to say that increasing intellectual property protection always (or ever) has a net benefit on the public domain. While increasing intellectual property protection may act as a further incentive for the creation of new expression, it also expands protection for existing works. Thus, although expanding intellectual property protection, for instance by increasing the term of copyright, may result in new works being created (making certain uses of those works, such as fair dealing, immediately available as part of the public domain), it also extends the period of time in which other uses of existing works will not be available as part of the public domain.

---

38 *Ibid.*

39 For instance, see Diane Leenheer Zimmerman, "Can Our Culture Be Saved? The Future of Digital Archiving" (2007) 91 Minn L Rev 989.

40 This material, once lost, would be unavailable for use in ways that would be encompassed by the fair use or fair dealing defences, and would not be available for unrestricted use upon expiry of the copyright in the work.

As well, at a certain point, it can be assumed that the incentive function mentioned above will cease to operate. At this point, expanding intellectual property protection will not result in the creation and dissemination of any new works (works that would not have been created or disseminated absent the expanded intellectual property protection). Said differently, any expansion of intellectual property protection at or past this point will not provide any benefit to the public domain. Instead, it will only result in a contraction of the public domain.

In applying the precautionary principle in the intellectual property context, the risks posed to the public domain by expanding intellectual property protection must be balanced with the benefits to the public domain that flow from expanding intellectual property protection. This is a complicated calculus. However, the complicated nature of this calculus should not bar the application of the precautionary principle in the intellectual property context. Given the significant degree of uncertainty with respect to the impact of any expansion of intellectual property rights on the public domain, and the possibility that expansions in intellectual property might negatively impact the public domain, it can be argued that if the public domain is seen as valuable and worth protecting (an assumption upon which this chapter is built), preventative measures should be taken, and some version of the precautionary principle ought to be applied.

The application of the precautionary principle in the intellectual property context can also be justified by reference to the values that may be seen to underlie the precautionary principle. Feintuck, for instance, has suggested that the precautionary principle has an "essentially collective orientation,"[41] and that it has "potential utility . . . . as an aspect and reassertion of the public domain in the face of private economic interests."[42] In referencing the public domain, Feintuck is referring broadly to the set of interests that belong collectively to the public and not specifically to the public domain in the intellectual property context. However, his statement is directly applicable in the intellectual property context. The application of the precautionary principle, in the intellectual property context, may provide some degree of protection for the set of collective interests and values that are furthered by the existence of a robust public domain in the face of

41 Feintuck, above note 16 at 398.

42 *Ibid* at 372.

private economic interests that may attempt to encroach upon the public domain through intellectual property reform.

2) In What Types of Situations is it Appropriate to Apply the Precautionary Principle in the Intellectual Property Context?

In considering the application of the precautionary principle in the intellectual property context, a second question that must be addressed relates to the types of situations in which the precautionary principle could be applied. In the environmental context, the precautionary principle is applied in two types of situations. First, parties that wish to initiate a project, engage in a behaviour, market a product, or use a substance that would otherwise be prohibited by law are required, in certain circumstances, to apply to a regulatory body or administrator for permission or for a licence. In determining whether to grant permission or a licence, the regulatory body or administrator may be required to apply the precautionary principle. Second, legislators may be required to consider the precautionary principle or to adopt a precautionary approach when developing legislation.

In the intellectual property context, a precautionary principle/approach could be applied in several ways. First, a precautionary approach could be applied by the relevant granting bodies in determining whether a patent ought to be granted[43] or whether a trademark ought to be registered. Second, the precautionary principle could be applied as an interpretive tool in determining whether an intellectual property right has been infringed;[44] whether a compulsory licence ought to be granted; or whether a defence to copyright infringement ought to apply. Third, the precautionary principle could be applied at the point at which proposals, the implementation of which may result in "important" effects on the public domain, are submitted to a minister or Cabinet for approval.[45]

43 In Europe, for instance, it can be argued that the "ordre public" or morality exclusion from patentability enshrined in Article 53(a) of the *EPC* embodies a precautionary approach. See *Convention on the Grant of European Patents* (5 October 1973) 13 ILM 268 (*European Patent Convention*, as amended) (*EPC*).

44 See, for instance, Timothy Endicott & Michael Spence, "Vagueness in the Scope of Copyright" (2005) 121 Law Q Rev 657.

45 This suggestion is modelled upon Strategic Environmental Assessment, "a tool that contributes to informed decisions in support of sustainable development by incorporating environmental considerations into the development of public policies and strategic

Fourth, and the subject of this chapter, another situation in which the precautionary principle could be usefully applied is at the point at which proposals for intellectual property reform are introduced. The application of the precautionary principle in the context of intellectual property reform could require legislative bodies, when evaluating proposed amendments to their intellectual property legislation or new intellectual property legislation, to explicitly consider the impact of any such proposals on the public domain. In the following section, I will consider one possible instantiation of the precautionary principle in the context of intellectual property reform, namely in the form of a PDIA.

3) Applying the Precautionary Principle in the Context of Intellectual Property Reform: Towards a Public Domain Impact Assessment

In considering how the precautionary principle might be applied in the context of intellectual property reform, it is informative to look to existing works that have advocated for an approach to intellectual property reform that could be characterized as "precautionary." One commentator, Thomas F Cotter, has explicitly suggested the application of the precautionary principle in the context of copyright, stating that "policymakers would be wise to incorporate something analogous to the Precautionary Principle, in order to minimize the risk that aggressive copyright laws will decimate the cultural environment."[46]

Cotter proposes several ways in which the application of the precautionary principle could impact intellectual property reform. First, he suggests that the principle could "shift the burden of justifying a proposed, but potentially harmful, rule to the affected industry."[47] Cotter states that the burden of proof could vary depending on factors such as the "magnitude of the potential harm, its irreversibility, and the current state of scientific understanding of its probability."[48] Second, Cotter suggests that "advocates of further copyright expansion" could be required to demonstrate, through "some meaningful degree of proof that further expansions are necessary to

---

decisions": Canadian Environmental Assessment Agency, online: www.ceaa-acee.gc.ca/default.asp?lang=En&n=A4C57835-1.

46 Thomas F Cotter, "Memes and Copyright" (2005) 80 Tul L Rev 331 at 409.

47 *Ibid* at 404.

48 *Ibid*.

maintain incentives, and are likely to do no harm to the other relevant goals of copyright."[49]

Modifying the intellectual property reform process in such a manner as to require evidence demonstrating the probability and seriousness of harm that may result to the public domain from the adoption of proposed reforms, and demonstrating the consistency of proposed reforms with the goals of intellectual property laws, could be of significant benefit to the public domain. It is unclear, however, how the burden shift suggested by Cotter might function should multiple industries propose the same reform or should reform be proposed by parties other than industry. As well, questions could be raised as to whether it is in the public interest to permit the industry proposing legislative reform to act as the party providing evidence justifying this same reform. Cotter, acknowledging the potential for abuse inherent in such an approach, notes that "affirmative findings [could be required] from the Copyright Office or from Congress."[50]

Building on Cotter's approach, I will conclude this chapter by proposing another possible instantiation of the precautionary principle in the context of intellectual property reform. Specifically, I will propose the creation of a PDIA. I envision the PDIA as a process through which proposals for intellectual property reform, prior to their enactment, are evaluated by an independent review panel in order to determine their potential impact on the public domain. Given the space constraints of this edited text, I will not describe the PDIA in exhaustive detail. Instead, I will introduce the framework of the PDIA, leaving the specific details to be expanded upon in a future work.

---

49 *Ibid* at 406.

50 Cotter, above note 46 at 406. Although Cotter's paper is the only work to explicitly suggest the application of the precautionary principle in the context of copyright, other works can be seen as supporting, in principle, the call for the adoption of a precautionary approach in the intellectual property context. For instance, see two "companion studies" prepared by Ian Kerr for the Copyright Policy Branch of the Department of Canadian Heritage: Ian Kerr, "Technical Protection Measures: Part I — Trends in Technical Protection Measures and Circumvention Technologies" (Ottawa: Minister of Public Works and Government Services Canada — Department of Canadian Heritage, 2004); Ian Kerr, "Technical Protection Measures: Part II — The Legal Protection of TPMs" (Ottawa: Minister of Public Works and Government Services Canada — Department of Canadian Heritage, 2004). Cotter, above note 46, also suggests that the proposal developed by Neil Netanel in Neil Weinstock Netanel, "Locating Copyright Within the First Amendment Skein" (2001) 54 Stan L Rev 1 at 47–54 can be characterized as an application of the precautionary principle in the context of copyright law.

My proposed PDIA is modelled on the *Canadian Environmental Assessment Act* (*CEAA*).[51] The *CEAA* can be seen as an instantiation of the precautionary principle in the context of Canadian environmental law. As in the case of intellectual property, in which private rights are balanced with the public interest, the *CEAA* attempts to achieve a balance between economic development and environmental concerns.

I envision the PDIA process as an open, public process, conducted by an independent review panel. Individuals, groups, and industry could have the opportunity to submit documents and provide oral testimony to the review panel with respect to the impact of certain legislative proposals on the public domain. Documents and testimony under consideration by the panel could then be published online, giving the public the opportunity to examine and comment on the submissions, the evidence contained in the submissions, and the methodology employed by parties that have submitted evidence.[52] Structuring the process in such a manner, as opposed to relying on the party desiring a specific reform to provide evidence justifying that reform, reduces the risk that the party desiring the specific legislative reform might, as Cotter states, make "rosy predictions" or engage in "sleight of hand."[53]

As is the case in the procedure set out under the *CEAA*, a number of mandatory factors could be considered under the PDIA process, including:[54]

---

51 *Canadian Environmental Assessment Act*, SC 1992, c 37 (*CEAA*), as repealed by *Jobs, Growth and Long-Term Prosperity Act*, SC 2012, c 19. On 29 March 2012, Bill C-38, *An Act to Implement Certain Provisions of the Budget Tabled in Parliament on March 29, 2012 and Other Measures*, 1st Sess, 41st Parl, was introduced by Canadian Finance Minister Jim Flaherty. Among other measures, Bill C-38 proposed to repeal the *CEAA* and replace it with a new environmental assessment act (the *CEAA 2012*). *Jobs, Growth and Long-Term Prosperity Act*, SC 2012, c 19 received Royal Assent on 29 June 2012. Given uncertainty as to how the *CEAA 2012* will operate in practice, I have chosen to base my approach, and the PDIA, on the *CEAA*.

52 In many ways, the PDIA process proposed in this chapter can be seen as an extension of current legislative practices. For instance, in Canada, the public is already given the opportunity to comment on proposed regulations. As well, in Canada, Parliamentary Committees considering legislative changes have the power to call experts to give evidence. The main difference between the PDIA and current legislative practices would be the explicit focus of the PDIA on the potential impact of proposed legislative reforms on the public domain.

53 Cotter, above note 46 at 406.

54 The following factors are drawn from and based on s 16(1) of the *CEAA*, above note 51. Some of these factors are also suggested by Cotter, above note 46.

- The projected impact of the proposed legislative reform on the public domain, including the cumulative effects on the public domain that are likely to result from the proposed reform in combination with existing legislation or other reforms that have been or will be undertaken.
- The significance of this impact.
- Comments from the public received during the course of the PDIA process.
- Measures that might mitigate any adverse impacts of the proposed legislative reform on the public domain.[55]
- The purpose(s) of the legislative reform.
- Alternative means of achieving this/these purpose(s) and the effects of such alternative means on the public domain.
- Evidence demonstrating that the proposed reform will (or will likely) achieve the desired result.[56]
- The impact that the proposed reform might have on groups.[57]

While the factors noted above may already have been considered by bureaucrats and politicians in the legislative drafting process,[58] several advantages flow from formalizing their consideration in a public manner through a PDIA. First, formalizing these factors and mandating their review through a PDIA would ensure that each factor is explicitly considered. Second, formalizing these factors and mandating their review through a PDIA would increase openness and transparency within the legislative process, ensuring that the factors are not simply analyzed by bureaucrats and politicians, but that they are seen, by the general public, to have been analyzed. Third, formalizing these factors and mandating their review through a PDIA would create a record of evidence that could be helpful for courts

55 For instance, if a bill proposes to increase the period of copyright protection (an act that might have an adverse impact on the public domain), additional defences or exceptions to copyright infringement could mitigate any adverse impact.

56 A detailed analysis comparing and contrasting the application of the precautionary principle in the intellectual property context with an evidence-based approach to law-making in the intellectual property context is beyond the scope of this chapter, and will be the subject of another paper.

57 See Siva Vaidhyanathan, "The Anarchist in the Coffee House: A Brief Consideration of Local Culture, The Free Culture Movement, and Prospects for a Global Public Sphere" (2007) 70 Law & Contemp Probs 205.

58 For instance, these factors may have been considered in a Regulatory Impact Analysis or a Regulatory Impact Assessment.

and others seeking to interpret the legislation. This record could also be relied on in future years in seeking to further reform, develop, and shape intellectual property legislation and policy.

The consequences of determining, through the PDIA process, that proposed legislative reforms might negatively impact the public domain could vary. One possible approach could be for legislative bodies to bind themselves to the determination arrived at through the PDIA process.[59] This approach would represent the strongest instantiation of the precautionary principle of the options outlined in this chapter. Under this approach, if the PDIA process concludes that proposed intellectual property reforms might negatively impact the public domain beyond a certain threshold (for instance, might have a "severe impact" on the public domain), the legislative body would not be permitted to pass the legislation as proposed.

Several criticisms of this approach could be raised. First, this approach could raise democratic legitimacy concerns, as elected officials would be prevented from passing legislation by a decision made by an unelected body of individuals (the PDIA review panel). Second, adopting an approach that limits the ability of the legislative body to expand intellectual property protection (if one assumes that expanding intellectual property protection, at least past a certain point, negatively impacts the public domain) could create the risk of harm in other areas, for instance with respect to foreign relations, international trade, or the development of a nation's cultural industries.

A second option that could be pursued in the event that the PDIA process concludes that proposed legislative reforms might negatively impact the public domain beyond a certain threshold could be to require the legislative body to take steps to mitigate the potential impact of their proposals on the public domain. One step that could be taken is the creation of a body that has the authority to take certain steps to mitigate harm that might be done to the public domain should certain legislative reforms be enacted into law. This body could be given the authority to create or recommend the creation of additional defences to copyright infringement or to grant specific licences in order to partially (or completely) offset potential harm to the public domain that might result from the enactment of the proposed intellec-

59 This suggestion goes beyond what is prescribed in the *CEAA*, which provides the administration with discretionary power to approve or not approve a project (see *CEAA*, above note 51, s 37).

tual property reforms.[60] Depending on how this mechanism is structured, democratic legitimacy concerns could arise under this approach, as well.

A third option that could be pursued in the event that the PDIA process concludes that proposed legislative reforms might negatively impact the public domain beyond a certain threshold could be to permit the legislative body to pass the legislation as proposed, without mandating any of the mechanisms outlined above. The legislative body could choose, however, to implement any or all of the proposed mechanisms.

Although representing the weakest instantiation of the precautionary principle of all of the options described in this chapter, numerous positive benefits, for the public domain, would flow from the adoption of this approach. As is the case with the first two approaches, the public, open, and transparent nature of the PDIA process would bring attention to the risks to the public domain that might flow from the proposed intellectual property reforms; individuals would have the opportunity to give testimony to an independent body about the potential impact of the proposed reforms on the public domain, creating opportunities for discussion and deliberation; any evidence presented in support of the proposed reforms could be scrutinized; and lack of evidence provided to support any proposed reforms could be noted.

Additionally, while under this approach the legislative body would not be compelled to make changes to proposed legislative reforms as a result of the conclusion reached in the PDIA process, legislators could be held to account in future elections for their decision to pass the proposed intellectual property reforms notwithstanding the determination of the PDIA process. Given these benefits, and the democratic legitimacy concerns mentioned above with respect to the first two options, I would advocate for legislative bodies to consider adopting this approach.[61]

In a manner similar to the way in which the implementation of the procedure outlined in the *CEAA* guards against certain risks to the environ-

---

60 A model for such a mechanism can be found in 17 USC §1201(a)(1), which permits the Librarian of Congress to determine "whether there are any classes of works that will be subject to exemptions from the statute's prohibition against circumvention of technology that effectively controls access to a copyrighted work": see James H Billington, "Statement of the Librarian of Congress Relating to Section 1201 Rulemaking" (2010) US Copyright Office, online: www.copyright.gov/1201/2010/Librarian-of-Congress-1201-Statement.html.

61 Before any approach is formally adopted, however, more detailed consideration of the constitutional impediments to introducing a mandatory review of proposed legislation would be required.

ment, the introduction of a PDIA into the context of intellectual property reform would guard against certain risks to the public domain. First, the introduction of a PDIA into the context of intellectual property reform would provide some measure of assurance that legislative reform is "considered in a careful and precautionary manner" with respect to the possible impact of legislative proposals on the public domain.[62] Second, introducing a PDIA would also "ensure that there are opportunities for timely and meaningful public participation" on the issue of the potential impact of intellectual property reform on the public domain.[63] Third, incorporating a PDIA into the legislative reform process in the area of intellectual property law might also "encourage" parties to "take actions" that maintain a healthy public domain.[64] Lastly, the mere presence of the PDIA (and the public nature of its process) would serve as an affirmation of the importance of the public domain, of the public values that underpin intellectual property, and of the interconnectedness of private rights and the public interest.

Certain issues with respect to the PDIA would need to be addressed prior to its implementation in any jurisdiction. For instance, the legislative body would need to determine what types of consequences it wishes to have flow from a determination that the proposed reforms negatively impact the public domain beyond the applicable threshold; what ought this threshold to be; what limitations, if any, would need to be placed on the ability of individuals, groups, or industry to give testimony or to comment on testimony in order to ensure that the legislation can be considered within a reasonable time frame; who ought to bear the cost for a PDIA; how ought the selection process for the independent review panel proceed; whether (and/or to what extent) the PDIA would be conducted a second (or third) time in the event that amendments to the proposed legislation are introduced; and what steps could be taken if the PDIA process determines that there is no way to mitigate potential harm to the public domain that might arise from proposed legislative reforms.

D. CONCLUSION

This chapter assumes the importance of the public domain. If this assumption is correct, then it is necessary to explore different ways through which

62 *CEAA*, above note 51 at s 4(1)(a).

63 *Ibid*, s 4(1)(d).

64 *Ibid*, s 4(1)(b).

the public domain can be protected. Concepts, tools, and techniques developed by the environmental movement and drawn from environmental law and policy-making can play (and have played) an important role in this project. In this chapter, I have considered whether one concept originally developed in the context of environmental law — namely the precautionary principle — might usefully be applied in the intellectual property context in order to protect the public domain.

I have suggested both that it is appropriate to apply a precautionary principle in the intellectual property context, and that the precautionary principle could be applied in the intellectual property context at the point at which proposals to reform intellectual property legislation are introduced. In the final section of this chapter, I have drawn upon the *CEAA* to suggest one possible instantiation of the precautionary principle in the context of intellectual property reform. Specifically, I have proposed the creation of a PDIA: a process through which proposals for intellectual property reform, prior to their enactment, are evaluated by an independent review panel in order to determine their potential impact on the public domain.

The adoption of such an approach by legislative bodies would signal broad acceptance of the idea that the public domain is important; that it is valuable; and that, like the environment, action must be taken to ensure that it is protected. While the adoption of a PDIA may not prevent legislative bodies from enacting legislation that negatively impacts the public domain, it would, at a minimum, help to clearly articulate what is at stake (and what might be lost) should proposed reforms to intellectual property legislation be enacted into law.

CINQ

Abus et Propriété Intellectuelle ou du Bon Usage des Droits

PIERRE-EMMANUEL MOYSE[1]

ABSTRACT (EN): Intellectual property is ubiquitous, is the cause of all things, and we often blame it when problems arise. Its omnipresence is a measure of its sophistication, which can make it particularly harmful. It is embroiled in everything and is difficult to explain. This is in part due to its specialized and highly inaccessible nature, traits that are encouraged and maintained by those who have a vested interest, such as lawyers, and because of it, legal norms become meaningless. The law, in intellectual property, serves many masters and many interest groups. This law is truly a "balancing act." Intellectual property, therefore, is not in charge, and its normative function is reduced to functional arbitration of conflicts. Law is not a means to an end other than compromise. Yet, at the beginning of the twentieth century, an era during which we sought to enrich the law with contributions from other disciplines, we cling to a belief in functional rights and the possible instrumentalisation of intellectual property law in the public interest. This chapter attempts to rehabilitate the idea of the "spirit of the rights," with the goal, perhaps, of preventing antisocial uses of intellectual property rights.

RÉSUMÉ (FR): La propriété intellectuelle s'immisce dans toutes les matières, elle est de toutes les causes et on lui attribue tous les maux. Son omniprésence est désormais à la mesure de sa sophistication, ce qui peut la rendre

1 Ce projet a pu être mené à terme grâce au soutien du Fond de recherche du Québec sur la société et la culture.

particulièrement nocive. Elle se mêle de tout et s'explique mal. Et ceci est en partie dû à sa spécialité, trait entretenu par ceux qui y ont intérêt, juristes compris, et qui conduit à une perte de sens. La loi, en propriété intellectuelle, sert plusieurs maîtres, plusieurs groupes d'intérêts, elle est un acte d'équilibre dit-on, « a balancing act ». De ce fait, elle n'est plus guère directrice et sa fonction normative se réduit à des vertus fonctionnelles arbitrales. La loi n'est pas un moyen vers une fin autre que le compromis. Pourtant, au début du vingtième siècle, à une époque où l'on cherchait à enrichir le droit des apports des autres sciences, on croyait encore aux droits-fonctions, à sa possible instrumentalisation à des fins d'intérêt public. Ce texte tente de réhabiliter l'idée d' « esprit des droits » afin, peut-être, de prévenir les usages asociaux des droits intellectuels.

Les droits intellectuels, par la variété et la multiplicité des objets qu'ils visent, sont de plus en plus souvent invoqués à l'appui de prétentions infondées ou d'actions qui auraient dû trouver leur base juridique ailleurs que dans les recours choisis. Dans le premier cas, on parlera d'abus ou de détournement de droits intellectuels; dans le second de cumul de droits intellectuels. Le langage de l'abus[2] nous transporte naturellement vers la théorie civiliste du même nom, l'abus de droit. De nombreuses causes intéressant notre matière, la propriété intellectuelle, y font désormais référence[3]. Les études sur les chevauchements des droits de propriété intellectuelle, « intellectual property overlaps », se multiplient également[4]. Envahissante, la propriété intellectuelle s'immisce dans toutes les matières : informatique, biotechnologie, commerce, etc. On lui reproche d'ailleurs son appétit. Elle s'ingénie à transformer toute chose, toute impulsion créative, en bien juridique. Son omniprésence ne peut être ignorée.

Au Canada comme ailleurs, les projets de réforme législative se succèdent, transposant son insatiable ambition en autant de lois et d'amendements. Mais son expansion n'occupe pas seulement les recueils de lois. L'expansion est également conceptuelle. Elle détourne le régime de la pro-

---

2 Voir Jason Mazzone, *Copyfraud and Other Abuses of Intellectual Property Law*, Stanford, Stanford University Press, 2011.

3 Au Canada, deux jugements récents en propriété intellectuelle font expressément référence à la théorie de l'abus: *Euro-Excellence Inc c Kraft Canada Inc*, 2007 CSC 37 [*Kraft CSC*]; *Philip Morris Products SA c Malboro Canada Limited*, 2010 CF 1099; *Assessment Technologies of WI LLC v Wiredata, Inc*, 350 F 3d 640 (7e Cir 2003).

4 Estelle Derclaye et Matias Leistner, *Intellectual Property Overlaps: A European Perspective*, Londres, Hart Publishing, 2011.

priété ordinaire, elle met en question le droit de la concurrence, force le droit des contrats, s'immisce dans les relations de travail, etc. Bien entendu, cette typologie sommaire des pathologies de la propriété intellectuelle qui nous fait osciller entre détournement et interférence repose en réalité sur le matériel que nous livre l'actualité juridique et jurisprudentielle. Qu'il nous suffise de mentionner les agissements des flibustiers des brevets (*patent trolls*)[5] ou l'imposture du droit d'auteur dans des commerces auxquels il n'appartient pas[6]. Il faut ainsi garder à l'esprit que les questions difficiles, celles qui ont trait aux contours fuyants de la propriété intellectuelle, nous sont données par une casuistique singulière. Toute tentative de généralisation à partir de ce matériel collecté peu à peu par la jurisprudence est évidemment risquée.

Nous ne prétendons pas ici proposer une méthode scientifique capable de corriger les déviances de notre matière. Notre but est plus modeste. Il s'agira d'exposer certaines idées empruntées à la théorie de l'abus de droit et, partant d'elle, à la philosophie morale et politique, afin de tenter d'expliquer la crise actuelle de légitimité que traverse la propriété intellectuelle et de montrer la récurrence de certains discours sur le droit.

Discuter de l'abus revient en effet à s'interroger sur le domaine des prérogatives réservées à l'individu dans l'espace public[7]. Un vaste programme qui, dans le langage civiliste, s'exprime par le rapport entre l'idée de droit privé et celle de droit public. La sociologie juridique et la philosophie politique sont familières avec ce thème. « On attribue trop d'importance aux lois, trop peu aux mœurs . . . . », écrivait le clairvoyant Tocqueville[8]. Tout

---

5 Voir à ce sujet l'excellente analyse critique de G. Resta qui reprend certaines idées de Polanyi afin de dénoncer la privatisation du savoir par l'utilisation excessive des brevets d'invention, Giorgio Resta, « The Case against the Privatization of Knowledge: Some Thoughts on the Myriad Genetics Controversy », dans Roberto Bin, Sara Lorenzon et Nicola Lucchi, dir, *Biotech Innovations and Fundamental Rights*, New York, Springer, 2012 à la p 11.

6 Nous avons déjà mentionné la cause Kraft où il était question de la protection de la marque graphique Côte d'Or. Une affaire similaire occupe les tribunaux américains, cette fois concernant le logo Omega apposé à même les montres: *Costco Wholesale Corp v Omega, SA*, 131 S Ct 565 (2010).

7 On renverra à la fameuse description des droits individuels de Wolff. Ce dernier les décrivait comme des ballons. Robert Paul Wolff, « Beyond Tolerance » dans Robert Paul Wolff, Barrington Moore Jr et Herbert Marcuse, dir, *A Critique of Pure Tolerance*, Boston, Beacon Press, 1969 à la p 28 (o).

8 Alexis de Tocqueville, *Tocqueville au Bas-Canada*, Montréal, Éditions du jour, 1973, en ligne : les classiques des sciences sociales http://classiques.uqac.ca/classiques/De_tocqueville_alexis/au_bas_canada/tocqueville_au_bas_canada.pdf. (« [j]e suis convain-

comme les mœurs prédisposent les lois, des valeurs partisanes du droit mais non nécessairement juridicisées guident le travail des juges dans la prise de décision. Les tribunaux ont certes la fonction d'appliquer la règle de droit (au sens strict), c'est-à-dire d'établir la justice formelle, mais également celle de veiller aux principes d'équité. Ces principes placent le juriste sur un plan normatif différent, en marge d'une trame textuelle. Ils enrichissent l'univers du discours du droit puisqu'ils ouvrent nécessairement sur une conception laissant encore la place à la philosophie et aux sciences sociales.

Le droit est parfois, on le sait, en rupture avec l'idée de justice : l'abus permet de rendre compte de ce phénomène. Bien avant les idées de « Justice as fairness » de Rawls[9] et de « equal respect and concern » de Dworkin[10], les théoriciens de l'abus avaient tenté non seulement d'expliquer les luttes du droit, mais aussi de les apaiser[11]. Dans le vocabulaire de Josserand, le droit est soumis à un principe de *superlégalité* qui soumet donc son exercice à un examen de conformité[12]. Il y aura abus lorsque le droit, bien qu'inattaquable dans sa forme, est exercé de manière asociale. La théorie de l'abus révèle ainsi l'injustice. Elle résulte de cette interrogation sur la justice dans l'exercice des droits et la coordination des intérêts individuels dans le du droit privé. L'abus fait présumer l'interdépendance et l'interrelation des deux ordres de réflexion — l'un formel, l'autre que nous nommerons, faute d'autre qualificatif, métaphysique — de sorte que le droit dans sa réalité positive ne peut être totalement désolidarisé d'un ensemble de principes

---

cu que la situation la plus heureuse et les meilleures lois ne peuvent maintenir une constitution en dépit des mœurs . . . . L'importance des mœurs est une vérité commune à laquelle l'étude et l'expérience ramènent sans cesse. Il me semble que je la trouve placée dans mon esprit comme un point central ; je l'aperçois au bout de toutes mes idées » à la p 107); on relira également avec attention le discours prononcé par Portalis devant le Corps législatif le 17 janvier 1804, Jean-Étienne-Marie Portalis, « Exposé de motifs », dans Jean-Guillaume de Locré, *La législation civile, commerciale et criminelle de la France*, vol 8, Paris, Treuttel et Würtz, 1827 aux p 142 et s.

9 John Rawls, *A Theory of Justice*, Cambridge, Harvard University Press, 1971.

10 Ronald Dworkin, *Taking Rights Seriously*, Cambridge, Harvard University Press, 1977.

11 Rudolph Von Jhering, *La lutte pour le droit*, Paris, Dalloz, 2006.

12 Louis Josserand, *De l'esprit des droits et de leur relativité: théorie dite de l'abus des droits*, 2e éd, Paris, Dalloz, 2006 à la p 2 [Josserand]. L'œuvre de Josserand doit être replacée dans le contexte de la pensée juridique, éveillée comme elle l'a été par l'émergence des sciences sociales : David Deroussin, dir, Le *renouvellement des sciences sociales et juridiques sous la IIIe République*, Paris, Édition La Mémoire du Droit, 2007 et plus précisément au sujet de la contribution de Josserand, David Deroussin, « L Josserand : le droit comme science sociale ? », *ibid* à la p 63.

supérieurs de justice. Voilà ce qui explique que Josserand termine son exposé en faisant référence à l'équité et à la morale. S'exprimant au sujet de la « vaste construction de l'abus des droits », il écrit : « c'est elle qui moralisera, qui harmonisera le droit, qui lui donnera son véritable sens en assurant son « individualisation judiciaire, » en faisant passer jusque dans ses moindres réalisations le grand souffle d'équité qui doit l'animer et sans lequel il ne serait qu'une froide abstraction, sans réalité, sans moralité et sans vie »[13].

Si, comme Tocqueville a pu l'écrire, les mœurs, plus que l'habilité du législateur, forment les bonnes lois, le sentiment de justice est l'indice des bons jugements. C'est en partant de cette idée que nous présenterons nos réflexions sur la justice dans le droit. Le sentiment de justice est tout à la fois personnel et collectif — culturel et social. Et c'est auprès du juge, en raison de sa charge, mais aussi de son humanité que l'on retrouve cette tension entre l'individu et la société, entre la décision particulière et la règle générale. Rejaillissent alors les discours sur le rôle du juge dans la production normative, c'est-à-dire dans une conception politique, dans l'établissement de l'ordre et la poursuite du bien social : le juge peut-il être *colégislateur*? Le thème du social, récurrent dans la pensée juridique, est d'une facture particulière en droit privé puisqu'il donne les moyens d'une soumission des intérêts privés à l'intérêt général. Et c'est là d'ailleurs tout le programme de l'abus et de l'idée de solidarité dans le droit.

Nous en présenterons les principaux éléments dans une première partie (A). Ce rapport entre la force des lois et l'autorité des juges a occupé la pensée juridique moderne. Il est mis en relief dans les écrits sur l'abus d'une manière fort originale. L'abus, dans la théorie du même nom, est l'usage asocial d'un droit — par exemple le droit de propriété ou l'obligation contractuelle. Lorsqu'il en retient le principe, le juge repousse la prétention en droit pour introduire un principe de responsabilité dans l'exercice d'un droit. L'essentiel de notre argument est qu'il existe une similarité troublante entre la pensée juridique formelle contre laquelle l'abus s'était dressé, pensée défendue par l'école de l'exégèse, et les effets sclérosants d'une lecture moderne qui veut voir dans les lois spéciales la source unique de la propriété intellectuelle. La théorie de l'abus est ainsi apparue dans le contexte d'une codification devenue stérile; cette défaillance du droit codifié réapparaît désormais dans des disciplines très réglementées. Le discours actuel sur les législations de propriété intellectuelle et la pauvreté des mécanismes

13 Josserand, *supra* note 12 à la p 442.

d'interprétation soulèvent des problématiques identiques; celle d'une crise de légitimité du droit positif. En insistant sur les vertus moralisatrices ou pacificatrices du droit, les tenants de l'abus avaient voulu réinscrire le droit dans une projection idéale. Surtout, ils offraient une version moderne de l'approche finaliste et fonctionnelle du droit au moment où des théories à saveur plus libérale apparaissaient. L'une d'elles, la doctrine des intérêts conflictuels, laissait déjà présager l'emprise des théories économiques sur le droit privé. On fera là encore l'analogie avec l'évolution récente de la propriété intellectuelle, discipline qui se targue d'établir l'équilibre entre intérêts opposés. La réminiscence de cette notion d'intérêt peut être vue, si l'on se replace dans la perspective de l'abus, comme un signe d'une déficience politique, l'état et ses institutions étant incapables d'établir la fonction sociale des droits en cause. Ce sera le sujet de notre seconde partie (B).

A. L'ABUS COMME PRINCIPE DE SOLIDARITÉ

La théorie de l'abus de droit apparaît dans le contexte du renouveau de la pensée juridique au contact des sciences sociales. Le rapprochement avec la sociologie politique en particulier est perçu comme particulièrement fécond puisqu'il permet de mettre en relief, voire en opposition, la complexité du droit et le droit positif, c'est-à-dire tel qu'exprimé par la loi; le droit immanent, un droit naturel qui se dégage des rapports sociaux, et le droit formel, ce dernier n'étant toujours que la révélation imparfaite du premier[14]. La théorie de l'abus se nourrit de ces ouvertures de sens créées à partir de la polysémie du mot droit. La loi n'étant pas tout le droit, la réalisation des droits prévus par la loi doit encore être conforme à l'esprit qui les anime, c'est-à-dire à leur fonction sociale.

Nous commencerons par situer brièvement les travaux de Josserand sur l'abus de droit et leur relativité dans le contexte de la pensée juridique européenne du début du XIXe siècle (1). Nous verrons ensuite que l'abus procède d'une critique de l'interprétation littérale ou grammaticale du droit, et plus généralement de la législation (2), et réintègre la notion fondamentale d'équité dans la méthode du droit (3).

---

14 François Gény, *Méthode d'interprétation et sources en droit privé positif, Essais critiques*, vol 1, 2e éd, Paris, Librairie générale de droit et de jurisprudence, 1954 à la p 6 [Gény, *Méthode d'interprétation*]; un point similaire est défendu plus récemment par le philosophe Gerald Allan Cohen dans Gerald Allan Cohen, *Rescuing Justice and Equality*, Cambridge, Harvard University Press, 2008.

1) L'esprit des Droits

À lire les auteurs de la fin du XIXe et les témoignages qu'ils nous ont laissés, la science juridique vit à cette période une véritable renaissance. Un esprit nouveau se répand sur tout le continent européen. Enviant l'optimisme scientifique ambiant et la jeunesse des sciences nouvelles, le juriste s'interroge sur la méthode juridique. On veut désormais croire en un droit plus flexible[15], plus dynamique, bref à un droit *inspiré*. Il doit pour cela cesser d'être une science verbale, pour « redevenir ce qu'il est, et ce qu'il doit être, une science purement sociale »[16]. Ce puissant élan vers les sciences sociales se traduit du même coup par le refus, par la nouvelle doctrine, de la méthode qui leur avait été enseignée; celle de logique syllogistique et dogmatique. Au-delà de sa forme, on recherche désormais l'esprit du droit, l'esprit des droits, l'esprit de l'institution[17]. On critique le projet des codificateurs. On veut un droit vivant, réaliste, et sorti des abstractions. Gény écrira ainsi que :

> [l]'effort principal des jurisconsultes, au XIXe siècle, visait à faire rendre aux modes d'expression du droit positif, — notamment, et parfois même exclusivement, au plus formel d'entre ces modes, la loi écrite, prise comme manifestation d'une volonté contraignante, — tout ce que l'on pouvait en tirer. Cet effort parvenu au terme extrême de ses résultats possibles, il fallait bien, pour poursuivre le progrès nécessaire, chercher, derrière l'enveloppe formelle du texte légal, la réalité dont celui-ci n'était que le symbole, et, soit accepter de la loi écrite une notion plus objective et plus vivante, soit admettre, à côté d'elle, des sources moins formelles et plus plastiques, la coutume, la jurisprudence, soit même s'adresser plus haut encore et chercher à pénétrer l'essence propre de la vérité juridique, vérité insaisissable d'un coup et en son entier, fuyante et variable à raison des modalités infinies qui la conditionnent, mais à laquelle nous ramène inéluctablement une aspiration instinctive vers le but suprême du droit[18].

---

15 Jean Carbonnier, *Flexible droit : pour une sociologie du droit sans rigueur*, 10e éd, Paris, Librairie générale de droit et de jurisprudence, 2001; voir également Marie-Claire Belleau, « Les Juristes inquiets : Classicisme juridique et critique du droit au début du vingtième siècle en France » (1999) 40 C de D 507.

16 Raymond Saleilles, Préface dans Gény, *Méthode d'interprétation*, *supra* note 14 à la p XXIII.

17 Josserand, *supra* note 12 aux pp 414-15.

18 François Gény, *Science et technique en droit privé positif : nouvelle contribution à la critique de la méthode juridique*, Paris, Sirey, 1913 à la p 27.

Cette idée de finalité dans le droit que l'on doit à Jhering[19] va être le connecteur entre le droit et ce que nous appellerons les idées socialisantes : la logique juridique doit opter pour une rationalité empirique[20]. Il ne s'agit pas encore de pluralisme mais d'une réinitialisation de la pensée juridique à partir d'une compréhension plus éclairée des phénomènes sociaux qu'elle prend pour objet. L'étude des travaux de Josserand sur l'abus permet de prendre la mesure de ce mouvement. Pour lui, comme pour ses contemporains, la législation formelle est nécessairement imparfaite. Il décide donc de soumettre le droit formel à un principe de conformité qui deviendra, dans son langage, le *motif illégitime* en droit et dont il dégagera un principe de *superlégalité*. On peut donc, selon lui, avoir pour soi le droit et contre soi tout le droit; satisfaire les présuppositions d'un texte et pourtant s'en voir refuser le bénéfice. Regroupant pour les fins de son exposé une jurisprudence éparse, Josserand va vanter les vertus pratiques d'une telle approche. Dès lors que la réalisation des droits est soumise à un tel examen, l'acte abusif peut toujours être réprimé. L'abus de droit devient un principe de responsabilité sociale sorti des mécanismes traditionnels de la faute aquilienne: l'existence d'un droit n'immunise plus son titulaire. On peut alors respecter la lettre de la loi ou du contrat et être en situation d'illégalité. Influencé par la théorie des risques[21], Josserand voit dans l'abus de droit un moyen de pacification du droit; un moyen de faire justice et de s'opposer à la tyrannie des droits subjectifs, ceux du propriétaire, du patron ou du syndicat. Il reprend ainsi à son compte l'idée déjà en vogue des droits-fonctions, pour faire plier les actes, d'ordinaire soumis aux seules contraintes de la loi, à un principe supérieur d'équité ou, si l'on veut, pour insuffler une conscience morale aux prérogatives individuelles. L'abus de droit se définit alors comme le détournement d'un droit de sa fonction sociale. Josserand avait acquis la conviction que les tribunaux devaient contribuer à *socialiser* le droit en neutralisant les déviations dont il pouvait faire l'objet. Josserand

---

19 Rudolph Von Jhering, *L'esprit du droit romain*, Paris, A Marescq, 1880; François Gény, *Méthode d'interprétation et sources en droit privé positif : Essai critique*, vol 1, 2e éd, Paris, Librairie générale de droit et de jurisprudence, 1954 à la p 144.

20 C'est d'ailleurs le positivisme de Herbert LA Hart, *The Concept of Law*, Oxford, Clarendon Press, 1961.

21 Josserand s'était beaucoup investi dans la doctrine de l'époque au sujet de la responsabilité du fait des choses inanimées. Daniel Jutras, « Louis and the Mechanical Beast, or Josserand`s Contribution to Objective Liability in France », dans Ken Cooper-Stephenson et Elaine Gibson, dir, *Tort Theory*, Toronto, Captus University Publications, 1993, 317, en ligne : Social Science Research Network http://ssrn.com/abstract=1551359, aux pp 334–39.

recueille les critiques de ses contemporains quant à la méthode du droit : l'enseignement du droit ne peut plus être l'enseignement de la loi. Il opte pour un positivisme jurisprudentiel; « par la jurisprudence; mais au-delà de la jurisprudence », clame Josserand[22]. Ces idées sont perçues comme particulièrement progressistes puisqu'elles remettent en cause le principe de sécurité juridique, principe découlant essentiellement d'une théorie de la législation[23]. Ce principe est désormais la cause des lacunes et de la fixité des lois. Josserand fait alors du juge le principal acteur du changement dans et par le droit.

Appelé à s'expliquer sur la mise en application de sa théorie de l'abus, Josserand proposera le critère du motif illégitime, une notion qui lui permet de sortir de la compréhension classique de la faute comme révélatrice d'illégalité et de proposer la thèse du détournement des droits. Le concept de faute est réformé et élargi. La faute devient dans les travaux de Josserand l'usage d'un droit contraire à sa destination sociale ou économique. Les contemporains de Josserand ne seront pas sourds à ces idées. Certains accepteront volontiers d'ailleurs qu'il puisse y avoir faute dans l'exercice d'un droit en cas d'agissements excessifs; l'existence d'un droit ne confère pas une immunité absolue. Et puis la notion de faute avait considérablement évolué, effet des temps modernes et de la mécanisation. On émet déjà à l'époque l'idée d'une possible responsabilité sans faute et on souligne la nécessité de socialiser le risque. Reste que les règles traditionnelles de la responsabilité civile seront généralement jugées inadéquates pour intégrer des questions dépassant le simple règlement de conflit privé.

En définitive, si les systèmes de droit civil reconnaîtront l'autonomie et la complémentarité des principes de l'abus, soit par une reconnaissance jurisprudentielle, soit par sa consécration dans la loi[24], c'est une version modérée de la théorie de Josserand qui sera généralement retenue. Au Québec, les rédacteurs du Code civil retiendront le principe de l'exercice déraisonnable ou excessif d'un droit mais refuseront d'étendre l'application de l'abus à l'exercice asocial ou contraire à sa fonction économique comme l'avait suggéré Josserand.

---

22 Louis Josserand, *Cours de droit civil positif français*, vol 1, 3e éd, Paris, Sirey, 1938 à la p 74.

23 Voir les réflexions de Demogue à ce sujet, René Demogue, *Les notions fondamentales du droit privé : essai critique pour servir d'introduction à l'étude des obligations*, Paris, Rousseau, 1911 à la p 63 [Demogue].

24 *Code Civil du Québec*, LQ 1994, c 64, art 7.

2) L'abus : Une Critique de la Législation

La pensée allemande a conquis le continent juridique européen dès la seconde moitié du XIXe siècle avec une efficacité redoutable[25]. Les aspirations téléologiques de la doctrine française du début XXe siècle y trouvent ses sources. Les civilistes doivent également aux juristes allemands, et notamment à Savigny, l'idée du droit à formation spontanée. Appelé à se prononcer sur le projet allemand de codification, Savigny avait mis en garde contre le caractère statique, voire régressif d'un droit promulgué[26]. Régressif, car l'ordre formel peut rapidement faire oublier les objectifs sociaux que présupposent les situations juridiques. Les droits établis par la loi, les droits promulgués, sont occupés entièrement par les intérêts personnels du titulaire sans qu'il soit possible d'y retrouver l'objectif collectif auquel ils étaient prédestinés. La notion de droit pourtant éminemment sociale est alors vidée de toute obligation sociale, de son sens collectif. Elle n'est plus que le vecteur libre des aspirations personnelles. La théorie de l'abus, quant à elle, tente de réintégrer la notion de devoir social dans l'exercice des droits. Selon cette doctrine, le droit ne peut pas toujours être fécondé par la logique juridique et ses modes déductifs. Elle avait à l'esprit l'œuvre magistrale mais combien paralysante des codificateurs français. Mais l'Europe des lumières n'était plus, la réalité des années 1900 allait être différente.

Les premières causes de jurisprudence sur l'abus montrent bien cette rupture historique : elle est affaire de différends entre patrons et ouvriers[27]. Les travaux des juristes réformateurs doivent ainsi être relus dans le contexte de l'époque. Le début du XXe siècle est une période de forte industrialisation mais aussi de grande instabilité politique. L'Europe politique découvre les défaillances du système parlementaire. Le solidarisme juridique n'est pas étranger non plus à la montée du socialisme. Les travaux de Marx et d'Engels sont désormais largement diffusés. Ils annoncent en France la percée du

---

25 Voir le texte très intéressant d'Olivier Jouanjan, *De la vocation de notre temps pour la science du droit : modèles scientifiques et preuve de la validité des énoncés juridiques*, (2003) XLI-128 Revue européenne des sciences sociales 129 en ligne : Revue européenne des sciences sociales http://ress.revues.org/398 [Jouanjan].

26 Code civil allemand, promulgué le 18 août 1896, entré en vigueur le 1er janvier 1900, traduit et annoté par C Bufnoir, et al, t 1, Paris, Impr. Nationale, 1904, en ligne : Gallica http://gallica.bnf.fr/ark:/12148/bpt6k504246c/f16.image, préface de Raymond Saleilles, p 10.

27 Alexandre Lunel, « L'abus de droit et la redéfinition des rapports juridiques entre patrons et ouvriers en droit français (seconde moitié du XIXe - premier quart du XXe siècle) » (2009) 4 RHD 515.

Front populaire. Bref, c'est l'avènement du social et d'une société aux prises avec d'importantes mutations que le droit doit désormais épouser.

On s'interroge alors nécessairement sur le rôle de l'État. Sans surprise, le droit public prend une place de premier ordre, car le droit privé, avec son langage limité, semble bien incapable de mener le débat social. Le droit privé se fige, se replie. L'abus, dans ce contexte, est une réaction des privatistes pour se réapproprier le discours du droit et pour s'accorder avec une réalité que sa méthode technicienne avait tenue loin de lui. Le droit privé, largement auto-poëtique, avait fini donc par s'enrayer[28]. On n'osait plus toucher au Code ou alors avec une attitude révérencieuse et pleine de retenue : la doctrine elle-même avait fini par être éblouie et dominée par lui[29]. Dirigeant son regard vers l'Angleterre, Saleilles semblait envier l'approche législative d'outre-manche : « C'est une habitude acquise en Angleterre de voter des lois à révision, en se réservant de les corriger successivement, et presqu'immédiatement, par des additions législatives ultérieures ». Et il poursuit :

> Les esprits formés à l'école d'autrefois s'en étonnent un peu; ils y voient la preuve d'une fabrication défectueuse. Ils devraient s'en réjouir; car c'est la marque d'un assouplissement de l'appareil législatif, qui n'a plus la prétention d'opérer pour l'éternité, mais uniquement d'obvier à un besoin, peut-être uniquement temporaire et en tous cas très circonscrit, par des mesures qui ne puissent prouver leur valeur qu'à l'épreuve de la pratique[30].

Devant le statisme des lois et leur incomplétude, Josserand voyait dans l'activité judiciaire les garanties de la transformation du droit privé. Sa position était justifiée d'une part en raison du fait que l'intervention législative n'est pas toujours souhaitable en matière de droit privé et, d'autre part, parce que l'intervention du juge ne remettait pas en cause la cohérence de l'ordre juridique, puisque celui-ci ne légifère pas véritablement. Il suspend l'application de la loi et déboute le demandeur dans les cas exceptionnels où le droit est mésusé[31]. Et c'est là la formidable force de la théorie de l'abus de droit, réintégrant la fonction normative de l'équité, elle ne prétend pas

---

28 Voir Anna Di Robilant, « Abuse of Rights: The Continental Drug and the Common Law » (2009-10) 61:3 Hastings LJ 687 (pour une analyse de l'abus comme d'une mesure corrective cosmétique d'un droit privé romain bourgeois et d'une expérience au temps d'un capitalisme d'avant-garde).

29 Gény, *Méthode d'interprétation*, *supra* note 14, vol 1 à la p 28.

30 *Ibid*, préface, à la p XXIII.

31 Pierre-Emmanuel Moyse, « L'abus de droit : l'anténorme », (2012) 57 RD McGill 859 aux p 910 et s.

proposer autre chose que la destitution du titulaire. L'abus est un principe normatif curatif, non législatif.

3) Le Sentiment de Justice

L'équité et la référence au sentiment de justice sont des thèmes consubstantiels et récurrents dans les théories réformatrices. Bien qu'elle ouvre sur un vaste domaine de philosophie du droit et nous ramène à l'atemporel discours d'Aristote dans l'Éthique de Nicomaque[32], on tente, en ce début de XIXe siècle, de théoriser l'équité de manière à l'inclure dans une méthode scientifique. Et la raison en est fort simple : la loi et les méthodes traditionnelles d'interprétation n'ont apporté que l'illusion de stabilité. Qu'il s'agisse d'interprétation grammaticale ou littérale, que l'on cherche l'intention du législateur ou que l'interprète y substitue la sienne, le mode de rationalité mis en œuvre ne peut pallier l'insuffisance de la loi. Une fois la relativité du droit admise, il faut étudier sa plasticité et non plus sa géométrie[33]. De sorte que le sentiment de justice, auquel on associe l'équité, appartient à la méthode juridique.

C'est chez le contemporain de Josserand, François Gény, que l'on trouve les développements les plus intéressants à ce sujet. Gény semble tourmenté par cette idée d'équité. Il finit par lui reconnaître une place de premier ordre, car elle est, écrit-il, « irréductible aux opérations de la raison proprement dite »[34], elle est « une sorte d'instinct, qui, sans faire appel à la *raison raisonnante*, va, de lui-même et tout droit, à la solution la meilleure et la plus conforme au but de toute organisation juridique »[35]. Il rejette par contre la notion d'équité individuelle, « celle qui détermine l'influence des circonstances particulières à une situation concrète et déterminée »[36]. Ce que Gény semble vouloir indiquer, c'est que le principe d'équité ne permettrait pas de

---

32 Aristote, Éthique *de Nicomaque*, Paris, Flammarion, 1992, livre 5 (le chapitre X concerne les rapports de l'équité avec la justice).

33 Et Ripert de s'insurger contre cette position: « Plasticité. Élasticité ce sont des mots flatteurs dont on pare l'arbitraire » : Georges Ripert, « Abus ou relativité des droits : À propos de l'ouvrage de M. Josserand : De l'esprit des droits et de leur relativité, 1927 » (1929) 49 Revue critique de législation et de jurisprudence 33 à la p 41.

34 Gény, *Méthode d'interprétation*, *supra* note 14, vol 2 à la p 111.

35 *Ibid* aux pp 109-10.

36 *Ibid* à la p 112.

déroger à la règle de droit proprement dite, aussi stricte soit-elle[37]. C'est là le dilemme des classiques. Josserand, Gény et leurs contemporains veulent s'affranchir de la loi alors même qu'ils lui prêtent encore, malgré tout, allégeance. La position de ces juristes du progrès est intenable : l'idée motrice des constructions socialisantes est de dynamiser le droit formel en le redirigeant sur les voies tracées par le droit immanent, un droit *informé* par le social et non plus par le texte et son exégèse.

Cette tension est palpable chez Gény. Il cite le « système des Cours d'équité, qui naguère encore jouait un rôle si capital en Angleterre » pour enjoindre aux juges français de ne pas s'en servir à l'encontre d'une règle de droit « à moins que celle-ci ne renvoie expressément à l'équité ainsi comprise, soit même qu'elle se dégage de la libre recherche scientifique, à moins que les éléments mêmes de celle-ci (justice, nature des choses,) ne commandent de lui laisser place »[38]. On fera le rapprochement de ces propos avec l'esprit des travaux de Josserand. Pour lui aussi, la notion d'équité est centrale. Seulement, elle ne le tourmente point, car Josserand, contrairement à Gény, a choisi de se détacher de la loi, de la banaliser.

On peut comprendre pourquoi la référence à des notions aussi floues et équivoques dérange. Le sentiment de justice est une donnée essentielle du droit, mais n'appartient pas totalement à son épistème notamment en raison des airs scientifiques qu'il a voulu se donner. Cet élément donc, bien qu'essentiel, a été rejeté de son système, hors des barrières formées par son langage. L'abus retrouve ici sa cible : la méthode déductive ne comble qu'à moitié l'idéal de justice. La légalité ne peut pas être entièrement contenue dans le texte de loi. Pour cela, et pour ne pas avoir à répondre aux mises en échec des principes du droit par ceux de justice, le juriste préfèrerait se tenir loin des « sentiments », épousant plutôt l'illusoire rationalité de sa méthode. Mais cela, on le sait, n'est guère possible. La science juridique n'est pas la science mathématique et le rejet du sentiment de justice n'a jamais pu être complet. Le droit prend sa source dans les faits, puis devient fait à son tour. Il se construit dans un mouvement de valeurs, alternatif et incessant, du fait au droit, c'est-à-dire de modélisation des conduites. Le sentiment de justice

37 La relation difficile entre *common law* et l'*equity* permet d'illustrer également l'antinomie sur laquelle se prononce Gény, mais également, dans le système de *common law*, leur complémentarité. Voir les travaux de Michelle Cumyn sur la notion d'équité en *common law* et en droit français: Michelle Cumyn, « L'équité : définitions et concepts » dans Pierre-Claude Lafond et Benoît Moore, dir, *L'équité au service du consommateur*, Cowansville, Yvon Blais, 2010 à la p 1

38 Gény, *Méthode d'interprétation*, *supra* note 14, vol 2 à la p 112.

n'est pas seulement une figure poétique du droit, ni une vague formule métaphysique, psychologique ou sociologique, mais il constitue, à notre avis, une mesure de la légitimité dans le droit.

Le droit de la preuve et de la procédure et son principe contradictoire mettent en scène ce sentiment : le procès est un exercice de conviction. Le plaideur expérimenté cherchera d'ailleurs à s'informer sur les goûts et humeurs du juge. L'élément qui emporte la décision n'est pas toujours rationnel; la reconstruction des faits par la preuve très souvent incomplète. Ainsi, au même titre que les mœurs forment les lois, pouvons-nous avancer qu'il existe un sentiment commun de justice qui permet d'établir des échelles de valeurs permettant d'apprécier la force et l'autorité d'une décision de justice. Il existe ainsi dans l'imaginaire collectif des bons et des mauvais jugements. Ce sentiment est déterminant pour le juge qui doit convaincre à son tour et rendre intelligible l'adéquation de son opinion au droit. Ainsi, nous semble-t-il, le sentiment de justice est une valeur idéale, structurante et surtout, correctrice. C'est là aussi l'enseignement de la théorie de l'abus. L'abus peut en effet se concevoir comme un impératif de la conscience morale et, à ce titre, le sentiment de justice ou d'injustice guide le juge dans la détermination de l'acte illégitime : il identifie des points de dissidence et de rupture dans la mesure d'égalité censée être représentée par le droit[39]. De sorte que la théorie de l'abus est l'impulsion du droit mais doit se traduire en droit et user de son langage pour se faire entendre. La formule de l'abus est son porte-voix.

Le sentiment de justice établit également le niveau de tolérance et d'acceptabilité de la règle de droit, qu'elle soit comprise dans la loi ou un jugement. Le droit vaut droit, en partie parce qu'il est perçu et accepté comme tel. Le sentiment de justice est la mesure approximative de la règle juste, de sa légitimité, une sorte d'intuitionnisme moral[40]. Sous ce dernier trait, il fait voir comment le droit use de la rhétorique, non seulement pour établir

---

39 Il est intéressant de comparer cette thèse à celle d'Adorno. Selon ce dernier, le sentiment d'inconfort lors de certaines expériences est le meilleur moyen d'identifier un problème éthique ou encore politique. « The splinter in your eye is the best magnifying glass »: Theodor Adorno, *Minima moralia : Reflections on a Damaged Life*, traduit par E F N Jephcott, London, Verso, 1974 [1951]; Voir également les débats sur la méthode du jugement intuitif : Joseph C Hutcheson, « Le jugement intuitif, la fonction du « hunch » dans la décision judiciaire », traduit par Gabriel Marty, dans *Recueils d'études sur les sources du droit en l'honneur de François Gény*, Paris, Recueil Sirey, 1934 à la p 531.

40 Pour une présentation classique de l'intuitionnisme moral, voir George Edward Moore, *Principia ethica*, Mineola NY, Dover, 2004.

des proportions dans les situations juridiques, mais aussi pour provoquer l'assentiment. La forme des jugements, on le sait, est souvent essentielle. Le sens de la formule, la concision et l'éloquence sont, au regard de l'idée de justice, tous aussi importants que la solution elle-même.

C. L'ABUS DANS LA THÉORIE DES DROITS INTELLECTUELS

Les réflexions que nous avons posées plus haut nous donnent les moyens d'exprimer dans un langage déjà aguerri certains phénomènes de la propriété intellectuelle moderne. Le premier de ceux-là est l'hermétisme de ses lois et la panne de ses moyens d'interprétation (1). Si le rotor de l'abus se remet en mouvement, c'est justement qu'il exprime une aspiration naturelle de la matière vers des solutions qui veulent s'affranchir du droit formel (2).

1) Hermétisme

Les réflexions sur le droit formel et le droit immanent, sur l'équité, sont des réminiscences des antinomies du droit. Celles qui préoccupaient les théoriciens du droit naturel et qui allaient mener à un compromis avec les positivistes : la distinction simplificatrice entre droit subjectif et droit objectif, distinction qui fait apparaître les multiples facettes du droit, l'une métaphysicienne, l'autre praticienne, mais toutes deux politiques. Et ces discussions politiques qui ramènent le droit à sa fonction de liaison entre individus et société, n'ont jamais véritablement pris pied en propriété intellectuelle. La matière s'est en quelque sorte exclue de la réflexion fondamentale en revendiquant très tôt un statut d'exception pour communiquer franchement sa constitution formelle, celle d'une législation particulière[41]. Il faut voir ici la cause d'une radicalisation et d'un appauvrissement des discours sur sa propre méthode. Les juristes, les privatistes surtout, n'ont retenu des classiques que ce qui permettait de justifier l'emploi du langage de la propriété privée et son économie. L'agitation doctrinale s'est faite essentiellement

41 Ce particularisme prend un relief encore plus prononcé dans les pays de *common law*. Alain Strowel décrit les systèmes de *common law* comme étant des systèmes « fermés », détaillant, dans un catalogue exhaustif, des droits précis : Alain Strowel, *Droit d'auteur et copyright, divergences et convergences*, Étude de droit comparé, Bruxelles, Bruyant, 1993 à la p 146.

sur le terrain des théories justificatrices[42]. Mais peu nombreux sont les auteurs qui ont su rapporter à la propriété intellectuelle les enseignements de la science politique ou de la philosophie morale, réduisant le champ de prospection généralement à la question de la propriété. Même l'intérêt public demeure une notion indéfinie, très citée mais peu étudiée. Le juriste de droit privé, sélectif dans ses références, aura tendance à isoler, chaque fois qu'il le peut, les travaux de Locke sur la propriété privée, de sa conception politique du droit qu'il délaisse aux publicistes. Les théoriciens de l'abus se feront une mission de réhabiliter ce discours politique laissé pour compte.

L'intrusion récente de l'abus en propriété intellectuelle, dans son langage autant que dans son procédé juridique, est donc un rappel à l'ordre. Les accords ADPIC font références aux « usages abusifs », une formule qui est reprise dans la Loi canadienne sur les brevets[43]. L'abus se manifeste également dans la jurisprudence canadienne autant qu'américaine. En effet, l'engouement pour la théorie du *misuse* en droit américain ne se dément pas. Cette tendance est certainement attribuable à l'usure du modèle « propriété » de la propriété intellectuelle et à la surchauffe évidente de l'activité législative et réglementaire. Voilà pourquoi on cherche réconfort dans les modes de pensée plus ouverts. On redécouvre aussi, à côté de l'abus, le vieux discours du constitutionalisme. Christophe Geiger voit la possibilité de constitutionaliser la propriété intellectuelle et ce dans le but de lui donner une direction dont elle serait dépourvue, de lui faire justice[44]. Ce mouvement constitutionaliste, au même titre que les théories classiques sur la justice, élargissent les perspectives de l'interprète et oblige notamment à ce que l'on s'interroge sur le rôle du juge dans notre matière.

La pensée du droit elle aussi a son cycle. Le droit privé se fait miroir du jeu des procédés démocratiques d'une nation. On y lit tantôt la confiance accordée à l'État et à son rôle régulateur, tantôt la menace qu'il représente pour les libertés. Le droit alterne ainsi dans sa méthode entre droit réactionnel — que l'on associe plus volontiers à la common law — et droit institutionnel — qui sied mieux aux formes d'un droit écrit, c'est-à-dire entre positivisme jurisprudentiel et positivisme formel, entre *rule of law* et État

---

42 Notamment Peter Drahos, *A Philosophy of Intellectual Property*, Aldershot, Dartmouth, 1996.

43 *Loi sur les brevets*, LRC 1985, c P-4, art 65.

44 Christophe Geiger, « 'Constitutionalising' Intellectual Property Law? — The Influence of Fundamental Rights on Intellectual Property in the European Union » (2006) 37:4 IIC 371.

de droit, entre déréglementation et régulation. L'abus, on l'a vu, est une formule correctrice qui vise à délester le pouvoir législatif dont la production normative doit être minimale. Gény avait bien résumé la pensée de l'époque sur ce point. Répondant à ceux qui voyaient le principe de sécurité juridique et de primauté de la loi en péril, il écrit :

> L'objection pourrait nous arrêter, si le système traditionnel donnait ici plus de garanties en faveur de la vérité objective. Il n'en est rien. Ce n'est qu'une illusion, purement décevante, qu'on s'imagine trouver, dans une étroite interprétation des textes légaux, étayée des raisonnements d'une logique abstraite, une base vraiment ferme de solutions juridiques[45].

Ces propos vantent les vertus universalistes de l'abus. Surtout qu'en propriété intellectuelle, la déception quant aux productions normatives se vit quotidiennement. Le cycle ininterrompu des réformes, aux effets souvent mitigés, ainsi que la facture souvent absconse des textes, doublée chez nous des difficultés linguistiques[46], lui donnent encore raison. D'autant que le législateur sait faire, mais rarement défaire.

La déficience de la règle, puisque c'est là où l'abus nous mène, renvoie le juriste à replacer le droit dans sa complexité politique et éthique. Soit que le droit, en tant qu'ordre construit, contienne toute la justice soit, au contraire, qu'il ne puisse jamais totalement se réaliser dans sa légalité formelle. Dans la théorie de l'abus, les prescriptions du droit étatique sont sans cesse soumises à un examen de conformité à l'idée de justice. La distinction entre le droit positif et le droit subjectif, on l'a mentionné, a été particulièrement utile pour exprimer cette idée puisqu'elle fait voir un droit dynamique, tendu entre l'intérêt individuel (droit subjectif) et l'État (droit positif), entre l'individu et la collectivité. De là une attention nourrie sur la fonction des droits dans le droit. Mais entre les principes angéliques de justice et les propriétés stables du droit positif, les sociétés modernes ont vite privilégié le second. L'idée d'un droit *statutaire* est naturellement une formule apaisante pour les civilistes en particulier et les privatistes en général. Ceux du droit d'auteur, par exemple, y voient une véritable sinécure. On décrit alors la loi sur le droit d'auteur comme un *code complet* pour éviter l'épanchement de sens et accommoder l'interprète. Dans notre système, se plaît à répéter la

---

45 Gény, *Méthode d'interprétation*, *supra* note 14, vol 2 à la p 224.

46 Nicholas Kasirer, « L'ambivalence lexicographique en droit d'auteur canadien » dans Marie Cornu et al, dir, *Dictionnaire comparé du droit d'auteur et du copyright*, Paris, CNRS, 2003 à la p 313.

Cour suprême du Canada « le droit d'auteur tire son origine de la loi, et les droits et recours que celleci prévoit sont exhaustifs »[47]. Il faut cependant s'interroger, depuis quand la législation particulière vide le droit de toute sa matière? Depuis quand les arguments dits *philosophiques* contiendraient moins de droit que la loi elle-même?[48]

La dérive à laquelle mène une telle formule se rencontre encore dans la reprise de déclarations atones au sujet de la méthode actuelle d'interprétation : « Selon la méthode « moderne » ou « téléologique », a-t-on l'habitude de lire, les termes de la Loi doivent être lus « en suivant le sens ordinaire et grammatical » qui s'harmonise avec les objets de la Loi »[49]. Cette méthode n'en est pas une ; la généralité de ses termes rend la formule creuse. Au contraire, dès lors que l'on tente de faire valoir qu'un droit qu'elle prévoit est détourné des objectifs qu'on peut lui prêter, la vague formule est agitée d'un camp à l'autre. Voilà qui met en perspective les positions contrastées des juges Rothstein et Bastarache dans l'affaire Kraft et dans laquelle l'abus de droit avait été invoqué mais rejeté malgré les suggestions du juge Bastarache. S'exprimant pour la majorité, Rothstein réplique :

> Je crains que l'approche du juge Bastarache en l'espèce soit incompatible avec la méthode d'interprétation législative adoptée par notre Cour. Selon la méthode « moderne » ou « téléologique », les termes de la Loi doivent être lus « en suivant le sens ordinaire et grammatical » qui s'harmonise avec les objets de la Loi. Toutefois, les juges ne sont pas pour autant autorisés à substituer leurs préférences en matière de politique générale à celles du législateur. La Cour a constamment jugé que « le droit d'auteur tire son origine de la loi, et les droits et recours que prévoit la *Loi sur le droit d'auteur* sont exhaustifs . . . . J'estime, en toute déférence, que les motifs du juge Bastarache dérogent à cette théorie[50].

De son côté, le juge Bastarache adopte une position toute josserandienne. Il ne manque que la référence au motif illégitime. Faisant allusion

---

47 *Théberge c Galerie d'Art du Petit Champlain inc*, 2002 CSC 34 au para 5; *CCH Canadienne Ltée c Barreau du Haut-Canada*, 2004 CSC 13 au para 9 [*CCH*]; *Bishop c Stevens*, [1990] 2 RCS 467 à la p 477; *Compo Co Ltd c Blue Crest Music*, [1980] 1 RCS 357 aux pp 372–73.

48 Dans le jugement de première instance de l'affaire Kraft (*supra* note 3), les arguments relevant des principes généraux du droit ou de l'idée d'équité avaient été qualifiés, non sans une certaine connotation péjorative, de « philosophiques », *Kraft Canada Inc c Euro Excellence Inc*, 2004 CF 652 au para 47, [2004] 4 RCF 410.

49 *Kraft CSC*, *supra* note 3 au para 3.

50 *Ibid*.

à la stratégie qui consiste à substituer une base d'action pour une autre et à jouer ainsi sur la duplicité des formes de protection (droit des marques, droit d'auteur), il écrit :

> il faut éviter de lui donner une interprétation incompatible avec la *Loi sur les marques de commerce*, L.R.C. 1985, ch. T13. La législation sur les marques de commerce protège les parts de marché des biens commerciaux; le droit d'auteur protège les gains économiques résultant de l'exercice du talent et du jugement. Si la législation sur les marques de commerce ne protège pas une part de marché dans un cas particulier, il n'y a pas lieu de recourir à la législation sur le droit d'auteur pour offrir cette protection si cela oblige à sortir le droit d'auteur de son champ d'application normal[51].

C'est à travers la jurisprudence que l'on peut observer cette éclipse toujours partielle du droit et de la justice. C'est là, dans l'ouvrage du juge, que se trouve l'intérêt de cette discussion. Nous l'avons écrit, si l'on persiste à confondre légalité et justice alors le simple respect des lois suffira à remplir les exigences d'une déontologie juridique minimale et peu exigeante. La physionomie des droits intellectuels encourage naturellement cette approche. L'argument est puissant et prend pour inévitables mais acceptables l'imperfectibilité et l'insuffisance des lois[52]. De la sorte, le sentiment d'injustice éprouvé à la suite de l'application intransigeante d'un texte trouve immédiatement sa raison d'être et sa solution dans le texte. La difficulté du droit injuste est en partie évacuée par la place que tiennent dans cette conception les mécanismes de révision ou de réforme législative. Les imperfections du système légal sont traitées à partir des mécanismes parlementaires et du contrôle de légalité. Mais le positivisme légal n'épuise pas la question. Ces propos de Gény prennent tout leur sens : « Mais vraiment, on ne peut se fier à lui [le législateur], pour satisfaire à tout. Son intervention doit rester relativement rare, en matière de droit privé. Il n'est même pas désirable, que les plus menues règles, destinées à satisfaire des intérêts nouvellement reconnus ou mieux compris, soient, toujours et de suite, rédigées en article de lois »[53].

---

51 *Ibid* au para 83.

52 On voit clairement comment cette position a pu être celle des tenants de la philosophie libérale : tout ce qui n'est pas interdit est donc permis et la justice dans sa compréhension politique devient aussi bien le fait du législateur que des mécanismes de régulation naturels dans un milieu de concurrence.

53 Gény, *Méthode d'interprétation*, *supra* note 14, vol 2, à la p 228.

2) La Jurisprudence des Intérêts : le Péril Libéral

L'impression générale est effectivement que le traitement spécial des droits intellectuels soustrait au juge une partie de son appréciation. Leur administration dépendrait d'autres instances, spécialisées elles aussi, la loi ne suffisant plus pour rendre compte de la multiplicité grandissante des intérêts. Carbonnier avait d'ailleurs évoqué la « pulvérisation du droit en droits subjectifs »[54].

De plus, cette centralité du discours des intérêts qui atteint aussi la façon dont les cours abordent les questions de propriété intellectuelle a pour effet de minorer la fonction judiciaire et de lui imposer un rôle subalterne. La recherche de l'équilibre des intérêts, objectif annoncé des récentes décisions de la Cours suprême du Canada en propriété intellectuelle, maintient le droit dans la règle textuelle et non dans le principe. Elle devient le signe d'une justice affaiblie qui refuse de remettre le droit en question et de revenir à des solutions que dicterait pourtant l'équité. Olivier Jouanjan a très bien saisi le premier paradoxe fondamental du droit qu'il appellera le tourment de l'interprétation, car très vite l'interprète doit se situer hors du texte :

> Mais l'interprétation et ses méthodes font exploser le cadre formel de la logique. Car elle se présente comme :« libre activité spirituelle », « art » . . . , c'est-à-dire activité *créatrice*. C'est à l'intuition qu'elle s'en remet en dernier ressort. Or, la création non plus que l'intuition n'ont à rendre compte de leurs fondations. Le fruit de la création n'a pas à être *prouvé* et ne saurait l'être. Sa source n'est autre que la souveraineté de l'artiste, de l'interprète. L'art de l'interprétation recèle donc un *pouvoir*, une puissance que l'idée de l'État *de droit*, dans lequel les décisions doivent être *fondées en droit*, refoule[55].

Le second de ces paradoxes met en cause l'abus dans son projet politique. Si aujourd'hui il nous semble avoir à faire à une propriété intellectuelle si dense, si peu plastique, si indécise qu'elle en devient un tissu synthétique de lois, c'est que la notion de droit elle-même n'est plus irradiée par une conception forte de l'État, du Souverain. Avec Raynaud, nous sommes donc bien fondés à nous demander si nous n'entrons pas « dans une ère où le droit s'émancipe de l'État, où s'éclipse la figure du souverain et où la fonction judi-

---

54 Jean Carbonnier, *Droit et passion du droit sous la Ve République*, Paris, Flammarion, 1996 à la p. 106.

55 Jouanjan, *supra* note 25 au para 30.

ciaire devient en droit première dans l'ordre juridique [notes omises]»[56]. Cette perdition ou élévation du droit à travers l'autorité du juge, par ailleurs si crainte, Josserand l'a soutenue sans aucune retenue. Le politique cherchant à tout prix à s'exprimer, la voix législative étant perdue dans la polyphonie des représentations, il le ferait plus naturellement par le prononcé judiciaire. La position des tenants de l'abus est une reformulation de la justice aristotélicienne selon laquelle l'équitable peut dépasser la loi écrite[57].

On a fait remarquer que la théorie de l'abus reposait sur une trame plus littéraire que juridique. D'où son ambigüité, d'où son impossible instrumentalisation. La formule de l'abus envoûte par son esthétisme, par sa puissance évocatrice. Elle se fait entendre non dans les assemblées mais dans les prétoires et désigne ainsi ces autres chantiers de construction juridique que sont les tribunaux[58]. La propriété intellectuelle a refusé d'ouvrir les prétoires et entend demeurer entièrement modelée par les lois. Voilà peut-être l'origine des déboires de notre matière lorsqu'il s'agit de redresser le détournement de ses droits. « Les changements incessants de la réalité sociale et la tolérance liée au pluralisme empêchent le législateur d'enfermer encore l'écrit normatif dans la formulation implacable de lois immuables. S'il légifère plus que jamais, le législateur s'attache plus aux détails qu'aux principes et s'il touche à ceux-ci, c'est sur le ton de la directive, non du commandement »[59]. Et on entend la complainte lancinante de ceux qui reprochent aux lois de propriété intellectuelle leur manque d'aspiration, de sens. Cette lacune est encore soulignée par le discours des intérêts conflictuels. Le législateur autant que le juge recherchent le compromis. L'approche téléologique cède alors le pas à une méthode de computation des valeurs et des intérêts. Teresa Scassa avait montré par exemple comment le contentieux judiciaire en droit d'auteur s'exprime à partir de la notion d'équilibrage des intérêts et pourquoi l'approche n'est pas sans faille :

> Most recently copyright law in Canada has been referred to as a balance between the interests of creators and users of works. Other iterations of the balance have made reference to a broader societal interest as well. Yet such

---

56 Philipe Raynaud, *Le juge et le philosophe*, Paris, Colin, 2008 à la p 121.

57 Chaïm Perelman, Éthique et droit, Bruxelles, Éditions de l'Université de Bruxelles, 1990 notamment aux pp 51 et s, et 198 et s.

58 Paul Martens, « Thémis et ses plumes — Réflexions sur l'écriture juridique » dans *Nouveaux itinéraires en droit — Hommage à François Rigaux*, Bruxelles, Bruylant, 1993 à la p 346 [Martens].

59 *Ibid* à la p 347.

> statements are far from being an adequate articulation of the interests in the balance. Little attention has been given to defining who "creators" and "users" are, or to identifying the societal interests at play. Further, the expression of balance between users and creators overlooks another important — if not crucial — interest: that of owners [60].

Cette didactique des intérêts fige considérablement la pensée juridique moderne et limite l'impact d'un intérêt « public » ou « social » qui n'est plus alors qu'un facteur parmi d'autres. On ne peut s'empêcher de lire dans ce mouvement les effets des forces libérales puisqu'il aboutit à considérer les intérêts comme autant de valeurs particulières et échangeables, c'est finalement le retour au subjectivisme, à l'atomisme.

Étonnement, l'idée de réduire l'analyse juridique à une méthode de conciliation n'est pas nouvelle; elle est même contemporaine à l'apparition de la théorie de l'abus. Heck[61] en Allemagne et Demogue[62] en France, notamment[63] en sont les précurseurs. Ils avaient, tout comme leurs contemporains, adressé une critique sévère à ceux qui croyaient encore au perfectionnement de la législation. Mais plus cyniques, et refusant toute pensée téléologique, ils ont réduit la mécanique du droit privé à la computation des *masses* d'intérêts à considérer. L'office du juge est la pesée. Or, dans ce contexte, si le droit est désormais sorti de la théologie, les forces extérieures du lobbying en font une matière tout autant pétrie d'arbitraires. Et après avoir relu le texte de la Loi sur la modernisation du droit d'auteur[64], qui vient d'être adoptée au Canada, jamais ne nous sommes nous sentis plus proches des conclusions de Martens pour qui « l'image du droit mûri dans les assemblées, coulé dans des lois dont le juge n'aurait qu'à exécuter les commandements, n'est plus pertinente »[65]. Le même auteur rappelle, en fin d'analyse, la force salvatrice de la formule de l'abus de droit. Par elle,

---

60 Teresa Scassa, « Interests in the Balance », dans Michael Geist, dir, *The Public Interest: The Future of Canadian Copyright Law*, Toronto, Irwin Law, 2005 à la p 41. L'expression "juste équilibre" est désormais consacrée par la Cour suprême; voir *CCH*, *supra* note 47 au para 48

61 Philipp Von Heck, *Die Entstehung der Lex Frisionum*, Stuttgart, Verlag von W Kohlhammer, 1927.

62 Demogue, *supra* note 23.

63 Oliver Wendell Holmes, *The Common Law*, Boston, American Bar Association, 2010 et « Law in Science, and Science in Law » (1899) 12 Harv L Rev 443; Benjamin Cardozo, *The Paradoxes of Legal Science*, Clark, The Lawbook Exchange, 2000 [1928].

64 *Loi sur la modernisation du droit d'auteur*, LC 2012, c 20.

65 Martens, *supra* note 58 à la p 369.

écrit-il, « les émotions troubles de l'équité purent se structurer dans des arcatures objectives et se donner un aspect de validité juridique. Alors les juges purent user des ressources de l'énoncé performatif et de la magie illocutoire : ils osèrent manifester l'idée de justice qui jusque-là avait dormi en eux dans un état d'insuffisance littéraire »[66].

D. CONCLUSION

Finalement, la formule de l'abus n'est pas moins vide ou pleine de sens que celles des législations particulières de la propriété intellectuelle et d'un code complet ou que celle de la méthode moderne de l'interprétation, refrain repris ces dernières années par la Cour suprême du Canada. L'interprétation est une lecture contextuelle et globale de la loi « en suivant le sens ordinaire et grammatical qui s'harmonise avec l'esprit de la loi, l'objet de la loi et l'intention du législateur »[67]; une formule que les sophistes auraient appréciée et qui, en fin de compte, paraît bien plus comme une logomachie. On y lit pourtant une expression qui a une signification particulière dans la pensée juridique : « l'esprit de la loi ». Le débat est là, à savoir si tout le droit est contenu dans la loi ou s'il peut être cherché ailleurs dans une dimension plus abstraite, celle de « l'esprit » des choses.

L'idée de sentiment de justice a bien servi en droit mais elle a également été reçue dans d'autres domaines des sciences humaines. On la retrouve en économie. Selon Amartya Sen[68] par exemple, l'interprétation populaire de l'œuvre d'Adam Smith[69] oublie la centralité du sentiment de justice en économie. En s'étant départie de l'aspect normatif, l'économie se serait appauvrie considérablement. Il est de notre avis que ce métadiscours normatif est nourricier dans toutes les sphères d'étude portant sur le comportement humain. La théorie de l'abus, on le sait, demeure un principe actif et libérateur. Il s'agit désormais de ne plus craindre son emploi[70].

---

66 *Ibid* à la p 353.

67 *Rizzo & Rizzo Shoes Ltd (Re)*, [1998] 1 RCS 27 à la p 41.

68 Amartya Sen, « Comportement économique et sentiments moraux » dans Amartya Sen, Éthique *et économie*, Paris, Presses Universitaires de France, 2008 à la p 1.

69 Adam Smith, *The Wealth of Nations*, New York : Knopf, 1991 [1776]; Adam Smith, *Théorie des sentiments moraux*, Paris, Presses Universitaires de France, 2003.

70 Christophe Caron, *Abus de droit et droit d'auteur*, Paris, Litec, 1998.

SIX

Biopatenting and Industrial Policy Discourse: Decoding the Message of Biomedia on the Limits of Agents and Audiences

BITA AMANI

ABSTRACT (EN): Patent law has yet to recognize the agency of multiple creators acting jointly with so-called inventors. It operates on the romantic myth of individual creation, ignoring the agency of plants, animals, people, and their genetic substrates. Invention is, according to the law, a singular deliberative act completed in isolation. The legal doctrine of "products of nature" provides only a partial challenge to the legitimacy of biopatent claims and is contingent on human agency for meaning. In Canada, the Supreme Court has recognized the agency of non-humans with its concern over "reproducibility" of mice in the Harvard mouse case and has used this understanding to inform its perhaps unduly criticized reasons against the patentability of the oncomouse. A socio-cultural approach to law using actor network theory may inform our understanding of biology and biotechnology as discourse, always in performativity, adaptation, mutation, and translation. It may provide a means to challenge the normative assumptions implicit in claims of legal entitlement to patents in language familiar to the patent bar, paving the way for recognition of the agency of others while helping define the necessary limits on patentability and patent rights in biomedia. An interdisciplinary approach may generate the necessary conceptual shift and create, in the words of Stuart Hall, a critical "moment of collective self-clarification."

RÉSUMÉ (FR): Le droit de la propriété industrielle n'a toujours pas reconnu les capacités d'agir « agency » de nombreux créateurs qui collaborent avec les prétendument inventeurs. Ce droit fonctionne sur la base du mythe romantique de la création individuelle, ignorant la contribution des plantes, des animaux, des personnes et de leur substrat génétique. En droit, une invention est un acte délibéré singulier achevé de façon isolée. La théorie juridique du « produit de la nature » ne constitue qu'un défi limité à la légitimité des revendications de biobrevetabilité et dépend de l'intervention humaine pour lui donner une signification. Au Canada, la Cour suprême, dans l'affaire de la souris Harvard, a reconnu l'immixtion de facteurs non humains en prenant en considération le problème de la « reproductibilité » des souris et a utilisé cette perspective pour justifier son raisonnement peut-être indûment critiqué pour ne pas breveter la souris. Une approche socioculturelle du droit, recourant à une théorie des réseaux d'acteurs, peut éclairer notre compréhension du discours concernant la biologie et la biotechnologie, toujours en performativité, en adaptation, en mutation, et en traduction. Cela peut donner un moyen de mettre en question les présupposés normatifs implicites dans les revendications de droits aux brevets, dans un langage plus familier aux praticiens en brevets, pour ainsi ouvrir la voie à la reconnaissance de l'apport des autres agents, tout en aidant à définir les limites nécessaires à la brevetabilité et aux droits des brevets en biomédia. Une approche interdisciplinaire peut apporter une réorientation conceptuelle nécessaire et créer, pour reprendre les mots de Stuart Hall, un « moment d'autoclarification collective » critique.

A. INTRODUCTION

Spring 2012 witnessed a perfect storm in media, a merger of art with life. A science fiction thriller, *Prometheus* was released in theatres and featured two archaeologists on board the *Prometheus* spaceship on a mission to find the "engineers" of the human race. At the same time, the United States Supreme Court (USSC), in *Mayo v Prometheus*,[1] was confronted with the contested scope of ownership claims and doctrinal limits to the legal meaning of "invention" for biotechnology patents (biopatents). Patent law has allowed the appropriation of labour and agency from multiple creators and users acting in collaboration with so-called inventors. Dutfield notes

> [w]hether we have God or natural processes alone to thank, much of the difficult work has been done — in many cases millions of years earlier. Putting it in its bluntest terms, genetic engineers are really just free-rid-

1 *Mayo Collaborative Services v Prometheus Laboratories Inc*, 566 US __ (2012) [*Prometheus*].

> ers who tinker half-knowingly with what they have got and actually create nothing that was not there before.[2]

"Invention" is reduced in common law jurisdictions to the mythology of a single creator engaged in a deliberative act of ingenuity. Insofar as courts have upheld the view that life is patentable, the law reinforces the romantic myth of individual creation, and ignores the agency of plants, animals, even human actors in maintaining their genetic and biological substrates. Patent protection is rationalized on the utilitarian view that patents incentivize new inventions that in the long term will lead to welfare gains. As a matter of policy, offering a short-term monopoly is a rational trade-off for encouraging research and development in the life sciences. But, can the claim to inventorship be justified given the unique capacity for life, from whole organisms to the genes coded by deoxyribonucleic acid (DNA), to self-replicate, adapt, and mutate in response to a (host) environment? The mutability of life in a discursive process is known to science and is a central tenet of epigenomics.[3] It features also in the film *Prometheus*.

This chapter reviews the 2012 USSC's *Prometheus* decision regarding patent ineligibility for natural processes and draws some parallels with the Supreme Court of Canada's (SCC) Harvard mouse decision[4] on the patentability of products that result from the *reproducibility* phenomenon in nature. Both decisions imply that the patentees' claims to entitlement simply cannot be made out. *Harvard* initiates a necessary conceptual shift towards a broader understanding of non-human actor agency in the context of product claims while *Prometheus* serves this function in terms of *natural* processes. The chapter is divided into four parts. Section B examines the Prometheus myth as metaphor to help inform our reading of *Prometheus*. Actor Network Theory (ANT) is introduced to register its potential as a theoretical framework. Section C reviews the concept of reproducibility

---

2 Graham Dutfield, "Who Invents Life: Intelligent Designers, Blind Watchmakers or Genetic Engineers?" (2010) 5:7 J Intell Prop L & Practice 531 at 533.

3 See National Human Genome Research Institute, *Epigenomics Fact Sheet* (7 May 2012), online: National Human Genome Research Institute www.genome.gov/27532724. "Derived from the Greek, epigenome means 'above' the genome. The epigenome consists of chemical compounds that modify, or mark, the genome in a way that tells it what to do, where to do it and when to do it. The marks, which are not part of the DNA itself, can be passed on from cell to cell as cells divide, and from one generation to the next."

4 *Harvard College v Canada (Commissioner of Patents)*, 2002 SCC 76 [*Harvard*]; see also Bita Amani, *State Agency and the Patenting of Life in International Law: Merchants and Missionaries in a Global Society* (Aldershott: Ashgate Publishing Company, 2009).

endorsed by the majority of the SCC as a basis for rejecting patent claims over a higher life organism. Considered through the ANT lens, the concept of *reproducibility* as a basis for determining patentability may be applied to reconsider the law on lower life, genes, and even DNA. Section D examines the historical treatment of DNA, from its origins in the scientific literature as a "discovery" to its subsequent judicial treatment as chemicals, purified and isolated, and therefore patentable. The final stage in our understanding of DNA would be to give legal effect to DNA as biomedia. As we move from the hardware of the knowledge economy to the wetware[5] of the bio-economy,[6] decoding the message of DNA may help us understand our relationship with non-human actors.[7] Section E returns to the Prometheus metaphor. Modern science reveals we are all chimeras; transgenics comprised of aliens within. Some of these actors are essential to our survival. The impulse towards greater human agency, to colonize and impose proprietary mappings on inner space as the new frontier, may be strong. Yet these boundary-bending "foreign" bodies force us to interrogate the legal concept of discrete interventions as *inventions*, the scope and limits of property, and the concept of what is "human" and, by corollary, what is "nature." Rather than a piecemeal and incremental approach to the patentability of biological and biochemical claims, a principled understanding is needed to inform doctrinal analyses. This is where interdisciplinarity holds promise.

---

5 Dennis Bray, *Wetware: A Computer in Every Living Cell* (New Haven, CT: Yale University Press, 2009). Bray defines wetware as "the sum of all the information-rich molecular processes inside a living cell . . . . Cells are built of molecules that interact in complex webs, or circuits . . . . The computational units of life — the transistors, if you will — are its giant molecules, especially proteins. Acting like miniature switches, they guide the biochemical processes of a cell this way or that. Linked into huge networks they form the basis of all of the distinctive properties of living systems" at x.

6 Matthew Herder & E Richard Gold, "Intellectual Property Issues in Biotechnology: Health and Industry" Report delivered at the Third Meeting of the Steering Group of the OECD International Futures Project on the Bioeconomy to 2030: Designing a Policy Agenda, Paris (7–8 February 2008).

7 See, for example, Feris Jabr, "Microbial Mules: Engineering Bacteria to Transport Nanoparticles and Drugs" (2012) 306:6 Scientific American 20, reporting on research taking non-pathogenic *Escherichia coli* and saddling it with beads, rods, and crescents made from nickel and tin coated in gold that is heated by infrared light to destroy surrounding diseased tissue. Other projects are focused on engineering bacteria to deliver medical packages directly to diseased cells.

B. *PROMETHEUS* AND THE ORIGIN OF ORIGIN STORIES

What can *Prometheus* teach us? Stories of creation or evolution are origin stories. Origin stories are authorship[8] stories, born from the normative narrative of those who give expression to an articulation that claims sovereignty over competing narratives and interpretations. According to Leeming,

> [h]uman beings have traditionally used stories to describe or explain things they could not explain otherwise . . . . In this sense, myth is related to metaphor, in which an object or event is compared to an apparently dissimilar object or event in such a way as to make its otherwise inexplicable essence clear . . . to read a culture's myths is to gleam information about that culture . . . . In a real sense, the world reveals its inner self through its common mythology.[9]

Semiotics[10] helps explain how each (re)iteration of Prometheus as myth and metaphor captures and modifies its social meaning, encoding a new narrative to be decoded by the audience. Prometheus is credited with creating humanity (from clay) and Zeus for punishing him, but who authors Prometheus? Leeming tells us that

> [a] question that inevitably arises in connection with mythology is that of authorship. Who wrote the myths or, more accurately, who first told them? Almost invariably the answer must be the people themselves. The myth, like its close relative the fairy tale, has its origins in the collective "folk" mind.[11]

When we seek to locate an individual author, we run into trouble as "[p]ower and authorship fabricate reality."[12] It is axiomatic in western intellectual

---

8 See, for example, Michel Foucault, "What is an Author" in Josué V Harari, ed, *Textual Strategies: Perspectives in Post-Structuralist Criticism* (New York: Cornell University Press, 1979) at 141. Foucault asserts that the idea of an atomistic author as the "sole creator" of unique works is a relatively recent invention; see also Martha Woodmansee & Peter Jaszi, eds, *The Construction of Authorship: Textual Appropriation in Law and Literature* (Durham: Duke University Press, 1994).

9 David Adams Leeming, *The World of Myth: An Anthology* (New York: Oxford University Press, 1990) at 3–6.

10 See, for example, Susan W Tiefenbrun, "Semiotic Definition of Lawfare" (2011) 43 Case W Res J Int'l L 29, wherein the author defines semiotics as "the exchange between two or more speakers through the medium of coded language and convention" at 32 [footnotes omitted].

11 Leeming, above note 9 at 6–7.

12 Donna J Haraway, *Simians, Cyborgs, and Women: The Reinvention of Nature* (New York: Routledge, 1991) at 74.

property law that whoever tells the tale owns it. And, what of the contribution of "others"?

The politics of ownership and control are an integral part of media studies but also attract much scrutiny in intellectual property literature, where the law is sometimes seen as having independent agency in meaning (myth) making:[13] treating corporations as persons and life as proprietary "invention." The law prioritizes the patent as readable text and so recognizes the agency of some actors, inventors in patent law, while alienating the "other" whose voiceless agency renders them invisible as actants in the law. But who is an inventor and what is an "invention"?

The relationship between law and science is political.[14] The USSC in a 5-4 split decision in *Diamond v Chakrabarty* found living micro-organisms patentable as a "nonnaturally occurring manufacture or composition of matter — a product of human ingenuity."[15] The focus was not so much on life as patentable subject matter *per se* but on human agency. That "anything under the sun that is made by man" [16] is patentable — reflects the view that no distinction is to be drawn on the basis of whether the claim extends to the living or inanimate.

Beineke v USPTO[17] addressed whether discovered superior oak trees, each over 100 years old, were patentable. Plants and animals have long been patentable in the United States.[18] Yet, the Federal Circuit upheld the Patent Office's rejection of the claims on the basis that these were unpatent-

---

13 Leeming, above note 9. The term "myth" may be understood as "a generally accepted belief unsubstantiated by fact" at 3.

14 For example, the characterization of Ephedra, now banned, as a natural substance rather than as a drug situated its use as a weight loss supplement outside the need for FDA approval. Over 800 law suits were later launched on the view that use of Ephedra use led to heart attacks and strokes; see Hon Jed S Rakoff, "Science and the Law: Uncomfortable Bedfellows" (2008) 38 Seton Hall L Rev 1379, online: Seton Hall http://38.113.83.199/Students/academics/journals/law-review/Issues/archives/upload/Rakoff-final.pdf.

15 *Diamond v Chakrabarty*, 447 US 303 (1980).

16 *Ibid* at 309, citing S Rep No 1979, 82d Cong, 2d Sess, 5 (1952).

17 *Beineke v USPTO*, 12-580 (2012) [*Beineke*], online: Justicia http://docs.justia.com/cases/federal/appellate-courts/cafc/11-1459/11-1459-2012-08-06.pdf; petition for writ of *certiorari* (5 November 2012) denied by the US Supreme Court, 19 February 2013, online: US Sup Ct www.supremecourt.gov/Search.aspx?FileName=/docketfiles/12-580.htm.

18 *JEM Ag Supply v Pioneer Hi-Bred International*, 534 US 124 (2001); "Transgenic non-human mammals," US Patent No 4736866 (22 June 1984); but see *Ex Parte Latimer*, 1889 Dec Com Pat 123, rejecting the application over a fibre found in pine tree needles and not known in the prior art as "invention"; see *Parker v Flook*, 437 US 584 (1978) [*Flook*], where it was held that "[e]ven though a phenomenon of nature or mathematical formula may be well known, an inventive application of the principle may be patented. Conversely, the

able discoveries of products of nature. The Court found no evidence to support the patentee's claim; the trees were not, from inception, created or contributed to by "human activity."[19] The Court also found that "the statute required some "exercise of the inventive faculty"[20] and that this view was consistent with *Chakrabarty*. *Chakrabarty*'s distinction between the natural and non-natural was affirmed as the central question in this case. Yet, law is as much a social construct, an artifact of cultural production — a myth — as the nature it seeks to govern.

At issue in *Mayo v Prometheus*,[21] were the contested patents of Prometheus Laboratories relating to the use of thiopurine drugs to treat autoimmune diseases. These drugs were metabolized by the ingesting body differently, producing variable levels of metabolites that must be "read" and measured before the medication is adjusted by the doctor overseeing treatment: "[t]he patent claims at issue here set forth processes embodying researchers' findings that identified these correlations with some precision . . . . The patent claims seek to embody this research in a set of processes."[22]

Did Prometheus Laboratories invent this process? Prometheus, as exclusive licensee of the contested patents, sold the diagnostic blood tests embodying the processes to Mayo Clinic et al. In 2004, Mayo announced its intention to use and sell its own tests, with higher metabolite metrics for determining toxicity. The District Court found that Mayo's tests were infringing; the toxicity levels were too similar to those of Prometheus to be considered different tests. Based on the claim language, the Court also endorsed Prometheus' view that the medical expert using the Mayo test could also violate the patent even if no change was made in treatment decisions after test results.[23] Summary judgment was granted to Mayo, however, on the basis that "the patents effectively claim natural laws or natural phe-

---

discovery of such a phenomenon cannot support a patent *unless* there is some *other inventive concept* in its application" at 594 [emphasis added].

19 *Beineke*, above note 17 at 4.

20 *Ibid* at 9. The 35 USC § 161 provides that "[w]hoever invents or discovers and asexually reproduces any distinct and new variety of plant, including cultivated sports, mutants, hybrids, and newly found seedlings" may be eligible for a plant patent. The Federal Circuit rejected the patent, finding "no indication in the text of the amendments or in the legislative history that Congress intended to ignore the longstanding view that, to be patentable, a new and distinct invention (including a new and distinct plant) must be the product or result of man and his inventive efforts" at 18.

21 *Prometheus*, above note 1.

22 *Ibid* at 5.

23 *Ibid* at 6.

nomena — namely the correlations . . . — and so are not patentable."[24] The Federal Circuit reversed on appeal and found that the patents claimed more than natural correlations. The process claims specify the steps of administering the drug to a patient and determining the resulting metabolite level. These steps were said to involve the transformation of the human body or of blood taken from the body. "Thus, the patents satisfied the Circuit's 'machine or transformation test.'"[25] The USSC granted Mayo's petition for *certiorari* and vacated the judgment, remanding the case for reconsideration in light of *Bilski*,[26] which had clarified that the "machine or transformation test," although helpful, was not definitive of patent eligibility. The Federal Circuit on remand reaffirmed its earlier decision that the patent claims "do not encompass laws of nature or pre-empt natural correlations."[27] Mayo filed another petition for *certiorari* which was granted. In a unanimous decision the USSC held that the process claims were not patent eligible:

> Prometheus' patents set forth laws of nature — namely, relationships between concentrations of certain metabolites in the blood and the likelihood that a dosage of a thiopurine drug will prove ineffective or cause harm . . . . While it takes a human action (the administration of a thiopurine drug) to trigger a manifestation of this relation in a particular person, the relation itself exists in principle apart from any human action. The relation is a consequence of the ways in which thiopurine compounds are metabolized by the body — entirely natural processes. And so a patent that simply describes that relation sets forth a natural law.[28]

Implicit in the rationale for patent ineligibility is the recognized difficulty of claiming inventorship where the level of human agency is insufficient to warrant a twenty year grant of exclusive rights.[29] When phrased in relation to the laws of nature, the distinction may appear arbitrary; from the lens of agency, it becomes principled. That is, we might move beyond the

---

24 *Ibid* at 7.

25 *Ibid*.

26 *Bilski v Kappos*, 561 US __ (2010) [*Bilski*].

27 *Ibid* at 8.

28 *Prometheus*, above note 1 at 8.

29 *Ibid*. Citing *Flook*, above note 18 and *Bilski*, above note 26, Justice Breyer, writing for the Court found that the authorities "insist that a process that focuses upon the use of a natural law also contain other elements or a combination of elements, sometimes referred to as an 'inventive concept,' sufficient to ensure that the patent in practice amounts to significantly more than a patent upon the natural law itself" at 3.

"natural/non-natural" distinction in *Chakrabarty* to the analysis of what is "man-made."

Prometheus and *Harvard* happened to draw the right line, but without a more stable underpinning, such decisions are vulnerable to the composition of the bench,[30] and so *eternally* contingent[31] on the particular subjectivities of individual judges when reading "nature" as the subtext of the patent text. So much depends on language for "preferred readings"[32] and dominant meanings of patent texts. Dominant or preferred meanings, insofar as they are ideological, function to transform the real into the imaginary,

30 In *Bowman v Monsanto Co*, No. 11-796, writ for *certiorari* granted by the US Supreme Court (5 October 2012), the Federal Circuit rejected the farmer's claim to his right to save commodity seeds purchased from a grain elevator that embodied the glyphosate resistance of Monsanto's Roundup Ready patented soybean variety, finding that to apply the "first sale doctrine to subsequent generations of self-replicating technology would eviscerate the rights of the patent holder." Matthew Alan Chivvis, Rachel Krevans, & Michael R Ward, "Sound the Alarm? — The Supreme Court's Renewed Interest in Life Sciences Patents Could Create Additional Hurdles Across the Field" (16 November 2012), online: Morrison & Foerster www.mofo.com/files/Uploads/Images/121116-Life-Sciences-Patents.pdf. Chivvis, Krevans, & Ward conclude that the USSC's decision to review the Federal Circuit's decision "suggest[s] that the Court is unhappy with the Federal Circuit's articulation of the law in this area." On 13 May 2013, the USSC affirmed that the doctrine of exhaustion only limits the patentees rights to the particular article sold and does not apply to allow farmers to harvest patented plant seed from a legitimately acquired plant for future replanting without the permission of the patentee: see *Bowman v Monsanto*, 569 US___ (2013), online: www.supremecourt.gov/opinions/12pdf/11-796_c07d.pdf.

31 Quentin Meillassoux, "Iteration, Reiteration, Repetition: A Speculative Analysis of the Meaningless Sign" (20 April 2012), translated by Robin Mackay, online: http://cdn.shopify.com/s/files/1/0069/6232/files/Meillassoux_Workshop_Berlin.pdf?100796. "The contingency of which we speak is speculative, not physical. It designates the possible being-otherwise of every entity, even entities that cannot be modified by any human means" at 36.

32 Stuart Hall, "Encoding/Decoding" in Stuart Hall et al, eds, *Culture, Media, Language* (London: Hutchinson, 1980) at 128. Hall writes that "[a]ny society/culture tends, with varying degrees of closure, to impose its classifications of the social and cultural and political world. These constitute a *dominant cultural order*, though it is neither univocal nor uncontested. This question of the 'structure of the discourses in dominance' is a crucial point. The different areas of social life appear to be mapped out into discursive domains, hierarchically organized into *dominant* or *preferred meanings* . . . . [W]e say 'dominant' because there exists a pattern of 'preferred readings'; and these both have the institutional/political/ideological order imprinted in them and have themselves become institutionalized" at 134 [emphasis in original][footnote omitted].

"History into Nature."[33] What then is *nature*?[34] Can the reductive dichotomy between nature and culture be sustained any longer?

Stengers, in discussing the natural versus the supernatural, contends that the distinction "relies on a disastrous definition [of] the 'natural,' namely: that which Science will eventually explain."[35] And, what is to come *after* nature? Bruno Latour observes "there is no way to devise a successor to nature, if we do not tackle the tricky question of *animism* anew."[36] One can contest the idea of nature as stasis; "*always already assembled*, since nothing happens but what comes from before."[37]

Thus, the main issue in biopatent cases can be seen as an issue of animism/inanimism understood more technically through the ANT lens:

> [A]lthough every state of affairs deploys associations of *mediators*, everything is supposed to happen as if only chains of purely passive *intermediaries* were to unfold. Paradoxically, the most stubborn realism, the most rational outlook is predicated on the most unrealistic, the most contradictory notion of an *action without agency*.[38]

Latour is one of the founders of ANT. John Law, another founder, contends that ANT "may be understood as a *semiotics of materiality*."[39] ANT was originally "developed by sociologists of science as a response to the methodological and theoretical dilemmas these scholars encountered as they explored how scientists produced and circulated scientific facts."[40]

ANT theory "insists that performance creates the relations and the objects/people/actants constituted by these relationships. Networks and actors do not exist prior to performance, but are constituted by perform-

---

33 Roland Barthes, "Myth Today" in Roland Barthes, *Mythologies*, translated by Annette Lavers (New York: Hill & Wang, 1984) at 10.

34 See, for example, Eduardo Kac, ed, *Signs of Life: Bio Art and Beyond* (Cambridge: Massachusetts Institute of Technology, 2007) [Kac, *Signs of Life*].

35 Isabelle Stengers, "Reclaiming Animism" 36 *e-flux* (July 2012), online: e-flux www.e-flux.com/journal/reclaiming-animism/.

36 Bruno Latour, "An Attempt at a 'Compositionist Manifesto'" (2010) 41:3 New Literary History 471 at 481 [emphasis in original].

37 *Ibid* at 482 [emphasis in original].

38 *Ibid* [emphasis in original].

39 See John Law, "After ANT: Complexity, Naming and Topology" in John Law & John Hassard, eds, *Actor Network Theory and After* (Oxford: Blackwell, 1999) at 4 [emphasis in original].

40 Ilana Gershon, "Bruno Latour (1947–)" in Jon Simons, ed, *From Agamben to Žižek: Contemporary Critical Theorists* (Edinburgh: Edinburgh University Press, 2010) at 161.

ance."[41] From this critical lens we begin to appreciate how other doctrines of patent law may be conceptually incomplete in the biotechnology context. They cannot adequately deal with the rupture to the legal claim of title that biological matter introduces. The law should not sanction appropriations from "nature" not least because the conceptual view of nature as a separate entity from man who claims sovereignty over it is no longer tenable. Sometimes nature is seen as co-optor of the agency of other actors.[42] More often, nature is an effective co-author/co-inventor, and sometimes intended collaborator, in a complex performance of discursive agencies called Life.[43] ANT's recognition of these activities and agencies will force patent law to reconsider the doctrinal limits to the patentee's claim as "owner." In short, ANT asks us to consider the subtle difference between concluding: "these are not *inventions*" and "even if these are *inventions*, they are not *yours* alone."

The distinction between author/creator/inventor and owner is fundamental in IP law.[44] Recent changes to US patent law further entrench the distinction between human agents/inventors and owners of such claimed inventions:

> Metaphysically, the rules serve to crystallize the US patent system's *shift in focus* away from inventors and toward corporate owners . . . . Up to now, corporations were never considered patent applicants. Rather, inventors were the applicants. Even when the ultimate rights were owned by a corporate entity, the USPTO still focused on the inventors as the patent applicants. Under the new rules . . . the status of "patent applicant" will no longer be keyed to inventorship but instead ownership. Thus, any juristic entity who can show a proprietary interest will be permitted to file and prosecute a patent application *as the patent applicant* . . . .[45]

If non-human, non-living manufactured corporate actors can find representation in the judicial world as juristic persons, why not other non-hu-

---

41 *Ibid* at 166.

42 Robert H Carlson, *Biology is Technology: The Promise, Peril, and New Business of Engineering Life* (Cambridge: Harvard University Press, 2010) at 1.

43 See, for example, Eduardo Kac, "Life Transformation — Art Mutation" in Kac, *Signs of Life*, above note 34 at 164 [Kac, "Life Transformation"].

44 See Dennis Crouch, "AIA Shifts USPTO Focus from Inventors to Patent Owners" *PatentlyO* (14 August 2012), online: PatentlyO www.patentlyo.com/patent/2012/08/aia-shifts-usptos-focus-from-inventors-to-patent-owners.html.

45 *Ibid* [emphasis in original]; it is worth noting that while Canada is a first to file system, until recent patent reform, the US had a first to invent system.

man yet animate actants? Performance artists and common lay-persons[46] challenge any inclination for conflation in the law's asymmetrical recognition of labour and agency. They seem to recognize, as Latour has, that "[i]t is inanimism that is the queer invention: an agency without agency constantly denied by practice."[47]

In *Prometheus*, the USSC asked: "[D]o the patent claims add *enough* to their statements of the correlations to allow the processes they describe to qualify as patent-eligible processes that *apply* natural laws?" The three step process recited in the claims,

> tells doctors interested in the subject about the correlations that the researchers discovered. In doing so, it recites an "administering" step, a "determining" step, and a "wherein" step. These additional steps are not themselves natural laws but neither are they sufficient to transform the nature of the claim.[48]

In reading the claims, the Court speaks directly to the issue of audience:

> [T]he "administering" step simply refers to the relevant audience, namely doctors who treat patients with certain diseases with thiopurine drugs. That audience is a pre-existing audience; doctors used thiopurine drugs to treat patients suffering from autoimmune disorders long before anyone asserted these claims.[49]

The Court, in examining the "wherein" clauses, concludes that these "simply tell a doctor about the relevant natural laws."[50] The Court recognizes that there is a discourse — "these clauses tell the relevant audience about the laws while trusting them to use those laws appropriately where they are relevant to their decision-making."[51]

Through their use of language in claims drafting, patent lawyers and agents inscribe new texts on the "state of nature." Judges adjudicating such

---

46 See, for example, patent GB Application No 0000180.0 (5 January 2000) (application terminated 9 March 2001). Donna MacLean, a British waitress and poet, applied to patent herself, claiming she had reinvented herself, was new, useful, and non-obvious; see: Bita Amani & Rosemary J Coombe, "The Human Genome Diversity Project: The Politics of Patents at the Intersection of Race, Religion, and Research Ethics" (2005) 27:1 Law & Pol'y 152 at 159.

47 Latour, above note 36 at 482–83.

48 *Prometheus*, above note 1 at 9.

49 *Ibid*.

50 *Ibid*.

51 *Ibid*.

cases may be more competent and comfortable reading the patent text than its underlying science, but the exercise of reading law is complicated by the reading of the science.[52] In *Prometheus*, the USSC held unanimously that the patent text as written could not be interpreted to support the claim of patentability:

> Our conclusion rests upon an examination of the particular claims before us in light of the Court's precedents. Those cases warn us against interpreting patent statutes in ways that make patent eligibility "depend simply on the draftsman's art" without reference to the "principles underlying the prohibition against patents for [natural laws]" . . . . If a law of nature is not patentable, then neither is a process reciting a law of nature unless that process has additional features that provide practical assurance that the process is more than a drafting effort designed to monopolize the law of nature itself.[53]

According to the judgment, the combination of these three steps in order "adds nothing to the laws of nature that is not already present when the steps are considered separately."[54] *Prometheus* is to be applauded and coheres with *Harvard* where even the "added" contribution of the scientists who "engineered" the mouse was not enough to create sovereignty over "nature."[55]

C. LIFE IN PERFORMANCE: THE REPRODUCIBILITY PHENOMENA

The SCC's finding that a mouse genetically modified to carry a cancer-causing gene was patent-ineligible was highly controversial and set Canada apart from other common law jurisdictions. The Court found that while bacteria and yeasts were patentable, non-human higher life, namely plants and animals, were not. The oncomouse was neither a manufacture nor a composition of matter within the definition of "invention." Of key

---

52 Philip J Hanes, "The Advantages and Limitations of a Focus on Audience in Media Studies" (April 2000), online: www.aber.ac.uk/media/Students/pph9701.html. "[A] text does not have a single meaning but rather a range of possibilities which are defined by both the text and by its audiences. The meaning is not in the text, but in the *reading*" [emphasis in original], quoting Hart (1991, 60).

53 *Prometheus*, above note 1 at 3 and 8–9.

54 *Ibid* at 10.

55 *Harvard*, above note 4.

concern was the patentee's lack of control over the reproducibility of the mouse.

At trial, Nadon J found that:

> the question of reproducibility is related to the scope of the respondent's invention . . . . [B]ecause the respondent is . . . claiming . . . the entire mammal, and the respondent has not made any claims to even minor control over any aspect of the mammal except the presence of the transgene, [thus] the respondent can make no claim to being able to reproduce the mammal at will by doing anything other than ordinary breeding.[56]

Justice Rothstein, for the Court of Appeal, found the oncomouse patentable, holding:

> The definition of "invention" in the *Patent Act* does not expressly exclude discoveries that follow the laws of nature. It would thus appear that the reason creations or discoveries that *only* follow the laws of nature do not meet the requirements of patentability is because they are not considered new and unobvious. Rather, such creations or discoveries are considered to have existed and only to have been uncovered by man. Something more is required for patentability, namely, a non-naturally occurring "composition of matter" arising from the application of inventiveness or ingenuity.[57]

The distinction between unpatentable discoveries and patentable inventions was valid and remains undisturbed by the SCC decision that overturned Rothstein J's finding. In the SCC's summary of the appeal decision, it was noted that Rothstein J had

> also disagreed with the Commissioner's approach of dividing the invention into two phases on the basis that, once it is accepted that most inventions involve the laws of nature, "there can be no valid basis for splitting an invention between the portion that is the result of inventive ingenuity and the portion that is not."[58]

Was the human ingenuity in this case enough to support a patent claim over the *whole* animal? Claim 1 was even more ambitious in staking claim to all transgenic *mammals*. Though the Harvard scientists who "made" the

56 *Ibid* at para 134.

57 *Harvard College v Canada (Commissioner of Patents)*, [2000] 4 FC 528 (CA) at para 126 [emphasis in original].

58 *Harvard*, above note 4 at para 139.

mouse demonstrated inventive faculty, theirs was not the sole contribution to the existence of the mouse; why should it be credited as such? This is the "reproducibility" problem the Court grappled with:

> [T]he Commissioner determines that there are two distinct phases. The first phase involves the preparation of the genetically engineered plasmid. The second involves the development of a genetically engineered mouse in the uterus of the host mouse. The Commissioner concluded that while the first phase is controlled by human intervention, in the second phase it is the laws of nature that take over to produce the mammalian end product. He was therefore unwilling to extend the meaning of "manufacture" or "composition of matter" to include a non-human mammal. In his view, *the inventors do not have full control over all of the characteristics of the resulting mouse, and human intervention ensures that reproducibility extends only so far as the cancer-forming gene.*[59]

The material distinction for patentability in Canadian law is now between higher and lower life. But, can lower life remain patentable applying the *reproducibility* analysis as a test for agency? Any affirmation of the patentability of lower life was *obiter* since the issue was not before the Court. The Court's reasoning, however, invites us to revisit the arbitrary line between higher and lower life[60] with a less arbitrary (ANT) framework. Despite any judicial urge to converge with legal norms of other jurisdictions that hold higher life patentable, the SCC's analysis recognizes that not all labour and agency ought to be legally rewarded with title. The distinction between higher and lower life was rendered moot after the SCC majority decision in *Schmeiser*, where unpatentable higher life embodying the patented subcomponent was found to be an infringing use.[61] According to Haraway,

> patent status reconfigures an organism as a human invention, produced by mixing labor and nature as those categories are understood in Western

---

59 *Ibid* at para 130 [emphasis added].

60 See *Re Application of Abitibi Co* (1982), 62 CPR (2d) 81 (Pat App Bd), where the claim was for both product and processes that resulted from new mixed fungal yeast culture. The fungi were isolated and subjected to increasing concentrations of sulphites and nutrients, surviving yeast were functionally adapted to consume and digest paper mill waste product. The Patent Commissioner accepted the Patent Board's recommendation to allow the claims over these micro-organisms as invention so long as they could be recreated uniformly on large scale and at will.

61 *Monsanto Canada v Schmeiser*, 2004 SCC 34; see also Amani, above note 4 at ch 3.

> law and philosophy, patenting an organism is a large semiotic and practical step toward blocking nonproprietary and nontechnical meaning from many social sites — such as labs, courts, and popular venues.[62]

Common law jurisdictions may well have the most experience in determining where to draw the lines between unpatentable discoveries and patentable inventions[63] but the determination is "both fuzzy and arbitrary."[64] The remaining question is whether DNA could be patentable under an ANT lens. As Dutfiled aptly states, "[n]o legal distinction is scientifically trustworthy."[65]

D. LAW, SCIENCE, AND BIOMEDIA: CODE, CHEMICALS, AND COMMUNICATION

The discovery of the double helix structure of DNA in 1953 by James Watson and Francis Crick and the subsequent development of mapping technologies were essential for the advancements made in molecular genetics and the intensification of the biotechnology industry.[66] Watson and Crick "appropriate[d] the metaphors of 'information' and 'coding' to describe their elucidation of the structure of DNA."[67] The "coding problem" became a central concern for molecular biology.[68] The metaphors stuck[69] as DNA paved the way for subsequent decryption projects, as the Human Genome Project (HGP), Human Genome Diversity Project, and the HAPMAP project.[70] DNA

---

62 Donna J Haraway, *Modest_Witness@Second_Millennium.FemaleMan©_Meets_Oncomouse™: Feminism and Technoscience* (New York: Routledge, 1997) at 82.

63 Dutfield, above note 2 at 531.

64 David Vaver, *Intellectual Property Law: Copyright, Patents, Trade Marks*, 2d ed (Toronto: Irwin Law, 2011) at 294.

65 Dutfield, above note 2 at 539–40.

66 Carlson, above note 42 at 10, citing examples such as farming, breeding, biofuel production and bioremediation, etc.

67 Eugene Thacker, *Biomedia* (Minneapolis: University of Minnesota Press, 2004) at 146.

68 *Ibid.*

69 Kevin Davies, *Cracking the Human Genome: Inside the Race to Unlock Human DNA* (New York: The Free Press, 2001).

70 The HGP, an international public collaborative scientific research project launched in 1988, met with private competition from Craig Venter, an abdicator from the project. The completion of the mapping was announced in 2003. Already more than 4,000 of the approximately 24,000 genes had been claimed in US patents. See generally Amani, above note 4.

gave new legitimacy for the use of science in the law,[71] importing a certain indisputability, authority, and complexity into the law while simultaneously mediating its relationship with science. In some areas, such as the use of DNA in the criminal context, we listen to the claims of science regarding what DNA *communicates* as informational code[72] — even if our reception of the message is flawed or leads to unsupported genetic determinism, errors in human translation, and potential manipulation. As one judge put it, "[l]ike aliens from outer space, then, science has invaded the courtroom . . . . Nevertheless, judges frequently find it difficult, and sometimes bewildering, to come to grips with science . . . ."[73]

The genetic revolution prompted the revolution in biopatenting. The view of DNA as code was rewritten judicially with articulation of "DNA as chemical"[74] and has since gained hegemony. As chemicals, DNA is patentable because of its isolation and purification — criteria that mythologically rewrite DNA as "invention" rather than "discovery." The 1995 case *Howard*[75] found that "[i]t is established patent practice to recognise novelty for a natural substance which has been isolated for the first time and which had no previously recognised existence."[76] On appeal, the Technical Board of Appeal affirmed that, "[i]t is worth pointing out that DNA is not 'life,' but a chemical substance which carries genetic information and can be used as an intermediate in the production of proteins."[77]

Myriad Genetic's controversial BRCA1 and BRCA2 gene patents associated with a propensity to develop breast and ovarian cancer further tested this concept in *Ass'n for Molecular Pathology v United States Patent and Trademark Office*. On petition for certiorari, the USSC vacated the Federal Circuit's

71 See Neil Gerlach et al, *Becoming Biosubjects: Bodies, Systems, Technologies* (Toronto: University of Toronto Press, 2011).

72 See Thacker, above note 67 at 64.

73 Rakoff, above note 14 at 1380.

74 In *Parke Davis and Co v HK Mulford and Co*, 189 F 95 (SDNY 1911), aff'd 196 F 496 (2d Cir 1912), Justice Learned Hand had to address the patentability of adrenaline as a purified form of a natural product that was extracted from the other gland tissue in which it was found; see also Dutfield, above note 2 at 534 for analysis of the significance of this decision in enabling the patentability of natural products.

75 *Re Howard Florey Institute-Relaxin*, [1995] EPOR 541 (Opp Div). The product claims were characterized by their chemical structure and disclosed a use of the protein encoded by the DNA. All charges for invalidity were dismissed: "until a cDNA encoding human H2-relaxin and its precursors was isolated . . . the existence of this form of relaxin was unknown" at para 4.3.1; though pregnant bodies are natural producers of this hormone.

76 *Ibid* at para 4.3.1.

77 *Ibid* at para 6.3.4.

decision reversing the District Court finding[78] and remanded the matter to the Federal Circuit for reconsideration of the validity question in light of the USSC *Prometheus* decision. On 16 August 2012, a two to one panel of the US Federal Circuit Court of Appeal reaffirmed the view that both isolated DNA and cDNA are patent eligible and ruled in favour of Myriad's gene patents. The majority found that "[e]verything and everyone comes from nature, following its laws. But the compositions here are not natural products. They are the products of man, albeit following, as materials do, laws of nature."[79] The majority drew a distinction between unauthored "native" DNA and "invention":

> [T]he challenged claims are drawn to patent-eligible subject matter because the claims cover molecules that are markedly different — have a distinctive chemical structure and identity — from those found in nature. It is undisputed that Myriad's claimed isolated DNAs exist in a distinctive chemical form — as distinctive chemical molecules — from DNAs in the human body, *i.e.*, native DNA. Natural DNA exists in the body as one of forty-six large, contiguous DNA molecules. Each of those DNA molecules is condensed and intertwined with various proteins, including histones, to form a complex tertiary structure known as chromatin that makes up a larger structural complex, a chromosome . . . . Isolated DNA, in contrast, is a free-standing portion of a larger, natural DNA molecule. Isolated DNA has been cleaved . . . or synthesized to consist of just a fraction of a naturally occurring DNA molecule.[80]

Simply cleaving covalent (chemical) bonds to isolate the BRCA1 and BRCA2 genes from the rest of the DNA was now sufficient to gain a patent. For the dissent, genes could not be patented simply because they were isolated from the body; this would be like recognizing snapping a leaf from a tree as worthy of a patent. Though chemically different in structure once severed and with potential new uses, the leaf is no less a leaf found in nature. Though the majority agreed that snapping a leaf would not make the leaf patentable, they rejected the analogy to the DNA context: "Snapping a leaf from a tree is a physical separation, easily done by anyone. Creating a

78 *The Association for Molecular Pathology v United States Patent and Trademark Office*, 653 F 3d 1329 (2011).

79 *The Association for Molecular Pathology v United States Patent and Trademark Office*, 2010-1406 (Fed Cir 2012) at 51–52 [*Assn Molecular Pathology*].

80 *Ibid* at 44–45.

new chemical entity is the work of human transformation, requiring skill, knowledge, and effort."[81] It is not clear why, in deciding patentability, the change in the structure of DNA should be decisive when the isolated DNA continues to function as information in the same manner as the native DNA.[82] James Watson's brief opposed gene patenting and expressed concern over the misapprehension by the court of the unique nature of DNA:

> It is a chemical entity, but DNA's importance flows from its ability to encode and transmit the instructions for creating humans. Life's instructions ought not be controlled by legal monopolies created at the whim of Congress or the courts.[83]

The panel's decision was subject to a new petition for *certiorari*, granted by the USSC on 30 November 2012 and heard on 15 April 2013.[84] Twenty-four *amici* briefs were filed, indicating significant public interest in this issue. In the tradition of prior human biopatent cases, the Federal Circuit failed to consider the agency of the person in maintaining her body, her creative contribution was rendered public domain for private appropriations[85] and allowed the law to intextuate the body by inscribing new meanings and socializing stories for exerting inordinate control over the potential for private personhood.[86] Insofar as patents confer exclusive property rights, they create monopolies that limit access and use, and mediate human relations:

> [A]s a legal term property denotes not material things but certain rights. In the world of nature apart from more or less organized society, there are things but clearly no property rights . . . . [W]e must recognize that a prop-

---

81 *Ibid* at 52.

82 Andrew Bowman, "Genes 101: Are Human Genes Patentable Subject Matter?" (2012) 18:4 Rich JL & Tech 15 at 21–23.

83 Interest of Amicus Curiae James D Watson in Support of Neither Party, United States Court of Appeals for the Federal Circuit — *Association of Molecular Pathology v USPTO*, No 2010-1406 (15 June 2012) at 2, online: DocStoc.com www.docstoc.com/docs/123708444/2012_06_15_-_james_d__watson_brief_on_remand.

84 *Assn Molecular Pathology*, above note 79.

85 See *Moore v Regents of the University of California*, 271 Cal Rptr 146 (1990); Karla Holloway, *Private Bodies, Public Texts: Race, Gender, and a Cultural Bioethics* (Durham: Duke University Press, 2011), regarding the HeLa cell line developed from tissue taken from Henrietta Lacks' cervical tumour.

86 See, for example, Holloway, *ibid*.

> erty right is a relation not between an owner and a thing, but between the owner and other individuals in reference to things.[87]

Indeed, "dominion over things is also *imperium* over our fellow human beings."[88]

On 13 June 2013, in a decision written by Thomas J for a unanimous Court,[89] the USSC held "a naturally occurring DNA segment is a product of nature and not patent eligible merely because it has been isolated, but that cDNA [complementary DNA] is patent eligible because it is not naturally occurring."[90] The Court's analysis was informed by policy considerations; namely, the need to ensure balance in the patent regime so as not to impede the flow of information necessary to spur important inventions.[91] Isolated DNA fragments are not patentable because unlike cDNA, it was found, they are naturally occurring and severance of chemical bonds is insufficient human agency to render them otherwise. Isolating DNA from the human genome does not create "a nonnaturally occurring molecule"[92] and is insufficient to warrant a patent. Moreover, Myriad's claims "are simply not expressed in terms of chemical composition, nor do they rely in any way on the chemical changes that result from the isolation of a particular section of DNA."[93]

The Myriad litigation emphasizes how contentious—and variable—determinations of patentability are, and how contingent on conceptions of nature and degree of "inventive faculty":

> The location and order of the nucleotides existed in nature before Myriad found them. Nor did Myriad create or alter the genetic structure of DNA . . . . Myriad did not create anything. To be sure, it found an important and useful gene, but *separating that gene from its surrounding genetic material is not an act of invention*.[94]

---

87 Morris R Cohen, "Property and Sovereignty" (1927-28) 13:1 Cornell LQ 8 at 11-12, online: University of Texas at Austin https://webspace.utexas.edu/ob242/www/cohen.pdf.

88 *Ibid* at 13 [emphasis in original].

89 *Association for Molecular Pathology v Myriad Genetics Inc*, 569 US __(2013) at 11, [*Assn Molecular Pathology* USSC]; Justice Scalia wrote a separate opinion, concurring in the judgment.

90 *Ibid* at 1.

91 *Ibid*.

92 *Ibid* at 14.

93 *Ibid*.

94 *Ibid* at 12 [emphasis added].

The judicial adoption of the view of DNA as chemical enabled the patentability of life as a fragmented, disarticulated, and disembodied part of the self. Yet, it ignored that DNA is also information, something that may well make it analogous to other exclusions such as abstract theorems and scientific principles. While DNA fragments and genes remain patentable in Canada, in the US, ambiguity persists: What is "naturally occurring" and the degree of human intervention necessary to constitute "invention"? Isolation is insufficient but removing introns to create exons-only strands is enough to characterize the resulting cDNA as not naturally occurring but "synthesized," and therefore patent eligible even if the sequence is "dictated by nature." Will law remain beholden to lawyers' particular abilities to evidence "nature"?[95]

DNA is not simply unidirectional code—a linear simplification of genes as encoding for proteins and prescribing protein function and phenotypes. Nor is DNA *merely* chemical (though chemicals themselves can demonstrate a "life cycle").[96] DNA is, rather, a communication medium in a complex biological and biochemical systems network with other actants. There are reading, coding, translating, and all sorts of other familiar communicative processes engaged in by DNA, RNA, mRNA, etc.[97] The conceptual shift alone to the communicative and discursive view of DNA as biomedia would be a major milestone towards more diversified analyses of the legal issues in biopatenting. Normative understandings operating in the law have broader consequences for us all. Biotechnological intervention is characterized by human conceit; the intervention is irreversible, notes Habermas, in a self-regulated process, and will lead to consequences

95 See, for example, Brief for Amicus Curiae Eric S Lander in Support of Neither Party, No. 12-398, noting that the Federal Circuit assumed, without citing evidence, that isolated fragments of the human genome do not occur in nature but that in fact these are present in the human body and thus are products of nature.

96 Dutfield, above note 2. "In the article announcing their breakthrough, the polio-makers commented as follows: 'if the ability to replicate is an attribute of life, then poliovirus is a chemical . . . with a life cycle'" at 535 [footnote omitted]; see also Pier Luigi Luisi, *The Emergence of Life: From Chemical Origins to Synthetic Biology* (Cambridge: Cambridge University Press, 2006) at 25.

97 Bray, above note 5. The author contends that "the distinction between chemistry and mechanics is a human invention and not one that concerns a cell. At the atomic level, all movements entail a chemical change and all chemical changes create movements. The difference is one of degree rather than kind" at 93.

we cannot control.[98] In short, "patent law needs to evolve to recognize that biotechnology is different from all other technologies."[99]

Marshall McLuhan famously stated that the "medium is the message."[100] He, amongst other media theorists such as Walter Benjamin and Martin Heidegger, discussed "the ways in which the human subject and the human body are transformed in the interactions with different technologies."[101] For McLuhan, the "message" is "the change of scale or pace or pattern" that a new invention — new media — "introduces into human affairs."[102] Indeed, do-it-yourself biology proliferating as biohacking becomes the new play for a young generation of biopunks[103] no longer willing to trust in the "pretense of professionalism and the cult of the expert."[104] Such interventions may prove problematic but no more so than when conducted in research labs without necessary regulatory oversight.[105] Yet, as a democratic movement to open access to biology and therefore technology, these actors see themselves more as co-actors than inventors and so are willing to co-labour wittingly in everyday grassroot performances[106] that test the capacity for property to enclose biology. Insofar as patent law is a spur or drag on biomedia's broader social and structural meanings — the unintended or anticipated impact on how society relates — it would help to remain mindful that "patent law is there for human beings in general. They may not read it as

---

98 See Hans Jonas, "Lasst uns einen Menschen klonieren" in Hans Jonas et al, *Zur Praxis des Prinzips Verantwortung* (Frankfurt am Main: Suhrkamp, 1985) as discussed in Jürgen Habermas, *The Future of Human Nature* (Cambridge, UK: Polity Press, 2003).

99 Stuart Laidlaw, "Monsanto Decision Hurts Equity, Innovation Expert Ruling Sows Seeds of Conflict; Court Treats Genes like any Old Widget Richard Gold Thinks that's a Big Mistake" *Toronto Star* (21 June 2004) D01 at 1, quoting Richard Gold; see generally, Amani, above note 4.

100 Marshall McLuhan, *Understanding Media: The Extensions of Man* (New York: McGraw Hill, 1964) at 9, online: http://beforebefore.net/80f/s11/media/mcluhan.pdf.

101 Thacker, above note 67 at 7.

102 McLuhan, above note 100 at 8.

103 Marcus Wohlsen, *Biopunk: Kitchen-Counter Scientists Hack the Software of Life* (Toronto: Penguin Books, 2011).

104 *Ibid* at 6.

105 See, for example, Martin Enserink, "Scientists Brace for Media Storm Around Controversial Flu Studies" *Science Insider* (23 November 2011), online: Science Insider http://news.sciencemag.org/scienceinsider/2011/11/scientists-brace-for-media-storm.html; see also Carlson, above note 42 at 19.

106 Kac, *Signs of Life*, above note 34. Kac notes that "[i]n art, to work with biomedia is to manipulate life, and . . . is part of the global network known as evolution" at 3.

avidly as they read literature, but they are nevertheless touched by the law at least as — if not more — significantly, whether they know it or not."[107]

E. ON *COLON*-IZATION AND INDIGINEITY: TRANSGENICS AND YOU, A MODERN DAY MASH-UP

This paper began with the space adventure of *Prometheus* and travelled to inner space with the 2012 *Prometheus* decision; "[t]he two new investment frontiers, outer space and inner space, vie for the futures market."[108] The final frontier may be the colon-ization via fecal transplants currently contemplated as a means to restore the destroyed flora, the "natural ecosystem," of the gut. The transplants would reintroduce what were indigenous bacteria. These natives did not survive our over-consumption of prescription antibiotics.[109] The aliens within are not simple imaginings of science fiction authors contending "we are all *aliens* until we get to know one another."[110] Rather, scientific advancements evidence our hybrid selves as transgenic.[111] Our survival and destruction is contingent on the agency of these non-human actors. Some of these boundary penetrating aliens are friendly, others hostile. Their presence renders us the material of modern day mash-ups, generated discursively with the "other" content-providing, sometimes process-abiding, user-generated actants.

Jennifer Ackerman reports that bacterial cells in the body outnumber human cells by a factor of ten to one. She also reports that the number of genes distributed among the friendly bacteria that live in people's bodies (3.3 million in gut microbiome) outnumber the genes inherited from our

---

107 David Vaver, "The Problems of Biotechnologies for Intellectual Property Law" (2004) Hors Série Les Cahiers de Propriété Intellectuelle: Mélanges Victor Nabhan 375 at 392.

108 Donna Haraway, "The Promise of Monsters: A Regenerative Politics for Inappropriate/d Others" in Lawrence Grossberg, Cary Nelson, & Paula Treichler, eds, *Cultural Studies* (New York: Routledge, 1992) 295 at 319, citing the work of Sarah Franklin [Haraway, "Promise of Monsters"].

109 Jennifer Ackerman, "The Ultimate Social Network" (2012) 306:6 Scientific American 36.

110 Expressed by Commander John Koenig (Martin Landau) in *Metamorph*, the first episode in the second season of the 1999 television series *Space*.

111 Kac, "Life Transformation," above note 43. "The Human Genome Project (HGP) has made it clear that all humans have in their genome sequences that came from viruses, acquired through a long evolutionary history. This means that we have in our bodies DNA from organisms other than human. Thus we too are transgenic. Before deciding that all transgenics are 'monstrous,' humans must look inside and come to terms with their own 'monstrosity'" at 180.

parents (20,000–25,000). Some of these bacterial genes encode for compounds that the body cannot make while others "train the body not to overreact to outside threats."[112] Advances in computing and gene sequencing have enabled the development of detailed catalogues of bacterial genes that make up the "microbiome."[113]

Biotechnology will also force us to redefine the "self" and what constitutes our humanness. In *Harvard*, the majority found that

> a judicially crafted exception from patentability for human beings does not adequately address issues such as what defines a human being and whether parts of the human body as opposed to the entire person would be patentable.[114]

We are all bio-objects, with alterable genetic identities, but also biosubjects; our biosubjectivity

> alter[s] the field of social relations . . . and troubles traditional modernist dualisms between natural and artificial, human and animal, private and public, and present and future. The subject is both alienated from and dependent upon a fragmented body. It is a subject outside of humanist ethics and firmly within capitalist relations.[115]

Using contemporary immune system discourse, Haraway examines what counts as a self and an actor in a context where images of war and defense against invasions are dominant metaphors. The immune system has "a vast array of circulating acellular products . . . . These molecules mediate communication among components of the immune system, but also between the immune system and the nervous and endocrine systems, thus linking the body's multiple control and coordination sites and functions."[116] Immunity is discursive; the body is not passive audience but essential to the performance of the microbe. Moreover,

---

112 Ackerman, above note 109 at 38.

113 The law will be forced to mediate these issues as we move into the realm of biobots (biological robots with active biological elements in its body). See, for example, Kac "Life Transformation," above note 43, for a discussion of Eduardo Kac's *The Eight Day* art exhibit, featuring transgenic bioluminescent plants, amoeba, fish, and mice that seek to expand biodiversity within "a self-contained artificial ecology" at 176.

114 *Harvard*, above note 4 at para 206.

115 Gerlach, above note 71 at 6.

116 Haraway, "Promise of Monsters," above note 108 at 323.

> [t]he genetics of the immune system cells, with their high rates of somatic mutation and gene product splicings and rearrangings to make finished surface receptors and antibodies, makes a mockery of the notion of a constant genome even within "one" body. The hierarchal body of old has given way to a network-body of amazing complexity and specificity.[117]

To conclude, the body produces not only networks of value but also networks of meaning. Yet, "invention" in biotechnology remains, according to the law, a singular deliberative act unless confronted with a law of nature, as iterated and conceived by the laws of man. Title as an explicit ground for invalidity is not assessed. Still, our composition and capacity for agency is due to the "active 'de-composition' of many invisible agents" [118] performing with(in) "us." Can the mythological Prometheus claim credit for his own healing, his resistance against decay that perpetuated his suffering, any more than Prometheus Laboratories can claim credit for a metabolite process within the body or Harvard for the reproduction of a whole mouse? The failure of the law to address the broader social dynamics in the construction of institutional facts generates the risk of patent law being labelled a fetishized fantasy of active myth makers. The lack of interdisciplinarity in law may well reflect a paucity of interdisciplinarity in legal scholarship and legal education. Where it exists in biopatenting law and industrial policy discourse, the focus has been on a law and economics approach, rather than critical readings of text and language use in law.[119] ANT teaches us that

> [n]ature is not a thing, a domain, a realm, an ontological territory. It is (or rather, it was during the short modern parenthesis) a way of organizing the division . . . between appearances and reality, subjectivity and objectivity, history and immutability . . . . a fully *political* way of distributing power. [120]

Since "ecology seals the end of nature,"[121] it may serve society well to recognize the coercive power of authority; if we be Gods, so too we are monsters.

---

117 *Ibid*; see also Robert Esposito, *Immunitas: The Protection and Negation of Life* (Cambridge: Polity Press, 2011). "[I]f, finally, the immune system is now the cutting edge in this performative dynamic, then a decisive game is played in defining it, not only on the ground of biology but also specifically on the ground of politics" at 153–54.

118 Latour, above note 36 at 474 [citation omitted].

119 Peter M Tiersma, "What Is Language and Law? And Does Anyone Care?" in Frances Olsen, Alexander Lorz, & Dieter Stein, eds, *Law and Language: Theory and Society* (Düsseldorf: Düsseldorf University Press, 2008).

120 Latour, above note 36 at 476 [emphasis in original] [footnotes omitted].

121 *Ibid*.

THEME TWO(A)

New Windows — New Insights

A DIFFERENT DISCIPLINARY LENS

SEVEN

Historical Institutionalism and the Politics of Intellectual Property[1]

BLAYNE HAGGART

ABSTRACT (EN): All intellectual property law is political and cannot be understood outside of the political forces that shape it. Understanding the power relations of IP — who makes the rules, how they do so, and who wins and loses — is essential to our understanding of what IP is, how it is perpetuated, and even if it is necessary. Treating IP as politically and historically contingent also allows academics and policy-makers to avoid considering IP law only in terms of itself. This chapter outlines how a specific theoretical approach — historical institutionalism — can contribute to our understanding of IP's development and potential future changes, both topics of interest to IP scholars across all disciplines. Historical institutionalism focuses on the changes over time in the relationship among the ideas underpinning IP, the actors involved in policy-making, and the institutions structuring their interactions. Its concept of path dependence suggests why a socially suboptimal policy like IP has persisted in the face of criticisms regarding its utility. Applying it to the history of Canadian copyright policy, this chapter also demonstrates how historical institutionalism can allow researchers to analyze systematically IP policy outcomes, and to evaluate situations in which change is likely or possible.

1 Thanks to all the participants at the IP Scholars Workshop and two anonymous reviewers for their helpful comments.

RÉSUMÉ (FR): Toute législation en propriété intellectuelle est politique et ne peut être comprise sans l'étude des forces politiques qui la forgent. Comprendre les relations de pouvoir de la propriété intellectuelle — qui établit les règles, comment les établit-il, qui gagne et qui perd — est essentiel afin de la connaître, de savoir comment elle se perpétue, et si elle est nécessaire. Analyser la propriété intellectuelle d'un angle historique et politique permet aussi aux universitaires et aux responsables politiques de ne pas seulement examiner le droit de la propriété intellectuelle en lui-même. Ce chapitre décrit comment une approche théorique spécifique — l'institutionnalisme historique — peut contribuer à notre compréhension du développement de la propriété intellectuelle et de ses changements potentiels futurs, tous deux sujets d'intérêt pour les spécialistes de la propriété intellectuelle de tous les domaines. L'institutionnalisme historique se concentre sur les changements qui s'opèrent au fil du temps, dans les rapports entre les idées à la base de la propriété intellectuelle, les acteurs impliqués dans les prises de décision, et les institutions structurant leur interaction. Le concept de « dépendance au chemin emprunté » « path dependence » peut expliquer pourquoi une politique sociale sub-optimale comme celle de la propriété intellectuelle s'est tout de même perpétuée malgré les critiques sur son utilité. L'appliquant à l'histoire de la politique canadienne sur le droit d'auteur, ce chapitre démontre aussi comment l'institutionnalisme historique peut aider les chercheurs à analyser de façon systématique les conséquences des politiques sur la propriété intellectuelle, et à évaluer les situations où le changement est souhaitable ou possible.

A. INTRODUCTION

January and February 2012 offered indisputable proof that intellectual property is inherently political. On 11 February 2012, tens of thousands of Europeans took to the streets to protest the *Anti-Counterfeiting Trade Agreement*,[2] a US-led agreement designed to strengthen intellectual property rights that critics said would erode citizens' privacy rights and impede access to

2 *Anti-Counterfeiting Trade Agreemen*, 1 May 2011 (signed by Australia, Canada, the European Union, Japan, the Republic of Korea, Mexico, Morocco, New Zealand, Singapore, Switzerland, and United States) [*ACTA*], online: Office of the United States Trade Representative www.ustr.gov/acta; Wikipedia, "INT: Teilnehmerzahlen" (25 February 2012), online: Wikipedia http://wiki.stoppacta-protest.info/INT:Teilnehmerzahlen (concerning the number of protesters).

affordable medicines.[3] A month earlier and a continent away, on 18 January, millions of Americans signed petitions or contacted their elected representatives to protest against a far-reaching copyright bill, the *Stop Online Piracy Act*,[4] that experts warned would damage the underlying architecture of the Internet itself. So many people tried to contact their senators that it crashed the Senate's online contact page.[5]

These mobilizations are merely the latest evidence that intellectual property has become politicized in the public consciousness. The public involvement in an area traditionally considered to be a technocratic backwater dominated by large commercial interests has the potential to move intellectual property in new directions, but it also obscures the more basic point that intellectual property has *always* been political. This reality was strongly suggested by one of the main recommendations of the May 2011 report into intellectual property's role in enabling or constraining innovation prepared for the British government by Professor Ian Hargreaves.[6] Its first recommendation, that the United Kingdom adopt an evidence-based intellectual property regime,[7] was an implicit recognition that the UK's intellectual property policy is driven by politics, and not by empirical evidence.

Intellectual property law, in short, is the outcome of historically contingent processes and cannot be understood outside of the political forces that shape it. Although the importance of politics to intellectual property policy is becoming increasingly obvious, and despite intellectual property's increasingly central role in the global political economy as a means of appropriating value within global production chains, it remains a field understudied by political scientists, and political scientists remain underrepresented in the intellectual property field. As Sebastian Haunss and Kenneth C Shadlen remark, intellectual property studies are "insufficient-

---

3 Amnesty International, "EU Urged to Reject International Anti-Counterfeiting Pact" (10 February 2012), online: Amnesty International www.amnesty.org/en/news/eu-urged-reject-international-anti-counterfeiting-pact-2012-02-10.

4 US, Bill HR 3261, *Stop Online Piracy Act*, 112th Cong, 2012, online: The Library of Congress http://thomas.loc.gov/cgi-bin/query/z?c112:H.R.3261:.

5 Nathan Ingraham, "On SOPA Blackout Day, Senate Web Sites Experience 'Technical Difficulties'" *Washington Post* (18 January 2012), online: Washington Post www.washingtonpost.com/business/technology/on-sopa-blackout-day-senate-websites-experience-technical-difficulties/2012/01/18/gIQABWkh8P_story.html.

6 UK, *Digital Opportunity: A Review of Intellectual Property and Growth* (An Independent Report to the Department for Business, Innovation, and Skills) by Ian Hargreaves (May 2011), online: UK Intellectual Property Office www.ipo.gov.uk/ipreview-finalreport.pdf.

7 *Ibid* at 8.

ly theorized in a political sense: not enough attention is given to how the politics of IP may be informed by distinct dynamics and logics."[8] This lack of attention is regrettable, and not only because political scientists and political economists are ignoring an important and fascinating corner of the world. Political science, at its core, involves the study of power. To the extent that intellectual property is perpetuated by the exercise of power, understanding the power relations of intellectual property policy — who makes the rules, how they do so, and who wins and loses — is absolutely essential to our understanding of what intellectual property is, how it is perpetuated, and even if it is necessary. Focusing on intellectual property as something that is politically and historically contingent — and not necessarily sustained by logic or evidence — allows the researcher to avoid considering intellectual property law only in terms of itself, of "reifying" its subject: "abstracting . . . a particular set of relations into an ahistorical naturalised (and hence non-political) set of occurrences."[9] Focusing too intently on the law in itself rather than situating the law in its larger political (and economic) context can lead the researcher to ask the wrong question, such as: "how can we reform copyright law to deal with our modern reality?" rather than asking, "given that copyright emerged out of a particular situation to deal with a particular problem, is it the best policy response to our current reality, and if not, what is?"

This paper outlines a specific theoretical approach — historical institutionalism — that can contribute to our understanding of intellectual property's development and potential future changes. Historical institutionalism focuses on the changes over time in the relationship among the ideas underpinning intellectual property, the actors involved in policy-making, and the institutions structuring their interactions. Crucially for intellectual property studies, historical institutionalism's concept of *path dependence* suggests why a socially suboptimal policy like intellectual property has persisted in the face of criticisms regarding its utility. The following sections outline the four elements — institutions, interests, ideas, and change over time — of a

8 Sebastian Haunss & Kenneth C Shadlen, "Introduction: Rethinking the Politics of Intellectual Property" in Sebastian Haunss & Kenneth C Shadlen, eds, *Politics of Intellectual Property: Contestation Over the Ownership, Use, and Control of Knowledge and Information* (Cheltenham: Edward Elgar, 2009) at 2.

9 Christopher May, *The Global Political Economy of Intellectual Property Rights: The New Enclosures*, 2d ed (New York: Routledge, 2009) at 149; see also A Claire Cutler, "Gramsci, Law, and the Culture of Global Capitalism" (2005) 8:4 Critical Review of International Social & Political Philosophy 527.

historical-institutionalist approach to intellectual property studies, illustrated through an examination of the protracted Canadian copyright debate from 2001 to 2012. The three main branches of intellectual property — patents, copyrights, and trademarks — each involve different constituencies and somewhat different logics. While this chapter focuses on copyright for clarity's sake, historical institutionalism's logic can also be used to analyze intellectual property policy development more generally.

Canada offers a fascinating illustration of how historical institutionalism can be applied to copyright policy-making. On 29 June 2012, the *Copyright Modernization Act*[10] received Royal Assent. A bill seven years in the making — successive governments had been trying to pass similar legislation since 2005 — included both new user rights and strong legal protection for technological protection measures (TPMs), which are digital locks placed on works like MP3s and ebooks to control their use and access. Far from being a "natural" extension of Canadian copyright law, the bill was the outcome of political and institutional processes. While space precludes a full analysis of the issues raised by digital locks and user rights, and the complex nature of Canadian copyright policy-making, it is hoped that this brief discussion will demonstrate historical institutionalism's general utility for students of intellectual property policy development.[11]

B. THEORIZING THE POLITICS OF INTELLECTUAL PROPERTY

Politically, copyright (like intellectual property generally) is defined by three characteristics. First, it has persisted, in one form or another, over several hundred years. Copyright's birth is usually dated to the United Kingdom's 1709 *Statute of Anne*,[12] although it has earlier antecedents and regulation of the market in creative works — focusing on attribution — dates at least

---

10 SC 2012, c 20.

11 For a more complete account through mid-2011, see Blayne Haggart, *North American Digital Copyright, Regional Governance, and the Potential for Variation* (PhD Thesis, Carleton University, 2011), online: http://blaynehaggart.files.wordpress.com/2011/08/deposit-copy-north-american-digital-copyright-policy-governance-and-the-potential-for-variation.pdf [Haggart, "North American"].

12 *An Act for the Encouragement of Learning, by Vesting the Copies of Printed Books in the Authors or Purchasers of such Copies, During the Time therein Mentioned*, 1710 (UK), 8 Anne, c 19.

to Ancient Rome.[13] Second, copyright has changed in response to pressure from existing and new groups, often in parallel with technological changes. Third, and most striking to copyright neophytes, empirical evidence that it is either necessary to achieve its overt societal objectives — for copyright, the maximization of the production and dissemination of creative works[14] — or that it actually accomplishes these objectives, is shockingly thin on the ground for such a long-lived social policy.[15] Saying that copyright is the basis for the well-being of several industries and thousands of individual creators and (more often) intermediaries, and has led to certain forms of creative production, is not the same as saying that copyright is *necessary* for creative production, yet this is usually the extent of the "evidence" offered in copyright's defence in policy discussions.

A political theory of copyright must therefore account for its constrained evolution over a long period of time, its persistence despite a lack of evidence that it achieves its societal objectives, and evidence that it may actually impair these goals.

Historical institutionalism allows us to address all three characteristics. Historical institutionalism emerged from the comparative politics subfield of political science as one of the (now-not-so-) "new institutionalisms" of the 1980s and 1990s.[16] The new institutionalisms offered a way to strike a middle ground between overly structuralist theories in which actors had no agency and overly atomistic behaviouralist theories that "often obscured the enduring socio-economic and political structures that mould behaviour

13 Graham Dutfield & Uma Suthersanen, *Global Intellectual Property Law* (Cheltenham, UK: Edward Elgar, 2008) at 64.

14 Copyright also has a unique "moral rights" dimension that justifies property rights in creative works in the language of human rights, protecting the integrity of the individual author. This chapter focuses on copyright's economic dimension, as this is the focus of current copyright debates.

15 See, for example, Michele Boldrin & David K Levine, *Against Intellectual Monopoly* (Cambridge: Cambridge University Press, 2008); Robert M Hurt & Robert M Schuman, "The Economic Rationale of Copyright" (1966) 56:1 The American Economic Review 421; Raymond Shih Ray Ku, Jiayang Sun, & Yiying Fan, "Does Copyright Law Promote Creativity? An Empirical Analysis of Copyright's Bounty" (2009) 63 Vanderbilt LR 1669; Arnold Plant, "The Economic Aspects of Copyright in Books" (1934) 1:2 Economica, *New Series* 167; Ruth Towse, Christian Handke, & Paul Stepan, "The Economics of Copyright Law: A Stocktake of the Literature" (2008) 5:1 Review of Economic Research on Copyright Issues 1.

16 See generally Peter A Hall & Rosemary CR Taylor, "Political Science and the Three New Institutionalisms" (1996) 44:5 Political Studies 936; James G March & Johan P Olsen, *Rediscovering Institutions: The Organizational Basis of Politics* (New York: The Free Press, 1989) [March & Olsen, *Rediscovering Institutions*].

in distinctive ways in different national contexts."[17] Historical institutionalism focuses researchers' attention on the interaction of three key variables — institutions, interests (or actors), and ideas — and how they change over time.[18]

1) Institutions

Humanity lives within a world of institutions, both formal and informal. Institutions can be thought of as semi-persistent "formal or informal procedures, routines, norms and conventions embedded in the organizational structure of the polity or political economy. They can range from the rules of a constitutional order or the standard operating procedures of a bureaucracy to the conventions governing trade union behaviour or bank-firm relations."[19] Copyright can thus be considered an institution, as it provides people with rules about how to conduct their affairs. Different institutional set-ups can lead to different outcomes, even when facing similar social situations.[20]

In a historical institutionalist approach, institutions and policies do not necessarily represent efficient, unique equilibria, or socially objective "best practices." They are created, sustained, and changed by purposeful actors with varying degrees of material and ideational resources, and under conditions of imperfect information and something less than perfect foresight. They can also persist beyond their "best before" date. Institutions favour some groups and policies over others. Outcomes depend on actors' skills, resources, and technical expertise deployed in public and private debates.[21]

Finally, institutions are not wholly self-contained, internally consistent entities. They exist within a universe of other institutions, some with

17 Kathleen Thelen & Sven Steinmo, "Historical Institutionalism in Comparative Politics" in Sven Steinmo, Kathleen Thelen, & Frank Longstreth, eds, *Structuring Politics: Historical Institutionalism in Comparative Analysis* (Cambridge: Cambridge University Press, 1992) at 1.

18 For an institutionalist, if not explicitly historical institutionalist, analysis of Canadian intellectual property policy making, see G Bruce Doern & Markus Sharaput, *Canadian Intellectual Property: The Politics of Innovating Institutions and Interests* (Toronto: University of Toronto Press, 2000).

19 Hall & Taylor, above note 16 at 938.

20 Colin Hay, "Contemporary Capitalism, Globalization, Regionalization and the Persistence of National Variation" (2000) 26:4 Review of International Studies 509 at 512.

21 Frank R Baumgartner & Bryan D Jones, *Agendas and Instability in American Politics* (Chicago: University of Chicago Press, 1993) at 9.

overlapping jurisdictions that may complement or contradict the rules set forth in the particular institution being studied. Furthermore, the relevant institutions in a given policy area can be located on any "level," from the subnational to the global. Just as, for example, US copyright policy-making institutions can have a disproportionate effect on international intellectual property treaties, so can international institutions influence domestic policy outcomes, and institutional creation, maintenance, and change in other countries.[22]

a) Canadian Copyright Institutions

Canadian copyright policy is made within an overlapping framework of international, regional, and domestic institutions. International institutions, including the *Agreement on Trade-Related Aspects of Intellectual Property Rights*,[23] Chapter 17 (the IP chapter) of the *North American Free Trade Agreement*,[24] the various treaties administered by the World Intellectual Property Organization (WIPO),[25] as well as (given their influence on global copyright policy) US copyright and trade institutions,[26] set the overall parameters for Canadian copyright debates. In particular, Canadian (and global) conceptions that define digital copyright reform have been largely shaped by the two 1996 WIPO treaties, namely the *Copyright Treaty* and *Performances and Phonograms Treaty*, collectively known as the *Internet Treaties*. For example, both treaties require that signatories provide legal protection TPMs.[27] Jeremy F de Beer and others call such rules "paracopyright," entirely new rights within copyright law.[28] There is nothing inherent in copyright

---

22 Susan K Sell, *Private Power, Public Law: The Globalization of Intellectual Property Rights* (Cambridge: Cambridge University Press, 2003).

23 *Agreement on Trade-Related Aspects of Intellectual Property Rights*, 15 April 1994, 1869 UNTS 299, 33 ILM 1197.

24 *North American Free Trade Agreement Between the Government of Canada, the Government of Mexico and the Government of the United States*, 17 December 1992, Can TS 1994 No 2, 32 ILM 289 (entered into force 1 January 1994) [*NAFTA*].

25 *Copyright Treaty*, 20 December 1996, 36 ILM 65 (entered into force 2 March 2002) [*Copyright Treaty*]; *Performances and Phonograms Treaty*, 20 December 1996, 36 ILM 76 (entered into force 20 March 2002) [*Performances and Phonograms Treaty*].

26 Sell, above note 22.

27 See *Copyright Treaty*, above note 25, art 11; *Performances and Phonograms Treaty*, above note 25, art 18.

28 Jeremy F de Beer, "Constitutional Jurisdiction Over Paracopyright Laws" in Michael Geist, ed, *In the Public Interest: The Future of Canadian Copyright Law* (Toronto: Irwin Law, 2005) at 89.

that requires regulating such locks within copyright law. Regardless, TPM protection was a central element in all of the proposed copyright bills.

Institutions are not monoliths. Inter- and intra-institutional rules often conflict, with significant effects on policy development. Domestically, the Canadian *Copyright Act*,[29] like copyright itself, embodies the central political intellectual property paradox: it seeks to encourage both the "protection" and the "dissemination" of creative works,[30] even though stronger protection by definition will inhibit innovation and the spread of creative works. Similarly, much of the difficulty in passing copyright law is attributable to the diametrically opposed mandates of the two departments responsible for developing copyright policy — the Department of Canadian Heritage (which generally favours protection-focused interests) and Industry Canada (which generally favours dissemination). The institutionalization of copyright's fundamental tension makes it that much more difficult for any government to even reach a decision about what type of reforms to undertake. In the words of one government official who was involved in the law-making process, were copyright the responsibility of one department, "life would be a thousand times easier."[31]

These domestic institutions had a significant effect on the Canadian copyright debate of the early 2000s. Between 2005 and 2012 successive governments attempted four times to pass a bill that would adapt Canadian copyright law for the digital age (finally succeeding in 2012).[32] Domestically, inter-departmental fighting between the Canadian Heritage and Industry Canada departments contributed to the slow process of crafting legislation, while the existence of minority governments between 2005 and 2011 made it difficult to pass what had become very contentious legislation. Because these minority Parliaments required the government to negotiate with opposition parties to pass legislation, they also opened the government to influence by individual voters, as will be discussed below. Only after the Conservative government won a majority government in May 2011 was it able to get its bill through Parliament.

Beyond the two main departments, the highly centralized nature of political power (in the hands of the Prime Minister) in the federal government allowed the Prime Minister's Office (PMO) to decide, for political reasons,

---

29 RSC 1985, c C-42.

30 Doern & Sharaput, above note 18 at 18–19.

31 Haggart, "North American," above note 11 at 251, n 188.

32 See *Copyright Modernization Act*, above note 10.

that the government would follow the US lead on TPMs, rather than maintain the compromise position that the departments had previously reached. Where the departmental position would have effectively maintained the protection/dissemination status quo (by making it illegal to break a digital lock only if it were done for the purposes of violating an underlying copyright), the US (and PMO) position did not link TPM protection to actual infringement, and required that trafficking in lock-circumvention devices be prohibited.

2) Ideas

Although theorists have argued that the role of ideas in historical institutionalism has remained underdeveloped, historical institutionalism's incorporation of their constraining and enabling effects represents one of its primary contributions to policy studies.[33] Ideas play two important roles in the policy-making process, along the lines of what Campbell refers to as "background" and "foreground" ideas.[34] "Foreground" ideas are those that are linked to specific policy proposals. Lying behind these foregrounded ideas are what Campbell refers to as "background" ideas. Background ideas are the assumptions about how the world works that constrain the range of acceptable policy solutions available to policy-makers and, in a democracy, the public. Even more interestingly, actors often internalize background ideas; these ideas become the lens through which they view policy and politics, predisposing them toward some solutions over others, and shaping their policy preferences.

Background ideas represent the primary link between institutions and the deep structures that undergird the political and economic system. Ideas are embedded within institutions, which are maintained by "a powerful supporting idea . . . generally connected to core political values which can be communicated directly and simply through image and rhetoric."[35] While whatever are considered to be the "best" ideas will differ from society to society, investigating which are the fundamental ideas underpinning insti-

33 Stephen Bell, "Do We Really Need a New 'Constructivist Institutionalism' to Explain Institutional Change?" (2011) 41:4 British Journal of Political Science 883.

34 John L Campbell, *Institutional Change and Globalization* (Princeton: Princeton University Press, 2004) at 93–94.

35 Baumgartner & Jones, above note 21 at 7.

tutions and policies, both as they are and how they ebb and flow over time, provides a way to highlight dominant social structures.

The effective use of foregrounded ideas depends not only on the material resources deployed by actors to support them, but also on the fit between these foregrounded ideas and background ideas, which Campbell divides into policy paradigms (elite ideas) and public sentiments (public ideas). For example, foundational concepts like "freedom," "individuality," and "property" represent powerful concepts embedded within institutions and which policy-makers will seek to use to frame their proposals.

Just as institutions can embody sometimes-conflicting rules, various types of background ideas rarely exist uncontested. Institutions can embody conflicting paradigms. *Liberté, egalité, fraternité* may be foundational ideas in French society (and in Western society generally), but they exist in tension with each other. Often, a successful challenge to a dominant institution will involve reworking dominant paradigms, including a redefinition of an issue, expressed in a way that deploys powerful symbols. Policy proposals do best when they are linked to a "strong" paradigm[36] that makes institutions seem natural, rather than "socially contrived arrangements."[37]

Building off this point, copyright as a form of regulation of the marketplace in creative works is anchored in core Enlightenment ideas of property and individuality: powerful ideas that are often deployed to defend a particular form of copyright. Proponents of stronger copyright, including collection societies like the Access Copyright collection society in Canada and motion picture and music producers worldwide, couch their arguments in favour of stronger copyright laws, written to maximize their material interests, in these terms. However, the positive idea of ownership is in tension with the negative idea of copyright as a "monopoly" (i.e., copyright prevents someone who has lawfully acquired a work to do whatever they wish with it). "Monopoly" implies not only that control is vested in only one person, but also that this control is unfair (a monopoly is typically regarded as societally destructive). Those who do not benefit from current copyright laws can use this argument to challenge them. Together these two ideas — property and monopoly — form the "protection-dissemination" paradox at the heart of

---

36 *Ibid.*

37 Ira Katznelson, "Periodization and Preferences: Reflections on Purposive Action in Comparative Historical Social Science" in James Mahoney & Dietrich Rueschemeyer, eds, *Comparative Historical Analysis in the Social Sciences* (Cambridge: Cambridge University Press, 2003) at 296 [Katznelson, "Periodization"] [footnote omitted].

copyright policy. Proponents of "balanced" copyright (itself a loaded term), such as the telecommunications industry, researchers, consumers, and future creators, invoke notions of fairness and—yes—balance intended to emphasize the "dissemination" side inherent in all copyright laws to promote their own material interests.

a) Canadian Copyright Ideas

The Canadian copyright debate continues to take place within this familiar protection/dissemination frame. During the debate over the WIPO implementation bills, content owners emphasized the need to crack down on "pirates," while advocates for greater user rights called on the government to undertake a "balanced" approach.[38] Furthermore, despite the lack of strong empirical evidence, referred to above, that copyright actually maximizes the production and dissemination of creative works, and despite the way digital technologies have upended existing copyright-based business models, the basic question of whether copyright is necessary was never seriously raised. If one pole of the debate was defined by the copyright industries' arguments for stronger copyright protection, the other was defined by the argument—associated with Michael Geist, Professor at the University of Ottawa, Faculty of Law—that user rights should be taken into consideration when crafting copyright law. While he has been vilified in some circles for his views—one Canadian artist refers to him as "he who shall not be named"[39]—Geist's overriding argument, that copyright should balance both protection and dissemination, is hardly radical. That Geist and those who hold similar views can pass for "radical extremists," in the words of Conservative Heritage Minister James Moore,[40] suggests the power and strength of the ideas in which copyright is grounded in Canada.

---

38 As can be seen in the title of the edited volume in Michael Geist, ed, *From "Radical Extremism" to "Balanced Copyright": Canadian Copyright and the Digital Agenda* (Toronto: Irwin Law, 2010).

39 Jeff Gray, "Changing Canada's Tune on Copyright Law" *Globe and Mail* (20 April 2010), online: The Globe and Mail www.theglobeandmail.com/report-on-business/industry-news/the-law-page/changing-canadas-tune-on-copyright-law/article1211543/.

40 The quote is taken from a comment about critics of the government's copyright bill made by Heritage Minister James Moore to industry executives: Peter Nowak, "Copyright Debate Turns Ugly" *CBC* (24 June 2010), online: CBC www.cbc.ca/news/technology/story/2010/06/23/copyright-heritage-minister-moore.html.

3) Actors/Interests

Historical institutionalism holds that actors are purposeful agents acting under conditions of constrained agency. Actors act strategically, seeking to realize complex, contingent, and often changing goals, in a context that favours certain strategies over others, and must rely upon incomplete (possibly inaccurate) perceptions of context, seen primarily in institutional terms. In other words, actors' strategic actions are limited cognitively by the ideas and identities promoted by their institutional context.[41] Actors exhibit a "situated . . . rationality,"[42] "operating within relational structural fields that distinguish the possible from the impossible and the likely from the less likely."[43]

Actors both shape and are shaped by the institutions within which they operate, as well as the institutions that they either sustain or change (often in unforeseen ways) through their actions. Institutions can affect actors in two ways. They provide the rules governing their interactions, based on the "background" ideas discussed above. Through their rules and propagated norms, institutions shape their strategies by privileging some strategies and actors over others. Institutions also provide actors with "rules of appropriateness,"[44] partially constituting actors' identities. Institutions "create categories and 'realities' that seem natural,"[45] comprising of "actors with particular identities, values, interests, and strategies — that is, preferences — who seek to manage and solve problems."[46]

Actors vary not only in their objectives, but also in their access to material and ideational resources: better-resourced actors, all else being equal, will have a greater effect on institutional and policy outcomes than those lacking resources, as will those privileged by an institution's rules. As a consequence

---

41 Colin Hay & Daniel Wincott, "Structure, Agency and Historical Institutionalism" (1998) 46:5 Political Studies 951.

42 Ira Katznelson, "Review: The Doleful Dance of Politics and Policy: Can Historical Institutionalism Make a Difference?" (1998) 92:1 The American Political Science Review 191 at 196.

43 Ira Katznelson, "Structure and Configuration in Comparative Politics" in Mark Irving Lichbach & Alan S Zuckerman, eds, *Comparative Politics: Rationality, Culture, and Structure* (Cambridge: Cambridge University Press, 1997) at 83.

44 James G March & Johan P Olsen, "The New Institutionalism: Organizational Factors in Political Life" (1984) 78:3 The American Political Science Review 734 at 741; Hall & Taylor, above note 16.

45 Katznelson, "Periodization," above note 37 at 294.

46 *Ibid*.

of this state of affairs, institutions, themselves shaped by actors with different resource levels, will favour some actors and policies over others; as noted above, institutions do not represent socially optimal equilibria.

A historical institutionalist analysis requires identifying the relevant actors and their underlying interests. The actors involved in the Canadian copyright debate can be divided in several, somewhat artificial, ways. Most crudely, they can be sorted into users (such as consumers, researchers, or even future creators, who draw on existing works for inspiration), creators (such as musicians and writers), and intermediaries (such as the various industry lobby groups), each of which interacts with copyright law in different ways. These distinctions, however, ignore the reality that any one actor can be a creator, user, and/or distributor of creative works, and that different types of actors within these categories can have different material interest in copyright law.[47] Politically, though, actors tend to pursue reforms that emphasize copyright's "protection" or "dissemination" roles.[48]

Copyright offers a perfect example of how institutions shape "not just actors' strategies . . . but their goals as well, and by mediating their relations of cooperation and conflict, institutions structure political situations and leave their own imprint on political outcomes."[49] The legal creation of scarcity in creative works — copyright — is but one possible way to regulate the market in creative works. Yet, debates focus on *copyright* reform, not on the underlying market. From the establishment side, at a time in which technology makes maintaining this legal scarcity increasingly difficult, the music and motion picture industries, for example, have continued to concentrate their efforts almost exclusively on strengthening domestic copyright laws and promoting ever-stronger copyright provisions in treaties such as the aforementioned ACTA, rather than modify their business models to minimize their dependence on the artificial/legal maintenance of scarcity in digital products. The goal for these firms has become not the maximization of profits, but the preservation of their right to copy. This focus on means, rather than ends, is the result of an inability to think past the institutionalized model of copyright. These ideational barriers also impose a significant

---

47 Yochai Benkler, "A Political Economy of the Public Domain: Markets in Information Goods Versus the Marketplace of Ideas" in Rochelle Cooper Dreyfuss, Diane Leenheer Zimmerman, & Harry First, eds, *Expanding the Boundaries of Intellectual Property: Innovation Policy for the Knowledge Society* (Oxford: Oxford University Press, 2001).

48 Doern & Sharaput, above note 18 at 18–19.

49 Thelen & Steinmo, above note 17 at 9 [footnote omitted].

social cost: discussing only copyright reform precludes the issue of whether copyright is actually necessary to accomplish objectives like maximizing the production and dissemination of creative works. This second, more important, conversation is cut off before it even gets started.

a) Canadian Copyright Interests

On the "protection" side of the Canadian copyright debate we tend to find copyright-based industries (most of which are foreign-based) such as the motion-picture industry, the United States government, and several traditional creator groups, notably collection societies such as Access Copyright. On the "dissemination" side, we find groups such as the telecoms industry (companies such as Rogers and Bell), consumers, researchers, up-and-coming artists, and public-interest organizations. "The public" is also important, both as individual voters and as a group that various smaller interest groups claim to represent.[50] Lobbyists and advocates within academia also work to promote specific views of copyright.

During the 2000s, the Canadian copyright debate was particularly notable because it saw the emergence of individuals as an important force on the dissemination side of copyright policy. Influential copyright-based interest groups and research institutions such as universities previously dominated the Canadian copyright agenda. Social-networking technology, notably Facebook, allowed individuals across the country to network and lobby the government for greater user rights. Its greatest accomplishment occurred in December 2007, when Michael Geist created the "Fair Copyright for Canada" Facebook page.[51] Tens of thousands of Canadians joined the page, and thousands used it to organize local chapters to lobby their Members of Parliament.[52] This lobbying led directly to the inclusion of new user rights in the Conservative government's eventual 2012 legislation.[53]

---

50 Sara Bannerman, "Canadian Copyright Reform: Consulting with Copyright's Changing Public" (2006) 19:2 IPJ 271.

51 Michael Geist, "The Fair Copyright for Canada Facebook Group" (2 December 2007), online: Michael Geist www.michaelgeist.ca/content/view/2428/125.

52 Michael Geist, "Canadians for Fair Copyright" *Facebook* (2 December 2007), online: Facebook www.facebook.com/groups/6315846683; Michael Geist, "Fair Copyright for Canada" *Facebook* (25 April 2010), online: Facebook www.facebook.com/FairCopyright-Canada/info.

53 Haggart, "North American," above note 11 at ch 4; see Michael Geist, "The Battle Over C-11 Concludes: How Thousands of Canadians Changed the Copyright Debate" (18 June 2012), online: Michael Geist www.michaelgeist.ca/content/view/6544/99999, on the provenance of these new user rights.

4) Consistency and Change in Historical Institutionalism

a) "Constrained Innovation"

Historical institutionalism scholars continue to debate the conditions under which change happens in historical institutionalism, and the mechanisms that drive it. In most accounts, existing institutions structure and shape the direction of reform along a certain *path*. Change in historical institutionalism is thus the consequence (whether intended or unintended) of strategic action (whether intuitive or instrumental), filtered through perceptions (however informed or misinformed) of an institutional context that favours certain strategies, actors, and perceptions over others. Actors then appropriate a structured institutional context which favours certain strategies over others and they do so by way of the strategies they formulate or intuitively adopt.[54]

Because actors, pursuing their own partial interests, lack perfect information, resulting institutions do not represent societally optimal results. These postulates lead to historical institutionalism's famous notion of *path dependence*, which is based on the observation that institutions, once established, are difficult to change, and can outlive their objective utility. Institutions structure future actions, resulting in "constrained innovation"[55] and institutional persistence: "preceding steps in a particular direction induce further movement in the same direction . . . ."[56]

One of the main points of contention among historical institutionalism scholars is how to account for periods of radical change. One influential school of thought[57] holds that institutional histories can be divided into periods of stability and change, divided by "critical junctures" when, for various reasons (such as an external economic shock), institutions and policies can be knocked onto a new "path." This view has been criticized for being logically inconsistent, that "institutions explain everything until they explain nothing."[58] In contrast to the "critical junctures" approach, what we can call an *unstable institutions* view, sees institutions as constantly being made and remade by actors when they follow or deviate from in-

54 Hay & Wincott, above note 41 at 955.

55 Campbell, above note 34 at 8.

56 Paul Pierson, "Increasing Returns, Path Dependence, and the Study of Politics" (2000) 94:2 The American Political Science Review 251 at 252.

57 Stephen D Krasner, "Sovereignty: An Institutional Perspective" (1988) 21:2 Comparative Political Studies 66.

58 Thelen & Steinmo, above note 17 at 15.

stitutional rules.[59] The unstable institutions approach argues that there is almost always a degree of continuity between periods.[60] Such continuity, even between two seemingly disparate institutional periods, becomes more obvious if one sees institutions as historically contingent and as temporary responses to "enduring problems."[61]

The invention and evolution of copyright offers a perfect example of path dependence within an unstable institutions framework. The formal history of copyright may begin in 1709, but it emerged from, and was shaped by, the monopoly granted by the British Crown to the Stationers' Guild. Canadian copyright law is directly influenced by this British tradition. Before Confederation, Canada was ruled by a succession of British copyright laws, and its first *Copyright Act* (passed in 1924) was essentially a replica of the UK *Imperial Copyright Act* of 1911.[62] Subsequent laws have been based in the Anglo-American tradition, although in some areas it follows the Continental moral rights tradition, reflecting the French influence (via Quebec) on Canadian law.

Since then, we have seen constrained innovation at work in wave after wave of copyright reform. Challenges to copyright law, in Canada as elsewhere, which emerged as a response to technological change — from the phonogram to the Internet — have all been subsumed within copyright law as a result of actors' decisions to do so. Even technologies that have little in common with physical book publishing have been treated as if copyright, a

---

59 This is a variation on the famous agent-structure debate. For a useful elaboration, see Margaret S Archer, *Realist Social Theory: The Morphogenetic Approach* (Cambridge: Cambridge University Press, 1995).

60 Campbell, above note 34, notes that change "rarely starts from scratch. Typically, institutional change involves the recombination of old institutional elements and sometimes the introduction of new ones as well" at 28.

61 Jeffrey Haydu, "Making Use of the Past: Time Periods as Cases to Compare and as Sequences of Problem Solving" (1998) 104:2 American Journal of Sociology 339 at 354 and 358; see Paul Pierson, "Not Just What, but *When*: Timing and Sequence in Political Processes" (2000) 14:1 Studies in American Political Development 72, for a description and defence of dividing "path dependence" into "open" and "closed" stages; on the uneasy fit between path dependence and critical junctures, see also Chris Howell & Rebecca Kolins Givan, "Rethinking Institutions and Institutional Change in European Industrial Relations" (2011) 49:2 British Journal of Industrial Relations 231; James Mahoney, "Path Dependence in Historical Sociology" (2000) 29:4 Theory and Society 507.

62 1911 (UK), 1 & 2 Geo V, c 46; Sara Bannerman, *Canada and the Berne Convention, 1886–1971* (PhD Thesis, Carleton University, 2009); Canada, Royal Commission on Patents, Copyright, Trade Marks, and Industrial Designs, *Report on Copyright* (Ottawa: Queen's Printer and Controller of Stationary, 1957) at 8–10 (Chair: James Lorimer Ilsley), online: Privy Council Office http://epe.lac-bac.gc.ca/100/200/301/pco-bcp/commissions-ef/ilsley1957a-eng/ilsley1957a-eng.htm.

regulatory regime developed for physical books, is appropriate to their regulation. A historical institutionalist analysis reminds us that these developments are the result of historical accidents and the exercise of political will by interested actors.

In historical institutionalism, actors can exploit ideational and material resources, as well as potentially conflicting institutional rules in order either to maintain or change — incrementally or radically — an institution or a policy. Some resources and institutions are more potent than others. For example, in Canada's highly centralized federal government, the PMO has much more discretion in setting copyright policy than does the US President; in the United States, power is split between the Executive and Congress. Prime ministerial approval is thus a powerful resource for those who receive it. Some ideational resources, similarly, carry particular weight. Policies that can be framed as supporting Canadian artists will tend to resonate more than those that are framed as primarily benefiting foreign multinational record companies.

Actors also differ in their access to these resources, with those that benefit from the status quo often using their resources and influence to perpetuate the institution; that is, to promote path dependence. As a result, institutions and policies can persist even in the face of a changing external environment. Change-seeking actors, for their part, can use their resources and exploit rules that favour them in order to pursue their preferred policies.

b) How Change Can Happen: Bricolage

Change, ultimately, depends on the actions of actors. Scholars have elaborated numerous strategies for effecting change, such as "layering" ("grafting of new institutions onto old ones"), "conversion" ("changes in function" of the institution), and "drift" (change through a "loss of relevance" of the current institution).[63] Change also depends on the relative strength of institutional rules (including the extent to which actors follow these rules and what outcomes result from following the rules).[64] This chapter focuses on one strategy in particular, *bricolage*, which involves the active combination

---

63 Steven Levitsky & María Victoria Murillo, "Variation in Institutional Strength" (2009) 12 Annual Review of Political Science 115 at 127; Wolfgang Streeck & Kathleen Thelen, "Introduction" in Wolfgang Streeck & Kathleen Ann Thelen, eds, *Beyond Continuity: Institutional Change in Advanced Political Economies* (New York: Oxford University Press, 2005).

64 Levitsky & Murillo, above note 63.

of various sources of material, ideational, and regulatory power. Bricolage is the act of recombining "locally available institutional principles and practices in ways that yield change . . . ."[65] Bricolage can be either *substantive*, where "the recombination of already existing institutional principles and practices to address these sorts of [substantive] problems and thus follows a logic of instrumentality" or "symbolic," which "involves the recombination of symbolic principles and practices . . . ," or a combination of both. Both types of bricolage refer to the recombination of already-existing elements, not the introduction of new elements.[66] When actors emphasize a particular combination of copyright's protection and dissemination roles, they are engaging in a form of bricolage.

The common conception of intellectual property (including copyright) as a trade issue emerged from a process of bricolage. There is nothing inherent in intellectual property that requires it to be defined as a trade issue rather than, for example, a purely domestic regulatory policy. As Drahos and Braithwaithe document, the link between trade and intellectual property was the result of lobbying by US intellectual property firms in the 1970s and 1980s, who argued that maximizing international intellectual property protection would maintain US global economic dominance at a time when this hegemony was being threatened by the rising star of Japan, among others.[67] There was nothing "natural" or inevitable about this linkage, but once made, it exerted, and continues to exert, a powerful hold on our conceptions of how to address copyright and intellectual property issues.

As with all types of institutionally-based change, the form that bricolage takes, and whether it is successful, will depend on the material, ideational, and institutional resources available to actors, both domestic and international, and the constraints under which they operate. Even this type of change, however, is dependent on the willingness and ability of actors to work to effect change.

c) Change in the Canadian Copyright Debate

As this chapter suggests, a historical institutionalist analysis can help account for the development of Canadian copyright law in the 2000s. Institu-

---

65 Campbell, above note 34 at 69 [endnote omitted].

66 *Ibid* at 69–73, citing March & Olsen, *Rediscovering Institutions*, above note 16.

67 Peter Drahos & John Braithwaite, *Information Feudalism: Who Owns the Knowledge Economy?* (London: Earthscan Publications Ltd, 2002). All intellectual property owners, including patent and copyright holders, have exploited this trade-IP nexus.

tionally, the articles of the 1996 WIPO Internet treaties also largely defined the terms of the digital-copyright debate. Domestically, as the author has set out elsewhere,[68] the *Copyright Modernization Act* reflected the particular nature of the Canadian copyright-policy-making regime, including the divided responsibility for copyright policy and the highly centralized nature of power in the Canadian federal system. Ideationally, the debate itself took place within the well-defined boundaries of copyright law, even though the digital technologies' near-zero marginal cost of reproduction fundamentally challenges the logic of using a regime that regulates copy-making designed for a world in which copying was difficult. Within these parameters, interest groups engaged in bricolage.

Canadian user-rights activists, for example, displayed both the willingness and the ability to influence government copyright policy, engaging in substantive bricolage to advance the objective of greater user rights. Specifically, they reinterpreted the tension between dissemination and protection inherent in the *institution* of copyright to emphasize the need for greater attention to user (i.e., dissemination) rights, arguing that the changes demanded by the United States and copyright-based industries would be harmful to this fundamental part of copyright policy. Claiming that the bill was made in the United States, as some critics did, also played to anti-American sentiments that are rarely far below the surface in Canadian political life.[69] While the TPM provisions were the result of American lobbying, other parts of the bill, such as its more-balanced approach to the issue of ISP liability (relative to US policies), departed from the US position to stake out a "made in Canada" approach to copyright reform.

With respect to interests, despite the tendency in the 1980s and 1990s for Canadian policy-makers to emphasize copyright's protection function, and despite the material and institutional advantages of traditional copyright interests, new interest groups — including public-interest groups and individual voters — were able to advance "user interests" by exploiting new social-media technologies that made it easier to organize, emphasizing copyrights in pursuit of new user rights and against strong protection for

68 Blayne Haggart, "International Copyright Treaties and Digital Works: Implementation Issues in Canada and Mexico" (2011) 38:3 Australian Journal of Communication 33.

69 In actuality, many parts of the bills reflected a "made in Canada" consensus. New rules on ISP liability, for example, codified an already-established informal institution between important segments of copyright-based industries and the politically and economically important telecoms industry. In contrast, there were no existing rules for TPMs: it is always easier to create a new rule or institution than change one.

digital locks. While they were unsuccessful in preventing the inclusion of strong, US-demanded rules for digital locks, the final bill included several new user rights that represent a change from the previous status quo, within copyright's well-established protection/dissemination dichotomy and the ideational parameters set in 1996 by WIPO.

While this short overview of a decade's worth of highly contentious copyright politics cannot do justice to the debate, it does highlight several points. First, the outcome was a highly political contest among Canadian and foreign (notably the US government) interests, with the outcome determined by the institutional structure of the Canadian policy-making regime (particularly the central role of the PMO), and the amount and effectiveness with which actors deployed material and ideational resources (arguments in favour of protection/dissemination; the highly effective use of social media by individuals and user-interest groups). The victory, in other words, went to the best political argument in the context of existing institutions, not necessarily the best argument.

C. CONCLUSION

Historical institutionalism provides researchers with a useful way to think about the politics of intellectual property and to understand how it has changed and adapted as it has for over 300 years. Rather than focusing on the law itself, historical institutionalism involves identifying relevant institutions, interests, and ideas — be they domestic, regional, or international — and how they interact. Understanding if change is likely, or where change might emerge, is a matter of considering their relative strength and whether anything has happened that might upset the status quo, such as the introduction of a means to simplify the organization of disparate individuals around a specific policy demand. Historical institutionalism analyses, done well, can provide us with a better and more nuanced understanding of how institutions and public policies emerge and develop. It can provide us with a framework for thinking about where, when, and how policies can be shaped and who is shaping the laws under which we live. For those interested in copyright and intellectual property reform, such an analysis offers a guide about how best to think about successfully influencing policy-making.

Historical institutionalism analyses also serve as a reminder of the historically and politically contingent nature of intellectual property. This focus on the politics of intellectual property and its contingent nature, somewhat ironically, has the potential to expand the debate from a focus on reforming intellectual property laws as an end in itself toward considering intellectual property as part of a larger puzzle, seeing intellectual property as a contestable form of regulation that can be changed or discarded if conditions warrant. Intellectual property, like all institutions, is maintained by the actions of purposeful actors. Being conscious of the political forces that support intellectual property is a necessary step toward having a complete debate, not just on the limited question of how to reform intellectual property law, but also on the more interesting and fundamental question of how society should best regulate the market in intellectual products, concepts, and ideas.

EIGHT

Feminist Anthropology and Copyright: Gauging the Application and Limitations of Oppositions Models[1]

B COURTNEY DOAGOO

ABSTRACT (EN): The purpose of this brief chapter is to explore the application of interdisciplinarity to intellectual property law, specifically copyright law, through the lens of feminist critiques. The paper attempts to demonstrate how the application and limitation of the two oppositions models offered by feminist anthropology intersect with copyright law. Specifically, drawing on examples from what is considered to be traditionally feminine areas of creativity, the paper broadly examines the values we associate with women, what they create, and how it is perceived and valued before the law.

RÉSUMÉ (FR): Le but de ce court chapitre est d'explorer l'application de l'interdisciplinarité au droit de la propriété intellectuelle, plus particulièrement au droit d'auteur, d'un angle critique féministe. Cet article essaie de démontrer comment les applications et les limites de deux modèles opposés offerts par l'anthropologie féministe s'entrecroisent avec le droit d'auteur. Plus spécialement, en se basant sur des exemples de ce que l'on considère comme des domaines traditionnels de créativité féminine, cet article exa-

1 I would like to express my sincere gratitude to the Intellectual Property Workshop Committee (Professor Mistrale Goudreau, Professor Teresa Scassa, and Executive Director of the Centre for Law, Technology and Society, Madelaine Saginur) for encouraging me to participate in this tremendous project, and also for all of their help, patience, and guidance. I would also like to thank the participants at the conference for their feedback, the two peer reviewers, the student editors, and committee editor for all of their hard work, dedication, and assistance.

mine globalement les valeurs associées à la femme, la façon dont elle crée et comment cette création est perçue et évaluée par le droit.

A. INTRODUCTION

In recent years, scholars have revealed an interest in unravelling the inherently patriarchal underpinnings of copyright law.[2] Why certain kinds of art, culture, and knowledge receive mainstream economic and legal protection while others do not is an important question that has far ranging implications beyond law.[3] Copyright protection — or the lack thereof — for creativity traditionally considered "feminine" such as decorative crafts, needlework, and clothing[4] is illustrative.[5]

While examining intellectual property, specifically copyright, from a traditional legal approach might yield a justification based on Lockean, Hegelian, or utilitarian theories,[6] an inquiry through the lens of interdisciplinarity allows for an alternate approach to understanding the origins of the

---

2 See, generally, Ann Bartow, "Fair Use and the Fairer Sex: Gender, Feminism, and Copyright Law" (2006) 14:3 Am U J Gender Soc Pol'y & L 551; Shelley Wright, "A Feminist Exploration of the Legal Protection of Art" (1994) 7 CJWL 59; Debora Halbert, "Feminist Interpretations of Intellectual Property" (2006) 14:3 Am U J Gender Soc Pol'y & L 431; Carys J Craig, "Reconstructing the Author-Self: Some Feminist Lessons for Copyright Law" (2007) 15 Am U J Gender Soc Pol'y & L 207; Dan L Burk, "Feminism and Dualism in Intellectual Property" (2006) 15 Am U J Gender Soc Pol'y & L 183; Rebecca Tushnet, "My Fair Ladies: Sex, Gender, and Fair Use in Copyright" (2007) 15:2 Am U J Gender Soc Pol'y & L 273.

3 Wright, above note 2, states that "[t]he apparent gender neutrality of copyright is therefore questionable because of its association with the public world of the marketplace which has, in European history, consistently marginalized or excluded women" at 70; Tushnet, above note 2, asserts that "[c]opyright's economic focus and the expense of litigation will systematically lead to case law undervaluing non-market production, including historically female creative practices" at 304; Tushnet also contends that although seemingly neutral, the law is "entangled in ideas about gender and sexuality" at 304.

4 While clothing was produced by men and women, both prior to and after the eighteenth century, these roles were not recorded with accuracy: see, generally, Madeleine Ginsburg, "The Tailoring and Dressmaking Trades, 1700–1850" (1972) 6:1 Costume 64. "In 1859, there are 23,517 London tailors. There is no eighteenth century estimate of professional needlewomen or dressmakers but a high proportion of the women mentioned in the Old Bailey Sessions Papers, a good cross section of London artisan life, so describe their occupation" at 64.

5 Tushnet, above note 2, suggests that there is a tendency to compensate masculine activities whereas traditionally feminine activities such as "fashion, cooking, and sewing," do not garner the same level of economic security at 303–4.

6 See, generally, Daniel J Gervais & Elizabeth F Judge, *Intellectual Property: The Law in Canada*, 2d ed (Toronto: Carswell, 2011) at 34.

law. This is particularly true of feminist critiques, which have contributed relevant insights about gender and the socio-cultural inequalities present within the intellectual property law system.[7]

This chapter considers the contributions and limitations of feminist anthropology to an understanding of how traditional "feminine" creativity fits into the Canadian copyright framework.[8] The goal of this piece is to provoke dialogue about the values that we associate with creativity by examining the economic security we grant to certain kinds of cultural production and deny to others.[9] This chapter will attempt to expand further on the idea that the marginalization of feminine activities from the scope of intellectual property protection is intimately tied to the gender values associated with the producer of the work.[10] In the first part, I will briefly introduce the "oppositions" models associated with feminist anthropology in order to offer context for the social treatment of feminine cultural production. Section C will relate the concepts to historical examples of cultural production, and Section D will attempt to highlight these implications from within the Canadian legislative context.

B. EXAMINING THE "OPPOSITIONS" APPROACH

The feminist critique of copyright law has gained impressive ground in the past few decades.[11] Scholars have mostly written about the "other side" of the economic security granted by intellectual property law, namely those areas of cultural production that have been excluded (either entirely or partially) from the framework of legal protection.[12] Although there are num-

---

7 See, generally, above note 2; Halbert, above note 2, contends that "applying a feminist framework gives us a different way of looking at the world" at 432.

8 This topic has been well documented in Wright, above note 2, a paper that articulates the gendered history of copyright and design laws; see also Rozsika Parker & Griselda Pollock, *Old Mistresses: Woman, Art and Ideology* (New York: Pantheon Books, 1981), who make the connection between the feminist anthropology oppositions models and feminine cultural production that I will discuss in this paper; the examination of oppositions models in intellectual property is not new, as it has previously been explored in Burk, above note 2.

9 This paper does not take the view that copyright law should be expanded to include additional protection for various industries; rather, it seeks to help identify the possible biases inherent in the system stemming from gender inequalities.

10 See, generally, above note 2.

11 *Ibid.*

12 *Ibid.*

erous feminist theories relevant to this discussion, the section below will examine the application and limitations of two specific oppositions models[13] in order to explore the treatment of feminine cultural production and its relationship with copyright.

Broadly described, feminist anthropology is a discipline that "formulates its theoretical questions in terms of how economics, kinship and ritual are experienced and structured through gender . . ."[14] and further asks "how gender is structured and experienced through colonialism, through neo-imperialism and through the rise of capitalism."[15]

In an instrumental piece explaining the construction of gender and its corresponding inequalities, Sherry Ortner proposed an analytical framework that explored what she felt was the universally accepted view that women hold a secondary status to men.[16] Ortner rejected the suggestion that "biological determinism"[17] dictated the subordination of women and instead pointed to the "universals of the human condition" (i.e., the physical, social, and psychological realms) for an answer.[18] She identified *nature*, in its most generalized sense, as something that was devalued, manipulated into, and controlled by *culture* (what she largely defined as the products of human consciousness and thought processes), and compared this relationship between women and men.[19]

---

13 While there are many theories within feminism and feminist anthropology, this article will focus on the two opposition models as proposed by Sherry Ortner and Michelle Zimbalist Rosaldo.

14 Henrietta L Moore, *Feminism and Anthropology* (Cambridge: Polity Press, 1988) at 9 [Moore, *Feminism*].

15 *Ibid* at 10.

16 Sherry B Ortner, "Is Female to Male as Nature Is to Culture?" [Ortner, "Is Female to Male"] in Michelle Zimbalist Rosaldo & Louise Lamphere, eds, *Woman, Culture, and Society* (Stanford: Stanford University Press, 1974) at 67 [Rosaldo & Lamphere, *Woman, Culture, and Society*].

17 *Ibid*. Biological determinism only gains significance in the "framework of culturally defined value systems" at 71; Moore, *Feminism*, above note 14. Moore summarizes Ortner and distills what she calls *asymmetries* at the "level of cultural ideologies and symbols" at 14.

18 Ortner, "Is Female to Male," above note 16 at 71. For example, Ortner looks for answers in the universals that exists in every culture: everyone is born to a mother, engages in society, strives for survival, dies, etc.

19 *Ibid* at 72. Although *nature* and *culture* are social constructs, Ortner "maintain[s] that the universality of ritual betokens an assertion in all human cultures of the specifically human ability to act upon and regulate, rather than passively move with and be moved by, the givens of natural existence" at 72; Moore, *Feminism*, above note 14 at 14; Burk, above note 2. Dualisms, i.e., mind/body have been used to "naturalize domination" and to support dominance over women, at 192.

As a result of these cultural beliefs, Ortner proposed that women have merely been considered *closer* to nature than men, while men have been considered *closer* to culture.[20] She outlined three general levels that contribute to the association of women with nature, concerning the "female body and its function" (i.e., procreative function), which were all at tension with her simultaneous participation with culture, thereby suspending her status between the two oppositions.[21] Finally, Ortner concluded that the ensuing position of women — being considered closer to nature — was also perpetuated in the "institutional forms that reproduce her situation."[22]

Connected to Ortner's framework — and important to the analysis of the devaluation of cultural production — was the idea that the socially systematic division of gender (nature/culture) is mirrored in societal institutions (i.e., private versus public spheres).[23] The private/public model had been considered important because "it provides a way of linking the cultural valuations given to the category 'woman' to the organization of women's activities in society."[24] This model, as observed by Michelle Zimbalist Rosaldo, outlined a "structural framework necessary to identify and explore the place of male and female in psychological, cultural, social, and economic aspects of human life."[25] For example, she observed that women, in their role as mother and nurturer of children were relegated to the domestic sphere, while men attended to "extra-domestic" activities.[26]

Further, Rosaldo claimed that this dualism "underlies" the "cultural stereotypes . . . in the evaluation of the sexes" rather than "determine[s]" it.[27] One of the consequences of women's "ascribed status" to womanhood (as opposed to men's "achieved status" to manhood), she observed, was that their activities were "relatively uninvolved with the articulation and expression of social differences."[28] Rosaldo concluded in suggesting that women

---

20 Ortner, "Is Female to Male," above note 16 at 73.

21 *Ibid* at 73–74.

22 *Ibid* at 87.

23 *Ibid*; Moore, *Feminism*, above note 14 at 21; Michelle Zimbalist Rosaldo, "Woman, Culture, and Society: A Theoretical Overview" in Rosaldo & Lamphere, *Women, Culture, and Society*, above note 16 at 23 [Rosaldo, "Woman, Culture, and Society"].

24 Moore, *Feminism*, above note 14 at 21.

25 Rosaldo, "Woman, Culture, and Society," above note 23 at 23.

26 *Ibid* at 24; but see Michelle Zimbalist Rosaldo, "The Use and Abuse of Anthropology: Reflections on Feminism and Cross-Cultural Understanding" (Spring 1980) 5:3 Signs 389 at 400 [Rosaldo, "The Use and Abuse"].

27 Rosaldo, "Woman, Culture, and Society," above note 23 at 23.

28 *Ibid* at 29.

relegated to the domestic sphere experienced oppression due largely to their alienation from society, and that the opportunity to interact within the public sphere instead provided them with "power and a sense of value."[29]

Even though these models provide a useful framework for understanding the subordination of women, they have important limitations. Both Ortner and Rosaldo cautioned against relying on universalisms to frame the questions and to explain the complexities of gender dynamics in society, because doing so oversimplified and overlooked the nuances and contradictions that actually existed across and within different cultures.[30] In her later work, Rosaldo suggested that applying universalisms (i.e., the public/private model) to account for concrete cases "assume[s]—where it should rather help illuminate and explain—too much about how gender really works."[31] Similarly, Ortner acknowledged concerns about these cultural particulars at the very beginning of her piece, asserting that although certain universals existed (such as the secondary status of women), they were at tension with cultural variances, stating that "the specific cultural conceptions and symbolizations of woman are extraordinarily diverse and even mutually contradictory."[32]

These opposition models were also criticized by scholars,[33] however, as Henrietta Moore observed, they served an important purpose at the time

---

29 *Ibid* at 41.

30 Ortner "Is Female to Male," above note 16 at 67; Rosaldo, "The Use and Abuse," above note 26 at 395 and 415.

31 *Ibid* at 399. "[B]y linking gender, and in particular female lives, to the existence of domestic spheres, we have inclined, I fear, to think we know the 'core' of what quite different gender systems share, to think of sexual hierarchies primarily in functional and psychological terms . . . to minimize such sociological considerations as inequality and power" at 400.

32 Ortner, "Is Female to Male," above note 16 at 67; Sherry B Ortner, *Making Gender: The Politics and Erotics of Culture* (Massachusetts: Beacon Press, 1996). In a response to her earlier work, Ortner addresses the issues concerning universalisms, stating that "[t]he biggest substantive 'error' in the paper may be the main point, that is, the point that a linkage between female and nature, male and culture 'explains' male dominance, whether universal or not" at 177; rather, she finds that male dominance can be due to the "result of some complex interaction of functional arrangements, power dynamics, and bodily effects" at 177.

33 Henrietta Moore, "'Divided We Stand': Sex, Gender, and Sexual Difference" (1994) 47 Fem Rev 78 [Moore, "Divided"]. "The categories of nature, culture, public and private were themselves found to be historically and culturally variable . . . and the categories of gender difference were revealed to be far from universal" at 80; Moore, *Feminism*, above note 14 at 16 and 21; see, for example, Carol P MacCormack "Nature, Culture, and Gender: A Critique" in *Nature, Culture, and Gender* (Cambridge: Cambridge University Press, 1980).

they were introduced because they endeavoured to explain the devaluation of women based on social and not biological terms.[34] Moore also suggested that the use of universalisms had since opened the door to their "critical reinterpretation" by feminist scholars, resulting in unique and diverse accounts of what being a "woman" meant, and further challenging what these accounts entailed.[35]

Notwithstanding these limitations, the models do offer interesting insights about the dynamics of contemporary society, specifically in the context of cultural production, which is arguably tied to the social status of its producer. The relevance of these models is grounded in the fact that much of the language used to describe the subordination of feminine cultural production makes references to the nature of the work as tied to its producer and the place in which it is created.[36] For example, Parker and Pollock suggest that the language used in the Victorian era to describe women's work perpetuated themes of nature and the separation of spheres to denote the division of labour between the sexes.[37]

Importantly, the subordination of women affects the social, economic, and legal valuation of their cultural production.[38] For example, women have been excluded from certain activities, their work has been devalued, and, finally, their exclusion from equal participation in cultural production tends to perpetuate masculine ideologies.[39] Having identified the param-

---

34 Moore, "Divided," above note 33 at 80.

35 *Ibid* (i.e., through the lens of sexual orientation, race, culture, etc.).

36 Parker & Pollock, above note 8 at 9–10, 12, and 70; Rozsika Parker, *The Subversive Stitch: Embroidery and the Making of the Feminine*, 3d ed (New York: I B Tauris, 2010) at 5.

37 Parker & Pollock, above note 8 at 10 and 12–13.

38 See, generally, Bartow, above note 2. Most creative sectors are "dominated and controlled" by men at 578; also labelling cultural production female "commands less attention and less money than the creative works of men" at 552; see, generally, Tushnet, above note 2 at 303–4; Burk, above note 2, suggests that patterns of subordinating "feminine labour" — which goes unrecognized — are arguably present in "our system for rewarding innovation and creativity" at 192–93.

39 See Sally Hagaman, "Feminist Inquiry in Art History, Art Criticism, and Aesthetics: An Overview for Art Education" (1990) 32:1 Studies in Art Education 27. Hagaman identifies these three levels of inequality in knowledge for women in academic disciplines at 28; Gill Perry, "The Parisian Avant-Garde and 'Feminine' Art in the Early Twentieth Century" in Gill Perry, ed, *Gender and Art* (London: Yale University Press, 1999) at 199 [Perry, *Gender and Art*]. Perry discusses the exclusion of women from public Parisian art academies until the late nineteenth century. They were permitted to attend private schools, but were often segregated and charged higher fees than male students; Ortner, "Is Female to Male," above note 16 at 80. Cooking is considered a woman's natural domestic role; in contrast, at a professional level, such as haute cuisine, it is mostly the domain of men;

eters of the oppositions models — the association of women to nature and the private sphere — the following will attempt to explain the devaluation of feminine cultural production socially and legally.

C. GENDERING CULTURAL PRODUCTION

This section will briefly examine two examples of cultural production prevalent between the end of the Renaissance and Victorian eras in Britain. This temporal and geographical period is of particular interest since Canadian copyright law is based on the 1911 British *Imperial Copyright Act*, and was therefore influenced by the corresponding social and cultural context leading up to that period.[40] Taking into consideration the application and limitations of the two oppositions models discussed above, the following will attempt to link the binary themes of nature/culture and private/public to the general socio-cultural context of this period.

1) Arts and Crafts

The devaluation of female cultural production is perhaps best seen comparatively, in relation to masculine cultural production. An interesting example is the distinction between the arts and the crafts: craft is valued differently than art.[41] However, this was not always so. Art and craft were

---

Carol M Rose, "Woman and Property: Gaining and Losing Ground" (1992) 78 Va L Rev 421. Rose addresses traditional feminine crafts, noting that "[m]odern feminism has interested the art world in the aesthetic merit of such crafts, suggesting that such cooperative forms of creativity may attain very high levels, despite the often strained circumstances of their creation and the disdain with which our legal institutions have treated them," at 455; Burk, above note 2 at 192: feminine labour is largely devalued and unrecognized; see, generally, Shulamith Firestone, *The Dialectic of Sex: The Case for Feminist Revolution* (New York: William Morrow & Company, 1970) at 178: masculine domination of culture has caused all creations of culture to be seen via the lens of masculine ideas of aesthetic and beauty — women artists even painted the female body based on its masculine interpretation; Parker & Pollock, above note 8 at 135–36.

40 1911 (UK), 1 & 2 Geo V, c 46; see, generally, Sara Bannerman, "Copyright: Characteristics of Canadian Reform" in Michael Geist, ed, *From "Radical Extremism" to "Balanced Copyright": Canadian Copyright and the Digital Agenda* (Toronto: Irwin Law, 2010) at 17, for a general discussion on the evolution of Canadian copyright law and reform.

41 Mark Banks, "Craft Labour and Creative Industries" (2010) 16:3 International Journal of Cultural Policy 305 at 312; see, generally, Sally J Markowitz, "The Distinction between Art and Craft" (1994) 28:1 Journal of Aesthetic Education 55.

equally valued until the Renaissance period, during which time a cultural shift occurred, creating an "intellectual separation" between the two.[42]

This shift resulted in art (and consequently artists) assuming a status superior to craft (and consequently craftspeople), which in turn also affected the way the arts were perceived, appreciated, and taught.[43] It has been suggested that the division between arts and crafts could roughly be equated with the division between the sexes during this period: men began to associate themselves with *superior* activities, such as the politics, business, or arts, while women were encouraged to participate in *menial* activities such as the domestic crafts.[44] It should be noted that men also participated in craftwork; however, their involvement was predominantly with industrial, and not domestic crafts.[45]

The division of masculine art and feminine craft mirrored the status of women during that time; craft, like embroidery, was considered inferior to art and therefore "accorded lesser artistic value."[46] Further, women's association with embroidery became symbolic of, and eventually synonymous with, their natural femininity.[47] Parker and Pollock suggest that "the act of embroidering, the hours a woman spent sitting stitching for love of home and family, symbolized the domestic virtues of tireless industry, selfless ser-

---

42 Edward Lucie-Smith, *The Story of Craft: The Craftsman's Role in Society* (Ithaca: Cornell University Press, 1981). It was the stage after the Renaissance where an "intellectual separation between the idea of craft and that of fine art" occurred, at 11; Anthea Callen, "Sexual Division of Labor in the Arts and Crafts Movement" (1984) 5:2 Woman's Art Journal 1. The split between the (fine) arts and (lesser) crafts occurred during the Renaissance period, "when artists began to shun the practical and manual aspects of their craft in order to gain the social status accorded to intellectuals" at 3.

43 Parker & Pollock, above note 8 at 17; Lucie-Smith, above note 42 at 11; Markowitz, above note 41 .Markowitz suggests that one of the key justifications for the distinction between art and craft can be attributed to the mind-body dualism, which proposes that society places a higher value on the products of the mind (art) in contrast with products of physical labour (craft). "This dualism has shaped the way we regard morality, politics, [and] gender; now we must ask as well how it has shaped our view of art" at 68); Burk, above note 2. The valuations attributed to labour are reflected in the way creativity is rewarded, for example Burk observes that "mental effort" is awarded a higher value than the "corporeal [or] material development" at 192–93.

44 See, generally, Wright, above note 2 at 87–88; Lucie-Smith, above note 42 at 182–83; Parker & Pollock, above note 8 at 50–51: women did participate in the arts, albeit on a restricted level; Parker, above note 36 at 5 (art/craft).

45 Callen, above note 42 at 4; Lucie-Smith, above note 42. Lucie-Smith holds that few men also engaged in domestic craft activities although it was uncommon and was considered "eccentric" at 182.

46 Parker, above note 36 at 5.

47 *Ibid* at 11; Wright, above note 2 at 88.

vice and praiseworthy thrift"[48] and that it "played a crucial part in maintaining the class position of the household."[49]

Further, much of feminine cultural production took place within the private sphere.[50] Women were largely hindered from enrolling in public art institutions. [51] However, when women did successfully participate in the arts, it was mostly because they were able to circumvent the barriers to access and not because it was socially or institutionally facilitated.[52] The following passage is telling:

> Women artists were, it became clear, usually either trained as part of household workshops of artists by their fathers, and belonged to the skilled craft worker class, or they might be noblewomen, whose fathers paid for them to be tutored by professional artists.[53]

Finally, the artistic subject matter that women practised perpetuated their association with nature, compared to the wide range of subject matter available to men.[54] It seems that in addition to the hierarchy between art and craft, women were also subordinated within the domains of art and craft.

---

48 Parker & Pollock, above note 8 at 61: needlework became an accepted female stereotype.

49 *Ibid* at 60–61: embroidery gradually went from being a leisurely activity associated with aristocracy to a marginalized feminine activity; Lucie-Smith, above note 42. "[F]ancy work" akin to ornamentation provided an outlet for women who were prevented from joining other industries at 182–83; spinning was considered to be traditional female employment at 183–84.

50 Parker & Pollock, above note 8 at 70, considering Ortner's oppositions model.

51 *Ibid* at 33 and 35. Parker, above note 36 at 120.

52 Parker & Pollock, above note 8 at 17–18. While men from all backgrounds were able to access the arts, mostly noblewomen were able to do the same; Gill Perry, "Women Artists, 'Masculine' Art and the Royal Academy of Art" in Perry, *Gender and Art*, above note 39 at 88–89 [Perry, "Women Artists"]. Art historians have signalled the necessity of looking beyond traditional institutions "to uncover some other enabling strategies adopted by women artists, who more often worked on the fringes of official or professional art practices" at 100.

53 Catherine King, "Made in Her Image: Women, Portraiture, and Gender in the Sixteenth and Seventeenth Centuries," in Perry, *Gender and Art*, above note 39 at 33 [King, "Made in Her Image"]: female artists in the sixteenth and seventeenth centuries.

54 Parker & Pollock, above note 8 at 51 and 58; Parker, above note 36 at 120; Catherine King, "What Women Can Make" in Perry, *Gender and Art*, above note 39. "[G]endering of genres" is used to describe the hierarchical and gendered division of seventeenth century Western art. Men were permitted to engage in the creation of all genres of art, whereas women participated in areas that "symbolize[d] . . . her relative weakness" at 61; Perry, "Women Artists," above note 52, refers to alternate types of art that women participated in such as "flower painting, miniature painting or embroidery" which were deemed lesser arts, at 100.

2) Weaving and Spinning

A further example of the devaluation of feminine cultural production is apparent in the case of needlework.[55] Parallel to the segregation between art and craft, women were discouraged from participating in economically important sectors of production such as the silk and wool weaving industries.[56] Weaving and masculine activities were deemed to require a higher level of skill and thus granted a higher status than women's work.[57]

The marginalization of women's work was justified based on what was deemed their natural abilities.[58] For example, Joanne Entwistle observes that women were deliberately labelled with "natural" characteristics such as "nimble fingers," which were considered well adapted to spinning.[59] These justifications (i.e., natural thus effortless) coupled with the fact that the work was often performed in the home also operated to strip the act of spinning from association with "real art or technique."[60]

Shelley Wright suggests that the devaluation of feminine cultural production could be associated with women's role as "homemaker and caregiver."[61] She suggests that women were confined to the home (or sweatshops), silently contributing to the economy, without recognition, "turning this cloth into wearing apparel for themselves and their children and creating artistic work with needle and thread."[62] In contrast, men concerned themselves with important public sphere activities such as creating "real art."[63]

Drawing attention to the fact that the description of women's cultural production was imbued with references to nature, natural ability, the feminine, and the domestic sphere establishes a noteworthy connection with the models theorized by Ortner and Rosaldo.[64] Simply acknowledging the

---

55 Wright, above note 2 at 87. Wright observes that with the decline in women's status in the monastic communities, women were relegated to activities such as spinning while men dominated the weaving industry. By the seventeenth century needlework became a highly feminized and devalued activity.

56 *Ibid*; Joanne Entwistle, *The Fashioned Body: Fashion, Dress, and Modern Social Theory* (Cambridge: Polity Press, 2000) at 212. Male weavers established a guild in the eighteenth century which would work to exclude women and children from the weaving industry.

57 *Ibid* at 212–13.

58 *Ibid*.

59 *Ibid* at 213 [endnote omitted].

60 *Ibid* [endnote omitted].

61 Wright, above note 2 at 89.

62 *Ibid* at 91.

63 *Ibid* at 88.

64 See Parker & Pollock, above note 8 at 69–70, making reference to Ortner's theory.

parallels between the oppositions theories and the historical accounts of feminine cultural production could provide a general framework to help explain why certain areas of cultural production may have been overlooked by legislation. However, as mentioned above, important limitations exist in applying the models as they might not take into account the variances and exceptions that exist within the domains of art, craft, needlework, and weaving. Variances may include factors such as geography, class, ethnicity, or the fact that female artists did exist,[65] as did male tailors, designers, and dressmakers.[66]

D. GENDERING THE LAW

The inception of copyright law, beginning with the *Statute of Anne*,[67] was based on the protection of public sphere, economically important male-dominated industries and has since expanded in scope to encompass numerous new ones.[68] Although the Canadian *Copyright Act*[69] is derived from and has evolved since the 1911 British *Copyright Act*,[70] the legislative framework remains largely the same.[71]

The oppositions models offer a useful perspective for examining the gendered origins of copyright law. Quite logically, economically important activities carried out by men in the public sphere would have an influence on the marketplace, which would in turn influence Parliament to legally secure them.[72] By contrast, women, whose vocational activities were often performed in the home, were largely excluded from the public sphere, and consequently from the scope of the legislative decision-making process.[73]

65 Perry, "Women Artists," above note 52 at 100; Parker & Pollock, above note 8 at 17.

66 Ginsburg, above note 4; Callen, above note 42. Callen observes that designing embroidery was considered masculine because it required "both intellect and creative powers" at 4.

67 1710 (UK), 8 Anne, c 19; Bartow, above note 2: copyright originated from male-centric ideals of "creativity and commerce" at 557; Wright, above note 2, notes that "it is clear that this legislation was for the benefit of 'learned men,' their publishers, and 'their families,' e.g. women and children" at 70.

68 For example, software and architecture.

69 RSC 1985, c C-42.

70 See above note 40.

71 David Vaver, *Intellectual Property Law: Copyright, Patents, Trade-marks*, 2d ed (Toronto: Irwin Law, 2011) at 55–56; Gervais & Judge, above note 6 at 36.

72 See, generally, Wright, above note 2 at 70; Tushnet, above note 2 at 304.

73 Bartow, above note 2, states that "[c]ertain kinds of works, those best suited for industrialized commoditization, have been heavily propertized through a symbiotic blend of copyright and contract law precepts, while other forms of arts and crafts, those that have

The section below will examine several provisions in the Canadian *Copyright Act* that correspond to the protection of craft and needlework (clothing), and attempt to trace the marginalization of these industries within the law. The two relevant provisions that will be discussed in the following segment are the "works of artistic craftsmanship" under the definition of *artistic works*, and the *useful article* provision in section 64 of the *Copyright Act*.

1) Works of Artistic Craftsmanship

Copyright law protects artistic, dramatic, and musical subject matter.[74] Artistic works encompass a broad range of visual arts (such as paintings, sculpture, and drawings), but also include the more obscure category "works of artistic craftsmanship."[75] While copyright protection for any artistic work does not require an artistic or aesthetic qualification, craftwork seems to require a qualitative artistic element. The term also reproduces the unfortunately masculine reference to its origins with a "craftsman."

First, as Wright points out, the subject matter of copyright law does not neatly incorporate feminine craft.[76] "Works of artistic craftsmanship," a subcategory of *artistic works* defined in the *Copyright Act*[77] may be used to protect certain types of craft, although the scope of protection has never clearly been defined by legislation or the courts.[78] Further, she argues that the enactment of this subcategory was explicitly intended to protect craftsmen, and not craftswomen.[79] Examples of *feminine* crafts included fanciful or decorative activities such as embroidering, decorative or applied arts, performed predominantly in the home, as opposed to *masculine* crafts such as architecture, stonework, and ironwork, which were performed in trade.[80]

---

been relegated to the domestic realm, are less often the subject of rigorous copyright protections or restrictions" at 559; Wright, above note 2 at 70.

74 *Copyright Act*, above note 69, s 2.

75 *Ibid* [artistic works].

76 Wright, above note 2 at 91.

77 *Copyright Act*, above note 69, s 2.

78 Wright, above note 2 at 91.

79 *Ibid* at 91, n 102. Works of artistic craftsmanship were meant to protect craftsmen, not women, because women would not have been designated as craftsmen during the time that the provision was enacted in the British *Copyright Act* of 1911.

80 Callen, above note 42 at 4; King, "Made in Her Image," above note 53; Cheryl Buckley, "Made in Patriarchy: Toward a Feminist Analysis of Women and Design" (1986) 3:2 Design Issues 3. Women are considered to have sex-specific skills that relegate them to areas of design that are "naturally suited" to them such as "decorative arts" at 5.

An interesting example of the treatment of feminine cultural production (in this case, clothing), illustrated by Wright, is in the language used by the court in *Burke & Margot Burke Ltd v Spicers Dress Designs:*[81]

> I can conceive it possible that Mrs. Burke might design a frock and make it all herself, and if she did that I can well understand she might be the author of an original work of artistic craftsmanship, but that is not what has happened in this case. *I do not want it to be assumed that, even so, I should feel able to hold that a lady who designed a frock and made it all herself was necessarily entitled to copyright* . . . . Does a designer who herself designs and makes a frock cultivate one of the fine arts in which the object is mainly to gratify the aesthetic emotions by perfection of execution whether in creation or representation? A possible view is that what she does is merely to bring into being a garment as a mere article of commerce. If that is the right view there may be a difficulty in holding *that even a lady who designs and executes a beautiful frock is necessarily the author of an original work of artistic craftsmanship* . . . .[82]

The language used by the court permeates the social and cultural attitudes directed towards women, and subsequently feminine cultural production.

Second, as Wright also observes, the originality requirement for "works of artistic craftsmanship" involves showing an elevated aesthetic merit that is not required for other artistic works protected by copyright.[83] These heightened requirements are present in the language used by the courts when evaluating "works of artistic craftsmanship" in British, and more subtly in Canadian, caselaw.[84] This requirement has been taken to mean that the author must prove an artistic intent in creating the work.[85]

---

81 *Burke & Margot Burke Ltd v Spicers Dress Designs*, [1936] Ch 400 [*Burke*] as quoted in Wright, above note 2 at 92.

82 *Ibid* at 408 [emphasis added].

83 *DRG Inc v Datafile Ltd*, [1988] 2 FC 243 at 13–15 [*DRG*]; Wright, above note 2 at 92.

84 See, generally, *George Hensher Ltd v Restawhile Upholstery (Lancs) Limited*, [1976] AC 64 [*Hensher*]. The courts required that a level of intellectual or emotional satisfaction had to be invoked by the work; *Burke*, above note 81; *Merlet and Another v Mothercare*, [1986] RPC 115 at 126. The test to determine whether a work of art was artistic lies in the intent of the artist and will also take into consideration whether the craftsman — breaking into the arts — was already an artist. In this case, the aesthetic value of the work was not aesthetic enough on its own merits and was not copyrightable; *DRG*, above note 83.

85 *Ibid*. Note that not all of the lords in *Hensher*, above note 84, took this view; Vaver, above note 71. Vaver suggests that "[w]hat the producer intended (appropriately discounted for self-interest), how she proceeded, and what resulted are key issues" at 84.

In Canada, clothing design may not yet qualify for copyright protection under the subcategory of "works of artistic craftsmanship,"[86] and the question remains unresolved by the courts.[87] In *DRG v Datafile*, the Federal Court pronounced that although artistic works do not require an elevated threshold of aesthetic merit, the sentiment remained unclear for works of artistic craftsmanship.[88]

> To turn then to the definition of "artistic work" as set out in s. 2 of the *Copyright Act*, I forbear from stating whether "artistic"-ness must be determined by the courts for works of craftsmanship and architecture. It is not necessary to discuss this issue, although it must be noted that the text of Canadian statute mirrors that of the 1911 Act of the United Kingdom [*Copyright Act*, 1911 (U.K., 1 & 2 Geo. 5), c. 46] where jurisprudence has seemed to indicate that such is required. Also the *Hay* case, noted above, has accepted this view and struggled to find an appropriate test.
>
> Even if works of craftsmanship and architecture must be measured against some test of "artistic"-ness (as set out in the *Hensher, Merlet* or *Hay* cases) I do not accept that the category of artistic works in general must meet such a test. *I do not accept that the word "artistic" in reference to "artistic work" is being used in the same sense as the word "artistic" in reference to "works of artistic craftsmanship," that is, if in the latter case "artistic"-ness requires a determination along the lines of that attempted in Hensher, Merlet or Hay* . . . . It [artistic work] is used as a general description of works which find expression in a visual medium as opposed to works of literary, musical or dramatic expression.[89]

Traditional arts such as painting and sculpture, which were once predominantly masculine activities (public sphere) enjoy straightforward protection under the *artistic works* section of the *Copyright Act* while predominantly feminine activities such as "domestic" crafts (private sphere) float somewhere between copyright and industrial design protection, thereby reinforcing the gendered distinction between art and craft.

---

86 *Ibid*.

87 See, generally, *Magasins Greenberg Ltée c Import-Export René Derhy (Canada) Inc* (2004), 37 CPR (4th) 305; *Pyrrha Design Inc v 623735 Saskatchewan Ltd*, 2004 FCA 423.

88 *DRG*, above note 83 at 13–15.

89 *Ibid* at 14–15 [emphasis added].

2) "Useful Articles" and Industrial Design Protection

At the height of the textile boom in the United Kingdom, Parliament responded to lobbying from within the (male dominated) weaving industries by enacting the first copyright protection for printed designs called the *Designing & Printing of Linen Act* in 1787.[90] Design laws eventually expanded to include articles beyond its original scope of textile design to subject matter such as articles of manufacture.[91]

The foundation of industrial design protection in Canada, now the *Industrial Design Act*,[92] is based largely on British legislation, and has since evolved from protection for specific classes of goods, to a single definition of design.[93] Clothing design is categorized under the *Industrial Design Act* as a class of good, and if a clothing or craft designer wishes, they may receive protection once the design has been registered.[94] However, there are rigorous registration requirements,[95] the term is ten years,[96] and the scope of protection has been criticized as quite narrow.[97]

Clothing design and crafts that do qualify for copyright protection may be protected as an artistic work until more than fifty copies are made based on the "useful article" provision (section 64) of the *Copyright Act*.[98] Once this threshold is surpassed, then it is no longer considered infringement

---

90 Lara Kriegel, "Culture and the Copy: Calico, Capitalism, and Design Copyright in Early Victorian Britain" (2004) 43:2 Journal of British Studies 233 at 240; "History of Design" *UK Intellectual Property Office*, online: www.ipo.gov.uk/types/design/d-about/d-whatis/d-history.htm. The 1787 Act provided protection for "arts of designing and printing linens, cottons, calicos and muslin."

91 *Ibid*. The 1839 *Copyright and Design Act* extended protection to various types of materials such as "wool, silk or hair and to mixed fabrics" and also evolved to expand protection to articles of design in the spirit of modern design laws; Amy Muhlstein & Margaret Ann Wilkinson, "Whither Industrial Design" (2000) 14 IPJ 1 at 8–9; Wright, above note 2, suggests that the shift from domestic to factory production (owned and controlled by men) is the point at which the legal protection for "some forms of needlework" became significant at 91.

92 RSC 1985, c I-9.

93 Muhlstein & Wilkinson, above note 91 at 9, 12, and 16.

94 Clothing is categorized under Class Code 006 [APPAREL] "Canadian Industrial Design Database" *Canadian Intellectual Property Office* (last update 13 December 2012), online: CIPO www.ic.gc.ca/app/opic-cipo/id/dsgnSrch.do;jsessionid=0001vdheRb4wga0A40Y-2Gap53v8:24RD3DMHMH; *Industrial Design Act*, above note 92, s 4(1).

95 *Ibid*, s 6(1); Muhlstein & Wilkinson, above note 91 at 19.

96 *Industrial Design Act*, above note 92, s 10(1).

97 Muhlstein & Wilkinson, above note 91 at 23.

98 *Copyright Act*, above note 69, ss 64 and s 64(2); Gervais & Judge, above note 6 at 1152; Vaver, above note 71 at 86.

to reproduce the designs either substantially or entirely.[99] The end result is that if the creator intends on protecting their design once the fifty-copy threshold is surpassed, then the design should be registered under the *Industrial Design Act*.[100]

The rationale behind the enactment of section 64 based on the 1988 amendment was to prevent commercially mass-produced works that were also useful items from receiving the extended protection of copyright in the interest of promoting competition in the marketplace.[101] As a result, the *Copyright Act* was amended in order to dovetail with the *Industrial Design Act* based on section 64, creating the threshold for commercially produced useful articles. However, exceptions were also enacted in subsection 64(3) that would allow for certain traditional copyrightable (artistic) elements to retain protection for the entire copyright term.[102]

David Vaver suggests that the "attempt to draw a bright line between fine art and industrial design is unfortunately undermined by the list of bric-à-brac that is specifically allowed to retain full copyright: trade-mark designs, labels, architectural works, textile designs, character merchandising items . . . and anything else the government feels like adding by regulation."[103] For example, based on paragraph 64(3)(c) of the *Copyright Act*, full copyright protection extends to "material that has a woven or knitted pattern or that is suitable for piece goods or surface coverings or for making wearing apparel,"[104] but does not extend protection to clothing design.[105] Further, textiles receive both copyright and industrial design protection concurrently, irrespective of the fifty-copy threshold,[106] which perhaps emanates from the gendered history of the weaving industry.

---

99 *Copyright Act*, above note 69, s 64(2)(c); Muhlstein & Wilkinson, above note 91 at 19–20.

100 *Industrial Design Act*, above note 92, s 5(1); Gervais & Judge, above note 6 at 1152.

101 *Copyright Amendment Act*, SC 1988, c 15; *House of Commons Debates*, 33rd Parl, 2nd Sess, Vol 6 (26 June 1987) at 7689 and 7692 (Sheila Finestone and Lynn McDonald, respectively); Myra J Tawfik, "When Intellectual Property Rights Converge — Tracing the Contours and Mapping the Fault Lines 'Case by Case' and 'Law by Law,'" in Ysolde Gendreau, ed, *An Emerging Intellectual Property Paradigm: Perspectives from Canada* (London: Edward Elgar, 2008) 267 at 270.

102 *Industrial Design Act*, above note 92, s 10(1); *Copyright Act*, above note 69, s 64.

103 Vaver, above note 71. Since the nineteenth century there has been differential treatment between fine arts and "design" artwork at 89 [footnotes omitted].

104 *Copyright Act*, above note 69, s 64(3)(c).

105 Vaver, above note 71 at 89.

106 See also "Canadian Industrial Design Database," above note 94 at Class Code 026.

Arguably, one might suggest that the distinction lies in the utilitarian (hence "useful articles") nature of the craft and clothing articles;[107] yet this argument is undermined since protection for architecture — both useful and previously a male dominated enterprise — is also exempt from the commercial quantity threshold.[108]

Copyright protection is therefore limited for craft and clothing in some circumstances based on the number of copies produced, while at the same time craftspeople bear the burden of demonstrating a higher threshold of originality under the *Copyright Act*, compared to other works of art. Commentators attribute the lack of clear, definitive protection for feminine industries to the fact that these works were created by and associated with women working in the private sphere.[109] At the same time, rationalizing the legal treatment of cultural production based on the oppositions models does not fully account for variances such as class and race, and their application should therefore be limited in scope and in light of relevant historical and empirical evidence.

E. CONCLUSION

Interdisciplinarity provides an interesting means of exploring the various facets of intellectual property law. The feminist anthropology critique is particularly useful as it allows us to critically deconstruct the inequalities based on gender, race, and class, and enables us to appreciate a deeper and dynamic understanding of the underlying social values we place on cultural producers. The association of certain forms of creativity with *nature* and the *domestic* sphere, as described in the literature concerning the devaluation of feminine cultural production, provides a relevant contribution to understanding the socio-cultural framework and context surrounding the inception and enactment of copyright law.

Although reliance on the universalisms present in the oppositions models risks oversimplifying and excluding the diverse experiences of women from various backgrounds and are therefore limited in application,

107 Thalia Gourma-Peterson & Patricia Mathews, "The Feminist Critique of Art History" (1987) 69:3 The Art Bulletin 326 at 333. The authors suggest that the distinction of craft as low art and art as high art is partially because crafts "could not transcend utilitarianism" hence art is valuated solely for aesthetic purposes while craft is for practical use.

108 *Copyright Act*, above note 69, s 64(3)(d).

109 Wright, above note 2 at 91 and 94; Bartow, above note 2 at 559.

they do offer an interesting perspective on the apparent gender neutrality of intellectual property law. Finally, while it is true that intellectual property laws — copyright law in this case — were not initially created with gender neutrality in mind,[110] questioning and acknowledging the social and institutional inequalities that women face is an important step in acclimatizing and democratizing the way we value and attribute economic security to feminine creativity today.

---

110 Wright, above note 2 at 70.

NINE

Intellectual Property, Employment, and Talent Relations: A Media Studies Perspective

MATT STAHL

ABSTRACT (EN): This chapter considers twentieth century contests over the terms of creative employment in the United States film and music industries. The sites of creative employment are pre-eminently sites of power relations; cultural industry employers' dependence on continuous streams of novel intellectual property correlate to contrasting forms of struggle in "talent relations" (a sectorial adaptation of "labour relations") at the star and rank-and-file levels. This chapter offers brief accounts of Olivia de Havilland's and Olivia Newton-John's court disputes over the duration of their contracts (as well as a related change of relevant employment law), and of the American Federation of Musicians' and the American Federation of Radio Artists' collective bargaining efforts to stem and compensate for the technological displacement of their members. It argues that, surveyed together, these very different forms of contest reveal distinct logics of corporate control in core copyright industries. The management of the entertainment industries' constitutive tension between innovation and control has produced regimes of highly constrictive star contracts but it has allowed openings for extraordinary gains by organized creative craftspeople. Stars' great economic rewards can come at the expense of radical constraint; the AFM, AF(T)RA, and other organizations have been able to significantly democratize their employment.

RÉSUMÉ (FR): Ce chapitre étudie les luttes du vingtième siècle concernant les conditions d'emploi créatif dans les industries américaines du film et de la musique. Les domaines d'emploi créatif sont de façon prédominante des lieux de relations de pouvoir; les employeurs dans l'industrie de la culture dépendent de courants continus de propriété intellectuelle originale, ce qui est en corrélation avec les formes de conflits en « relations de talents » (une adaptation sectorielle des « relations de travail ») au niveau des vedettes et des créateurs ordinaires. Ce chapitre donne un compte rendu succinct des poursuites judiciaires d'Olivia De Havilland et d'Olivia Newton-John pendant la durée de leurs contrats respectifs (de même que des changements pertinents apportés au droit du travail), ainsi que des efforts de négociation collective de l'American Federation of Musicians et de l'American Federation of Radio Artists dans le but de freiner le remplacement technologique de leurs membres et leur obtenir compensation. Il soutient que ces très différentes formes de contestations révèlent des logiques distinctes de contrôle corporatif dans les industries centrales du droit d'auteur. La gestion des tensions entre l'innovation et le contrôle dans les industries du spectacle a produit des régimes restrictifs de contrats pour les vedettes, mais elle a aussi permis aux professionnels organisés de la création d'en retirer des bénéfices importants. Les récompenses astronomiques des vedettes peuvent être versées, mais seulement aux frais de contraintes importantes; le AFM (American Federation of Musicians of the United States and Canada), l'AF(T)RA (American Federation of (Television and) Radio Artists (AFTRA)) et d'autres organismes ont réussi à démocratiser de façon significative ce type d'emploi.

> *"[T]he work site is where we often experience the most immediate, unambiguous, and tangible relations of power that most of us will encounter on a daily basis."*[1]

A. INTRODUCTION

Intellectual property rules allocate proprietary rights to some people and groups and correspondingly dispossess or exclude others; in addition to allocating (intellectual) property rights,[2] employment also assigns rights to command to some people and finds in others a duty to obey.[3] The distinctive

---

1 Kathi Weeks, *The Problem with Work: Feminism, Marxism, Antiwork Politics, and Postwork Imaginaries* (Durham: Duke University Press, 2011) at 2.

2 David P Ellerman, *Property and Contract in Economics: The Case for Economic Democracy* (Cambridge: Blackwell, 1992) at 20.

3 Carole Pateman, *The Sexual Contract* (Stanford: Stanford University Press, 1988) at 146–51 [Pateman, *The Sexual Contract*].

logics of intellectual property and employment routinely intersect in the creative workplaces found in many of the "core copyright industries . . . wholly engaged in the creation, production, performance, exhibition, communication or distribution and sales of copyright protected subject matter."[4] In a foundational social-scientific analysis, DiMaggio and Hirsch observe that "[c]ultural production systems are characterized by a constant and pervasive tension between innovation and control."[5] Troublous intersections of intellectual property and employment in these systems express this tension. Consumers' demand for new cultural material requires innovation at all levels: from idiosyncratic performances and works by star creators to expert contributions by rank and file creative workers. Forms of control are correspondingly distributed, for example, over production processes, workers' time and effort, and rights to resulting intellectual properties.[6] This characteristic tension between innovation and control frequently boils over into conflict regarding the terms of creative employment, including lawsuits and (threatened) strikes. Employers' intellectual property concerns often influence the conditions of employment; creative workers — as individual employees and as members of unions, able to mobilize varying kinds and amounts of bargaining power in distinctive social contexts and at different historical moments — repeatedly come up against and sometimes contest the workplace corollaries of this influence, in typically patterned ways. On the one hand, established stars struggle against their employers' desire and power to bind them to long-term contracts that assign present and future performances and works of potential long-term value. On the other hand, skilled rank and file creative workers contesting casualization have been able to withhold their labour to exploit their employers' dependence on streams of novel, marketable intellectual property. In both of these contexts, "relations of power become more apparent and make the contested terrain of struggle more visible."[7] The efforts of star and rank and file

4 WIPO, "Copyright-Based Industries: Assessing Their Weight" (May 2005) 3 *Wipo Magazine*, online: WIPO Magazine www.wipo.int/wipo_magazine/en/2005/03/article_0012.html.

5 Paul DiMaggio & Paul M Hirsch, "Production Organizations in the Arts" in Richard A Peterson, ed, *The Production of Culture* (Beverly Hills: Sage, 1976) at 79 [endnote omitted].

6 See, generally, Matt Stahl, "Privilege and Distinction in Production Worlds: Copyright, Collective Bargaining, and Working Conditions in Media Making" in Vicki Mayer, Miranda J Banks, & John T Caldwell, eds, *Production Studies: Cultural Studies of Media Industries* (New York: Routledge, 2009) [Stahl, "Production Worlds"].

7 Danae Clark, *Negotiating Hollywood: The Cultural Politics of Actors' Labor* (Minneapolis: University of Minnesota Press, 1995) at 38.

creative workers to exercise control over their labour make more visible the socially problematic nature of employment and intellectual property, giving rise to questions about the affordances and politics of both institutions.

Today, scholars from numerous disciplines take increasing interest in the practices, institutions, and individuals involved in cultural production; differing scholarly approaches illuminate contrasting questions and priorities. Critical legal studies of media and cultural production have long approached intellectual property rights as a problem, identifying ways in which they intervene in the production and circulation of media texts;[8] media studies scholars have also contributed to this tradition.[9] Particularly under the banner of the "cultural industries" approach, media scholars have focused on creative labour, closely examining the unusual social relations of creative workplaces and the occupational identities of writers, singers, artists, journalists, musicians, television producers, and other such workers.[10] Here too, legal and legal-historical research is making significant contributions.[11]

However, with few exceptions,[12] studies of cultural production rarely give the institution of employment the kind of critical attention devoted to intellectual property. Exemplary cultural industries research into creative work has targeted exploitive "bad work,"[13] sometimes invoking the "liberal-democrat-

---

8 See, for example, Jane M Gaines, *Contested Culture: The Image, the Voice, and the Law* (Chapel Hill: University of North Carolina Press, 1991); Peter Jazsi & Martha Woodmansee, eds, *The Construction of Authorship: Textual Appropriation in Law and Literature* (Durham: Duke University Press, 1994).

9 See, for example, Siva Vaidhyanathan, *Copyrights and Copywrongs: The Rise of Intellectual Property and How it Threatens Creativity* (New York: New York University Press, 2001).

10 See, for example, Bernard Miege, *The Capitalization of Culture* (New York: International General, 1989); Bill Ryan, *Making Capital from Culture: The Corporate Form of Capitalist Cultural Production* (New York: Walter De Gruyter, 1992); Mark Banks, *The Politics of Cultural Work* (New York: Palgrave Macmillan, 2007); David Hesmondhalgh & Sarah Baker, *Creative Labour: Media Work in Three Cultural Industries* (New York: Routledge, 2011).

11 See, for example, Catherine L Fisk, *Working Knowledge: Employee Innovation and the Rise of Corporate Intellectual Property, 1800–1930* (Chapel Hill: University of North Carolina Press, 2009) [Fisk, *Working Knowledge*]; Steve Greenfield & Guy Osborn, *Contract and Control in the Entertainment Industry: Dancing on the Edge of Heaven* (Brookfield: Ashgate, 1998) [Greenfield & Osborn, *Contract and Control*]; Giuseppina D'Agostino, *Copyright, Contracts, Creators: New Media, New Rules* (Northampton, MA: Edward Elgar, 2010), examines the contracting practices of freelance independent contracting writers.

12 See, for example, Fisk, *Working Knowledge*, above note 11; see also Greenfield & Osborn, *Contract and Control*, above note 11.

13 Hesmondhalgh & Baker, above note 10 at 36.

ic"[14] context of such work, understood to set limits on such work's exploitive badness. While these analyses are rich and rigorous in sociological terms, they tend to eschew challenges posed by democratic theorists[15] or by critical political economists,[16] who suggest, for example, that "exploitation" does not analytically exhaust the politics of work.[17] However, recent work on writers in North America and Europe has begun to take up these challenges with respect to problems associated with independent contracting. D'Agostino argues, for example, that under current copyright conditions, the freelancer's purported freedom is essentially illusory.[18] This salutary contribution does much to bridge these diverging perspectives. Along with the prospect D'Agostino's observation illuminates, the democratic-theoretical challenge demands that scholarship touching on work confront not only exploitation but also *domination*; this chapter suggests that forms of creative work central to the production of profitable intellectual properties reveal distinctive patterns along these lines.

Approaching the social relations of creative workplaces by way of a media studies framework, extended through insights drawn from social scientific, democratic theoretical, and critical legal studies, this chapter offers a brief account of twentieth century contests over the terms of creative employment in the American film and popular music industries. Taking employment as pre-eminently a system of power relations, it argues that cultural industry employers' economic dependence on intellectual property has political effects in "talent relations" (a sectorial adaptation of "labour relations") at different strata. The nature and extent of rights of property and command, as well as the definitions governing what sorts of working people enjoy or endure and their respective benefits or obligations, differ in various sectors and at various moments: an activity once legally recognized as authorship may at some later time not be recognized as such;[19] an activity once classified as mere execution may at some later time come to be linked with intellectual property rights;[20] an activity recognized as authorial in one sector may not be

14 Banks, above note 10 at 100.
15 See, for example, Weeks, above note 1.
16 Nicole S Cohen, "Cultural Work as a Site of Struggle: Freelancers and Exploitation" (2012) 10:2 TripleC: Cognition, Communication, Cooperation 141.
17 Pateman, *The Sexual Contract*, above note 3 at 149.
18 D'Agostino, above note 11 at 244–45; see also Cohen, above note 16.
19 Fisk, *Working Knowledge*, above note 11.
20 Robert A Gorman, "The Recording Musician and Union Power: A Case Study of the American Federation of Musicians" (1983) 37:4 Sw LJ 697 at 739–40.

treated as such in another.[21] The examples examined here bring into relief patterns in the ways that Hollywood-based film and popular music industry employers and their creative employees have vied over the terms on which the tension between innovation and control will be managed. The chapter does not consider freelance independent contractors, though many of the working people involved in the examples are freelance employees who work under union employment contracts, nor does the chapter explicitly engage theories of intellectual property or copyright. The argument is that these characteristic flashpoints reveal how corporate dependence on commercially exploitable intellectual property affects talent relations at the star and rank-and-file levels.

B. CONTRACTS

Cultural industry firms demand control of copyrights so that their licences have maximum value and minimal competition.[22] Control over copyright, in turn, requires control over labour and workplace creation: star creators are often subject to long-term, restrictive, exclusive contracts,[23] other creators to regimes of work for hire or market-based pressures toward maximal rights assignment.[24] Employers achieve control of labour and property through the intersecting instruments of employment, independent contracting, and copyright's doctrine of work for hire, which are themselves continually adjusted by lobbying and regulatory capture, and mediated by the market or bargaining power of the different players.[25] These forces interact at the point of the employment contract for creative labour, with differing outcomes at the levels of individual and collective bargaining. Individuals' bargaining power, even that of stars, is rarely great enough to overcome norms of dispossession; recording artist attorney Jay Cooper testified

---

21 Stahl, "Production Worlds," above note 6 at 54.

22 Martin Kretschmer & Friedemann Kawohl, "The History and Theory of Copyright," in Simon Frith & Lee Marshall, eds, *Music and Copyright*, 2d ed (New York: Routledge, 2004) at 43.

23 Gaines, above note 8 at 148.

24 See generally Johanna Fisher Stewart, "The Freelancer's Trap: Work for Hire under the Copyright Act of 1976" (1984) 86:3 W Va L Rev 1305; D'Agostino, above note 11.

25 See, generally, Fisk, *Working Knowledge*, above note 11; Stewart, above note 24; D'Agostino, above note 11; see also Marci A Hamilton, "Commissioned Works as Works Made for Hire Under the 1976 Copyright Act: Misinterpretation and Injustice" (1987) 135:5 U Pa L Rev 1281.

before United States lawmakers that despite representing some of the most commercially successful artists in popular music, he has never been successful in striking a work for hire provision from a recording contract.[26] On the other hand, collective bargaining power supports surprisingly strong claims of non-star employed creators. As I recount below, agreements between Hollywood cultural industry employers and their unionized creative employees have long enshrined significant workers' rights, including what Fisk calls "private intellectual property rights."[27]

Gaines writes that "it is the transferability of rights that is the basis of the mass marketing of the human image and the human voice in the communications industries."[28] In the organizations and relations at issue here, it is the employment contract that enables these transfers of rights; yet in so doing the contract creates not equal parties exchanging goods but regimes of private rule. In Pateman's words, "a form of government that is seen in democratic countries as 'intolerable' in governing the state is seen as desirable in enterprises." She maintains that "[t]he enterprise, like the state, is a political system where power is exercised over the governed."[29] In the disciplines of labour studies, critical political economy, and democratic political theory, the idea that the employment contract transfers both property *and* command rights is less controversial than in sociology, media studies, and communication, the disciplinary homes of much empirical creative work research. The virtue of a democratic-theoretical perspective for the study of intellectual property and employment is that, in rendering workers' surrendering of rights of self-determination legible and controversial, it provides a framework to connect the concerns of critical scholars of intellectual property to broader themes of work, dispossession, and subordination in contemporary society.

The questions this line of research poses include: On what terms are those rights transferred? What kinds of (historical, social, cultural, legal, or economic) circumstances shape those terms and how? What accounts for

---

26 Matt Stahl, *Unfree Masters: Recording Artists and the Politics of Work* (Durham: Duke University Press, 2013) at 197-98 [Stahl, *Unfree Masters*].

27 Catherine Fisk, "The Role of Private Intellectual Property Rights in Markets for Labor and Ideas: Screen Credit and the Writers Guild of America, 1938–2000" (2011) 32:2 Berkeley J Emp & Lab L 215 [Fisk, "Markets for Labor"].

28 Gaines, above note 8 at 155.

29 Carole Pateman, "Self-Ownership and Property in the Person: Democratization and a Tale of Two Concepts" (2002) 10:1 Journal of Political Philosophy 20 at 46 [footnote omitted] [Pateman, "Democratization"]; see also Weeks, above note 1.

change in or persistence of these terms? How do the terms differ within the cultural industries, and between the cultural industries and other sectors? Representing early findings in an ongoing research project, this chapter suggests that patterns and themes are discernable in these arrangements and that an approach that highlights the politics of work has something of value to contribute to an understanding of intellectual property's role in the social relations of cultural production.

1) Individual Star Contracts

The star contracts of Hollywood's 1930s and '40s "studio system" era offer an Ur-example of how a firm dependent on steady flows of potentially valuable new intellectual properties may seek to cement its power over the labour of its most valuable star workers.[30] Stars present a linking of cultural and economic value, a "market strategy"[31]: their personae, voices, and bodies provide anchor points for consumers' imaginative identification and desire as well as their demand and willingness to pay for cultural goods. "In economic terms," writes Balio, "stars created the market value of motion pictures . . . . [A] distributor simply pointed to the past box-office performance of a star to justify the rental terms for his or her forthcoming pictures."[32] The long-term option contract characteristic of the studio system (and of the contemporary recording industry) provides a crucial foundation for profitability. It enables the employer to secure the services of a new or rising performer at a low initial rate and is constructed such that, at any of a series of predetermined points, the employer may either exercise the option or terminate the contract.[33] These contracts are typically written so that only the employer has an option; these are "take-it-or-leave-it" deals in which

---

30 See, generally, Emily Susan Carman "*Independent Stardom*: Female Film Stars and the Studio System in the 1930s" (2008) 37:6 Women's Studies 583.

31 Cathy Klaprat, "The Star as Market Strategy: Bette Davis in Another Light" in Tino Balio, ed, *The American Film Industry* (Madison: University of Wisconsin Press, 1985) at 354.

32 Tino Balio, *Grand Design: Hollywood as a Modern Business Enterprise, 1930–1939* (New York: Macmillan Publishing, 1993) at 144 &145 [footnote omitted].

33 See, for example, Donald S Passman, *All You Need to Know about the Music Business*, 6th ed (New York: Free Press, 2006) at 99. The logic of the "option" has been analyzed extensively by scholars of the recording industry in which it is also a central form.

the only option available to employees is to work as directed or be in violation of the contract.[34]

The laws of the state of California, home to the Hollywood studio system and to much entertainment industry activity, have come to play an important role in the establishment of norms of entertainment industry contracting; arguments over some of these laws bring some of the imperatives of entertainment industry employment relations into focus. The so-called "seven-year rule" — a section of the state's labour code originating in the late nineteenth century — limits the enforcement of employment contracts to that eponymous statutory maximum.[35] This rule was at the centre of a court battle between the film star Olivia de Havilland and her employing studio, Warner Bros. Pictures.[36] Her contract, like many during this period, had a clause providing that time spent "under suspension" during the life of the contract could be tacked on to the end of the contract's term. Over the course of her seven-year option contract, de Havilland had spent twenty-five weeks under suspension, some by her choice, some by the studio's. When the studio attempted to enforce the contract beyond its seventh anniversary in order to claim the twenty-five weeks' labour they considered they were owed, de Havilland and her lawyer sued under the seven-year rule.[37]

The published ruling of the Appellate Court decision is striking in its "absolute" reading of the statute[38] and its explicit conceptualization of employment as an object of public policy. However, the unpublished ruling of Los Angeles Superior Court Justice Charles S. Burnell in favour of de Havilland penetrates the politics of the standard option contract in a startling way. Justice Burnell dilates on the threat embedded in Warner Bros. Pictures' claim on seven years of actual service (as opposed to a contract covering seven calendar years). He finds that the studio's construction of the seven-year rule could "easily result" in a contract like de Havilland's "being indefinitely extended, even to the point of constituting life bondage for the employee."[39] Under the interpretation sought by the studio, wrote Burnell,

34 See, generally, Steve Greenfield & Guy Osborn, "Understanding Commercial Music Contracts: The Place of Contractual Theory" (2007) 23:3 Journal of Contract Law 248.

35 *California Labor Code*, §2855 (1937).

36 *De Havilland v Warner Bros*, 487685 Los Angeles County Sup Ct (1944); *De Havilland v Warner Bros Pictures*, 67 Cal App (2d) 225 (1944).

37 Jonathan Blaufarb, "The Seven Year Itch: California Labor Code Section 2855" (1983–84) 6:3 Comm/Ent LJ 653 at 666.

38 *Ibid* at 668.

39 LA Sup Ct, above note 36 at 14.

"the life of the contract might at the option of the producer be extended . . . indefinitely, thus precluding [the actor] from ever working for any other employer. It was to prevent such a condition of peonage or serfdom that the statute was enacted."[40] Justice Burnell's perception of the profoundly unequal — feudal, even — relations established in the contract sensitizes him to the need for the exercise of the "police powers of the state"[41] in protecting the rights of employees against the private power of employers, and to the potentially perverse results of expansive freedom of contract between manifestly unequal parties.

The seven-year rule was codified in the 1870s, a period in the state's history when employment took the form of relations of master and servant, when employees — particularly non-white employees — had few rights, and when conditions of labour shortage predominated in California.[42] It must have appeared as a reasonable protection for workers whose employers had incentives to hold them under contract for long periods. When economic growth outpaces population, contractually assured rights in people's labour and to their obedience can be very valuable.[43] While the balance of economy and population in California had changed markedly by the 1930s, the Hollywood film studios shared something with the state's early employers: they depended heavily on and were in competition for the labour of a scarce population, in this case bankable stars: a small number of actors whose names and likenesses constituted much of the value of the firms' intellectual property.[44]

The argument here is not that Warner Bros. Pictures fought to keep de Havilland from challenging the studio's intellectual property rights, or that de Havilland should be considered an author under law, rather, it is that de Havilland's intellectual property-producing performance labour was so crucial to the company's value and profitability that they would fight vigorously

---

40 *Ibid*.

41 *Ibid* at 7.

42 Donna R Mooney, "The Search for a Legal Presumption of Employment Duration or Custom of Arbitrary Dismissal in California 1848–1872" (2000) 21:2 Berkeley J Emp & Lab L 633.

43 Maurice Dobb, *Studies in the Development of Capitalism* (London: Routledge & K Paul, 1963) at 23.

44 See, generally, Tom Kemper, *Hidden Talent: The Emergence of Hollywood Agents* (Berkeley: University of California Press, 2010), on varying ways in which stars and their agents sought to turn individual monopolies to their advantage.

to keep her (and her other star colleagues) under contract for as long as possible. As Balio writes,

> [a] star's popularity and drawing power created a ready-made market for his or her pictures, which reduced the risks of production financing. Because a star provided an insurance policy of sorts and a production value, as well as a prestigious trademark for a studio, the star system became the prime means of stabilizing the motion-picture business.[45]

The Hollywood studio system depended on stars; option contracts grounded their salaries in their low initial rates and, until de Havilland's court victory, secured their services for potentially interminable durations. The efforts of Warner Bros. Pictures to keep de Havilland (and other stars such as Bette Davis[46]) under potentially interminable contracts can be read as evidence of the stars' importance to the ongoing profitability of intellectual property-dependent cultural industries.

Today, few workers have to worry about being held to overlong contracts. Yet, some core copyright industries still rely on their capacity to capture the labour and output of creative workers through long-term contracts. The recording industry of the late twentieth and early twenty-first centuries poses a particularly striking example.

Four decades after the unambiguous resolution of the de Havilland suit, another group of Hollywood employers was surprised by a similar lawsuit, this time by Grammy-winning singer Olivia Newton-John, who sought release from her contract with MCA Records. The Appellate Court ruling here was as decisive, if not as lyrical, as those of the de Havilland courts: it reaffirmed the right of employees to freedom from contract at seven years.[47] This 1979 decision inspired numerous other artists to pursue their own freedom under the seven-year rule,[48] provoking panic on the part of record companies.[49] Seeking to stabilize at a moment of perilous profit slump, the industry soon reorganized around a new blockbuster model that would intensify companies' dependence on the new releases and back catalogue of

---

45 Balio, above note 32 at 144.

46 *Ibid* at 150 and 159–61; Greenfield & Osborn, *Contract and Control*, above note 11 at 12–14.

47 *MCA Records Inc v Olivia Newton-John*, 90 Cal App (3d) 18 (1979).

48 Ben McLane & Venice Wong, "Practice Tips: How Recording Artists Have Broken Their Contracts" (1999) 22:2 Los Angeles Lawyer 27 at 27.

49 Stahl, *Unfree Masters*, above note 26 at 109 and 124.

shrinking numbers of more profitable stars.[50] In this context, the ability to hold such artists to effectively interminable contracts was of paramount importance, and the Recording Industry Association of America (RIAA) lobbied the California legislature to carve out recording artists from the seven-year rule's protection.[51] They were concerned that they would be unable to reap "full benefits" from stars' existing and potential intellectual property. The RIAA's 1985 position paper argued that the

> current law in California has been used as a weapon by prominent, highly successful recording artists to force their record company employer/financiers into renegotiating contracts under circumstances in which the record company is not even sure it will get the benefit of the new bargain . . . . The record company . . . is deprived of the full benefits of its bargain just at a point where the investment seems about to pay off.[52]

In 1987, after two years of deliberation, and despite opposition from labour unions, prominent artist attorneys and artists, and many lawmakers, the bill proposed and sponsored by the trade association became law. The industry is heavily concentrated in California; ever since the carve out, North American recording artists have been subject to contracts that are only effectively terminable by the employer.[53]

In 2002, a committee of the California State Legislature held a hearing on a bill to repeal the 1987 carve out.[54] Speaking in opposition to the proposed legislation, Jeff Ayeroff (an executive of Warner Bros. Records with contract signing powers) made it clear that long-term control over actual and potential artist-created intellectual property is a primary impetus toward effectively interminable contracts. He testified that when he and his colleagues succeed in recruiting and marketing a profitable act "we're entitled to hav[e] a long-term relationship to be able to recoup those kinds of

---

50 Reebee Garofalo, "From Music Publishing to MP3: Music and Industry in the Twentieth Century" (1999) 17:3 American Music 318 at 342–43.

51 From a distance, recording artists appear as independent contractors. Indeed, federal copyright law appears to treat them as such. Yet, their numerous struggles with record companies in courts and before legislators show that they are employees under state law.

52 Gang, Tyre, and Brown and JLA Advocates Inc, "Background Paper in Support of Senate Bill 469 (Dills)" (Industrial Relations Committee Bill File SB 469, California State Archive) at 4.

53 See, generally, Stahl, *Unfree Masters*, above note 26.

54 US, California State Senate Committee on the Judiciary, *Hearing on California Labor Code Section 2855: Informational Hearing SB 1246*, Cal (19 March 2002) (Kevin B Murray).

investments."[55] Ayeroff averred that by virtue of his company's contractual relationship with artists he shares "a certain portion of [the artists'] revenues": "I have a relationship with the records that I've bought from them, that I own, because the only way the record industry survives is by ownership of catalogue, and by owning a certain portion of the relationship to an artist's career."[56] Ayeroff's personal claim of ownership may be controversial, but his rationale is clear: long-term control of artists' labour is positively correlated to the value to the firm of the intellectual property created by the artist.

With the advent and normalization of the encompassing "360" or "multi-rights" recording contract in the last several years, recording artists are subject to more company demands than they had been up through the early 2000s. These contracts typically grant companies access to significant portions of formerly off-limits artist incomes, including touring, licensing, and other non-recording activities. Many of these contracts even grant companies decision-making power in these areas. Recording artists' ability to support themselves through these non-recording activities had given them a real degree of bargaining leverage: a credible ability to withhold their labour. Under the 360 deal, such options are effectively foreclosed.[57]

2) Collective Bargaining and Employees' Quasi-Proprietary Rights

At times, star creators working in core copyright industries organized around the existing and anticipated market value of star talent have found themselves subject to binding, long-term contracts that reveal virtually feudal degrees of domination. For recording artists, this logic has only ratcheted up under digitalization.[58] But where the rank and file of creative workers is concerned, the prevailing employment dynamic has been an emphasis on casualization rather than stiffening. Over the course of the

55 Stahl, *Unfree Masters*, above note 26 at 165.

56 *Ibid* at 164.

57 See, generally, Matt Stahl & Leslie M Meier, "The Firm Foundation of Organizational Flexibility: The 360 Contract in the Digitalizing Music Industry" (2012) 37:3 Canadian Journal of Communication 441; Lee Marshall, "The 360 Deal and the 'New' Music Industry" (2013) 16:1 European Journal of Cultural Studies 77; Ian Brereton "The Beginning of a New Age?: The Unconscionability of the '360-Degree' Deal" (2009) 27:1 Cardozo Arts & Ent L J 167.

58 Stahl & Meier, above note 57.

twentieth and early twenty-first centuries, technological and political-economic changes have enabled the Hollywood cultural industries to reduce their dependence on the reliably expert labour of relatively anonymous "creative crafts[persons],"[59] while at the same time extracting greater amounts of profit from the products of their work.[60] In particular, cultural industries' application of the new technologies of sound film, network radio broadcasting, radio transcriptions, and television video-recording threatened to, and in some cases did, destroy employment for large groups of creative workers. Corporate policies enabled by these technologies resulted in large-scale processes of casualization: the conversion of the work of many professional musicians, actors, and other creative personnel from relatively stable and well-paid occupations to increasingly outsourced, highly competitive and stratified contingent systems. Similar processes of casualization have been at work in the wider society since at least the rise of Thatcherism and Reaganism. Yet these creative workers were able to turn their employers' dependence on their skilled labour to their advantage and impede these processes, institutionalizing durable regimes of private, quasi-proprietary rights not only in their jobs (as have many other organized workers)[61] but in *the products of their labour*, a range of rights unparalleled (to my knowledge) in other fields.

From the 1930s through the 1950s and early 1960s, the American Federation of Musicians (AFM), the American Federation of Radio Artists (AFRA), and other Hollywood unions fought against their technological displacement and the casualization of their occupations. Conceptually linking the erosion of their opportunity structures and the undermining of their social mobility with the expansion of their employers' ability to use and reuse their recorded performances and written work, these highly organized, skilled, and motivated workers exploited cultural industries' dependence on continuous streams of new cultural material to secure rights to additional, extra-salary "residual" or "reuse" payments. Whereas stars' individual monopolies could only rarely overcome the bargaining power of their film

59 Jack Gould, "Video Brings Hollywood Closer to Dream of Never-Ending Pay" *New York Times* (4 July 1955) 1.

60 See also D'Agostino, above note 11, on the experience of independent contracting writers along these lines.

61 William Gomberg, "Featherbedding: An Assertion of Property Rights" (1961) 333 Annals of the American Academy of Political and Social Science 119. From the AFM's contractual perspective, "what is featherbedding to an employer is protection of a property right to a worker and his union" at 120.

studio or record company employers, the collective monopolies of expert side musicians, supporting and commercial actors, script writers, and other creative workers, poised at industrial choke points, compelled these employers to bear some of the burden of casualization, to accept limits to their ability to reuse recorded performances, and to share profits in ways that reshaped the entertainment industries. Today, Fisk argues, "[r]esiduals are foundational to the Hollywood labor market . . . ."[62]

First pursued by radio voice talent and musicians as a means of stemming workers' technological displacement and protecting occupations and employment, these private intellectual property rights regimes soon came to be understood rather in terms of what creative workers experienced as authorship. This section sketches the emergence of these regimes in the American broadcasting industry, prior to their (re)conceptualization as rooted in creative workers' creative practices.

The AFM and its members had benefited mightily from the explosion of silent film in the United States. Unlike other industrial workers in the first decades of the twentieth century, as Kraft writes, musicians "faced no innovative job-threatening machinery, no strong employer associations and no efficiency experts speeding up the pace of work."[63] In the world of motion picture exhibition, "[d]emand for musical workers was high and rising while the supply of skilled instrumentalists was relatively low."[64] Yet, by the late 1920s, sound film "enabled theater owners to discharge pit musicians in wholesale fashion, a classic case of substituting capital for labor. By 1934 about twenty thousand theater musicians — perhaps a quarter of the nation's professional instrumentalists and half of those who were fully employed — had lost their jobs."[65]

At the same time — the late 1920s — radio was looming as a major threat: "Local employment opportunities were . . . seriously undermined in 1926 and 1927 when the NBC and CBS radio networks were formed, allowing transmittal of a single program through local stations to the entire nation."[66] Having failed to arrest the hemorrhage of movie theater employment, the

62 Fisk, "Markets for Labor," above note 27 at 263; see also Alan Paul & Archie Kleingartner, "Flexible Production and the Transformation of Industrial Relations in the Motion Picture and Television Industry" (1994) 47:4 Indust & Lab Rel Rev 663.

63 James P Kraft, *Stage to Studio: Musicians and the Sound Revolution, 1890–1950* (Baltimore: Johns Hopkins University Press, 1996) at 32.

64 *Ibid* at 33.

65 *Ibid*.

66 Gorman, above note 20 at 700.

musicians sought in the early 1930s to preserve radio employment through two approaches: by trying to control the use of records by radio stations and by trying to maintain minimum staffing levels in radio stations. These efforts met with some success in contracts with radio and record companies in the late 1930s, yet the staffing minima were struck down legally, as were the efforts of bandleaders to enforce restrictive labelling on records. As Gorman writes, the effect of that latter failure "was that radio broadcasters were legally entitled, upon payment of the price of a phonograph record, to exploit and re-exploit for their own commercial advantage the public's desire to hear the major recording artists of the day."[67]

In 1940, the famously aggressive Chicago local officer James C. Petrillo became the union's president, and in August of 1942 he announced that AFM members would cease their recording work. This first national "recording ban" took over two years to resolve, and was immediately followed by pointed anti-AFM and anti-union legislation (the *Lea Act*[68] and the *Taft-Hartley Act*[69]), and then by a second ban.[70] The result of this activity was the establishment of several AFM "trust funds" over the course of the 1940s. These funds would collect fees in a number of circumstances where recorded performances of music were used and reused, and use those monies to pay un- and under-employed musicians around North America to present free concerts for the public. By 1952, there were four trust funds, jointly administered by the union and the companies, drawing contributions based on 1) percentages of sales of records and revenues of transcription use, 2) percentages of revenues from the use and reuse of films made for television, 3) fees for the use of jingles and advertisements, and 4) percentages of revenues from the exhibition of theatrical films on television. The 1952 version of this latter agreement "permitted producers to use an original soundtrack upon making a one-time payment to the original film musicians of one-half of the 1952 scale" while also making trust fund contributions of 5 percent

67 *Ibid* at 704.

68 *Lea Act*, c 138, 60 Stat 89 (1946) (codified at 47 USC § 506 (1976), amending *Communications Act of* 1934, c 652, 48 Stat 1064), as repealed in 1980, Pub L No 96-507, 94 Stat 2747 [*Lea Act*].

69 *Labor Management Relations Act*, c 120, 61 Stat 136 (1947) (codified as amended at 29 USC §§ 141–67, 171–87 (1976 & Supp V 1981)) 29 [*Taft-Hartley Act*].

70 Kraft, above note 63 at 148; Gorman, above note 20; see also Tim Anderson, "'Buried Under the Fecundity of His Own Creations': Reconsidering the Recording Bans of the American Federation of Musicians, 1942–1944 and 1948" (2004) 22:2 American Music 231.

gross revenues.[71] Kraft points out that in accepting contracts that gave the union the right to impose extra costs on recordings, "recording companies had acquiesced in, even if they did not positively agree with, the principle that technological change imposed social costs that employers had a responsibility to share."[72]

AFRA was formed in the midst of the commercial organization of radio under the nascent network system, around the same time that the AFM was beginning to contest the accelerating displacement of radio musicians. In 1937 AFRA became the "autonomous union of all radio talent except musicians."[73] The union focused on wages and working conditions, but also was concerned with transcriptions, recorded radio programs distributed in disc form to radio stations. In the late 1920s, independent transcription producers had begun to supply recorded programming to radio stations in areas of the country not well served by the networks. Advertisers embraced transcriptions, which enabled them to target local and regional markets, supplementing their national network campaigns. So also did smaller radio stations, whose audiences often preferred pre-recorded to live programming, and, "[b]y the end of 1930 . . . [approximately] 75 percent of the nation's radio stations used transcriptions,"[74] mainly produced and distributed by independent companies. A number of factors propelled the networks themselves to get into the transcription business in the ensuing years,[75] and by the late 1930s AFRA had become convinced that transcriptions posed a dire threat to the employment of radio talent.

In 1939, on the eve of negotiating their first nationwide contract for advertiser-supported programming, the union made it clear that, in addition to higher contract minimums and payment for rehearsal time (which stations had been requiring performers to undertake without pay), additional payment for the use of transcriptions was one of its central demands. The broadcasters' trade journal reported that the "[t]hreat of a nationwide strike of radio talent that might conceivably throw every commercial network

71 Gorman, above note 20 at 730.

72 Kraft, above note 63 at 160.

73 "Single Union to Embrace Radio Talent Is Organized; Actors' Equity Withdraws" (1 August 1937) 13:3 Broadcasting at 12.

74 Alexander Russo, "Defensive Transcriptions: Radio Networks, Sound-on-Disc Recording, and the Meaning of Live Broadcasting" (2004) 54:1 The Velvet Light Trap 4 at 8 [footnote omitted].

75 *Ibid.*

program off the air," [76] involving the "withdrawal of all [radio] talent save musicians,"[77] was a real possibility. As Cole and Holt argue, "[m]ore than many industries, broadcasting suffers a nearly irretrievable loss when work stoppage occurs."[78] AFRA was in a powerful position: shutting down advertiser-supported program production would most likely result in increased production of network-supported programs, providing more work for striking commercial talent. Moreover, Actors Equity and the Screen Actors Guild promised not to work struck programs.[79] With this threat looming, the networks conceded, and within a month virtually all network programming was covered by another two-year contract.

However, it was not until May of 1941 that the union and employers arrived at an acceptable set of terms regarding the general use of transcriptions by larger and smaller radio stations, known from that moment on as the Transcription Code. According to the Code, "[i]n the event [a] sponsor repeats the use of [a transcription]"—on a station of greater than 1,000 watts in power, beyond the first use allowed under the contract—"the artist shall receive for each repeated use, a fee equal to the compensation paid for the original performance . . . ."[80] This clause grants compensating payments to those performers who had been accustomed to multiple performances for networks reaching multiple time zones. Smaller stations could reuse transcriptions without additional payments, but should such a transcription be used by a station of greater than 1,000 watts, it would be reclassified and accordingly generate reuse payments. AFRA's 1941 Transcription Code appears to be the first entertainment industry collective bargaining agreement to require additional payments for the reuse of recorded performances.

As do many other collective bargaining agreements, the 1941 AFRA contract codified significant degrees of union control over the terms and condi-

---

76 "AFRA Threatens Net Talent Strike" (15 January 1939) 16:1 Broadcasting at 14 [AFRA Threatens].

77 "AFRA Contract Covers Broad Scope" *Broadcasting* (1 November 1940) at 28.

78 Robert L Cole & Darrell Holt, "The Effects of Unionism on Broadcasting: A Mathmatical Analysis" in Allen E Koenig, ed, *Broadcasting and Bargaining: Labor Relations in Radio and Television* (Madison: University of Wisconsin Press, 1970) at 38.

79 AFRA Threatens, above note 76.

80 AFRA, *Code of Fair Practice for Transciptions and Recordings for Radio Broadcasting Purposes: Minimum Terms and Conditions for Radio Recording Artists* (New York: American Federation of Radio Artists, National Office, 1941); see also AFRAOfficial Bulletin, 2:8 (April 1941); see also Robert W Gilbert, "'Residual Rights' Established by Collective Bargaining in Television and Radio" (1958) 23:1 Law & Contemp Probs 102.

tions of members' conveyance of labour to their employers. An increase in worker control represents an instance of democratization, an incremental contribution to the ongoing modern project of "reducing subordination and creating a more democratic society."[81] However, what appears as a turning point in American labour relations was the union's achievement of rights to additional compensation based on the subsequent use of their recorded performances which would impose limits on, and defray the social costs of, technological displacement of workers. Over the subsequent two decades, the Screen Actors Guild,[82] the Writers Guild of America,[83] the Directors Guild,[84] and the numerous guilds affiliated with the International Alliance of Theatrical Stage Employees (IATSE) would also gain residual rights (although the rights of the IATSE guilds would take a different form).[85] It is in large part these very systems of profit sharing (and the regimes of attribution that ground them[86]) that have enabled Hollywood's talent guilds to remain so effective and relevant in an era of widespread union decline.[87]

Both AFRA and the AFM had acted against the technological evisceration of their occupational power by their (former) employers' ability to mass produce, circulate, and profit from symbolic forms protected by intellectual property rules. Each achieved significant degrees of participation in the governance of their work, as well as forms of remuneration based on the reuse of recorded performances. Yet soon ideas of authorship and copyright — particularly conceptions of the nature of royalties, which their forms of extra-salary remuneration resembled — began to colonize and stratify what had begun as a solidaristic effort of resistance. While this is a topic of ongoing and future research, initial findings suggest that authorial discourse may flow into and (re)define areas of practice that could be and sometimes were otherwise conceived. Since the 1950s, understandings of residuals as primarily serving labour market functions or securing work-

81 Pateman, "Democratization," above note 29 at 22.
82 David F Prindle, *The Politics of Glamour: Ideology and Democracy in the Screen Actors Guild* (Madison: University of Wisconsin Press, 1988).
83 Fisk, "Markets for Labor," above note 27 at 262.
84 "New Contract Boosts Film Directors Pay" (16 May 1960) 18 Broadcasting at 94.
85 Paul & Kleingartner, above note 62 at 670.
86 Fisk, "Markets for Labor," above note 27 at 244–48 (outlined with respect to writers).
87 *Ibid* at 277–78: a more complete account of the development of the residual right in Hollywood is an anticipated outcome of this research project; see, generally, Paul & Kleingartner, above note 62.

place rights appear to have been effectively banished from Hollywood creative labour discourse.

C. CONCLUSION

The intersections of intellectual property and employment in the social relations of creative labour are not exceptional: intellectual property is a factor in many workplaces,[88] obedience a norm in most. In fact, the employment relationship, in which employers' property rights and employees' duty to obey appear virtually as facts of nature, "is accepted as part of the furniture of the social universe."[89] What is unusual is the immediacy of the connection between the social relations of work and the innovative generation of new intellectual property: contests at these hinge points highlight problems of workplace autonomy and property that characterize but are obscure in the run of North American workplaces.

This chapter has suggested that the fraught social logics of intellectual property and employment intersect acutely in certain of the core copyright industries, and that their intersections ramify in different but patterned ways in different sectors, times, and occupational clusters. Bringing a media studies perspective into dialogue with other disciplinary perspectives, it has suggested that the "constant and pervasive tension between innovation and control"[90] characteristic of the Hollywood film and music industries of the twentieth century has had paradoxical effects in the employment of star and rank-and-file creative workers: regimes of highly constrictive individual contracts for even the most eminent stars appear on the one hand, and extraordinary workplace powers achieved by organized creative craftspeople on the other.

The realities of long-term star contracts, and the arguments that emerge when those contracts come under scrutiny, impel our consideration of basic questions about the politics of employment: If long-term contracts can be seen to effect forms of serfdom and peonage, does that not also throw into question their short-term siblings? How, and at what point in its duration, might an employment contract become (experienced or understood as) an indenture? Organized musicians, actors, and other creative workers not only exploited their position at industry choke points but gained rights to

88 See, generally, Fisk, *Working Knowledge*, above note 11.

89 Ellerman, above note 2 at 106.

90 DiMaggio & Hirsch, above note 5 at 79 [endnote omitted].

profit participation (that have come to appear very much like the intellectual property rights so zealously protected and enforced by their employers) in the name of stabilizing the market for creative labour and compensation for lost employment. Moreover, they have sustained and been sustained by these rights well into an era of spectacular union-busting. But how might the capacity of workers in other sectors as well as policy-makers to fight for similar rights be hampered by conceptions of cultural creation and intellectual property that obscure the ways in which not just creative cultural industry employment but employment in general resists democratization? Indeed, it appears that conceptions of residuals as royalty-like systems of reward based on intellectual property creation crowded out conceptions of them as instances of work's democratization or embodiments of employer obligation around technological displacement and compensation for lost employment.

Creative workers of the kinds discussed here bring to points of cultural production heightened (authorial) consciousness of the value of their work and of its place in the systems that employ them. These organizational contexts are characterized by employers' contradictory requirements of control of labour and ownership of intellectual property (on the one hand) and the accentuated employee creative autonomy on which continuous innovation depends (on the other). Creative workers in different positions find themselves differently able to participate in the governance of and revenues associated with their work; thus far, this research suggests that workers' capacity to claim participation and exercise control and ownership (or at least quasi-ownership) is not something easily achieved through individual bargaining, and that workers' claims of rights of authority and property are best supported by a credible strike threat.

TEN

A Gramscian Analysis of the Public Performance Right

LOUIS D'ALTON

ABSTRACT (EN): This chapter briefly traces the historical establishment and expansion of the public performance right in musical works within those countries united by the Anglo-American legal tradition, with a focus on the Canadian experience. Viewing the issue of the public performance right in musical works within a critical Marxist frame, the essential problem leading to the creation of the public performance right in musical works is seen as an outgrowth of the struggle between the author/composers and the dominant publishing interests which dictated their employment and terms of recompense. Within this frame, the analysis utilizes Antonio Gramsci's theoretical conceptions of hegemony to provide the structural basis on which the analysis rests. Ultimately the struggle is seen as an example of the dominant publishing interest's effective absorption of the desires and goals of the creator interests, but reiterated in such a way as to achieve the primary goals of the publishing interests within an evolving hegemonic order.

RÉSUMÉ (FR): Ce chapitre trace brièvement l'établissement historique et l'expansion du droit de représentation publique des œuvres musicales dans les pays de traditions anglo-américaine, avec une attention particulière portée à l'expérience canadienne. En étudiant, d'un œil marxiste critique, la question de la représentation publique des pièces musicales, le problème essentiel menant à la création de ce droit est vu comme la conséquence de la lutte entre les auteurs-compositeurs et les intérêts dominants des éditeurs qui ont dicté leur emploi et les termes de leur compensation. Les concepts théoriques de l'hégémonie utilisés dans l'analyse d'Antonio Gramsci fournissent une base structurelle à cette analyse. Ultimement, cette lutte semble un exemple de l'absorption par les intérêts dominants des éditeurs, des désirs et des buts des intérêts des créateurs, réitérée de façon à ce que les objectifs premiers des intérêts des éditeurs soient atteints à l'intérieur de l'ordre hégémonique en évolution.

A. INTRODUCTION

The success of performance rights organizations has been responsible for the massive growth of copyright collectives, particularly in Canada. Prior to the 1988 *Phase I* revisions to the *Copyright Act*,[1] there was only a single type of copyright collective authorized under Canadian law — those collecting on the public performance right in music. Since the *Phase I* revisions came into law, more than thirty-four copyright collectives[2] have been registered with the Copyright Board of Canada. With thirty-four registered collectives, Canada has more than double the copyright collectives of any of the key nations listed in Daniel Gervais's 2002 study.[3]

Despite the fact that a public performance right in music was first explicitly granted under the 1842 *Copyright Act*,[4] it was actively ignored by the industry of the day, and as a result, the first performance right collective in the United Kingdom, the Performing Right Society, would not be formed until 1914. This chapter views the subsequent adoption and successful expansion of the public performance right as an example of a hegemonic process as delineated by Antonio Gramsci.

B. GRAMSCI

Antonio Gramsci (1891–1937) was a leading member of the Italian Communist party as well as a highly critical journalist. Gramsci was arrested by the Italian Fascist state in November of 1926 and would remain in prison until

---

1 *Copyright Amendment Act*, SC 1988, c 15.

2 *Copyright Act*, RSC 1985, c C-42, s 2 [collective society]. A copyright collective is an agency created under the terms of the *Copyright Act*, which collects royalties or licensing fees on behalf of registered copyright owners.

3 Daniel J Gervais, "Collective Management of Copyright and Neighbouring Rights in Canada: An International Perspective" (2002) 1 Can J L & Tech 21 at 38 (table 3).

4 *Imperial Copyright Act of 1842* (UK), 5 & 6 Vict, c 45.

he was transferred to a clinic in 1935 and then a hospital where he would die in April of 1937. His theoretical work, and the contribution of his conception of hegemony in particular, have been adopted and championed by a wide range of social theorists with differing interpretations, but it is important to note that Gramsci's hegemonic theory is fundamentally a theory of class struggle. However, the theory as Gramsci develops it is so encompassing, it is not surprising that it has been widely adopted within other discrete frames of social analysis.

With the aforementioned in mind, it seems appropriate and necessary at this point to place this Gramscian analysis of the public performance right within the context of political class struggle. While the analysis focuses on a single aspect of copyright, it is essential to remember that copyright as a process controls the flow, distribution, use, and reuse of information throughout society. Within that context, copyright can and has been used as a tool of capital within business and publishing dimensions. Copyright has provided those interests with a means to deny or limit the use of information by society, and in particular those members of society who make up the working class/users of the information. The successful imposition of the public performance right created the precedent for the establishment of further owners' rights across a spectrum of information and not merely the public performance of musical works. The contemporary discourse surrounding the Canadian copyright collective known as Access Copyright is a direct result of the success of the hegemonic order.

C. GRAMSCI'S THEORETICAL CONCEPTIONS OF HEGEMONY

Gramsci's concept of hegemony is situated within a political economic view of society, and is formulated in relation to some fundamental Marxist positions. Key amongst these is the Marxian concept of economic determinism. Within orthodox Marxist formulations, economic relations form the bedrock upon which other hierarchical spheres of culture depend. Economic relations are the base in a base-superstructure hierarchy and, within the historical processes delineated by Marx, determine derivative structures that form the superstructure (the realms of the political, the social, and the intellectual). The base level is composed from the elements of material production: money, things, the relations of production, as well as the stage of development of productive forces which can be thought of more simply as the physical world as well as the forces of economic relations that capital creates. Located within the superstructure are political and ideological institutions, social relations, and cultures. An orthodox interpretation holds that the movements and goals of the independent units of society are a result of these established and inherited property structures, and within these units of organization, cultural activity is an expression of controlling economic interests.

For Gramsci, society is the sum of all its cultural and ideological parts and is not simply driven by economic divisions. Therefore the dialectic nature of the social order, with its varying influences and exchanges, can and does have political outcomes regardless of class status. In his analysis of the French revolution, Gramsci makes it clear that the upheaval was not simply determined by economic inequalities:

> In any case, the rupture of the equilibrium of forces did not occur as the result of direct mechanical causes — i.e. the impoverishment of the social group which had an interest in breaking the equilibrium, and which did in fact break it. It occurred in the context of conflicts on a higher plane than the immediate world of the economy; conflicts related to class "prestige" (future economic interests), and to an inflammation of sentiments of independence, autonomy and power. [5]

Thus, in his analysis of the French revolution, Gramsci rejects a rigid base-superstructure model because it relies too heavily upon class status, and does not sufficiently appreciate the intellectual and philosophical impact of the culture and individuals within it.

Within a Gramscian hegemonic framework, the dominant class relies not only upon coercion and naked power to subvert the subordinate class to their goals, but also manufactures consent through the creation of cross-class alliances. This theory assumes a consent given by the majority in a particular direction as suggested by those in power. Consent is not always peaceful and may also be induced by means of coercion through physical, legal, or cultural processes. The consent is taken to be "common sense," but is in reality an ideology of dominance that has become so widespread, powerful, and increasingly unnoticeable that over time society's members no longer question it: "The 'spontaneous' consent given by the great masses

5 Antonio Gramsci, *Selections from the Prison Notebooks of Antonio Gramsci* (New York: International Publishers, 1971) at 184.

of population to the general direction imposed on social life by the dominant fundamental group; this consent is 'historically' caused by the prestige (and consequent confidence) which the dominant group enjoys because of its position and function in the world of production." [6]

For Gramsci there were no absolutes, but only possibilities for which each person could strive. Though he recognized the fundamentally political economic nature of class struggle, Gramsci also realized that a society was the sum of all its cultural and ideological parts, not simply its class status. Therefore, the dialectic nature of the social order, and its interrelationships with their varying influences and exchanges, could and would have political outcomes regardless of class status: "A third moment is that in which one becomes aware that one's own corporate interests, in their present and future development, transcend the corporate limits of the purely economic class, and can and must become the interests of other subordinate groups too."[7] Gramsci does not simply say that their interests must be imposed on the subordinate group, but rather that the dominant group's interests *become the interests of the subordinate*. Herein lies the notion of consent that is at the heart of hegemony.

Within Gramsci's view of society as a hegemonic order, the subordinate class participates in and consents to the historical processes of change. The subordinate members of society are empowered through a participatory process, and because of this they experience a sense of agency and involvement when changes take place. While the system is participatory, it is not equal, and the very nature of the hegemonic order ensures that the values of the dominant order will perpetually be inculcated into the culture as a whole.[8]

Gramsci recognized that at various times within society, crises develop, and while some are insignificant, others are indicative of deep pockets of discontent within society. Such crises create the opportunity for new classes to overthrow the established order. "If the ruling class has lost its consensus, i.e. is no longer 'leading' but only 'dominant,' exercising coercive force alone, this means precisely that the great masses have become detached from their traditional ideologies, and no longer believe what they used to believe previously, etc." [9] If unsuccessful, the class attempting to wrest

6 *Ibid* at 12.

7 *Ibid* at 181.

8 *Ibid*.

9 *Ibid* at 275–76.

control would simply fade back into the social frame until such time as another opportunity arose. The fundamental disconnect of the masses from the ruling ideologies is characterized as an organic crisis that could lead to an overthrow of the dominant order. These moments represented what Gramsci referred to as moments of *organic crisis*, a crisis so fundamental and so widespread that it creates the possibility of overthrowing the ruling hegemony.

Viewing the public performance right issue from a historical perspective we see that the fundamental problem lay in the disparity between publishers and composers. The publishers and the new emerging middle class controlled the means of production and distribution and they would choose to invest in those works they believed would sell. For the composers it was a closed system. If you could convince a publisher of the potential value of your work they might choose to publish it, but if so they would in all likelihood offer you a lump sum in exchange for the copyright. An article from the *Evening Standard* of September 1902 points out the significant disparity between the profits of composers and the publishers.[10] They note that the composer Johann Strauss was paid forty pounds for his *Blue Danube* waltz, which sold 400,000 copies in a single year in America and England and generated over 100,000 pounds for the publisher. Put another way, for every pound the composer received, the publisher received 2,500 pounds. Nonetheless these two oppositional classes had to forge an alliance to create the successful hegemonic order.

D. THE PUBLIC PERFORMANCE RIGHT

It is the *owner* of the work that enjoys all the economic rights delineated in subsection 3(1) of the *Copyright Act*, including the "sole right to produce or reproduce the work or any substantial part thereof in any material form whatever, to perform the work or any substantial part thereof in public or, if the work is unpublished, to publish the work or any substantial part thereof."[11] These economic rights provide the means of compensation for the owner of the work. With respect to the economic rights delineated in the *Copyright Act*, it is the right to "perform the work or any substantial part

10 James Coover, *Music Publishing, Copyright and Piracy in Victorian England: A Twenty-Five Year Chronicle, 1881–1906, from the Pages of the Musical Opinion & Music Trade Review and Other English Music Journals of the Period* (London: Mansell Publishing, 1985) at 89.

11 *Copyright Act*, above note 2, s 3(1).

thereof in public" that provides the basis of discussion for this chapter. This owner's right of public performance should not be confused with the more recently added neighbouring right of a "performer's performance." They are two separate economic rights, though they are related.

Historically, in the case of music, the copyright owner has always been the publisher, as the assignment of copyright to the publishing house has generally been a condition of publication.[12] It is also important to note that the public performance right is a particular form of recompense unique to cultural goods, and is fundamentally dominant in the area of musical goods. Though the costs of the public performance right are not transparently borne by the individual users, it nonetheless impacts significantly in the operating costs of the larger community. In 2009, the three major North American performing rights organizations, the Society of Composers, Authors and Music Publishers of Canada (SOCAN), the American Society of Composers, Authors and Publishers (ASCAP) and Broadcast Music International (BMI), collected a little over $2.1 billion. In Canada, given the current population of just under thirty-four million,[13] the SOCAN collection amounted to $7.55 per capita.[14]

What seems to be lacking in the discussion of the owner's public performance right is why the owners should receive an additional economic right beyond those for reproduction and distribution. This concept of paying to use something, after it has been purchased or rented, was unique in its application to musical works. While the first instance of copyright in the Anglo-American tradition appears in 1710 in the *Statute of Anne*,[15] an owner's public performance right does not appear until the *Dramatic Literary Property Act* of 1833,[16] and then only with respect to musical-dramatic

---

12 Joanna Demers, *Steal This Music: How Intellectual Property Law Affects Musical Creativity* (Athens, Georgia: University of Georgia Press, 2006) at 12.

13 Central Intelligence Agency, *The World Factbook* (January 2011), online: Central Intelligence Agency www.cia.gov/library/publications/the-world-factbook/geos/ca.html.

14 SOCAN, "2009 Financial Report," online: www.socan.ca/pdf/pub/FinancialReport2009.pdf. Note that in 2004 when this research was begun the total collection was one billion five hundred and fifty four million, and the SOCAN figure was $6.40 per capita. For all three groups as a whole that amounts to a 38 percent increase in collections during the period. For SOCAN alone it amounts to a little more than a 14 percent increase. The collection figures for the various agencies were obtained from their published financial reports. The SOCAN report also cites both BMI, and ASCAP's 2009 collections.

15 *An Act for the Encouragement of Learning, by Vesting the Copies of Printed Books in the Authors or Purchasers of such Copies, during the Times Therein Mentioned*, 1710, 8 Anne, c 19.

16 *Dramatic Literary Property Act*, 1833, 3 & 4 Will IV, c 15.

works such as theatre or opera. In 1842 the *Copyright Act* would establish an owner's right of public performance, but it would never be widely enforced. Only in 1914 would an owner's public performance right begin to be collected, 200 years after the *Statute of Anne*.[17] It is only within the last few decades that similar rights have been extended to books or other works.

Perhaps most intriguing is the question of why music has been treated differently. We do not pay additional fees to the engineer who designed our cars every time we take a drive. Surely the conception, realization, and designs that have been borne out in our vehicles are unique, creative, and original contributions. Arguably, our lives are enriched in significant ways by the end results of these efforts, and yet there is no payment made to these creators, nor to the industrial interests that support them, every time we start the engine and drive down our roads. If we wish to dismiss the automobile as simply a mechanical contrivance, then let us consider the other professions that might be deemed more creative or artistic. The architect who designed our homes does not receive a royalty for each night we spend in them, or for each party we hold. Even if the building were commercial and not a private home, royalties are not paid. When the portrait artist paints his work and sells it to a buyer, his economic interest in it ends there. The portrait artist receives no royalty when it is put on display, nor are the visitors to the home where it hangs counted so that a royalty might be returned to recompense for their viewing. We have struck our economic bargain between artist (be it automotive designer, architect, or portrait artist) and end user when we purchased or rented their creation. No further rents are paid. Nonetheless, it has somehow become accepted that it is perfectly reasonable for an author/composer, or more specifically the copyright owner (who is often not even the original creator), to be paid for each use beyond the point of sale or rental.

There is no obvious logic or model for an additional economic right to be collected following the initial economic transaction. The standard economic arguments proffered such as incentive for creation would not apply to this additional right,[18] as the creator would have been paid when they

17 A public performance right in music was successfully imposed in France beginning in 1851 with the establishment of the Société des Auteurs, Compositeurs et Éditeurs de Musique [SACEM].

18 Such arguments are questionable in any case when applied to artistic creation since artists create for many reasons beyond simple economic recompense. The annals of artistic creation are filled with artists who left huge bodies of work despite little if any financial success in their own time e.g., Charles Ives, Lead Belly, Van Gogh.

sold the container in which the work was held. Though large scale uses such as broadcasting[19] may not appear on the surface to adequately recompense the creator given their broad dissemination of the work, broadcast of some kind has always been absolutely necessary for the creation and expansion of markets, as evidenced by the long historic practice of payola in the industry.[20] Not only is the owner's public performance right an additional economic right added to the existing reproduction right, it is an economic right collected on something that has no physical existence: a performance.

E. THE NATURE OF PERFORMANCE

Like a thought or conversation, a performance exists only in the moment and later as a memory. If it is fixed in a medium, then it is no longer a performance, but a recording and, as such, can be sold or traded. Within this context, the thought of a unique owner's right of public performance seems even more problematic when applied specifically to music. If we consider music as an abstract object, or even simply as a commodity form, its only purpose is performance. Textual or manuscript manifestations serve only as guideposts in the creation or re-creation of a performance. Indeed, if performance were not the intent, the composer would not have released the work to the world.

More importantly, unlike a recording or a broadcast, a performance is not a one-way transmission. Performers respond, react, and interact with their audiences. A performer can play the same song on every night of a tour and each performance will be different and unique. Much of the difference in those performances will come from the audience and their reac-

---

19 Note that the advent of the public performance right predated broadcasting technology by a significant margin. SACEM was formed in France in 1851. Radio broadcasting does not become commonplace until the mid 1920s.

20 New York State Office of the Attorney General, Press Release, "Sony Settles Payola Investigation" (25 July 2005) online: www.ag.ny.gov/press-release/sony-settles-payola-investigation. In 2005 the attorney general's office of New York State investigated a number of the music industry's largest corporations. In the *Assurance of Discontinuance*, it was noted that "Sony BMG had illegally provided radio stations with financial benefits to obtain airplay and boost the chart position of its songs . . . . through such deceptive and illegal practices as: (a) on occasion, bribing radio station employees . . . (b) providing a stream of financial benefits to radio stations . . . (c) providing vacation packages . . . and other valuable items . . . (d) using independent promoters as conduits for illegal payments . . . ." at para 4.

tions to the performance. It is an ephemeral and transitory state that is to a large degree mutually constituted by performer and audience.

It is also of the utmost importance to recognize that despite our contemporary conception (both legal and social) of what may constitute a performance now, and perhaps more significantly what the performing rights organizations might believe constitutes a performance, historically, during the period of its inception and for a significant time period to follow, the *only* type of performance that existed with respect to music was a live in the moment transmission between audience and performer(s). Thus, to reiterate, the public performance right is not only an additional economic right unique to musical works beyond the traditional rights of reproduction and distribution, but in its historic inception it was attached to something that had no physical manifestation, a performance.

F. A CHRONOLOGICAL REVIEW OF THE GRAMSCIAN HEGEMONIC ORDER

Within the context of the struggle between composers and publishers, the publishers held the balance of power. Although there existed an explicit performance right in the United Kingdom as early as 1842, the publishers made it clear that they had no intention of observing it. In fact they were able to overcome their own internal competitive class interests to form an association in 1881 primarily to oppose the right at the national level in their opposition to the *Berne Convention for the Protection of Literary and Artistic Works*.[21] Their lack of success in opposing the *Berne Convention* was likely due to the larger capital interests beyond their own which held more influence with the various governments involved and whom would benefit from an increased level of trade brought about by an international agreement. "[W]hile Berne may have been a response to the claims and work of the International Literary Association (or, looked at from a purely British perspective, the Copyright Association), it was equally a strategic instrument for the extension and maintenance of trade interests."[22] However, despite the advancement of the *Berne Convention*, the British publishers still ignored the public performance right. "William Boosey was generally accepted as

21 *Berne Convention for the Protection of Literary and Artistic Works*, 9 September 1886, 1161 UNTS 30 [*Berne Convention*]; Coover, above note 10 at 9–11.

22 Lionel Bently & Brad Sherman, "Great Britain and the Signing of the *Berne Convention* in 1886" (2001) 48:3 J Copyright Soc'y USA 311 at 339–40.

the industry's leader, but neither he nor most of his colleagues in the Music Publisher's Association were yet committed to performing right or the importance of the gramophone."[23]

The necessity of expansion led to the first cross-class alliance with the composers. Without the public face of the composer, the publishers would not have been able to collect the performance right. Presumably this would have been a simple decision for the composers, since it would provide a new revenue stream. However the creation of a right of public performance did not address the core issue of disparity between publisher and composer in terms of both recompense and power. Instead of the imbalance being addressed, the issue was deflected with the advocacy of a public performance right, the costs of which would be borne by the users.

The British music industry's opposition to a public performance right was extreme. Consider the following: despite the fact that the United Kingdom's *Copyright Act* of 1842 had established a public performance right for musical works, a collective would not be formed until 1914. The French performance right society, Societé des Auteurs, Compositeurs et Éditeurs de Musique (SACEM), had pursued their rights on British soil since 1881 but, without the support of the Music Publishers Association, they achieved only minimal success. The Music Publishers Association (MPA) was formed in part to oppose the imposition of a public performance right, or as the Chairman of the MPA referred to it the "vexatious rights of performance."[24] Great Britain signed the *Berne Convention* in 1886, and though there was an attempt to form a British performing rights society in 1890, it failed without the support of the MPA.[25]

The *Berne Convention* was the first international treaty to establish a public performance right in music. Article 9[26] of the *Berne Convention* of 1886 stated "[t]he stipulations of Article 2 apply equally to the public performance of unpublished musical works, and of published works as to which the author has expressly declared upon the title-page or at the commencement of the work that he forbids their public performance."[27] The 1908 Berlin revision to

---

23 Cyril Ehrlich, *Harmonious Alliance: A History of the Performing Right Society* (New York: Oxford University Press, 1989) at 14.

24 Coover, above note 10 at 38.

25 *Ibid* at 43.

26 Following the 1908 revisions to the *Berne Convention* this stipulation would move to article 11 where it remains in the most recently amended version.

27 "*Berne Convention*, Berne (1886)," in Lionel Bently & Martin Kretschmer, eds, *Primary Sources on Copyright (1450–1900)*, online: Arts & Humanities Research Council www.copyrighthistory.org.

the *Berne Convention* recognized a mechanical right for the copyright owner due to the success of the mechanical music business (piano rolls, gramophones, melodeons).[28] The new mechanical rights would also provide new areas for the expansion of the performance right hegemony.

G. THE ESTABLISHMENT OF THE ANGLO-AMERICAN PERFORMANCE RIGHT COLLECTIVES

The Performing Right Society (PRS) incorporated in 1914 and began its attempts to enforce the public performance right in the United Kingdom. The failures of previous attempts to start a British collective were not due to any lack of desire from composers, who were always looking for new sources of income, but rather the lack of support from the Music Publishers Association. Once the publishers saw the economic value in the union with creators, the partnership was established, thereby forming the *historic bloc*[29] as delineated by Gramsci and the first infant steps of the ruling hegemony. The American Society of Composers, Authors and Publishers (ASCAP) would also form in 1914 but in New York City. The PRS and ASCAP would eventually establish the first successful performing rights organization in Canada in 1925.

The PRS was the first cross-class alliance between composers and their traditional opponents, publishers, within the Anglo-American tradition. As Gramsci noted with respect to the establishment of any hegemonic order, the basis was purely economic. For the publishers to successfully establish the PRS they needed the public face of the composers. It was this public face that allowed the public inculcation of the *justness* of the performance right. Had the attempts been made to collect purely on the basis of the publishers' right it would likely not have succeeded. The pattern of establishment was similar in the United States and Canada. Considering the tone of the debates in Canada's Parliament, it was only marginally accepted in Canada even with the composers as the focus.[30]

---

28 *Berne Convention*, above note 21, revised in Berlin, 13 November 1908.

29 Gramsci, above note 5 at 181.

30 *House of Commons Debates*, 18th Parl, 1st Sess, No 1 (28 February 1936) (Hon CH Cahan). The Parliamentary debates of 1936 in Canada are quite vivid in their descriptions of the Canadian Performing Right Society as "evil," and that some form of control was needed to "put an end to price-fixing and extortion" at 644.

Gramsci noted that throughout the course of the hegemonic order the dominant group leading the order would face various moments of crisis. Despite winning a significant victory establishing their right to collect from cabarets in *Herbert v Shanley Co*,[31] ASCAP continued to face an uphill battle. The American Federation of Musicians (AFM) advised its members not to perform any works by ASCAP members out of fear that the increased costs might adversely effect their employment in hotels and lounges.[32] In addition to the AFM, the Hoteliers Association,[33] and the Motion Picture Exhibitors Association[34] actively opposed ASCAP's right to license their use of music. Similarly, many music publishers intuitively felt that a successful application of the performing right would in effect mean that users would have to pay for music twice: once when purchased from the publisher and again when used. Shortly after the *Herbert* ruling of 1917, the music publishers would form their own association, the Music Publishers Protective Association (MPPA), in response to concerns about the impact that ASCAP might have on their industry.[35] However, similar to the British experience, the economic depression of the 1920s, coupled with technological changes, saw the sales of sheet music plummet and the publishers' need to find alternate ways to profit from their copyrights.[36] Ultimately, a deal was struck and the majority of publishers joined ASCAP and brought their catalogues along with them.

The emergence of radio broadcasting also created opportunities for the growth of the hegemonic order. It was not immediately apparent in either Canada or the US if the performance right extended to broadcasting. In the US, ASCAP decided that broadcasting might be a very lucrative source of funding and in an obvious attempt to establish its territory offered temporary licences. The licences waived any fee, but admitted ASCAP's jurisdic-

---

31 *Herbert v Shanley Co*, 242 US 591 (1917) established that cabaret — bars, nightclubs, hotels — performances were a performance for profit regardless of whether or not there was a door charge.

32 Bennie L DeWhitt, *The American Society of Composers, Authors, and Publishers 1914–1938* (Atlanta: Emory University, 1977) at 25.

33 *Ibid* at 23–24 and 34.

34 *Ibid* at 37–38.

35 *Ibid* at 35.

36 That was in fact cited as one of the justifications for the expansion of the performance right in the report of the Canadian Royal Commission chaired by Justice Parker. Similar rationales can be found in pleas made for the blank media levy relative to cassette copying, and the current request for increased intellectual property rights in the wake of perceived losses due to downloading.

tion.[37] In 1923 the National Association of Broadcasters (NAB) was formed from the ranks of private broadcasters in the United States. It was the position of the NAB that broadcasting music on the radio did not constitute a performance for profit.[38] In 1925 the performance right was extended to broadcasting in the United States following the ruling in *Jerome H Remick & Co v American Automobile Accessories Co*.[39] This move to expand into new related territories would become habitual within the hegemony.[40]

Possibly, as a result of their experience with the broadcasting tariff, ASCAP realized the value of lobbying and by 1927 had become an effective presence in Washington, illustrating clearly that it intended to influence policy decisions.[41] This period marks the first efforts of the hegemonic order to inculcate their ideology beyond their membership and target markets. By virtue of influencing directly at the policy level, ASCAP helped to enable the expansion of its regimes with less recourse to individual legal actions. It was also at this time that ASCAP began to expand into Canada in association with the PRS in their joint establishment of the Canadian Performing Right Society (CPRS) in 1927.

In an echo of its forming partners, the CPRS also faced hostility at its inception, ultimately resulting in Royal Commissions to investigate its actions in 1932 and 1935. Enough concerns were raised during the 1935 Commission that a permanent tribunal, the Copyright Appeal Board, was formed in 1936, specifically to deal with issues related to the performance right. Meanwhile, by 1939 the United States broadcast licensing revenues rose to 4.5 million dollars and were set to reach 9 million dollars in the proposed new contract.[42] As a result, the broadcast industry, in conjunction with its trade

37 William Randle, *History of Radio Broadcasting and its Social and Economic Effect on the Entertainment Industry, 1920–1930* (Western Reserve University, 1966) at 369.

38 *Ibid* at 370.

39 5 F(2d) 411 at 411–12 (1925).

40 Given the success of ASCAP in this instance, one cannot help but wonder if their contemporary descendants, Access Copyright (AC), might have fared better in the current tariff process had they merely extended their control (their proposed tariff included areas not previously under licence, such as web links and image displays, and also lacked exclusions for fair dealing) via their contracting, without simultaneously increasing their licence fees. While they likely would have still faced opposition, it probably would not have been as widespread or heated. In fact, given university administrators' overall concern with the bottom line, it might just simply have gone through. Once AC had established their territory, they could have gradually raised the rates.

41 DeWhitt, above note 32 at 120.

42 Marc Hugunin, "ASCAP, BMI and the Democratization of American Popular Music" (1979) 7:1 Popular Music and Society 8 at 9.

association, the NAB, formed their own licensing agency, Broadcast Music International (BMI). Following the Second World War, and following the pattern of the other performing rights organizations, BMI expanded into Canada and set up a Canadian office to collect on the performance right. While the NAB had initially been established in opposition to ASCAP, after its failure in the courts the NAB adopted the ideology of the dominant order and while still in competition with elements within the hegemony (ASCAP). They nonetheless had become proponents of the dominant ideology of the hegemonic order (the public performance right).

Surviving the attacks and crises of the Royal Commissions, opposition from broadcasters and the public, the hegemony continued to move forward and simultaneously began the political process of lobbying to influence policy outcomes. The Ilsley Commission of 1959 devoted an entire chapter of its report solely to the issue of performance rights, though the tone had changed markedly from the earlier Royal Commissions. Not only were the performance rights regimes being generally treated with less suspicion (which is interesting given that two previous commissions had been specifically called to investigate them), but they had reached a level of confidence that allowed them to suggest that the government regulation via the Copyright Appeal Board was inconsistent with obligations under international agreements.[43] By this time the hegemony was firmly established and confident. It had continued to expand, moving into radio, and now began its encroachment into the emerging medium of television.

By the time the performance right hegemony entered the 1960s it was so thoroughly entrenched that it was no longer questioned, in fact just the opposite began to occur. The publications of the Economic Council of Canada (ECC), which had been charged with investigating a new copyright policy for Canada, began to reflect the effectiveness of the hegemonic order surrounding the public performance rights regimes upon the policy process. In a series of reports, *Copyright in Context: the Challenge of Change*,[44] *Re-*

43 Royal Commission on Patents, Copyright, Trade Marks and Industrial Designs, *Report on Copyright* (Ottawa: E Cloutier Queen's Printer, 1957) at 100–1 (Chair: James Lorimer Ilsley), online: Library and Archives Canada http://epe.lac-bac.gc.ca/100/200/301/pco-bcp/commissions-ef/ilsley1957a-eng/ilsley1957a-eng.htm. The Commission noted that "Canada is therefore perfectly free, so far as the conventions are concerned, to enact such provisions as it thinks fit to prevent or deal with any abuse of the rights centralized in performing rights societies" at 100–1.

44 Bruce C McDonald, *Copyright in Context: The Challenge of Change* (Ottawa: Economic Council of Canada, 1971).

port on Intellectual and Industrial Property,[45] the ECC strongly recommended the adoption of copyright collectives modelled on the performance rights regimes for the purposes of collection in other areas. Perhaps the ultimate indicator of the extent to which the hegemony surrounding the performance right was successful is the fact that the Minister of Culture supported the idea that the two separate performing rights agencies in Canada, the Composers, Authors, and Publishers Association of Canada (CAPAC) and the Performing Rights Organization of Canada (PROCAN),[46] should amalgamate into a single monopoly.[47] Following the changes to the *Copyright Act* in 1988, they did so, forming the Society of Composers, Authors and Music Publishers of Canada (SOCAN). At the same time the hegemonic order reached its full maturation with the extension of copyright collectives across a broad spectrum beyond the public performance right with the Phase I revisions to copyright in 1988.

In observing the extension of copyright collective management regimes across a broad base of interests, it is imperative to stress the "natural outcome" and the "common sense" with which this direction was perceived. The policy changes appeared to be the natural evolution of the policy process. However the concept of a separate economic right (the public performance right itself) within the larger copyright frame was anything but a natural outcome. In fact, the very people who subsequently championed the right for their own economic interests, the publishers, were at the outset vehemently opposed to the right.

H. HEGEMONIC RESISTANCE

Gramsci recognized that at various times within the hegemonic process, crises would develop, and while some would be insignificant others would be organic, representative of deep pockets of discontent within society. Such organic crises create the opportunity for new classes to overthrow the established order: "If the ruling class has lost its consensus, i.e. is no longer 'leading' but only 'dominant,' exercising coercive force alone, this means

45 Economic Council of Canada, *Report on Intellectual and Industrial Property* (Ottawa: Information Canada, 1971).

46 SOCAN, "Our History," online: www.socan.ca/jsp/en/pub/about_socan/history.jsp. BMI Canada had divested itself from its American parent corporation in 1969 and established itself as a solely Canadian entity operating under the name PROCAN.

47 Jan V Matejcek, *History of BMI Canada Ltd and PROCAN: Their Role in Canadian Music and in the Formation of SOCAN (1940–1990)* (Toronto: Matejcek, 1996) at 96.

precisely that the great masses have become detached from their traditional ideologies, and no longer believe what they used to believe previously."[48]

Within the performance rights framework there were numerous instances of such resistance ranging from the publishing class themselves at the outset, through various trade and social unions as well as larger media interests. British and American publishing interests challenged the idea of a public performance right from the outset. Even after they had been formed, the performance right collectives continued to face opposition from the musicians union, hoteliers associations, cabarets, and motion picture exhibitors. Even after most of these issues had been settled in favour of the collectives, the onset of broadcasting would result in another adversarial standoff. The establishment of the Canadian Performing Right Society faced similar opposition, but in addition the CPRS had to appear before two Royal Commissions called to investigate its operation. The Royal Commissions would eventually lead to the establishment of the Copyright Appeal Board (now simply the Copyright Board) to deal with complaints. Despite the ongoing opposition, none of the adversaries have ever successfully challenged the dominant group, though they have influenced some outcomes. In fact, as Gramsci theorized would happen, most adversaries to the hegemony established by the performing rights collectives have ultimately been assimilated into the hegemony itself and have become part of that which they opposed. Indeed, that has been the overwhelming success of the hegemonic order.

As part of the working class, composers and performers have been dependent upon the labour of their bodies to forge an existence. Despite their historic lack of control over the processes of production and distribution, composers and performers have continued to participate in the industrial process even in the face of overwhelming evidence that industrial capital will take advantage of them at every opportunity. Paul McGuinness, manager of the pop band U2, noted in a speech to an international managers summit in 2008 that the music industry had a long history of abusing artists, and that both the band and McGuinness were consciously aware of that: "We were never interested in joining that long, humiliating list of miserable artists who made lousy deals, got exploited and ended up broke and with no control over how their life's work was used, and no say in how their names

48 Gramsci, above note 5 at 275–76 [footnote omitted].

and likenesses were bought and sold."[49] The music industry continues such practices today, even as it complains bitterly about "piracy" and "theft" with respect to downloading and digital music issues. In the same speech, McGuinness cites the "360" deals being pushed by the current industry as evidence of the continued exploitation of the artist: "It's ironic that, at a time when the majors are asking the artists to trust them to share advertising revenue they are also pushing the dreadful '360 model.'"[50]

The current crisis surrounding the downloading of digitized music and copyright generally seems to reflect a new mode of thought with respect to the conception of copyright, owning, and sharing, notions which were certainly not those being advocated by the dominant order. This new mode of thought can be seen to be much more reflective of the social classes that actually make use of the works. The way in which our contemporary society views copyright with respect to reuse and sharing within our social frames is very different from the way in which industrial concerns would like it to be seen. It is now quite common for young children to create works in various media and post them to the web. The author's thirteen year-old son regularly creates various types of creative media on his smart phone and shares/reuses it with friends and strangers online. Contemporary theorists such as Lawrence Lessig, Siva Vaidyanathan, James Boyle, and Joanna Demers (to name just a few) have made clear that there is a distinct clash between the evolving user-generated culture and established industrial interests. The simple fact that intellectual property issues and policies have become an increasingly common source of debate and point of discussion in the popular media indicates a general awareness that simply did not exist twenty years ago. This new mode of thinking has led to a new discourse, which has begun to question the foundations of the dominant order and place the hegemony in question.

The prevalence of this new copyright discourse and the continued questioning of the dominant order's ideology in regard to copyright seem

---

49 Paul McGuinness, Address (Keynote address delivered at the Midem Music Industry Convention, Cannes, keynote address 28 January 2008), online: Digital Cowboys: Hired Hands for the 21st Century http://digitalcowboys.com/2008/01/29/paul-mcguinness-u2s-manager-speaks-out-at-cannes.

50 The term "360 deal" refers to an increasingly common practice in the music industry to sign an artist to deals that provide the industry label with a proportion of income from all aspects of the artist's income, not simply those related to the music or recording. As such, the industry interests can also collect on any uses of the artist's likeness, touring income, merchandise sales, and/or expansion into new fields (such as film or TV).

indicative of the organic crisis which Gramsci noted would be necessary for the overthrow of a dominant order. Given the prevailing social behaviours with respect to copyright it seems clear that "the great masses have become detached from their traditional ideologies . . . ."[51] The response to the proposed colleges and universities tariff request of Access Copyright seems a particularly poignant example of the masses having become disconnected from the traditional ideologies of the ruling hegemony. The July 2012 copyright pentalogy rulings of the Supreme Court of Canada may also be seen to indicate the disconnection between the ruling hegemony and the changing copyright discourse.[52] As Raymond Williams has noted, "[a] lived hegemony is always a process. It is not, except analytically, a system or a structure. It is a realized complex of experiences, relationships, and activities, with specific and changing pressures and limits."[53] Thus, hegemony is a dialectic process, the "push and pull" of relationships and cultures within the social structure which impact, and are impacted by, the processes surrounding it — cultural, social, legal, and political. It is constantly shifting, changing, and negotiating, yet fundamentally driven by the ideology of the dominant group as it responds to challenges and crises. However, the detachment of the masses that seems to be taking place may lead to the organic crisis necessary to displace the ruling hegemony. Only time will tell.

51 Gramsci, above note 5 at 275–76 [footnote omitted].

52 *Entertainment Software Association v Society of Composers, Authors and Music Publishers of Canada*, 2012 SCC 34; *Rogers Communications Inc v Society of Composers, Authors and Music Publishers of Canada*, 2012 SCC 35; *Re:Sound v Motion Picture Theatre Associations of Canada*, 2012 SCC 38; *Society of Composers, Authors and Music Publishers of Canada v Bell Canada*, 2012 SCC 36; *Alberta (Education) v Canadian Copyright Licensing Agency (Access Copyright)*, 2012 SCC 37.

53 Raymond Williams, *Marxism and Literature* (Oxford: Oxford University Press, 1977) at 112.

ELEVEN

Branding Culture: Fictional Characters and Undead Celebrities in an Era of "Transpropertied" Media

DANIEL DOWNES

ABSTRACT (EN): This chapter explores changes in intellectual property law as part of a changing media ecology that began during the 1970s in which IP law is a medium of control in the digital age. It will be shown that the extension of copyright, trademark, and rights of publicity to fictional characters and authors helps set the boundaries of economic and social expression in the global media environment of the twenty-first century in a process defined by the author as transpropertization, whereby different types of IP protection overlap.

The mechanism or communicative practice associated with this new ecology of information is branding, which is evolving from a technique of marketing to an informal medium of control alongside these changes in the law.

RÉSUMÉ (FR): Ce chapitre explore les changements du droit de la propriété intellectuelle en tant qu'écologie changeante des médias, débutant dans les années 1970 au cours desquelles le droit de la propriété intellectuelle devient un moyen de contrôle dans l'ère numérique. Il sera démontré que l'expansion du droit d'auteur, des marques de commerce et des droits de publicité sur les personnages fictifs et les auteurs aide à créer les limites de l'expression économique et sociale dans l'environnement médiatique mondial du 21e siècle dans un processus défini par l'auteur comme « la transpropriation », qui se produit lorsque différents types de propriété intellectuelle se chevauchent.

Le mécanisme ou la pratique communicative associée avec cette nouvelle écologie de l'information est la création de l'image de marque, qui s'est développée à partir d'une technique de marketing jusqu'à devenir un moyen informel de contrôle en parallèle aux changements du droit.

A. INTRODUCTION

On 28 October 2009, a public reading of a unique literary collaboration was staged at Toronto's Bathurst Street Theatre.[1] Expatriate Canadian Dacre Stoker and American screenwriter Ian Holt took elements from Stoker's great-uncle Bram Stoker's unpublished notes to his 1897 novel *Dracula* and wrote an *official* sequel entitled *Dracula the Un-dead*.[2]

The publication of *Dracula the Un-dead* and its public performance by the authors and various actors in period costumes is of particular interest to both media and intellectual property (IP) scholars because the sequel was written, in part, "to right the wrongs done to Bram's original classic."[3] To answer the question of what wrongs had been committed, the authors apologize to their literary audience for "losing the copyright and control of Bram's magnificent and immortal story for almost a century."[4]

While it may seem counterintuitive to hear a writer reclaiming ownership of copyrighted and, indeed un-copyrightable material, Stoker's use of the language of ownership and control in describing both his own and his ancestor's work is consistent with what might be described as the contemporary ecology of IP.

There is a deeply ingrained tendency to talk about various forms of expression as property, to think of the free market as a natural environment, and to think of many, perhaps all, forms of human interaction as fungible and translatable to economic relations. But, we must ask, in what ways is our understanding of IP historically contingent and how is that understanding related to social, economic, and technological conditions in the creative industries?

---

1 "Dracula the Un-Dead — A Dramatic Reading w/ Original Music Premieres in Toronto" *MODA Entertainment* (28 October 2009), online: http://modaentertainment.blogspot.ca/2009/10/dracula-un-dead-dramatic-reading-w.html; see also *Dracula the Un-dead: The Official Site for the Sequel to the Original Classic*, online: www.draculatheun-dead.com/Dracula_the_Un-Dead/Home.html.

2 Dacre Stoker & Ian Holt, *Dracula the Un-dead* (Toronto: Viking Canada, 2009).

3 *Ibid* at 413.

4 *Ibid*.

In what follows, I argue that as changes in the technologies of communication mediate, shape, or determine the nature of human interaction, IP law can be understood as a technology or technique of mediation between creative expression and the propertization of information. I suggest that the extension of copyright, trademark, and rights of publicity to fictional characters and authors helps set the boundaries of economic and social expression in the global media environment of the twenty-first century in a process of transpropertization whereby different forms of IP protection overlap. Transproperty claims are made and maintained in this mediated environment, in part using a specialized form of communicative activity — branding.

B. MEDIA ECOLOGY AND TRANSPROPERTIZATION

Media ecology is an approach to the study of communication that focuses on the social and psychological effects of new communication technologies. From this perspective, each communication technology (or medium) has the potential to influence the relationship between technology, representations, and society.[5] For media ecologists, the dominant technology of communication in a society functions as a transformative agent. Indeed, it is common in histories of communication to partition history into periods governed, respectively, by oral tradition, print media, electronic media, and digital technology. The media ecological perspective, also known as *medium theory*, traces its origins to Canadian geographer and economist Harold Adams Innis, and was later popularized by Marshall McLuhan.

Innis wrote that different societies were shaped to a large extent by the particular space-binding or time-binding nature of their dominant medium of communication. Space-binding technologies, such as papyrus, parchment, and paper, helped create empires that needed to exert control over great expanses, while time-binding media, such as stone and clay, were dominant in traditional societies whose control extended not over territory but through time.

Electronic media have changed the media ecology dramatically. Technological tools extend human activity, and shape and control the scale

---

5 See Harold Innis, *The Bias of Communication* (Toronto: University of Toronto Press, 1951) and Marshall McLuhan, *Understanding Media: The Extension of Man* (New York: McGraw-Hill, 1964). Other writers associated with media ecology are Walter Ong, Edmond Carpenter, James Carey, Neil Postman, and Mark Poster.

of human association and action. McLuhan argued that as the world was wired into a planetary-wide information grid, it also contracted, becoming a global village. Yet, while McLuhan identified electronic communication with an oral tradition of dialogue and dialectic, traditional values, and philosophical speculation, Innis recognized that the speed and distance covered by electronic communication would likely enhance the process of centralization and imperialistic power, rather than fulfill McLuhan's hope of a new tribal society. Innis also recognized the strong connection between media industries and markets. For Innis, the commercialization of communication created "new oligopolies of knowledge as corporate media acquired increased power to manipulate and direct public opinion."[6]

Political scientist Ronald Diebert adopts a media ecological approach in his analysis of the influence of global communications on international politics. For Diebert, media ecology provides "an open-ended, nonreductionist, thoroughly historicist view of human existence that emphasizes contingency over continuity both in terms of the trajectory of social evolution and the nature and character of human beings."[7]

In the cultural sphere, Henry Jenkins[8] explores how storytelling across different media platforms is emerging as a dominant characteristic of the digital, global entertainment industries. Jenkins describes how media characters appear in film, television, publishing, and promotional outlets as components of an expanded fictional universe. Jenkins calls such cross-platformed cultural properties *transmedia*. He also explores the role of fan communities in supporting media franchises and shaping the meaning of media texts. Optimistically, Jenkins claims that new digital media help create a participatory culture.[9]

Elsewhere, I have argued that the metaphors we use to describe technology, processes of communication, and our sense of communal and per-

---

6 Stephen Kline, Nick Dyer-Witherford, & Greig de Peuter, *Digital Play: The Interaction of Technology, Culture, and Marketing* (Montreal: McGill-Queen's University Press, 2003) at 32.

7 Ronald J Deibert, *Parchment, Printing, and Hypermedia: Communication in World Order Transformation* (New York: Columbia University Press, 1997) at 17–18.

8 Henry Jenkins, *Convergence Culture: Where Old and New Media Collide* (New York: New York University Press, 2006) at ch 3.

9 *Ibid* at 3; Lawrence Lessig also discerns the possibility of a participatory RW (read-write) culture emerging in contrast to the R/O (read only) culture dominated by the advocates of the current copyright regime: see Lawrence Lessig, *Remix: Making Art and Commerce Thrive in the Hybrid Economy* (New York: Penguin Press, 2008) at 28 [Lessig, *Remix*].

sonal identity serve as tools that set boundaries for possible interactions.[10] The terms *media* and *mediation* in this sense refer to various technologies and techniques of formalization; media contain or embody the normative social rules that bound the horizon of human interaction[11] and involve various sets of power relations. If we think for a moment of the past 125 years of mass media-created content as the resource pool from which contemporary cultural texts, images, and artifacts are created, we can see the transformation of that cultural pool into an enclosed, privatized space defined and regulated by IP laws and practices that limit our use and, more importantly from my perspective, our understanding of cultural properties.

Following Diebert's analysis of the historically contingent nature of the media landscape, and the use of language and metaphor as a medium of social construction, I will explore an ecological shift in IP law that began at the same time as a shift in the communication mediascape in which elements of fictional properties and their owners are governed by a net of legal protection including copyright, trademark, and the common law right of publicity.[12] Just as Jenkins argues that transmedia cultural texts make no sense unless we examine them across each of the media platforms they occupy, I suggest that in the contemporary communication context it makes sense to see cultural properties as *transpropertied*, where the multi-faceted

---

10 Daniel M Downes, *Interactive Realism: The Poetics of Cyberspace* (Montreal: McGill-Queens University Press, 2005); see also Jonathan Zittrain, *The Future of the Internet and How to Stop It* (New Haven: Yale University Press, 2008) and Lawrence Lessig, *Code and Other Laws of Cyberspace* (New York: Basic Books, 1999) for similar discussions of the ways that Internet architecture and computer software "regulate" and mediate human interactions.

11 Other researchers have focused on particular media as the agents of change, and on a broad understanding of "media." From Parsons and Habermas comes the debate over money as a medium of human interaction. Sociologists look at power as a mediating force and, in his insightful discussion of the transformation of the public sphere by the institutionalization of "professional communications" practiced by public relations firms and political spin doctors, Leon Mayhew posits a notion of influence as a concept that mediates human interactions: see Talcott Parsons, "On the Concept of Influence" in Talcott Parsons, ed, *Sociological Theory and Modern Society* (New York: Free Press, 1967); see also Jurgen Habermas, *The Theory of Communicative Action. Lifeworld and System: A Critique of Functionalist Reason*, translated by Thomas McCarthy, vol 2, 3d ed (Boston: Beacon Press, 1985) at 178–85 and Leon H Mayhew, *The New Public: Professional Communication and the Means of Social Influence* (Cambridge: Cambridge University Press, 1997). The common thread in these writers is the understanding that language, technology, and communicative practices shape and limit our actions with regards to the social construction of reality.

12 As my concern is with expression in the creative economy, I will not include a discussion of patent laws here.

character of such intellectual artifacts requires the interaction and protection of formerly distinct forms of IP protection.

C. CHANGING ORGANIZATION OF THE MEDIA INDUSTRIES

Critical media ecology demonstrates that changes to the mediated environment happen over time and in relation to changes in other aspects of social, economic, and political life. While many argue that dramatic changes to the creative economy and the media environment occurred in the last decade of the twentieth century, it can be shown that change was underway as early as the 1970s. It was during this period that IP legislation and caselaw showed a shift in the nature and language of IP protection.

Political economist Ronald Bettig describes how in the United States "there has always been a tension between the monopolistic character of intellectual property and its normative goal of enhancing the flow of information and ideas."[13] Indeed, the United States began as a pirate nation, promoting various versions of the free flow of information, and the democratic importance of education, until the second half of the twentieth century when culture came to be seen as exportable and the foundation of an intangible, information economy.[14] Bettig argues that to eliminate competition and to reduce risks associated with the unpredictable nature of media success, companies in the media sector seek "to increase their control over production, distribution, and sales within their market sector, and to increase their economic and political power"[15] in the following ways: through horizontal mergers — characteristic of turn-of-the-twentieth-century mergers; through vertical integration — dominant in the 1920s and 1930s and best demonstrated by the Hollywood studio system and the concentration of film under the control of a few major studios; through conglomeration between the end of World War II and the mid-1970s during which period companies diversified holdings to stabilize incomes without worrying about in-

---

13 Ronald V Bettig, *Copyrighting Culture: The Political Economy of Intellectual Property* (Boulder: Westview Press, 1996) at 7–8.

14 See James Boyle, *The Public Domain: Enclosing the Commons of the Mind* (New Haven: Yale University Press, 2008); see also Lewis Hyde, *Common as Air: Revolution, Art, and Ownership* (New York: Farrar, Straus, & Giroux, 2010) on the transformation of copyright from the late eighteenth century to the present.

15 Bettig, above note 13 at 37.

dustry-specific business cycles; and, finally, through cross ownership after the 1970s with a focus on core businesses and related lines.[16]

This last type of industrial organization begins to blur the distinctions between different media and characterizes them all as communications or information industries. To Bettig's periodization we could add a fifth. Since the 1990s global media industries have emerged — first in synergistic conglomeration, then later in a reshuffling in response to technological developments and global economic shocks.

The technological convergence of various forms of media content through digitization is linked to economic globalization in the cultural industries as well as a shift in regulations affecting those industries, including IP laws. Thus, the conditions interacting in a transmediated environment of propertied information were being developed in the 1970s — twenty years before the existence of the commercialized Internet, digital downloading, and the *Digital Millennium Copyright Act*.[17] IP has been a blind spot in writing about the effects of convergence on the media industries.

D. CHANGING METAPHORS IN INTELLECTUAL PROPERTY

Since the 1970s both policy discussions and copyright cases have used the language of property. Before transformations to IP came to a sort of confluence during that decade, a number of similar ideas about the relationship between creators and the public can be discerned. For Litman, copyright was a bargain between the creator and the public; for Boyle, copyright was a limited monopoly granted in exchange for access to the intellectual or cultural commons; for Hyde, intellectual property actually took the form of a cultural commons (rather than the view that the commons was that which remained after propertization) that allowed for stinted property rights.[18] Each of these views of cultural material was transformed by the practices of the entertainment industries in the twentieth century and by the rise of the information economy which can be categorized by the following conditions: work-for-hire; and the propertization of culture and information and

16 *Ibid*.

17 *Digital Millennium Copyright Act*, Pub L No 105-304, 112 Stat 2860 (1998).

18 Jessica Litman, *Digital Copyright* (Amherst, NY: Prometheus Books, 2001) [Litman, *Digital Copyright*]; see also Boyle, above note 14; Hyde, above note 14.

the resulting net of overlapping IP protection, which has been applied to cultural and other forms of expression as though they were fungible.

For Hyde, the transformation in IP since the seventies is the result of three factors. First, the rise of a knowledge economy means that it matters for a variety of companies that they be able to control their know-how and their goods: "it matters that the law help them guard the rights that ownership is supposed to bring, especially the exclusive right to charge fees for access."[19] Second, "[i]n the 1990s, digital copying and the global Internet appeared almost simultaneously, and all of a sudden many of the useful old fences simply disintegrated."[20] Finally, following the fall of the Soviet Union as an oppositional force to free market capitalism,

> the West entered a period of unabashed market triumphalism, during which many things long assumed to be public or common — from weather forecasting to drinking water, from academic science to the "idea" of a crustless peanut butter and jelly sandwich — were removed from the public sphere and made subject to the exclusive rights of private ownership.[21]

For Bettig, IP became a strategic asset in the information economy. For the entertainment industries, copyright laws, in particular rights of copy, distribution, and performance, permit the transfer of ownership claims in information and cultural goods.[22] Increasingly in the entertainment industries it is the transfer of such claims that monetizes IP.

The contemporary media sector is made up of content producers, distributors, and companies that deal in the purchase and exchange of copyrights and trademarks for films, television programs, sound recordings, and books. Kembrew McLeod calls this new commodity cultural software.[23] I refer to this new revenue stream as the cultural industries' *back catalogue*, a term derived from the recording industry that refers to the previously released stock of recordings owned or controlled by the major record labels. Control of cultural software is tied to consolidation of media ownership as large, globally-situated firms have the resources to purchase and trade the back catalogues of other companies.

---

19 Hyde above note 14 at 10.

20 *Ibid*.

21 *Ibid* at 12.

22 Bettig, above note 13 at 81.

23 Kembrew McLeod, *Owning Culture: Authorship, Ownership, and Intellectual Property Law* (New York: Peter Lang, 2001) at 2.

By the mid-1990s, IP generated close to $240 billion USD, over 20 percent of world trade.[24] Since our concern here is with the fictional characters that make up a substantial portion of the cultural resource pool, some comic-book-related figures are instructive. By the late 1970s, Marvel generated most of its business through the licensing of Marvel characters for merchandise. Of the $800 million the movie *Spider-Man* generated, Marvel received more than $50 million. Similarly, DC Comics generated several billion dollars in income related to Superman between 1969 and 1984.[25] Comic-book-based superhero films are well represented in the top grossing films of all time. Of the top twenty films, Marvel's *Avengers* (2012) ranks third while *Spider-Man* (2002) and *Spider-Man 2* (2004) rank thirteenth and eighteenth. DC Comics's property Batman appears in the *Dark Knight* (2008) at fourth and the *Dark Knight Rises* (2012) at eighth.[26]

The copyright system allows copyright holders to take legal action against unauthorized users of their works (traditionally companies that made unauthorized or unlicensed copies of books, sound recordings, or films for commercial distribution); to transfer rights to other parties; and to recycle their existing stock of properties in derivative works in new mediated forms as a source of royalties. These activities allow copyright owners to recover the costs of initial production, to generate revenue over time, and to monetize in new and innovative ways those works they control. The assumption that copyright is necessary to the smooth functioning of the media has a long history in the US entertainment industries.[27]

E. COPYRIGHT

Litman suggests that in the late seventies advocates of copyright owners "began to come up with different descriptions of the nature of copyright, with an eye to enabling copyright owners to capture a greater share of the

24 *Ibid* at 6; see Jeremy Rifkin, *The Age of Access: The New Culture of Hypercapitalism: Where All of Life is a Paid-For Experience* (New York: Putnam, 2000) at 8. Jeremy Rifkin notes that by the end of the 1990s cultural production in the world was beginning to eclipse physical production in commerce and trade.

25 Britton Payne, "Super Grokster: Untangling Secondary Liability, Comic Book Heroes and the DMCA, and a Filtering Solution for Infringing Digital Creations" (2006) 16:3 Fordham Intell Prop Media & Ent LJ 939 at 944, n 20.

26 IMDB, "All-Time Box Office: USA," online: IMDB www.imdb.com/boxoffice/alltimegross.

27 Litman, *Digital Copyright*, above note 18 at 23–25.

value embodied in copyright-protected works."[28] She argues that the shift in metaphors for copyright protection, from the bargained limited monopoly granted to creators to a model of incentives without which the creator will withhold their work, led, ultimately, to a transformation of copyright "into the right of a property owner to protect what is rightfully hers."[29] According to Litman, "by changing metaphors, we somehow got snookered into believing that copyright had always been intended to offer content owners extensive control, only, before now, we didn't have the means to enforce it."[30]

In addition to a shift in the way stakeholders characterize copyright, two new ideas that proved fundamental to the current global IP landscape emerged from changes in the 1976 US revision of copyright. First, the fundamental unit of copyright became the ephemeral copy of information in RAM. An unforeseen consequence of this seemingly minor provision of the statute has come to mean that all computer-mediated communication must conform to copyright rules.[31] Further, the 1976 revision eliminated the registration requirement, meaning that since that date *no new* creations have entered the public domain. According to Hyde, this means that every creative work comes with a presumptive right to exclude. He argues that it is impossible for a work *not* to be thought of as property: "[T]here is no statutory provision whereby a work can be given to the public domain . . . . [T]he law includes a 'termination of transfer' provision whereby rights revert to the creator after a certain number of years no matter what licenses or contracts have been signed."[32]

These two changes to copyright at the dawn of the information economy create what Hyde calls the *second enclosure* wherein "the law grants nearly perpetual private rights to nearly every creative expression appearing in any media now known or yet to be discovered!"[33]

Technology changes the copyright landscape: previously, copyright focused on the relationship between creators of works of authorship and disseminators of them. Computers and the Internet make each computer a potential publisher — copyright must be enforceable to all or it becomes obsolete. It makes sense for copyright holders to argue that unlicensed, pri-

---

28 *Ibid* at 79.
29 *Ibid* at 81.
30 *Ibid* at 86.
31 *Ibid* at 28.
32 Hyde, above note 14 at 58.
33 *Ibid* at 59.

vate copying is piracy because all activities in the digital age of technological, economic, and regulatory convergence can be seen as *commercial* activities that fall under the umbrella of the expanding IP regime.

Writers like McLeod and Lessig argue that IP law misunderstands the nature of creative activity[34] (a position I also take), but it is clear that copyright, trademark, and publicity rights are being used in a coherent way in the United States in cases that posit creative work and celebrities as propertized. Let us turn to the two other prongs of cultural propertization: trademark and publicity rights.

F. TRADEMARK

Trademark is a very different kind of instrument than copyright because there is no "bargain" between the creator and society. Copyright, in the American context, is based in the US Constitution,[35] whereas trademark comes from the regulation of commercial activity first codified in the US *Commerce Act*.[36] The trademark is a sign of ownership and the intent to sell and is outlined in the *Lanham Act*.[37] In particular, Section 43(a) of the *Lanham Act* creates a civil cause of action against any person who identifies his product in a way that is likely to cause consumer confusion regarding the product.[38]

The basis of trademark infringement is that someone else's use of a particular trademark can confuse consumers, thereby directing profits away from the trademark owner and, potentially, diffusing the impact of the trademark itself. By the 1980s trademark cases under the *Lanham Act* were launched to protect fictional characters, which traditionally fell outside the bounds of copyright law.[39] Unlike copyright, trademarks are valid as long as

---

34 McLeod, above note 23; see also Lessig, *Remix*, above note 9.

35 US Const art I, § 8, cl 8.

36 *Act of 4 February 1887*, Pub L No 49-41, c 104, 24 Stat 379 (*Interstate Commerce Act*).

37 *Lanham (Trade-Mark) Act of 1946*, c 540, 60 Stat 427 (codified as amended in 15 USC ch 22) [*Lanham Act*].

38 *Ibid*, s 1125 (a); see also Stephanie Dotson Zimdahl, "A Celebrity Balancing Act: An Analysis of Trademark Protection Under the Lanham Act and the First Amendment Artistic Expression Defense" (2005) 99:4 Nw UL Rev 1817 at 1823.

39 See Lawrence L Davidow, "Copyright Protection for Fictional Characters: A Trademark-Based Approach to Replace *Nichols*" (1984) 8:4 Colum VLA Art & L 513, for an early attempt to show that a trademark theory of character protection might be more suitable than copyright in dealing with fictional characters.

they remain in use, strengthening the sense that trademarks are the property of their owners.

G. PUBLICITY RIGHTS

The right of publicity has its roots in the right of privacy, articulated by Samuel Warren and Louis Brandeis.[40] As originally conceived, the right of privacy was intended to protect private individuals from intrusion into their lives by the press. Writing seventy years later, William Prosser identified four distinct torts included within the right of privacy: (1) intrusion upon the plaintiff's seclusion; (2) public disclosure of embarrassing private facts; (3) publicity which places the plaintiff in a false light in the public eye; and (4) appropriation of the plaintiff's name or likeness.[41] What has become known as the right of publicity evolved from Prosser's fourth category. Prosser recognized that right of publicity cases generally involved the wrongful or unauthorized use of a celebrity's likeness or name. The focus of the right of publicity is on protecting the celebrity's identity from economic exploitation and providing an incentive for creativity and achievement. "This has led some commentators to observe that a *Lanham Act* claim for false endorsement is practically the federal equivalent of the state protected right of publicity."[42]

Over time, a number of states enacted right of publicity legislation. In some, led by Indiana and Tennessee and a case initiated by the estate of Elvis Presley, a celebrity's publicity rights extend after the death of the celebrity and are "descendible"; that is, they can be exploited by heirs or, as in the case of Presley, companies who purchase those rights.[43]

H. TRANSPROPERTIED FICTIONAL CHARACTERS

Historically, it was very difficult to obtain IP protection for fictional characters. The test was generally based on the distinctiveness of the characters, and generally the answer was negative. Courts ruled that there was no copyright protection for characters like Sam Spade unless it could be shown that

40 Samuel D Warren & Louis D Brandeis, "The Right to Privacy" (1890) 4:5 Harv L Rev 193.

41 William L Prosser, "Privacy" (1960) 48:3 Cal L Rev 383.

42 Zimdahl, above note 38 at 1825 [footnote omitted].

43 Mark Bartholemew, "A Right is Born: Celebrity, Property, and Postmodern Lawmaking" (2011) 44:2 Conn L Rev 301 at 315–17.

the stories were about the characters to the extent that that the character constituted the story. However, as commentator Leslie Kurtz points out, an author may be free to use his or her characters in new stories (which was the issue between author Dashiell Hammett and Warner Brothers in the Sam Spade case), but so is everyone else.[44]

Things changed in the 1970s. Following a DC Comics case,[45] trademark started to be applied to these fictional characters; names, nicknames, physical appearances, and costumes of the superheroes could now be trademarked. For example, George Lucas was able to trademark the Darth Vader, R2D2, and C3PO characters. A new kind of convergence occurred where courts viewed copyright, trademark, and unfair competition claims as though they were coequal and necessarily interrelated.[46] According to Helfand:

> Courts have replaced the great uncertainty previously facing character owners with an equally problematic, overly protective doctrine for fictional characters. The distinctions between, and goals of, intellectual property laws that have existed in other contexts have become nonexistent when applied to fictional characters. As a result, the role of public domain doctrine is uncertain.[47]

With greater protection possible for fictional characters, a shift has occurred in the nature of characters considered for protection. Copyright law affords protection for the "expression" of a graphic character. This expression may refer to its appearance or the "pattern" that identifies it. With literary characters the inquiry ordinarily focuses on whether a character is sufficiently distinctive or well-developed to command protection, and whether such distinctive development has been copied.[48] With visual characters, on the other hand, like animated cartoons or comic book heroes, copyright

---

44 Leslie A Kurtz, "The Methuselah Factor: When Characters Outlive Their Copyrights" (1994) 11:2 U Miami Ent & Sports L Rev 437 at 455 [Kurtz, "Methuselah Factor"].

45 Robert E Anderson, "Alternatives to Copyright Law Protection of Graphic Characters: The Lanham Act and Antidilution Statutes" (1991) 13:2 Hastings Comm & Ent LJ 179. In 1978 Filmation was sued by DC Comics for using a character very like Plastic Man. As Robert Anderson writes,"[p]rotectable 'ingredients' recognized in this circuit include the names and nicknames of entertainment characters, as well as their physical appearances and costumes, but not their physical abilities or personality traits" at 185.

46 See Michael Todd Helfand, "When Mickey Mouse Is as Strong as Superman: The Convergence of Intellectual Property Laws to Protect Fictional Literary and Pictorial Character" (1992) 44 Stan L Rev 623 at 623.

47 *Ibid* [footnote omitted].

48 Kurtz, "Methuselah Factor," above note 44 at 438.

already finds it easier to afford protection. In the case of visual characters, the test is to compare "the plaintiffs' and defendants' characters to see if the similarity between them is sufficient for infringement."[49] According to Kurtz, "[t]he more an audio-visual character resembles a cartoon character in its physical existence, the more it should be treated as a cartoon character for the purposes of determining copyright infringement."[50] By the early 1990s the law had become much more hospitable to character protection than it used to be.[51]

According to Moffat, "[t]rademark law now protects much more than just names, words, and logos. Instead, a wide variety of designs, product configurations, and even the overall 'look and feel' of a product . . . function as indicators of source [that the 'look and feel' points to a particular owner] and are, therefore, protectable under the Lanham Act."[52]

The tension between expression and property can be seen in the growing importance of trademark and publicity rights cases that challenge aspects of cultural expression that would seem to fall under the umbrella of copyright. Significantly, whereas (at least until the 1970s) the dominant view of copyright was in the form of a bargain between creators and the broader society, trademark was not based on such a bargain — it was commercial policy designed to protect consumers from misleading claims made by commercial entities in the marketplace.

For example, *Universal City Studios v Nintendo Co* involved a dispute over two gorillas — Donkey Kong and King Kong. The various owners of the King Kong mark had diluted the character to the point where the gorilla was too indistinct to be protected. Unfortunately for Universal, multiple parties over the years had granted licences in the character of King Kong for a variety of uses.[53]

A few years earlier in a different action, Universal had argued that King Kong and his story were in the public domain. Now Universal was asserting

49 *Ibid* at 439.

50 See Leslie A Kurtz, "The Independent Legal Lives of Fictional Characters" (1985) 1986:3 Wis L Rev 429 at 471 [Kurtz, "Legal Lives"].

51 Jessica Litman, "Mickey Mouse Emeritus: Character Protection and the Public Domain" (1994) 11:2 U Miami Ent & Sports L Rev 429 at 430.

52 Viva R Moffat, "Mutant Copyrights and Backdoor Patents: The Problem of Overlapping Intellectual Property Protection" (2004) 19:4 Berkeley Tech LJ 1473 at 1495 [footnote omitted].

53 *Universal City Studios Inc v Nintendo Co Ltd*, 746 F2d 112 (1984); see also Kurtz, "Legal Lives," above note 50; also see Anderson, above note 45, for discussions of *Universal v Nintendo*.

rights in King Kong, claiming it had acquired these rights through a settlement with the son of the original story's author and claiming secondary meaning and distinctiveness for the character. The court found that the confusion among licensors made it difficult to argue that any consumer could attribute King Kong products to a single source. Universal failed to establish secondary meaning. In a later development in the same case, the district court found that Universal's *Tiger* video game infringed Nintendo's *Donkey Kong* because the tone and feel of Donkey Kong was closely replicated in *Tiger*.[54] Still, even though Universal lost in its attempts both to poach and then to protect King Kong, other companies have also practiced manipulative strategies to propertize fictional characters and elements.

For example, in an unusually collaborative move, publishing rivals DC Comics and Marvel jointly registered the terms *superhero* and *supervillain* in 1979. Even though the terms were so commonly used as to be unsupportable by trademark claims, no one challenged the trademark registration and it was approved two years later.[55]

Superhero costumes can also be protected — cases involving Superman, Wonder Woman, and Marvel character suits as "skins" in computer games have all been decided in favour of the owners of the trademarks.[56] The issue in such cases is "whether the author has added new, protectable expression to a derivative work not in the public domain. When the author adds such expression, those aspects of the character are still a protected derivative work."[57] Thus, the development of new costumes, changing the race or gender of a character, or changing relationships in the storyline can either be judged derivative works belonging to the copyright holder or new works that can be afforded protection.[58] Such rights are of significant commercial value.

Take the case of Superman. While the heirs of Jerry Siegel and Joe Shuster will reclaim the copyright to Superman in 2013, these rights do not necessarily extend to the Man of Steel's appearances in other media. In a protracted and complicated legal battle, the heirs reclaimed copyright of characters and story elements, while the defendants (DC Comics and its parent

---

54 *Universal City Studios v Nintendo*, 615 F Supp 838 (1985). Nintendo also was awarded damages on its claim for tortious interference with contract, punitive damages, and attorneys' fees; see Kurtz, "Legal Lives," above note 50 at 492, n 349.

55 Payne, above note 25 at 952–53, n 64.

56 *Ibid* at 952–53 and 992–93.

57 Helfand, above note 46 at 654.

58 Compare the situations of Marv Wolfman and Neil Gaiman.

company Time Warner Inc) were found not guilty of sweetheart deals that diminished the revenues owed the estates of Siegel and Shuster. Siegel's heirs won a 2008 ruling that entitled them to profits earned by DC Comics.[59] However, once the rights revert to the heirs, they would be able to exploit the transmedia potential of Superman in competition with Time Warner.[60] However, two appeal cases in October 2012 and January 2013 saw the 2008 ruling overturned and the claim for copyright termination by the Shuster estate denied.[61]

Similarly, the estates of comic book artists Jack Kirby and Joe Simon sued Marvel for control of characters including the Fantastic Four, the Hulk, and Captain America, all subjects of Hollywood films in the past decade.[62] Such copyright cases create an additional layer of complexity for media companies whose business depends on the exploitation of fictional characters and their transfer between companies engaged in different forms of media.[63] For instance, one can certainly see how *articulations of corporate authorship* play into fan debates over whether or not the Siegel and Shuster estates should regain their rights to Superman, with many fans expressing concern that the quality of the character's representations would inevitably suffer due of their lack of institutional resources and managerial acumen. Sampling fan posts on the web, Santo reports that comic book fans accept the corporate role in producing and maintaining characters over time: "the only reason the Superman character is what it is today (and worth all that

---

59 Dave McNary, "Warner Bros. wins 'Superman' case" *Variety* (8 July 2009), online: www.variety.com/2009/biz/news/warner-bros-wins-superman-case-1118005806.

60 Die Trich Thrall, "The Final Fate of SUPERMAN: Lawsuit Settled in Favor of Creators Heirs — DC and Warner Brothers Will Lose All Rights in 2013" *Variety* (14 August 2009), online: Die Trich Thrall http://dietrichthrall.wordpress.com/2009/08/14/the-final-fate-of-superman-lawsuit-settled-in-favor-of-creators-heirs-dc-and-warner-brothers-will-lose-all-rights-in-2013.

61 Eriq Gardner, "Warner Bros. Wins Blockbuster Victory in Legal Battle for Superman" *Hollywood Reporter* (10 January 2013), online: The Hollywood Reporter www.hollywoodreporter.com/thr-esq/warner-bros-wins-blockbuster-victory-410871.

62 Jay Goldberg, "King Kirby and the Amazin' Terminatin' Copyrights: Who Will Prevail?!?" (Summer 2010) 2:1 American University Intellectual Property Brief 10, online: Digital Commons http://digitalcommons.wcl.american.edu/cgi/viewcontent.cgi?article=1011&context=ipbrief; see also John Molinaro, "Who Owns Captain America? Contested Authorship, Work-For-Hire, and Termination of Rights under the Copyright Act of 1976" (2004) 21:2 Ga St U L Rev 565.

63 Mike Fleming Jr, "Fox Insiders: No Galactus Talks with Marvel" *Deadline* (6 August 2012), online: Deadline.com www.deadline.com/2012/08/fox-insiders-no-galactus-talks-with-marvel

money)," writes one poster, "is because of DC's work shepherding him over the past 70 years." Another fan writes "Superman didn't become the major property he is today because of [Siegel and Shuster]. He became this property because DC used and marketed him in this way."[64]

I. TRANSPROPERTIED PERSONALITIES

Where publicity rights come into conflict with other forms of IP, celebrities can invoke the *Lanham Act* and claim that their economic rights have been affected by the offending work.

In 1993, under the California right of publicity,[65] game show hostess Vanna White sued Samsung Electronics America on the grounds that a Samsung ad depicting a blond wigged robot standing at a *Wheel of Fortune* wheel constituted an appropriation of her likeness. When White won the case in 1994, it became possible for celebrities to assert property rights in the attributes that constitute their personae.[66]

Another *Lanham Act* case, involving musicians Edgar and Johnny Winter, who appeared in a comic book as mutated and depraved worm-creatures called the Autumn Brothers, was decided in favour of the comic book because the work was deemed suitably transformative such that the brothers' right of publicity was not challenged by the portrayal. "[T]he California Supreme Court held that the comic book's use of the Winter Brothers' image was protected by the First Amendment guarantee of freedom of expression. To arrive at its holding, the court utilized, for only the second time, a test that it developed in 2001 — a copyright based 'fair use' test for the right of publicity."[67]

Common law and state laws around publicity rights have shifted from personal to proprietary rights. In addition, publicity rights have been treated as descendible rights that can be protected after the death of a celebrity. These changes in IP laws as they affect creative works have, in effect, created a loose net of IP protection that forms the enclosure that legal scholars

---

64 Avi Santo, "The Lone Ranger and the Law: Legal Battles over Corporate Authorship and Intellectual Property Management, 1939–1942" (2012) 29:3 Critical Studies in Media Communication 185 at 199–200 [endnote omitted].

65 *California Civil Code*, § 3344.

66 See John R Braatz, "*White v Samsung Electronics America*: The Ninth Circuit Turns a New Letter in California Right of Publicity Law" (1994) 15 Pace L Rev 161 at 221.

67 Gil Peles, "The Right of Publicity Gone Wild" (2004) 11:2 UCLA Ent L Rev 301 at 310 [footnotes omitted].

have described on the information and cultural commons. These protections have also changed the way that cultural goods are characterized in the marketplace. Indeed, a specialized form of communicative action has developed with the express purpose of guaranteeing (or at least encouraging) property claims in the intangible economy. This form of communication is branding.

J. BRANDING: THE LANGUAGE OF TRANSPROPERTIZATION

The value added to cultural entities is encased, enclosed, and enforced in the concept of the "brand." As culture increasingly became the battleground of business competition, the frenzied obsolescence of fashion was introduced into all manner of cultural endeavours, providing "a means to accelerate the pace of consumption not only in clothing, ornament, and decoration but also across a wide swathe of life-styles and recreational activities (leisure and sporting habits, pop music styles, video and children's games, and the like)."[68] Starting in the 1960s with advertising's realization that marketing the experience was as important as, if not more important than, advertising the specific and unique qualities of particular products, the slow process of reifying IP began.[69] If the culture industry worked largely through the commodity, argue Lash and Lury, the global culture industry works through brands.[70]

Some writers consider the brand as "the good name of a product, an organization or a place; ideally, linked to its identity."[71] From this perspective, a brand is a "promise of value."[72] Others see branding as a creative tool with which to create emotional links between audience/consumers and companies/products. Marc Gobé calls this emotional branding.[73] More central to this discussion is the recognition that brand stories are constructions

---

68 Thomas Frank, *The Conquest of Cool: Business Culture, Counterculture and the Rise of Hip Consumerism* (Chicago: University of Chicago Press, 1997) at 25 [footnote omitted].

69 Jim McGuigan, *Cool Capitalism* (London: Pluto, 2009).

70 Scott Lash & Celia Lury, *Global Culture Industry: The Mediation of Things* (London: Polity, 2007) at 25.

71 Robert Govers & Frank Go, *Place Branding. Glocal, Virtual and Physical Identities, Constructed, Imagined and Experienced* (London: Palgrave MacMillan, 2009) at 12.

72 *Ibid.*

73 Marc Gobé, *Emotional Branding: The New Paradigm for Connecting Brands to People* (New York: Allworth Press, 2001) at 8–15.

that appeal to a variety of senses and whose intent is, like Pavlovian psychology or social engineering, to influence our behaviour. As marketing guru Scott Bedbury puts it, "[t]he concept of the brand — the Platonic idea, if you will — creates a response in its audience without the audience's seeing the product or directly experiencing the service."[74]

Yet, as Rifkin writes, "[m]arketing is the means by which the whole o f the cultural commons is mined for valuable potential cultural meanings that can be transformed by the arts into commodifiable experiences, purchasable in the economy."[75] Further, he observes, "the culture, like nature, can be mined to exhaustion."[76]

The roles and nature of branding have changed over the past generation as branding evolves into a new kind of commercial speech, not geared to describing goods in the marketplace nor the reputation of a supplier of goods, services, or lifestyles, but as a mark of property and as the very process through which forms of expression and culture are deemed property. Branding is the activity for establishing and maintaining a reputation in the marketplace, thereby asserting one's property rights in image, attributes, name, etc. One of the tests that US courts use to decide whether a particular person's publicity rights are descendible is whether that person asserted her publicity rights as property during her lifetime.

Companies have emerged in the past twenty years whose specific purpose is to propertize celebrities, using the language of branding and the conflated assumptions shared by copyright, trademark, and publicity rights cases that "image" is property. These companies claim that resources like classic films and Hollywood icons deserve "our attention and respect."[77] While companies are willing to pay extraordinary sums for the rights to commercially exploit celebrities such as Elvis or Muhammad Ali,[78] others exploit the knowledge and contacts of their heirs in order to control the new publicity rights as property and to brand those celebrities as products.[79]

---

74 Scott Bedbury & Stephen Fenichell, *A New Brand World: 8 Principles for Achieveing Brand Leadership in the 21st Century* (New York: Viking, 2002) at 12–13.

75 Rifkin, above note 24 at 171.

76 *Ibid* at 247.

77 MODA Entertainment, "About," online: http://modaentertainment.com/about.html.

78 Richard Verrier, "Elvis Will Live On — At Least Digitally" *Los Angeles Times* (7 June 2012) online: Los Angeles Times http://articles.latimes.com/2012/jun/07/business/la-fi-ct-virtual-elvis-20120607.

79 For example, Stephen Humphrey Bogart sued MODA claiming that the company exploited his knowledge of Hollywood and his contacts over a three-year period. "Bogart and

K. STOKER AND HOLT: RE-ESTABLISHING THE FAMILY BUSINESS

Returning to our point of origin, how can we look at an event like the publication of Stoker and Holt's novel as an example of convergence era, transpropertied media? Recall the conditions described earlier that characterize the new IP environment: works-for-hire, the propertization of culture using branding, and overlapping IP protection. How do these appear in the Stoker story?

Bram Stoker died before his work became popular. His widow successfully sued the makers of *Nosferatu*, but, failing to see all copies of the film destroyed and having her control of the property rejected by Universal Studios as they prepared a sequel to *Dracula*, she gave up her battles to assert control over the work in the United States by the mid-1930s. The German film, produced in 1922 by Prana Films, tried to avoid the copyright suit by changing character names (Count Dracula becomes Count Orlock) and plot elements (the death of Orlock by exposure to daylight) to distance the film from Stoker's novel. A British court ordered all copies of the film destroyed, although a print survived and surfaced in the United States. The lawsuit bankrupted Prana Films.[80]

Dracula entered the public domain in the United States in 1899 due to an error in the registering of the work. It entered the public domain in the UK and other countries bound by the *Berne Convention* in 1962.[81] Dacre Stoker and Ian Holt wrote the *Un-dead* sequel in 2009 based on a 125-page manuscript appearing in Stoker's papers. Stoker the younger also prepared a book with scholar E Miller, editing a "lost" notebook by the elder Stoker.[82] While not working for hire, the collaborations characteristic of Dacre Stoker's endeavours suggest a corporatized method of cultural production.

Bacall's Son Sues Bosses" *Contact Music* (28 January 2009) online: Contact Music www.contactmusic.com/news/bogart-and-bacalls-son-sues-bosses_1093112.

80 Jonathan Bailey, "Dracula vs. Nosferatu: A True Copyright Horror Story" *Plagiarism Today* (17 October 2011), online: Plagiarism Today www.plagiarismtoday.com/2011/10/17/dracula-vs-nosferatu-a-true-copyright-horror-story.

81 See *Lugosi v Universal Pictures*, 603 P 2d 425 (Cal Sup Ct 1979) at n 4; see also Kathryn M Foley, "Protecting Fictional Characters: Defining the Elusive Trademark-Copyright Divide" (2009) 41:3 Conn L Rev 921, for a recent discussion about the difficulties in protecting fictional characters using copyright claims.

82 Elizabeth Miller & Dacre Stoker, eds, *The Lost Journal of Bram Stoker: The Dublin Years* (London: Biteback Publishers, 2012).

Regarding the propertization of culture, Stoker claims to give the original novel the "respect" it deserves. He has "rescued" the orphaned novel from the public domain and has started to mine his ancestor's cultural pool for gold. Indeed, Stoker offers the kind of respect that custodial ownership affords. He uses the web and licensing firms to manage the estate of the writer, to manage the brand, and to create a chill on future work based on the writer's characters.[83] In 2009, in the months leading up to the publication of *Dracula the Un-dead*, promotion and licensing were handled by MODA Entertainment.[84] Bram Stoker LLC is based in the United States and represents the direct descendants of the author in the United Kingdom. The company has consolidated the international rights and trademarks of the Bram Stoker Estate. Dacre Stoker manages the company for rights in the US and South America, while Stoker's grandson, Robin MacCaw, manages them for the UK, Europe, and the Far East. Bram Stoker Estate LLC treats "all things Stoker" as a family business, freely applying US common law publicity rights to establish Bram Stoker as a brand.[85]

Through these activities the Stoker family business directs its activities to each of the forms of IP we have described. The performance of the work in Toronto echoes a live reading staged by Bram Stoker to demonstrate his copyright over the original Dracula. Dacre Stoker continues to publish, to make live appearances as the custodian of the estate, and to work in other media, including documentary film. Assuming the validity of descendible publicity rights, the Stokers operate on behalf of the financial interests of a celebrity who died a hundred years ago.

---

83 The Stoker estate has several websites active, including: Dracula meets Stoker, online: www.draculameetsstoker.com; Stoker & Holt, above note 2; Bram Stoker: Official Website for the Bram Stoker Estate, online: www.bramstokerestate.com; a Facebook page, online: www.facebook.com/BramStokerEstate; and a Tumblr page, online: www.tumblr.com/tagged/bram-stoker-estate.

84 MODA Entertainment handled the book launch, the public reading in Toronto, a screening of the 1931 film starring Bela Lugosi, and a *Dracula the Un-dead* credit card. As of 2012, licensing of Stoker merchandise is handled by Cribbs Consulting, a New York City firm who, according to *Forbes* magazine, specialize in managing dead celebrities; see Jake Paine, "Managing the Dead Celebrities Corporations Love" *Forbes* (25 October 2011), online: Forbes www.forbes.com/sites/dorothypomerantz/2011/10/25/managing-the-dead-celebrities-corporations-love.

85 In the afterword to *Dracula the Un-dead*, co-author Ian Holt promotes the re-establishment of Dracula and Bram Stoker as Stoker-controlled brands by stating, "if you don't see the bat-logo, it's not *official* Bram Stoker Dracula merchandise": Stoker & Holt, above note 2 at 423 [emphasis added].

L. CONCLUSION

Understanding changes in IP law as part of a changing media ecology allows us to connect changing practices in the creative and intangible economy and to see the role of IP in a new light. Intellectual property law is a medium of control in the digital age. It helps set the boundaries of interaction and, to a degree, reality definition. From this, we can make two claims.

First, it is possible, and, I would argue appropriate, to talk of an ecology of IP based on the propertization of information that began in law reform and in caselaw during the 1970s. As copyright, trademark, and the right of publicity converge, it makes sense to talk about the objects of their protection as transpropertied goods. Second, the mechanism or communicative practice associated with this new ecology of information is branding, which has changed from a technique of marketing to an informal medium of control alongside these changes in law.

A final warning, dear reader. The success of claims made under the new climate of overlapping IP protection is not the pertinent issue. In fact, the results of such cases have been mixed — *White v Samsung* established property rights in personality, while the Winter brothers lost their case on the basis that freedom of expression, particularly where creative transformation has occurred, trumps both the right to publicity and the *Lanham Act*. The estates of Siegel, Shuster, Kirby, and Simon have had mixed results. The important point to remember is that the practice of branding personalities (fictional, living or dead) presupposes their status as property and, over time, cases and law reform will reflect the practice.

TWELVE

Punishment, Private Style: Statutory Damages in Canadian Copyright Law

JOÃO VELLOSO & MISTRALE GOUDREAU

ABSTRACT (EN): Copyright infringement is a widespread contemporary behaviour of commercial enterprises and private individuals. To restrain such infringements, legislators and courts have used punitive and statutory damages to sanction infringing activities and, in doing so, have incorporated the punitive aspects of criminal law into the private sphere without the procedural guarantees generally associated with criminal law. This chapter provides a detailed analysis of the courts' decisions on statutory damages in the Canadian copyright context. The authors argue that such a punitive path is fundamentally based on utilitarian and behaviourist approaches. Based on social sciences scholarship, the authors question the effectiveness of such approaches to reduce copyright violations (deterrence). The authors also situate this process of private style punishment in a more general trend of asymmetric incorporation of criminal justice norms (Legomsky, 2007) and discuss the systemic incoherencies created by such practices.

RÉSUMÉ (FR): La violation du droit d'auteur est un comportement contemporain très répandu chez les entreprises commerciales et les individus. Afin de mettre fin aux violations, les législateurs et les tribunaux ont recouru à des dommages punitifs et préétablis pour sanctionner les actes de contrefaçon et, ce faisant, ont incorporé les aspects punitifs du droit criminel dans la sphère privée sans les garanties procédurales généralement associées au droit criminel. Ce chapitre procède à une analyse détaillée des décisions ayant accordé des dommages préétablis dans le contexte du droit d'auteur canadien. Les auteurs soutiennent qu'une telle voie punitive se base fondamentalement sur des approches utilitaristes et comportementales. Se basant sur les enseignements des sciences sociales, ils questionnent l'efficacité de telles approches pour freiner les violations du droit d'auteur (théorie de la dissuasion). Les auteurs discutent de ce procédé, style de peine privée, dans une tendance plus générale à l'incorporation asymétrique des normes de justice criminelle (Legomsky, 2007) et montrent les incohérences systémiques créées par une telle pratique.

A. INTRODUCTION

In 1997, a statutory damages regime was introduced in the *Copyright Act*,[1] as part of the second major phase of copyright reform in Canada.[2] Under this regime, plaintiffs in copyright cases have the ability to elect to receive an award of statutory damages in lieu of actual damages and profits.[3] The copyright holder may make such election at any time before final judgment.[4]

The government has clearly stated the underlying reasons for the adoption of the regime:

> A copyright owner who commences proceedings for infringement must prove not only the infringement, but also the losses suffered as a result. However, it is often difficult, sometimes impossible, to prove such losses because evidence as to the extent of infringement is usually difficult and/or expensive to find. Statutory damages alleviate this difficulty by guaranteeing a minimum award of damages once infringement is established. They also ease the evidentiary burden on the plaintiff in proceedings for

---

1 RSC 1985, c C-42 [*Copyright Act*].

2 Phase I took place in 1988 [*An Act to Amend the Copyright Act and to Amend Other Acts in Consequence Thereof*, RSC 1985, c 10 (4th Supp)] and Phase II in 1997 [*An Act to Amend the Copyright Act*, SC 1997, c 24] [*An Act to Amend the Copyright Act (1997)*]. After that, the government announced that it was embarking on a permanent process of copyright reform and introduced a series of bills, some of which resulted in legislative modifications, while others died on the order paper after the dissolution of Parliament: see Industry Canada, *A Framework for Copyright Reform* (Ottawa: Industry Canada, 2002), online: Industry Canada www.ic.gc.ca/eic/site/crp-prda.nsf/eng/rp01101.html. The last Bill C-11, which modifies the statutory damages regime, received royal assent on 29 June 2012 and became the *Copyright Modernization Act*, SC 2012, c 12.

3 *An Act to Amend the Copyright Act (1997)*, above note 2, introducing s 38.1.

4 *Ibid*.

infringement, deter future infringements, reduce the cost of litigation and encourage the parties to settle matters out of court.[5]

The Canadian legislature, in enacting section 38.1, clearly had in mind the presumed deterrent purpose of statutory damages. The statute itself includes "the need to deter other infringements of the copyright in question" among the relevant factors that the court should take into consideration when setting the award.[6] The alleged deterrent effect of statutory damages is also one of the reasons why the United States *Copyright Act* allows for such remedy.[7] In this paper, we will first provide an overview of the Canadian legislative scheme and the courts' implementation of the regime. In the second part, we will use a socio-legal studies approach to question the basis of deterrence theory and to show how inadequate it is to use such discourses in a copyright regime. We conclude that the Canadian statutory damages regime is fairly outbalanced and insufficient to compensate for commercial violations and for excessively punishing non-commercial infringements.

---

5 Industry Canada, *Fact Sheet on Copyright Remedies* (Ottawa: Industry Canada, 2011), online: Industry Canada www.ic.gc.ca/eic/site/ippd-dppi.nsf/eng/ip00090.html.

6 See *Copyright Act*, above note 1, s 38.1(5); the other factors are the good faith or bad faith of the defendant and the conduct of the parties before and during the proceedings.

7 It has been said that the Canadian regime was modelled on the US provisions: Malcolm E McLeod, "Recent Copyright Developments: the Canadian Perspective" (1998) 15 CIPR 39 at 49. The US *Copyright Act of 1909*, Pub L No 60-349, 35 Stat 1075 provided that statutory damages "shall not be regarded as a penalty" at 101(b). However, this provision was repealed in 1976 and now courts stress the deterrent purpose of statutory damages; see *FW Woolworth Company v Contemporary Arts Inc*, 344 US 228 (1952): "Moreover, a rule of liability which merely takes away the profits from an infringement would offer little discouragement to infringers. It would fall short of an effective sanction for enforcement of the copyright policy. The statutory rule, formulated after long experience, not merely compels restitution of profit and reparation for injury, but also is designed to discourage wrongful conduct. The discretion of the court is wide enough to permit a resort to statutory damages for such purposes. Even for uninjurious and unprofitable invasions of copyright, the court may, if it deems it just, impose a liability within statutory limits to sanction and vindicate the statutory policy" at 233; see also *St Luke's Cataract & Laser Inst, PA v Sanderson*, 573 F 3d 1186 at 1206 (11th Cir 2009); *E & J Gallo Winery v Spider Webs Ltd*, 286 F 3d 270 at 278 (5th Cir 2002); *FEL Publications, Ltd v Catholic Bishop of Chicago*, 754 F 2d 216 at 219 (7th Cir 1985). For a deeper analysis, see Pamela Samuelson & Tara Wheatland, "Boundaries of Intellectual Property Symposium: The Boundaries of Copyright and Trademark/Consumer Protection Law: Statutory Damages in Copyright Law: a Remedy in Need of Reform" (2009) 51:2 Wm & Mary L Rev 439 at 461.

B. THE CANADIAN STATUTORY DAMAGES REGIME

Certainly the amounts of statutory damages set in the legislation are meant to discourage future infringers. The court may award an amount between $500 and $20,000 in respect of each work or subject matter infringed by the defendant. The award covers each separate infringement with respect to each work. Subsection 38.1(2) of the *Copyright Act* allows for a smaller award when the defendant had acted in good faith: the award may be reduced to between $200 and $500 if the defendant "was not aware and had no reasonable grounds to believe that [he or she] had infringed copyright." The courts will not often consider that a person had no reasonable ground to believe a work was not protected since "no person is entitled to assume, without inquiry, that a work published anonymously is not the subject of copyright."[8] It has been said that "it may be relatively difficult for a defendant to take advantage of this subsection . . . ."[9]

There is a possibility for further reductions if more than one work or subject matter is involved.[10] Furthermore, the 2012 legislative modifications, adding paragraphs 38.1(1)(a) and (b) to the Act, make the amount of statutory damages contingent upon the commercial or non-commercial purpose of the infringement. For non-commercial infringers, the damages range between $100 and $5,000 for all infringements in a single proceeding for all works.

There could be situations where even the minimum award would be grossly disproportionate to the infringement. For example, the regime reserved to statutory damages claimed by collective societies shows that the goal is not compensatory; they can ask for an amount not less than three times, nor more than ten times the amount of applicable royalties.[11]

The regime is also very severe for a one-time infringer. In 2012, iTunes charged $1.29 CAD for the downloading of a single Justin Bieber song[12] and his CDs were on sale at HMV for $12.99 CAD.[13] Assuming that a song is a single work, the minimum award, even taking into account the good faith

8 See *Slumber-Magic Adjustable Bed Co v Sleep-King Adjustable Bed Co* (1984), 3 CPR (3d) 81 at 118 (BCSC) referring to *Gribble v Manitoba Free Press Co*, 40 Man R 42, [1931] 3 WWR 570 at 575, [1932] 1 DLR 169 (Man CA) at paras 28–30.

9 John S McKeown, *Fox Canadian Law of Copyright and Industrial Designs*, 3d ed (Scarborough: Carswell, 2000) at 661; for a rejection of this defence in the context of s 38.1(2), see *Nicholas v Environmental Systems (International) Ltd*, 2010 FC 741 at para 104 [*Nicholas*].

10 *Copyright Act*, above note 1, s 38.1(3).

11 *Ibid*, s 38.1(4).

12 Apple iTunes, online: http://itunes.apple.com/us/album/boyfriend-single/id513122978.

13 HMV, online: www.hmv.ca/Products/Detail/665016.aspx.

of a non-commercial infringer and the range set in the 2012 legislative modifications, would be $100 per proceeding, so seventy-seven times the actual damages. In practice, even the criminal regime can be more lenient for the offender. Let us take the example of a first-time shoplifter of a CD. It is true that a "theft under $5,000" (shoplifting) conviction can lead to fines and possibly jail time (up to two years if an indictable offence or up to six months if charged as a summary offence),[14] but many judges will not inflict any sanctions to a first-time shoplifter and, usually, the charges will be withdrawn if the offender successfully completes a diversion program. In this regard, Crown attorneys may conditionally drop the charges or choose to use other extrajudicial measures such as imposing community service, donation to a local charity, or attendance at a lecture dissuading people from shoplifting.[15]

In other words, in some cases, the statutory damages regime may (and more likely will) impose a harsher sanction than the criminal law regime. It is to be noted that the maximum set by the legislation may also be insufficient to cover all the unauthorized profits made by the defendant and the actual damages suffered by the plaintiff.[16] However, as the Act reserves the plaintiff's right to also ask for exemplary or punitive damages,[17] the courts have not pre-set maximum limits for the awards.

So what was the impact of the regime? How did the courts exercise this new discretion granted to compensate copyright holders?

To properly understand the impact of the legislative provision, one must first know that courts, when faced with the problem of an unproven scale of damages, did and still do resort to making rough quantification. In *Louis Vuitton Malletier SA v Singga Enterprises (Canada)*,[18] the Federal Court explained

14 See *Criminal Code*, RSC 1985, c C-46, ss 334(b) and 787(1).

15 On those diversion programs, see Public Safety Canada, *Adult Offender Diversion Programs*, No 3:1 (Ottawa: Public Safety, January 1998), online: www.publicsafety.gc.ca/res/cor/sum/cprs199801-eng.aspx.

16 *Copyright Act*, above note 1, s 35 allows the plaintiff to claim both an account of profits and damages. In *Microsoft Corporation v 9038-3746 Québec Inc*, 2006 FC 1509 [*9038-3746 Québec Inc*], the court doubted that the maximum of "$500,000 cover[ed] a full accounting of the profits the defendants have derived from infringing [the plaintiff's] rights" at para 115.

17 See *Copyright Act*, above note 1, s 38.1(7); McKeown, above note 9, questions the wisdom of the rule: "to the extent that deterrence has been considered by the court in exercising its discretion under section 38.1 punitive or exemplary damages should not be awarded" at 662.

18 2011 FC 776.

the strategy developed by the judiciary. For instance, when infringing sales had been proven after an execution of an Anton Piller order, the courts would evaluate the damages "in the amount of $3,000 where the defendants were operating from temporary premises such as flea markets, $6,000 where the defendants were operating from conventional retail premises, and $24,000 where the defendants were manufacturers and distributors of counterfeit goods."[19] Courts have also made some allowance for the effects of inflation[20] and have increased the amounts when the defendant was "engaged in continuous and blatantly recidivist activities over a period of time."[21] It was also accepted that courts could award punitive damages in cases of copyright infringement,[22] with amounts varying from $5,000 to $250,000.[23]

The principles underlying the regime of statutory damages, therefore, were not foreign to Canadian judges. Courts had granted lump sum awards in cases where the actual damages were hard to prove, and punitive damages in order to punish infringers and deter future violations. However the range of damages allotted by the *Copyright Act* and the integration of the regime in civil proceedings are, in our view, problematic.

1) The Problematic Range of Damages

From 1997 to 2011, there had been about twenty-two reported cases where statutory damages were awarded.[24] Some of them caught the legal commun-

---

19 *Ibid* at para 129, referring to *Nike Canada Ltd v Holdstart Desigh Ltd et al*, T-1951085 FC (unreported).

20 *Ibid* at para 130, referring to *Louis Vuitton Malletier SA v Yang*, 2007 FC 1179 at para 43 [*Yang*]; and *Louis Vuitton Malletier SA et al v 486353 BC Ltd et al*, 2008 BCSC 799 at paras 59–60 [*486353 BC Ltd*].

21 For example, by relying on the frequency of inventory turnover, *ibid* at paras 131–33 referring to *Yang*, above note 20 at paras 43–44; see also *486353 BC Ltd*, above note 20 at paras 67–72.

22 See, for instance, those early cases: *Durand et Cie v La Patrie Publishing Co*, [1960] SCR 649; *Hay & Hay Construction Co Ltd v Sloan et al* (1957), 12 DLR (2d) 397; *Pro-Arts Inc v Campus Crafts Holdings Ltd et al* (1980), 110 DLR (3d) 366 (Ont HC); *Schauenburg Industries Ltd v Borowski* (1979), 25 OR (2d) 737 (Ont HC); *Orbitron Software Design Corp v MICR Systems Ltd* (1990), 48 BLR 147 (BCSC).

23 See *France Animation SA c Robinson*, 2011 QCCA 1361 at para 249 and the decisions referred to. The Superior Court had awarded punitive damages at $1 million, the Court of Appeal reduced the amount to $250,000. Leave to the Supreme Court has been granted.

24 *Wing v Velthuizen* (2000), 9 CPR (4th) 449, 197 FTR 126 (TD); *Ritchie v Sawmill Creek Golf & Country Club Ltd* (2003), 27 CPR (4th) 220, 2003 CanLII 24511 (ON SC); *LS Entertainment Group Inc v Formosa Video (Canada) Ltd*, 2005 FC 1347; *9038-3746 Québec Inc*, above note 16; *Film City Entertainment Ltd v Chen*, 2006 FC 1150; *Film City Entertainment Ltd v Golden*

ity's attention because of the amount of damages involved.[25] For instance, the amount of statutory damages was set at about $300,000 in *Telewizja Polsat SA v Radiopol Inc*;[26] and in *Microsoft Corporation v 9038-3746 Québec Inc*, the award was $500,000 (that is, the maximum of $20,000 per work for twenty-five works), joint with an award of punitive damages of $200,000[27] and a lump sum representing solicitor/client costs and disbursements close to $1,600,000.00.[28] The maximum of $20,000 per work was also awarded in two cases, *Louis Vuitton Malletier SA v 486353 BC Ltd*[29] and *Louis Vuitton Malletier SA v Yang*.[30] Statutory damages in excess of $100,000 were granted in two more cases.[31]

In some decisions, the judges raised the issue of proportionality. In *Telewizja Polsat SA v Radiopol Inc*,[32] the defendants had decoded the signals of a television producer and had made them available to the public via the Internet. The evidence showed that 2,009 programs had been illegally decoded but that the plaintiff has suffered little damages. Justice Lemieux of the Federal Court stressed that there "should be some correlation between actual damages and statutory damages even though section 38.1 does not speak of actual damages"[33] and lowered the award to $150 per work, arguing

---

Formosa Entertainment Ltd, 2006 FC 1149; *Telewizja Polsat SA v Radiopol Inc*, 2006 FC 584 [*Telewizja Polsat*]; *Video Box Enterprises Inc v Lam*, 2006 FC 546; *Duclow v Atlantic Business Consultants Ltd*, 2006 NSSM 26; *Lari v Canadian Copyright Licensing Agency*, 2007 FCA 127 [*Lari*]; *Yang*, above note 20; *Don Hammond Photography Ltd v The Consignment Studio Inc*, 2008 ABPC 9 [*Don Hammond*]; *486353 BC Ltd*, above note 20; *Microsoft Corporation v PC Village Co Ltd*, 2009 FC 401; *Microsoft Corporation v 1276916 Ontario Ltd*, 2009 FC 849; *Nicholas*, above note 9; *Entral Group International Inc v MCUE Enterprises Corp*, 2010 FC 606 [*Entral Group*]; *Sixty Spa v 3127885 Canada inc*, 2010 QCCS 2754 [*Sixty Spa*]; *Louis Vuitton Malletier SA v Singga Enterprises (Canada) Inc*, 2011 FC 247; *Society of Composers, Authors, and Music Publishers of Canada v IIC Enterprises Ltd*, 2011 FC 1088; *Century 21 Canada Limited Partnership v Rogers Communications Inc*, 2011 BCSC 1196 [*Century 21*]; *Setanta Sports Canada Ltd v 840341 Alberta Ltd*, 2011 FC 709.

25 John Cotter & Tara James, "Microsoft Wins Maximum Award in Counterfeit Software Dispute" *The Lawyers Weekly* (9 March 2007), online: The Lawyers Weekly www.lawyersweekly.ca/index.php?section=article&articleid=439.

26 *Telewizja Polsat*, above note 24.

27 *9038-3746 Québec Inc*, above note 16.

28 *Microsoft Corporation c 9038-3746 Québec Inc*, 2007 FC 659.

29 *Yang*, above note 20.

30 *Ibid*.

31 See *Lari*, above note 24 (statutory damages $500,000, punitive damages $100,000, solicitor-client costs $100,000); see also *Entral Group*, above note 24 (statutory damages $105,000, punitive damages $100,000, solicitor-client costs $70,000).

32 *Telewizja Polsat*, above note 24.

33 The court was quoting McKeown, above note 9 at 660.

that subsection 38.1 (3) allowed him to reduce the per work statutory minimum. In other cases as well, the courts have been concerned that the minimum statutory damages appeared disproportionate to the actual damages and used their discretion accordingly.[34] These rulings show that the courts are concerned when the actual damages suffered by the plaintiffs are much lower than the statutory damages, which they can claim under the *Copyright Act*. In such cases, statutory damages are used much more as harsh sanctions than as civil compensation, which is fairly problematic.

2) The Punishment — Private Style of the Legislative Scheme

The available damages are problematic not only because of their range, but also because they are a form of punishment operating in a "private style" (paraphrasing Marc Galanter[35]). Statutory damages are primarily remedies in civil settings, but they are also aimed at punishing the defendant and deterring future infringements. In so doing, these damages are usurping the traditional primary goals of criminal law and the discourse of criminal law-based theories of punishment (deterrence, retribution, and denunciation). However, it has been established in criminal law that criminal punishment should be imposed only on those deserving the stigma of a criminal conviction.[36] Because of its punitive aspects, the stigma associated with a criminal conviction, and the potential abuses of the sovereign state, criminal law has historically developed a set of rights and safeguards for the defendant (*due process*), limiting consequently the range and strength of executive action in most democratic societies. For instance, the accused has a right against self-incrimination,[37] he or she is presumed innocent and, therefore, the state must prove the elements of the infraction beyond reasonable doubt, specific standards of fault (*mens rea*) are constitutionally required with respect of certain offences,[38] the accused is protected from

---

34 *Don Hammond*, above note 24; *Sixty Spa*, above note 24; *Century 21*, above note 24.

35 Marc Galanter, "Punishment, Civil Style: Punishment Outside the Criminal Law in the Contemporary United States" (1991) 25 Isr LR 759.

36 See, for a recent reaffirmation, *R v Roy*, 2012 SCC 26.

37 *Canadian Charter of Rights and Freedoms*, Part I of the *Constitution Act, 1982*, being Schedule B to the *Canada Act 1982* (UK), 1982, c 11, s 11(c) [*Charter*].

38 See, for example, *R v Beatty*, 2008 SCC 5, where the Court decided that, in the offence of dangerous operation of a motor vehicle causing death, "the requisite *mens rea* may only be found when there is a 'marked departure' from the standard of care expected of a reasonable person in the circumstances of the accused" at para 33.

cruel and unusual punishment,[39] and harsher penalties imply additional procedural guarantees.[40]

In civil law cases, those privileges or rights are diminished or inexistent. In civil proceedings, a defendant may be forced to testify[41] and the facts need only to be proven on a balance of probabilities. The defendant's intent is not relevant in principle and the defendant who in good faith believes he or she was authorized to use the copyrighted work will still be held liable for statutory damages. Of course, as mentioned in paragraph 38.1 (5)(a), the courts will take into account the good or bad faith of the defendant in setting the award of statutory damages, but the infringer still has to face the minimum rate. As it is sometimes three times what the normal royalties would have been, even the user acting in good faith may still be punished and in a relatively severe way.

Accordingly, the uses of statutory damages result in an *overpenalization* of non-commercial users acting in good faith, since the statutory damages imposed are disproportionately higher than the actual damages, which is even more problematic because of the lower standards of legal guarantees in civil proceedings. Paradoxically, this statutory approach is not enough to repair the injustice resulting from the commercial infringements (*underpenalization*). For instance, in *Microsoft Corporation v 9038-3746 Quebec Inc*,[42] the court doubted that the maximum of $500,000 was equivalent to the profits the defendants derived from infringing the plaintiff's rights.[43] So the maximum imposable statutory damages may also be significantly lower than the actual damages and plaintiffs often will also seek compensation via punitive damages.

When granting punitive damages, the courts have been very careful in identifying the function of those awards. The Supreme Court of Canada

---

39 *Charter*, above note 37, s 12.

40 *Ibid*, s 11(f) (right to trial by jury).

41 See, for example, *Code of Civil Procedure*, RSQ, c C-25, ss 302 and 309; see also Léo Ducharme & Charles-Maxime Panaccio, *Administration de la preuve*, 4e ed (Montréal: Wilson & Lafleur, 2010) at 240. In the context of *ex parte* Anton Piller orders related to copyright cases, the arguments based on the protection against self-incrimination were dismissed: see McKeown, above note 9 at 633–34. In some of the cases awarding statutory damages, the defendant had failed to produce documents and appropriate records: see *9038-3746 Québec Inc*, above note 16; *486353 BC Ltd*, above note 20. The courts felt that it was a factor, which weighed in favour of an award of statutory damages at the highest end of the scale.

42 *9038-3746 Québec Inc*, above note 16.

43 *Ibid* at para 115.

stated that "there has been 'a substantial consensus . . . that the general objectives of punitive damages are punishment (in the sense of retribution), deterrence of the wrongdoer and others, and denunciation.'"[44] Punishment, deterrence, and denunciation should be reserved for those cases where, borrowing Cory J's words, "the jury or judge expresses its outrage at the egregious conduct of the defendant."[45] Similar comments may be made concerning the statutory damages regime. However, by assuming those functions without integrating the due process safeguards of the criminal law and by imposing minimum awards, the regime may not be achieving the intended results. As criminologists and legal scholars have demonstrated, harsher punishment does not necessarily have an effect on crime rates.[46] In fact, severity and indiscriminate punishment may lead to more and worse deviant behaviour, as we will demonstrate later in this chapter.

This private style of punishment raises some issues, especially regarding the use of statutory damages to administer copyright conflicts. As discussed above, statutory damages overpenalize non-commercial infringements and are not enough to compensate the harm caused by commercial violations. Moreover, this penalization occurs administratively and not as a traditional criminalization process, or to use Stephen Legomsky's words: it is an "asymmetric incorporation of criminal justice norms,"[47] a technique that borrows punitive discourses, enforcement structures, and resources from criminal justice without the corresponding guarantees of criminal trials. The use of statutory damages is a problematic innovation in the penal field in this sense and the efficacy of their goal of deterring other infringements (as expressed in paragraph 38.1(5)(c)) is questionable.

---

44 *Whiten v Pilot Insurance Co*, 2002 SCC 18 at para 68, as quoted in *de Montigny v Brossard (Succession)*, 2010 SCC 51 at para 51.

45 *Hill v Church of Scientology of Toronto*, [1995] 2 SCR 1130 at para 196.

46 See, for instance, the *Archambault Report* (Canadian Sentencing Commission, *Report — Sentencing Reform: A Canadian Approach* (Ottawa: Minister of Supply and Services Canada, 1987)), a key Canadian reference on the topic that reviewed more than 900 studies on deterrence and concluded that none of them could prove or provide consistent evidence that deterrence theory achieved its goals of deterring crime. See also, in the same sense and more contemporary, Anthony Doob & Cheryl Webster, "Sentence Severity and Crime: Accepting the Null Hypotheses" (2003) 30 Crime & Justice 143.

47 Stephen H Legomsky, "The New Path of Immigration Law: Asymmetric Incorporation of Criminal Justice Norms" (2007) 64:2 Wash & Lee L Rev 469.

C. A SOCIO-LEGAL CRITIQUE OF THE STATUTORY DAMAGES SCHEME

We will criticize the regime in two parts: first, by questioning the basis of deterrence theory itself; and second, by setting out how counterproductive it may be to punish severely and indiscriminately all kinds of non-commercial infringements.

1) Beyond Rational Choice and Deterrence

Deterrence theory is based on utilitarian assumptions about human beings that are fairly anchored in an eighteenth and nineteenth-century humanist context. Philosophical ideas do not necessarily become obsolete over time and the Greek classics are a good reminder of this. However, the behaviour theory that is behind deterrence theory is very dated and quite simplistic. Utilitarianism basically argues that human beings are rationally and hedonistically driven, seeking to maximize pleasure and minimize pain. It is based on this assumption that Jeremy Bentham and many others after him (including contemporary judges) have argued that punishment deters certain behaviour because individuals rationally make utilitarian choices to minimize pain. Two hundred years later, utilitarian behaviour theory does not make a lot of sense, especially when you consider the rise of psychology and sociology as scientific discourses aiming, among other things, to explain human action from individual and societal points of view. Even the contemporary approaches that focus on individual and rational aspects of human behaviour (e.g., *behaviourism* and *routine active theory*) add other variables and learning elements to classical rational choice theory.[48]

Our critique of deterrence theory suggests that its assumptions about human behaviour (and human nature) are not supported by contemporary understandings of approaches of human agency (individual capacity to

48 Exception made to some economic models that are essentially theoretical and fairly qualitatively disconnected from reality, for example, Milton Friedman and the neo-utilitarianism of the Chicago School. For grounded critiques of rational choice approaches in economy see among others: Louis Dumont, *From Mandeville to Marx: the Genesis and Triumph of Economic Ideology* (Chicago: University of Chicago Press, 1977); Maurice Godelier, *Rationality and Irrationality in Economics* (New York: New Left Books, 1972); Karl Polanyi, *The Great Transformation* (Boston: Beacon Press, 1971); Marshall D Sahlins, *Stone Age Economics* (Chicago: Aldine-Atherton, 1972); Marshall D Sahlins, *Culture and Practical Reason* (Chicago: University of Chicago Press, 1976).

act independently, to make one's own choices). Literature reviews on deterrence studies overwhelmingly indicate that there is no evidence to support it.[49] Deterrence does not work because it is based on a bad behaviour theory, which assumes that it is part of human nature to maximize pleasure and minimalize pain, universalizing a particular set of behaviours as if they were applicable to all human beings in all cultural contexts. Multiple contributing factors influence how individuals behave in society and a utilitarian-hedonistic calculus is not often among them. There are many other variables playing an important role in human agency, which reduce considerably the real capacity of agents to act freely (free will). There is a consensus among twentieth century social theorists[50] that agency is somehow related to social structures and individuals will make their choices in a fairly limited universe of possibilities.

Pierre Bourdieu, for instance, suggests that human beings rely on different (symbolic) capitals (economic, cultural, political, relational, etc.) that will substantially affect individual choices.[51] Moreover, he demonstrates that even what we usually take as our most intimate choices (e.g., taste) are not the result of strictly individual choices, but of determinations at different levels.[52] He argues that actors who occupy a given social space will share, more or less, the same habitus, tastes, political opinions, etc., and that choices are often embodied (his notion of *habitus* borrowed from Norbert Elias) and not the result of rational calculations. In short, individuals learn how to behave and most of the time they will simply act without thinking of how they should interact in everyday life. While Anthony Giddens takes a more theoretical approach in his *structuration theory*,[53] his theory recog-

49 Above notes 46–48.

50 Just to list the most important scholars in the agency/structure debate: Norbert Elias, Talcott Parsons, Peter Berger and Thomas Luckmann, Pierre Bourdieu, Anthony Giddens, and Michel Foucault. The ways they conceptualize human agency are not exactly the same, but they share the idea that the distinction between free will and determinism is a false dichotomy, pointing to notions of agency that relate to both individual choices and determinations (conditions, limitations of choices).

51 Pierre Bourdieu, *Outline of a Theory of Practice*, translated by Richard Nice (Cambridge: Cambridge University Press, 1977); Pierre Bourdieu, *Practical Reason: On the Theory of Action*, translated by Randal Johnson et al (Stanford: Stanford University Press, 1998).

52 Pierre Bourdieu, *Distinction: A Social Critique of the Judgement of Taste*, translated by Richard Nice (Cambridge: Harvard University Press, 1984).

53 Anthony Giddens, *New Rules of Sociological Method: A Positive Critique of Interpretative Sociologies* (Stanford: Stanford University Press, 1976); Anthony Giddens, *Central Problems in Social Theory: Action, Structure and Contradiction in Social Analysis* (Los Angeles: University of California Press, 1979) [Giddens, *Central Problems*]; Anthony Giddens, *The*

nizes the practical aspects of the reflexivity of the actors (and the limited capacity of monitoring reflexively their actions) and also that structures are "both medium and outcome of the reproduction of practices"[54] (*duality of structure*). In short, human action is essentially action in structures and the reflexivity of agents is not exclusively rational calculation driven by hedonism as assumed by classic utilitarianism.

Giddens, Bourdieu, and other pillars of twentieth century social theory argue similarly: behaviour and human action happen through structures, through sets of norms and values that are already present in society before we are born and many of them continue to exist without major changes after we die. Individuals learn to behave through socialization and normalization processes (family, school, work, prison, etc.). Contemporary social scientists fairly agree on the existence of a process of introjection and/or incorporation of social norms and values into the body/self (individual subjectivity). However, they have obviously different positions on how such processes occur. Their positions on how human beings are socialized vary mainly from school of thought or research area to another as each will put more emphasis on his or her own approach. For instance, the way a sociologist will conceptualize it will not be the same as an anthropologist or a psychologist, but even in the same disciplinary context they will vary marginally (e.g., constructivists and interactionists in sociology or behaviourists and cognitivists in psychology). In other words, social scientists will agree that there is somehow a socialization (to use George H Mead's term)[55] or normalization process (to use Norbert Elias's and Michel Foucault's concepts),[56] but they disagree on how this happens. That hedonism is part of human nature and that individuals intrinsically make utilitarian calculi aiming to maximize pleasure and minimize pain is simply an assumption that is not backed by most contemporary behavioural theories. Certainly utilitarian reasoning is popular in Western cultures and fairly common in the legal

---

Constitution of Society: Outline of the Theory of Structuration (Cambridge: Polity Press, 1984).

54 Giddens, *Central Problems*, above note 53 at 5.

55 George H Mead, *Mind, Self, & Society from the Standpoint of a Social Behaviourist* (Chicago: University of Chicago Press, 1962).

56 Norbert Elias, "On Transformations of Aggressiveness" (1978) 5:2 Theory & Society 229; Norbert Elias, *The Civilizing Process* (Oxford: Blackwell, 2000); Michel Foucault, "Truth and Juridical Forms" in *Power: Essential Works of Foucault, 1954–1984* (New York: New Press, 1974); Michel Foucault, *Discipline and Punish: The Birth of the Prison* (New York: Vintage Books, 1995).

and economic fields. But this reasoning cannot be applied indiscriminately to all. Opposing utilitarianism rationality, we can argue that most people refrain from engaging in deviant activities because they adhere to social norms (e.g., "killing is not good") and not because of the potential sanctions involved. These socialization processes are so powerful that, for instance, when someone enters the army he or she will have to learn, will have to normalize, the killing of other people.[57]

Deterrence theory will generally disregard socio-anthropological scholarship on this topic. Deviance is a normal human behaviour present in every society as Emile Durkheim, one of the founding fathers of sociology, pointed at the end of the nineteenth century in *The Rules of Sociological Method*.[58] Actually, he goes even further and argues that deviance reinforces social norms and supports the progress and development of society (i.e., the role of individual genius). Fifty years later, Claude Lévi-Strauss argued analogously in the anthropological field,[59] pointing to the importance of the other, taboos, and interdictions to reaffirm the identity of a group (or of individuals). Social-constructivists and symbolic-interactionists in the 1960s and 1970s (labelling theory)[60] added that society creates deviancy since what is normal and deviant is ultimately a social construct and the result of different (institutional) processes that classify and reclassify a given act as acceptable or not. Back to the "killing is not good" example, labelling approaches taught us that the meaning of the act of killing is socially constructed depending on the social context, and is not derived only from the act itself. For instance, killing may be labelled as deviant (murder) or, in the other extreme, as a desirable behaviour (war hero). More contemporary critics like Jack Katz[61] examine how emotions and other non-utilitarian rationalities play a determinant role in deviance. Katz has shown that it is

---

57 Stanley Kubrick's *Full Metal Jacket* (1987) is a good cinematographic representation of this.

58 Émile Durkheim, *Les règles de la méthode sociologique*, 23d ed (Paris: Flammarion, 1987); the original edition was published in 1894.

59 See, especially, Claude Lévi-Strauss, *The Elementary Structures of Kinship* (Boston: Beacon Press, 1969) and Claude Lévi-Strauss, *Structural Anthropology* (New York: Basic Books 1963).

60 See, for example, Howard S Becker, *Outsiders: Studies in the Sociology of Deviance* (London: Free Press of Glencoe, 1963); Erving Goffman, *The Presentation of Self in Everyday Life* (London: Allen Lane, 1969); Erving Goffman, *Stigma: Notes on the Management of Spoiled Identity* (Englewood Cliffs: Prentice-Hall, 1963); David Matza, *Becoming Deviant* (Englewood Cliffs: Prentice-Hall, 1969).

61 Jack Katz, *Seductions of Crime: Moral and Sensual Attractions in Doing Evil* (New York: Basic Books, 1988).

cool to deviate, to do evil, especially when you are young,[62] and in that sense the poor and the rich alike are emotionally driven and can commit crimes when they are seduced in a given context.[63]

The bottom line is that no one has the *Criminal Code* as a pillow book, not even criminal law professors or practitioners. Supposedly, even if a potential offender knew the *Criminal Code* by heart, it would certainly not mean that she or he would rationalize the process of committing (or not) any criminalizable acts in function of the eventual sanctions that may be imposed. Thus, assuming that non-commercial users will stop to think about statutory damages before copyright infringement is simply naïve, and yet, it is a fiction or myth shared in the legal field.[64] Even if one can make a statistic relation between harsher statutory damages and conforming to IP and copyright regulations, there are so many other variables at play that it is virtually impossible to establish a causality link between these two variables.

We argue that users are adhering to a way of experiencing art and intellectual work that is shaped and driven by mass consumption since the beginning of the twentieth century. As Walter Benjamin argued in his famous essay, "The Work of Art in the Age of Mechanical Reproduction," "mechanical reproduction of art changes the reaction of the masses toward art."[65] It makes a lot of sense that users educated by a cultural industry favouring copies will end up copying as well.[66] We were socialized to consume copies as originals and today, in an age of electronic reproduction, consumers have

---

62 Men account for 80 percent of adults charged, and most accusations occur when people are aged sixteen to twenty-five, peaking around eighteen: see Shannon Brennan, *Police-Reported Crime Statistics in Canada, 2011* (Ottawa: Statistics Canada, 2012) at 20–21, online: Statistics Canada www.statcan.gc.ca/pub/85-002-x/2012001/article/11692-eng.pdf. These numbers are fairly stable when considering previous reports and they should not be interpreted essentially as deviant behaviour because young males are fairly over-policed and profiled, resulting in more charges to this population group.

63 Katz, above note 61.

64 For the uses of rational choice theories in criminal law and critiques to how such discourses are used by actors in the criminal justice system, see, for instance, Bernard E Harcourt, *Illusions of Order: The False Promise of Broken Windows Policing* (Cambridge: Harvard University Press, 2001); Bernard E Harcourt, *Against Prediction: Profiling, Policing, and Punishing in an Actuarial Age* (Chicago: University of Chicago Press, 2007); André Jodouin & Marie-Eve Sylvestre, "Changer les lois, les idées, les pratiques: Réflexions sur l'échec de la réforme de la détermination de la peine" (2009) 50:3-4 C de D 519; Marie-Eve Sylvestre, "Rethinking Criminal Responsibility for Poor Offenders: Choice, Monstrosity, and the Logic of Practice" (2010) 55:4 McGill LJ 771.

65 Walter Benjamin, *Illuminations* (New York: Schocken, 1968) at 234.

66 Professor Lawrence Lessig of Harvard Law School uses the term "Remix Culture" to describe the modern society where the creation through copying is not only permitted,

more than ever the means to copy on their own. Non-commercial users adhere to these norms, but they are not in accordance with the legal norms that regulate copyrights, making these users deviants. Users copy because they learn to copy and they see it as a normal, acceptable behaviour.[67] This being said, punishment is probably the least effective strategy to changing behaviour and educational strategies would be more effective to prevent infringements.[68] Finally, even if deterrence theory worked, its asymmetric incorporation in the copyright regime is highly problematic as we are going to explain in the next subsection.

2) The Mismeasure of Punishment: Limits and Effects of Unusual Punishment

Deterrence theory is related to criminal law, in that both examine how we can justify punishment and under what circumstances the state may inflict pain on its citizens. However, mandatory minimum damages for copyright infringement, as discussed in the first part of the chapter, are applied outside of a normative system with the same guarantees that were historically earned in criminal law. Moreover, it is always good to remember that deterrence theory emerged anchored in Humanistic/Enlightenment values, aiming to reduce or at least setting limits to the sovereign and in reaction to the doctrine of maximum severity.[69] The doctrine of maximum severity

---

but encouraged: Lawrence Lessig, *Remix: Making Art and Commerce Thrive in the Hybrid Economy* (New York: Penguin Press, 2008).

67 John Palfrey et al, "Youth, Creativity, and Copyright in the Digital Age" (2009) 1:2 International Journal of Learning & Media 79 at 86–89.

68 For instance, in the United States in 2003, the Recording Industry Association of America (RIAA) started a vast litigation campaign against some 3,500 individual peer-to-peer users. It was said that the campaign was quite effective in increasing awareness of the illegality of file sharing but that its deterrence effect was debatable. The campaign was quite unpopular among the public and RIAA did put an end to it in 2008. See Will Moseley, "A New (Old) Solution for Online Copyright Enforcement After Thomas and Tenenbaum" (2010) 25:1 Berkeley Tech LJ 311 at 331–34; Ben Depoorter, Sven Vanneste, & Alain Van Hiel, "Copyright Backlash" (2011) 84:6 S Cal L Rev 1251 at 1255; Ernesto, "Filesharing Report Shows Explosive Growth for uTorrent" (26 April 2008), online: TorrentFreak http://torrentfreak.com/p2p-statistics-080426/.

69 The concept of doctrine of maximum severity was coined by Leon Radzinowicz to describe the indiscriminate use of severe punishment and the proliferation of capital sentences in the eighteenth and early nineteenth century in Britain. See Leon Radzinowicz, *History of English Criminal Law and its Administration from 1750*, vol 1 (London: Stevens and Sons, 1948); see also Alvaro Pires, "La doctrine de la sévérité maximale au

states that the only way to control deviance is through severity and strict enforcement (to punish more and more and to punish all offenders).

Radzinowicz suggested that a good historical example of this reasoning is found in the set of norms known as the "The Bloody Code" in England. At the beginning, there were merely fifty offences punishable by death. Yet, it was not enough to deter deviance, and "crime" rates were increasing. The answer was to punish more and more and punish all offenders. A century later, 200 offences were punishable by death. As a result, not only was there more crime, but the crimes committed were also more serious. The classic politically incorrect joke usually told in criminology classes goes as follow: if almost every deviant act was punished by death and people followed the rational-choice frame of mind, the offender would not only steal a horse, but also kill the owner, burn the farm, and get rid of all the witnesses. Obviously, it does not make any sense, and today the doctrine of maximum severity is used much more as an example of how severe punishment simply does not work and has no deterrent effect beyond neutralizing the offender him/herself.

In response, deterrence theory interestingly suggested that what deters crime is a just measure of pain through proportional and prompt punishment.[70] By that we mean, proportional and prompt in criminal law terms: proportional to the responsibility of the offender and the nature of the offence, and assuming that individuals are punished in a timely fashion while having the right to a minimum set of legal guarantees before being punished. It is important to note that Bentham himself argued that unnecessary laws and excessive punishment could lead to more dangerous evils and that the utilitarian calculus should be made in societal terms.[71] This is not the case in copyright law, especially regarding the use of statutory damages. The range of damages is not proportional to the fault; individuals accused of infringements have less guarantees than they would have in criminal

---

siècle des lumières" in Christian Debuyst, ed, *Histoire des savoirs sur le crime & la peine*, vol 2 (Bruxelles: Larcier, 1998).

70 See Jeremy Bentham, *Introduction to the Principles of Morals and Legislation* (Oxford: The Clarendon Press, 1876) [Bentham, *Introduction*]; Jeremy Bentham, *Theory of Legislation* (London: Trubner, 1876); Cesare M di Beccaria, *An Essay on Crimes and Punishments* (London: F Newbery, 1769); Michael Ignatieff, *A Just Measure of Pain: The Penitentiary in the Industrial Revolution, 1750–1850* (New York: Pantheon Books, 1978); Nils Christie, *Limits to Pain* (Oxford: Martin Robertson, 1982).

71 See Bentham, *Introduction*, above note 70: the calculus should address if a given law and/or punishment is causing more pleasure or more pain for the collectivity.

law, and one can really question to what extent punishment of non-commercial minor copyright violations is bringing more pleasure or more pain for society. When analyzed cautiously, the overpenalization through statutory damages looks much more like the *doctrine of maximum severity* than *deterrence theory* and this excessive (non-proportional) and arbitrary (less legal guarantees) punishment may simply lead to an escalation of deviance (e.g., from illegal downloading to file sharing), either because individuals are hedonistic and rationally driven (utilitarianism) or because they are not adhering to copyright norms taken as illegitimate and/or not reasonable (contemporary behaviour theories).[72]

D. CONCLUSION

The Canadian statutory damages regime, while helping copyright owners to obtain compensation for their losses, also purports to deter future infringements. In reality, the effectiveness of the regime to deter copyright violations is questionable. Deterrence theory is based on outdated utilitarian assumptions of human behaviour and it has consistently been proved ineffective by empirical studies. The *Copyright Act* sets the minimum and maximum awards of statutory damages, which can result in overpenalization or underpenalization of defendants, punishing not proportionally either excessively or not enough to compensate copyright violations. Because the regime operates in civil settings, it ignores most of the safeguards and protective rights elaborated in the criminal proceedings. When dealing with non-commercial minor infringement, it operates more along the premises of the doctrine of maximum severity and could actually lead to an escalation of deviance and copyright violations. A more productive avenue could be to study how individuals internalize social norms and why this normalization of copyright compliance is not occurring in our electronic cultural age.

---

72 Two empirical studies conducted in the United States seem to confirm that stringent sanctions tend to increase the rate and frequency of infringing activities; Depoorter, above note 68 at 1267–72 and 1287–90.

THEME TWO(B)

New Windows — New Insights

DISCOURSES AND PARADIGMS

THIRTEEN

Information Society Discourse, Innovation, and Intellectual Property

MICHAEL McNALLY

ABSTRACT (EN): This paper examines the discursive relationship between intellectual property rights (IPRs), innovation, and theories of the information society. Using Norman Fairclough's method, Critical Discourse Analysis, this paper examines how the idea and rhetoric around an emerging information society have been used by neo-liberal policy-makers to strengthen IPRs. The paper argues that information society theorists such as Daniel Bell and Manuel Castells extol the benefits of innovation while failing to substantively address the issue of IPRs. Through their writings they present the process of innovation as a nominalized entity obscuring questions of agency and the power relations involved in production of information. More importantly, such writings have naturalized the concept of an information society making it appear as common sense and ideologically neutral while obfuscating the role of IPRs. In turn, policy-makers have used the positive and seemingly value-free discourse on the information age as a means of framing the need to strengthen IPRs. This paper includes a specific examination of two major policy documents produced by the Canadian government that were part of the recent copyright reform process.

RÉSUMÉ (FR): Cet article examine la relation décousue qui existe entre les droits de la propriété intellectuelle (DPI), l'innovation et les théories de la société de l'information. En utilisant la méthode d'«analyse de discours critique » de Norman Fairclough, cet article examine comment l'idée et la rhétorique autour d'une société de l'information émergente ont été utilisées par les responsables politiques néolibéraux pour renforcer les DPI. L'article soutient que les théoriciens de la société de l'information tels que Daniel Bell et Manuel Castells prônent les bénéfices de l'innovation tout en omettant d'aborder les problèmes de DPI de façon substantielle. Dans leurs écrits, ils présentent le processus d'innovation comme une entité nommée, ce qui cache les questions d'« agency » ou capacité d'agir, et de relations de pouvoir impliquées dans la production d'information. Plus particulièrement, ces écrits ont adapté le concept de « société de l'information » en le faisant paraître comme le bon sens et idéologiquement neutre, tout en masquant le rôle des DPI. En retour, les responsables politiques ont utilisé le discours sur l'ère de l'information, positif et apparemment ne reflétant aucune valeur, pour donner un cadre au besoin de renforcer les DPI. Cet article comprend un examen particulier de deux importants documents de politiques produits par le gouvernement canadien qui firent partie du récent processus de réforme du droit d'auteur.

A. INTRODUCTION

Over the past forty years an increasing number of commentators from academia, industry, the media, and government have declared that broad political, economic, and social changes taking place demonstrate the emergence of a new type of society generally called the "information society/age."[1] Information society theorists point to the declining role of manufacturing in advanced economies and the corresponding rise of service and informational industries as evidence of a shift away from industrial capitalism. Concomitant with the increasing economic importance of the informational sector has been an increased emphasis on the part of governments and industry to provide greater protection for intellectual property, which has resulted in a series of international initiatives including the *Agreement on Trade-Related Aspects of Intellectual Property Rights*[2] and the World Intellectual Property Organization Internet treaties.[3] More importantly, information society dis-

1 Kenneth Carlaw et al, "Beyond the Hype: Intellectual Property and the Knowledge Society/Knowledge Economy" (2006) 20:4 J Econ Surveys 632. The authors list thirteen different names used by a variety of authors to describe the information age/knowledge economy at 669–90.

2 *Agreement on Trade-Related Aspects of Intellectual Property Rights*, 15 April 1994, 1869 UNTS 299, 33 ILM 1197 [*TRIPS*].

3 *WIPO Copyright Treaty*, 20 December 1996, 36 ILM 65 (entered into force 2 March 2002) [*WCT*]; *WIPO Performance and Phonograms Treaty*, 20 December 1996, 36 ILM 76 (entered

course has facilitated neo-liberal policy-making by creating a body of discourse that obscures questions of agency, obfuscates power relations, and masks crucial, ideologically loaded assumptions about the nature of innovation and the information age. This paper explores the relationship between discourse and intellectual property policy and highlights the importance of critical discourse analysis as a method in intellectual property scholarship.

This paper examines the treatment of intellectual property within the writings of information society theorists Daniel Bell and Manuel Castells, and contrasts their work with that of David Harvey, whose scholarship is critical of the idea of the emergence of an information age. The paper employs the methodology of Critical Discourse Analysis (CDA) developed by Norman Fairclough and argues that at the textual level, information society discourse obscures questions of agency in emphasizing innovation. Discursively, Bell's work has created an intertextual chain linking it with other information society theorists. Most importantly, information society discourse serves a specific ideological purpose by hiding the assumptions that underpin the concept of an information society and makes such a vision of the future appear as common sense. Using CDA, the paper specifically examines how Canadian policy-makers have used information society discourse to strengthen copyright law by looking at recent science and technology policy documents.[4]

B. INFORMATION SOCIETY THEORY AND DISCOURSE

Discussions about information society theories tend to start with Daniel Bell's 1973 book, *The Coming of Post-Industrial Society: A Venture in Social Forecasting*,[5] despite the fact that more critical works on the subject predate Bell's.[6] While scholars such as Machlup and Porat had previously identified

into force 20 March 2002) [*WPPT*].

4 Industry Canada, *Mobilizing Science and Technology to Canada's Advantage* (Ottawa: Industry Canada, 2007), online: Industry Canada www.ic.gc.ca/eic/site/icgc.nsf/vwapj/SandTstrategy.pdf/$file/SandTstrategy.pdf [Industry Canada, *Mobilizing Science*]; Government of Canada, *Improving Canada's Digital Advantage: Strategies for Sustainable Prosperity* (Ottawa: Industry Canada, 2010), online: Government of Canada Publications http://publications.gc.ca/collections/collection_2010/ic/Iu4-144-2010-eng.pdf [Canada, *Digital Advantage*].

5 Daniel Bell, *The Coming of Post-Industrial Society: A Venture in Social Forecasting*, anniversary ed (New York: Basic Books, 1999) [Bell, *Coming of Post-Industrial*].

6 Samuel E Trosow, "The Ownership and Commodification of Legal Knowledge: Using Social Theory of the Information Age as a Tool for Policy Analysis" (2004) 30 Man LJ 417 at 420–21.

the increasing economic importance of the information industries,[7] Bell extended this idea by arguing that the changes affected not only economics but also culture and society.[8] Although the idea of a new information age has been approached by numerous academics,[9] common themes permeate the literature: a social revolution comparable to the social changes experienced in the Industrial Revolution, the emergence of a new post-industrial/information economy, a shift in political practices and the nature of community, and the decline of the state.[10] To support their claims, theorists often point to changes in the prevalence of *information and communications technologies* (ICTs), occupational shifts away from manufacturing, the increasing economic value of information, the pervasiveness and importance of networks (both social and technological), and an increased emphasis on the production and interpretation of signs and symbols.[11] While a number of scholars emphasize the degree to which the modern society represents a break from industrial capitalism, a diverse body of critical literature suggests that many of the overarching and most significant themes of industrial-capitalism are still present in the information society.[12] Information society proponents tend to engage in naïve technological determinism and information exceptionalism, which overemphasizes the role of information in modern society while downplaying the fact that information has been significant throughout history.[13]

Despite the contested academic discourse, the concept of an information society has had a powerful influence on policy-makers from Japan,[14] to

7 Fritz Machlup, *The Production and Distribution of Knowledge in the United States* (Princeton: Princeton University Press, 1962); Marc Uri Porat, *The Information Economy: Definition and Measurement* (Washington DC: US Department of Commerce, Office of Telecommunications, 1977).

8 Robert Babe, *Telecommunications in Canada: Technology, Industry, and Government* (Toronto: University of Toronto Press, 1990) at 248.

9 Frank Webster, *Theories of the Information Society*, 3d ed (London: Routledge, 2006), provides an overview discussion of the range of information society theories, at 8–31; see also Christopher May, *The Information Society: A Skeptical View* (Cambridge: Polity, 2002) at 1–12; Carlaw, above note 1 at 669–90.

10 May, above note 9 at 12–16.

11 Webster, above note 9 at 8–21.

12 May, above note 9 at 149–50; Webster, above note 9 at 6–7 and 270–73.

13 Trosow, above note 6 at 440; Webster, above note 9 at 12.

14 Webster, above note 9 at 10.

the European Union,[15] the United States,[16] and Canada.[17] Information society rhetoric was used by Thatcher and Reagan in the 1980s as a part of their neo-liberal policies that transferred increased power from the state to private enterprise through deregulation and privatization.[18] Information society rhetoric has been popular in Canada for decades. In 1981, a Canadian Department of Communications report entitled *The Information Revolution and Its Implications for Canada* noted, "the information revolution is unavoidable."[19] A 1996 Canadian policy document on the Internet entitled *Building the Information Society* stated, "[t]he first challenge facing Canadians is to facilitate Canada's transition into the knowledge society."[20] Globally, the International Telecommunications Union hosted two world summits on the information society in 2003 and 2005.[21] Though the idea of an information society is conceptually rich, policy-makers, like information society advocates, have tended to adopt a narrow and simplistic, technologically determinist approach privileging information and communications technologies.[22] More importantly, information society discourse has

---

15 European Commission, *Digital Agenda for Europe*, online: European Commission https://ec.europa.eu/digital-agenda.

16 United States, "U.S. Delegation Cites Consensus on Key Information Society Issues" (10 December 2003), online: America.gov Archive www.america.gov/st/washfile-english/2003/December/20031210163112rellufj0.6401483.html.

17 Industry Canada, *European Union — Canada Joint Statement: Electronic Commerce in the Global Information Society* (Ottawa: Industry Canada, 2008), online: Industry Canada www.ic.gc.ca/eic/site/ecic-ceac.nsf/eng/gv00386.html; Industry Canada, *Canada — United Kingdom Joint Statement on Global Electronic Commerce and E-Government* (Ottawa: Industry Canada, 2008), online: Industry Canada www.ic.gc.ca/eic/site/ecic-ceac.nsf/eng/gv00387.html; Industry Canada, *Canada — Costa Rica Joint Statement on Global Electronic Commerce* (Ottawa: Industry Canada, 2008), online: Industry Canada www.ic.gc.ca/eic/site/ecic-ceac.nsf/eng/gv00382.html; Industry Canada, *Convergence Policy — Backgrounder* (Ottawa: Industry Canada, 2010), online: Industry Canada www.ic.gc.ca/eic/site/smt-gst.nsf/eng/sf05267.html.

18 Nick Dyer-Witheford, *Cyber-Marx: Cycles and Circuits of Struggle in High-Technology Capitalism* (Urbana, IL: University of Illinois Press, 1999) at 22.

19 Canada, *The Information Revolution and Its Implications for Canada* by Shirley Serafini & Michel Andrieu (Hull, QC: Department of Communications, 1981) at 13.

20 Canada, Information Highway Advisory Council Secretariat, *Building the Information Society: Moving Canada into the 21st Century* (Ottawa: Industry Canada, 1996) at 3.

21 International Telecommunications Union, *World Summit on the Information Society* (2012), online: International Telecommunications Union www.itu.int/wsis/index.html.

22 Ajit Pyati, "WSIS: Whose Vision of an Information Society?" 10:5 *First Monday* (2 May 2005), online: First Monday http://firstmonday.org/htbin/cgiwrap/bin/ojs/index.php/fm/article/view/1241/1161.

been employed to advance neo-liberal policies including ratcheting up intellectual property protection.

Discursive analyses of both information society literature and intellectual property cases are not new. Numerous articles have examined the general connection between information society discourse and neo-liberalism,[23] but these articles do not focus specifically on the role of intellectual property. Conversely, discursive analyses focusing on intellectual property have also been conducted. These studies have investigated the rise of the term *intellectual property* itself[24] and the rhetorical shift of describing infringement of intellectual property rights as "piracy" and "theft."[25] James Boyle has identified the role of romanticized rhetoric on authorship in supporting the ratcheting up of intellectual property protection within information society discourse.[26] Christopher May has examined the connection between information society discourse and neo-liberalism, noting that these two use the promise of innovation and the potential for economic growth as a means to justify greater intellectual property protection.[27] While the analyses of both May and Boyle are useful in revealing the discursive connection between intellectual property, innovation, information society discourse, and neo-liberalism, the subject remains understudied and under-theorized. CDA is particularly well suited to theorizing how discursive practices are both influenced by and influence the productions of texts, as well as examining the dialectical relationships between discursive practices and social practices. There have been some studies specifically theorizing the connec-

23 See, generally, Norman Fairclough, *Language and Globalization* (Routledge: London, 2006) at 47–50; Norman Fairclough, "Language in New Capitalism" (2002) 13:2 Discourse & Soc 163; John M Budd & Douglas Raber, "Discourse Analysis: Method and Application in the Study of Information" (1996) 32:2 Inf Processing & Mgmt 217 at 217; Bernd Frohmann, "Discourse Analysis as a Research Method in Library and Information Science" (1994) 16:2 Lib & Inf Sci Res 119 at 122–26; Ian Goodwin & Steve Spittle, "The European Union and the Information Society: Discourse, Power and Policy" (2002) 4:2 New Media & Soc 225 at 233–42; Leah A Lievrouw, "Our Own Devices: Heterotopic Communication, Discourse, and Culture in the Information Society" (1998) 14:2 The Inf Soc 83.

24 Harry First, "Controlling the Intellectual Property Grab: Protect Innovation, Not Innovators" (2007) 38:2 Rutgers LJ 365; Mark A Lemley, "Property, Intellectual Property, and Free Riding" (2005) 83:4 Tex L Rev 1031 at 1033–39.

25 Siva Vaidhyanthan, *Copyrights and Copywrongs: The Rise of Intellectual Property and How it Threatens Creativity* (New York: New York University Press, 2001) at 11–12; Jessica Litman, *Digital Copyright* (Amherst, NY: Prometheus, 2001) at 85–86.

26 James Boyle, *Shamans, Software, and Spleens: Law and the Construction of the Information Society* (Cambridge: Harvard University Press, 1996) at 107.

27 May, above note 9 at 165–66.

tion between information society discourse and the resultant policy changes in New Zealand[28] and Romania using CDA,[29] but the Canadian situation remains understudied. Critical discourse analysis is a useful mechanism for not only investigating why information society proponents fail to fully account the role of intellectual property in their theories, but also examining how and why information society discourse has proved so effective in advancing neo-liberal policies. The following section briefly describes Norman Fairclough's approach to CDA with a focus on the role of ideology and assumptions in discourse.

C. ASSUMPTIONS AND IDEOLOGY IN CRITICAL DISCOURSE ANALYSIS

Though there are a wide variety of approaches to studying language, Norman Fairclough's approach to CDA is particularly useful for studying discourse surrounding the information society.[30] CDA does not suggest that "everything is discourse" and posits a dialectical relationship between language and society where each is co-constitutive of the other.[31] Importantly, Fairclough's approach is critical in that it seeks to address social wrongs,[32] which make it particularly useful for focusing on how entrenched political and economic powers use discourse to advance their own interests through hegemony.[33] Furthermore, CDA is methodologically reflexive in acknowledging that no textual analysis can be objective, but more importantly in allowing interpretations of text to be connected into larger areas of social life.[34]

---

28 Shirley Leitch & Sally Davenport, "The Politics of Discourse: Marketization of the New Zealand Science and Innovation System" (2005) 58:7 Human Relations 891.

29 Norman Fairclough, *Critical Discourse Analysis: The Critical Study of Language*, 2d ed (Harlow, UK: Pearson Education, 2010) at 505–20 [Fairclough, *Critical Discourse Analysis*].

30 Norman Fairclough, *Analysing Discourse: Textual Analysis for Social Research* (London: Routledge, 2003) at 4 [Fairclough, *Analysing Discourse*]; Goodwin & Spittle, above note 23 at 230.

31 Norman Fairclough, "Critical Discourse Analysis and the Marketization of Public Discourse: The Universities" (1993) 4:2 Discourse & Soc 133 at 134 [Fairclough, "Marketization"]; Norman Fairclough, *Language and Power*, 2d ed (Harlow, UK: Pearson Education, 2001) at 19 [Fairclough, *Language and Power*].

32 Norman Fairclough, "A Dialectical-Relational Approach to Critical Discourse Analysis in Social Research" in Ruth Wodak & Michael Meyer, eds, *Methods of Critical Discourse Analysis* (Los Angeles: Sage, 2009) at 163.

33 Fairclough, "Marketization," above note 31 at 136.

34 Fairclough, *Analysing Discourse*, above note 30 at 14–15.

Fairclough's approach to CDA employs a three-dimensional framework that facilitates both a micro-level analysis of text and a macro-level examination of how discourse affects social practices.[35] The three hierarchical dimensions of CDA are text, discursive practices, and social practices whereby texts, discursive practices, and social practices are connected through dialectical relationships.[36] With regard to texts, analysis focuses on vocabulary, grammar, syntax, and sentence coherence with specific attention to how texts represent or obfuscate agency.[37] The specific element of textual analysis that is the focus of this paper is Fairclough's idea of nominalization where processes are represented entities.[38] For example, when globalization is depicted as an entity rather than a process it obscures the agents at work in globalization. With regard to the second dimension of CDA, discursive practices examine how texts are produced and consumed. This paper will focus specifically on the concepts of intertextuality and interdiscursivity, which examine how texts and orders of discourse are used to shape the production of texts.[39] Intertextuality is a discursive practice whereby pieces of previous texts are assimilated into the creation of new texts.[40] An extension of the concept of intertextuality is the idea of interdiscursivity where discursive practices established in one order of discourse influence a second order of discourse.[41] For example, Fairclough notes that some university job advertisements are interdiscursive, blending the discourse of education with commodity advertising discourses.[42]

The final element of CDA is an examination of how discursive practices influence social practices. Fairclough's approach to the role of assumptions and ideology in discourse are particularly useful in this regard. Assumptions play a central role in influencing social practice. When texts (and their authors) contain assumptions that are not made explicit, they convey value systems and as such can be seen as doing ideological work.[43] Fairclough argues, "[i]deologies are closely linked to language, because using language is the commonest form of social behaviour, and the form of social behaviour

35 Norman Fairclough, *Discourse and Social Change* (Cambridge, UK: Polity, 1992) at 86.

36 *Ibid* at 73.

37 *Ibid* at 75.

38 *Ibid* at 182.

39 *Ibid* at 84–85.

40 *Ibid* at 84.

41 *Ibid* at 85.

42 Fairclough, *Critical Discourse Analysis*, above note 29 at 102–04.

43 Fairclough, *Analysing Discourse*, above note 30 at 58.

where we rely most on 'common-sense' assumptions."[44] Fairclough argues that the way through which ideological assumptions are conveyed in discourse is through a process known as *naturalization*.[45] He states, "in the naturalization of discourse types and the creation of common sense, discourse types actually appear to *lose* their ideological character."[46] Thus, when texts contain assumptions that are not made explicit they contribute to a body of discourse that appears over time to be "common sense" and value free; however, when such discourse is taken for granted as neutral it succeeds in hegemonically conveying the ideological position of entrenched elites.[47] Fairclough's approach to discourse analysis is particularly well suited for assessing how information society proponents' lack of attention to intellectual property issues naturalizes particular ideological assumptions and provides a discourse tool for advancing neo-liberalism.

The next part of this chapter examines the information society theories of Bell and Castells with a specific focus on how these authors extoll the information age for ushering in a new wave of innovation, but fail to account for intellectual property. Their implicit assumptions about the benefits of innovation, without an analysis of intellectual property, are contrasted with the work of Harvey who is critical of the idea of the emergence of an information society. In particular, this section will emphasize how, at the textual level, the process of innovation is nominalized in the work of Bell and others, and how, through intertextuality, Bell's work goes on to influence the writings of Castells. Following this discussion, the chapter concludes by examining how the nominalized concept of innovation is interdiscursively used in recent Canadian policy documents, and ultimately how the naturalized information society discourse is used to advance the strengthening of copyright in Canada.

D. DANIEL BELL'S POST-INDUSTRIAL SOCIETY

Although Bell was not the first to broach the subject of the emergence of a new society and a break with industrialism, his work represented a substantive break with previous efforts due to its size and systematic nature,

---

44 Fairclough, *Language and Power*, above note 31 at 2.
45 *Ibid* at 76.
46 *Ibid* [emphasis in original].
47 Fairclough, *Analysing Discourse*, above note 30 at 58.

and has had considerable influence on policy-makers.[48] Bell's work was not a prediction of where society was headed, but a forecast based on extrapolating existing trends in the late 1960s and early 1970s.[49] While he has accumulated numerous critics over the past forty years, Bell continues to remain relevant and was one of the top ten most cited living social science authors in the past decade.[50]

Bell claims that post-industrial society is characterized by a fundamental shift in the treatment of knowledge. Unlike the industrial era where knowledge is used to coordinate the production of goods, he argues that society will move towards a system where codified theoretical knowledge is used to determine and direct change, noting that in modern science-based industries such as computers and electronics, production of goods is dependent on theoretical advances in scientific knowledge.[51]

Bell is aware that intellectual property rights are an issue in the information society, though he describes them as "mundane."[52] For Bell, patents and copyrights provide an incentive to undertake intellectual work, but these rights are weak given the relative ease with which they are infringed upon or circumvented.[53] Bell is cognizant of the public good nature of information, but underappreciates how easily this public good becomes commodified or of the role played by governments in facilitating such commodification. He correctly predicts the rise of new knowledge-based industries, but crucially does not account for the role of intellectual property in the production and distribution of intellectual goods.[54] While he views information as a source of power, his analysis is weakened by failing to see that informational power is greatly influenced by intellectual property.[55] Bell's writings also nominal-

48 Webster, above note 9 at 31–33; Robert Hassan, *The Information Society: Cyber Dreams and Digital Nightmares* (Cambridge: Polity, 2008) at 52; Bell, *Coming of Post-Industrial*, above note 5 at ix–x.

49 *Ibid* at 4.

50 "Relative Ranking of a Selected Pool of Leading Scholars in the Social Sciences by Number of Citations in the Social Science Citation Index, 2000–2011" (n.d.) online: University of Southern Carolina Annenberg http://annenberg.usc.edu/Faculty/Communication/~/media/73EE18E8CC9140A28F46C8E49F85C78D.ashx.

51 Bell, *Coming of Post-Industrial*, above note 5 at 20 and 25.

52 *Ibid* at 176; Daniel Bell, "The Social Fabric of the Information Society" in Tom Forester, ed, *The Microelectronics Revolution: The Complete Guide to the New Technology and its Impact on Society* (Oxford: Basil Blackwell, 1980) at 537 [Bell, "Social Fabric"].

53 *Ibid* at 512.

54 Bell, *Coming of Post-Industrial*, above note 5 at 79.

55 Bell, "Social Fabric," above note 52 at 515.

ize the process of innovation. For example, Bell writes, "[t]he post-industrial society, it is clear, is a knowledge society in a double sense: first, the sources of innovation are increasingly derivative from research and development . . . ."[56] In this statement Bell obfuscates the human agents involved in innovating. The combination of the uncritical treatment of intellectual property and the nominalization of innovation serve a specific ideological purpose. They create a body of discourse in which the process of innovation is nominalized. By nominalizing innovation, the role of a system of exclusionary rights is obscured.

In addition to nominalizing the term innovation, Bell's work contains assumptions that assist in naturalizing information society discourse. He assumes a technologically determinist viewpoint and a naïve optimism.[57] Bell vehemently rejects the suggestion that he is a technological determinist;[58] however, his claim is undermined by his own writing, for example, "[t]echnology has created a new class . . . ."[59] and "[t]echnology has created a new definition of rationality . . . ."[60] Even innovation is technologically determined as he posits, "economic innovation and change are directly dependent upon new technology,"[61] again eliminating the human element in innovation. Bell's technological determinist framework precludes critical questions from scrutiny such as who selects the new technologies to be developed and who benefits from their diffusion. In turn, his determinism facilitates naïve optimism. Bell's optimistic assessment of the role of the knowledge elite has proven a powerful mechanism at garnering adherents as well as critics.[62] In claiming that the political, economic, and cultural spheres are separate and distinct entities, Bell is able to focus on the technological changes while ignoring the pervasiveness of capital across all areas of life.[63]

However, it is specifically because of these shortcomings that Bell's analysis has proven so palatable for policy-makers. He assumes that because

---

56 Bell, *Coming of Post-Industrial*, above note 5 at 212.

57 *Ibid* at 41 and 43.

58 *Ibid* at xviii.

59 *Ibid* at 189.

60 *Ibid*.

61 *Ibid*.

62 Michael H Harris, Stan A Hannah, & Pamela C Harris, *Into the Future: The Foundations of Library and Information Services in the Post-Industrial Era*, 2d ed (Greenwich, CN: Ablex, 1998) at 11–12.

63 Dan Schiller, *How to Think about Information* (Urbana, IL: University of Illinois Press, 2007) at 20; Webster, above note 9 at 37–38.

patents and copyrights are easily circumvented they are not a significant source of economic power for rights holders. Bell's general optimism and his technological determinism appear to suggest that for whatever problems post-industrial society may engender, some technological innovation exists to solve such problems. Furthermore, in addition to nominalizing innovation and naturalizing the idea of an information society, Bell creates a discursive foundation on which both scholars and policy-makers will borrow, further naturalizing the concept of the information society. The next section examines the discursive connection between Bell's writings and that of Manuel Castells.

E. MANUEL CASTELL'S NETWORK SOCIETY

Although Manuel Castells's writings on the network society and informational capitalism are different from Bell's conception of a post-industrial society, the two are intertextually linked, despite Castells's clear rejection of Bell's thesis.[64] Castells's writing has a commanding scope, with *The Information Age* trilogy spanning nearly 1,500 pages. Of all authors on the topic, his work is the most encyclopedic and to the uncritical eye, it appears the most persuasive.[65] Castells places technological innovation and information at the centre of his theory of the emergence of a network society stating that innovation is the "primordial function" of the new economy.[66] Like Bell, the process of innovation is nominalized, demonstrating the intertextual link between the two authors. Though Bell contends that theoretical knowledge is displacing capital and labour in post-industrial society as the axial principle in society, Castells adopts a slightly different approach arguing that entrepreneurial innovation, not capital, is driving the Internet economy.[67] By placing innovation at the centre of his theory, Castells makes an implicit assumption that innovation is overwhelmingly positive, and that the mechanisms that facilitate innovation, including intellectual property, are also beneficial by extension.

---

64 Manuel Castells, *The Information Age: Economy, Society and Culture, Volume I — The Rise of the Network Society*, 2d ed (Oxford: Blackwell Publishing, 2000) at 218–19 [Castells, *Network Society*].

65 Webster, above note 9 at 98 and 265.

66 Manuel Castells, *The Internet Galaxy: Reflections on the Internet, Business, and Society* (Oxford: Oxford University Press, 2001) at 100 [Castells, *Internet Galaxy*].

67 *Ibid* at 56.

Castells provides several critical and valuable insights as a theorist. He recognizes the importance of the pursuit of profit in driving innovation, arguing that it is the primary motive in the Internet economy.[68] He is also critical of this facet of the information age, arguing that it is accompanied with a focus on immediate gratification, workaholism, superfluous consumption, and a diminished emphasis on family and personal relationships.[69] He highlights the dangers of growing inequality and most importantly the limitations of a culture of excess, centred on individual self-interest.[70] He also acknowledges the ideological hegemony of neo-liberalism in the 1990s.[71] While Castells offers some important insights, his under-analysis of intellectual property serves to naturalize the role of intellectual property in the information age.

Like Bell, Castells fails to analyze intellectual property in a substantive manner. His failure to include a discussion of intellectual property in his *Information Age* trilogy has been described as a fundamental flaw.[72] This omission is particularly troubling because innovation is a central topic in Castells's work. In *The Rise of the Network Society* he argues that the two factors driving innovation are research potential, the ability to engage in research, and specification ability; the application of research to a specific problem.[73] He does not address the role of intellectual property in incenting innovative activity. When he does address intellectual property his treatment is more passing than substantive. In *The Information Age* trilogy he notes that intellectual property "rights are a key factor in the development of the knowledge economy, but at the same time, their strict enforcement becomes a major obstacle for the redistribution of wealth in the planet."[74] Unlike Bell's analysis that assumes the weakness of intellectual property protection, Castells does identify a problem created by intellectual property, but it is his only analytical comment on intellectual property in a nearly 1,500-page theory of the information age. Besides this reference to how

---

68 *Ibid.*

69 *Ibid* at 58–59; Manuel Castells & Martin Ince, *Conversations with Manuel Castells* (Cambridge: Polity, 2003) at 37.

70 Castells, *Internet Galaxy*, above note 66 at 276 and 278.

71 Castells, *Network Society*, above note 64 at 143–44.

72 Felix Stalder, *Manuel Castells: The Theory of the Network Society* (Cambridge: Polity, 2006) at 204.

73 Castells, *Network Society*, above note 64 at 296–97.

74 Manuel Castells, *The Information Age: Economy, Society, and Culture, Volume II — The Power of Identity*, 2d ed (Oxford: Blackwell, 2004) at 363.

intellectual property rights inhibit wealth distribution, he makes only two other passing references to the subject in his trilogy.[75] He claims that innovation depends on access to knowledge that is openly available,[76] and that the primary issue around innovation is how to harness it without limiting creativity and research.[77] Though these are critical issues, he fails to see through these analyses by including a discussion of intellectual property. In omitting a substantive discussion of intellectual property, Castells's discourse undertakes ideological work by naturalizing the role of intellectual property in the information society.

Castells's later writings contain a few direct references to the role of intellectual property that are more critical in nature. He notes that intellectual property is central to profit making in the economy, and that the balance between users' and creators' rights is being lost.[78] He describes the debate over the role of intellectual property as a key battle, and also concludes that Internet business models based around intellectual property cannot succeed as they will be supplanted by some sort of alternative.[79] However, he fails to complete this analysis by demonstrating how alternatives will triumph. Castells's 2005 essay "The Network Society: From Knowledge to Policy," contains a critical paragraph on intellectual property:

> Creativity and innovation are the key drivers of value creation and social change in our societies — in fact in all societies. In a world of digital networks, the process of interactive creativity is contradicted by the legislation of property rights inherited from the industrial era.[80]

Castells's analysis of innovation is impaired by the fact that he stresses that it is innovation, not innovators (i.e., humans), that are the driving force behind creativity demonstrating an intertextual link to Bell's nominalized portrayal of innovation. While Castells's more recent writings demonstrate an increased awareness of the connection between intellectual property

75 Castells, *Network Society*, above note 64 at 114 and 120.

76 Castells, *Internet Galaxy*, above note 66 at 100.

77 Castells & Ince, above note 69 at 54.

78 Castells, *Internet Galaxy*, above note 66 at 182.

79 Manuel Castells, "The Cultures of the Internet" (2002) 109:3 Queen's Quarterly 333 at 341–42.

80 Manuel Castells, "The Network Society: From Knowledge to Policy" in Manuel Castells & Gustavo Cardoso, eds, *The Network Society: From Knowledge to Policy* (Washington, DC: John Hopkins Center for Transatlantic Relations, 2005) at 19 [emphasis in original].

and innovation, he still presents a nominalized view of innovation and his discourse helps to naturalize the idea of an information age.

Like Bell, Castells's work has been subject to a fair deal of criticism and in many respects lacks substantive differences with that of Bell's analysis.[81] Although he is less prone to overstating the case for an information age than other information society proponents, his work suffers from a degree of technological determinism, though lesser in degree than that of Bell. He claims that information technology largely determines innovative capacity.[82] His simplistic view of innovation is also a weakness. Even Bell is critical of Castells for failing to differentiate between invention, innovation, and the diffusion of innovation.[83] As with Bell, Castells offers a nominalized view of innovation, while his writings help to naturalize the idea of an information society where intellectual property rights and their effects on power and social relations do not play a significant role.

Castells goes further than any other information society theorist in not only analyzing the idea of a network/information society,[84] but also extolling the benefits of innovation. While he addresses the subject of innovation extensively, it is only in his more recent writings that he begins to reflect critically on the role of intellectual property. His failure to engage the topic at greater length, particularly given his relentless focus on innovation and entrepreneurialism, is a major shortcoming. Castells provides some useful insights on the negative trends that have occurred since the 1970s; however, like Bell, his overemphasis on the positive elements of innovation and lack of rigour in accounting for the role of exclusionary intellectual property rights contribute to the naturalization of information society discourse, which has been fruitfully employed by neo-liberal policy-makers to consistently expand and strengthen intellectual property protection.

F. DAVID HARVEY AND THE INFORMATION SOCIETY AS AN EXTENSION OF INDUSTRIAL CAPITALISM

David Harvey's analysis of the changes taking place in society is antithetical to the work of Castells and Bell. Juxtaposing Harvey's work with that of Bell and Castells is illuminating because though he deals with the same sub-

81 Webster, above note 9 at 121.

82 Castells, *Network Society*, above note 64 at 259.

83 Bell, *Coming of Post-Industrial*, above note 5 at xxiv.

84 Webster, above note 9 at 98 and 265; Hassan, above note 48 at 93.

ject matter as the others, his conclusions are significantly different. Most importantly, an examination of Harvey's writings, which do not display an intertextual link with the works of Bell and Castells, demonstrates the struggle that exists within orders of discourse.

Like Castells and Bell, Harvey acknowledges the crucial role played by innovation; however, drawing on Marx he views innovation as an essential and historical feature of capitalism and not a new phenomenon.[85] He is critical of how social inequality is used to encourage entrepreneurial risk taking.[86] While Harvey acknowledges that innovation has produced new goods and services, he is critical of how it can alter social relations in a destabilizing manner.[87] For capitalists, innovation is a necessary mechanism to ensure profitability and labour surpluses that weaken the position of workers and lower wages.[88] Harvey argues that innovation accounts for the majority of US job losses and twice as many losses as caused by firms relocating production sites to locales outside of the United States.[89] He further argues that such information technology is given a privileged status in neo-liberalism for its ability to facilitate speculative activity.[90] While Harvey provides a pervasive critique of capitalist innovation, his view of capitalism is not entirely negative. He does argue that capitalism on its own cannot be blamed for things like urban sprawl and increased meat consumption that arise from changes in socio-cultural preferences.[91] Furthermore, he also notes that without capitalism there may not have been a way to support the world's expanding population over the past three centuries unless alternative methods of providing goods had been developed.[92] Unlike Bell and Castells who assume the inherent benefit of innovation, Harvey casts a critical eye on the subject, which in turn leads his analysis to identify many of the problematic aspects of intellectual property.

---

85 David Harvey, *The Condition of Postmodernity: An Enquiry into the Origins of Cultural Change* (Cambridge, MA: Blackwell, 1990) at 111 [Harvey, *Condition of Postmodernity*].

86 David Harvey, *A Brief History of Neoliberalism* (Oxford: Oxford University Press, 2005) at 156 [Harvey, *Brief History*].

87 Harvey, *Condition of Postmodernity*, above note 85 at 27 and 106.

88 *Ibid* at 105; David Harvey, *Limits to Capital*, 2d ed (London: Verso, 2000) at xxiv; David Harvey, *The Enigma of Capital: and the Crises of Capitalism* (Oxford: Oxford University Press, 2010) at 14 and 59–60 [Harvey, *Enigma of Capital*].

89 *Ibid* at 93.

90 Harvey, *Brief History*, above note 86 at 157 and 159.

91 Harvey, *Enigma of Capital*, above note 88 at 73–74.

92 *Ibid* at 144.

Harvey is also much more attuned to the role of intellectual property than most information society advocates. Rather than viewing patents as a stimulant for innovation, he argues that monopoly rights help to limit the pace of innovation and lessen the ability of innovation to destabilize capitalism[93] — a similar view to that of Schumpeter who saw patents as a mechanism for stabilizing the economy in light of creative destruction. Intellectual property rights and the undermining of common property rights are seen as one mechanism through which neo-liberal governments have facilitated a transfer of wealth to elites.[94] He argues the commodification of information is not a generative wealth creating process, but instead a redistribution from the dispossessed (ranging from the holders of traditional knowledge to artistic labourers) to powerful rights holders.[95] He is critical of how commodification takes properties of things such as originality, uniqueness, and creativity and transforms them into commodities.[96] Harvey warns that increasing intellectual property rights may lead to the eventual patenting of human life.[97] Intellectual property is part of a broader pattern of commodification that has occurred under neo-liberalism where a range of common property rights have been converted into private property against the broad will of the general public.[98] Although he is highly critical of intellectual property and capitalist innovation, Harvey is not opposed to innovation *per se*; rather, he advocates for technological innovations that support the common good and not private gain.[99]

Harvey serves as a useful counter example to the positions of Bell and Castells. Harvey's writings are discursively disjunct — innovation is not nominalized and the ideological assumptions that underpin information society discourse are explicated — reflecting Fairclough's argument that discourse is a site of struggle.

93 *Ibid* at 91.

94 David Harvey, *Spaces of Global Capitalism: Towards a Theory of Uneven Geographical Development* (London: Verso, 2006) at 43 [Harvey, *Spaces*]; Harvey, *Brief History*, above note 86 at 159–60.

95 Harvey, *Spaces*, above note 94 at 44–45.

96 Harvey, *Brief History*, above note 86 at 166.

97 Harvey, *Enigma of Capital*, above note 88 at 221.

98 Harvey, *Brief History*, above note 86 at 159 and 161.

99 Harvey, *Enigma of Capital*, above note 88 at 230–31.

G. INFORMATION SOCIETY DISCOURSE, INTELLECTUAL PROPERTY, AND NEO-LIBERALISM

Information society discourse and neo-liberalism are intimately linked. Information society discourse with its embedded assumptions that under-estimate the importance and prominence of intellectual property and celebratory yet nominalized rhetoric on innovation has provided an invaluable discursive mechanism for the neo-liberal policy agenda to be advanced. At first glance the neo-liberal approach which favours deregulation and celebrates the virtues of competition unfettered by government interference would be at odds with monopoly intellectual property rights;[100] however, the fundamental principle behind neo-liberalism is not the complete diminution of the state but the use of state power to maximize the business climate for capital accumulation.[101] Both are premised on liberalism and the respect for property rights, and emphasize the "'free market' as the ideal allocative mechanism."[102] Although information society theorists often downplay the central role of intellectual property rights, information age discourse and neo-liberal economic logic combine and mutually reinforce the notion that intellectual property is necessary to advance innovation.[103] Bell's work had a direct influence on the Reagan administration[104] and also provided a conceptual underpinning to information society policies in Europe and the Clinton administration.[105] Bell's optimistic vision of a post-industrial future has not only influenced policy-makers at the highest level; it has also provided conceptual and rhetorical mechanisms that have been used to deploy neo-liberal policies. Bell's discourse has influenced both academics and governments not only in the past but currently as well. The recent strengthening of Canadian copyright provides a case study that demonstrates how Bell's writings have had an interdiscursive effect on policy-making literature in Canada, and how the nominalized conception

100 May, above note 9 at 166.

101 Harvey, *Spaces*, above note 94 at 25.

102 Trosow, above note 6 at 418; May, above note 9 at 164; James Boyle, "Fencing Off Ideas: Enclosure and Disappearance of the Public Domain" (2002) 131:2 Daedalus 13 at 24.

103 May, above note 9 at 165.

104 Harris, Hannah, & Harris, above note 62 at 58.

105 William H Dutton, "Introduction" in William H Dutton, ed, *Information and Communications Technologies: Visions and Realities* (Oxford: Oxford University Press, 1996) at 15; William H Dutton, Jay G Blumler, Nicholas Garnham, Robin Mansell, James Cornford, & Malcolm Peltu, "The Politics of Information and Communication Policy: The Information Superhighway" in William H Dutton, *ibid* at 387–405.

of innovation and naturalized assumptions of the information society provide a discursive means for ratcheting up intellectual property protection.

In the lead up to the passing of Bill C-11,[106] the Canadian government released several significant policy documents that discussed the importance of strengthening copyright. These documents have a clear inter-discursive link with the writings of Bell and Castells. Most importantly, they import the nominalized view of innovation and rely on the naturalized, or common sense idea of the information society as a means of arguing for stronger copyright protection. In 2007, the Government of Canada released *Mobilizing Science and Technology to Canada's Advantage*, which explicitly stressed the need to increase copyright protection.[107] Although the government does not use the specific term "information society," the document repeatedly refers to the "knowledge economy,"[108] "knowledge-based economy,"[109] and "new economy."[110] The nominalized concept of innovation is present. For example, in the introductory message from the Minister of Finance, Jim Flaherty notes, "[t]he Government of Canada will do its part by creating a new climate of innovation and discovery in our nation."[111] The document also notes, "[i]mprovements in our quality of life and standard of living will depend on our increasing success in bringing scientific and technological innovations to life."[112] A similar sentiment is repeated when the government declares, "[s]cientific and technological innovations enable modern economies to improve their competitiveness and productivity, giving us the means to achieve an even higher standard of living and better quality of life."[113] In these passages the agents of innovation are obscured, while the benefits of innovation are extolled. More importantly, the government links its celebratory rhetoric on innovation to the need for copyright reform.[114] Because the concept of an information age (or knowledge economy as the government refers to it) has been naturalized through discourse, the government is more easily able to argue the need for greater copyright protection to facilitate higher levels of innovation.

---

106 *Copyright Modernization Act*, RSC 2012, c 20.
107 Industry Canada, *Mobilizing Science*, above note 4 at 52.
108 *Ibid* at 23.
109 *Ibid* at 25, 65, and 80.
110 *Ibid* at 53.
111 *Ibid* at 5.
112 *Ibid* at 22.
113 *Ibid* at 23.
114 *Ibid* at 52.

The use of a nominalized portrayal of innovation and the naturalized concept of the information society is also present in the more recent digital economy consultation paper.[115] While the government has shifted from calling the use of "knowledge economy" to "digital economy," the document has a clear intertextual link to *Mobilizing Science and Technology to Canada's Advantage*. The nominalized view of innovation is evident in quotes such as, "the critical role that technology and innovation will play in our future prosperity and quality of life . . . ."[116] It should be noted that while the process of innovation is presented in a nominalized fashion, the government is clear that innovation will be undertaken by the private sector.[117] Again, the strengthening of copyright is highlighted as a means for ensuring innovation with the government stating, "[a]n updated copyright framework . . . will help maximize creativity, innovation and economic growth."[118] The government also suggests, "[i]nnovation and creativity will grow where investments of time, energy and money are secure and fairly rewarded."[119] This passage explicitly links a nominalized view of innovation with the idea of stronger (more secure) copyright. These passages are couched within a document rich in information society discourse. The government states, "we all have a vested interest in a dynamic and flourishing digital economy."[120] The document goes on to argue, "[a] strong digital economy will be the backbone of Canada's future prosperity and success."[121] Similar to the 2007 science and technology strategy paper, the Canadian government has employed seemingly neutral information society discourse as a means of advancing a neo-liberal political agenda aimed at increasing the protection for copyright holders. While the government did have two failed copyright bills, information society discourse has been an important mechanism through which the government achieved its goal of copyright reform.

H. CONCLUSION

Starting with Bell's work in the early 1970s and continuing with texts such as Castells, information society discourse has paved the way for policies

115 Canada, *Digital Advantage*, above note 4.
116 *Ibid* at 9.
117 *Ibid* at 11, 15, 17, 22, and 25.
118 *Ibid* at 14.
119 *Ibid* at 28.
120 *Ibid* at 8.
121 *Ibid*.

that have ratcheted up intellectual property policies. By extolling innovation, such discourse has naturalized the idea that in an information age it is necessary to have strong intellectual property protection to facilitate economic growth, while obscuring the ideological fact that such policies disproportionately benefit rights holders by limiting access to information. The recent policy documents by the Canadian government demonstrate how naturalized information society discourse has been used discursively to frame changes to Canadian copyright. Discursive analyses of information society rhetoric provide a useful mechanism for intellectual property scholars to examine how intellectual property policies are ideologically naturalized through discourse. More study is needed to further examine the relationship between theories of the information society, intellectual property, and policy-making.

FOURTEEN

Seeking the Margins—Fair Use and Copyright, Harold Innis, and Israel

MEERA NAIR[1]

ABSTRACT (EN): This paper seeks to combine elements from the fields of law and communication to address contemporary challenges concerning the use of exceptions within the system of copyright. The debate surrounding copyright exceptions often seems intractable, with a key point of dispute being the vagueness of the language of the law. That vagueness has merit — exceptions which facilitate the pursuit of creativity must necessarily be as indeterminate as creativity itself. Returning to the work of Harold Adams Innis (1894–1952) reminds us of the value of language that invites thoughtful deliberation. Innis' work has further relevance as a contemporary evaluation of how nation states are adopting and functioning with indeterminate language—this paper sets the stage for a long-term research study concerning Israel's adoption of fair use into domestic copyright. Modern copyright is increasingly set by a global template, leaving little room for individuality; with recourse to Innis the author suggests that Israel has the potential to

1 Azrieli International Postdoctoral Fellow (2012–2013), Hebrew University of Jerusalem. I wish to thank the Azrieli Foundation for supporting my interest in Israel; their enabling of a postdoctoral year has set the stage for long-term research. Ricki Newman was invaluable, not merely for translation services but for being the willing sounding board throughout. Gratitude is due to Michael Birnhack and Menahem Blondheim; their help from afar was critical to moving this project from a theoretical state to an active undertaking. And thanks must go to two anonymous reviewers whose remarks improved this paper immeasurably.

adhere to twenty-first century copyright principles without compromising their own particular culture of reading and knowledge development.

RÉSUMÉ (FR): Ce texte combine des éléments de droit et de communication afin d'aborder les défis contemporains touchant à l'utilisation des exceptions en droit d'auteur. Les débats entourant les exceptions au droit d'auteur semblent souvent insolubles, mettant l'accent sur l'imprécision du langage utilisé dans la loi. Ce manque de précision comporte aussi des avantages: les exceptions qui facilitent la recherche de la créativité doivent être tout aussi imprécises que cette créativité. Le travail d'Harold Adams Innis (1894-1952) nous rappelle la valeur du langage qui invite aux réflexions judicieuses. L'œuvre d'Innis est des plus pertinentes pour évaluer de façon contemporaine comment les États-nations adoptent un langage indéterminé et comment ils fonctionnent avec ce langage. Ce texte prépare le terrain pour une étude à long terme sur l'adoption par Israël de l'usage équitable du droit d'auteur en droit interne. Le droit d'auteur moderne se bâtit de plus en plus à partir d'un modèle universel, qui laisse peu de place à l'individualité; en ayant recours à Innis, l'auteur estime qu'Israël pourrait adhérer aux principes de droit d'auteur du vingt-et-unième siècle, et ce, sans compromettre sa culture particulière du développement de la lecture et du savoir.

A. INTRODUCTION

In the late twentieth century, citing the disruptions caused by digital technology set upon worldwide networks, copyright holders pressed for greater control of copyrighted works; these arguments have only continued in intensity and force.[2] This paper seeks to contribute to discussion in the fields

---

2 The scope of control desired is illustrated in Pamela Samuelson, "The US Digital Agenda at WIPO" (1996) 37 Va. J Int'l L 369. Ongoing pressure emanates from the United States via the annual process known as "Special 301" where countries are ranked in terms of their disfavour by American judgment with respect to intellectual property control. See US Trade Representative, *2012 Special Report 301* (Washington, DC: 2012), online: Office of the United States Trade Representative www.ustr.gov/sites/default/files/2012%20Special%20301%20Report_0.pdf.

Furthermore, global trade negotiations have moved beyond the relative transparency of the World Intellectual Property Organization to closed-door agreements reaching for ever more stringent intellectual property control; a recent illustration being the TransPacific Partnership Agreement: see Carolina Rossini, "Professor Michael Geist on TPP and its Effects on Canadian Internet Users" (14 September 2012), online: Electronic Frontier Foundation www.eff.org/deeplinks/2012/09/professor-michael-geist-tpp-and-its-effects-canadian-users.

of communication and law by positioning the work of an early twentieth century scholar against the twentieth century challenge of *balance* in the system of copyright.

The intersection of communication and copyright is not new — Patricia Aufderheide, Kembrew McLeod, and Siva Vaidhyanathan were among the vanguard addressing the challenges and opportunities wrought when creativity and distribution are both enhanced via technology.[3] But communications scholars themselves may question the guide I have chosen: Harold Adams Innis (1894–1952). Once considered the most influential man in Canadian academia,[4] his name enters conversation only through occasional historical references in undergraduate textbooks. Innis's legacy has become largely confined to his early works in political economy and later

---

3 Patricia Aufderheide, Professor of Communication at American University, founded their Center for Social Media and served as Director since its inception in 2001. She has worked tirelessly to promote fair use in documentary film production and beyond, and recently co-authored *Reclaiming Fair Use* with Professor Peter Jaszi of Washington College of Law: see Patricia Aufderheide & Peter Jaszi, *Reclaiming Fair Use: How to Put Balance Back in Copyright* (Chicago: University of Chicago Press, 2011). Kembrew McLeod, documentarian and Associate Professor in Communication at the University of Iowa, captures with biting prose the absurdity that follows in the wake of excessive application of copyright: see Kembrew McLeod, *Freedom of Expression®: Overzealous Copyright Bozos and Other Enemies of Creativity* (New York: Doubleday, 2005). Siva Vaidhyanathan, formerly a professional journalist and now a cultural historian and media scholar, is the Robertson Professor in Media Studies at the University of Virginia. Vaidhyanathan's early work bridged the disciplines of law and communication with deceptive ease: see Siva Vaidhyanathan, *Copyrights and Copywrongs: The Rise of Intellectual Property and How It Threatens Creativity* (New York: New York University Press, 2001).

4 Innis was known not only for his scholarship, but also for his efforts to foster intellectual development in Canada: see Vincent Wheeler Bladen, "Harold Adams Innis (1953) 43:1 American Econ Rev 1 at 5. Innis's efforts went beyond the academy; he served as a Royal Commissioner on three occasions. Upon Innis's death Prime Minister Louis St. Laurent and Transport Minister Lionel Chevrier each sent a telegram of condolence to Innis's widow Mary Quayle Innis commending Innis's service to his nation. See Toronto, University of Toronto Archives/B72-0003/Box 005, file 17. Regard for Innis extended beyond national borders; Joseph Willits of the Rockefeller Foundation penned these words to Sidney Smith, President of University of Toronto:

> . . . The highest purpose of the Rockefeller Foundation is to serve and to strengthen the scholars and scientists of quality who are seeking to raise the levels of intellectual processes in society. Harold Innis was one of the greatest of these. Wherever his influence extended, there was quality as a result.

(24 November 1952), see Toronto, University of Toronto Archives/B72-0003/Box 005, file 43.

works in communication; few people are aware that Innis had a lifelong interest in the study of law.[5]

Innis's writings concerning the rule of law illustrate his appreciation of the conjoining of principle and practice in early systems of law, to the benefit of individual freedom.[6] Such freedom was central to Innis' lifetime of work and is directly relevant to the system of copyright. Copyright, deemed to be an incentive to creativity, too often impedes the individual freedom necessary to foster intellectual activity by invoking a "culture of fear and doubt."[7] The measure that began as a trade mechanism now has a sweep-

---

5 I am indebted to Alexander John Watson for his definitive biography of Innis. First published as a doctoral dissertation in 1981 and updated twenty-five years later to include reference to recent scholarship, Watson uncovers the pursuit of law that lay at the foundation of Innis's entire body of intellectual endeavour: see Alexander John Watson, *Marginal Man: the Dark Vision of Harold Innis* (Toronto: University of Toronto Press, 2006) [Watson, *Marginal Man 2006*]; see also Alexander John Watson, *Marginal Man: Harold Innis' Communications Work in Context* (PhD Thesis, University of Toronto, 1981) [unpublished] [Watson, *Marginal Man 1981*]. Working without recourse to Watson's work, only a handful of other scholars noted the importance of law to Innis: see William Christian, ed, *The Idea File of Harold Adams Innis* (Toronto: University of Toronto Press, 1980); see Richard Noble, "Innis' Conception of Freedom" in Charles R Acland & William J Buxton, eds, *Harold Innis in the New Century: Reflections and Refractions* (Montreal: McGill-Queen's University Press, 1999) 31; and see William Pencak, "Canada as a Semiotic Society: Harold Innis, Roberta Kevelson, and the Bias of Legal Communications" (2005) 18:2 Int'l J Sem L 207.

6 Meera Nair, "Copyright and Ethics: An Innisian Exploration" 2009 2:1 Global Media J—Canadian Edition 23 [Nair, "Copyright and Ethics"].

7 Aufderheide and Jaszi begin with close attention to the problem of thwarted cultural engagement: see Aufderheide & Jaszi, above note 3 at 1–15; ironically, copyright was described as the "engine of free expression" by the United States Supreme Court as the Court chose to suppress publication of a new work on the grounds of copyright infringement: see *Harper & Row Publishers, Inc v Nation Enterprises*, 471 US 539 at 558 (1985). The court reasoned that the marketplace ensures production of creative effort and copyright's inherent structure of protecting expression, not ideas, serves as the safeguard against censorship. Yet, this seeming safeguard has been called into question many times, for instance, see David Fewer, "Constitutionalizing Copyright: Freedom of Expression and the Limits of Copyright in Canada" (1997) 55 UT Fac L Rev 175; see Jonathan Griffiths & Uma Suthersanen, eds, *Copyright and Free Speech: Comparative and International Analyses* (Oxford: Oxford University Press, 2005); and see also Neil Weinstock Netanel, *Copyright's Paradox* (Oxford: Oxford University Press, 2008). Even if the safeguard had worked according to theory, utilizing protected expression is foundational to creativity, in particular the "imagery of commerce is a rich source for expressive activity": see Rosemary J Coombe, *The Cultural Life of Intellectual Properties: Authorship, Appropriation, and the Law* (Durham: Duke University Press, 1998) at 6. In terms of private, consumer copying, despite the role such copying plays in facilitating media development, there is little assurance that such behaviour can seek shelter under fair use: see Fred von Lohmann, "Fair Use As Innovation Policy" (2008) 23:1 Berkeley Tech LJ 1 at 6. In terms of Canadian law, while some educational and consumer copying is protected through recent amendments,

ing ambit and intrudes on private activity. Whether such activity occurs through learning, teaching, research, journalism, the fine arts, consumption of popular culture, or a creative response within that culture, increased anxiety over copyright law denies people the benefits available from legitimate exceptions to the law.

The exception of focus here is fair use and this exploration concerns its adoption into Israeli copyright law in 2007.[8] While fair use's antecedents lie in England, it is most often identified with judicial development in the United States.[9] Codified in 1976, American fair use is described illustratively; a set of possible uses is listed and prefaced with the phrase "for purposes such as."[10] The elasticity of language allows some as-of-yet unimagined shelter from the charge of infringement — provided the conditions of the use are deemed fair. Fair use has endured some challenging years, often charged with being unstable and inhospitable.[11] Those years may also be seen as the growing pains that ensue as a legal doctrine develops, with the comforting knowledge that growth will yield to stability. Literature indicates that fair use has matured and offers some modest patterns of predictability.[12]

Fair use is recognized as central to the story of innovation in the United States[13] — copyright's exceptions must be robust in order to create a space where individuals are free to tinker in thought. But exceptions are met with

---

those protections are coloured by an obedience to digital locks: see *Copyright Act*, RSC 1985, c C-42 s 41. When these measures were proposed, Ian Kerr noted there were "no countervailing provisions that would set limits or impose obligations concerning the use of locks, and certainly no provisions that prohibit particular uses of them or require them to be unlocked." See Ian Kerr, "Digital Locks and the Automation of Virtue" in Michael Geist, ed, *From Radical Extremism to Balanced Copyright: Canadian Copyright and the Digital Agenda* (Toronto: Irwin Law, 2010) 247 at 297 [Geist, *From Radical Extremism*].

8 *Copyright Act*, 5768-2007, 2007 LSI 34 (2007)(Isr.) [*Israeli Copyright Act*].

9 The conceptual basis of fair use developed from English precedents concerning fair abridgment and principles of fair use were recognizable in 1839 American caselaw; nevertheless, the language of fair use as it is recognized today is often attributed to *Folsom v Marsh* 9 F Cas 342 (CCD Mass 1841), see William F Patry, *The Fair Use Privilege in Copyright Law*, 2d ed (Washington, DC: The Bureau of National Affairs, Inc, 1995) at 3–19.

10 17 USC § 107.

11 Matthew Sag, "Predicting Fair Use" (2012) 73:1 Ohio St LJ 47 at 48–51.

12 Barton Beebe, "An Empirical Study of U.S. Copyright Fair Use Opinions: 1978–2005" (2008) 156:3 U Pa L Rev 549; see also Pamela Samuelson, "Unbundling Fair Uses" (2009) 75 Fordham L Rev 2585; see also Neil Weinstock Netanel, "Making Sense Out of Fair Use" (2011) 15 Lewis and Clark L Rev 715; see also Sag, above note 11.

13 von Lohmann, above note 7; see also Ian Hargreaves, "Digital Opportunity: A Review of Intellectual Property and Growth" (May 2011), online: UK Intellectual Property Office, www.ipo.gov.uk/ipreview-finalreport.pdf.

hostility; Justice Laddie's remarks concerning UK copyright law in 1996 are apropos to the global discussion of copyright in 2012:

> Rigidity is the rule. It is as if every tiny exception to the grasp of copyright monopoly has had to be fought hard for, prized out of the unwilling hand of the legislature and, once conceded, defined precisely and confined within high and immutable walls.[14]

Closer to home, when the Canadian government solicited public opinion for copyright amendment in 2009, a coalition of rights holders took great pains to denounce fair use.[15] In the face of formidable global intransigence,[16] a new perspective may help. To that end, I offer Innis's paradigm for fostering creativity and Israel as contemporary illustration.

This paper endeavours to sketch the contours of a project in its infancy. Section B begins by sifting out some of Innis's work that enhances a dis-

---

14 Justice Laddie, "Copyright: Over-Strength, Over-Regulated, Over-Rated?" (1996) 18:5 Eur IP Rev 253 at 259.

15 "The fair use model is not a panacea for solving difficult problems resulting from digitization and the internet. 'Fair use' has been described as an 'astonishingly bad' system amounting to little more than 'the right to hire a lawyer'": see Access Copyright et al, "Why Canada Should Not Adopt Fair Use: A Joint Submission to the Copyright Consultation" (15 September 2009), online: Industry Canada www.ic.gc.ca/eic/site/008.nsf/eng/02524.html at 2; for a rebuttal, see Meera Nair, "Fair Dealing at a Crossroads" in Geist, *From Radical Extremism* above note 7 at 102–8 [Nair, "Fair Dealing at a Crossroads"].

16 Perhaps one of the most poignant illustrations is the slow pace of permitting access to works for visually impaired people. During the most recent round of negotiations, the World Intellectual Property Organization claimed progress; following meetings in early October 2012 Director General Francis Gurry praised the engagement of member states in "setting timetables for concluding negotiations on international instruments on access to copyrighted work by the visually impaired"; see "WIPO Assemblies Agree Roadmaps for New International Instruments," *World Intellectual Property Office* (9 October 2012), online: World Intellectual Property Office www.wipo.int/pressroom/en/articles/2012/article_0022.html. Left unsaid was that these negotiations began twenty years ago and current stakeholders were pressing for access for the blind to be used as leverage to increase new global enforcement norms: see Manon Ress, "Timeline: Addressing Copyright Related Barriers to Overcoming Reading Disabilities," Knowledge Ecology International (5 October 2009), online: Knowledge Ecology International, http://keionline.org/timeline-reading; see Jamie Love, "October 19 WIPO negotiations on copyright exceptions for disabilities," Knowledge Ecology International (20 October 2012), online: Knowledge Ecology International, http://keionline.org/node/1571. When the treaty was concluded in June 2013, with favorable terms for visually impaired people, it was hailed as nothing less than miraculous; see Catherine Saez, "Miracle in Marrakesh: 'Historic' Treaty For Visually Impaired Agreed," International IP Policy (26 June 2013), online: Intellectual Property Watch, www.ip-watch.org/2013/06/26/miracle-in-marrakesh-historic-treaty-for-visually-impaired-agreed.

cussion of copyright and balance. Then, as the essence of balance requires flexibility within the language and interpretation of law, Section C delves into Innis's explorations of language in law. Section D sets the stage for this project by examining Innis's overall thesis concerning sites of creative endeavour. Finally, since no conclusion can be drawn from work yet to be done, I consider what lies ahead.

B. CUES FROM HAROLD INNIS

Innis did not directly address the system of copyright. Yet, evidence indicates that he was aware of copyright's role in developing publishing industries, and also the political ramifications (domestic and international) of copyright in the nineteenth century.[17] Innis's untimely death cut short his scholarship, but given his explorations of staple commodities and systems of communication I cannot resist musing that intellectual commodities with the attendant copyright implications would eventually have come into sharper focus for Innis. That said, it is not my aim to continue the work of Innis — such a claim would be both grandiose and absurd — but merely to consider how his writings concerning communication lend themselves to contemporary efforts to find balance in the system of copyright.

The concept of balance was dear to Innis: "I have attempted to show elsewhere that in Western civilization a stable society is dependent on an appreciation of a proper balance between the concepts of space and time."[18] Space denoted an inclination to expansion, innovation, and the individual, whereas time focused on heritage, custom, and community. Innis's writings illustrate his efforts to understand and explain how elite groups within a so-

---

17 Copyright makes frequent appearances throughout Innis's writings, for instance: "American authors with lack of copyright protection turned to journalism . . . . Publishers demand great names and great books if no copyright is involved": Harold A Innis, "Minerva's Owl" [Innis, "Minerva's Owl"] in Harold A Innis, ed, *The Bias of Communication*, 2d ed (Toronto: University of Toronto Press, 2003) at 28–29 [Innis, *Bias*]; "American copyright legislation in 1890 created a new series of rights and the literary agent emerged to interpret them . . . the absence of copyright [meant] large scale piracy of English books in the United States, and a smaller-scale piracy of American ones in England": see Harold Innis, "An Economic Approach to English Literature in the Nineteenth Century" in *Political Economy in the Modern State* (Toronto: The Ryerson Press, 1946) at 53 [Innis, *Political Economy*]; "Emerson reported the remark of an Englishman: 'As long as you do not grant us copyright, we shall have the teaching of you'": see Harold A Innis, "Technology and Public Opinion in the United States," in Innis, *Bias* above note 17 at 171.

18 Harold Innis, "Plea for Time" in Innis, *Bias*, *ibid* at 64 [footnote omitted].

ciety may exploit these inclinations of media to meet particular objectives.[19] I have described elsewhere how the structure of copyright itself can be interpreted via space and time — space is represented by the grant of rights to a copyright holder to control distribution to the advantage of the individual and time is represented by the exceptions to control which sustain the creative community.[20] What I suggest here is to incorporate another aspect of Innis's work, namely his thoughts on empires and margins.

In his explorations of empires and communication, Innis argued that empires were sustained by the cultural activities found at its margins. Margins were those far-flung realms that received lesser attention and control from the centre of the empire, and whose inhabitants exploited that laxness by innovation and creativity, to the betterment of the very empire itself. Yet margins could not survive on their own; they needed the protection of their patron and master. I suggest applying the paradigm of margin and empire, not only in terms of geography but also in terms of legal structure. In the contemporary setting of the Information Age, if the system of copyright constitutes the empire, its own success is dependent on the preservation of its margins.[21] Said another way, margins delineate the limits of the grant of control offered through copyright.

Of course, by its very structure, copyright has a set of explicitly defined limits: (1) copyright is not perpetual, so time eventually gives access to works; (2) the inadmissibility of copyright upon facts or other building blocks of knowledge means raw data is available to all; and (3) the distinction between idea and expression is deemed to safeguard against excessive control.[22] But in order to maximize conditions for creativity, creative material must be available to seed future creativity, during the term of protection. Herein lies the necessity of marginal spaces offered through fair dealing and fair use. Like the empires of the past, these margins are not

---

19 Harold A Innis, *Empire and Communications* (Toronto: Dundurn Press, 2007) [Innis, *Empire*].

20 Nair, "Copyright and Ethics," above note 6.

21 My application of Innis to copyright shares some affinity with Jessica Litman's argument that copyright is dependent upon the existence of the public domain. Litman convincingly argues that it is the implicit authorization contained in the public domain that allows copyright to be spared the challenge of dissecting the contributions of the many authors that coalesce into a singly attributed creation: see Jessica Litman, *The Public Domain* (1990) 39:4 Emory LJ 965 at 969. As the public domain includes all materials unprotected by copyright, fair dealing and fair use are critical to accessing this larger body of material.

22 Nair, "Fair Dealing at a Crossroads," above note 15 at 92.

clearly delineated. But in these spaces, cultural traditions mingle, thereby enabling the creative sparks Innis would later document.

Fortunately, recent pronouncements by the Canadian Supreme Court offer encouragement for a healthy margin of copyright in Canada.[23] But more attention is due to another nation. In 2007 Israel went to the fullest extent possible with exceptions, by moving from a closed regime of fair dealing[24] to the open-ended exception of fair use.[25] Intriguingly, this returns the notion of margin to Innis's invocation in the geographic sense. Israel, as a modern developing nation located at an intersection of East and West, is well-suited as a case study in which to situate Innis's writings.

Interdisciplinary work spread across law and communication is not without challenge — the risk of pleasing neither community looms large. But the pleasure of an interdisciplinary piece is that it allows one to tell a story, with plot and subplot accepted as intermingling in less than tidy fashion. In this story, national dreams, questions of black letter law, heroic protagonists, and narration provided through Innis offer engaging non-fiction.

C. LAW AS A MEDIUM OF COMMUNICATION

Innis saw communication where others might not. His writings present *medium* as anything that influences human relationships, shapes our conceptions of time and space, and has the potential to affect civilization.[26] But

23 The Supreme Court remains keenly aware that copyright is a system perched upon a delicate balance: see Michael Geist, "How the Supreme Court of Canada Doubled Down on Users' Rights" (23 July 2012), online: Michael Geist www.michaelgeist.ca/content/view/6599/125/; see also *Entertainment Software Association v Society of Composers, Authors and Music Publishers of Canada*, 2012 SCC 34; *Society of Composers, Authors and Music Publishers of Canada v Bell Canada*, 2012 SCC 36; *Alberta (Education) v Canadian Copyright Licensing Agency (Access Copyright)*, 2012 SCC 37.

24 Fair dealing was not intended to be interpreted restrictively. Until its codification in the *Copyright Act 1911* [UK], fair dealing was judge-made law with a measure of elasticity embedded within. And codification need not have instilled rigidity, as "the interpretative convention at the turn of the 20th century was that except where and so far as the statute is plainly intended to alter the course of the common-law statutes should be construed in conformity with the common-law rather than against it": see Arial Katz, "Fair Dealing's 100 Years of Solitude" (16 December 2011), online: Ariel Katz http://arielkatz.org/2011-the-fair-dealing-year.

25 *Israeli Copyright Act*, above note 8.

26 Robert E Babe, "Innis and the Emergence of Canadian Communication/Media Studies" (2008) 1:1 Global Media Journal — Canadian Edition 9 at 11; see also Catherine Frost, "How Prometheus Is Bound: Applying the Innis Method of Communications Analysis to the Internet" (2003) 28:1 Canadian Journal of Communication 9 at 12.

Innis does not make such a conclusion easy—his thoughts are scattered among an assortment of vast, seemingly arcane details; and he eschews a clear enunciation of his central thesis. However, this avoidance of scholarly rigour works to the advantage of new scholars. Unshackled by overt awareness of Innis's intentions, opaque texts prompt inspiration and inquiry. One such gem is: "Law was found, not made."[27]

To find as compared with *to make* conveys a very different connotation—the former carries an air of serendipity, whereas predictability exudes from the latter. Serendipity is anathema to many copyright holders, and some copyright users, who prefer a precise set of rules to govern the use of copyrighted work.[28] But it is because of the imprecision of the creative process that exceptions to copyright must be similarly imprecise. No politician, researcher, artist, teacher, or individual of any kind can say with certainty what manner of exposure, what combination of input copyrighted material, may be necessary to sustain the fine arts, education, and innovation. If copyright is deemed an incentive to creativity, it must not inhibit creativity—the language of exceptions must invite broad consideration of how a work contributes to creative effort.

Innis's writings illustrate his view that prose in general cannot be assumed to be so inviting. He is unambiguous in his appreciation for well-crafted prose that lends itself to dynamic conversation instead of stagnant edict.[29]

---

27 "In France and particularly in England the weakness of the written tradition favoured the position of custom and the common law. Law was found, not made, and the implications were evident in the jury system, the King's Court, common law, and parliament": see Innis, "Minerva's Owl," above note 17 at 21. To a fair dealing enthusiast, Innis's remark immediately brings to mind an instruction from our Supreme Court in 2004; specifically, that practices are relevant to a decision of fair dealing: see *CCH Canadian Ltd v Law Society of Upper Canada*, 2004 SCC 13 at paras 53–60 [*CCH*].

28 In 2004, the Supreme Court of Canada emphasized in *CCH*, *ibid*, the importance of a multi-faceted approach to evaluating fair dealing, called for a liberal interpretation of research, and went so far as to position fair dealing as a user's right. Following these pronouncements, the studied denigration of fair dealing by collective licensing organizations in Canada was matched only by the disinterest in protecting fair dealing on the part of Canada's educational community: see Nair, "Fair Dealing at a Crossroads," above note 15 at 97–102.

29 Innis made particular reference to the power of Plato's (written) dialogues:

> Plato attempted to adapt the new medium of prose to an elaboration of the conversation of Socrates by the dialogue with its question and answer, freedom of arrangement, and inclusiveness. A well-planned conversation was aimed at discovering truth and awakening the interest and sympathy of the reader . . . .

See Innis, *Empire*, above note 19 at 79.

His exploration of legal language was rooted in that of the culture of Ancient Greece;[30] Innis's admiration for Greek culture stemmed neither from hostility to modern technology, nor a romantic inclination to pastoral times, but from the view that Greek culture represented an inclination to justice and democracy: "'the democracy of Athens was the first great instance which the world ever saw of the substitution of law for force.'"[31] Playing a key role in the cultivation of this language of law was its uniquely oral culture.

Alexander Watson explains the central distinction between Greek oral culture and the oral traditions of other Eastern empires; Greek oral tradition carried the cultural mindset of developing a consensus, and not of "legitimizing oppression."[32] Greek practice drew strength from what Watson terms, "their intellectual backwardness [in the employment of script]," a handicap that ensured the adoption of writing began as subordinate to the oral tradition. Innis saw the advantage this brought to a system of law:

> The flexibility of law shown in the major reforms centring around the names of Dracon (621 B.C.), Solon, and Cleisthenes was possible before a written tradition had become firmly entrenched .... When Athens became the centre of the federation the way was opened to greater flexibility in the law through the contributions of orators to the improvement of prose from 420 to 320 B.C.[33]

The constraints of written language upon law show again in Innis's work, but this time with a modern interlocutor:

> Codes and statutes impose a heavy burden on language .... Changes in language necessitate the constant attention of the courts. "A word is not a crystal, transparent and unchanged; it is the skin of a living thought and

---

30 One element of Innis's work that is relatively transparent is his appreciation for the culture of Ancient Greece. Innis was keenly aware that Greek culture was the cradle of both Western and Eastern civilizations. With the Cold War looming, Innis saw that the cultural heritage of the United States and the Union of Soviet Socialist Republics originated from the Roman and Byzantium empires respectively. Each being a variant of Greek heritage, Innis hoped for rapprochement between the two superpowers by renewing the cultural traditions of their former unity. See Harold A Innis, "Reflections on Russia" in Innis, *Political Economy* above note 17 at 263–66.

31 EA Freeman, quoted in Innis, *Empire*, above note 19 at 78.

32 Watson, *Marginal Man 2006*, above note 5 at 371; see also Watson, *Marginal Man 1981*, above note 5 at 535.

33 Innis, "Minerva's Owl," above note 17 at 7–8.

may vary greatly in the colour and content according to the circumstances and times in which it may be used" (Holmes).[34]

The reference to Oliver Wendell Holmes Jr raises a question: how did Innis view Holmes's contribution to jurisprudence? A Civil War veteran wounded in battle, a philosopher at heart who pursued a career in law following the end of the war; there are parallels to Innis's life. Holmes's reputation as the Great Dissenter might also have intrigued Innis.[35] An enigmatic entry from Innis's *Idea File* provides some answers: "[Oliver Wendell] Holmes—background of interest in common law—oral tradition—refusal to be bound by black letters—common law is experience."[36]

Holmes's unwillingness to yield interpretation of the law to dogma may have appealed to Innis. Another interlocutor—this time for Holmes himself—appears in Innis's notes; Innis's invocation of Holmes comes via Max Lerner's *The Mind and Faith of Justice Holmes*, a work combining a brief personal history of Holmes together with a selection of his speeches, essays, letters, and judicial opinions. To Lerner's eyes, Holmes opposed the dominant strain of thought:

> It was not a brilliant Court nor an enlightened one .... The main outlines of judicial strategy had already been laid down ... [The] whole duty of a Supreme Court Justice lay in filling in the outlines of [due process and laissez-faire] decisions and in using constitutional law as a way of entrenching the system of economic power. Holmes refused to live up to the rules of the game so conceived. He had no intention of conscripting the legal Constitution as he saw it to the uses of the economic Constitution, any more than he would conscript it to the uses of a political program.[37]

---

34 Harold A Innis, "Roman Law and the British Empire" in *Changing Concepts of Time* (Lanham: Rowman & Littlefield Publishers, 2004) at 70.

35 Holmes participated in fewer dissents than the average United States's justice but the sincerity with which he wrote, coupled with the deference he showed to the majority, gained him both the title and the respect of the nation: see Catherine Drinker Bowen, *Yankee from Olympus: Justice Holmes and his Family* (Boston: Little Brown and Company, 1945) at 372–73. Like Holmes, Innis is described as a dissenter: see Robert E Babe, *Canadian Communication Thought: Ten Foundational Writers* (Toronto: University of Toronto Press, 2000) at 54.

36 See Christian, above note 5 at 22.

37 Max Lerner, ed, *The Mind and Faith of Justice Holmes* (New York: Modern Library, 1943) at xxxvii–xxxviii.

Holmes set interpretation of the law not merely against the events of the times, but in consideration of the future. New ideas often came to the court in shackles with the judiciary charged to decide the legality of the idea: "the accident of our finding certain opinions natural and familiar or novel and even shocking ought not to conclude our judgment . . . ."[38]

That such interpretation is a necessary part of law now seems only natural. But what we take for granted today needed champions to lead the way. As with his work in political economy and communication, Innis was ahead of his time with his views on law. He might have been pleased at the twentieth century Canadian development of interpretation — reaching what is known as *purposive interpretation* where interpretation must follow in light of the broader purpose of a statute. This development was facilitated through the work of Elmer Driedger; in 1998 Iaobucci J stated:

> Although much has been written about the interpretation of legislation . . . Elmer Driedger in *Construction of Statutes* (2nd ed. 1983) best encapsulates the approach upon which I prefer to rely. He recognizes that statutory interpretation cannot be founded on the wording of the legislation alone . . . he states: "Today there is only one principle or approach, namely, the words of an Act are to be read in their entire context and in their grammatical and ordinary sense harmoniously with the scheme of the Act, the object of the Act, and the intention of Parliament."[39]

Closer inspection of Driedger's work reveals some reliance on the work of a contemporary of Innis's, a prominent legal scholar by the name of James Alexander Corry:

> It will be urged here, with supporting evidence, that literal interpretation of a statute by no means always reveals a clear, precise meaning for application to particular cases. It will also be urged that it needs to be supplemented, in particular circumstances and under sober safeguards, by judicial reference to the broad object and social purpose of the statute, as a guide to the intention of the legislature in cases of doubt.[40]

---

38 Holmes in Lerner, *ibid* at 149.

39 Elmer A Driedger, *Construction of Statutes*, 2d ed (Toronto: Butterworths, 1983) at 87 [*Construction of Statutes*], cited in *Rizzo & Rizzo Shoes Ltd (Re)*, [1998] 1 SCR 27, 1998 CanLII 837 (SCC) at para 21.

40 See *Construction of Statutes*, above note 39, Appendix 1 at 252. The Appendix is an amended version of an earlier work by JA Corry, "Administrative Law and the Interpretation of Statutes" (1936) 1 UTLJ 286. Corry went on to become principal of Queen's University; his

The language of "sober safeguards" brings to mind *CCH* and its multi-faceted framework with which to judge unauthorized reproduction of copyrighted work. The Supreme Court of Canada saw fit to remove the straitjacket that had bound fair dealing through much of the twentieth century,[41] yet ensured that their interpretation could not be reinterpreted as sanction for piracy. Israel too had such a moment but in an ill-fated case. In 1993, the Israeli Supreme Court, while denying a satirical use of copyrighted work as fair dealing, offered a more expansive interpretation of the category of "criticism" within their regime of fair dealing, and introduced fair use's multi-faceted framework into Israeli copyright dialogue.[42] Israel's later adoption of fair use into law is credited to this judicial starting point.[43]

D. AN OWL IN ISRAEL?

The 2007 Israeli amendments to copyright were framed with specific goals that gave prominence to advancing the public good, and included a very striking phrase, *freedom of creativity*:

> The objective of the laws of Copyright is to establish an arrangement that will protect creative works while striking a balance between various interests of the public good. The balance required is mainly between the need to provide a sufficient incentive to create, which is in the form of granting general financial rights in the creations, and between the need to enable the public to use the creations for the advancement of culture and knowledge. This balance must be obtained while safeguarding the freedom of

---

correspondence illustrates that Innis was aware of Corry's work and in 1951 Innis invited Corry to join the University of Toronto; see Frederick W Gibson, *Queen's University, Volume II, 1917–1961: To Serve and Yet Be Free* (Montreal: McGill-Queen's University Press, 1983) at 261.

41 Prior to *CCH*, above note 27, Canadian courts tended to evaluate fair dealing with an uncompromising rigidity, suggesting unease "with the flexibility inherent in the concept of fairness": see Carys Craig, "The Changing Face of Fair Dealing in Canadian Copyright Law" in Michael Geist, ed, *In the Public Interest: The Future of Canadian Copyright Law* (Toronto: Irwin Law, 2005) at 443.

42 CA 2687/92 *Geva v Walt Disney Company*, 48(1) PD 251 (1993) [*Geva*].

43 Tony Greenman, "Fair Use Under Israel's New Copyright Act," online: Tony Greenman Law Offices www.tglaw.co.il/en/article.php?id=109. For a broader examination of the events leading to the adoption of fair use in Israel, see Meera Nair, "Canada and Israel: Cultivating Fairness of Use" (2012) Program on Information Justice and Intellectual Property (PIJIP) Research Paper no.2012-04, online: American University Washington College of Law, Digital Commons http://digitalcommons.wcl.american.edu/research [Nair, "Canada and Israel"].

> speech and freedom of creativity and while preserving free and fair competition.[44]

The advancement of culture and knowledge is not merely a platitude. Initial study suggests that Israel fosters a competitive, entrepreneurial atmosphere, with emphasis upon widespread social and creative well-being.[45] It is logical that a country with little in the way of natural resources should seek to cultivate its intellectual resources, namely its human capital. In such a setting, freedom of creativity is not a luxury but a necessity. Israel's creative aptitude emulates a pattern of behaviour described by Innis regarding *where* creativity is likely to flourish.

Readers of Innis may remember an essay titled "Minerva's Owl." Minerva, also known as Pallas Athena, was the patron saint of Athens. The persona of the goddess included the couplet of wisdom and the warrior. The owl, the familiar of Minerva, represents the search for knowledge but must continually return to the safety of his patron. Given as an address to the Royal Society in 1947, "Minerva's Owl" was something of an anomaly among Innis's writings. As he did not usually rely on literary devices, the metaphor invites scrutiny:

> [I]n a sense the flowering of the culture comes before its collapse. Minerva's owl begins its flight in the gathering dusk not only from classical Greece, but in turn from Alexandria, from Rome, from Constantinople, from the republican cities of Italy, from France, from Holland, and from Germany .... In the regions to which Minerva's owl takes flight the success of organized force may permit a new enthusiasm and an intense flowering of culture incidental to the migration of scholars engaged in Herculean efforts in a declining civilization to a new area with possibilities of protection.[46]

Innis's thesis is not easy to sift out; fortunately, Watson probes and then distills Innis' thoughts: "Western civilization can be renewed only by intellectual developments on a periphery that, in turn, becomes a new centre

44 Draft Bill Amending the Copyright Act (No 196), 2005, HH (Isr).

45 Dan Senor & Saul Singer, *Start-Up Nation: The Story of Israel's Economic Miracle* (New York: Twelve, 2009); Nimrod Kozlovski et al, "Fair Use in Israel" in Jeremy Malcolm, ed, *Access to Knowledge for Consumers — Reports of Campaigns and Research 2008–2010*, (Kuala Lumpur: Consumers International, 2010) 141.

46 Innis, "Minerva's Owl," above note 17 at 5.

for cultural florescence."[47] Innis did not despair over the migration of the owl; the collapse of one empire and the birth of another offer the potential for cultural renewal. Such renewal sustains civilization as a whole. Innis was not naïvely suggesting that the cultural effort of one empire would be duplicated in another, more hospitable, region. Instead, cultural traditions intermingle, creating a synergy capable of producing different avenues of thought and forms of expression. Extrapolating such ideas beyond cultural expressions in the conventional sense, to considering law as equally porous to a mingling of cultural tradition, invites consideration of how fair use took root in Israel, how it will meld with Israeli culture and, perhaps most important of all, can that undefinable entity we call *culture* be maintained in the face of pressures to conform to a global standard of copyright governance?[48]

E. What Lies Ahead?

To answer such a question requires a broader understanding of Israeli culture. No small task for an outsider. But to an Innis enthusiast — the project is irresistible. Orality, margins, multi-jural systems of law, education, and nation building — these were the hallmarks of Innis's work and all resonate within Israel. There are many points of entry into a project of this magnitude; what I seek are clues to the cultural atmosphere of intellectual property. A starting point has emerged from a pattern within the judiciary.

In a study of caselaw concerning fair dealing prior to 2007, it was observed that if attribution was reasonably expected but not present, the exception was denied.[49] While this trend raised some concerns,[50] it is not

---

47 Watson, *Marginal Man 2006*, above note 5 at 7; see also Watson, *Marginal Man 1981*, above note 5 at 16.

48 Israel has shown some determination to maintain its autonomy on matters of copyright; see Nair, "Canada and Israel," above note 43. Whether this can continue remains to be seen. At the time of this writing, the World Trade Organization has concluded a fourth review of Israel's trade policies and practices, including its treatment of intellectual property. The expansion of fair dealing to fair use did not go unnoticed. Thirukumaran Balasubramaniam, *WTO Trade Policy Review of Israel covers new developments on fair use, data exclusivity and parallel importation* (2 November 2012), online: Knowledge Ecology International http://keionline.org/node/1576.

49 Kozlovski et al, above note 45 at 150–51.

50 In a case concerning the Dead Sea Scrolls, the deciphering and reconstruction of one of the scrolls was deemed worthy of authorship and, thus, a reproduction of the work was denied fair dealing when attribution was not accorded to that author: see Michael Birnhack, "The Dead Sea Scrolls Case: Who Is an Author" (2001) 23:3 Eur IP Rev 128 at 5–6. Further discussion concerning the implications of awarding authorship, and with it

surprising given a cultural background which emphasizes recognition of the author. However, that recognition should not be blithely attributed to notions of the Romantic author; Neil Netanel writes:

> The Talmudic prohibition of plagiarism and its concomitant requirement of source attribution, moreover, aimed as much or more at ensuring that readers could assess the accuracy and force of a proffered ruling or argument than at protecting a personal right of individual authors.[51]

This turning on its head of a Western canonical principal is but one illustration of a non-Western cultural foundation of a law providing a fuller justification for the same law. Arguably, the very secular Platonic-like question/answer dialogue that shapes decisions and practices of fair use resembles the rabbinical tradition of inquiry. An acclaimed Israeli father-daughter team writes: "In the Jewish tradition, every reader is a proof-reader, every student a critic, and every writer, including the Author of the universe, begs a great many questions."[52] With such regard accorded to recipients of intellectual effort, the culture of reading, while still lacking precise definition, is clearly different. It permeates the very existence of the Israeli people; those same authors begin with a simple statement that speaks volumes: "Ours is not a bloodline but a textline."[53] To that end, it seems only to be expected that a system of law whose presumed objective is to facilitate the creation and diffusion of text should reflect this distinctiveness. How this will play out may only be seen through the fullness of time and research.

---

a means to limit access, to historical artifacts is cited in Guy Pessach, "Israeli Copyright Law: A Positive Economic Perspective" (2006) 39:3 Isr LR 123 at 139.

51 Neil Weinstock Netanel, "*Maharam of Padua v Giustiniani*: The Sixteenth-Century Origins of the Jewish Law of Copyright" (2007) 44 :4 Houston L Rev 821 at 852 [footnote omitted].

52 Amos Oz & Fania Oz-Salzberger, *Jews and Words* (New Haven: Yale University Press, 2012) at x.

53 *Ibid* at 1.

FIFTEEN

Intellectual Property: The Promise and Risk of Human Rights[1]

CHIDI OGUAMANAM

ABSTRACT (EN): The intersection of intellectual property and human rights is a relatively new site in the search for balance in intellectual property law and policy. Although this intersection opens up intellectual property to a unique kind of interdisciplinary analysis, only the human rights system appears to have seized the opportunity, while its intellectual property rights counterpart remains reluctant to engage. There are, so far, different competing first impressions over the nature of the intersection between intellectual property and human rights. Despite empirical credence of the conflict narrative, the co-existence or complementary thesis of the intellectual property and human rights interface has greater prospects for a meaningful and balanced rapprochement between the two. This chapter argues for a critical scrutiny of the human rights appeal of intellectual property rights in order to avoid its potential for being hijacked by stronger stakeholders at the expense of their weaker opponents for whom intellectual property rights have strong paradoxical ramifications.

RÉSUMÉ (FR): L'intersection entre la propriété intellectuelle et les droits de la personne est un point relativement nouveau dans la recherche d'un équi-

1 Thanks to Professor Tesh Dagne for reading and commenting on this paper in draft. I am grateful to Professor Scassa, Professor Goudreau, Madelaine Saginur, and B Courtney Doagoo, the conveners of the 2012 Intellectual Property Scholars Workshop, for inviting me to speak, and to the members of the academy and anonymous reviewers of this contribution for their helpful feedback.

libre en droit et en politique de la propriété intellectuelle. Même si cette intersection ouvre la porte à une analyse interdisciplinaire unique pour la propriété intellectuelle, le système des droits de la personne semble être seul à en avoir saisi l'occasion, tandis que son homologue en droit de la propriété intellectuelle demeure réticent à se lancer. Jusqu'à maintenant, il existe plusieurs premières impressions sur la nature de l'intersection entre la propriété intellectuelle et les droits de la personne. Malgré les croyances empiriques concernant le narratif du conflit, la thèse de la coexistence ou de la complémentarité dans l'interface entre la propriété intellectuelle et les droits de la personne donne un plus grand espoir de rapprochement sérieux et équilibré entre les deux. Ce chapitre plaide pour un examen critique minutieux de l'attrait des droits de la personne pour la propriété intellectuelle, pour empêcher que le potentiel des premiers soit détourné par des parties prenantes aux dépens de leurs opposants plus faibles pour qui les droits de la propriété intellectuelle ont des fortes ramifications paradoxales.

A. INTRODUCTION

Striking a just balance between rights holders and users of innovations and creativity is a constant quest of intellectual property (IP) law and policy. Both in their statutory and common law derivations, intellectual property rights (IPRs) have built-in mechanisms for negotiating this balance. However, the complexity and multiplicity not only of various claimants to IPRs but also of IP regimes make the quest for balance contentious and elusive. These factors have also yielded diverse conceptual frameworks for the discourse of balance in IP jurisprudence. That discourse challenges the adequacy of so-called built-in mechanisms in IP law to respond to public policy considerations and diverse renditions of the balance narrative.

Aside from when the analysis focuses on specific statutory accommodations in national IP laws,[2] the diverse conceptual frameworks for broaching

2 See, for example, copyright statutes' accommodation or lack thereof of freedom of expression under the *Canadian Charter of Rights and Freedoms*, Part I of the *Constitution Act, 1982*, being Schedule B to the *Canada Act 1982* (UK), 1982, c 11 and the *Fourth Amendment of the United States Constitution*, US Const amend IV; see Ysolde Gendreau, "Copyright and Freedom of Expression in Canada" in Paul LC Torremans, ed, *Copyright and Human Rights: Freedom of Expression, Intellectual Property, Privacy* (The Hague: Kluwer Law, 2004) 21–36 [Torremans, *Freedom of Expression*]; Wendy Gordon, "Do We Have a Right to Speak in Another's Language? *Eldred* and the Duration of Copyright" in Torremans, *Freedom of Expression*, *ibid*.

the issue of balance include discourse on IP and development, IP and economic empowerment, IP and access to knowledge (A2K), and, lately, IP and human rights (HRs). These binary configurations are overlapping and are distinguished in regard to conceptual emphasis. After all, at least on a rhetorical level, A2K is integral to realization of HRs and, when optimized, both can yield favourable development outcomes.

The focus of this chapter is on the intersection between HRs and IPRs at global policy-making levels.[3] We approach the HRs-IP discourse as a fairly new site in the search for balance in IP law and policy. In trying to understand the tenor of the emerging interface between HRs and IP, an interesting question is how to characterize the nature of that engagement from an *interdisciplinary* perspective, with a view to reflecting on the lessons to be learned therefrom, and hinting at the dangers thereto, especially the prospects and implications of HRs' ratchet of IP.

This chapter is divided into five sections. The first explores the context for the entente between HRs and IP. The second examines the one-sided nature of the rapprochement as driven by the international HRs system amidst a cold reception by its IP counterpart. The third identifies Article 15 of the *International Covenant on Economic, Social, and Cultural Rights*[4] as articulating a direct connection between IP and HRs. The section notes, however, that too much emphasis on Article 15 appears to undermine the general depth of *ICESCR* provisions and their ramifications in regard to core areas of "conventional HRs." This narrow approach is fatal in framing the interface between IP and HRs, especially as the two increasingly collide.

In a tripartite framework, section four examines the paradox, the attraction, and the danger of an uncritical conception of IP as HRs, with emphasis on the potential boomerang effect on indigenous peoples' rights, specifically traditional knowledge (TK). The concluding segment adopts a *disciplinary* analysis, reflecting on the competing and complementary conceptions of the nature of the relationship between IP and HRs. It argues that despite empirical evidence of a conflict approach, the co-existence/complementary thesis has prospects for a meaningful and balanced HRs-IP rapprochement.

3 *Ibid*. There are few safety nets for mitigating the negative impacts of international intellectual property law in contrast to the national systems, especially in developed countries.

4 GA Res 2200A (XXI), UNGAOR, 1966, Supp No 16, UN Doc A/6316, 993 UNTS 3 at 49 (entered into force 3 January 1976) [*ICESCR*].

B. HUMAN RIGHTS AND INTELLECTUAL PROPERTY: ANATOMY OF RAPPROCHEMENT

Though HRs and IP laws may have followed different paths in their development,[5] they evolved in shared contexts. According to Grosheide, both evolved amidst inequalities occasioned by rapid industrial and economic advances in Europe in the eighteenth and nineteenth centuries and the consequential expansion of international trade by economically and technologically dominant countries.[6] That expansion in international commerce called attention to IP as a mechanism for negotiating access[7] to innovation by less technologically endowed countries.

The foundational multilateral IP instruments came into being in the second half of the nineteenth century,[8] a period that symbolized the foundation of the modern HRs regime.[9] In terms of developments in HRs and IP in the twentieth century, Grosheide suggests that the legislative histories of the 1948 *Universal Declaration of Human Rights*[10] and the 1994 *Agreement on Trade-Related Aspects of Intellectual Property Rights* (*TRIPS*)[11] are equally indicative of identical socio-economic circumstances.[12]

Despite the foregoing insinuations, HRs and IP remained "strangers."[13] This is so for diverse reasons, not the least of which is the continuing historical subjugation of economic, social, and cultural rights, notably by the US, a leading champion of IP, which has failed to ratify the *ICESCR*. In addition, there is no *direct* involvement of institutions with true IP credibility on the

5 See Laurence R Helfer, "Human Rights and Intellectual Property: Conflicts or Coexistence?" (2003) 5 Minn Intell Prop Rev 47 [Helfer, "Conflicts"].

6 See Willem Grosheide, ed, *Intellectual Property and Human Rights: A Paradox?* (Cheltenham, UK: Edward Elgar, 2010) at 3–5.

7 Developing countries also perceive IP as a stumbling block to access to innovation.

8 For example, the *Paris Convention for the Protection of Industrial Property*, 20 March 1883, 828 UNTS 305; *Berne Convention for the Protection of Literary and Artistic Works*, 9 September 1886, 1161 UNTS 3.

9 Grosheide, above note 6 at 4, n 4, and n 6.

10 GA Res 217 (III), UNGAOR, 3d Sess, Supp No 13, UN Doc A/810, (1948) [*UDHR*].

11 15 April 1994, 1869 UNTS 299, 33 ILM 1197 [*TRIPS*].

12 See Grosheide, above note 6 at 5 and n 6; compare Helfer, "Conflicts," above note 5; Laurence R Helfer, "Toward a Human Rights Framework for Intellectual Property" (2007) 40:3 UC Davis L Rev 971 [Helfer, "Framework"]; Peter K Yu, "Reconceptualizing Intellectual Property Interests in a Human Rights Framework" (2007) 40:3 UC Davis L Rev 1039 at 1041 [Yu, "Reconceptualizing"]; Philippe Cullet, "Human Rights and Intellectual Property Protection in the TRIPS Era" (2007) 29:2 Hum Rts Q 403 at 430, noting that human rights and intellectual property evolved separately.

13 See Helfer, "Conflicts," above note 5 at 47.

subject of interface between IP and HRs. Recently, however, "international standard setting activities have begun to map previously uncharted intersections between intellectual property law on the one hand and human rights law on the other."[14] The neglected rights of indigenous peoples in international HRs processes and the consequences of the *TRIPS*-instigated seismic shift of IP into the trade arena have been identified as the sparks that dissipated the fog separating HRs and IP.[15] Perhaps, more important is the expansion of HRs and IP in the past several decades in directions that have made their collision inevitable.

Indigenous peoples' pressure on the international system over the reclamation of their cultural and traditional knowledge was, in part, a response to IP's facilitation of exploitation of those knowledge forms.[16] Indigenous peoples have made modest progress after decades of rough and tumble politics of the international HRs system. This is evident, in part, through the *United Nations Declaration on the Rights of Indigenous Peoples*,[17] and the progressive induction of indigenous knowledge onto the agenda of not only IP law and policy but also the overall global knowledge and cultural governance.[18]

Although the *UNDRIPs* takes a holistic approach to indigenous peoples' rights, those rights are largely rooted in HRs. The document makes a strong link between TK and IP in its elaboration of indigenous peoples' rights.[19] Within the four decades of the making of the *UNDRIPs*, TK has found traction in diverse regimes such as biodiversity, medicine, agriculture, cultural property, and intangible cultural heritage, linking them with IP in furtherance of the HRs of indigenous peoples.[20]

TRIPS also provoked severe backlash on a number of fronts with HRs implications. The impacts of *TRIPS* on public health, especially on access to medicines, became the flashpoint for linking IP with HRs from a con-

---

14 *Ibid.*

15 *Ibid.*

16 See Toshiyuki Kono, ed, *Intangible Cultural Heritage and Intellectual Property: Communities, Cultural Diversity and Sustainable Development* (Antwerp: Intersentia, 2009).

17 GA Res 61/295, UNGAOR, 61st Sess, Supp No 49, UN Doc A/61/295 (2008) [*UNDRIPs*].

18 See Michael F Brown, "Can Culture be Copyrighted?" (1998) 39:2 Current Anthropology 193; see also Chidi Oguamanam, "Local Knowledge as Trapped Knowledge: Intellectual Property, Culture, Power and Politics" (2008) 11:1 Journal of World Intellectual Property 29.

19 See *UNDRIPs*, above note 17, art 31.

20 See, generally, Charles R McManis, ed, *Biodiversity & the Law: Intellectual Property, Biotechnology & Traditional Knowledge* (London: Earthscan, 2007).

flict paradigm.[21] Stronger IP protection in the wake of the digital and biotechnology revolutions of the mid-twentieth century removed the leverage which less-developed countries had to tailor their policies in areas of innovations in agriculture and plant genetic resources to national economic exigencies.[22] It was not long before *TRIPS* attained notoriety as a catalyst for the aggravated North-South development gap, and the principal reason for the negative link between IP and a broad range of HRs, including the rights to food, health, education, and the freedom of expression.[23]

The global public health crisis sparked by the HIV/AIDS pandemic forced a reluctant but inchoate attempt to recalibrate *TRIPS*. Attempts by the US and a coalition of pharmaceutical corporations to shut down the Mandela-led post-apartheid South Africa's legislative response to facilitate access to patented HIV/AIDS medicines sparked a global outrage.[24] A few years later, that outrage gave impetus to the 2001 Ministerial Declaration on *TRIPS* Agreement and Public Health (*Doha*).[25] The latter sought to pave the way for World Trade Organization (WTO) member countries with no, or insufficient, pharmaceutical manufacturing capacity to access patented medicines through a process that purports to abridge the rights of patent holders.[26] The *Doha Declaration* was a symbolic pushback by the WTO process against criticisms from the UN on the negative HRs impact of *TRIPS*. Article 4 of the *Doha Declaration* reads:

> We agree that the TRIPS Agreement does not and should not prevent members from taking measures to protect public health . . . . we affirm that the

---

21 See Cynthia M Ho, "Current Controversies Concerning Patent Rights and Public Health in a World of International Norms" in Toshiko Takenaka, ed, *Patent Law and Theory: A Handbook of Contemporary Research* (Cheltenham, UK: Edward Elgar, 2008); James Thuo Gathii, "Rights, Patents, Markets and the Global AIDS Pandemic" (2002) 14:2 Fla J of Int'l L 261.

22 See Peter Drahos & John Braithwaite, *Information Feudalism: Who Owns the Knowledge Economy?* (London: Earthscan, 2002); Tzen Wong & Graham Dutfied, eds, *Intellectual Property and Human Development: Current Trends and Future Scenarios* (New York, NY: Cambridge University Press, 2011).

23 See JH Reichman, "The TRIPS Agreement Comes of Age: Conflict or Cooperation with the Developing Countries?" (2000) 32:3 Case W Res J Int'l L 441.

24 Gathii, above note 21; Ho, above note 21.

25 WTO, Ministerial Conference, *Doha Declaration on the TRIPS Agreement and Public Health*, WTO Doc WT/MIN(01)/DEC/2, 4th Sess, (2001), online: WTO http://wto.org/english/thewto_e/minist_e/min01_e/mindecl_TRIPS_e.htm [*Doha Declaration*].

26 See Frederick M Abbott & Jerome H Reichman, "The DOHA Round's Public Health Legacy: Strategies for the Production and Diffusion of Patented Medicines under Amended TRIPS Provisions" (2007) 10:4 J of Int'l Econ L 921.

> Agreement can and should be interpreted and implemented in a manner supportive of WTO members' right to protect public health and, in particular, to promote access to medicines for all.[27]

A year before the *Doha Declaration*, the United Nations Sub-Commission on the Protection and Promotion of Human Rights adopted *Resolution 2000/7: Intellectual Property and Human Rights*.[28] Paragraph 2 of the Resolution declares:

> [S]ince the implementation of the TRIPS Agreement does not adequately reflect the fundamental nature and indivisibility of all human rights, including the right of everyone to enjoy the benefits of scientific progress and its applications, the right to health, the right to food and the right to self-determination, there are apparent conflicts between the intellectual property rights regime embodied in the TRIPS Agreement, on the one hand, and international human rights law, on the other.[29]

The Resolution sets a tone for a collaborative scrutiny by UN HRs actors and IP institutions, including the World Intellectual Property Office (WIPO), the World Health Organization (WHO), the United Nations Development Program (UNDP), the United Nations Conference on Trade and Development (UNCTAD), and the Convention on Biological Diversity (CBD), to explore and deepen their analysis of the impacts of *TRIPS* on HRs. The UN High Commissioner for Human Rights urged the "Committee on Economic, Social and Cultural Rights [CESCR] to clarify the relationship between intellectual property rights and human rights . . . through the drafting of a general comment on this subject."[30]

The following year, in 2001, the CESCR issued a statement on *Human Rights and Intellectual Property*,[31] in which it identified "the key human rights principles deriving from the *Covenant* that are required to be taken into account in the development, interpretation and implementation of contemporary intellectual property regimes."[32] The CESCR outlines the context in which HRs are implicated in IP[33] and notes that

27 *Doha Declaration*, above note 25.

28 E/CN 4/Sub 2/Res/2000/7, UNHCHR, 52nd Sess, (2000).

29 *Ibid* at para 2.

30 *Ibid* at para 11.

31 CESCR, *Human Rights and Intellectual Property: Statement by the Committee on Economic Social and Cultural Rights*, E/C 12/2001/15, UNHCHR, 27th Sess, (2001).

32 *Ibid* at para 2.

33 *Ibid* at para 1.

> [t]he allocation of rights over intellectual property has significant economic, social and cultural consequences that can affect the enjoyment of human rights. The contemporary importance of intellectual property for human rights reflects two developments. The first is the expansion of the areas covered by intellectual property regimes to include, for example, patenting of biological entities, copyright print protections in the digital domain, and private intellectual property claims with respect to cultural heritage and traditional knowledge. The second is the emergence of universal rules on intellectual property protection in the global trading system.[34]

In the document, the CESCR enunciated the HRs principles[35] that would guide its interpretive functions when HRs come into contact with IP.[36] It counsels that the principles are subject to refinements and elaborations.[37]

Like the CESCR, the WHO seized the momentum to galvanize opposition to *TRIPS* on the basis of its negative impact on the HR to health.[38] Indeed, the WHO was one of the principal actors that gave life to the *Doha Declaration*.[39] It assumed responsibility for pushing back on *TRIPS*'s impact on access to medicines, an issue that was topical in a few flashpoint developing countries.[40] The WHO was charged by its governing body in 1999 to "examine the impact of the WTO on national drug policies and essential drugs and to make recommendations for collaboration between the WTO and WHO."[41] It adopted proactive strategies, including provision of technical advisory support for developing countries both in regard to exploiting various flexibilities in *TRIPS* and on the issues of exercise of compulsory licences and par-

34 *Ibid* at para 1. They are universality, indivisibility and interdependence of human rights, equality and non-discrimination, participation, accountability, general legal obligations, core obligations, international cooperation and assistance, self-determination, and balance.

35 See above note 31 at para 2.

36 *Ibid.*

37 See, generally, Susan K Sell, "TRIPS and the Access to Medicines Campaign" (2002) 20:3 Wis Int'l LJ 481 at 504–6; Susan K Sell, "The Quest for Global Governance in Intellectual Property and Public Health: Structural, Discursive, and Institutional Dimensions" (2004) 77:2 Temp L Rev 363 at 389.

38 Susan K Sell, "TRIPS-Plus Free Trade Agreements and Access to Medicines" (2007) 28:1 Liverpool Law Review 41 at 48.

39 For example, South Africa, Brazil, Namibia, Malawi, Zimbabwe.

40 WHA, *Revised Drug Strategy*, Res 52.19 WHO, 52nd World Health Assembly (Geneva: WHO, 1999), online: WHO www.who.int/phi/WHA52.19.pdf.

41 *Ibid* at 92–93. In addition, the WHO occasionally issues a world drug strategy, an instrument oriented toward an anti-free market approach to drug procurement that assists mainly less developed countries in fashioning their national drug plans.

allel importation of patented drugs.[42] The WHO maintains that *TRIPS* and, for that matter, IP as a whole is a burden on the HR to health, insisting that "access to essential drugs is a human right"[43] and that "essential drugs are not simply another [trade] commodity."[44]

Not only have the UN HRs system and other bodies such as the WHO initiated a rapprochement between HRs and IP, part of their approach is to penetrate the IP policy-making arenas in order to infuse them with HRs consciousness. For instance, the High Commissioner for HRs has sought observer status with the WTO in order to engage in the review of *TRIPS*.[45] Similarly, the High Commissioner, the WHO, and many NGOs have observer status at the WIPO Intergovernmental Committee on Intellectual Property and Genetic Resources, Traditional Knowledge and Folklore (WIPO-IGC).

The pressure on IP by several actors helps to highlight its jurisdictional perviousness:

> [T]he nature of the UN human rights system and the WHO's interest [i]n intellectual property call into question what it actually means to say that an organization, such as WIPO or the WTO, has a special jurisdiction, mandate, or competence in regard to intellectual property matters. That claim is certainly in need of critical and urgent revision. Intellectual property issues are complex, and they transcend the competence or jurisdiction of a few organizations.[46]

This observation is equally true in relation to open-ended disciplinary interests around IP. *TRIPS* is the source of the festering of the "relatedness" concept in the IP narrative within the UN system and institutions, and in the contexts of several relevant subject matters and disciplines.

---

42 WHO, *Network for Monitoring the Impact of Globalization and TRIPS on Access to Medicines* (2002) (Meeting Report, 19–21 February 2001, Bangkok, Thailand) at 20, online: World Health Organization http://apps.who.int/medicinedocs/en/d/Js2284e/.

43 *Ibid* at 21.

44 Helfer, "Framework," above note 12 at 987.

45 See Chidi Oguamanam, *Intellectual Property in Global Governance:A Development Question* (London: Routledge, 2012) at 101.

46 See Helfer, "Framework," above note 12 at 979.

C. UNIDIRECTIONAL OVERTURE AND QUESTIONABLE PRIMACY OF HUMAN RIGHTS

HRs instruments such as the *UDHR* and the CESCR accommodate IPRs. However, HRs' rapprochement "has not been reciprocated in the international intellectual property system. No references to 'human rights' appear in multilateral treaties such as the Paris, Berne, and Rome Conventions, nor do they appear in the more recently adopted TRIPS Agreement."[47] What we have is a unilateral effort at provoking an interdisciplinary conversation between HRs and IP. In other words, there is "a visible imbalance insofar as the language of human rights has not penetrated intellectual property rights institutions, while the language of intellectual property rights is regularly addressed in human rights institutions."[48]

IP's indifference to HRs is unsurprising for several reasons. First, the inchoate nature and lack of textual precision on the details of HRs, especially under the CESCR, is not well-matched to a texted-based statutory regime like IP. Perhaps most important, even though HRs and IP are both underpinned by *rights* jurisprudence, the principal justifications for the invocation of *rights* in IP are hardly rooted in "deontological claims" on the fundamental and inalienable attributes of HRs.[49] Instead, rights claims in IP are largely driven by "economic and instrumental benefits."[50] Thirdly, HRs' overture to IP can easily be perceived as an "affirmative strategy" by the global South to use HRs for *subsidized* access to intellectual products of the industrialized world.

The foregoing review demonstrates a new consciousness and active rapprochement but reluctant disciplinary engagement between HRs and IP. So far, the outcome of the HRs-IP interface is hard to measure in any concrete way. First, given the ubiquitous manifestations of HRs considerations in diverse degrees across equally diverse sites of IP discourse, precision in identifying HRs-driven changes in IP discourse may be elusive. Secondly, the nascent status of the conversation suggests that any form of assessment may be premature.

---

47 Cullet, above note 12 at 414 [footnote omitted].

48 Helfer, "Framework," above note 12 at 980.

49 *Ibid*.

50 *Ibid* at 981; see also Yu, "Reconceptualizing," above note 12; Laurence R Helfer, "Regime Shifting in the International Intellectual Property System" (2009) 7:1 Perspectives on Politics 39; see generally Graeme B Dinwoodie, "The International Intellectual Property Law System: New Actors, New Institutions, New Sources" (2004) 98 Am Soc'y Int'l L Proc 213.

Nonetheless, it is evident that pressures from the WHO, the UN HRs system, and elsewhere have resulted in a more tempered approach to IP law and policy. IP's supposed negative impact on public health has emboldened a trend in the decentralization of forums in which IP issues are raised outside the traditional ones. From biodiversity, indigenous peoples' rights, A2K, to broader development discourse — each with elements of HRs considerations — "the international intellectual property system has morphed . . . into a 'conglomerate regime' or a 'regime complex'"[51] resulting in a chessboard approach to norm creation in the IP arena.

Without underemphasizing the modest impact of HRs overture on IP, suggestions of primacy of HRs over IP by the UN HRs system or allegations of *TRIPS* violations of HRs have yet to be rigorously scrutinized through the principles of customary international law. Alluding to that gap, Helfer argues that the efforts by the UN HRs system "fail to provide a detailed textual analysis of a human rights framework for intellectual property and how that framework interfaces with existing intellectual property protection standards in national and international law."[52] Rather, he argues that Resolution 2000/7 set "an ambitious new agenda for reviewing intellectual property issues within the U.N. human rights system" based on the "principle of human right primacy" over IP.[53]

The CESCR assumed responsibility for championing the principle of HRs primacy over IP. This was evident in its first interpretative foray into the HRs-IP interface through General Comment 17 issued in 2005: the right of everyone to benefit from "the protection of the moral and material interests resulting from any scientific, literary or artistic production of which he or she is the author."[54] This provision is perhaps the most direct link in treaty jurisprudence between HRs and IP.

The significance of *GC17* cannot be overstated in regard both to the CESCR's previous work in areas relevant to HRs and IP, and its influence on emerging HRs frameworks for IP.

According to *GC17*:

---

51 Helfer, "Framework," above note 12 at 987.

52 *Ibid* at 986.

53 See CESCR, *General Comment No 17, The Right of Everyone to Benefit from the Protection of the Moral and Material Interests Resulting from any Scientific, Literary or Artistic Production of which He or She is the Author*, 35th Sess, UN Doc E/C 12/GC/17 (2005) at para 47 [*GC17*]. The same provision takes its life from Article 27(2) of the *UDHR*, above note 10.

54 *Ibid* at para 1.

- Article 15(1)(c) rights derive their force from "inherent dignity and worth of all persons."[55] As such, they are basically HRs, and are apart from and transcend general IPRs.[56] Modalities for protection of those rights need not equate to the ones obtainable under copyright, patent, and other IP forms in so far as they secure the moral and material interest of authors.[57] While IPRs are mostly alienable, temporary, and limited in time and scope, HRs "are timeless expressions of fundamental entitlements of the human person."[58]
- References to moral and material interests[59] speak respectively to: a) recognition of moral rights of authors in their works as an expression and extension of their personality; b) commensurate remuneration, which supports an adequate standard of living of creators. Such recompense need not necessary be in tandem with what obtains in conventional IP, such as statutory copyright or patent accommodations.[60]
- Rights under Article 15(1)(c) are subject to balancing in relation to other rights pursuant to indivisibility and interrelatedness of HRs. Thus, "the private interests of authors should not be unduly favoured and the public interest in enjoying broad access to their productions should be given due consideration."[61]
- Article 15(1)(c) (which includes IPRs such as copyright, patent, plant breeder rights, etc.) ought not constrain states' abilities to discharge their core obligations in relation to the rights to "food, health and education," rights to participate "in cultural life and to enjoy the benefits of scientific progress."[62]
- Yet on the principles of interrelatedness of HRs and core obligations, GC17 notes:

> Ultimately, intellectual property is a social product and has a social function. States parties have a duty to prevent unreasonably high costs for

55 *Ibid* at para 3.
56 *Ibid* at para 10.
57 *Ibid* at para 2.
58 *Ibid* at paras 12–16.
59 One-off payments or alternative remuneration schemes for creators of intellectual work as opposed to conventional royalties are feasible under this interpretation.
60 See *GC17*, above note 53 at para 35.
61 *Ibid*.
62 *Ibid*.

> access to essential medicines, plant seeds or other means of food production, or for schoolbooks and learning materials, from undermining the rights of large segments of the population to health, food and education. Moreover, States parties should prevent the use of scientific and technical progress for purposes contrary to human rights and dignity, including the rights to life, health and privacy, e.g. by excluding inventions from patentability whenever their commercialization would jeopardize the full realization of these rights.[63]

Like all HRs, Article 15(1)(c) rights are subject to three levels of obligations for their implementation by states, namely: a) to respect, i.e., to avoid direct or indirect interference with authors' freedom to enjoy their rights; b) to protect, i.e., to initiate positive measures to stop third parties from interfering with those rights; and, c) to fulfill, i.e., to proactively adopt diverse measures to facilitate optimal realization of the rights.

GC17 is the first major effort in the ongoing attempt to map an HRs' framework for IP. It is not only animated by the principle of primacy of HRs over IP as set by the sub-commission, but also by the 2001 CESCR's statement of key HRs principles for IP. In addition, it highlights the principle of indivisibility and interdependence of HRs. On that premise, Article 15(1)(c) rights are linked with the rest of the *ICESCR*, but more emphatically with other Article 15 rights, including rights to take part in cultural life and to enjoy the benefits of scientific progress, and freedoms associated with scientific research and creativity. The relationship between these rights and Article 15(1)(c) "is at the same time mutually reinforcing and reciprocally limitative."[64]

GC17 opened up space for incorporation of group rights generally, and the rights of indigenous and local communities within the intersection of HRs and IP.[65] Counterintuitively, it excludes corporations from making HRs claims over Article 15(1)(1)(c).[66]

Further, the tendency to cast Article 15(1)(c) rights both in terms of scope and the nature of rights[67] opens a window to accommodate TK in the

---

63 *Ibid* at para 4.

64 *Ibid* at paras 7 & 8.

65 *Ibid*, noting that "under the existing international treaty protection regimes, legal entities are included among the holders of intellectual property rights. However . . . their entitlements, because of their different nature, are not protected at the level of human rights" at para 7.

66 *Ibid* at paras 1 and 3.

67 Cullet, above note 12 at 430.

context of HRs.[68] *GC17* recognizes a broad construction of "authors" to include rights holders in virtually all regimes of IP, including copyright, patent, and plant breeders' rights.[69] Yet, it warns that the nature of IP under the HRs rubric of Article 15 and the entire *ICESCR* is neither absolute, nor fundamental. Rather, it is unequivocally qualified.[70]

Audrey Chapman observes that "[t]o be consistent with the full provisions of Article 15, the type and level of protection afforded under any intellectual property regime must therefore facilitate and promote cultural participation and scientific progress and do so in a manner that will broadly benefit members of society both on an individual and collective level."[71] In *GC17*, we glimpse the nuances of HRs' framework for IP, at least in their preliminary conceptualization.

Since the release of *GC17* in 2005, the CESCR has issued only one more GC that bears direct relevance to IP as a component of Article 15. That is *GC21* titled *The Right of Everyone to Take Part in Cultural Life* (article 15, paragraph 1(a)).[72] Like *GC17*, it applies (with appropriate modifications) the 2001 principles in enunciating the right to take part in cultural life. For instance, on the basis of indivisibility and interrelatedness, the rights are linked to the provisions of Article 15, other HRs categories (including the rights to education, self-determination, and adequate standard of living) as well as all the *ICESCR* rights.[73] It elaborately provides for indigenous peoples as part of categories for special protection. As well, it recognizes the communal or group-oriented nature of indigenous peoples' rights.[74]

---

68 See Rochelle Cooper Dreyfuss, "Patents and Human Rights: Where Is the Paradox?" in Grosheide, above note 6 at 72. Analysts of Article 15(1)(c) tend to isolate patent from its ambit; compare Peter K Yu, "Ten Common Questions About Intellectual Property and Human Rights" (2007) 23:4 Ga St U L Rev 709 [Yu, "Ten Questions"].

69 See *GC17*, above note 53 at paras 1–4.

70 Audrey R Chapman, "The Human Rights Implications of Intellectual Property Protection" (2002) 5:4 J Int'l Econ L 861 at 868 [Chapman, "Implications"].

71 CESCR, *General Comment No 21, The Right of Everyone to Take Part in Cultural Life*, 43rd Sess, Un Doc E/C.12/GC/21 (2009) [GC21].

72 *Ibid* at para 2.

73 *Ibid*, see for example, paras 3, 7, and 36.

74 They are also known as rights in intellectual creations; see below note 81.

D. ARTICLE 15 RIGHTS[75] AND CONVENTIONAL HUMAN RIGHTS CATEGORIES

Article 15 of the *ICESCR* demonstrates direct connection between HRs and IP.[76] It is, however, far from being the only article to do so. Arguably, only a fraction of the *ICESCR* articles can be distanced from IP, especially as the expansion of IP is felt in every area of life. Keeping our focus on core HRs, specifically the right to adequate food (art 11),[77] the right to education (art 13),[78] the right to the highest attainable standard of health (art 12),[79] the CESCR has already issued GCs on these rights in 1999 and 2000.

A review of the GCs on these core HRs shows that the CESCR shied away from making a direct link between them and IP. This approach is perhaps in strict compliance with the text of the *ICESCR*. Interestingly, issues around access to health, food, and A2K, with emphasis on information technologies and educational materials have been the touchstone of the HRs-IP interface.[80] These GCs predate the 2001 principles. Since those principles were meant for development, interpretation, and implementation of contemporary IP regimes, it is hard to justify the exclusion of core HRs from the understanding of extant IP regimes.[81]

The failure of the CESCR to directly raise IP concerns in its GCs on the core HRs most relevant to IP is a fundamental flaw in the current rapprochement between the two regimes. The narrow analytical confines which focus the HRs framework for IP on Article 15 of the *ICESCR* are far from helpful. Admittedly, direct reference to IP is missing in the *ICESCR* provisions for these core rights. Also, GCs on Article 15(1)(c), and Article 15(1)(a) indicate that the comments are applicable to the *ICESCR* as a whole. As well, the two

---

75 See Yu, "Ten Questions," above note 68 at 711.

76 CESCR, *General Comment No 12, The Right to Adequate Food*, 20th Sess, UN Doc E/C.12/1999/5 (1999), art 11 [*GC12*].

77 CESCR, *General Comment No 13, The Right to Education*, 21st Sess, UN Doc E/C.12/1999/10 (1999), art 13 [*GC13*].

78 CESCR, *General Comment No 14*, (2000), *The Right to the Highest Attainable Standard of Health*, 22nd Sess, UN Doc E/C.12/2000/4 (2000), art 12 [*GC14*].

79 See, generally, Laurence R Helfer & Graeme W Austin, *Human Rights and Intellectual Property: Mapping the Global Interface* (New York: Cambridge, 2011); Grosheide, above note 6.

80 Indeed, these core HRs regimes are among the critical animators of contemporary intellectual property law and policy-making.

81 See, for example, *GC17*, above note 53 at para 35; *GC21*, above note 71 at para 2.

Article 15 GCs make references to aspects of those core HRs,[82] but they are bereft of direction and clarity on the dynamics of contemporary IP.

HRs are dynamic, evolving, and even contingent.[83] The CESCR elaboration of 2001 principles and its recent focus on Article 15 are responsive to the contingent nature of the contemporary challenges which IP poses for HRs. Those challenges are also increasingly raised at the sites of core HRs. Therefore, it is expected that any attempt to invoke the GCs, especially those relevant to key HRs identified above, after 2001 ought to take into account the 2001 principles in order to accommodate IPRs and specific HRs issue linkages.

There is a decade between the first GC on a core HR (right to food) and the very last one on Article 15(1)(b) issued in 2009. The 1999 *GC12* (right to adequate food (art.11))[84] states that the right is violated when a party adopts legislation or policies, including international agreements, which are inconsistent with its pre-existing legal obligation on the right to food.[85] In 2000, the CESCR shied away from even making reference to IP under *GC14* (right to highest attainable standard of health (article 12)).[86] Similar to the provision of *GC12*, there is a violation when states undertake legal obligations capable of undermining the right to health.[87] The overall tenor and features of *GC14* brings it closer to the language of the 2001 principles.[88] This is perhaps because of the closeness in time of the two and the general consciousness of IP at the CESCR at that time. More important, it also shows a progressive shift by CESCR to engage HRs intersection with IP.

The ramifications of *TRIPS* and the WTO system on HRs raise difficult challenges for less developed states given that *TRIPS* predates some rel-

82 See Jack Donnelly, *Universal Human Rights in Theory and Practice*, 2d ed (Ithaca, NY: Cornell University Press, 2003) at 1 (cited in Yu, "Ten Questions," above note 68 at 718 and n 27).

83 *GC12*, above note 76.

84 *Ibid* at para 19.

85 *GC14*, above note 78.

86 *Ibid* at para 50.

87 *Ibid* at para 27: for example, the accommodation of indigenous knowledge in HRs-IP narrative.

88 See Chapman, "Implications," above note 70. Respect for state sovereignty is often the alibi for weak international enforcement of human rights. However, Chapman rightly notes that "[s]omewhat ironically, the same scrupulous concerns . . . do not seem to concern the member nations of the WTO" at 866.

evant GCs.[89] Less developed states have blamed their food insecurity, public health crises, and lack of access to medicine, new information technologies, and educational resources on the WTO-*TRIPS* system.[90] Put differently, depending on their specific experiences, there is a basis to plead a conflict between IP rules as an integral part of the new global trade system and the HRs obligations of states under the CESCR. Yet, for some reason, the CESCR has shied away from giving this proposition legal imprimatur, lending credence to Helfer's observation that the thesis of HRs primacy over IP has yet to attain normative validity under customary international law.

However, recognizing the CESCR's determination to engage the HRs-IP intersection through its GCs since 2001 and the evolutionary rapidity of that discourse, it is not clear how best it could upgrade its pre-2001 GCs in which IPRs are implicated to the post 2001 module. Nonetheless, it is obvious that the new tempo and interest in HRs-IP interface by the CESCR creates some sense of inconsistency in its earlier work.

E. INTELLECTUAL PROPERTY AS HUMAN RIGHTS: SEDUCTION OF STRANGE BEDFELLOWS

Analysts struggle with the question of whether IP is an HR.[91] A more pointed question is whether the recognition of IP as a HR pursuant to Article 15 of the *ICESCR* extends to IP the same fundamental status as other HRs.[92] From the foregoing analysis of the GCs, it is clear that even though rights arising from "scientific, literary or artistic production" (author/creators' rights)[93] are recognized as HRs, they do not enjoy such fundamental status as other HRs categories. This position seems to infringe the principle of indivisibility of HRs. Yet, because of the simultaneous location of authors' rights within economic (material) and non-economic (moral) interests, it is hard

---

89 See Jerome H Reichman, "Intellectual Property in the Twenty-First Century: Will the Developing Countries Lead or Follow?" (2009) 46:4 Hous L Rev 1115.

90 See Robert L Ostergard Jr, "Intellectual Property: A Universal Human Right?" (1999) 21:1 Hum Rts Q 156; see also Yu, "Ten Questions," above note 68 at 713.

91 *Ibid.*

92 *Ibid.* Yu refers to these as "the right to the protection of moral and material interests in intellectual creations," which is the same as the *ICESCR* text reference to right in "scientific, literary and artistic production" at 711.

93 See Cullet, above note 12 at 407–9; see also Chapman, "Implications," above note 70 at 867–68; Audrey R Chapman, "Core Obligations Related to ICESCR Article 15(1)(c)" in Audrey R Chapman & Sage Russell, eds, *Core Obligations: Building a Framework for Economic, Social and Cultural Rights* (New York: Intersentia, 2002) at 314.

to conceive of them with the full complement of fundamental HRs for many reasons outside the scope of the present analysis.

Commentators on the drafting history of the *UDHR* argue that the rights arising from intellectual creations—IPRs—were not intended to have equal status as fundamental HRs.[94] This is borne out by *GC17* which clearly states that the realization of Article 15(1)(c) rights is dependent on the enjoyment of other guaranteed HRs. The HRs-IP intersection is an amorphous and often paradoxical relationship, the untangling of which is a complex exercise. But the direct nesting of IPRs in crucial HRs instruments, no matter how weakly conceived, is a warrant to broach the subject of IP's HRs status even within the confines of the *ICESCR*'s textual prescriptions.[95]

The attraction of the HRs narrative is now such that even opposing stakeholders in both the HRs and IP enterprise are willing to explore the moral authority of HRs to advance their interests. Specifically, indigenous and local community advocates have always linked cultural production to self-determination, which is at the core of indigenous rights in international law.[96] Given the open-ended nature of self-determination, indigenous peoples' rights claims to the protection of their knowledge constitutes a matter of self-determination and consequently of HRs.[97] The urgency of such protection increases with the recent expansion of IPRs and rampant appropriation of TK.

At the same time, corporations are also hedging their bets on HRs to IPRs, and are not willing to be excluded from the narrative. IP-based industries would not hesitate to "invoke the authors' rights and property rights provisions in human rights treaties to further augment existing standards of protection."[98] As we have noted, *GC17* excludes corporations from Article 15(1)(c) of the *ICESCR*. Yet, the same GC clearly recognizes indigenous communal or group rights within the ambit of Article 15(1)(c).

In regard to indigenous claims, the first question, then, is what is the normative framework for identifying non-HRs aspects of indigenous know-

---

94 Compare Yu, "Ten Questions," above note 68 at 716, suggesting that accommodation IP in HRs instrument seem to settle the question of HR status of IP.

95 See Rosemary J Coombe, "Intellectual Property, Human Rights & Sovereignty: New Dilemmas in International Law Posed by the Recognition of Indigenous Knowledge and the Conservation of Biodiversity" (1998) 6:1 Ind J Global Legal Stud 59.

96 See Darrell A Posey & Graham Dutfield, *Beyond Intellectual Property: Toward Traditional Resource Rights for Indigenous Peoples and Local Communities* (Ottawa: IDRC, 1996).

97 Helfer, "Framework," above note 12 at 976.

98 *Ibid* at 976.

ledge and IP? It is tempting to gloss over indigenous rights claims with little constructive scrutiny. That scrutiny is important because unbridled triggering of the HRs' alarm on the IP sanctuary can drown the urgency for more serious attention to real HRs components of IP, even of indigenous knowledge and broader indigenous contexts.

Second, and perhaps more important, the attraction of the doctrine of HRs' primacy in ongoing attempts to map the HRs-IP interface is a potential ladder for proponents of stronger IP protection to step into HRs' moral high ground. Easily, "the rhetoric of human rights [is deployed] to bolster arguments for or against revising intellectual property protection standards in treaties and in national laws."[99] Similarly, when IP latches onto the HRs anchor, it is easy to weaken the traditional leverage to moderate IPRs on public interest grounds. Helfer notes, for example, that "[i]f the moral and material interests of authors and creators are fundamental rights, then the ability of governments to regulate them — either to protect other human rights or to achieve other social objectives — ought to be exceedingly narrow."[100]

Third, still on indigenous knowledge, an uncritical HRs capture could potentially cut short the needed conversation around the limits of rights, the feasibility of TK's immemorial status, and the nature of appropriate scrutiny for objectionable traditional cultural practices. One of the major hurdles for proponents of fixing the gap between conventional IP and TK is to account for some of the IPRs' inherent public-oriented mechanisms such as term limits, a concept not supported in indigenous circles. When TK is *located*, unquestionably, on the HRs landscape for IP purposes, the gulf between it and conventional IP may increase. This is because HRs' inherent moral edge limits the leverage for negotiating public interest compromises.

Fourth, how would weaker stakeholders, such as indigenous and local communities, fare in what an analyst calls the "'human rights ratchet' of intellectual property protection?"[101] HRs' ratchet of IP has a tendency to escalate extant disequilibrium in the IP system and "would ultimately backfire on those who seek to use the human rights forum to enrich the public

99 *Ibid* at 994.

100 See Yu, "Ten Question," above note 68 at 738 [footnote omitted]; see generally Yu, "Reconceptualizing," above note 12, on the notion of human rights ratchet.

101 *Ibid* at 1125.

domain and to set maximum limits of intellectual property protection."[102] According to Rochelle Dreyfuss, allowing HRs to shape IP discourse can be counterproductive as it fuels adversarial struggle for rights that pitches one group against the other in the nature of a zero sum game.[103] Without caution, framing IPRs as HRs is akin to bestriding an unruly horse, with no guarantee of desired destination. As the most vulnerable of the human family, indigenous and local communities have the direst need for HRs protection. Yet, they are least empowered to engage in the zero sum game of HRs ratchet of IP.

F. HUMAN RIGHTS AND INTELLECTUAL PROPERTY RIGHTS: REFLECTIONS ON THE NATURE OF ENGAGEMENT

As new developments continue to bring IP and HRs into contact,[104] preliminary literature on HRs-IP interface focuses largely on characterizing the nature of the relationship. Three prominent but hardly exhaustive schools of thought shape the discourse. The first suggests that HRs and IP are in "fundamental conflict."[105] The second perceives the two regimes as complementary and mutually supportive.[106] The third (which is located at the intersection of the first two) adopts an instrumental approach. It is prescriptive in nature and proposes that HRs can serve the objective of moderating expansive IP systems as insurance for safeguarding multifarious public-oriented considerations in IP.[107]

Clearly, the conflict approach is most popular. It derives momentum from the institutional fillip provided by the UN HRs system. There is some sense that the conflict narrative is self-evidently justified by the empirical reality of the negative and sobering impacts of *TRIPS*. From a jurisprudential perspective, the conflict approach is borne out by the conflicted disciplinary

---

102 See Dreyfuss, above note 68 at 89–90.

103 See Peter K Yu, "Intellectual Property and Human Rights in the Nonmultilateral Era" (2012) 64:4 Fla Law Rev 1045, focusing on the Anti-Counterfeiting Trade Agreement (ACTA) as one of the developments that warrant increased conversation over the HRs implications of IP.

104 See Helfer, "Conflicts," above note 5 at 48 [footnote omitted].

105 *Ibid.*

106 See Christophe Geiger, "Fundamental Rights, a Safeguard for the Challenge of Intellectual Property?" (2004) 35 International Review of Intellectual Property and Competition Law 268 at 277.

107 See Cullet, above note 12 at 415 [footnote omitted].

orientations of HRs and IP. Without undermining their fluidity, the former are within the realm of public law, whereas IP is *essentially* a private right and a subject of private law; albeit with strong public interest content. While HRs are publicly protected rights inuring from human dignity, IP consists *largely* of private rights animated by utilitarian material considerations for both creators and the public. Thus, the inherently conflicted conceptual orientation of the public and private law binary lends credence to the thesis of conflict.

According to the complementary approach, even though HRs and IP are located within the public and private law arenas respectively, they share a largely reconcilable objective: the promotion and protection of human well-being. According to Philippe Cullet, "intellectual property protection must serve the objective of human well-being, which is primarily given legal expression through human rights."[108] This view dovetails with the third approach, which conceives of the two regimes as instruments for achieving shared objectives. However, the emphasis of this approach is in the deployment of HRs considerations to moderate IP. According to Okediji, "human rights can be used instrumentally to deflect the moral appeal of certain affirmative rights of intellectual property holders, e.g. by justifying compulsory licenses for public health, or requiring national exceptions to copyright laws in the interests of freedom of expression."[109]

What is the nature of the contact between HRs and IP? So far, we have noted an intense conversation across the two. However, that conversation has barely begun, and it has yet to acquire a distinct identity. Nor have the two areas metamorphosed into a cohesive field of study. The language of HRs is being foisted upon IP, but the latter is reluctant to engage. Even though they are located under law's broad ambit, both HRs and IP do not easily lend themselves to precision in disciplinary classification. There are multiple layers involved in deconstructing the two from a disciplinary analysis. For example, HRs and IP are subcategories within the umbrella discipline of law even though they have morphed into separate specialities, each having its own language and research tools, methodologies, and idiosyncrasies. Yet, as indicated above, both HRs and IP are nested within more established broader legal categories, i.e., public and private law respectively.

---

108 Above note 12 at 415.

109 As quoted in Grosheide, above note 6 at 22–23.

As HRs and IP each continue to expand drawing in subject matters from diverse disciplines, the bases for their contact will only intensify. Not many themes underscore or unmask the multidisciplinary character of IP better than its interface with HRs. Buffeted by the demands of diverse disciplines, IP has yet to respond to its now obligatory multidisciplinarity. Yet, as a preliminary outcome, one major effect of multidisciplinarity in IP is gradual jurisdictional disaggregation or decentralization of IP regulatory and policy-making sites at least at the global level.

Notwithstanding the pre-eminence of the conflict approach, the co-existence thesis has greater prospects for HRs-IP rapprochement. First, quite unlike the coexistence approach's focus on problem resolution, which is an important objective of interdisciplinarity, the conflict approach freezes appetite for solution. Even then, resolutions emanating from the conflict narrative are less rigorous and are easily found in the doctrine of HRs supremacy. Second, a coexistence option not only highlights the fact of historic neglect of HRs in conventional IP, it also nuances the theme of commonality of objectives for the two disciplines. Third, as a consequence, the first and second conditions warrant the need for both HRs and IP to engage in a purposive rapprochement via an interdisciplinary experience to bridge their historical gap. Compared to HRs, the challenges of both interdisciplinarity and mutidisciplinarity are new to IP. However, HRs' recent engagement with IP provides the circumstance and opportunity for IP to bridge its long-standing indifference towards engaging other disciplines.

SIXTEEN

Merges on Just IP: Are IP Rights Basic?

GREGORY HAGEN

ABSTRACT (EN): This chapter criticizes Robert Merges's attempts to show that current IP law is just on Rawls' politically liberal theory of justice as fairness. Merges argues that IP law is just because IP rights are basic rights that enjoy a priority over distributive concerns and, therefore, that the inequalities created by the current IP system are irrelevant to whether it is just. IP rights are basic, he says, because they are necessary to provide the career options for creative professionals that would further their autonomy and self-ownership. But such a strong right to an occupation is not necessary to the exercise and development of the moral powers necessary for social cooperation which, on Rawls's view, is a necessary condition for basic rights. So, IP rights are not basic rights on Rawls's view. This chapter suggests that, at most, a very small subset of current IP rights would qualify as basic within a politically liberal IP regime because a strong set of IP rights would generate inequalities that would strain people's commitment to society and to its IP rules. Most IP law would, thus, need to satisfy a principle of distribution in order to be just.

RÉSUMÉ (FR): Ce chapitre critique les tentatives de Robert Merges visant à démontrer que le droit de la PI actuel est juste au sens de la théorie politique libérale de Rawls, selon laquelle justice équivaut à équité. Merges soutient que le droit en matière de PI est juste parce que les droits reconnus par la PI sont des droits fondamentaux ayant préséance sur les préoccupations de nature distributive et que, par conséquent, les inégalités créées par le système actuel de la PI ne sont pas pertinentes pour déterminer si ce dernier est juste ou non. Les droits de la PI sont fondamentaux, dit-il, parce qu'ils sont nécessaires pour offrir des perspectives de carrière à des professionnels créatifs en leur permettant d'accroître leur autonomie et leur réalisation de soi. Cependant, un droit aussi fort à une activité professionnelle n'est pas essentiel à l'exercice et au développement des pouvoirs moraux nécessaires à la coopération sociale qui, selon le point de vue de Rawls, est une condition indispensable pour les droits fondamentaux. Ainsi, les droits de la PI ne sont pas fondamentaux selon le point de vue de Rawls. Le chapitre indique qu'au mieux, on pourrait qualifier un très petit sous-ensemble des droits actuels de fondamentaux dans le cadre d'un régime politiquement libéral de PI, parce que sinon un vaste ensemble de droits de PI entraînerait des inégalités susceptibles de compromettre l'engagement de la population envers la société et ses règles en matière de PI. Le droit relatif à la PI doit ainsi, dans une large mesure, satisfaire à un principe de distribution afin de demeurer juste.

A. INTRODUCTION: POLITICAL PHILOSOPHY AND IP LAW

As intellectual property ("IP") rights have gradually seeped into virtually every area of our lives, the seemingly intractable disputes about the nature and justifiable scope of IP rights have become more polarized, hardened, and vitriolic and the stakes have become larger.[1] A key dispute is about what justice demands of IP law. Some would resolutely say that the grant of a right to exclude others from exploiting works, inventions, and other "intellectual" objects is just, without regard to its effects on the distribution of social goods. Others would say that justice would be done merely by granting an IP right to creators so long as it benefits the least advantaged in society. Still others would say a right of remuneration is more just than an IP right. The problem is not merely a moral one, as our Supreme Court does not give a consistent interpretation of what is just in IP law. [2] Does political

1 As a sample, consider the heated debates over the legal protection of technological protection measures in copyright law; the ratcheting up of IP protection in bilateral trade agreements; the scope of fair dealing; P2P file sharing; the harmful use of trademarks by advertisers; the emerging right of association with an event; and the patenting of the human genome, DNA, stem cells, higher life forms, software, business methods, and pharmaceuticals.

2 See *Théberge v Galerie d'Art du Petit Champlain inc*, 2002 SCC 34. The Supreme Court of Canada explained that one of the objectives of copyright, "obtaining a just reward for the

philosophy offer any insight about whether IP is just? John Rawls, perhaps the most famous political philosopher of the twentieth century, hoped that political philosophy could play a practical role in our political culture.[3] That role could be to diminish the philosophical and moral differences at the base of political conflict to an extent that "social cooperation on a footing of mutual respect among citizens" could be attained despite the existence of irreconcilable comprehensive moral views.[4]

Rawls never wrote anything on IP rights, but Robert Merges, in his thoughtful book, *Justifying Intellectual Property*, attempts to justify IP rights as a just form of a property right granted by government.[5] Although Merges was initially an advocate of a utilitarian justification for IP law, he became dissatisfied with utilitarianism as a theory of IP and, in this book, attempts to develop a rights-based theory of IP.[6] In developing his theory, Merges draws upon ideas from the philosophers Locke and Kant in order to justify current IP law as a system of basic property rights grounded in self-ownership and autonomy respectively, rather than welfare. Although his argument is based on abstract political philosophy, he argues that the ability of creative professionals to earn a living by selling copies of their products is "the practical, workaday manifestation of the abstract-sounding value of 'autonomy' that philosophers (especially Kant and Hegel) have long associated with property rights."[7]

Drawing upon Locke and Kant to justify IP rights is, of course, not new, but Merges simultaneously addresses what may be the most serious challenge to his property-based foundation for IP: that it conflicts with principles of distributive justice. In a nutshell, the challenge is that a grant of IP

---

creator," was more accurately described as "[preventing] someone other than the creator from appropriating whatever benefits may be generated" at para 30. This free-riding interpretation of "just reward" is clearly an "economic" or consequentialist type of justification of copyright rather than a deontological type as found in Locke; *CCH Canadian Ltd v Law Society of Upper Canada*, 2004 SCC 13. The Supreme Court implies, without stating, that the appropriate standard of originality must conform to "a natural rights or Lockean theory of 'just desserts' [*sic*], namely that an author deserves to have his or her efforts in producing a work rewarded" at para 15.

3 John Rawls, *Justice as Fairness: A Restatement* (Cambridge: Harvard University Press, 2001) at 1–2 [Rawls, *Justice as Fairness*].

4 *Ibid* at 1–3.

5 Robert P Merges, *Justifying Intellectual Property* (Cambridge: Harvard University Press, 2011) [Merges, *Justifying Intellectual Property*].

6 *Ibid*, ch 1 and 4.

7 *Ibid* at xi.

in an object is not just when that IP right does not work to the benefit of the least advantaged position in society. So, on Merges's view, while IP rights are founded on self-ownership and autonomy, they are also constrained by principles of justice. In order to show that IP law is just, Merges draws on Rawls's theory of justice as fairness, while making certain modifications,[8] in order "to combine this traditional emphasis on the importance of property with Rawls's solicitude for social justice, particularly the plight of the most destitute."[9] While Merges adopts Rawls's theory of justice as fairness as a political conception, in order to justify current IP law, Merges is forced to provide a radically different interpretation of its principles than does Rawls. Merges's interpretation elevates IP rights to basic rights within the system, which have a priority over concerns regarding the distribution of goods.[10] Thus, on his view, IP rights are just because distributional concerns are ruled out.

How can Merges's perplexing view — a stated concern for the plight of the most destitute, together with the claim that justice does not require that IP rights work to their benefit — be motivated, apart from a dire need to justify current IP law? On my view, Merges has, in effect, adopted a hybrid political theory which has been called "market democracy," a kind of theory which attempts to reconcile classical and modern or "high" liberalism, two views which are generally regarded as inconsistent.[11] The central claim of market democracy is that economic rights and liberties are basic.[12] This view adopts the justificatory framework and constructed rights[13] of high liberalism (elaborated in its greatest sophistication by Rawls), but rejects the diminished status of economic rights (including property rights) within it.[14] Instead, it seeks to retain and justify the importance of economic liberty (and

8 *Ibid*. Merges does not understand the resources that must be fairly distributed as Rawlsian primary goods — such as rights, liberties, powers, opportunities, income, and wealth — but as "tickets to an autonomous life," at 106.

9 *Ibid* at 308.

10 *Ibid* at 117.

11 John Tomasi, *Free Market Fairness* (Princeton, N.J: Princeton University Press, 2012), develops market democracy as a hybrid between classical liberalism and high liberalism; Samuel Freeman, "Capitalism in the Classical and High Liberal Traditions" (2011) 28:2 Soc Phil & Pol'y 19, for a comparison of the role of the market in classical and high liberalism.

12 Tomasi, above note 11 at 121.

13 See Liam Murphy & Thomas Nagel, *The Myth of Ownership: Taxes and Justice* (Oxford: Oxford University Press, 2002).

14 Tomasi, above note 11 at ch 4.

related notions of autonomy, desert, self-ownership, and property rights) of the classical liberals but rejects their justificatory machinery of natural rights and utilitarianism.[15] While this classification of Merges's view helps one to understand its motivation, it does not greatly assist his main claim. I will argue that IP rights, like other economic rights, are not, in general, basic rights on Rawls's view since they are not essential for persons to cooperatively engage with others throughout their lives. I suggest, without much argument in this paper, that a much smaller subset of IP rights may be basic, but the remainder of these rights would have to be justified in accordance with a principle of distribution, such as Rawls's difference principle.

Section B describes Merges's defence of contemporary IP law. It first describes Merges's view that IP rights are basic property rights grounded in autonomy and self-ownership; second, it very briefly describes Rawls's theory of justice as fairness and the role of property rights in it; and, third, it describes Merges's argument that IP rights are basic rights and, so, IP law is a just institution. Section C evaluates Merges's view.

B. MERGES'S DEFENCE OF CONTEMPORARY IP LAW

1) Merges: IP Rights Are Basic Property Rights

Merges takes his task to be to justify contemporary IP law by providing normative foundations for it.[16] Why have IP rights? For Merges:

> The reason is that creative labor is valuable and important. It is noble work, work that is worthy of recognition and reward. It is work that should be dignified with the grant of a small dollop of state power — a property right.[17]

Merges thus starts with the (controversial) idea that patents, copyrights, and trademark rights are property rights. Of course, the idea that there are property rights in intangible objects has been strongly criticized as an

---

15 *Ibid*.

16 Merges is speaking of contemporary US IP law. While Canadian IP law is similar to US IP law, in many ways, Canadian IP law possesses "stronger" IP rights than those found in the US: see Howard Knopf, "The Annual '301' Show — USTR Calls for Comment — 21 Reasons Why Canadian Copyright Law Is Already Stronger Than USA's" (17 February 2010), online: Excess Copyright http://excesscopyright.blogspot.com/2010/02/annual-301-parade-ustr-calls-for.html.

17 Merges, *Justifying Intellectual Property*, above note 5 at 293.

inapt extension of property rights in tangible objects,[18] but Merges dismisses such "historical-essentialist" concerns as too narrow an understanding of the concept of property, which is not bound to its historical uses.[19] Setting aside such criticisms, it is natural for Merges to look to those who have attempted to justify property rights, such as Locke and Kant. Very briefly, from Locke, Merges takes the conditions under which initial appropriation is justified.[20] In order to make use of our resources for our benefit, we must appropriate them without common consent.[21] Since we own ourselves and our labour, therefore, we own those things that, subject to provisos, we appropriate.[22] For Locke, governments come together to protect this pre-political right to appropriation.[23] From Kant, he takes the idea that "extensive interaction with objects" is essential to developing a person's full potential as an autonomous individual.[24] Merges claims that, for Kant, "[s]table possession permits the imprinting of some aspect of a person, what Kant called his will, onto objects so as to enable the person to more fully flourish."[25]

There have been extensive critiques of Locke's theory of appropriation in the context of IP law[26] and Merges's interpretation of Kant has been questioned.[27] Much of the criticism of a Lockean view of IP rights has focused on the idea that, even assuming that Lockean theory justifies appropriation of (rivalrous) physical objects, which require property rights for their effective use, it does not apply well to intellectual objects, which are non-rivalrous.[28] As Seana Shiffrin concludes, "[t]he fully effective use of an

---

18 See Mark Lemley, "Property, Intellectual Property, and Free Riding," (2005) 83 Texas L Rev 1031, for sophisticated arguments against IP rights as property rights.

19 Merges, *Justifying Intellectual Property*, above note 5 at 4–5.

20 *Ibid* at 305.

21 *Ibid* at 34.

22 *Ibid* at 35.

23 *Ibid* at 35.

24 *Ibid* at 305.

25 *Ibid* at 75–76.

26 See, for instance, Carys J Craig, "Locke, Labour and Limiting the Author's Right: A Warning against a Lockean Approach to Copyright Law" (2002) 28 Queen's LJ 1 at 16, and references cited therein.

27 Anne Barron, "Kant, Copyright, and Communicative Freedom" (2012) 31:1 Law & Phil 1, contests Merges's representation of Kant on the grounds that it is inconsistent with both the letter of Kant's texts and the spirit animating his philosophical system, at 9; Arthur Ripstein, *Force and Freedom: Kant's Legal and Political Philosophy* (Cambridge: Harvard University Press, 2009) for a recent exposition of Kant's legal and political philosophy.

28 Intellectual objects like a book are non-rivalrous in the sense that reading a copy of the book (i.e., a particular book) does not interfere with another person reading another token of the book. By contrast, eating a particular apple or reading a particular book

idea, proposition, concept, expression, method, invention, melody, picture, or sculpture generally does not require, by its nature, prolonged exclusive use or control."[29]

Merges responds directly to Shiffrin's critique saying, amongst other things, that "exclusive rights in creative works are necessary to permit creative professionals to thrive."[30] One could go on at great length examining Merges's views on Locke and Kant and whether IP rights are a form of property right within those justificatory frameworks. For the purposes of this paper, however, it is not necessary to do so. As Merges emphasized, his aim in developing his theory was to "translate these foundational writings of Kant, Locke and Rawls into the IP context — to write a liberal theory of intellectual property law . . . ."[31] He summarizes his view as follows:

> This theory's foundational components, as described by Locke, Kant, and others, are a commitment to individual ownership as a primary right, respect for third-party interests that conflict with this right, and, from the philosophy of John Rawls, an acceptance of redistributive policies intended to remedy the structural hardships caused by individual property rights.[32]

Thus, whatever rationale Merges might advance for the ownership of IP rights-based autonomy and self-ownership, the question that remains is whether IP rights are just based upon Rawls's justificatory framework.

Merges's way of melding together the views of Locke, Kant, and Rawls can be succinctly summarized in his claim that IP rights are basic rights.[33] Put more broadly, it is an attempt to retain the importance of economic rights and liberties (including private property rights in productive assets) of classical liberalism, with the justificatory apparatus of high liberalism. Thus, the defence of IP rights as basic rights faces a two-pronged challenge. From classical liberals, it faces the challenge that his approach abandons the forms of justification of property rights given by Locke and Kant because these views are, in Rawls's terminology, comprehensive doctrines,

---

will interfere with someone else eating the same apple or reading the same book (at the same time).

29 Seana Shiffrin, "Lockean Theories of Intellectual Property" in Stephen R Munzer, ed *New Essays in the Political Theory of Property* (Cambridge: Cambridge Univ. Press, 2001) 138 at 156.

30 Merges, *Justifying Intellectual Property*, above note 5 at 321.

31 *Ibid* at 13.

32 *Ibid*.

33 *Ibid* at 117.

views which not all members of a pluralist society affirm.[34] From high liberals, the attack concerns the elevated value of property since, for high liberals, economic rights, such as property rights, are of lesser value than other rights.[35] As John Tomasi puts it, for high liberals "property rights are not guardians of equality but obstacles to its achievement."[36] While the equal freedoms of Adam Smith's market destroyed the "feudal practices of a status-based economic preferment," the great concentration of property rights in a small number of private hands in the industrial age turned out to be "another device by which inequalities of status were coercively imposed upon the people."[37] Today, similar concerns exist regarding IP rights.

2) Rawls's Theory of Institutional Justice and IP

The challenge for Merges is how to fit his view that IP rights are basic within Rawls's theory of justice as fairness. In order to explain how Merges attempts do this, it is necessary to describe Rawls's theory of justice in very brief and selective terms in the context of IP.[38] To start with, Rawls's philosophy of political liberalism acknowledges the fact of pluralism, that citizens will have diverse and conflicting world views bearing on whether IP is just.[39] For Rawls, IP laws would be legitimate only when they are exercised in conformity with principles "which all citizens as free and equal may reasonably be expected to endorse in the light of principles and ideals acceptable to their common human reason."[40] Fortunately, despite profound disagreement on world views, reasonable citizens are ready to abide by principles and standards given the assurance that others will as well.[41] On a politically liberal view, the justification of IP rights is accomplished not through determining the truth of various possible comprehensive principles, such as

34 *Ibid* at 3.

35 Tomasi, above note 11, ch 2.

36 *Ibid* at 27.

37 *Ibid* at 32–33.

38 For useful overviews of Rawls's mature views, see Leif Wenar, "John Rawls" in Edward N Zalta, ed, *The Stanford Encyclopedia of Philosophy* (Fall 2008 Edition), online: http://plato.stanford.edu/archives/fall2008/entries/rawls; see also, Samuel Freeman, *Rawls* (London: Routledge, 2007); and see, Thomas Pogge, *John Rawls: His Life and Theory of Justice*, translated by Michelle Kosch (Oxford: Oxford University Press, 2007).

39 John Rawls, *Political Liberalism* (New York: Columbia University Press, 1996) at xviii–xix [Rawls, *Political Liberalism*].

40 *Ibid* at 137.

41 *Ibid* at 49.

those of Locke or Kant on property, but on the basis of a political conception of justice, a conception that is generated from the fundamental ideas implicit in the public political culture.[42] An "overlapping consensus" on such principles exists when each citizen supports a political conception of justice for (moral) reasons that are internal to that persons' own comprehensive moral doctrine.[43]

Rawls's theory of justice as fairness is a political conception of justice in the above sense. It is about the basic structure of society: the arrangement of its basic institutions, such as the constitution, the economic structure, recognized forms of property, and the family.[44] In a well-ordered society, "everyone accepts, and knows that everyone else accepts, the very same political conception of justice."[45] This conception is that society is a "fair system of social cooperation over time from one generation to the next."[46] In order to engage in social cooperation during a complete life, citizens must possess two moral capacities or powers to be so engaged.[47] First, they must have a sense of justice: "the capacity to understand, to apply and to act from . . . the principles of political justice that specify fair terms of cooperation"; and, second, persons must have a conception of the good: "the capacity to have, to revise, and rationally to pursue a conception of the good."[48] Citizens are equal in that they regard each other as having the necessary moral powers for social cooperation.[49] They are free insofar as they regard each other as having the moral powers that are necessary to possess a conception of the good and the right to make claims on their institutions in order to further their conceptions of the good.[50]

For Rawls, the question that a theory of distributive justice must address is, "how are the institutions of the basic structure to be regulated as one unified scheme of institutions so that a fair, efficient, and productive system of social cooperation can be maintained over time, from one generation to the next?"[51] This question is answered by the idea of the origin-

---

42 Rawls, *Justice as Fairness*, above note 3 at 32–33.

43 *Ibid* at 32–38.

44 *Ibid* at 10–12.

45 *Ibid* at 8.

46 *Ibid* at 5.

47 *Ibid* at 18–24.

48 *Ibid* at 18–19.

49 *Ibid* at 20.

50 *Ibid* at 21–24.

51 *Ibid* at 50.

al position, a thought experiment in which free and equal representative members of society come together to freely make an agreement on principles of justice.[52] It is because citizens do not agree on any moral authority, whether it be a sacred text, religious institution, or natural law, that justice as fairness sets the fair terms of social cooperation by *agreement*.[53] Fairness requires that this agreement be made under conditions where no one may have an unequal bargaining position.[54] In the original position, persons are veiled from knowledge of their various natural endowments, such as strength, intelligence, and *talents*.[55] The original position, therefore, represents the idea that fairness demands that persons do *not* deserve their intellectual talents, such as inventiveness, originality, and creativity, the use of which are sometimes necessary for obtaining IP rights in various intellectual objects.[56] Merges believes that persons *do* deserve their intellectual talents,[57] but his discussion confuses moral desert (in one's talents) with desert of rights (e.g., patent rights) in the results of the application of our talents. According to Rawls, people *are* rewarded in an institution that satisfies the difference principle for educating and training their talents and exercising them in a way that contributes to the good of others and themselves.[58]

Within the original position, persons have a fundamental interest in developing and exercising their moral powers for the purpose of social cooperation; satisfying this interest is one of the main aims in coming to an agreement within the original position.[59] Citizens (or their representatives) would choose two principles of justice as fairness in the original position: the first sets out that each person has the same entitlement to "a fully adequate scheme" of basic rights and liberties (compatible with the same rights and liberties for all), and the second adds equality of opportunity and the distributional requirement that any social and economic inequalities are "to be to the greatest benefit of the least advantaged members of society

52 *Ibid* at 14–18.

53 *Ibid* at 15.

54 *Ibid*. Thus, there is no force, fraud, coercion, or deception nor do the representatives have any knowledge of the particular circumstances of the basic structure of society such as one another's social positions, particular comprehensive moral beliefs, race, ethnicity, or sex.

55 *Ibid*.

56 *Ibid* at 74–75.

57 Merges, *Justifying Intellectual Property*, above note 5 at 107–9.

58 Rawls, *Justice as Fairness*, above note 3 at 75.

59 Rawls, *Political Liberalism*, above note 39 at 74.

(the difference principle)."[60] One reason for choosing the difference principle in the original position, though not the only one, is that individuals behind the veil of ignorance would want to ensure that they maximize their position in the worst off possible socio-economic scenario.[61] These principles are ordered so that the claims to basic liberties have priority over distributional concerns. As Merges recognizes,[62] though, on Rawls's view, the right to private, productive property is not a basic right.[63] Thus, assuming that IP rights are property rights, on Rawls's view, IP rights are *not* basic rights either. Rather, Rawls limits basic rights and liberties to include only *personal property* such as dwellings, but not *productive property*.[64] For Rawls, "the right to private property in natural resources and means of production generally, including rights of acquisition and bequest" are not basic rights.[65]

For Rawls, the issue of the ownership of productive property cannot be settled through philosophical discussion.[66] In short, Locke's and Kant's ideas about property are not shared fundamental ideas of our political culture that can be a common basis of agreement. Rather, they are highly contested ideas that need to be resolved in conformity with our political conception of justice. For Rawls, a necessary criterion of a basic right or liberty is being "essential for the adequate development and the full and informed exercise of [the] two moral powers" (so that persons can cooperate).[67] However, for Rawls, the rights to ownership of the means of production and natural resources are not "necessary for the development and exercise of the moral powers."[68] At the same time, Rawls says that "among the basic liberties of the person is the right to hold and to have the exclusive use of personal property . . . [so as] to allow a sufficient material basis for a sense

---

60 Rawls, *Justice as Fairness*, above note 3 at 42–43.

61 This maxim in principle has been subject to criticism by some game theorists, but a discussion of this point is beyond the scope of this paper.

62 Merges, *Justifying Intellectual Property*, above note 5 at 105.

63 Rawls, *Justice as Fairness*, above note 3 at 114.

64 *Ibid*. Productive property rights are usually considered to be rights in certain physical inputs, such as factories and tools that produce tangible products that can be sold. IP rights are also productive in the sense that their exercise can result in royalties paid to the IP owner.

65 *Ibid* at 114. Nor is the equal right to participate in the control of the means of production and of natural resources taken to be a basic right.

66 Rawls, *Political Liberalism*, above note 39 at 338–39.

67 Rawls, *Justice as Fairness*, above note 3 at 112–13.

68 Rawls, *Political Liberalism*, above note 39 at 298.

of personal independence and self-respect, both of which are essential for the development and exercise of the moral powers."[69]

This is not to say that justice as fairness does not permit property rights in productive assets, including IP rights. Justice as fairness, Rawls says, favours either a property-owning democracy or a form of democratic socialism, both of which permit ownership of productive assets.[70] A property-owning democracy encourages broad ownership of productive assets, whereas liberal democratic socialism emphasizes collective ownership and worker-managed firms.[71] In justice as fairness as espoused by Rawls, property rights are not basic rights (that are not subject to distributive considerations but only to other basic rights) but *are* justified only to the extent that they satisfy the difference principle *and* the first principle of justice.[72] Satisfying the first principle is important, since even if the grant of a property right in a work, for example, benefited the least advantaged, it would still have to do so in a way that does not violate the basic rights and liberties of persons.[73]

3) Merges's Argument for Basic IP Rights

Merges's aim is to show that the current IP system conforms to Rawls's theory of justice as fairness. However, Merges *denies* that IP can meet the difference principle[74] and his main move is to claim that IP is a basic right that is not subject to the requirements of the second principle of justice — it need not benefit the least advantaged.[75] Merges cannot merely argue, of course, from Locke's or Kant's comprehensive views about self-ownership, autonomy, and property rights directly, since they are particular moral views

---

69 *Ibid.*

70 Rawls, *Justice as Fairness*, above note 3 at 138–40.

71 *Ibid.*

72 *Ibid* at 135–38.

73 Speratua Dumitru, "Are Rawlsians Entitled to Monopoly Rights?" in Axel Gosseries, Alain Marciano, & Alain Strowel, eds, *Intellectual Property and Theories of Justice* (Palgrave MacMillan: New York, 2008), on the liberty to imitate.

74 Merges, *Justifying Intellectual Property*, above note 5. "From a Rawlsian perspective, the question is whether IP rights represent incentives designed solely to encourage the development of native endowments in a way that will benefit the least well off. In honesty, I do not think that IP can meet the stringent justificatory standards of Rawls's second principle" at 354.

75 *Ibid* at 117.

that are not widely shared. Instead, Merges argues that rational persons in the original position would agree to the current IP system.[76] As he puts it:

> The argument flows from Rawls's first principle: IP is a basic liberty for those who would most benefit from creative independence and the career fulfillment that follows. Everyone in the original position faces the possibility that he or she will have the talent to enjoy these benefits.[77]

Of course, in the original position, persons are tasked to choose principles of justice, not whether they would agree to the current IP system or not. They don't even have enough information to do that. Regardless, taking the argument as it is given, Merges emphasizes that IP is a basic right because it furthers personal autonomy and the development of an overall life plan.

> Property, including IP, forms a much larger part of the "total system of basic liberties" than Rawls himself believed. Because at least some form of property is essential to the development of a person's unique individual life projects, or overall life plan, it forms part of the system of basic liberties that any fair society must guarantee. Even if the broadest and most sweeping types of property are not required under Rawls's first principle — even if, that is, only a subset of all potential property rights are truly essential for the sake of fairness — IP surely forms part of the subset of property rights that *are* basic and essential. This is due to its more personal nature, and its close relationship to individual personalities and the need for individual autonomy.[78]

IP is essential to those who want to become creative professionals because it gives them career options which would not otherwise exist.[79] Merges comments that IP functions like the incentives that are necessary to attract well-positioned persons into socially beneficial roles.[80] Although Merges believes that such basic IP rights will create inequalities, "[p]eople in the original position would permit the 'inegalitarian' distribution resulting from the incentives offered by an IP system, because these incentives . . . give creative people career options, which in turn affect the overall distribution of society's resources."[81]

---

76 *Ibid* at 109–12.

77 *Ibid* at 110.

78 *Ibid* at 117.

79 *Ibid* at 111.

80 *Ibid* at 110.

81 *Ibid* at 111.

But why have IP rights as basic rather than non-basic? For one thing, Merges would say in response that the interest that creative professionals have in their careers morally "outweighs the operation of the 'difference principle.'"[82] Secondly, "[w]idespread redistribution of economic resources simply creates massive disincentives for people to work hard and improve their individual lives."[83] While one might think that non-basic rights (those that guarantee that the worst off benefit from any inequalities) might be regarded as more economically valuable than basic rights that do not have such a guarantee, it could be argued that this view ignores the magnitude of the effect of economic growth over the last century on the well-being of individuals.[84] Ironically, the prosperity that results from economic growth makes the exercise of economic rights, such as IP rights, more valuable to their holders; [85] more valuable, Merges could say, than distributional guarantees.

As mentioned, Merges does not believe that current IP law conforms to the difference principle.[86] He provides no evidence for his view, but there is a consensus that strengthening IP rights is positively correlated with income inequality in developing countries,[87] and given the increase in inequality amongst many OECD countries during the last decades,[88] a period when the value of international royalty and licensing fees and receipts has dramatically increased[89] and economies have grown,[90] it is a credible view.[91] Nevertheless, Merges argues that current IP law is justified because

---

82 *Ibid.*

83 *Ibid* at 106.

84 Tomasi, above note 11 at ch 3.

85 *Ibid* at 61.

86 Merges, *Justifying Intellectual Property*, above note 5 at 354.

87 Samuel Adams, "Globalization and Income Inequality: Implications for Intellectual Property Rights" (2008) 30:5 J Pol'y Modeling 725 at 730–31.

88 Organisation for Economic Co-operation and Development, *Growing Unequal? Income Distribution and Poverty in OECD Countries* (21 October 2008) at ch 1, online: www.oecd.org/social/socialpoliciesanddata/growingunequalincomedistributionandpovertyinoecdcountries.htm.

89 World Intellectual Property Office, *World Intellectual Property Report: The Changing Face of Innovation* (14 November 2011) at 60–61, online: WIPO www.wipo.int/econ_stat/en/economics/wipr.

90 World Bank, *GDP growth (annual %)*, online: http://data.worldbank.org/indicator/NY.GDP.MKTP.KD.ZG.

91 Recent studies have emphasized the positive correlation between the strength of IP rights and economic growth in high and low (though not middle) income countries; see Rod Falvey, Neil Foster, & David Greenaway, "Intellectual Property Rights and Economic Growth" (2006) 10:4 Review of Development Economics 700.

it has provided "significant benefits,"[92] such as television, the telephone, agricultural technology, air conditioning, cellphones, and pharmaceuticals to the poor.[93] He concludes:

> So the extremely high salaries at the top of the entertainment industry, the profits of consumer electronics companies, and the like, may benefit the poorest members of society enough to justify the way that these industries are set up — including, of course, the availability of IP rights and the profits that flow from them.[94]

Further, the justice of the IP system is evidenced by the internal structure of the rights themselves[95] and externally by the taxation system which redistributes income from IP right exploitation.[96] In terms of their internal structure, Merges relates this theory of IP back to the role of desert by saying that:

> . . . [E]very IP right includes two separate components: an inviolable individual contribution, which I call the "deserving core" of the work covered by the right; and a component that can best be thought of as owing its origins to social forces and factors, which I call "the periphery."[97]

Given this notion of the core, it seems that Merges intends all and only IP rights in the core to be basic rights, because neither basic rights nor the core deserved rights are subject to redistribution.[98]

C. EVALUATION OF MERGES'S THEORY OF IP

The main task that Merges faces is to establish that IP rights are basic rights. On his view, IP rights are basic because they are necessary for self-ownership and autonomy.[99] The biggest problem for Merges in this regard is to show how these robust, property-generating, moral conceptions of self-ownership and autonomy are relevant to justice as fairness, a political conception of justice. The point of a political conception of IP (which Merges purports

92 Mergers, *Justifying Intellectual Property*, above note 5 at 120.
93 *Ibid* at 118–20.
94 *Ibid* at 118.
95 *Ibid* at 121–23.
96 *Ibid* at 132–33.
97 *Ibid* at 121.
98 *Ibid*.
99 *Ibid* at 117 and ch 2–3.

to be developing) is not that it is morally legitimate, but that people will accept it despite the existence of irreconcilable moral views on IP rights. According to Rawls's theory, there is moral disagreement regarding the value of autonomy and self-ownership, so, these ideas cannot be a basis upon which persons in the original position would make decisions about the choice of principles of justice. Rather, the basis for decisions is the (less robust) shared idea that persons are free and equal and that a well-ordered society is a "fair system of social cooperation" in the senses defined earlier.

As discussed above, for Rawls, determining what rights are basic is done on the basis of elements from our public political culture, particularly the shared ideals of freedom, equality, and social cooperation.[100] In political liberalism, rights are basic only if they are a necessary condition of the "full and informed exercise" and "adequate development" of the moral powers of *all* citizens.[101] As Samuel Freeman points out, generally, it is not the case that merely because a particular right or liberty is an essential condition for *a class of persons* (say creative professionals) to pursue and develop *their* particular choice of life plan that it is a sufficient reason to make them basic rights and liberties for everyone. [102] The fact that IP rights further the self-ownership and autonomy of creative persons is not determinative of whether they are basic rights. Merges could counter, at this point, that if the freedom to choose an occupation is necessary for *everyone* to develop their moral powers, then this is also true of the ownership of productive property, such as IP rights.[103] As Tomasi has argued, further, economic rights provide all persons with the chance for responsible self-authorship and identity, economic independence from the state, and personal security.[104]

Merges's interpretation of the original position suggests that the right to a career as a creative professional could rest upon a basic right to a choice of occupation[105] that is much stronger than the traditional understanding that no one should be forced to work in a particular job. The stronger principle is that society should create job opportunities which match the aspirations of each individual. But many individual career aspirations may

100 Rawls, *Justice as Fairness*, above note 3 at 5.

101 *Ibid* at 112–13.

102 Samuel Freeman, "Can Economic Liberties Be Basic Liberties?" *Bleeding Heart Libertarians* (13 June 2012) online: Bleeding Heart Libertarians http://bleedingheartlibertarians.com/2012/06/can-economic-liberties-be-basic-liberties.

103 Tomasi makes the more general point in Tomasi, above note 11 at 77.

104 *Ibid* at 77–81.

105 See John Rawls, *A Theory of Justice* (Cambridge: Harvard University Press, 1971) at 274.

be unworkable, like the choice of a three-day workweek or seasonal work with strong unemployment benefits during a long off-season. More to the point, the basic right of IP would require creating a market of artificially scarce "intellectual" goods to create the opportunity for creative professionals. This principle would justify much broader IP rights than does the current system, so as to benefit talented home gardeners, buskers, and others whose creations would otherwise be uncompensated positive externalities.

Even if IP rights could be regarded as basic on some workable conception, their very alienability would appear to undermine their importance, as would the alienability of voter rights, and other political and civil rights and liberties.[106] Further, basic IP rights would operate regardless of potential massive inequalities resulting from them. Merges's answer, that there is no need to justify unequal distributions of the benefits of IP rights given that it is a basic right,[107] is inadequate. Economic rights are unlike basic civil or political rights since a basic right by itself offers no guarantee of the distribution of social goods. On the one hand, without such a guarantee, the commitment to society of hard-working creators, both talented and untalented, who could not earn a living from exploiting their IP rights, would become strained,[108] causing them to dishonour their agreement, believing that their life prospects have been sacrificed to make the advantaged even better off. On the other hand, creators, both talented and untalented, whose works are highly marketable, could make a fortune, with little redistribution of their gains to others, straining the commitment of those who use the creations, and resulting in widespread infringement of IP rights through the use of disruptive technologies, such as peer-to-peer file sharing. Given these economic implications, it is suggested that it is doubtful that those in the original position would choose principles which would result in anything but a small and weak subset of existing IP rights as basic rights. These basic rights would at most allow for a decent living rather than the fortune of JK Rowling, a heroine of Merges's book.[109]

---

106 Merges, *Justifying Intellectual Property*, above note 5, argues that alienability to corporations is in the interests of persons, at 206–13.

107 *Ibid* at 117.

108 Rawls, *Justice as Fairness*, above note 3 at 103–4.

109 It is beyond the scope of this paper to describe in detail the nature of non-basic IP rights that would be justified. My hunch is that such "property" rights would be much weaker in scope, duration, and excludability than those that exist currently, in order to conform to an egalitarian principle of distribution.

Merges's answer to the problem of distributional inequity, recall, was to point to evidence that IP has provided significant benefits to the poor, even if it does not satisfy the difference principle.[110] But an advocate of a market democratic theory of IP need not concede that the difference principle is not satisfied by IP law. Indeed, the difference principle is premised upon the idea that social and economic inequalities can work to the advantage of the least advantaged because the incentive structures involved will increase growth, which can then benefit the least advantaged through state-operated social services and "an aggressive system of redistributive taxation."[111] But market democracy need not take such a direct approach to the satisfaction of the difference principle. Instead, as Brenner and Tomasi have argued, a market democracy can seek to benefit the least advantaged by "creating the conditions for a robustly growing commercial society"[112] using individual incentives rather than state coercion.[113] The result on their view is that, paradoxically, a society that aims at benefitting the worst off position (e.g., high liberalism) ends up worse off over time because less economic freedom slows the growth of the economy.[114] Still, the basic problem with the market democracy approach is that it assumes the possibility of future economic growth, which is becoming more questionable given the increasing cost of extracting oil.[115] Rawls himself dismissed as unreasonable a theory of justice which requires continual economic growth.[116] Moreover, while conventional wisdom was that economic growth resulted in greater income equality, recent studies show a positive correlation between economic growth and income inequality.[117]

D. CONCLUSION

In his book *Justifying Intellectual Property*, Robert Merges attempts to show that IP rights grounded in autonomy and self-ownership are just on Rawls's

110 Merges, *Justifying Intellectual Property*, above note 5 at 120.
111 Tomasi, above note 11 at 231.
112 *Ibid* at 232.
113 *Ibid* at 231–33.
114 *Ibid* at 233–37.
115 Jeff Rubin, *The End of Growth* (Toronto: Random House, 2012) at 43–45.
116 Rawls, *Justice as Fairness*, above note 3 at 63–64. Of course, much of the discussion that criticizes the goal and possibility of future economic growth is based upon the assumption of the scarcity of tangible resources, rather than intangible resources.
117 Kristin J Forbes, "A Reassessment of the Relationship Between Inequality and Growth" (2000) 90:4 Am Econ Rev 869.

politically liberal theory of justice as fairness. His failure to do so is illuminating. First, he fails to appreciate sufficiently that a politically liberal theory of IP does not attempt to *morally* justify IP rights, but rather to provide principles of *political* justice that provide a basis for social cooperation involving intellectual objects, despite irresolvable conflicts about the moral justification of IP rights. Second, on Rawls's view, basic rights, like the right to vote, enjoy a priority over distributive principles, and must be necessary to enable persons to engage in mutually beneficial social cooperation using their moral powers. Merges argues that current IP law is just because IP rights are basic rights and, therefore, that the inequalities created by the current IP system are irrelevant to whether it is just. IP rights are basic, Merges says, because they are necessary to provide the career options for creative professionals that would enhance their autonomy and self-ownership. But such a strong right to an occupation — and the autonomy and self-ownership it seeks to further — is not necessary to develop the moral powers necessary for social cooperation. So, IP rights are not basic rights on Rawls's view. Furthermore, at most, a very small subset of current IP rights would be justifiable as basic rights within a politically liberal IP regime because an overly strong IP right could generate inequalities that would strain people's commitment to society and its IP rules. Thus, most IP rights would need to satisfy a principle of distribution, such as, perhaps, the difference principle, in order to be just.[118]

118 I offer my sincere thanks to the editors, and to Maria Lavelle and two anonymous reviewers for comments on an earlier draft.

SEVENTEEN

Appropriation Appropriated: Ethical, Artistic, and Legal Debates in Canada

LAURA J MURRAY & KIRSTY ROBERTSON

ABSTRACT (EN): Although Appropriation Art is often used to illustrate how freedom of speech can be constrained by expansionist copyright, such a framing oversimplifies the complex and often contested ways visual culture is used, borrowed, and stolen. Using Canadian examples to unsettle the centrality of US-centred copyright debates, the authors examine Appropriation Art from three interlinked perspectives: first, as a historical phenomenon within the Euro-American, and specifically the Canadian, art world; second, as a term that came to prominence during the Canadian copyright debates of 2006, and became entangled with a history of artist activism as practiced by Canadian Artists' Representation (CARFAC); and third, as a heretofore unexamined tension between appropriation championed as an act of resistance to the US entertainment industry and government, and appropriation vilified a decade earlier in Canada during controversies about cultural appropriation and "appropriation of voice" from Indigenous and racialized people. Ultimately, appropriation, whether as an art practice or an object of potential copyright regulation, is not the same in Canada as it is in the US, or for that matter, in theory. It has a history, which must be recognized if the interests of the various parties involved are to be accommodated or at least adequately described.

RÉSUMÉ (FR): Même si l'art de l'appropriation est fréquemment utilisé pour illustrer la façon dont la liberté d'expression peut être limitée par le droit d'auteur expansionniste, cette vision simplifie démesurément les façons complexes et souvent contestées par lesquelles la culture visuelle est utilisée, empruntée et volée. À l'aide d'exemples canadiens, pour perturber la trop grande concentration sur les débats de droit d'auteur propres aux États-Unis, les auteurs examinent l'art de l'appropriation sous trois angles interconnectés : premièrement, sous l'angle d'un phénomène historique du monde de l'art euro-américain, et plus spécialement canadien; deuxièmement, en tant que terme ayant occupé une place importante lors des débats sur le droit d'auteur canadien en 2006, et qui est devenu indissociable de l'histoire de l'activisme artistique tel que pratiqué par le Front des artistes canadiens (CARFAC); troisièmement, en tant que tension — jamais examinée jusqu'ici — entre l'appropriation, défendue comme acte de résistance contre l'industrie du divertissement et le gouvernement américains, et l'appropriation vilipendée il y a une décennie au Canada lors des controverses à propos de l'appropriation culturelle et « l'appropriation de la voix » des autochtones et autres personnes « racialisées ». Finalement, l'appropriation n'est pas, en tant que pratique artistique ou objet de réglementation potentielle du droit d'auteur, la même au Canada qu'aux États-Unis, ni d'ailleurs sur le plan théorique. Son histoire doit être reconnue pour que les intérêts des différentes parties impliquées soient pris en considération, ou tout au moins exprimés adéquatement.

A. INTRODUCTION

It may seem ironic that the United States, the main engine behind stronger intellectual property protections in the international arena, should also be the site of the most conspicuous critiques of copyright. And yet the two phenomena are connected: with their strong individual rights tradition (extending past security of the person to the famous "pursuit of happiness"), Americans have a potent discourse with which to engage intellectual property from within and without. In addition to this unifying ideology, a common platform for debate as it were, the United States also has ample economic motivation, and institutional and media resources, to develop and express opposing positions on intellectual property. Thus, the United States produces both the most forceful corporate and popular assertions of intellectual property in terms of the right to property, as well as the most proliferating critiques of intellectual property in terms of the right to freedom of expression. As the US entertainment industry flexes its lobbying and legal muscles to defend or expand its rights, a remix aesthetic also bolstered by rights claims flourishes not only in hip hop but also in design, software, fashion, cuisine, and the visual arts. Some of this activity is actually incentivized by a sense of resistance to copyright.

Despite the power and volume of this remix or "free culture" activity, its subtlety and range of application can be limited by its tendency to represent creative production and identity as disembodied and non-located, even while conceptualizing creative production and identity in specifically embodied and located ways. For example, an article reviewing the resistance in early 2012 to the proposed US *Stop Online Piracy Act* [SOPA] describes its proponents as "citizens of the Internet," and challenges those who would control the Internet to meet their adversaries "where they live — online, in chat rooms and user forums and social networks, on Twitter and Facebook and Tumblr and Reddit and whatever comes next."[1] This virtualization or universalization of a debate over a US Act may be politically effective in the short term and within that nation, but, whether it be polemical or inadvertent, it must be noted as problematic. These issues concern not only place or nation. More generally, as several scholars have observed, the celebration of the ease of creation in the discourse of "free culture" tends to efface labour, gender, environmental, and social justice issues.[2] Champions of digital freedoms represent creativity as an individual act of industry, intellect, inspiration, or rebellion, and, thus, without apparently recognizing the common ground, share with many champions of authors' rights a rather metaphysical idea of individual genius.

Appropriation art — that is, art built with images or parts of images from popular culture or other artists — has often been invoked in these arenas as an example of the way freedom of speech can be constrained by expansionist copyright.[3] We argue, however, that such a framing of appropriation over-

---

1 Larry Downes, "Who Really Stopped SOPA, and Why?" *Forbes* (25 January 2012), online: Forbes.com www.forbes.com/sites/larrydownes/2012/01/25/who-really-stopped-sopa-and-why/3.

2 See Laura J Murray, "Review of *RiP: A Remix Manifesto* by Brett Gaylor" (June 2009), online: Culture Machine www.culturemachine.net/index.php/cm/article/view/372; Boatema Boateng, "Whose Democracy? Rights-Based Discourse and Global Intellectual Property Rights Activism" and Richard Maxwell & Toby Miller, "The Environment and Global Media and Communication Policy," both in Robin Mansell & Marc Raboy, eds, *The Handbook of Global Media and Communication Policy* (Oxford: Wiley-Blackwell, 2011) 261 and 467; Kathy Bowrey & Jane Anderson, "The Politics of Global Information Sharing: Whose Cultural Agendas Are Being Advanced?" (2009) 18:4 Soc & Leg Stud 479.

3 In his speaking engagements in the 1990s, slides and videos of appropriation were central to Lawrence Lessig's assertions about the problems with expansionist copyright,

simplifies the complex and often contested ways in which visual culture is used, borrowed, and stolen. In this article, we seek to situate appropriation art both as a practice and a discourse in worlds outside US copyright debates. First, we look at it as a historical phenomenon within the Euro-American art world, and specifically the Canadian art world. Second, we examine how the term "appropriation art" fared when it came to prominence during the Canadian copyright debates of 2006, and became entangled with a history of artist activism as practiced by Canadian Artists' Representation (CARFAC). And third, we discuss a heretofore unexamined tension between appropriation championed as an act of resistance to the US entertainment industry and government as it was in the 2006 copyright debates, and appropriation vilified a decade earlier in Canada during controversies about cultural appropriation and "appropriation of voice" from Indigenous and racialized people. Ultimately, appropriation, whether as an art practice or an object of potential copyright regulation, is not the same in Canada as it is in the United States, or, for that matter, in theory. As would be the case anywhere, it has a history that must be recognized if the interests of the various parties involved are to be accommodated or at least adequately described.

B. APPROPRIATION ART: A VERY BRIEF HISTORY

Within the art world, and removed from intellectual property debates, appropriation has a long and storied history. Though it is occasionally traced back to copying and training practices in Renaissance studios,[4] more often its beginnings are placed at the start of the twentieth century, with the collage works of Pablo Picasso, Georges Braque, and others, who inserted the detritus of daily life — newspaper clippings and posters — into works that already unsettled traditional art in their abstraction.[5] A few years later,

---

although he more often used examples of direct political critique than specifically artistic examples; see also Negativland, "Negativland's Tenets of Free Appropriation," online: www.negativland.com/news/?page_id=10; commentaries on *Rogers v Koons*, 960 F 2d) 301 (2d Cir 1992) [*Rogers*] often argued that copyright was unduly constraining art: see James Traub, "Art Rogers vs. Jeff Koons" *Observatory* (21 January 2008), online: The Design Observer Group http://observatory.designobserver.com/entry.html?entry=6467.

4 The tradition of copying in art history should not be confused with appropriation or with forgery or theft. For more, see Sherrie Irvin, "Appropriation and Authorship in Contemporary Art" (2005) 45:2 British Journal of Aesthetics 123, especially 137.

5 They also tapped into the longer history of copying. Harry S Martin writes that "Raphael's Judgment of Paris (c1515) triggered one of the most sustained and substantial sequences of copying and counter-copying in Western Art. Raphael's painting became

Marcel Duchamp began to undermine the dominance of the elite art world by bringing "readymades" or already existing objects (among them a urinal, a snow shovel, and a wine rack) into the gallery. Through the years of the Second World War and into the 1960s, collage gained a political edge, in the anti-Fascist posters of John Heartfield, for example, or in the *détournement* practices of the French Situationists in Paris in 1968 (their work is often seen as a precursor of 1990s culture jamming). The word *appropriation* itself, however, was largely unused until it came to be associated with a kind of cutting-edge art practice popular in the 1980s that involved reworking mass and high culture for different ends. At this point, at least in terms of how appropriation was discussed by artists, questions of intellectual property were a far distant backdrop.

As Heidi Zuckerman Jacobson writes of Jeff Koons, who appropriated actual consumer objects (such as vacuum cleaners or basketballs) into his art:

> In the 1980s, the anxious question around Koons was whether the difference between art and commodity had completely collapsed. The concept of appropriation, however, signaled that the artist had been granted the potential to assimilate popular culture and yet still intervene, thereby allowing art to be art and not something inherently corrupted.[6]

Artist Karl Haendel expands on Jacobson's statement:

> I was taught that appropriation artists took images from mass culture, thus freeing them from their original contexts and meanings, and re-presented them anew so that we could see how such images work to reinforce this or that dominant ideology. I got the sense that these artists were dutifully following a political imperative, clinically treating images around them with

---

lost but his employee, Marcantonio Raimondi, made an etched copy of it which survived. A few years after the copy was made, the general demand for copies of the original work was so great that Marco Dente da Ravenna made a slavish copy of it. Three centuries later, Manet used part of Raphael/Raimondi's original as the basis for his work Le Déjeuner Sur L'Herbe. Manet used the group of three figures in the bottom right-hand corner of the original work as the heart of his new work, updating their clothing to contemporary garb and adding the naked women. Nearly a century later, Picasso paraphrased Manet's work in an extensive series of paintings, drawings, sculptures and linocuts he executed between 1959 and 1961, Les Dejeuners": *Harvard Law School, Image Rights*, online: www.law.harvard.edu/faculty/martin/art_law/image_rights.htm.

6 Heidi Zuckerman Jacobson, "Steal This Essay" in Juan Roselione-Valadez et al, *Beg, Borrow, and Steal* (Miami: Rubell Family Collection, 2009) at 13.

> the detachment and cool irony that such an important mission deserved. This seemed fine by me.[7]

In other words, appropriation was a way to challenge consumer norms and dominant ideologies, but it did not specifically thumb its nose at the law.

Nonetheless, authorship and originality were important elements to these artworks. In a recent article, Nate Harrison notes that in the early 1980s, artists such as Sherrie Levine (who photographed and displayed identical copies of the work of well-known photographers)[8] or Richard Prince (who used, among other popular culture items, photographs of the Marlboro Man) may not have even been aware of any elements of the 1976 (US) *Copyright Act*.[9] He suggests, however, that such artists benefitted from the Act's use of the phrase "original works of authorship fixed in any tangible medium of expression" to define which sorts of expression are covered by copyright.[10] As he proposes, "*the work* displaced the author as the central determining character in copyright doctrine."[11] There was a parallel, that is, between the way that authorship was understood in the *Copyright Act* (where the actions leading up to the production of the work are obfuscated by the work itself), and the way it was understood in the art world, where the work of Sherrie Levine, Richard Prince, and others from the so-called Pictures Generation specifically set out to undermine ideas of originality, authenticity, and the centrality of a romanticized (male) author.[12]

Though appropriation art in the form of the recycling of popular culture, or the remaking of already existing artworks, was largely a US phenomenon, it had corollaries elsewhere, including Canada. In Canada,

---

7 Karl Haendel, "Complicated Sneakers" in Juan Roselione-Valadez et al, *Beg, Borrow, and Steal* (Miami: Rubell Family Collection, 2009) at 84.

8 Though Levine began by photographing the work of Edward Weston whose copyright belonged to his estate before being transferred to the University of Arizona (who broadly encourage fair use and tacitly approve of Levine's work), her career took off when she began "copying" the well-known photographs of Walker Evans, whose photographs of the Depression were in the public domain.

9 *The Copyright Act of 1976*, 17 USC § 101-810 (1976) [*Copyright Act*].

10 Nate Harrison, "The Pictures Generation, the Copyright Act of 1976, and the Reassertion of Authorship in Postmodernity," online: Art & Education www.artandeducation.net/paper/the-pictures-generation-the-copyright-act-of-1976-and-the-reassertion-of-authorship-in-postmodernity.

11 *Ibid.*

12 *Ibid*; for more on this topic, see also Craig Owens "The Discourse of Others: Feminists and Postmodernism" and Douglas Crimp "On the Museum's Ruins" both in Hal Foster, ed, *Postmodern Culture* (London: Pluto Press, 1985) 57 and 43.

General Idea's take on *LIFE Magazine* (titled *FILE Megazine*) (just one of the art trio's works using appropriation) and, somewhat later, Natalka Husar's paintings on Harlequin Romance novel covers attracted considerable interest. One might also look to Douglas Coupland's tongue-in-cheek *Canada Pictures* still lifes, which specifically use examples of Canadian corporate popular culture (Jos. Louis cakes, Capitaine Crounche cereal, Maple Leaf bologna), photographer Roy Arden's "economic landscapes" showing the recognizable interiors and products of big-box stores, or Colwyn Griffith's photos of dollar-store products and landscapes made from easily identified foodstuffs (Tic tacs, Rice Krispies, and so on). Additionally, Canada was the home of extremely popular and widespread "appropriations" in the numerous popular culture jamming campaigns of the 1990s. Though not part of the art world, Vancouver-based *Adbusters* magazine caught the public imagination with its subversive ads: taking the iconic Absolut Vodka outline and changing it to Absolut AA; changing the glossy black and white photograph of a sculpted male model used for the Calvin Klein "Obsession for Men" ads to one showcasing the torso of an overweight and hairy man, complete with the tag line "Reality for Men"; putting the famous Joe Camel character in a hospital gown, obviously dying from cancer. *Adbusters* has addressed questions of copyright and trademark violation by noting repeatedly that it would welcome any court cases as a chance to publicize the labour records of each company,[13] but apparently nobody has ever taken them up on the offer.

Returning to the art world, if one were to cite a trend in appropriation art in Canada, one might point to a certain self-referentiality. For example, while Diana Thorneycroft has perhaps received the most attention for her drawings of the violent deaths of Disney and other cartoon characters, her more recent work appropriates iconic Group of Seven paintings as a backdrop to a series of "awkward moments," including Santa and his sleigh trapped in a pine tree, and Winnie the Pooh surrounded by grizzlies. There is, in fact, a whole subset of the Canadian art world that creates works by recycling, commenting on, or critiquing the famous (at least in Canada) landscape art of the Group of Seven.[14] In 1996, artist Jin Me Yoon created

13 Kalle Lasn, *Culture Jam* (New York: Harper Collins, 2000). *Adbusters* also faced a great deal of criticism for aping the slick advertising techniques of the companies they hoped to critique.

14 The Group of Seven was a group of Canadian painters working primarily in Ontario in the 1920s and 1930s. They were known for painting seemingly uninhabited Northern

A Group of 67, including 67 passport-like portraits, front and back, of Korean immigrants in front of paintings by Lawren Harris (Group of Seven) and Emily Carr; in 2005 the Plug In Gallery in Winnipeg held a fundraiser where seventy-five artists "re-interpreted" the Group of Seven in an exhibition called "Fabulous Fakes"; Steven Loft asks "Group of Who?" in a series of talks attempting to dislodge the Group's centrality and to create an alternate Aboriginal art history. In other words, while appropriation art in Canada is certainly present, the material used often operates as commentary on issues of identity, national representation, and so on. Such targets redefine the parameters of appropriation, revealing a quite different set of cultural and political circumstances than the standard (US-focused) account of appropriation art might acknowledge.

C. APPROPRIATION ART AND CANADIAN COPYRIGHT

Until the copyright reforms of 2012, the status of parody and satire in Canadian copyright law was quite unclear. While one might suppose that these artistic modes are essentially a form of criticism, one of the stated purposes of fair dealing, and hence eligible for consideration as such, a Federal Court ruled emphatically in 1997 that the parodic use of the Michelin man figure on a union poster constituted infringement. It stated that "the defendants are not permitted to appropriate the plaintiff's private property . . . as a vehicle for conveying their anti-Michelin message."[15] The court noted the categorical nature of fair dealing and concluded that its provisions "should be restrictively interpreted as exceptions." The 2004 *CCH Canadian Ltd. v Law Society of Upper Canada* case at the Supreme Court challenged this position in its affirmation that "the fair dealing exception, like other exceptions in the *Copyright Act*, is a user's right. In order to maintain the proper balance

---

Ontario wilderness landscapes, and for working to develop a specifically "Canadian" form of painting. In more recent scholarship, the Group has been critiqued for forwarding a parochial and masculinist form of anti-modern nationality. Additionally, the supposedly empty landscapes were in fact occupied, both by indigenous groups and by the logging and tourism industries active at the time. Nevertheless, the Group of Seven is consistently mobilized by individuals and authoritative institutions (galleries, government, etc.) alike as exemplary of a certain kind of Canadian nationality. For more, see Lynda Jessup, "Bushwhackers in the Gallery: Antimodernism and the Group of Seven" in Lynda Jessup, ed, *Antimodernism and Artistic Experience: Policing the Boundaries of Modernity* (Toronto: University of Toronto Press, 2001) 130.

15 *Compagnie générale des établissements Michelin-Michelin et Cie v CAW-Canada*, [1997] 2 FC 306 at 366.

between the rights of a copyright owner and users' interests, it must not be interpreted restrictively."[16]

While it would appear that this assertion would instruct lower courts to interpret "criticism" broadly, *CCH* did not refer specifically to parody or satire, and lower courts continued to cause problems for those practices.[17] This situation differed in both legal and cultural terms from the US environment where parody had been explicitly acknowledged as free speech and fair use in *Campbell v Acuff-Rose Music*.[18]

In 2006, the Canadian government introduced Bill C-60,[19] a copyright reform bill that included provisions for the protection of TPMs (technological protection measures) or DRM (digital rights management) that would have made it an infringing act to circumvent these digital locks for any reason, including fair dealing. It was this extra-legal barrier to appropriation art that provoked artists and cultural workers Gordon Duggan and Sarah Joyce to circulate an open letter on the Internet and through email calling on their colleagues in Canada to ask for copyright legislation that would "respect the reality of contemporary artistic practice"[20] by eschewing protection for DRM. The letter resulted in the formation of the Appropriation Art Coalition, eventually numbering over 600 artists, curators, directors, educators, writers, associations, and organizations from the arts sector.[21] The coalition contended that appropriation had important art historical precedent and social use and, as such, should be enabled rather than prohibited under copyright legislation. Allowing DRM to block copying would, in the words of an activist ally of the coalition, "criminalize . . . a recognized and legitimate art form."[22]

---

16 *CCH Canadian Ltd v Law Society of Upper Canada*, 2004 SCC 13, [2004] 1 SCR 339 at para 48 [*CCH*].

17 Laura Murray & Craig Berggold, "See You in Court: Can Canadians Practice Parody?" 32:2 *FUSE Magazine* (March 2009) 12.

18 *Campbell v Acuff-Rose Music*, 510 US 569 (1994).

19 Bill C-60, *An Act to Amend the Copyright Act*, 1st Sess, 38th Parl, 2005.

20 Appropriation Art Coalition, "Re: Canadian Copyright and Cultural Reform" (2006), online: Digital Copyright Canada www.digital-copyright.ca/node/2478.

21 For further information, see Appropriation Art Coalition, "Appropriation Art: Statement About" (2006), online: www.appropriationart.ca/statement/about.

22 Russell McOrmond, "Appropriation Art Coalition Condemns Proposed Copyright Bill C-61" (2008), online: Russell McOrmond's Blog www.digital-copyright.ca/node/4716. Collage and pastiche are not illegal if done with physical objects; the copyright implications arise when they are done using reproductions of images or objects rather than the original artifact.

While the Appropriation Art Coalition noted the historical lineage of the use of already existing work outlined above, the more immediate backdrop to the open letter and later deposition was an international constellation of artists shut down or taken to court in recent years for reproducing the work of others in their own work without permission. Despite the US Supreme Court's affirmation of the legitimacy of parody, many cases arose in which the nature of the unauthorized use could not be demonstrated to be parodic. Key figures included Jeff Koons, who lost the *String of Puppies* case brought by photographer Art Rogers because the judge felt that the work, a sculpture based on Roger's photograph, was satiric of a general culture of sentimentality rather than specifically parodic of the photograph.[23] The *Illegal Art Show*, an exhibition of "art and ideas on the legal fringes of intellectual property,"[24] was made up of works that repurposed iconic images and either anticipated or had already been met with accusations of IP infringement.[25] In the UK, Damien Hirst, whose sculpture *Hymn* replicated in giant form a children's anatomy set, paid an undisclosed sum to two children's charities in an out-of-court settlement.[26] Such cases created a cluster of examples on which artistic groups within and beyond the United States (advocating everything from fair copyright to copyleft or no copyright) drew to illustrate copyright's harmful effects on artistic expression.[27]

---

23 *Rogers*, above note 3.

24 Online: www.illegal-art.org (accessed 15 July 2009; website no longer operational); Art and Culture Center of Hollywood, "Illegal Art," online: http://artandculturecenter.org/illegal-art.

25 See Robert S Nelson, "Appropriation" in Robert S Nelson & Richard Shiff, eds, *Critical Terms for Art History*, 2d ed (Chicago: University of Chicago Press, 2003). Three of the artists in this exhibition, John Oswald, Natalka Husar, and Diana Thorneycroft, were Canadian. None of them were actually sued although in various ways their work was affected by threats or concerns about copyright. See also online: www.plunderphonics.com.

26 Hirst himself has also made claims of infringement — for example a case that saw a sixteen-year-old graffiti artist, Cartrain, ordered to cease and desist making collages with images of one of Hirst's infamous works — *For the Love of God*, a diamond encrusted skull (which was itself the target of another artist who claimed that Hirst was copying his crystal-encrusted skulls). In turn, three British artists responded to Hirst's accusations, by creating collages that copied Cartrain's collages (including the skull) with one change: a title of a book in the collage had been changed from *How To Be a Detective* to *Copyright and Intellectual Property Law*. See "Artists Flout Copyright Law to Attack Damien Hirst" *The Telegraph* (13 February 2009), online: The Telegraph www.telegraph.co.uk/culture/art/4609976/Artists-flout-copyright-law-to-attack-Damien-Hirst.html.

27 More recent cases include injunctions for Richard Prince's reworkings of photographer Patrick Cariou's images of Jamaican Rastafarians. Prince was ordered to destroy the

In this vein, the Appropriation Art Coalition asserted the special status and special needs of art. It promoted acknowledgement of art's exceptionalism through exceptions in the law to allow artists access to or latitude to reproduce otherwise protected material. "Lobbyists for the copyright industry claim that copyright owners need greater control over works," the coalition writes. "This is a misrepresentation of copyright. Copyright is meant to protect and encourage creativity not suppress and restrict it."[28] In effect, because "contemporary culture should not be immune to critical commentary,"[29] the coalition prioritized freedom of expression over owners' rights.

D. APPROPRIATION ART COALITION v CANADIAN ARTISTS' REPRESENTATION

This position brought the Appropriation Art Coalition in direct conflict with the copyright reform positions of CARFAC (Canadian Artists' Representation), a union established in the 1960s to represent Canadian artists. CARFAC has from its inception argued that artists deserve to be paid for their work, and that copyright is a key instrument for achieving this. CARFAC was arguing *against* fair dealing and other user rights, and in favour of protecting digital rights management. The argument was (and is) that all uses of artists' images ought to be cleared and paid for, and fair dealing ought to be minimized as, in fact, "unfair." To CARFAC, the Appropriation Art Coalition position that the freedom to make art be considered before livelihood was anathema. CARFAC and its copyright wing CARCC (the Canadian Artists Representation Copyright Collective, which is, unlike RIAA and other such pro-copyright bodies, associated with labour and union rights rather than big business) asserted that artists were already precarious, and that

---

images, though the case was overturned on appeal. See Charlotte Burns, "Patrick Cariou Wins Copyright Case Against Richard Prince and Gagosian" *The Art Newspaper* (21 March 2011), online: The Art Newspaper www.theartnewspaper.com/articles/Patrick+Cariou+wins+copyright+case+against+Richard+Prince+and+Gagosian/23387. A second instance involves an out-of-court settlement between Shepard Fairey and The Associated Press in a dispute over who owned the rights to the iconic Obama "Hope" poster: see David Kravets, "Associated Press Settles Copyright Lawsuit Against Obama 'Hope' Artist" *Wired* (12 January 2011), online: Wired www.wired.com/threatlevel/2011/01/hope-image-flap.

28 Gordon Duggan & Sarah Joyce, "Letter to Ministers 01_08" (2008), online: Government of Canada: Copyright Consultations www.ic.gc.ca/eic/site/008.nsf/eng/02734.html.

29 Above note 21.

the creation of art could not take place if the work of their hands was being, we could say, appropriated.[30]

For CARFAC, the crux of the argument was and is this: artists tend to be disadvantaged members of society. Statistics from 2005 show that, on average, artists in Canada earn 37% less than the average wage, coming in at $22,731 CDN, compared with $36,301 for the average Canadian worker.[31] Additionally, Karl Beveridge, then head of CARFAC, noted in an interview during this controversy that the work of artists is used in a number of venues — publications (museum and scholarly), classrooms, films, and elsewhere — but artists are not always (or even not often) compensated for these uses. For Beveridge, this constituted an exploitation of the artist that could be rectified through better protections.[32] The idea that artists could gain publicity through the free circulation of their images was, to him, just further exploitation.

The argument between CARFAC and the Appropriation Art Coalition erupted briefly. Emails were exchanged, articles were written, and then coverage died down. However, the positions of the two groups were clear, and suggest two distinct approaches to the relationship between copyright and art. Bill Patry takes note of the way that in the highly contested terrain of copyright, artists cannot even seem to agree among themselves:

> This division of opinion within the art community is interesting for another reason: artists have been the most fervent advocates of moral rights, which are based on the Romantic inseparability of the artist and his or her work. Appropriation art seems to deny that connection, and with it the concepts of author and originality. But can one have it both ways? Can one have moral rights without authors, works, and copies?[33]

30 CARCC, "About CARCC," online: www.carcc.ca. As their website states, "CARCC was established in 1990 by CARFAC, *Canadian Artists' Representation / Le Front des artistes canadiens*, a professional association that works for visual artists. CARCC was founded to put into practice the principles concerning artists' copyrights for which CARFAC continues to advocate — the professional practice of using written agreements (licences) and the payment of appropriate fees for the use of copyright. CARCC is a corporation separate from CARFAC, but controlled by CARFAC, which is CARCC's sole shareholder. Members of CARFAC's executive committee form CARCC's board of directors."

31 James Adams, "Starving Artists? Study Shows That's Not Far from the Mark," *Globe and Mail* (5 February 2009) R1.

32 Karl Beveridge, interviewed by Kirsty Robertson, Toronto, 30 September 2006.

33 William Patry, "Appropriation Art and Copies" (20 October 2005), online: The Patry Copyright Blog http://williampatry.blogspot.com/2005/10/appropriation-art-and-copies.html. Moral rights were not explicitly prominent in this controversy, where CARFAC

What CARFAC and the Appropriation Art Coalition had in common is the call for protection of the besieged artist. But to that end, CARFAC called for tighter regulation, and the Appropriation Art Coalition called for none. No doubt in private conversation many CARFAC members would acknowledge the need for fair dealing, and Appropriation Art Coalition members would want to reserve the right to make money from their work, but the debate became entirely binarized in this time and place.

The mobilization of appropriation discourse in Canada at a time when legal and technological protections were being proposed for corporate-owned cultural products, protections that threatened to reduce possibilities for collage, pastiche, parody, and satire, was powerful. It unsettled a previous binary geometry of copyright debates in which artists were conventionally positioned as owners defending their work against those who might appropriate it in unauthorized ways, and it tied arts issues into broader consumer rights discourses. Ultimately, if indirectly, the champions of appropriation art scored a legislative win with the inclusion of parody and satire as fair dealing purposes in Bill C-32,[34] the copyright reform bill passed in 2012. (The status of appropriation art that is not parody or satire remains unclear.) In 2006 such a victory would have been almost unimaginable. But although it has been achieved, conflicts between artists about what kind of copyright will serve them best have by no means been resolved.

E. APPROPRIATION AS COLONIALISM

The AAC/CARFAC controversy is not the only recent debate over appropriation in the Canadian art world. A search for "Appropriation Art and Canada" on Google brings up a huge number of results. Scrolling through the first few pages, one finds an equal number pointing to the Appropriation Art Coalition and to the cultural appropriation of Indigenous culture. Canada's passionate "appropriation of voice" debates of the 1980s and 1990s are an example even more telling than the AAC/CARFAC controversies of the tensions in Canada between different modes of understanding cultural pro-

---

emphasized economic rights and the Appropriation Art Coalition emphasized constitutional rights (freedom of expression) and borrowed US discourses in which moral rights have little place. And yet CARFAC has been a big promoter of moral rights, so this is one ground of difference between the two sides.

34 Bill C-32, *An Act to amend the Copyright Act*, 3d Sess, 40th Parl, 2010 (reintroduced as Bill C-11 in 1st Sess, 41st Parl, 2011).

duction. The conception of appropriation art mobilized by the Appropriation Art Coalition takes it as an article of faith that artists need free access to cultural goods, and sees the law as a means to ensure this, but the story of the earlier appropriation disputes reveals a rather different value system and set of tools for resolving differences. The connection between the controversies of the 2000s and those of the preceding decades goes beyond a shared word: they both manifest a conflict between a vision of the artist as an individual and a vision of the artist as part of a collective, between a vision of the artist as self-made and the artist as made by history.

As Jonathan Hart explains in a seminal definition, "cultural appropriation occurs when a member of one culture takes a cultural practice or theory of a member of another culture as if it were his or her own or as if the right of possession should not be questioned or contested."[35] In fact, several of the artists mentioned above in the context of the history of appropriation art (Picasso and Braque, for example) show up in this light as themselves appropriators of more than commercial mass culture. In the early twentieth century, avant-garde artists now central to canonical Western art history (the Cubists, the Fauves, and Die Brücke, for example), turned for inspiration to so-called "primitive" cultures, and specifically to the African masks at the Musée d'Ethnographie du Trocadéro in Paris. Though rarely given credit, the African works, always decontextualized, show up in a number of works, including one of Picasso's most famous paintings, *Les Demoiselles d'Avignon* (1907), in which a semi-abstract painted group of nude prostitutes crouch in a variety of uncomfortable positions, the two on the right-hand side sporting faces obviously influenced (if not copied) from the masks. Picasso, it is said, always denied the influence. The issue of his "copying"[36] came to a head in the controversy surrounding the 1984 Museum of Modern Art (New York) exhibition *Primitivism in Twentieth Century Art*, which certainly acknowledged that Picasso and others had drawn on African and other (including North American Aboriginal) cultures. The exhibition, however, was accused of valuing the non-European masks, artworks,

---

35 Jonathan Hart, "Translating and Resisting Empire: Cultural Appropriation and Postcolonial Studies" in Bruce H Ziff & Pratima V Rao, eds, *Borrowed Power: Essays on Cultural Appropriation* (New Brunswick: Rutgers University Press, 1997) 137 at 138.

36 Picasso's use of African masks is often remarked upon, but only since the 1980s has it been criticized. Often, Picasso's use of masks is taken as an extension of his use of "everyday" objects in his collages, and thus the words "copying," "stealing," and "misuse" often indicate the stance that the writer, rather than Picasso, was/is taking. Here it is used with the knowledge that the copying was not without consequences.

and artifacts only insofar as they were inspirational to European artists. In other words, the appropriation was legitimized even as it was revealed; the legacy of colonialism that had brought the objects to Paris was erased.[37]

In Canada and elsewhere in the 1980s and particularly in the 1990s, appropriation was a term much contested and mobilized primarily in connection with identity politics, stolen and misused Indigenous culture, and controversy over museum collections and displays. Appropriation came to be seen as a continuation in the present day of nineteenth- and early twentieth-century practices of illegitimate collection and salvage ethnography (the practice of collecting material from "disappearing" tribes).[38] Many of the collections of Aboriginal artifacts in North American, European, and Austral-Asian museums are the spoils of salvage collecting, itself the result of decimation of indigenous populations through disease, and the imposition of harsh punishments for the practice of culture (which, in several cases, such as potlatches on the Northwest Coast or sun dance ceremonies in the United States, was made illegal). The implementation of residential schooling and other assimilationist policies throughout North America, Australia, and New Zealand derived from and reinforced assumptions that Indigenous cultures had died or were dying out, and thus that their "remains" ought to be preserved behind glass.

Activism through the 1960s and 1970s on the part of groups like AIM (American Indian Movement) and those who organized the interventionist and critical Indian Pavilion at Expo 67 in Montreal did little to change these beliefs in mainstream North American culture. It was not until the late 1980s that concerted activism and a number of controversial exhibitions, conferences, artworks, writings, performances, blockades, and political actions (for example, the Oka Uprising) came together in a battle over representation, often focused on the idea (itself springing from identity politics) that Aboriginal peoples needed to be able to speak for and represent themselves.[39]

37 Simon Gikadi, "Picasso, Africa and the Schemata of Difference" in Sarah Nuttall, ed, *Beautiful/Ugly: African and Diaspora Aesthetics* (Durham: Duke University Press, 2006) 30 at 47–48.

38 See James Clifford, *The Predicament of Culture: Twentieth-Century Ethnography, Literature, and Art* (Cambridge: Harvard University Press, 1988), and Ruth Phillips & Christopher Steiner, eds, *Unpacking Culture: Art Commodity in Colonial Postcolonial* (Berkeley: University of California Press, 1999).

39 See Lee-Ann Martin, *The Politics of Inclusion and Exclusion: Contemporary Native Art and Public Art Museums in Canada: A Report* (Ottawa: Canada Council, 1991); Lynda Jessup & Shannon Bagg, eds, *On Aboriginal Representation in the Gallery* (Hull: Canadian Museum

In just two examples among many, Aboriginal groups protested the exhibition *The Spirit Sings* (1988) organized by the Glenbow Museum in Calgary alongside the Winter Olympics (also held in Calgary) for two reasons: first, the exhibition was sponsored by Shell Canada, which was then drilling on land under claim by the Lubicon Cree, and second because the exhibition was made up of only ancient native artifacts that refused to acknowledge a continued vibrancy of native life.[40] Aboriginal peoples had little to no say in how they were portrayed in this exhibition: no Aboriginal curators were involved. Not long afterwards, the exhibition *Into the Heart of Africa* opened in Toronto, showing artifacts gathered by Canadian missionaries and soldiers while in Africa.[41] This exhibition too drew extensive protests, including the formation of a Coalition for the Truth About Africa, that released a pamphlet stating: "Why, in the first seventy-seven years history of the ROM, does the first 'African' exhibit have to be from a colonial perspective?"[42]

Indigenous writers during this same period understood "voice" as the object of appropriation. In response, some white writers and artists articulated rights to imaginative freedom in absolute terms not dissimilar to the claims of free culture advocates. Novelist Russell Smith asserted that "appropriation of voice is what fiction is,"[43] and Erna Paris wrote "A Letter to the Thought Police."[44] Indigenous writers spoke back: Jeannette Armstrong invited non-Native people to

> [i]magine yourselves in this condition and imagine the writers of that dominating culture berating you for speaking out about appropriation of cultural

---

of Civilization, 2002); and Lee-Ann Martin, ed, *Making a Noise! Aboriginal Perspectives on Art, Art History, Critical Writing and Community* (Banff: The Banff Centre for the Arts, 2005).

40 Kirsty Robertson & J Keri Cronin, "Aboriginal Representation and the Canadian Art World" in J Keri Cronin & Kirsty Robertson, eds, *Imagining Resistance: Visual Culture and Activism in Canada* (Kitchener: Wilfrid Laurier University Press, 2011).

41 Carol Tator, Frances Henry, & Winston Mattis, "Into the Heart of Africa" in *Challenging Racism in the Arts: Case Studies of Controversy and Conflict* (Toronto: University of Toronto Press, 1998).

42 Coalition for the Truth About Africa, quoted in *ibid* at 41.

43 Russell Smith, quoted in Rosemary Coombe, "The Properties of Culture and the Politics of Possessing Identity: Native Claims in the Cultural Appropriation Controversy" (July 1993) 6:2 Can JL & Jur 249 at 251.

44 An excellent summary and reflection on these debates can be found in Richard Fung, "Working Through Cultural Appropriation" 16:5-6 *FUSE Magazine* (Summer 1993) 16. See also Kristjana Gunnars, "Transcultural Appropriation: Problems and Perspectives" in *Stranger at the Door: Writers and the Act of Writing* (Waterloo, ON: Wilfrid Laurier University Press, 2004).

> voice and using the words "freedom of speech" to condone further systemic violence, in the form of entertainment literature about *your* culture and *your* values and all the while, yourself being disempowered and rendered voiceless through such "freedoms."[45]

Such critiques of appropriation took on directly the liberal values that subtend celebration of appropriation today.

The interesting difference between these debates and the AAC/CARFAC controversy is that, by and large, it was the collective rights argument that won out over the individualist freedom of expression argument. The debates profoundly influenced museum culture in Canada (and also in varying ways in Australia, New Zealand, and parts of Europe and South America). And whereas in the United States, related activism took place in governmental arenas, leading to the passage of NAGPRA (*Native American Graves Protection and Repatriation Act*) in 1990,[46] changes in Canada were provoked by shaming, and negotiated through lengthy consultation, concerted activism, and the publication of academic and popular texts (fiction and non-fiction). Although Indigenous Canadians have since been active in advocating Indigenous intellectual property rights in International Law, in collaboration with non-Indigenous cultural workers,[47] legal reform and lawsuits were not an important tool for artists and other cultural workers attempting to halt cultural appropriation in the Canadian context. Instead, highly publicized cases of repatriation of stolen artifacts, organization of a series of exhibitions and workshops (such as *Indigena*, *Writing Thru Race*, and *Reservation X*), and the formation of the Aboriginal Curatorial Collective led to changes in funding, museum policy, and widespread awareness in the art world and beyond that appropriation was/is not always a positive encounter.

In the context of the history of appropriation art we sketched earlier, we can see from this wave of controversy and soul-searching that appro-

---

45 Jeanette C Armstrong, "The Disempowerment of First North American Native Peoples and Empowerment Through Their Writing" in Daniel David Moses & Terry Goldie, eds, *An Anthology of Canadian Native Literature in English* (Don Mills, ON: Oxford University Press, 2005) 242 at 243.

46 *Native American Graves Protection and Repatriation Act*, Pub L No 101-601, 104 Stat 3048 (1990).

47 The Creators' Rights Alliance (see online: www.cra-adc.ca) has been involved in WIPO negotiations on traditional knowledge, and in July 2010, the Assembly of First Nations passed *Support for an International Knowledge and Intellectual Property Rights Regime*, Resolution no 36/2010, Assembly of First Nations, Annual General Assembly (20–22 July 2010, Winnipeg, MB), online: AFN www.afn.ca/uploads/files/aga-res-10.pdf.

priation, while it claims to attack power, actually comes from a position of power. While artists such as Prince and Levine were engaging in postmodern attempts to unseat the centrality of the genius author, Indigenous artists were only beginning to have the privilege of occupying that position. A lengthy history of placing Aboriginal cultural objects in ethnographic rather than art museums, of failing to record or acknowledge the names of artists or the families and histories to which the objects belonged, coupled with a dismissal of work that had been "touched" by Western culture as thus "inauthentic" or "tourist art" profoundly influenced the ways that Aboriginal art was made, collected, confiscated, and suppressed in Canada.[48] Reclamation of past histories through repatriation and naming (for example, giving individual names to anonymous faces in the thousands of photographs collected of Aboriginal peoples, or to artists who created artifacts now held in museums)[49] manifested very different interactions with the idea of authorship than those of appropriation artists of the period. Harrison notes that "Levine and Prince took individual control of the mass-authored image, and in so doing, reaffirmed the ground upon which the romantic author stands,"[50] but this was not an option open to those for whom entire cultures had been simultaneously suppressed and appropriated.

In thinking through the way that appropriation as a right rubs up against appropriation as (mis)representation and oppression, the limited politics of the dominant "appropriation art" discourses become apparent. Indigenous artists and artists of colour fought hard to control certain forms of representation and demand their own right to represent themselves. For the most part, changes did not come about through copyright (although Indigenous artists have used copyright or trademark insofar as they were able), but rather through hard-won changes to institutional, organizational, and artistic practice. One can hope that one of the main things achieved by these labours by Indigenous and non-Indigenous cultural workers is a recognition that multiple conceptions of creative process and ownership

---

48 Ruth Phillips, *Museum Pieces: Toward the Indigenization of Canadian Museums* (Montreal & Kingston: McGill-Queens University Press, 2011). See also Ruth Phillips, *Trading Identities: The Souvenir in Native North American Art from the Northeast, 1700–1900* (Seattle: University of Washington Press, 1998).

49 See, for example, the work of photographer Jeff Thomas. See also Jeff Thomas & Anna Hudson, "Edmund Morris: Speaking of First Nations" in Lynda Jessup & Shannon Bagg, eds, *On Aboriginal Representation in the Gallery* (Hull: Canadian Museum of Civilization, 2002) 127.

50 Harrison, above note 10.

of culture exist and must coexist — an acknowledgment often missing in copyright discussions.

We give the final word to the recent appropriation art of two Aboriginal artists based in Canada — Sonny Assu and Brian Jungen. In his piece *Coke Salish*, Sonny Assu (Li'wilda'xw of the We Wai Kai First Nation [Cape Mudge]) uses the recognizable Coca-Cola font and red background for a billboard-like sign. Instead of spelling out "Enjoy Coca-Cola," however, the sign reads "Enjoy Coast-Salish Territory," an assertion that the city of Vancouver is built on disputed land. Assu's *Breakfast Series* of reworked cereal boxes (including *Treaty Flakes*/Frosted Flakes, *Bannock Pops*/Corn Pops, *Lucky Beads*/Lucky Charms, *Salmon Loops*/Fruit Loops, and *Salmon Crisp*/Sugar Crisp) is, according to his website "conceptually and aesthetically designed to challenge the authenticity of Indigenous art while simultaneously reflecting upon our western civilization's consumption culture."[51] Brian Jungen (Swiss-Dunn-Za heritage) is famous for his series *Prototypes for New Understanding*, a group of Nike Air Jordans deconstructed and re-sewn into Northwest Coast-style masks, which takes questions of consumption, authenticity, appropriation, and indigeneity even further. The Nike swooshes and jumping Jordan logos are clearly visible on Jungen's now much-sought works. The work of Assu and Jungen clearly references the multiple histories of appropriation acknowledged in this article. Perhaps one could say that these Indigenous artists have appropriated appropriation art, and thereby found considerable success in the art scene. While they make the classic move of appropriating corporate logos, their critiques have multiple targets — perhaps even including the glibness of anti-corporate appropriation art. Whatever their intentions, these artists have more agility in simultaneously defending and critiquing many sorts of rights than most copyright discourses and debates.

51 Sonny Assu, "General Artist Statement," online: http://sonnyassu.com/pages/general-artist-statement.

EIGHTEEN

The Story of My Life: Fiction, Ethics, and the Self at Law

ANDREA SLANE

ABSTRACT (EN): In *Cooper v Stockett*, a plaintiff unsuccessfully claimed that a central character in the 2009 novel *The Help* was based on her and that the depiction caused her emotional harm. By analyzing the documents filed by the parties, this article argues that the plaintiff is best understood primarily as a reader. From this perspective, the relationship between plaintiff and defendant parallels that between reader and author on several levels. The plaintiff-reader uses both textual and extratextual information to judge the author's moral fibre, especially her level of commitment to anti-racism, and attempts to engage the law to address what are essentially moral wrongs linked to race and representation. Textually, how the White author deploys literary strategies to convey moral messages within the novel generates a sense of moral dissonance in the Black plaintiff-reader, and extratextual factors, such as interviews with the author and legal arguments advanced by the defence team, work to exacerbate that sense of dissonance, undergirding the plaintiff's conviction that she has been wronged. While the substantive law of personality rights and invasion of privacy are not particularly sympathetic to her project, the procedural process of the lawsuit nonetheless provides a forum for it.

RÉSUMÉ (FR): Dans l'affaire *Cooper v Stockett*, la demanderesse a plaidé sans succès que le personnage principal du roman de 2009 intitulé "*The Help*" était inspiré d'elle et que cette représentation de sa personne lui avait causé un préjudice émotionnel. En analysant les documents déposés en cour par les parties, l'auteur soutient qu'on comprend mieux la demanderesse si on la considère d'abord et avant tout comme une lectrice. Vue sous cet angle, la relation entre la partie demanderesse et la partie défenderesse ressemble, à bien des égards, à celle qui unit le lecteur et l'auteur. La demanderesse-lectrice s'appuie sur des éléments d'information textuelle et extratextuelle pour juger la fibre morale de l'auteure, particulièrement son degré d'appui à la lutte contre le racisme, et tente de recourir au droit pour faire corriger ce que sont essentiellement des injustices morales associées à la race et aux représentations. Sur le plan textuel, la façon dont l'auteure de race blanche use de stratégies littéraires pour véhiculer des leçons morales dans la nouvelle crée, chez le demanderesse-lectrice noire, un sens de dissonance morale, et les facteurs extratextuels, comme les entrevues avec l'auteure et les arguments juridiques avancés par l'équipe de la défense, contribuent à exacerber ce sentiment de dissonance, renforçant chez la demanderesse la conviction qu'elle a été victime d'une injustice. Bien que le droit positif protégeant la personnalité et la vie privée n'ait pas été très favorable à son projet, le processus de la poursuite judiciaire fournit néanmoins une tribune pour ses revendications.

A. INTRODUCTION

> "When I was writing this book, I never thought anyone else would read it, so I didn't get real creative with the names . . . . I just used people I knew. Some of them aren't talking to me right now, but I feel like they'll come around."[1] (Kathryn Stockett, author of *The Help*)

> "I think she is just a racist. She claims she respects black people but she just ran all over me."[2]

1 Jennifer Brett, "Peach Buzz" *Atlanta Journal-Constitution* (26 October 2009). The same journalist repeated the quote in a 2011 article: Jennifer Brett, "The Buzz: Kathryn Stockett, Author of 'The Help,' Sued by Former Family Employee" *Atlanta Journal-Constitution* (18 February 2011).

2 Sharon Churcher, "Her Family Hired Me as a Maid for 12 Years but Then She Stole My Life and Made it a Disney Movie" *Mail Online* (4 September 2011), online: Daily Mail www.dailymail.co.uk/femail/article-2033369/Her-family-hired-maid-12-years-stole-life-Disney-movie.html, quoting Ablene Cooper plaintiff in lawsuit against Stockett.

"So ethical criticism does matter. It matters because who we become matters and because literature, or, rather, story in general, as an important midwife to our becoming, helps usher us into the world."[3]

In February 2011, Ablene Cooper filed a lawsuit in Hinds County Mississippi against Kathryn Stockett,[4] author of the bestselling 2009 novel *The Help*.[5] Cooper, a long-time maid and nanny to Stockett's brother, alleged in the lawsuit that the author had appropriated her name and likeness in the character "Aibileen" (one of the three central character-narrators in the novel), and in so doing had held Cooper up to the public eye in a false light, and intentionally or negligently inflicted emotional distress on Cooper.[6] Stockett denied all claims, including the claim that she had based the Aibileen character on Cooper in any way.[7] The suit was ultimately dismissed in August 2011 because the statute of limitations had run out before the suit was filed.[8]

This is a somewhat idiosyncratic example of lawsuits filed against authors of fictional works by real people upon whom the author allegedly based his or her work. In these suits, plaintiffs attempt to argue violations of personality rights, privacy rights, and/or defamation; however, they are nearly always unsuccessful.[9] Nonetheless, such suits arise on a regular basis in the

---

3 Marshall Gregory, "Ethical Criticism: What It Is and Why It Matters" (1998) 32:2 Style 194 at 215.

4 *Ablene Cooper v Kathryn Stockett* (9 February 2011), 251-11-134 CIV (Circuit Court of the First Judicial District of Hinds County Mississippi) (Statement of Claim of the Plaintiff) [*Plaintiff's Complaint*]; *Ablene Cooper v Kathryn Stockett* (14 April 2011), 251-11-134 CIV (Circuit Court of the First Judicial District of Hinds County Mississippi) (Memorandum of the Defendant in Support of Motion for Summary Judgment) [*Defendant's Motion*]; *Ablene Cooper v Kathryn Stockett* (27 April 2011), 251-11-134 CIV (Circuit Court of the First Judicial District of Hinds County Mississippi) (Plaintiff's Response to Defendant's Motion and Memorandum for Summary Judgment) [*Plaintiff's Response*]. The document contains a certificate of service dated 27 April 2011.

5 Kathryn Stockett, *The Help: A Novel* (London: Penguin Group, 2009).

6 *Plaintiff's Complaint*, above note 4.

7 *Defendant's Motion*, above note 4.

8 Matthew Belloni, "'The Help': Judge Tosses Lawsuit Claiming Character Stolen From Real-Life Maid" *The Hollywood Reporter* (16 August 2011), online: Hollywood Reporter www.hollywoodreporter.com/thr-esq/judge-tosses-the-help-lawsuit-223783; Kingfish, "Judge Green Dismisses *Help* Lawsuit" *Jackson Jambalaya* (16 August 2011), online: Jackson Jambalaya http://kingfish1935.blogspot.ca/2011/08/judge-green-dismisses-help-lawsuit.html (a video of the entire twenty-minute hearing as well as the court documents.

9 Some recent examples include *Tyne v Time Warner Entertainment Company LP*, 901 So (2d) 802 (Fla 2005), a case against the makers of the 2000 film *The Perfect Storm* brought by the families of the deceased fishermen whose demise the film depicts, where the defendants won; see also *Sarver v Hurt Locker LLC*, 39 Media L Rep 1204 (NJ 2010), a suit

United States, and their persistence begs the question of why plaintiffs continue to attempt such suits — is there something about a particular work of fiction that makes these plaintiffs believe that their case will be different? Is the lawsuit a useful forum for the plaintiff to voice moral complaints, even if the case will be unsuccessful before the court?

The following analysis will demonstrate that in cases like the one involving *The Help*, the plaintiff is best understood primarily as a *reader* who recognizes (or misrecognizes) herself in a novel. From this perspective, the relationship between plaintiff and defendant parallels that between reader and author on several levels. The plaintiff-reader uses both textual and extratextual information to judge the defendant-author's moral fibre. Textually, the defendant-author's moral choices — how she deploys literary strategies to convey moral messages (the "ethics of fiction") — generates a sense of moral dissonance in the plaintiff-reader, culminating in a lawsuit. Extratextual factors, such as interviews with the author and legal arguments advanced by the defence team, work to exacerbate the plaintiff-reader's sense of dissonance, acting as further evidence of the defendant-author's moral lassitude.[10]

This chapter will help clarify how law and morality intersect in this liminal legal domain, where plaintiffs continue to file lawsuits despite their general lack of success. It will apply the example of *The Help* to show how plaintiffs' moral judgments are informed by legal and extra-legal arguments, especially regarding the law's tendency to separate fiction from "truth" in the service of protecting creative licence. The plaintiff's legal arguments represent her attempt to recover her voice as a Black woman in a legal action that is not receptive to what she has to say — as a legal subject, if not as the subject upon whom a fictional character is based. She thereby seeks to remedy what she perceives as representational disenfranchisement at the hands of both a White author and the legal system. In the end, while the substantive law of personality rights and invasion of privacy are not particularly sympathetic to her project, the procedural process of the law-

---

brought by Sgt Jeffrey Sarver against the makers of the 2008 film *The Hurt Locker*, which the plaintiff also reportedly lost; see, for example, Henry Barnes, "Hurt Locker Lawsuit: Soldier must Pay $187,000" *The Guardian* (9 December 2011), online: The Guardian www.guardian.co.uk/film/2011/dec/09/hurt-locker-soldier-must-pay.

10 Sheldon Sacks, *Fiction and the Shape of Belief: A Study of Henry Fielding with Glances at Swift, Johnson, and Richardson* (Los Angeles: University of California Press, 1964); studying the ethics of fiction aims to answer the question posed by literary theorist Sheldon Sacks: "How can any novelist embody his beliefs in novels?" at 1.

suit — the filing of claims, answers and defences, and responses — nonetheless provides a forum for it.[11]

B. APPROPRIATION OF PERSONALITY, RECOGNITION, AND ETHICS: READERS JUDGING AUTHORS

Lawsuits like the one involving *The Help* are based on the shaky stance that a fictional character is essentially the "likeness" of a real person, and that this portrayal has caused this person harm.[12] Suits of this sort are difficult to win, mainly because freedom of expression guarantees in the US Constitution generally protect authors' rights to use real life as inspiration for fiction, except in very clearly maliciously intended circumstances where a character is overtly linked to its real life counterpart.[13]

Still, the plaintiff in this case argued that the character Aibileen was based on her in ways sufficient to add up to an actionable likeness: the complaint refers to the similarity between her given name (Ablene) and its phonetic equivalent in the character Aibileen,[14] along with two other sets of parallels. The first set involves strictly biographical comparisons: "Aibileen is described as black, middle aged, has a gold tooth, works for a white family in Jackson, Mississippi, and has a son who is deceased"[15] and "Ablene is black, middle aged, has a gold tooth, works for a white family in Jackson, Mississippi, and has a son who is deceased."[16] The second set involves how

11 See, for example, Sally Engle Merry, *Getting Justice and Getting Even: Legal Consciousness Among Working-Class Americans* (Chicago: University of Chicago Press, 1990). This study shares affinity with legal consciousness scholarship that has examined the dissonance between what litigants expect from the law and what they feel they get.

12 The defendant author denied these claims; *Ablene Cooper v Kathryn Stockett* (14 April 2011), Civil Action No 251-11-134 CIV (Circuit Court of the First Judicial District of Hinds County Mississippi) (Defendant's Answer and Defences, at para 29) [*Defendant's Answer and Defences*]. The caselaw on "likeness" mainly concerns a defendant's commercial use of "look-alike" or "sound-alike" actors (often along with other visual and aural cues) specifically intended to invoke a celebrity persona, rather than a written portrayal of a character not intended to specifically refer to an actual person; see *Allen v National Video Inc*, 610 F Supp 612 (SDNY 1985); *Waits v Frito-Lay Inc*, 978 F 2d 1093 (9th Cir 1992).

13 See *Polydoros v Twentieth Century Fox Film Corp*, 67 Cal App 4th 318 (2d Dist 1997).

14 *Plaintiff's Complaint*, above note 4 at para 19; *Defendant's Motion*, above note 4 (citing *People on Complaint of Maggio v Charles Scribner's Sons*, 130 NYS 2d 514 at 520 (NY Magis Ct 1954); the defence argues that caselaw holds that the name must "completely and exactly coincide" and "the context must also single her out and point to her 'as does a portrait or picture'" at 4–5.

15 *Ibid* at para 20.

16 *Ibid* at para 21.

the author came to know the plaintiff, namely as the nanny to her nephew and niece (also named Stockett): "The two white children, a boy and a girl, that Aibileen cares for call her Aibee"[17] and "the Stockett children, a boy and a girl, that Ablene cares for refer to her as Abie or Abi."[18]

For the most part, these similarities are rather general, given that the book is about Black maids working for White families in Jackson, Mississippi, in the early 1960s. Stockett's response is straightforward: *The Help* "is fiction and would not be understood by anyone as representing actual facts about any individual, much less Mrs. Ablene Cooper."[19] However, Stockett also marketed her book as particularly authentic, anchoring her credibility as a writer on the fact that she drew on her own biography.[20] For example, the dust jacket of the book states that Stockett was "born and raised in Jackson, Mississippi," and three of the six pages of a postscript to the novel describe Stockett's relationship with Demetrie, the real African-American maid who helped raise her.[21] Her statement in an interview, cited at the start of this article, demonstrates that while her characters were not intended to be *portraits* of real people, she admittedly used real people and situations as models or inspiration for characters in the book.[22]

It has been well established in US caselaw that authors are relatively free to draw inspiration from real life, but *Cooper v Stockett* provides an interesting example of a legal battle over the ethics of acknowledgement, accuracy, and sensitivity toward the real-life inspiration for fictional works. Much of Cooper's complaint rests not on the law *per se*, but rather on the implication that Stockett is essentially a hypocrite and therefore morally

---

17 *Ibid* at para 22.

18 *Ibid* at para 24.

19 *Defendant's Motion*, above note 4 at 4. The defence cites *Doe v Rowe*, 638 So (2d) 826 at 829 (Ala 1994), where the court held that the plaintiffs must lose because the book at issue "is clearly classified and represented as a novel, which the general public understands to be a fictitious work representative of real life" at 5.

20 Susan Tridgell, *Understanding Our Selves: The Dangerous Art of Biography* (Bern: Peter Lang, 2004) at 86. Tridgell's book features a chapter on "Moral Accountability and Narrating the Self" — that is, how a biographer uses a life story to create continuity regarding a subject's moral development, or to create discontinuity with a formerly amoral self. Stockett's invocation of her youthful failure to appreciate racial issues as motivation compelling her to make up for this blindness as an adult/author is an example of Stockett narrating her moral development through her writing.

21 Stockett, above note 5 at 447 ff (postscript to *The Help*).

22 *Defendant's Motion*, above note 4: "not only does the book say it is not attempting to convey facts about any real person, but it also identifies the real person from whom Ms. Stockett drew inspiration, and it is was Demetrie McLorn, not Mrs. Ablene Cooper" at 6.

blameworthy. In the plaintiff's eyes, Stockett is guilty of *some* wrong because she did not live up to her own professed moral code, and further did not meet her own reflexive ethics of fiction, as exemplified by the authorial ethics of the main White character in the novel, Skeeter Phelan, who enlists the help of a dozen maids to write a non-fiction "tell all" book about life as a Black maid working for a White family in Mississippi at that time. Finally, the plaintiff found further evidence of moral failure in Stockett's response to the lawsuit itself. The lawsuit is the plaintiff's attempt to take Stockett to task for these moral failures, loosely grounding the moral shortcomings in legally recognized wrongs.

At the core of these issues lies the problem of what readers perceive as "real" or "true" in fictional works, and how these determinations relate to an author's legal claims regarding the relationship between the novel and her own life. Literary scholar James Phelan wrote:

> [A]udiences will develop interests and responses of three kinds, each related to a particular component of the narrative: mimetic, thematic, and synthetic. Responses to the mimetic component involve an audience's interest in the characters as possible people and in the narrative world as like our own, that is, hypothetically or conceptually possible; responses to the mimetic component include our evolving judgments and emotions, our desires, hopes, expectations, satisfactions, and disappointments. Responses to the thematic component involve an interest in the ideational function of the characters and in the cultural, ideological, philosophical, or ethical issues being addressed by the narrative. Responses to the synthetic component involve an audience's interest in and attention to the characters and to the larger narrative as artificial constructs.[23]

Phelan went on to note that for most realistic narratives (like *The Help*), "the audience has a tacit awareness of the synthetic while it focuses on the mimetic and the thematic components . . . ."[24] The law, however, tends to focus on the synthetic component, and so favours defendants in these types of lawsuits.[25]

---

23 James Phelan, *Experiencing Fiction: Judgments, Progressions, and the Rhetorical Theory of Narrative* (Columbus: Ohio State University Press, 2007) at 5–6.

24 *Ibid* at 6.

25 Thomas M Clyde, "Trial Q&A: How Do Juries React When Creative Works Mix Fact with Fiction?" (2010) 27 Comm Law 18 at 18. The article discusses the unusual victory (by jury decision) of a plaintiff in a suit regarding a fictional character in the 2003 novel *The Red Hat Club*. The jury awarded damages for libel, mainly due to the large number of similar-

Philosophy scholar and fiction writer Claudia Mills is one of the few who have written explicitly about the more general professional ethics about appropriating the stories of other people, with a focus on fiction writing.[26] Like journalists, fiction writers must deal with the ethical problems associated with *using others as means* — which, drawing from Kant, Mills claimed is only *unjustified* if it is all that you are doing.[27] Fiction writers frequently justify using others in the service of their art, arguing that they, like other artists, serve some artistic higher good that outweighs any ethical breaches.[28] There are of course limits to this line of reasoning.[29] Additionally, some writers and literary critics have noted that "great" literature deserves more leeway than poor or otherwise deficient attempts at writing or making art: lawmakers have wisely avoided these quality distinctions.[30]

In crafting the character Skeeter in *The Help*, Stockett's plot development focuses on Skeeter's growth from an inexperienced and naïve young writer to a published author mindful of her ethical obligations. The plaintiff explicitly compares Stockett's conduct to Skeeter's:

> The irony of this lawsuit is inescapable. In *The Help*, the young white character, Skeeter Phelan, solicits the assistance of thirteen African-American maids to collaborate with her to write a book called *Help*. When the book is accepted for publication Skeeter receives an $800 advance. Skeeter then proceeds to give **all the money** to the maids, "the help," who made her book possible.
>
> Unlike Skeeter Phelan, Kathryn Stockett refuses to recognize Ablene Cooper, much less compensate her, for her role in *The Help*. Kathryn Stockett has reaped millions of dollars from this book, yet she denies Ablene

---

ities between the plaintiff and the character, who was also portrayed as a promiscuous alcoholic. The jury denied the plaintiff's privacy claims; see *Smith v Stewart*, 660 SE (2d) 822 (Ga App 2008), the Court of Appeals of Georgia decision on which causes of action could proceed in this case.

26 Claudia Mills, "Appropriating Others' Stories: Some Questions about the Ethics of Writing Fiction" (2000) 31:2 Journal of Social Philosophy 195 at 195.

27 *Ibid* at 202–4.

28 See, for example, Carolyn Anderson & Thomas W Benson, *Documentary Dilemmas: Frederick Wiseman's Titicut Follies* (Carbondale: Southern Illinois University Press, 1991) at 4. Documentary film raises similar issues regarding the interplay of art and ethics.

29 Cases dealing with the "artistic merit" defence in relation to making child pornography are a rich site of discussion of the limits of using others for artistic purposes. In Canada, see *R v Sharpe*, 2001 SCC 2; see also *R v Katigbak*, 2010 ONCA 411; in the United States, see *New York v Ferber*, 458 US 747 (1982).

30 June Ross, "*R v Sharpe* and the Defence of Artistic Merit" (2001) 12:1 Const F 23 at 27.

> Cooper is entitled to one dime in damages. With apologies to Oscar Wilde, life certainly does not imitate art, at least when it comes to *The Help*.[31]

In other words, because Stockett uses Skeeter's awareness of the ethics of writing as a means to foster reader identification with Skeeter as a hero (contributing to the ethics of fiction of the novel), she is particularly vulnerable to the charge that she is a hypocrite, or worse, that she deliberately exploited her subjects.

While Stockett admits to drawing on her memories of Demetrie, the maid (now deceased) who helped raise her, she denied using any currently living persons as inspiration.[32] In this way she sidestepped obligations that would arise from Cooper's accusation that she is mistreating the real maids she used as material for her novel. To the plaintiff, Stockett's denials served as an aggravating factor for the infliction of emotional distress claim. The complaint also implicitly accused Stockett of being a racist: "Just as the white characters in 'The Help' treated Aibileen in a reckless, careless, and indifferent manner, Kathryn Stockett's past conduct and her continuing and repeated conduct towards Ablene is outrageous, reckless, malicious, and grossly careless."[33] Cooper illustrated her amplified distress through her emotional statements as she left the courthouse upon dismissal of her suit: "She's a liar! She's a liar! You know she did it and everybody else knows she did it . . . she knows she did it! Tell her to tell the truth, she's a liar!"[34]

Other readers have also drawn conclusions about Stockett's racism based on what they see as her excessive denial of using Cooper as a model, especially because Stockett claims she barely knows Cooper. For example, the complaint states that "Ablene has, on occasion, served as a babysitter for Kathryn Stockett, keeping Stockett's daughter,"[35] but the defendant's answer states, "Ms. Stockett does not recall whether this allegation is true or not and so denies it."[36] Stockett has said in interviews that she has talked to Cooper only minimally over the course of her employment as her brother's maid.[37] But even this strikes some readers as evidence of moral weakness;

---

31 *Plaintiff's Response*, above note 4 at 10 [emphasis in original].

32 *Defendant's Answer and Defences*, above note 12 at para 29.

33 *Plaintiff's Complaint*, above note 4 at para 42.

34 "Ablene Cooper Reacts to Dismissal of 'The Help' Lawsuit" *WAPT News* (16 August 2011), online: YouTube www.youtube.com/watch?v=07F27VU4Ioc.

35 *Plaintiff's Complaint*, above note 4 at para 16.

36 *Defendant's Answer and Defences*, above note 12 at para 16.

37 "Author Hopes 'The Help' Lawsuit Thrown Out" *WAPT News* (15 August 2011), online: YouTube www.youtube.com/watch?v=D82NrKe5H2A&feature=relmfu. Stockett spoke

according to one comment on a *Forbes* blog discussing the lawsuit, "Kathryn Stockett is a liar. She states she met Ms. Cooper for 5 minutes? She has been the [maid] to her brother-in-law's [sic] family for YEARS. Just because Kathryn might have treated her like furniture in the room like the white women in her book, does not mean she was not there."[38]

Perhaps Stockett and her lawyers denied more than necessary in asserting that the contact between Stockett and Cooper was inconsequential.[39] Indeed, this line of argument also provides fodder for criticism of Stockett's choice to write her book in the first person via her three character-narrators (two of whom are Black). If she did not bother to take much notice, much less talk to her brother's maid, what research did she do on what it really feels like to be a Black maid working for a White family? In the postscript to the novel, Stockett acknowledges that:

> I'm pretty sure I can say that no one in my family ever asked Demetrie what it felt like to be black in Mississippi, working for our white family. It never occurred to us to ask . . . . I have wished, for many years, that I'd been old enough and thoughtful enough to ask Demetrie that question. She died when I was sixteen. I've spent years imagining what her answer would be. And that is why I wrote this book.[40]

As literary scholar Duchess Harris pointed out:

> It would have behooved Stockett to ask her burning question of another Black domestic, or at least read some memoirs on the subject, but instead

---

about the lawsuit at a panel discussion at the National Association of Black Journalists convention in 2011, where she stated: "If you add up the seconds that we've seen each other, it would be maybe 10 or 15. I've met her twice. Hello how are you? Goodbye. Have a nice day." This clip is incorporated into the WAPT-TV, Jackson, Mississippi, newscast the night before the hearing in *Cooper*.

38 Kiri Blakeley, "The Help: Maid Should Cash In Instead of Sue" *Forbes* (11 August 2011), online: Forbes www.forbes.com/sites/kiriblakeley/2011/08/11/the-help-maid-should-cash-in-instead-of-sue ("escarondito" commenting on Kiri Blakeley's blog). Note: Cooper worked for Stockett's brother, not her brother-in-law.

39 *Defendant's Answer and Defences*, above note 12, a further example of Stockett overstating how little she knew about the plaintiff at para 21; similarly, she denies knowing her niece and nephew refer to the plaintiff as Abie or Abi at para 24; *Plaintiff's Complaint*, above note 4 at para 21, in response to the Plaintiff's Complaint where she states that "Ablene is black, middle aged, has a gold tooth, works for a white family in Jackson, Mississippi, and has a son who is deceased," in that the answer states: "Ms. Stockett is without knowledge of this paragraph and therefore denies it."

40 Stockett, above note 5 at 451.

> she substitutes her imagination for understanding. And the result is that *The Help* isn't for Black women at all, and quickly devolves into just another novel by and for white women.[41]

With regard to the first-person narration, Harris noted,

> when the novel attempts to enter the mindset of the Black women, like Aib[i]leen or her best friend Minny, suddenly we enter the realm of the ridiculous . . . . So instead of incorporating a real Black woman's voice in a novel purported to being *about* Black domestics, the Skeeter/Stockett character is comfortingly centralized, and I can see why white women relate to her.[42]

In response to Cooper's claims of appropriation, the defence also quoted Stockett's statements in the postscript of the novel, but with the intent to demonstrate that Stockett was writing about a matter of public interest and so deserves strong expression rights protection, regardless of her appropriation of Black women's voices: "As Ms. Stockett puts it, what it felt like to be a black woman in Mississippi in the 1960s is not 'something any white woman on the other end of a black woman's paycheck could ever understand. But trying to understand is vital to our humanity.'"[43] In other words, the defence argued that Stockett has the right to imagine what it is like to be a Black maid to a White family and not do any empirical research. The courts have taken this position in the past, which explains why most cases are dismissed. However, for plaintiffs like Cooper, appropriation of voice and subject position without acknowledgement or compensation is the first layer of the moral wrong, and the second is the inaccuracy of the resulting portrait. The law may not validate this type of moral problem by awarding damages, but Cooper's suit successfully forced Stockett to answer the claims, and thereby to acknowledge the existence of a broader moral problem that includes the legal system as a whole.[44]

---

41 Duchess Harris, "Kathryn Stockett Is Not My Sister and I Am Not Her Help" *The Feminist Wire* (12 August 2011), online: The Feminist Wire www.thefeministwire.com/2011/08/kathryn-stockett-is-not-my-sister-and-i-am-not-her-help.

42 *Ibid* [emphasis in original].

43 *Defendant's Motion*, above note 4 at 6.

44 This strategy joins other efforts to use the law to affect social change. See Thomas B Stoddard, "Bleeding Heart: Reflections on Using the Law to Make Social Change" (1997) 72:5 NYU L Rev 967 at 970, examining the use of law to affect social change in the context of the gay rights movement in New Zealand.

C. FICTIONALIZATION, FALSE LIGHT PUBLICATION, AND THE ETHICS OF FICTION

False light publication is one of the four privacy torts recognized in the United States.[45] It addresses unwanted publicity that contains untrue information about a person, much like defamation.[46] Instead of focusing on damage to reputation, however, the privacy action protects against the mental or emotional harm caused by false or even misleading published information.[47] False light invasion of privacy is difficult to make out in relation to a work of fiction, precisely because works of fiction are not expected to adhere strictly to fact. Nonetheless, Cooper's claims again bring ethical issues into the legal forum, specifically the moral obligation for White authors to portray African-American characters accurately. For example, in citing the first category of demeaning false or misleading portrayals in *The Help*, the plaintiff referred to how the Aibileen character speaks in a heavy dialect, and what she says: "It has been emotionally upsetting and is highly offensive to Ablene to be falsely portrayed in 'The Help' as an African-American maid in Jackson, Mississippi who uses this kind of language and compares her skin color to a cockroach."[48] The second source of offensive falsehoods identified by the plaintiff was that the plot caused Aibileen to endure humiliating circumstances: "It has been emotionally upsetting and is highly offensive to Ablene to be falsely portrayed in 'The Help' as an African-American maid in Jackson, Mississippi who is forced to use a segregated toilet in the garage of her white employer's home."[49]

The plaintiff's discomfort at her historical displacement to the early 1960s (where she is subjected to Jim Crow style racism) is understandable, given her close identification with the Aibilene character. The defence, however, claimed that this historical displacement is further evidence that Aibileen is *not* Ablene: as the defence points out, the character Aibilene is

45 Richard A Posner, "The Right of Privacy" (1978) 12:3 Ga L Rev 393 at 411.

46 *Ibid* at 419–20.

47 Many false light publication cases deal with publication of images of the plaintiff, where the false or misleading aspect comes from the placement of the image in a publication or a misleading headline or caption; see, for example, *Peoples Bank & Trust Co v Globe International Inc*, 786 F Supp 791 at 792–93 (WD Ark 1992); *Jose Solano Jr v Playgirl Inc*, 292 F 3d 1078 (9th Cir 2002); *Braun v Flynt*, 726 F 2d 245 (5th Cir 1984); see *Time Inc v Hill*, 385 US 374 (1967), which deals with the story of a plaintiff, rather than a photograph.

48 *Plaintiff's Complaint*, above note 4 at para 34.

49 *Ibid* at para 36.

fifty-four in 1963, whereas the plaintiff Ablene is middle-aged today.[50] This defence is not particularly convincing, because it is certainly possible for an author to place a character modelled after a contemporary person in another historical moment. However, neither party can legally articulate the readerly source of the plaintiff's complaint, which is far more complicated in that it rests on the interplay between Stockett's writing and Cooper's reading. In other words, the plaintiff-reader here is in large part responding to the dissonant conditions the defendant-author created for contemporary Black readers.

Literary scholar James Phelan developed a useful approach for understanding the "feedback loop among authorial agency, textual phenomena (including intertextual relations), and reader response[,]" which "assumes that texts are designed by authors in order to affect readers in particular ways" and that "reader responses are a function, guide, and test of how designs are created through textual and intertextual phenomena."[51] In many ways, *Cooper* is about how this "feedback loop" gets tangled — that is, where Stockett's intentions for her readers' experiences go awry, particularly along racial lines. With regard to the false light publication claim, the snags occur in part at the intersection of realism and melodrama, an intersection that alternately supports and undermines the author's claims to an overall ethical project that is anti-racist.

Authors who employ the literary technique of realism are particularly vulnerable to complaints about inaccuracy, because realism stakes relatively strong claims to truth (as the name suggests), particularly with regard to portraying stories depicting social upheaval.[52] The genre of melodrama, on the other hand, employs techniques that enhance emotional impact, sometimes at the cost of realism, but no less likely to some ethical end.[53] With regard to *The Help*, critics have cited flaws in the realist depiction of the time period and the plight of its Black inhabitants, and have criticized Stockett's

50 *Defendant's Motion*, above note 4 at 6.

51 James Phelan, *Living to Tell About It: A Rhetoric and Ethics of Character Narration* (Ithaca: Cornell University Press, 2005) at 18.

52 Amy Kaplan, *The Social Construction of American Realism* (Chicago: University of Chicago Press, 1992) at 10.

53 See, generally, Linda Williams, *Playing the Race Card: Melodramas of Black and White from Uncle Tom to O.J. Simpson* (Princeton: Princeton University Press, 2001). Melodrama has been an object of intense study by feminist and critical race scholars, because it can both cement and undermine negative stereotypes.

use of melodramatic "Mammy" type characters, where both lines of criticism question the author's true dedication to anti-racism.

For example, some critics have pointed to historical evidence that Black women participated overtly in the Civil Rights movement, contrary to the fearfulness and timidity depicted in Stockett's characters.[54] This criticism is related to Cooper's complaint that Stockett's portrayal of how Aibileen talks and acts is "highly offensive."[55] Critics have also pointed out that the novel pays scant attention to the intense level of political activism actually going on in Mississippi at the time, and that when they are mentioned Stockett sometimes gets them wrong.[56] Historical inaccuracy or underemphasis are moral criticisms here, levelled at Stockett as a White author of a book set in the Civil Rights era where the characters engage in their own form of activism: writing a tell-all book to expose the racism among the middle-class White women who employ Black maids, in order to "change things."[57]

Further moral criticisms arise from the melodramatic features of the novel. The moral sympathies afforded to various characters are obvious: Skeeter, Aibileen, and Minny are heroes; Hilly and Elizabeth are villains, with other characters more mildly villainous or at least deserving some sympathy (for instance Skeeter's mother — where the readers' judgment of

54 Nicolaus Mills, "'The Help' I Knew Cared More About Voting Rights Than Getting Back at White Ladies" *Christian Science Monitor* (16 September 2011), online: The Christian Science Monitor www.csmonitor.com/Commentary/Opinion/2011/0916/The-Help-I-knew-cared-more-about-voting-rights-than-getting-back-at-white-ladies. "As in Stockett's novel, the help I knew had plenty of grievances against their white employers . . . . But getting back at the white families who hired them by helping a white author write a tell-all book (as Stockett's fictional black maids do) was the last thing any of the help I knew was going to try. Too much risk for too little payoff."

55 *Plaintiff's Complaint*, above note 4 at para 34.

56 See Onyx, "The Medgar Evers Error in The Help's First Edition" *A Critical Review of the Novel The Help* (9 April 2011), online: www.acriticalreviewofthehelp.wordpress.com/2011/04/09/medgar-evers-error-in-the-help. For instance, a historical error in the original printing of the book stated that civil rights activist Medgar Evers was bludgeoned in his front yard (he was actually shot). This error was reportedly repeated by Stockett in interviews before it was corrected in later editions; Onyx, "Challenging Kathryn Stockett's Spin on Segregation" *A Critical Review of the Novel The Help* (17 January 2011), online: www.acriticalreviewofthehelp.wordpress.com/2011/01/17/challenging-stockett-on-segregation. Onyx's site is entirely dedicated to criticism of the novel, movie, and extratextual issues (reviews, reception, and the lawsuit itself). Onyx further criticized Stockett for using civil rights events to humanize the White segregationist characters more than they deserved.

57 *The Help*, above note 5. The first section of the novel, written in Aibileen's voice, features a conversation between Aibileen and Skeeter wherein Skeeter stakes her moral claim on civil rights, asking Aibileen: "Do you ever wish you could . . . change things?" at 10.

her sexism and racism is tempered by the fact that she is dying of cancer; and Stuart, who is judged less harshly because he is the only man showing an interest in Skeeter).[58] As with the classic melodrama, most of the action in the novel takes place in families and homes and revolves around actual or threatened victimization, although these situations are complicated by the employment relationship between the nannies and the mothers of the children they care for. Nonetheless, as in the classic melodrama, threats to and within families create narrative tension (for example, Aibileen worries what will become of her White wards if she is fired or otherwise separated from them).[59]

Critics of *The Help* often target Stockett's use of stock characters, in particular Aibileen, a "Mammy" type character who is endlessly giving and affectionate to her White employers' children, yet tough on Black children.[60] In response to the plaintiff's claim that the appropriation of her name and likeness is "highly offensive" and has caused "outrage, revulsion, and severe emotional distress,"[61] the defence countered that the "book cover describes 'Aibilene Clark' as a wise, regal woman."[62] This response clearly misses the point that portraying a Black female servant as *wise* and *regal* rather than justifiably angry could be highly offensive, especially to those who see this type of figure as reinforcing racist stereotypes rather than breaking down racial barriers.[63] As literary scholar Michele Wallace wrote: "The Help glosses

---

58 Kathryn Stockett, *The Help: A Novel* (London: Penguin Group, 2011) ("Readers Guide for *The Help*" unpaginated back pages where reader sympathies are overtly courted for or against characters in the book, as reflected in book club study guides, such as the list of discussion questions the author poses to readers like: "Do you think that Skeeter's mother is a sympathetic or an unsympathetic character? Why?").

59 Sacks, above note 10. As literary scholar Sacks wrote, "[a]n action is a work organized so that it introduces characters, about whose fates we are made to care, in unstable relationships which are then further complicated until the complication is finally resolved by the removal of the represented instability" at 26.

60 See Onyx, "The Mommy/Mammy Issues in The Help" *A Critical Review of the Novel The Help* (2 March 2011), online: www.acriticalreviewofthehelp.wordpress.com/2011/03/02/mommy-mammy-issue; Touré, "Is *The Help* the Most Loathsome Movie in America?" *Time Ideas* (2 February 2012), online: *Time* http://ideas.time.com/2012/02/02/is-the-help-the-most-loathsome-movie-in-america.

61 *Plaintiff's Complaint*, above note 4 at para 31.

62 *Defendant's Answer and Defences*, above note 12 at para 31.

63 See Micki McElya, *Clinging to Mammy: The Faithful Slave in Twentieth-Century America* (Cambridge: Harvard University Press, 2007).

over the reality of African-American triumphs we bled and died for, in order to make a feel-good Hollywood story."[64]

The defence naturally sought refuge in the First Amendment, which affords especially strong protection to fiction "that addresses a matter of public concern, i.e., the relationship, between the races in Mississippi in the early 1960s."[65] In response, the plaintiff retorted that the novel is not really about race relations, and used criticism of the genre of melodrama to drive this point home:

> Ablene Cooper could not agree more with Stockett that race relations are indeed a matter of public concern. However, the problem for Stockett is *The Help* has absolutely nothing to do with race relations. According to the dust jacket on versions of *The Help* sold in the United Kingdom, the book is about "female love." Specifically, the entire accolade reads as follows: "A big, warm girlfriend of a book about female love [t]hat transcends race and class." Saying that *The Help* is about race relations in America would be akin to describing *The Da Vinci Code* as a book about Christianity.[66]

In other words, it is precisely because of how she deploys the ethics of fiction via melodrama that her authorial choices inspire moral outrage against her, casting doubt on her actual dedication to anti-racism. The lawsuit gave voice to these broader complaints via a claim to community support for the plaintiff's outrage: "Kathryn Stockett knows that Ablene is justified in the eyes of the community in Jackson, Mississippi in feeling seriously offended, aggrieved, and outraged by the conduct of Kathryn Stockett."[67] While the composition of the community is not specified, the plaintiff clearly casts herself as a spokesperson for its disgruntled members.[68]

---

64 Michele Wallace & Bridgette Bartlett, "The Help Love It Or Leave It?" (2011) 42:4 Essence 72 at 72.

65 *Defendant's Answer and Defences*, above note 12 at 4 (para 3 of the Affirmative Defences).

66 *Plaintiff's Response*, above note 4 at 9.

67 *Plaintiff's Complaint*, above note 4 at para 37.

68 *Ibid*. The same claim is also made under the infliction of emotional distress part of the complaint: "These facts when told to an average member of the community would cause that person to characterize the actions of Kathryn Stockett as being outrageous" at para 47.

D. CONCLUSIONS: AUTHORS, READERS, AND THE SELF AT LAW

The *Cooper* lawsuit ended up giving voice to Ablene Cooper's complaints, as ultimately representative of a broader set of issues regarding White authors depicting African-American characters. This set of concerns does not often find a legal forum.[69] Indeed, the exchange of court documents between plaintiff and defendant are a fascinating dialogue about authorial practices and reader experiences that do not fit easily within established legal principles.[70]

The dialogue centrally engaged what Wayne C Booth referred to as "ethical criticism," a mode of reading and analyzing literary work that the plaintiff insists is vital, although others, including the defence team, often malign it as a form of censorship.[71] Yet, using the lens of ethical criticism helps us understand the claims of the plaintiff, and explains her persistent resistance to a more dominant mode of reading fiction (mostly shared by the courts) that is largely anti-humanist: that is, not especially interested in how an author's life makes its way into the telling, but rather considering a fictional work to be a stand-alone text.[72]

Cooper's claims ran counter to this anti-humanist stance and demanded that the real people behind a fictional work be acknowledged and heard. In keeping with the circular nature of many of the claims, one of her final arguments was that, "By filing this motion for summary judgment and attempting to stifle the voice of Ablene Cooper, it appears that Stockett certainly does not have much interest in an 'uninhibited, robust, and wide open' debate taking place in the Circuit Court of Hinds County concerning this lawsuit."[73] The plaintiff thereby accused Stockett again of being self-serving, claiming that she valued freedom of speech only when it served her own

---

69 *Suntrust Bank v Houghton Mifflin Co*, 136 F Supp 2d 1357 at 1381 (ND Ga 2001), another interesting case with related issues which dealt with an African-American author, Alice Randall, who was sued for copyright infringement by the estate of a White author, Margaret Mitchell, regarding Randall's novel *The Wind Done Gone*, a rewriting of Mitchell's classic Civil War novel *Gone with the Wind* from the slaves' perspective; see David Roh, "Two Copyright Case Studies from a Literary Perspective" (2010) 22:1 Law & Literature 110, for an in-depth discussion of the case.

70 See *Geisler v Petrocelli*, 616 F 2d 636 (2d Cir 1980). This case suggests that claims against fiction writers are not *a priori* doomed to failure. However First Amendment arguments have generally prevailed in these types of cases.

71 Wayne C Booth, *The Company We Keep: An Ethics of Fiction* (Berkeley: University of California Press, 1988) at 3–4.

72 Tridgell, above note 20 at 12.

73 *Plaintiff's Response*, above note 4 at 9.

interests, and that she used the First Amendment to end the lawsuit and thereby perversely silenced the voices of real African-Americans. Although the legal arguments were presumably written by lawyers rather than Stockett herself, she is once again judged according to the ethics of her own position. She is painted as a hypocrite: morally (if not legally) in the wrong.

The plaintiff in *Cooper* thus relentlessly linked the experience of reading *The Help* with Stockett's statements — whether to the media, the public, or via the court documents in the lawsuit — and held the defendant-author accountable to a coherent ethical plan that cuts across all of these contexts. The plaintiff thereby reinscribed herself as a full subject into the novel and into the law, even as her case was not successful.[74]

---

74 My study of the *Cooper* lawsuit shares affinity with legal consciousness scholarship focused on how the actual people who are addressed by a law manage their dissonance with how they are characterized in law; see, for example, David M Engel & Frank W Munger, *Rights of Inclusion: Law and Identity in the Life Stories of Americans with Disabilities* (Chicago: University of Chicago Press, 2003).

NINETEEN

Structures of Sharing: Depropriation and Intellectual Property Law

MARCUS BOON

ABSTRACT (EN): Intellectual property law is concerned with control over the production and distribution of copies ("materially fixed expressions") of ideas. Copies are in fact ubiquitous and the attempt to situate copies within a certain discourse or discipline relies on particular philosophical decisions that can be shown, historically and otherwise, to be finally political and ideological. If the copy always evades and exceeds disciplinarity, including "multidisciplinarity" and law, what do we do about these copies that are ultimately depropriated, that is, lacking a "proper" place or location, yet nonetheless recognizably present? The author explores the work of French filmmaker Jean-Luc Godard as an example of an attempt to think and make a copy-based art that refuses the logic of IP, and argues that legal scholars need to consider broader issues of political economy when debating contemporary IP law.

RÉSUMÉ (FR): Le droit de la propriété intellectuelle s'intéresse au contrôle de la production et de la distribution de copies d'idées (« fixations matérielles de l'expression »). Les copies sont omniprésentes et la tentative de les situer à l'intérieur d'un certain discours ou discipline dépend de décisions philosophiques particulières dont on peut, de façon historique ou autre, finalement démontrer le caractère politique ou idéologique. Si la copie se soustrait toujours à la disciplinarité — y compris la « multidisciplinarité » — et au droit, et les dépasse, que pouvons-nous faire de ces copies qui sont ultimement désappropriées, c'est-à-dire auxquelles manquent une place ou un lieu « propre », mais qui sont toutefois visiblement présentes? L'auteur explore le travail du cinéaste français Jean-Luc Godard en tant qu'exemple d'une tentative de penser et de créer un art basé sur la copie qui refuse la logique du droit de la propriété intellectuelle et soutient que les spécialistes du droit doivent considérer des problèmes d'économie politique plus larges lorsqu'ils débattent du droit de la propriété intellectuelle contemporain.

A. INTRODUCTION

I wrote a book that was published about a year and a half ago called *In Praise of Copying*.[1] I wrote the book because it seemed to me that all around me, there was a proliferation of practices of copying, particularly by students I worked with, but very little by way of a justification of these practices, which tended to be engaged in with a sense of guilt, below the radar of the law. When they were justified, as in the case of the important work by Lawrence Lessig and James Boyle, it was through a quite cautious affirmation that stressed the importance of IP law, while arguing for quite modest adjustments that would allow certain kinds of sharing to happen, in the name of creativity.[2] The kinds of sharing, particularly of music, that people were and still are engaging in went far beyond what Lessig and Boyle argued in favour of. And I became fascinated by the radical gap between legal discourses concerning copying, and the actual practices of copying that people engage in today in everyday life. On closer inspection, the relatively limited framework of copying that is recognized as such, whether affirmatively in the case of hip hop sampling or literary citation, or negatively as in the counterfeiting of branded goods or the appropriation of indigenous cultural forms, appeared to me as part of a much broader set of practices or processes that could equally be described as copying. These would include: the generalized phenomenon of language acquisition by humans and non-humans; the principle of economic equivalence, by which one thing is established as having the same value as another thing (termed *economimesis* by Jacques Derrida[3]); the sexual (or asexual) reproduction of organic life forms as variations or permutations of the DNA molecule; and so on.

1 Marcus Boon, *In Praise of Copying* (Cambridge: Harvard University Press, 2010).

2 Lawrence Lessig, *Free Culture: How Big Media Uses Technology and the Law to Lock Down Culture and Control Creativity* (New York: Penguin Press, 2004); James Boyle, *The Public Domain: Enclosing the Commons of the Mind* (New Haven: Yale University Press, 2008).

3 Jacques Derrida, "Economimesis" translated by Richard Klein" (1981) 11:2 Diacritics 3.

I became intrigued by the relationship between laws that regulate copying and philosophical and anthropological descriptions of copying practices. I was particularly struck by the work of René Girard, who makes a grandiose but compelling argument that mimesis is the fundamental problem faced by human beings, who are constituted as such through a drive to imitate, but who at the same time struggle to establish their separate and individual identities. For Girard, violence is the result of this struggle for originality or authenticity or ownership (both of self and object of desire), and the law attempts to moderate claims to identity and ownership, while at the same time enacting the cathartic process of scapegoating certain individuals as being responsible for the evils of mimesis.[4] For my purposes, those who violate IP laws are scapegoated as engaging in illicit acts of "copying," so that the rest of society may enjoy the cathartically produced (but illusory) sense of being innocent of copying themselves.

Girard's work raises a fundamental question, one that is relevant to the topic of IP and interdisciplinarity: what is the place, field, or form in which the problem of imitation can be responded to in a human society? Law would be one structure that attempts to appropriate or organize mimesis. Art would be another. Economy would be a third. For Girard, only religion, and more specifically a Christian practice of counter-sacrifice, can respond adequately. I would like to radicalize or at least open up the problematic as set up by Girard, through the work of Georges Bataille, and his notion of "the accursed share" by which Bataille means the excess that is always present and must always be disposed of in some way by any human society.[5] This excessive "share" is "accursed" because it is generally forbidden or tabooed; yet, at certain key moments, the taboo is reversed and the share must be used up. For example, violence is forbidden in most societies, yet becomes mandatory when there is a war. There are reasons to question whether "excess" is the best word for this thing that can't be organized or

---

4 The simplest account of Girard's ideas concerning mimesis is probably the interview with him at the end of René Girard, *"To Double Business Bound": Essays on Literature, Mimesis, and Anthropology* (Baltimore: Johns Hopkins University Press, 1978). The fullest account is in René Girard, *Things Hidden since the Foundation of the World*, translated by Stephen Bann & Michael Metter (London: Athlone, 1987), particularly Book 1, ch 1, and Book 3, ch 1 & 2. The most well known account is in René Girard, *Violence and the Sacred*, translated by Patrick Gregory (Baltimore: Johns Hopkins University Press, 1977), in the chapter "From Mimetic Desire to the Monstrous Double" at 143.

5 Georges Bataille, *The Accursed Share: An Essay on General Economy, Volume 1: Consumption*, translated by Robert Hurley (New York: Zone Books, 1988).

framed, but if one thinks about mimesis and therefore copying in terms of the problematic set out by Bataille, the question is raised: is there indeed a generalized taboo on the excessive but inevitable proliferation of copies that is being enacted, or *contained*, at present through IP law? And what is the relationship between IP law and this more general taboo? One place to look for this connection is in the concept of moral rights, which is often raised, both legally and otherwise, as the justification of IP law. I hope you can see that the problem of interdisciplinarity is raised here: the law is only one of a number of structures by which humans seek to contain practices of copying in particular societies. Intellectual property law is itself only 300 years old, and belongs to a very particular set of cultural histories, specific to European and North American modernity, but is now being elevated to the status of a universal in the age of globalized capital.

Presenting this kind of material to legal scholars I feel naïve. I am not making an argument against the existence of the law either in general or specifically in the case of intellectual property. I am questioning whether the law can do what it ostensibly sets out to do, which is to regulate the production of copies. If the answer to this question is affirmative, then one needs to explain why copying proliferates to such a radical extent beyond the reaches of the law. Is this just a matter of a lack of fine tuning the law such that it is able to address all situations? Or is it a problem of enforcement such that there is simply a lack of political will to track down and prosecute all IP law violators? Of course, one could say that we are continually acting in a social and legal space in which our actions are made with only a general awareness of the actual nature of the legal code that governs that space. The entire range of legal mechanisms in our society come into play in articulating, testing, disputing, and enforcing the specific discursive/legal meaning of acts and events that remain opaque in the moment of their lived reality. If the answer is negative, meaning, to repeat, that there is something about the production of copies that will always remain beyond the capability of the law's ability to regulate, it would be important to unequivocally affirm that. Fair use and the public domain are ways of articulating a margin of unregulatability. They are typically justified with reference to the needs of the liberal subject, the affirmation of a public space tended by a liberal-democratic state. These needs and this affirmation are in turn limited by those of commerce and private interest. But the limits of fair use and the public domain are breached so regularly today, and the terms are so often invoked in situations where in fact the rights implied by these concepts no longer exist, that we should at least question whether they remain an appropriate vocabulary for enframing debate about IP.

In my book, I discuss this problematic in terms of appropriation and depropriation.[6] For many philosophers, appropriation is constitutive of being human and of the world more broadly. In order to survive, we eat, we build territories, we take, and we give. Marx in his early manuscripts spoke of man's entire relation to the world as one of sensory appropriation, and more broadly affirmed that all political-economic systems involve appropriation. Capitalism and colonialism are both particular regimes of appropriation then, as are feudalism and "primitive accumulation," while communism as presented in *The Communist Manifesto* involves a reappropriation of that which has been appropriated by the bourgeoisie.[7] A final appropriation if you like. Marx distinguished in the *Grundrisse* between property and private property, but insisted on the necessity of the former: "an appropriation which does not make something into property is a contradictio in subjecto."[8]

A question remains however about how fundamental appropriation is, and whether all entities can finally be defined as property, whether private or common. I argue that there is another position with respect to being, and that one name for it is depropriation. By depropriation I mean to suggest both certain things that are inherently unownable, that cannot be made property, and are therefore necessarily part of a public domain or commons, but also other things whose status outside of ownership is established by shared consensual protocols and practices. Legally speaking, depropriation takes at least two forms. One a positive form, which would include notions of public domain, open source, creative commons licensing, etc., in which the law is used to define a set of conditions under which access to ideas and their expressions is defined. The other a negative form, as in many file sharing communities and informal economies where local and sometimes more than local practices continue to exist outside of, or alongside, the law for various periods of time. Depropriation, and a set of related words that include "unbelonging," "decreation," etc., have a place in the history of thought, which might include the work of Simone Weil, Roberto Esposito,

---

6 Boon, above note 1 at 223–37.

7 Karl Marx & Friedrich Engels, *The Communist Manifesto* (New Haven: Yale University Press, 2012).

8 Karl Marx, *Grundrisse: Foundations of the Critique of Political Economy* (London: Penguin Books, 1993) at 87–88.

or more recently, Ranjana Khanna.[9] But what I want to emphasize here is not the curious philosophical pedigree of the term depropriation, but the way that contemporary situations are developing that require this kind of vocabulary and thought.

Today we increasingly encounter situations in which something like depropriation is recognizably occurring, especially in situations that concern intellectual property. IP, according to common wisdom, is one of the forms of property . . . but we should at least explore the inverse proposition: that property itself might only be a kind of intellectual property, in other words, property might be inseparable from the idea of property or even the ideology of property.

The main issue for me in thinking about intellectual property in interdisciplinary terms remains the relation between the law and the economy. Whenever I discuss copying with people, the principal argument against any substantial reform in IP law, allowing ordinary people to make and share copies of whatever kind, is that such a reform destroys people's ability to make a living from their creative work. Even if it can be proven that the creative work that they call their own is almost entirely reliant on images, ideas, words, and techniques that are taken from other people, there is still an intense belief that IP is the only way to guarantee economic survival. Thus, a recent book like Robert Merges's *Justifying Intellectual Property* can construct an argument in favour of IP whose "justification" is basically that it supports neo-liberal democratic capitalist economy. [10] Which indeed it does. You own something if you work on it (Locke),[11] you exist as a subject because you are capable of ownership (Kant and Hegel),[12] and the law and state exist in order to protect that right (ditto).[13] Merges makes no mention of Marx, or the vast history of the contestation of the rights of the bourgeois subject, which, via Kant again, Merges believes to be universal. There is a vast global underclass who own nothing, whose work does not result in

9 Simone Weil, "Decreation" in George A Manichas, ed, *The Simone Weil Reader* (Mt Kisco: Moyer Bell, 1985) at 350–56; Roberto Esposito, *Communitas: the Origin and Destiny of Community* (Stanford: Stanford University Press, 2010); Ranjana Khanna, "Unbelonging: In Motion" (2010) 21:1 Differences 109.

10 Robert P Merges, *Justifying Intellectual Property* (Cambridge: Harvard University Press, 2011).

11 *Ibid* at 31–67.

12 For Kant, *ibid* at 68–101; for Hegel, see George Friedrich Wilhelm Hegel, *Philosophy of Right*, translated by TM Knox (London: Oxford University Press, 1967).

13 Merges, above note 10.

their acquiring property rights, who do not benefit at all from IP law, and whose lives and cultural practices exist almost entirely within a pirate or black market economy that is illegal but affordable.[14]

I have to turn to French legal philosopher Bernard Edelman's remarkable book, *The Ownership of the Image*, for a different version of this history.[15] In this book, Edelman examines the historical relationship between the evolution of the photographic and cinematic images and the law that designates who owns them. Edelman astutely notes that when photographic images first appeared in the 1840s, they presented a problem for IP law. While a painting or a book might well be said to have a single author (regardless of Foucault's claims in "What Is an Author?"[16]), who is it that owns the photographic image? The person who takes the photo? The person whose image is used? The person who owns the camera? Who develops the photograph? These were new problems and Edelman tracks the way that at first the law has no consistent answer to them. It is only as photography emerges as an important form of economic activity that the question is resolved. The problems multiply with the arrival of the cinema, since now in addition to the cinematographer, etc., there is the director, the screenplay writer, the producers, the actors, and many more. Edelman shows the way that the evidently social character of movie making (it is a collective production, in terms of labour, subject matter, etc.) is pushed aside in order that cinema may be integrated as a form of capitalist economic activity. Edelman relates with delightful sarcasm the way that any Lockean ideas of labour resulting in ownership disappear with the evolution of large cartels of movie investors, who, despite the fact that they do not labour on the movie at all, other than investing in it, nevertheless become the copyright owners of the movie.

An orthodox Marxist response to this situation would be collective ownership, with laws that support it, as indeed happened in the early years of the Soviet Union. A collective appropriation. There is a surprising lack of historical scholarship on actually existing socialist societies and IP, and regardless of the failures of the broader system, it would be interesting to

---

14 See Ravi Sundaram, *Pirate Modernity: Delhi's Media Urbanism* (New York: Routledge, 2010); Brian Larkin, *Signal and Noise: Media, Infrastructure, and Urban Culture in Nigeria* (Durham: Duke University Press, 2008). These two works are remarkable ethnographies of IP in India and Nigeria, respectively.

15 Bernard Edelman, *Ownership of the Image: Elements for a Marxist Theory of Law*, translated by Elizabeth Kingdom (London: Routledge & Kegan Paul Books, 1979).

16 Michel Foucault, "What Is an Author?" in James D Faubion, ed, *Aesthetics, Method, and Epistemology: Essential Works of Foucault 1954–1984* (New York: New Press, 1999) at 205.

have more detailed case studies of modern, non-capitalist legal and political approaches to questions of IP.[17] I want to focus here however on examples of contemporary struggles involving depropriation that suggest other possibilities: the market for psychoactive substances, a.k.a., drugs; the increasingly complex production and distribution of music that samples and resamples itself, a.k.a., Tumblr tunes; WikiLeaks and other attempts to share private and/or national archives; the Occupy movements. I cannot discuss any of them in detail here but I want to at least point out that each of them challenges our idea of what *intellectual property*, or better, to use Hardt and Negri's term, *immaterial property*,[18] is. In each case there is something that resists becoming property, but which nonetheless is the object of active social engagement. Part of the engagement, in each case, is the development of practices of depropriation that maintain and affirm the status of the object of interest as unownable — and public.

With the struggle to decriminalize the use of various psychoactive substances (marijuana, psychedelics, etc.), we are in the realm of what Timothy Leary called the fifth freedom: the freedom to alter your own mind.[19] While this is often given a libertarian reading, in which my mind is my own private property and therefore I should be able to do what I please with it, one could equally think of it in terms of depropriation: that it is the possibility and practice of non-ownership, of sharing my mind with a plant or a chemical in a Latourian actor-network that is at issue here.[20] With music as the site of so many struggles over IP recently, there is the possibility that a sound cannot be owned, that because of what it is, a sound evades ownership and is easily, even necessarily shared. With WikiLeaks we have the possibility of contesting the ownership of national archives, and the emergence of new kinds of public space in which information cannot be or at least has not yet been controlled because of its almost instantaneous distribution across computer databases around the globe. With the Occupy protests, what is at issue is again a reinvigorated public space that is at once local and transnational, simultaneously private or state and public property, and yet none

17 Michael A Newcity, *Copyright Law in the Soviet Union* (New York: Praeger Publishers, 1978) and Serge L Levitsky, *Introduction to Soviet Copyright Law* (Leyden: AW Sythoff, 1964) are both useful but out of date in terms of methodology and perspective.

18 The term is first used in Michael Hardt & Antonio Negri, *Multitude: War and Democracy in the Age of Empire* (New York: Penguin Press, 2004) at 180–82.

19 Timothy Leary, *The Politics of Ecstasy* (New York: Putnam, 1968).

20 Bruno Latour, *We Have Never Been Modern*, translated by Catherine Porter (Cambridge: Harvard University Press, 1993).

of the above. It is an actively existent space: participatory, yet unowned (thus it is "occupied" through active practices of use of a space that accord with the ideals of a liberal democracy, but which are visibly and brutally crushed by the forces that dominate that same democracy).

I don't intend to solve the problem of what the relation between the law and depropriation is here. I would like to conclude by discussing some comments made by French filmmaker Jean-Luc Godard, who throughout his career has questioned ideas of property of various kinds. In recent years, Godard has gotten involved in IP disputes in France, contributing to the legal expenses of people accused of file sharing.[21] His most recent movie *Film Socialisme*[22] (translation: "filmed socialism," i.e., the film as an act of socialism) is, as with many of his films, full of appropriations from multiple sources who he lists at the beginning of the movie. In an interview published in the 1960s, he says regarding his early film *Breathless*:[23]

> People, in life, quote what pleases them. We have therefore the right to quote what pleases us. I show people "quoting" — only I arrange it so that the quote pleases me. In the notes I keep of what might be useful to me in a film I also put a sentence from Dostoievsky, if I like it. Why be constrained? If you want to say something, there is only one solution: say it. Moreover, the genre of *Breathless* was such that all was permitted, that was its nature. Whatever people might do — all this could be integrated into the film. This was even my point of departure.[24]

Quotation is a practice of appropriation, but the point here isn't to draw attention to the source of the image or its recontextualization, it is simply to acknowledge that such a circulation does already exist, and that it is also part of the practice of film making. In recent years, Godard has repeatedly insisted that: "il n'y a pas de droits d'auteur, il n'y a que des devoirs," — "there are no rights of authors, only duties." For example, in an interview in the *Nouvel Observateur* in 2001 we find the following exchange:

---

21 Xeni Jardin "Jean-Luc Godard Donates €1K for Accused MP3 Downloader's Defense: 'There is No Such Thing as Intellectual Property'" *Boing Boing* (13 September 2010), online: Boing Boing http://boingboing.net/2010/09/13/jean-luc-godard-dona.html.

22 *Film Socialisme*, DVD, directed by Jean-Luc Godard (Paris, France: Wildbunch Distribution, 2010).

23 *À Bout de Soufffle (Breathless)*, DVD, directed by Jean-Luc Godard (Paris, France: Carlotta Films, 1960)

24 Jean-Luc Godard, "Interview in Cahiers du Cinema" reprinted in Sallie Sears & Georgiana W Lord, eds, *The Discontinuous Universe* (New York: Basic Books, 1972) at 296.

NO: You've earned a proper living?

JLG: I've lived as a technician . . . That's why I don't understand these questions of paying rights to the whole world. It's an incredible abuse. One can't film a TGV train that's going by in the countryside, or the Eiffel Tower any more. It's Proudhon in reverse: "Property is theft." Here, theft becomes property. That's why I prefer to speak not of author's rights, but of author's duties. This right has no juridical basis, born in the organization of society. The author has only duties. When a poor man says he has the right to eat, what that means is that he has the duty. He has to live, to continue. Rights are the social organization of this duty.[25]

What does it mean to place duty before rights in this way? Godard was recently asked about a particular image used in *Film Socialisme* that was copied from Agnès Varda's recent film *Les Plages D'Agnès*.[26] He responded that he used Varda's image for his own purpose, without harming her use of the image, to develop a meaning that interests him.[27] If we think of authors (but not only authors) as fundamentally social beings, who live and work because of the network of structures of sharing that they inhabit, rather than as isolated individuals who own whatever they think or are involved in, then creative acts emerge not from the right to claim ownership of something and profit from it, but from a duty to contribute to the structures of sharing that one inhabits, and to develop the insights and work of others in a meaningful way.

Depropriation is a practice that might be associated with such structures of sharing, the possibility of acting and/or living without relying on a philosophy of rights, and a discourse of intellectual property. It is not necessarily beyond the law — indeed Godard vacillates between claiming that "there is no such thing as intellectual property" and acknowledging the limited right of familial inheritance in a work — or the economy: he recognizes Varda's right to receive some kind of payment for the use of "her" image. But

25 Interview of Jean-Luc Godard by Jacques Drillon, *Le Nouvel Observateur* (5 October 2001), online: Le Nouvel Observateur http://artsetspectacles.nouvelobs.com/p1905/a43503.html [translated by author].

26 *Plages D'Agnes*, DVD, directed by Agnès Varda (Paris, France: Les Films du Losange, 2008)

27 Interview of Jean-Luc Godard by J M L (18 May 2010) in J M L, "Le droit d'auteur? Un auteur n'a que des devoirs" *Les Inrockuptibles* (18 May 2010), online: les inRocks blogs http://blogs.lesinrocks.com/cannes2010/2010/05/18/le-droit-dauteur-un-auteur-na-que-des-devoirs-jean-luc-godard.

he knows that calling the image "hers" is merely provisional and that finally images do not belong to anyone, they are inherently social, collectively produced objects. The question today remains: how can we create structures that enable us to live in accord with that recognition?

A significant body of scholarship undertaken in the last decade, beginning perhaps with the publication of Antonio Negri and Michael Hardt's *Empire*, has attempted to elaborate the possibility of new kinds of social movement in the wake of globalization. The increased focus of scholars on an expanded notion of the commons, the common, or other terms for a shared, public world has so far involved relatively little focus on intellectual property issues, even though contemporary debates concerning IP are rich in new formulations of such structures of sharing. IP scholars similarly have paid little attention to Hardt and Negri's notions of multitude, immaterial labour, and the common.[28] Today, IP scholarship still tends to focus on the right to postmodern pastiche (and the postcolonial critique of the presumptions of postmodernism) even though broader theoretical debates about postmodernity have moved far beyond these questions, and the economic and political forces that are responsible for the "postmodernization of production" are all too obvious. At the same time, Hardt and Negri's celebration of the creativity of the multitude, and of a global society built around a notion of the common is perhaps symptomatic of what Slavoj Zizek sees as a refusal by leftist artists and activists to recognize the need to actually work with and change structures such as legal systems, rather than seeking out temporary or provisional spaces that are beyond the reach of the law.[29] To my mind, a question remains whether the word *structure* is a synonym for *law*.[30] Again, this is where the problem (or tool?) of interdisciplinarity is a crucial one. If, as I believe, structure and law are not synonymous, what is their relationship? Is the emerging, semi-autonomous practice of sharing

---

28 Michael Hardt & Antonio Negri, *Empire* (Cambridge: Harvard University Press, 2000), which has little or no discussion of IP; see also Michael Hardt & Antonio Negri, *Multitude: War and Democracy in the Age of Empire* (New York: Penguin Press, 2004), which devotes ten very interesting pages to the topic at 179–88; Michael Hardt & Antonio Negri, *Commonwealth* (Cambridge: Harvard University Press, 2009). Although this piece is built around an analysis of property and the common, it has no sustained analysis of IP.

29 Slavoj Zizek, "Resistance is Surrender" 29:22 *London Review of Books* (15 November 2007), online: London Review of Books www.lrb.co.uk/v29/n22/slavoj-zizek/resistance-is-surrender.

30 One could ask this question of any of the post-Lacanian critical theorists, including Zizek, *ibid*. Are all proposals of an alternative to the law merely evasions of the law unless they confront it?

merely awaiting its inevitable articulation within the law? Insofar as it continues to exist in a way that contradicts existing law, how can the "duty" that guides it be acknowledged or supported by legal scholars?

Either way, the possibilities for rethinking IP law, or indeed interdisciplinary scholarship on IP are severely limited, if such scholarship tacitly or explicitly accepts the order of the current political-economic system, and its affirmation of private enterprise as equivalent to the common good. If private ownership of immaterial labour is required in order to make wage labour viable, then the particular contemporary forms of IP law necessarily follow as a consequence. But the right to make certain kinds of copy cannot be treated justly without recognizing the broader challenges to "the common," to a public culture, or to a shared commons that we face today. In what ways can legal scholarship contribute to a broadening of the ways in which we think of political economy both historically and today in its emergent forms? What other branches of legal scholarship, and what other disciplines do IP scholars need to consider and dialogue with in order to open up the broader questions of IP's relation to political-economy?

Increasing recognition of this problematic may explain the rise of political parties such as Germany's Pirate Party, whose main focus appears to be IP law reform.[31] The apparently absurd "single issue focus" of such groups in fact recognizes that the new forms of freedom discovered via collective collaboration on the Internet require a full rethinking of our political and economic systems in order that they might be sustained or expanded. Of course, that's a tall order, and one that so far these emerging parties are not capable of responding adequately to, but it's precisely the fact that current practices of copying go so far beyond dominant legal, economic, and political models that makes them such powerful tools for modelling other, and hopefully better, forms of sociality.

---

31 Sven Becker et al, "The Grand Experiment: German Pirate Party Attempts to Reinvent Politics" *Der Spiegel* (25 April 2012), online: Spiegel Online International www.spiegel.de/international/germany/germany-s-pirate-party-seek-to-reinvent-politics-a-829451.html.

THEME THREE

Interdisciplinarity in Practice

TWENTY

Mapping the Outcomes of Multidisciplinary Intellectual Property Research: Lessons from the African Copyright Experience

JEREMY DE BEER[1]

ABSTRACT (EN): Multidisciplinary intellectual property research often involves large-scale collaborative projects. Such projects combine not just multiple research frameworks, methods, and perspectives, but also multiple individuals, institutions, and sources of funding. Demonstrating the results of financial and human resource investments into complex multidisciplinary projects is increasingly important. Experiences from one recent multidisciplinary project — the African Copyright and Access to Knowledge project — provide lessons for other intellectual property researchers trying to map outcomes from current and future projects.

RÉSUMÉ (FR): La recherche multidisciplinaire en propriété intellectuelle exige fréquemment la création de projets collaboratifs de grande envergure. Ces projets combinent non seulement de nombreux cadres, méthodes et perspectives de recherche, mais aussi un grand nombre de personnes, institutions et sources de financement. La démonstration des résultats des investissements en ressources financières et humaines dans des projets multidisciplinaires complexes devient de plus en plus importante. Les expériences tirées

1 The author gratefully acknowledges financial and strategic support from the International Development Research Centre, Genome Canada, and the Social Sciences and Humanities Research Council. Parts of this chapter are derived from C Armstrong, J de Beer et al, *Access to Knowledge in Africa: The Role of Copyright* (Cape Town: IDRC/UCT Press, 2010), and an unpublished report prepared for the World Intellectual Property Organization on copyright impact assessment methodologies.

d'un projet multidisciplinaire récent — le Projet africain sur le droit d'auteur et l'accès au savoir — peuvent fournir des leçons aux autres chercheurs en propriété intellectuelle tentant de tracer l'impact de projets actuels et futurs.

A. THE NEED TO MONITOR AND EVALUATE RESEARCH RESULTS

Research related to intellectual property often takes place in the context of large-scale projects. This is especially true of research related to the natural sciences and engineering, including such fields as genomics and related life sciences. But a similar pattern is apparent in the social sciences and humanities, involving, for example, law, philosophy, anthropology, management, economics, political science, and public policy. Common among these projects is a problem-based approach that draws heavily on multidisciplinary teams of academic researchers, as well as partners from government and industry. Rather than investigating an issue, for example copyright law, in the abstract, researchers are increasingly likely to look at legal issues applied to practical problems, such as access to scholarly publications and other learning materials. Applied research usually requires expertise beyond the capabilities of researchers in any single discipline: a multidisciplinary approach.

Multidisciplinary research projects face many challenges, from disparate literatures to methodological divides to disciplinary jargon. Another major challenge is proving that the project has made a practical difference in society. While this is perhaps an issue with all research projects, it is especially important for large-scale, multidisciplinary projects. For most multidisciplinary researchers of intellectual property issues, there is or soon will be a growing emphasis on results that demonstrate tangible returns on investments in research. The reasons vary: policy-makers are more often demanding pragmatic advice, granting councils are increasingly accountable for their use of public funds and more researchers are competing for less money.

Some funders of small- or medium-scale research programs that support multidisciplinary projects still leave researchers relatively free to administer funds without proving that they have achieved specific, promised results. Other established agencies, however, have more demanding procedures. Some hold mid-project meetings with peer reviewers, at which project managers, principal investigators, and research collaborators must report on progress, justify resource allocation, and earn satisfactory results to release further funding.

Increasingly often, multidisciplinary research projects are funded by multiple agencies or organizations, which can complicate matters considerably. Those funders include the traditional granting councils, but also new kinds of private and public sector donors, from philanthropic foundations to for-profit enterprises to government entities. For substantial investments of public funds, a result-oriented focus on applied research can be traced to the top levels of government, which clearly want to see "the translation of public research knowledge to the private sector" and "the commercialization of research into products and processes that create high-value jobs and economic growth."[2] Private-sector donors are rarely if ever less demanding.

Expectations like that might be well suited to some research in certain disciplines within the natural sciences or engineering, where the pressure to do applied research is familiar, albeit stronger now than in the past. But social sciences and humanities researchers are perhaps less accustomed to these pressures. Researchers at the boundary between natural and social sciences, for example in fields like Genomics, Economics, Ethics, Environment, Law and Society (GE^3LS), have been forced to fit into the reporting and evaluation rubrics typically applicable to the "hard" scientists, so they might be slightly better prepared than other researchers for a results-oriented funding paradigm.

One problem is that funders' investments are generally made in anticipation of a social, technical, or sometimes economic return that is attributable to expenditure. On occasion researchers and funders disagree on the success or failure of a research project because they have not agreed upon expectations at the outset.

But even when there is a clear agreement on expectations, appropriate tools to assess the human impacts of research projects are too rarely used. Examples of orthodox research evaluation techniques are numerous. Among the most common is an output-oriented approach, which involves counting things that the project has produced, like a number of articles, or a number of events, or a number of highly qualified personnel (so-called "HQPs"). Formally, that approach relies on a logical framework; outputs are logically connected to project's goals, which are logically connected to a project's purpose. It is sometimes referred to as a "logic model," a "log-frame" approach, or just "LFA." Some such models can encompass outputs

---

2 Government of Canada, *Jobs, Growth and Long-Term Prosperity: Economic Action Plan 2012* (29 March 2012) at ch 3.1, online: Government of Canada: Budget 2012 www.budget.gc.ca/2012/plan/chap3-1-eng.html.

as well as activities and short-, medium-, and long-term outcomes. But the basic flaw in this approach is that it is held together by assumptions that certain outputs are likely to lead — in a linear and isolated way — to certain outcomes. While that might work for simple studies, it rarely does so for complex, multidisciplinary research projects. It is difficult for logical models to capture external contextual influences, non-linear complexities of connectivity, and unintended outcomes.

For these reasons, monitoring and evaluating the results of major investments of human and financial resources into multidisciplinary research is a real and substantial challenge for which the familiar methods of any particular discipline are poorly suited. General reference works are essential starting points,[3] but there is no substitute for experience mapping outcomes from multidisciplinary projects and policy interventions. This chapter, therefore, will describe practical experiences and synthesize lessons from one recent, multidisciplinary, large-scale intellectual property research project — the African Copyright and Access to Knowledge Project (ACA2K)[4] — in order to propose an effective monitoring and evaluation method that might transcend disciplinary boundaries. It explains how monitoring and evaluation principles might be used to assess the outcomes of the research project, such as actual or proposed policy interventions, as well as to assess the subject matter of the research, which for many social scientific research projects might also be a particular policy intervention. In this way, monitoring and evaluation principles can help to establish a feedback loop between researchers and subjects. Better understanding this loop might not only improve the research, it might also improve outcomes.

"Outcome mapping" is a technique that has been used for many years by Canada's International Development Research Centre (IDRC), and several other organizations, to assess the contributions of its research projects and programming to international development.[5] While it is by no means the only method that might be used for monitoring and evaluation, nor is it suit-

---

3 Joseph S Wholey, Harry P Hatry, & Kathryn E Newcomer, eds, *Handbook of Practical Program Evaluation*, 3d ed (San Francisco: John Wiley & Sons, 2010); Peter H Rossi, Mark W Lipsey, & Howard E Freeman, *Evaluation: A Systematic Approach*, 7th ed (Thousand Oaks, CA: Sage Publications Inc, 2004).

4 See generally, *The African Copyright and Access to Knowledge Project (ACA2K)*, online: ACA2K www.ACA2K.org.

5 Sarah Earl, Fred Carden, & Terry Smutylo, *Outcome Mapping: Building Learning and Reflection into Development Programs* (Ottawa: International Development Research Centre, 2001), online: www.idrc.ca/en/ev-9330-201-1-DO_TOPIC.html.

able in all circumstances, it has been successfully adapted and implemented by a large group of multidisciplinary researchers to study the impacts of intellectual property laws, policies, and practices. The chapter first introduces the outcome-mapping framework, then describes how it was applied to monitor and evaluate the ACA2K research project, and concludes with lessons for assessing the impact of multidisciplinary research in general.

B. AN OUTCOME MAPPING FRAMEWORK ADAPTED FOR INTELLECTUAL PROPERTY RESEARCH

During 2005 and 2006 the IDRC recognized growing critical awareness among scholars, civil society, the private sector, and international policy-makers surrounding the untested assumptions about relationships among copyright and development. It sought to support large-scale, empirical research on this topic in order to gather evidence that could support international and national copyright policy-making processes. A proposal was received for a project to be led by several African researchers from Uganda, South Africa, and elsewhere. In consultation with IDRC staff and experts from other developing countries and from Canada, approximately eighteen months were spent custom designing a robust research methodology to implement the study project.

Implementing an ambitious, multinational research project in a relatively understudied area required the use of a robust monitoring and evaluation framework. Therefore, a custom-designed methodology was constructed using tools and systems that IDRC and other organizations had been working with for several decades. Specifically, the project was designed around the analytical framework of outcome mapping.

The distinction between "outcomes" and "impacts" is more than semantic. A variety of other words are sometimes used in this context too, such as "influence," "effect," or "consequence." Sometimes these words are synonymous, but there are sometimes subtle distinctions in meaning. Although assessing *impacts* of copyright policy research might, at a glance, seem the same as assessing *outcomes*, the term *impact* implies a but/for causal relation. Likewise, words such as *consequences* or *effects* suggest a direct causal relation (e.g., "cause and effect"), while a term such as *influence* implicitly allows consideration of multiple causal or correlated factors. Avoiding unjustifiable claims of causality is especially important in complex fields like intellectual property and development. The technique of outcome mapping consciously avoids claiming sole credit for results that are in fact attributable to a combination of interrelated variables, and instead attempts to describe the nature and degree of outcomes fairly attributed to one or more of these specific variables. The terms used in describing the exercise of outcome mapping matter less than this underlying principle.

Relations between research and/or policy interventions and human development are multi-faceted and non-linear. Consequently, the technique of outcome mapping focuses on monitoring sustained, incremental contributions to change. Assessments map dynamic rather than static outcomes. Moreover, because the changes that matter most in a development context are those that better people's daily lives, outcome mapping is most concerned with assessing changes in behaviour, not only changes in state. To put that in practical terms, the emphasis is on subtly assessing how organizations act and people live, rather than on single events or macroeconomic snapshots.

Outcome mapping methodologies can be unfamiliar and initially seem awkward to some people. But they have been applied successfully to assess the results of policy interventions in a wide variety of contexts, often but not always related to international development. Indeed, of course, monitoring and evaluating the impacts of projects or policies is generally not the sole domain of development practitioners. Valuable lessons might also be learned from environmental impact assessments commonly led by biologists, hydrologists, and other natural scientists (and lawyers),[6] or the social impact assessments pioneered in disciplines like sociology and cultural geography.[7]

But looking at techniques from the field of international development is nevertheless helpful for multidisciplinary intellectual property (or any social sciences) researchers because, as a practical matter, both areas share similar challenges. The areas of activity are not only complex but also dynamic, relationships between events are non-linear, and budgetary pressures increasingly require demonstrating results. A recently concluded research project at the intersection of intellectual and property and development, the ACA2K project assessing copyright's relationship with access to education and learning materials, is one example of outcome mapping used as a practical monitoring and evaluation tool.

6 Please see Chapter 4, "The Precautionary Principle and Its Application in the Intellectual Property Context: Towards a Public Domain Impact Assessment."

7 See Frank Vanclay, "International Principles for Social Impact Assessment" (2003) 21:1 Impact Assessment and Project Appraisal 5.

C. IMPLEMENTING OUTCOME MAPPING METHODS

Outcome mapping can be used to assess the contributions of a particular public policy intervention (such as intellectual property) on a societal issue (such as education or development). Or, on another level, outcome mapping can be used to determine the influence of an organization, program, or project (such as the ACA2K project or the IDRC) on a specific area of concern (such as copyright and educational materials, or education and development). The ACA2K project deployed outcome mapping in both ways. First, researchers used outcome mapping to assess the general influence of copyright laws, policies, and practices on education systems in Africa. Second, outcome mapping helped researchers design and monitor the contributions of the specific research project.

In those contexts, outcome mapping generally involves three elements: design, monitoring, and evaluation, depicted in Figure 20.1. The key aspects of these steps implemented by the ACA2K research project are discussed in the three subsections below.

Figure 20.1: Three Stages of Outcome Mapping

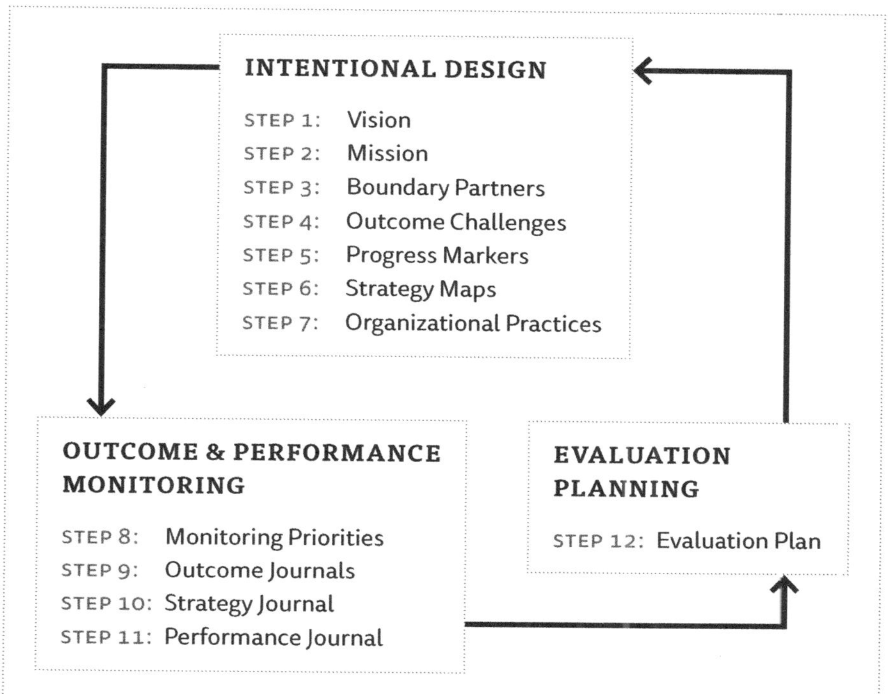

(Source: Sarah Earl, Fred Carden, & Terry Smutylo, *Outcome Mapping: Building Learning and Reflection into Development Programs*, above note 4. Reproduced with permission.)

1) Design

The starting point for the research project was the vision of a well-functioning copyright system contributing positively to human development in its economic, cultural, and social dimensions. Exclusive, private rights over original works are a means to this end, it is usually assumed, because such rights ultimately facilitate the creation of and access to knowledge for public benefit. The project's overarching mission was to better understand and influence — based on empirical evidence — the extent to which copyright is fulfilling its purpose of facilitating the creation of and access to knowledge for development.

To do that, a series of specific objectives were identified, including:

- building and networking the research capacity of African researchers to investigate copyright environments and access to learning materials (across all formats) within and across countries;
- developing methodological best practices around the relationship between copyright environments and access to learning materials;
- increasing the amount of published scholarship, such as technical reports and peer-reviewed publications, addressing this topic;
- raising awareness of the interface between copyright and access to learning materials and supporting copyright reform processes in relation to access to learning materials and access to knowledge in Africa; and
- building capacity for copyright policy engagement in universities and related institutions of higher learning regarding the impact of copyright on scholarly and research environments in their institutions.

The project's objectives demonstrate that the intention was not to conduct abstract or theoretical research into copyright. The project was geared from the outset towards practical, applied research to assess copyright's influence on an important development-related issue.

A broad investigation into copyright and access to learning materials in general, or even throughout all levels of a country's education system risked becoming conceptually unfocused, logistically unmanageable, and practically ineffective. So, while research teams were free to consider all aspects of their country's education system if it was deemed necessary to do so, emphasis throughout the project was placed on tertiary education.

There were three main justifications for this focus. First, studying the tertiary education sector allowed investigation of not only classroom learning but also advanced scholarly research. Second, tertiary education is primarily obtained in urban settings, and in contexts where non-copyright barriers (such as the lack of physical infrastructure or extreme poverty) will typically be lower. Third, anecdotal evidence available prior to the commencement of the project pointed to increasing support for access to learning materials and education in general at lower education levels (pre-tertiary) in most African countries, with students, researchers, and faculty at tertiary institutions typically not benefiting from government interventions aimed at improving materials access.

Initially, the concept was to conduct a baseline study aimed at understanding that issue in the context of the copyright legal framework in South Africa. As the demand for and opportunity to conduct more comprehensive yet still manageable research became clearer, the project evolved into a pan-continental, comparative analysis of not only copyright legal doctrines but also real-world practices. Research network nodes were first established with teams of researchers based in five countries: Egypt, Ghana, Senegal, South Africa, and Uganda. The number of country research nodes eventually grew to eight to include Morocco, Kenya, and Mozambique.

The countries studied represent Africa's geographic diversity, as well as its economic, linguistic, religious, cultural, and legal differences. The project encompasses some of Africa's most advanced economies, like South Africa and Egypt, as well as some its least developed, such as Senegal and Mozambique. There are former colonies of, and therefore copyright laws based on systems from, England (Egypt, Ghana, Kenya, South Africa, and Uganda), France (Egypt, Morocco, and Senegal), Spain (parts of Morocco), and Portugal (Mozambique). The legal systems in the study countries reflect common law and civil law traditions, and also Sharia law in some cases. Dominant languages in study countries include a wide variety of indigenous languages as well as English, French, Portuguese, and Arabic. Researchers held diverse occupations: full-time academics, librarians, graduate students, practising lawyers, consultants, civil servants, judges, and parliamentarians. Researchers also came from diverse backgrounds: law, economics, management, political science, development studies, international relations, education, library and information sciences, anthropology, and more. Almost all of the more than thirty people participating were from or based in Africa.

The research was designed to use three interrelated techniques: legal doctrinal analysis, qualitative assessment interviews, and comparative review.

The first of these methods, legal analysis, was at the heart of the research project. The state of the law in any particular jurisdiction is determined by a combination of legislative rules and their judicial or quasi-judicial application. Consequently, the first element of the research was to conduct a review of relevant statutes and decisions interpreting or applying them in each study country. Teams of researchers in each study country examined and reported on a variety of aspects of national laws. In addition to basic information, such as the titles and dates of relevant statutes, researchers situated national laws within the international copyright context of various treaties and agreements. Researchers investigated the criteria for obtaining copyright (the nature, scope, and duration of protection) and exceptions and limitations of various sorts. They also located, catalogued, and reported on relevant cases interpreting or applying the statutory provisions.

However, laws do not operate in a vacuum. Understanding what copyright law permits or prohibits *in theory* does not shed much light on what actually happens *in practice*. Acknowledging and acting on this realization was probably the most unique and, frankly, the most valuable aspect of the ACA2K project. Investigating copyright's real-world application is especially important in the African context, where anecdotal evidence surveyed prior to commencing the project supported the intuition that there is a tremendous gap between copyright law and practice.

This led to the project's second research method: qualitative data gathering with stakeholders. To obtain empirical evidence of copyright law's impact "on the ground," researchers adopted methodologies borrowed from non-legal social sciences and humanities, such as impact assessment interviews and focus group discussions, supported by thorough desk analysis of relevant literature.

To ensure a degree of consistency in data gathering across study countries, research teams structured their impact assessment interviews using general questionnaires adapted from guidelines that were custom designed for this research project. Interview questions were designed to elicit data regarding two general issues. First, what was/is the *intended* effect of copyright on access to learning materials? And second, what is the *actual* effect of the copyright environment on access to learning materials? Teams were particularly encouraged to hone in on two more specific subtopics: gender equity and information communications technologies.

Researchers used semi-structured oral interviews rather than written surveys. This reduced the number of people it was feasible to interview, but greatly enriched the interaction with each interviewee. Researchers kept meticulous records of the interviews, including notes, audio recordings, and often transcripts, so that data collected could be organized, reviewed, archived, and verified. All researchers followed codes of ethical conduct, with clear guidelines about obtaining informed consent, guaranteeing confidentiality, avoiding undue influence, and sharing the benefits of the research with participants.

Integrating qualitative research methods into the design of the framework provided an important, early opportunity to think about the project's "boundary partners." In outcome mapping lexicon, boundary partners are individuals or organizations with whom the project or policy program interacts directly and with whom there may be opportunities for influence.[8] By definition, the interviewees involved in the project were (among) its boundary partners. Boundary partners are a slightly smaller group than conventionally conceived stakeholders, who are influenced *by*, but may not necessarily have influence *on*, the policy intervention being assessed. By identifying early in the project who the boundary partners could be, researchers were both designing the project (figuring out who to interview for the research and who to target with the research results) and at the same time developing the monitoring and evaluation framework (these same boundary partners would be key to the success of the project in achieving its intended outcomes).

At national level, the boundary partner selections varied from country to country, but most research teams decided to engage with representatives of:

- government departments responsible for copyright law and policy-making;
- government departments responsible for education, arts, or culture;
- administrative or enforcement agencies and professionals;
- authors, copyright owners, collecting societies, and industry associations;
- educators, including administrators, teachers, and librarians;
- students and researchers; and
- intermediaries such as content distributors and telecommunications providers.

---

8 Earl, Carden, & Smutylo, above note 5 at 1.

Generally, most constituencies concerned about copyright and access to learning materials could be classified within one of three broad groups: (1) policy-making, government, or enforcement entities; (2) educational communities; and (3) rights holders or groups of rights holders.

The impact assessment interviews were complemented in every study country by a thorough review of relevant literature. Research teams located, catalogued, and synthesized books, academic articles, student dissertations, policy papers, newspaper reports, public relations materials, and online information. In combination, these data sources helped researchers understand how the law is being perceived and applied.

Together, the doctrinal and qualitative methods helped research teams to determine progress markers based on the behaviour changes they would expect to see, like to see, and love to see. Integrating those benchmarks into the project's design made ongoing monitoring and evaluation feasible. The next step was to develop strategies to achieve those changes. In essence, the strategies involved gathering and reporting on empirical evidence to inform better copyright-related policy-making and practices.

Conducting local-level research in the study countries was, of course, essential to this mission. But much of the value from the ACA2K research flowed from the fact that it was a pan-continental, comparative project. Results from all eight study countries (as well as scans of two more countries: Zambia and Zimbabwe) were compiled, synthesized, and analyzed in order to draw out generalizable themes and lessons from across Africa. Some of the substantive insights gleaned from the comparative review are described below in the context of project monitoring and evaluation.

2) Monitoring

Monitoring helps the project or program to conceive of itself as not simply an observer but also a part of the change process.[9] It also allows, if necessary, for responsive adjustments and improvements to ongoing interactions.

Diligence is needed to maintain effective project or policy monitoring practices. Monitoring need not be onerous, but does require work and should be regular. Processes ought to be integrated into the organization responsible for the project or policy intervention. To ensure that happens, experts point out that the system must be simple, light, useful, and rel-

9 *Ibid*, ch 4.

evant.[10] Though time and effort is inevitably required, monitoring must be a priority if an intervention is to be effective.

Periodic (for example, quarterly) meetings among key personnel, held either face-to-face or virtually, are valuable to ensure sustained focus on the challenges and opportunities arising throughout the duration of the project or program activities. In the interims between meetings, journaling is a technique well suited to monitoring performance and outcomes. This involves regularly documenting and reflecting on observations about behaviour changes taking place. Journals can be focused on monitoring changes in behaviour among boundary partners (outcomes), the project's or program's actions to achieve those outcomes (strategies), and generally the organizational practices to maintain relevance and influence (performance). Separate journaling activities are ideal to monitor each of these aspects.

The ACA2K project emphasized the importance of ongoing monitoring early in and consistently throughout its life cycle. Work was conducted on various levels. For example, country research teams conducted local monitoring activities, assessing the behaviour of national boundary partners in response to the evidence researchers were gathering and presenting, and adjusting activities accordingly. Moreover, on a project-wide level, researchers and management were monitoring the behaviour of the project teams, identifying how these teams themselves were integrating into the copyright environments of their respective jurisdictions. And perhaps most importantly, researchers continuously monitored the ways in which the project as a whole was having influence over the general state of copyright law, policy, and practice in respect of education throughout Africa and even globally. That does not mean that project participants influenced all developments in copyright or education, let alone that project participants monitored all such developments; rather, project participants monitored *their* influence as broadly as possible.

3) Evaluation

It is possible to evaluate the results of the ACA2K research project on two interrelated levels. First, what influence did the project itself have on copyright environments in the study countries? Second, and more substantively,

10 *Ibid.*

what does the evidence gathered suggest about the influence of copyright in the study countries on education?

Assessing *outputs* is a first step (too often the only step) in measuring a project's contributions to *outcomes*. By bringing together the findings of the doctrinal research with the findings of the qualitative interviews, each country team was able to develop a picture of the copyright environment in its country. Teams then described and analyzed that environment in a published report in each country, and later made regulatory and policy recommendations outlined in an executive policy brief. The result of just those activities was sixteen published documents reporting on copyright environments in the study countries.

Using country reports and executive policy briefs as dissemination tools, teams held national policy dialogue seminars to bring together boundary partners and other stakeholders to engage in a discussion of the evidence and recommendations for legal and practical reform. Between May 2009 and March 2010, nine national policy seminars were convened, in Nairobi, Accra, Kampala, Maputo, Marrakech, Cape Town, Johannesburg, Cairo, and Dakar. In total, hundreds of influential participants were involved in and affected by these meetings.

More broadly, the ACA2K's research into copyright and access to learning materials conducted in, and across, the eight study countries has yielded hundreds of pages reporting on statutory and doctrinal data and literature reviews, and dozens of hours of recorded engagement documenting people's and institution's actual experiences. Translating the data into meaningful conclusions and reporting those conclusions in a manner capable of achieving the project's overall objective of facilitating evidence-based policy-making were challenging tasks. Written research outputs have included:

- a detailed methodology guide to enable future research on this topic;
- comprehensive country reports documenting doctrinal and practical research results in each study country;
- executive policy briefs for each country, summarizing findings and making recommendations for legal reforms and pragmatic steps for improvement;
- briefing papers targeting official representatives, negotiators, and copyright policy-makers at key organizations working on international copyright policy issues;

- statements about ACA2K findings read to official sittings of WIPO committees (two statements at sittings of the WIPO Standing Committee on Copyright and Related Rights (SCCR) and one statement to a sitting of the WIPO Committee on Development and Intellectual Property (CDIP));
- a peer-reviewed journal article in Africa analyzing key findings across the eight countries;
- local and international media coverage of the project and its practical importance to contemporary issues and mainstream policy debates; and
- a multilingual website reporting on ACA2K activities and findings.

Project researchers have presented their research methods and findings at dozens of conferences, workshops, and symposia around the world, including the aforementioned national ACA2K policy seminars in each of the eight African study countries and forums in locations outside Africa including Quebec City, Ottawa, Milwaukee, London, Geneva, and Milan. Audiences at these events have included key representatives from international organizations, national governments, rights-holders associations, and educational communities.

Perhaps the most substantial output of all from this project is a book published by University of Cape Town Press, one of Africa's largest and most influential publishers, called *Access to Knowledge in Africa: The Role of Copyright*.[11] This book was also translated into French,[12] and distributed broadly in hard and soft copy under an open-access licence.

Outputs aside, the important thing from a project evaluation perspective is to gauge *outcomes*. This particular project has directed attention toward copyright's role in enabling or restricting access to learning materials. The project's principal contribution to the state of knowledge in this field is the rich empirical evidence generated by actually assessing the impact of copyright "on the ground" rather than merely "on the books." To the researchers' knowledge, such a pan-continental, multidisciplinary endeavour had never previously been undertaken. Empirical evidence gathered during almost three years of work by more than thirty researchers inves-

---

11 Chris Armstrong et al, eds, *Access to Knowledge in Africa: The Role of Copyright* (Cape Town: IDRC/UCT Press, 2010).

12 Chris Armstrong et al, eds, *L'accès au savoir en Afrique : Le rôle du droit d'auteur* (Laval: Les Presses de l'Université Laval/CRDI, 2012).

tigating copyright laws, policies, and practices in eight African countries has provided a valuable opportunity to assess how copyright environments really impact access to learning materials in the continent.

Perhaps the most important revelation from this research is that copyright laws in all study countries comply with international copyright standards. In many cases, the African countries studied provide even greater protection than international laws require. Thus, the countries studied do not need advice or assistance in drafting legislation to bring levels of legal protection up to par. Simply put, Africa does not need stronger copyright laws. This in itself is a very important finding, which urgently needs to inform African national copyright policy-making at a time when many countries — including ACA2K study countries Kenya, Ghana, and South Africa — are in the midst of revising or planning revisions to their copyright laws.

Throughout the continent, however, there is a lack of awareness, enforcement, and exploitation of copyright. A gap exists, to varying degrees, between copyright law and on-the-ground practices in all countries studied. Empirical evidence has confirmed the intuition and impression that copyright law in Africa is widely ignored, if even known about. And many of those who are aware of the concept of copyright are apparently unable to comply with it because of their socio-economic circumstances.

Access to learning materials in the study countries is obtained mainly through copyright infringement. When copyright enforcement begins in earnest (as research indicates it will), then, without mechanisms in place to promote and ensure non-infringing channels of access to knowledge, many learners, particularly at the tertiary level, will be in a precarious position. Entire systems of education will be vulnerable. Thus, maintaining the status quo is not a sustainable policy option. As well as representing an unreliable and unsustainable access mechanism, learners' systemic infringement of copyright in order to obtain necessary access to educational materials has a detrimental effect on the integrity of the entire copyright system. Copyright laws that cannot be followed by the vast majority of society only serve to generate resentment for their underlying principles, and ultimately undermine respect for copyright and the rule of law generally.

The consequences of maintaining unrealistic copyright systems are serious. Though the ACA2K research acknowledges that there are many other barriers to access to learning materials, such as the high prices of books and student poverty, copyright is an important and under-researched barrier. The evidence suggests that an appropriate and sustainable copyright environment, combined with other measures to make access to materials more affordable, could be one of the key components of a holistically well-functioning tertiary education system. Though all the countries studied have other public policy matters to address, from health crises to security and political or economic stability concerns, the importance of education in addressing these and related development challenges should not be understated.

For these reasons, the project's overarching recommendation is that all stakeholders throughout and beyond Africa work towards solutions that can help to bridge the gulf between national copyright laws and the prevailing practices used for accessing learning materials. There are essentially two ways to narrow this divide: modify behaviours and/or reform laws. Expanding copyright protection even further beyond international norms is almost certain to aggravate the existing compliance challenges. It is already impractical for most members of tertiary educational communities in the ACA2K study countries to adhere to existing legal requirements; compliance with even stronger laws is clearly unattainable. Evidence from the study countries strongly suggests that the copyright environment can be improved by legal reforms that make copyright more flexible and suitable to local realities. Paradoxically, less restrictive laws could provide more effective protection. Less restrictive laws would enable entire segments of the population currently operating outside of the copyright system altogether to comply with reasonably limited, realistic rules. This could, in turn, increase awareness of, and respect for, the concept of copyright, compounding in the longer term to bolster the effectiveness of the system for all stakeholders. Middle-ground models, such as collective management of copyright and collaboratively generated statements of best practices among stakeholders, hold significant promise to bridge the divide between law and practice.

Preliminary observation of the outcomes that this new evidence has contributed to at national, regional, and international levels suggests that this should be the beginning, not the end, of engagement with the issues at the intersection between copyright and access to learning materials in Africa. Already, this empirical research has found its way into the high-level policy debates examining intellectual property issues in the development context. Collaborative relationships have been formed between ACA2K and stakeholders on all sides of the copyright debate, including rights-holder and user groups, not to mention research centres, independent think tanks and non-governmental organizations (NGOs). The methods and findings of this project are already being taught in at least one university curriculum as a model for others to follow. National seminars have been held in every ACA2K study country, leading to meaningful engagement with lawmakers, policy-makers, and the stakeholders most directly impacted by tertiary educational access issues. The media have shown interest, with coverage of ACA2K finding its way into national and international outlets, including television, radio, print, and online. The book presenting the project's key findings has been positively reviewed by one of the world's leading scholars on the political economy of intellectual property in an influential academic journal.[13]

These outcomes demonstrate that this project has succeeded in achieving its objectives of increasing research capacity in Africa on matters of copyright and learning materials access, refining methodological practices for this kind of research, growing the body of published evidence in this area, and building researchers' awareness of the need to interrogate copyright in relation to educational development objectives and outcomes. And perhaps most importantly, it is apparent that the team that has been involved in executing this project has cross-fertilized to create a solid and sustainable human network of people who are passionate about these issues. The mission to create a network of African researchers empowered not only to study the impact of copyright environments on access to learning materials but also to use the evidence generated to assist copyright stakeholders to participate in evidence-based copyright policy-making has apparently succeeded. Some progress has thus been made towards the ultimate vision of people in Africa maximizing access to knowledge by influencing positive changes in copyright environments nationally and across the continent.

D. GENERAL LESSONS FOR LARGE-SCALE IP RESEARCH PROJECTS

Several relevant lessons from the ACA2K's project's experience can be brought to bear on the discussion and eventual design of general principles to design, monitor, and evaluate multidisciplinary intellectual property

---

13 Christopher May, "Access to Knowledge in Africa: The Role of Copyright" (2011) 110:441 African Affairs 664.

research. This final section of the chapter discusses two particular issues: potential indicators and implementation challenges.

In terms of potential indicators, the outcome mapping method relies heavily on qualitative as opposed to quantitative data. In order to be successfully adopted (or adapted) in the context of other intellectual property research projects, assessors would have to accept the legitimacy of this kind of data. This requires overcoming a degree of discomfort with the lack of precision and comparability of qualitative data. Those characteristics cannot be mistakenly perceived as implying a lack of rigour or reliability. This is a common challenge in multidisciplinary research, for example in projects connecting the natural sciences and engineering on one hand with social sciences and humanities on the other. But it can be overcome with sufficient open-mindedness.

Qualitative data *can* be measurable against appropriate, predetermined indicators or benchmarks. In the ACA2K project, for example, researchers in each study country predetermined measures of success based on changes in behaviour that they would "expect," "like," and "love" to see. Put another way, researchers continuously mapped over time whether the outcomes influenced by their intervention through the project met, exceeded, or greatly exceeded expectations. What those expectations are, specifically, would depend substantially on the aims and objectives of the intervention.

A related challenge is the ability of any metrics, qualitative or quantitative, to indicate *why* such behaviour took place. Was it the result of the research project or other factors? Obtaining qualitative data through, for instance, interviews or focus groups, might yield that kind of data. In a perfect world, monitoring and evaluation would also track what would have happened without the research project. The reality in the context of much intellectual property research, however, is that counterfactuals cannot be observed. Assessors might therefore speculate what might have happened but for the intervention.

Moreover, monitoring of behavioural changes that are attributable or at least correlated to a research project's intervention is a process, not an event. In this process, there is a differentiation between performance monitoring (ongoing through a project) and evaluation (analytical snapshots that can be done at the planning stage, at points during the project or at the end). Both require a baseline and then longitudinal data collection over a period of time — at the beginning of the research, while research is underway, and after research concludes. This also presents a potential problem for researchers, because results are not often observed until well after a project has finished, and reporting has been completed. In these circumstances, perhaps the best that researchers might do is to map trajectories of changes, looking for and reporting on signals that research stakeholders are beginning to behave differently or likely to do so in the future. Researchers, if possible, might also contemplate, at the design and proposal stage, post-project evaluation.

Generally, this entire process of data gathering about the research project itself, in addition to data about the subject matter being researched, can be labour and resource intensive. It need not be onerous, but it does require careful and deliberate thought, especially at the outset of the design phase. And it requires close monitoring by individuals, in direct contact with key stakeholders, over an extended period of time. It can generate considerable amounts of qualitative data, which requires not only collection but also organization and analysis. Those tasks can be time-consuming, and in some cases require significant investments of financial and human resources.

The general discussion of monitoring and evaluation also triggers deeper questions for multidisciplinary researchers managing the shift toward result-oriented research. One difficult issue involves research ethics. Especially on the subject of human behaviour, as is the focus of much intellectual property research, many researchers have been trained to respect a strict boundary between observation and intervention. Not only is it methodologically problematic to influence the behaviour of research subjects, it is in many circumstances unethical. Yet, that is precisely what research funders who demand demonstrable results expect. It leaves researchers in a delicate position, with potentially conflicting obligations to research funders and research subjects.

Such ethical dilemmas cannot be resolved in this chapter, but are nevertheless worth highlighting as an area where caution, and extensive discussion, is warranted. Adopting a monitoring and evaluation framework might, at least, force reflexive consideration of this sometimes-obscured issue.

Another key question moving forward is whether funders will in the future set rigid guidelines for assessments that will distill a single monitoring and evaluation methodology to be applied consistently, or rather accept a variety of methods that might be used together or separately as circumstances dictate. It may be that a single methodology better facilitates comparisons across projects, an objective that likely motivates many funding decisions. But allowing for different methods might yield richer and more nuanced data, which could be more appropriate for the highly qualitative comparisons in a wide variety of situations.

In conclusion, outcome mapping can be a valuable tool for designing, monitoring, and evaluating the influence of research projects and policy interventions in complex environments. That makes it potentially very useful in the context of methodologies for assessing multidisciplinary intellectual property research. Even if outcome mapping *per se* is not deployed as the assessment tool of choice, its underlying principles are valuable to inform the monitoring and evaluation process. Those principles include an appreciation for the validity of both qualitative and quantitative data, a longitudinal focus on changes in behaviour over time instead of static analysis of conditions or events, and care to avoid claiming credit for causality but rather recognizing inherent complexities and uncertainties. Proven experience with the IDRC-funded ACA2K research project demonstrates that the framework can be used to map the influence of a project or a policy intervention.

TWENTY-ONE

Evidentiary Problems of Multidisciplinarity in the Litigation of Business Method Patents

NORMAN SIEBRASSE

ABSTRACT (EN): It is now widely accepted that judicial decision making is not a neutral exercise in interpretation of established law and consequently decisions, particularly in novel areas, should take account of policy considerations. In this article the author uses the example of litigation over the patentability of business methods to problematize this line of reasoning. Sound policy typically turns on empirical evidence, and while there is a significant body of research on the question of whether business method patents promote innovation, such evidence has been introduced only indirectly, though academic articles. This does not allow adequate examination of the reliability of the evidence. Introducing empirical social science evidence directly in litigation faces a number of hurdles which are discussed. Ultimately the author argues that it is beyond the institutional competence of the courts to adequately take account of empirical social science evidence on the issue of whether business method patents are good for innovation. While the details of the arguments are specific to the context of business method patents, the author suggests that the issue of institutional competence should always be taken into account when considering whether empirical social science evidence should drive judicial decision making.

RÉSUMÉ (FR): Il est maintenant largement admis que le processus de décision judiciaire n'est pas un exercice neutre d'application de principes de droit établis et que, par conséquent, les décisions, particulièrement dans des nouveaux domaines, devraient tenir compte des considérations d'ordre politique. Dans ce chapitre, l'auteur s'appuie sur les arrêts qui se sont prononcés sur la brevetabilité des méthodes d'affaires commerciales pour étudier la problématique de cette ligne de pensée. Une politique rationnelle est normalement fondée sur des preuves empiriques, mais alors qu'il existe un important corpus de recherches sur la question de savoir si les brevets sur les méthodes d'affaires commerciales stimulent l'innovation, ces données empiriques ne peuvent être présentées en cour qu'indirectement, par le truchement d'articles scientifiques. Cela ne permet pas un examen adéquat de la fiabilité de ces études. La présentation directe de données de sciences sociales devant les tribunaux rencontre un certain nombre d'obstacles qui sont discutés dans ce chapitre. L'auteur conclut que le fait de tenir compte adéquatement des preuves empiriques des sciences sociales, lorsqu'il s'agit de décider si la brevetabilité des méthodes d'affaires est favorable à l'innovation, va au-delà de la compétence institutionnelle des tribunaux. Bien que le détail des arguments porte de manière spécifique sur la brevetabilité des méthodes d'affaires, l'auteur soutient que cette question de la compétence institutionnelle des tribunaux devrait toujours être prise en considération lorsqu'il faut décider si les preuves empiriques des sciences sociales seront déterminantes dans les prises de décision des tribunaux.

A. INTRODUCTION

The turn to policy in legal analysis that began with the Realists has undoubtedly been salutary in its overall effect on the law, but we have yet to fully come to grips with the evidentiary problems that this insight implies. The Realist insight is that legal doctrines are not neutral, but reflect particular policy considerations. Making these considerations explicit should therefore improve the quality of legal decision making. The difficulty is that while the correct decision from a policy perspective often turns on empirical social science evidence, the relevant evidence is typically not before the court. Focusing on *Amazon.com*[1] in Canada, and *Bilski*[2] in the United States, the following chapter illustrates this problem with the example of litigation

1 *Amazon.com Inc v Canada (AG)*, 2011 FCA 328 [*Amazon.com FCA*], rev'g 2010 FC 1011 [*Amazon.com FC*], *Re Amazon.com, Inc Patent Application No 2,246,933* (2009), 75 CPR (4th) 85 (PAB and Comm'r of Patents) [*Re Amazon.com's Application*].

2 *Bilski v Kappos*, 561 US ___, 130 S Ct 3218 (2010) [*Bilski*]; see Norman Siebrasse, "The Rule Against Abstract Claims: A Canadian Perspective on US Jurisprudence" (2010) 27 CIPR 3 [Siebrasse, "US Law in Perspective"], for a discussion of the US jurisprudence.

over the patentability of business methods. My premise is not novel: while the law should reflect policy considerations, the courts are not always the place to introduce policy concerns. More precisely, old-fashioned "black-letter" textual interpretation, which itself reflects the policy consideration of supremacy of the legislature, may be preferable to an expansively purposive approach to interpretation. I argue that properly assessing the policy evidence relevant to whether business methods should be patentable is beyond the institutional competence of the courts. While the same conclusion does not necessarily follow in all contexts, this example suggests that we should not simply assume that relevant empirical social science evidence should be judicially considered in litigation.

B. THEORY

The legal answer to the question of whether business methods are patentable turns on whether business methods are an "art" within the meaning of that term in the definition of "invention" in the *Patent Act*.[3] The modern approach to statutory interpretation requires consideration of the purpose of the statute as well as its text and context.[4] "When the words of a provision are precise and unequivocal, the ordinary meaning of the words play a dominant role in the interpretive process. On the other hand, where the words can support more than one reasonable meaning, the ordinary meaning of the words plays a lesser role."[5] The word "art" is open-ended on its face, so this seems to be a good case in which a purposive interpretation should be important. Given that the uncontroversial purpose of the Act is to promote innovation, this implies that "art" should be interpreted to include business methods if and only if patents would promote innovation in business methods. This is an empirical question. There is a substantial body of empirical research as to whether patents in particular fields, including business methods, would promote or impede innovation. From this research it would seem to follow that the interpretation of "art" should turn on this empirical evidence.

3 RSC 1985, c P-4, s 2.

4 *Rizzo & Rizzo Shoes Ltd (Re)*, [1998] 1 SCR 27 at para 21.

5 *Canada Trustco Mortgage Co v Canada*, 2005 SCC 54 at para 10.

C. PRACTICE

Despite this theory, consideration of whether patenting business methods would promote business innovation has not been central to the litigation. In *Amazon.com* Phelen J in the Federal Court decision expressly rejected consideration of policy in interpreting the term "art,"[6] while for both the Federal Court of Appeal in *Amazon.com* and for Kennedy J, writing the opinion of the United States Supreme Court in *Bilski*, the question turned solely on matters of legal principle.[7] The Patent Appeal Board in the decision under appeal in *Amazon.com* and the concurrence of Stevens J in the United States Supreme Court in *Bilski* recognized to some extent policy arguments in interpreting the term "art," but neither relied upon any of the crucial empirical evidence.

The entirety of the policy discussion in the Patent Appeal Board decision in *Amazon.com*, which was introduced only after the Board had concluded that business methods are unpatentable in Canada, was the following paragraph, quoted from an English High Court decision:

> Now let us consider business methods. What is the policy reason that lies behind the exclusion of those [under the *European Patent Convention* Article 52(2)(c)][8]? It is because, historically, patents for business methods were never granted yet business innovation went on very well without the benefit of that protection and without the red tape. Businessmen have been every bit as inventive as engineers. It was probably business administrators (and not poets or priests) who made the greatest "invention" of all time: phonetic writing. Consider as further examples: the invention of money; of double-entry bookkeeping; of negotiable bills of exchange; of joint-stock companies; of insurance policies; of clearance banking; of business name franchising; of the supermarket; and so on. None of these needed patent protection to get started.[9]

---

6 *Amazon.com FC*, above note 1 at para 36.

7 The decision of the Federal Court of Appeal in *Amazon.com* relied largely on its own prior decision in *Schlumberger Canada Ltd v Commissioner of Patents*, [1982] 1 FC 845 (CA) [*Schlumberger*]; see Siebrasse, "US Law in Perspective," above note 2, for a discussion of *Schlumberger* and *Bilski*.

8 *Convention on the Grant of European Patents*, 5 October 1973, 1065 UNTS 199 (entered into force 7 October 1977) [*European Patent Convention*].

9 *Re Amazon.com's Application*, above note 1 at para 149, quoting *CFPH LLC v Comptroller-General of Patents, Designs and Trade Marks*, [2005] EWHC 1589 (Pat) at para 41.

The observation that there have been many business innovations without patents is accurate, but it is not a good argument against granting business method patents. While the list of pre-patent business innovations is impressive, so is the list of pre-patent inventions in purely traditional fields of endeavour: the wheel, the spoked wheel, the bow and compound bow, bronze, the pulley, the mouldboard plow, rib and plank ship construction, the compass, brick, pottery, glass and porcelain making, and the printing press, to name a few. No one supposes that innovation would cease without patents.

The argument in favour of patents is that they may increase the speed of innovation. The patent system developed in its modern form during the British Industrial Revolution when the speed of innovation increased dramatically. It is unlikely that patents caused the Industrial Revolution, but they may have accelerated it.[10] Similarly, the argument for patenting business methods is not that there will be no business innovation without patents, but that patents will increase the pace of business innovation. The observation that there have been innovations in business methods even in the absence of patents fails to address this central point.

D. JUSTICE STEVENS IN *BILSKI*

The majority in *Bilski* held the patent in question to be unpatentable subject matter as claiming abstract ideas.[11] This is a general legal principle which, in the view of the United States Supreme Court at least, does not turn on empirical evidence. While Stevens J accepted this, he was of the view that business method patents should be excluded *per se*, whether or not the patent in question claimed an abstract idea or a specific application.[12] He relied expressly on the argument that ambiguous patent laws should be interpreted in a manner that encourages, rather than impedes, innovation,[13] and he dealt extensively with the policy arguments and evidence.[14] Justice

---

10 See, for example, Petra Moser, "How Do Patent Laws Influence Innovation? Evidence from Nineteenth-Century World's Fairs" (2005) 95 American Economic Review 1214, concluding at 1233 that the decision to strengthen patent laws "may have played an important role in encouraging the American focus on manufacturing machinery that spurred economic growth toward the end of the [nineteenth] century."

11 *Bilski*, above note 2 at 3229–30.

12 *Ibid* at 3232 and 3257 (Justice Stevens, Ginsburg, Breyer, & Sotomayor JJ, concurring).

13 *Ibid* at 3252–53.

14 *Ibid* at 3252–57.

Stevens's opinion fits closely with the approach implied by the Realist paradigm, and is therefore worth treating in more detail.

Justice Stevens began by noting that it is uncontroversial that the basic argument in favour of patenting is the need to provide an incentive to undertake "expensive" and "risky" investment in innovations that are "easily copied."[15] He referenced the economic scholarship, which "suggest[s] that these dynamics of cost, risk, and reward vary by the type of thing being patented."[16] This point can now be considered to be well-established in the scholarly literature.

From these general points, Stevens J turned to business methods specifically. Justice Stevens relied on the same historical point made by the Patent Appeal Board in *Amazon.com* that business methods innovation has occurred even without patents, though he acknowledged that "counterfactuals are a dubious form of analysis."[17] Apart from this anecdotal evidence, Stevens J relied on academic articles giving theoretical reasons, backed up by empirical evidence, as to why the residual non-patent incentives such as "various first mover advantages, including lockins, branding, and networking effects," provide adequate non-patent innovation incentives.[18] He also explained how business method patents might impede innovation, rather than encourage it, as when patent holders may use business method patents "to threaten litigation and to bully competitors, especially those that cannot bear the costs of a drawn out, fact-intensive patent litigation."[19]

The general difficulty with these arguments is that exactly the same may be said, as a matter of theory, about patents in many traditional areas. First-mover advantages and so on give some advantage in any field, and a substantial reward in some fields. Similarly, patents in any field may impede innovation. The threat of a larger company bullying a smaller one by the threat of protracted litigation is a problem of intellectual property law generally; after all, while many are concerned about business method patents encouraging patent trolls, the trolls that have appeared to date have exploited patents in traditionally patentable fields. And indeed, bullying tactics are a feature of law generally, which is a consequence of the cost of

---

15 *Ibid* at 3253.

16 *Ibid* [footnote omitted].

17 *Ibid* at 3254 [footnote omitted].

18 *Ibid*, citing Dan L Burk & Mark A Lemley, "Policy Levers in Patent Law" (2003) 89 Va L Rev 1575 at 1618.

19 *Ibid* at 3257 [footnote omitted].

litigation, rather than any feature of intellectual property law in particular. It is true that business method patents may impede innovation by needlessly restricting competition and raising prices of basic building blocks, and exposing true innovators to opportunistic actions. On the other hand, the fundamental theoretical justification for patent protection, and indeed intellectual property rights generally, is that innovation is fundamentally knowledge. Knowledge may require substantial investment to develop, and yet by its intangible nature is easily appropriated by free riders who can then undercut the innovator's price. Business method innovations fit this basic theoretical paradigm perfectly. This theory is not new. While modern scholars have added some refinements and associated jargon, like "patent thickets" and "opportunism," the horns of the intellectual property dilemma have been understood for centuries.[20] However, theory alone does not resolve the question. It is possible to support the case for or against patenting in any industry by selectively citing the theoretical considerations on one side or the other. Business method patents may indeed impede innovation; they may also promote innovation. The question is not whether they *may* impede innovation, but whether they *do*. This is an empirical question, not a theoretical one.

Justice Stevens relied particularly on an important article by Burk and Lemley, "Policy Levers in Patent Law," for the proposition that business methods in particular are different, as "companies have ample incentives to develop business methods even without patent protection, because the competitive marketplace rewards companies that use more efficient business methods."[21] However, Burk and Lemley's article is theoretical, and while it refers extensively to the empirical literature, it does not rely on empirical evidence to support this particular proposition.[22] This is because the thrust of their article is that different models of innovation are applicable to differ-

---

20 See *Sayre v Moore* (1785), quoted in *Cary v Longman* (1801), 1 East 358, 362 n (b), 102 ER 138, 140 n (b) (KB).

21 *Bilski*, above note 2 at 3254, Stevens J quoting Burk & Lemley, above note 18 at 1618.

22 Rochelle Cooper Dreyfuss, "Are Business Method Patents Bad for Business?" (2000) 16:2 Santa Clara Computer & High Tech LJ 263 at 274–77, which is another article quoted or cited at various points in Stevens J's opinion. Without engaging in a detailed discussion of this article, I will simply note that it makes an entirely theoretical point, for which there is a strong prima facie counter argument: see Norman Siebrasse, "The Structure of the Law of Patentable Subject Matter" (2011) 23:2 IPJ 167 [Siebrasse, "Structure"]. This is not to say that Dreyfuss's point is necessarily wrong, but rather that once again, the theoretical debate can only be resolved by empirical evidence.

ent industries and they argue that patent law should take "industry-specific variation into account explicitly in applying general patent rules to specific cases."[23] Their theoretical analysis is appropriate to support their thesis, as their ultimate conclusions are framed in general terms, which would be tailored to the facts of the specific case. They explicitly argue against different patent laws for different industries.[24] One of their main arguments on this point is that establishing industry patent laws specific policy requires information that goes beyond the current economic knowledge:

> [W]hile economics can make useful policy suggestions as to how patents work in different industries, we are skeptical of the ability of a statute to dictate in detail the right patent rules for each industry. Many of the predictions of economic theory are fact-specific — they suggest different factors that should bear on the outcome of particular cases, but that require case-by-case application that cannot easily be captured in a statute. Economic theory is more useful in making general suggestions about how the patent system can be adapted to particular factual contexts than as the basis for a whole series of new statutes.[25]

Consistently with this observation, they do *not* argue that business methods should not be patentable. Rather, they argue that business method patents "should be rare and very modest in scope."[26]

Justice Stevens did cite a leading empirical economic article on the industry specific nature of the patent incentive.[27] However, all that this study aimed to show is that the patent incentive varies by industry. Because the work was an early foray into this field of research, written before business method patents exploded onto the scene with *State Street Bank*,[28] it did not mention business method patents at all.[29]

Justice Stevens argued that "the functional case that patents promote progress generally is stronger for subject matter that has 'historically been

---

23 Burk & Lemley, above note 18 at 1579.

24 *Ibid* at 1631–37.

25 *Ibid* at 1634–35 [footnotes omitted].

26 *Ibid* at 1619.

27 Richard C Levin et al, "Appropriating the Returns from Industrial Research and Development" (1987) 3 Brookings Papers on Economic Activity 783 at 794–95, cited by Stevens J in *Bilski*, above note 2 at 3254, n 50.

28 *State Street Bank & Trust Co v Signature Financial Group Inc*, 149 F 3d 1368 (Fed Cir 1998).

29 Levin et al, above note 27, cited in *Bilski*, above note 2 at 3254, Stevens J.

eligible to receive the protection of our patent laws'. . . ."[30] This conclusion simply is not supported by the empirical evidence. This is not because the evidence shows that patents are important for promoting business method innovation; it is because the empirical evidence that patents are important in most traditional areas is also weak.[31] Because business method patents are a relatively recent phenomenon, there has been little empirical research directly on whether they have had a positive net effect on innovation, and it should also be recognized that this type of research is inherently difficult. Consequently, it is difficult to draw any firm conclusions. In a review article, Bronwyn Hall, one of the leading empirical researchers in this field, remarks wryly that "[t]he only conclusion that is certain is that allowing business method patents will cause an increase in the patenting of business methods."[32] She continues:

> Unfortunately . . . it is much more difficult to make predictions about the effects of this subject matter expansion on innovation that are not pure speculation. We know that patents are not considered essential for capturing the returns to innovation in many industries, and there seems no reason to think that this one is different. Casual observation suggests that business method patents are not being used to provide innovation incentives as much as they are being used to extract rents *ex post*, but this evidence could be misleading. We do not know whether there would have been as much entry into internet businesses or new financial offerings in the absence of the patent system, or even whether such entry is a good or a bad thing.[33]

We certainly cannot conclude that business method patents are good for innovation, but at this point we cannot conclude that they are particularly bad either.[34]

---

30 *Bilski*, above note 2 at 3253–54 [footnote omitted].

31 Siebrasse, "Structure," above note 22.

32 Bronwyn H Hall, "Business and Financial Method Patents, Innovation, and Policy" (2009) 56:4 Scottish Journal of Political Economy 443 at 459–60.

33 *Ibid* at 460 [emphasis in original]; see also Robert M Hunt, "Business Method Patents and US Financial Services" (2010) 28:3 Contemporary Economic Policy 322. The author concludes that "we still cannot determine whether these patents are creating value for the U.S. economy" at 349.

34 See Robert P Merges, "The Uninvited Guest: Patents on Wall Street" (2003) 88:4 Federal Reserve Bank of Atlanta: Economic Review 1. Merges is skeptical as to the value of patents in promoting innovation in finance, yet predicts that "[p]atents will not cause any real and lasting problems" as firms adapt to the new environment, at 12.

E. JUDICIAL NOTICE CRITIQUE

To this point I have argued that the theoretical case against business method patents is inconclusive and the empirical evidence by Stevens J in *Bilski* is inadequate to resolve the question. There is also a distinct objection to Stevens J's use of empirical evidence to conclude that business method patents would impede innovation. Justice Stevens's approach of citing academic articles that review or report on empirical research amounts to taking judicial notice of contested facts. Empirical social science evidence is a matter of fact. As such it should normally be introduced through expert witnesses at trial.

Indeed, evidence of the efficacy of patents in promoting innovations in business methods is of a nature that it must be introduced at trial. As McLachlin CJ held for a unanimous Court in *R v Find*:[35]

> Judicial notice dispenses with the need for proof of facts that are clearly uncontroversial or beyond reasonable dispute. Facts judicially noticed are not proved by evidence under oath. Nor are they tested by cross-examination. Therefore, the threshold for judicial notice is strict: a court may properly take judicial notice of facts that are either: (1) so notorious or generally accepted as not to be the subject of debate among reasonable persons; or (2) capable of immediate and accurate demonstration by resort to readily accessible sources of indisputable accuracy.[36]

Given the scholarly uncertainty reflected in Dr Hall's comments, quoted above, it is clearly impossible to say that the "fact" that business method patents are bad for innovation satisfies either of these tests.

Find articulated a relatively strict standard for judicial notice, which might be relaxed in certain circumstances in favour of an older and more flexible standard which would allow a court to take judicial notice of what "everybody knows."[37] However, statistical and survey evidence of the kind at issue in the debate over business method patents is not a candidate for a relaxed standard. In *Find* the information sought to be introduced through judicial notice concerned the existence of a widespread bias in the community, which ultimately would be established by statistical evidence sim-

35 *R v Find*, 2001 SCC 32 [*Find*].

36 *Ibid* at para 48.

37 *R v Spence*, 2005 SCC 71 at paras 49 and 56.

ilar in nature to that which would establish the incentive effect of patents. Chief Justice McLachlin in *Find* noted that

> [t]he scientific and statistical nature of much of the information relied upon by the appellant further complicates this case. Expert evidence is by definition neither notorious nor capable of immediate and accurate demonstration. This is why it must be proved through an expert whose qualifications are accepted by the court and who is available for cross-examination.[38]

Some relevant evidence might be judicially noticed under the more relaxed standard. For example, there is no doubt that "everybody knows" that business method innovation took place without patents. However, the evidence that might properly be judicially noticed is not sufficient to resolve the question of whether business method patents promote innovation.

This is not a technical point. While many people have strong opinions as to whether business method patents will spur innovation, it is ultimately a contested question of fact over which there is scholarly controversy. Even if Stevens J were to have conducted a thorough literature review of the empirical evidence in order to support his opinion, this approach would have amounted to deciding a crucial and contested matter of fact through judicial notice. Such an approach is not permitted in the Canadian legal system, which insists that the evidence must be tested by the parties, precisely in order to ensure that decisions are not made on the basis of supposed "facts" that are actually wrong.[39] No lawyer or legal scholar would suggest that a court could make a determination as to obviousness of a new pharmaceutical without extensive expert testimony, tested by cross-examination. The question of whether patents impede or encourage progress in a particular field of endeavour is at least equally complex and has far more far-reaching consequences than the validity of a single patent. To suggest that a court should decide a difficult empirical question on the basis of speculation and anecdote is just as absurd as suggesting that it should decide, without expert evidence, whether it is obvious to separate a racemate into its isomers using fractional crystallization.

38 *Find*, above note 35 at para 49.

39 *Ibid* at para 51.

F. RESPONSE

1) Introduce Fact Evidence at Trial

The most straightforward response to this problem would be to introduce the empirical evidence as to the incentive effect of business method patents at trial, through expert witnesses who could be cross-examined. However, there are significant practical impediments to this.

The first impediment is that it would be necessary to reconceptualize the interpretation of the definition of "invention" in section 2 of the *Patent Act* as turning directly on whether patents in the field in question would help or hinder innovation. At present, this is raised indirectly, as an aspect of a purposive interpretation of the Act, but the bulk of the effort and argument in both *Amazon.com* and *Bilski* were addressed to more traditional legal arguments over precedent and principle. A clear reconceptualization of the definition of "invention" is necessary as expert witness evidence is expensive to introduce and cross-examine and the parties are unlikely to undertake that expense unless it is clear that such evidence is likely to be determinative. This reconceptualization would be difficult, but is not unheard of. Competition law, for example, has been reconceptualized as turning on economic concerns, as opposed to the older emphasis on power relations.

Assuming that the necessary reconceptualization took place, a second problem is defining the scope of the exception. For example, it is not clear on the present evidence that business methods are the appropriate category for exclusion or inclusion. It might be that patenting would encourage innovation in financial services, but impede innovation in retail sales techniques. At a higher level of generality, it may be that patenting encourages innovation in "discrete product" industries, but not in "complex product" industries. What would be the appropriate question for the court? So, in *Amazon.com*, should the court be asked to decide whether inventions in complex products industries are patentable, or whether inventions in business methods are patentable, or whether inventions in retail sales methods are patentable?

It is not necessary to answer that question if the issue does not turn on the empirical evidence. For example, a decision that the application at issue in *Amazon.com* does not claim a patentable invention does not necessarily mean that business methods are not patentable; it only means that the particular method in question was not patentable. As the caselaw develops, lawyers can then extract generalizations representing their predictions as to whether a particular patent will be granted. However, if the court is to enunciate a general rule, the question of the appropriate level of generalization will arise.

If the court phrases the rule at a very high level of generality, the decision would run the risk of excluding patents in some sub-categories where they were important. That is, supposing that patenting would encourage innovation in financial services, a rule that patents are not available in complex product industries would wrongly exclude financial services methods from patentability. The other difficulty with a general rule of this type is that it is difficult to know whether a particular patent would be subject to a rule that is stated in such general terms. Which industries are "complex product" industries? How should a particular method be assigned to a particular industry? Should the assembly line, to pick an old example, be considered a mechanical method, an automotive industry method, an electronic industry method, or a manufacturing method? Correct categorization is particularly problematic because certainty is very important in patent law, which provides forward looking incentives through patents that are typically not litigated until years after the investment in the invention is made.[40]

The other extreme would be to draw the relevant category narrowly. The difficulty with this is that it would require repeated litigation of different categories. It would also undermine certainty, as we would not have confidence that any particular category was patentable, or not, until it was litigated. It would also make the empirical question more difficult, since there is typically less data available for a narrowly defined industry.

No doubt the optimal level of categorization is somewhere in the middle. However, it is not evident what that optimal level might be; indeed, that in itself is another empirical question. But that cannot be left to repeated litigation. The parties have to know what they are litigating before the litigation starts, so that they will know what evidence is relevant. The parties will no doubt call different evidence, and likely different experts, depending on whether the question is whether business method patents promote innovation, or whether retail sales patents promote innovation.

Another difficulty is that the empirical evidence is limited. If the category at issue is drawn too narrowly, there may be insufficient evidence to draw sound conclusions one way or the other, even if, in fact, patents ac-

---

40 *Human Genome Sciences Inc v Eli Lilly & Co*, [2011] UKSC 51, rev'g [2010] EWCA Civ 33, aff'g [2008] EWHC 1903 (Pat); *Bilski*, above note 2 at 3231.

tually have a major impact. But it is not satisfactory to let the categories be defined by the existing empirical research, as there is no reason to believe that the categories used in the research define optimal categories from an incentive perspective. The question of whether patents in a particular field promote innovation in that field is inherently difficult to answer, and particular studies are often tailored to the available data set. Further, the evidence itself may be affected by the litigation. A number of the leading studies involve survey evidence. Survey evidence in future studies is likely to become biased if survey participants realize that their answers are likely to determine whether inventions are patentable in their industry.

2) Presumption

The law typically deals with evidentiary difficulties through presumptions. The immediate question is whether the presumption should be in favour or against patenting in new fields, such as business methods.

There are a number of difficulties with a presumption against patenting in new fields. One is the narrowly legal point that this would be contrary to our obligations under *Agreement on Trade-Related Aspects of Intellectual Property Rights* to allow patents "in all fields of technology."[41]

There are also difficulties from a policy perspective. First, it is not clear how to define a field in order to say whether it is new or not. All patents must be new in a narrow sense, to satisfy the novelty requirement, so the nature of the invention claimed in a particular application does not tell us what new category that invention belongs in. Is an automobile gas pedal that uses an electronic linkage instead of a mechanical linkage in the old field of mechanical patents, or perhaps automotive patents, or is it in a new field of computer-controlled automobile controls, or perhaps computer-controlled automobile throttles?[42]

Secondly, a presumption against patenting in new fields would mean that patentability would turn on the vagaries of what has been patented in the past. Recent scholarship shows that roughly 8 percent of the earliest US patents were for business methods.[43] Should this establish that business

41 *Agreement on Trade-Related Aspects of Intellectual Property Rights*, 15 April 1994, 1869 UNTS 299, 33 ILM 1197 at art 27 (Annex 1C of the Marrakesh Agreement Establishing the World Trade Organization).

42 See the patent at issue in *KSR Int'l Co v Teleflex Inc*, 550 US 398 (2007).

43 Michael Risch, "America's First Patents" (2012) 64:5 Fla L Rev 1279 at 1320.

methods are patentable? Conversely, there is no suggestion that patents were granted in the field of nanotechnology until recently; does this mean that nanotechnology should be unpatentable? Software patents have been routinely granted in Canada for about thirty-five years.[44] Are software patents new or old?

The broader point here is that the question of whether patents were historically granted in a particular area does not map well onto the fields in which patents are likely to promote innovation. I have argued above that empirical evidence is needed to establish whether patents are good or bad for innovation in any particular field, but this is not to deny that research to date has shown that patents are more likely to be good in so-called simple product industries and less likely to be beneficial in complex product industries. While it is difficult to define these categories precisely, it is clear enough that historical patterns of patenting do not mirror this distinction even roughly. Many of the most traditional industries are complex product industries, and conversely, some of the new fields are at least arguably simple product industries.[45]

Further, truly new categories of invention will necessarily have the least empirical evidence. A presumption against patenting in new fields without empirical evidence would effectively preclude patenting in new fields since there will be no evidence that patenting helps innovation if such patents are not permitted. This is a peculiar result in patent law, because, as Binnie J noted in *Harvard College v Canada*, "by definition the *Patent Act* must contemplate the unforeseeable."[46] Presumably over time, as industrial patterns change, patents would become available in fewer and fewer industries of practical importance, so this presumption would amount to a gradual repeal of the *Patent Act*. It may be that the *Patent Act* should be generally repealed, and perhaps retained only in a few industries such as pharmaceuticals, but this is clearly a decision for the legislature and not one to be implemented surreptitiously by a judicial presumption.

---

44 While the Federal Court of Appeal in *Schlumberger*, above note 7, refused to allow a patent for a computer implemented invention in which the only novel element was an algorithm, the Patent Office has interpreted *Schlumberger* generously, and routinely granted such patents since the mid-1980s: see, for example, *Re Application for Patent of Batelle Memorial Institute* (1984), 8 CPR (3d) 133 (PAB and Comm'r of Patents) and *Re Application for Patent of Mobil Oil Corp* (1985), 24 CPR (3d) 571.

45 *Mayo Collaborative Services v Prometheus Labs, Inc*, 130 S Ct 3543 (2010), where the diagnostic correlations were found to be unpatentable.

46 *Harvard College v Canada* (Commissioner of Patents), 2002 SCC 76 at para 87.

G. CONCLUSION

There is a straightforward argument that the legal question of whether business methods should be patentable as falling within the meaning of the term "art" in the definition of "invention" should turn on the empirical evidence as to whether business method patents would be good for innovation. However, the courts in the recent high-profile cases have not considered that empirical evidence systematically. I have argued that rather than encouraging the courts to take such evidence into account, we should recognize that it is not within their institutional competence to do so. There is a good argument to be made that business method patents would be bad for innovation and should not be allowed, but the evidence that bears on this issue is of a nature that should be considered by the legislature, and not by the courts. Concerns of institutional competence are as much a valid policy consideration as concerns for encouraging innovation. I am *not* arguing that I believe that patenting is necessarily, or even likely to be beneficial in all new fields. My position is simply that making this determination is a question for the legislature, not the courts.

More broadly, the Realist insight that law inevitably implicates policy is not a licence for the courts to make policy based on guesswork and intuition. While I have used the example of business method patents and some of the arguments I have advanced in this chapter are specific to that context, the basic concern regarding institutional competence is a more general one. I do not suggest that this concern will lead to the same conclusion in every context, but I do suggest that it is always worth considering. I hope that this chapter may prompt a broader discussion about the appropriate use of social science evidence in litigation.

THEME FOUR

Impact of *Law* or *Impact* on *Law*?

TWENTY-TWO

Emerging Academic Scientists' Exclusionary Encounters with Commercialization Law, Policy, and Practice

MATTHEW HERDER

ABSTRACT (EN): Academic laboratories are, increasingly, sites of commercialization. While empirical evidence about the impact of the emphasis placed upon commercialization by governments, research funding agencies, and research institutions, and the attendant growth of commercialization activities in the academic sphere has been gradually accumulating, much of this evidence is tied to established academic scientists. Comparatively little empirical research has focused upon emerging academic scientists. Therefore, the purpose of this chapter is to identify a set of concerns flowing from emerging academic scientists' encounters with commercialization laws, policies, and practices. The chapter proceeds in three parts. In Section B, I describe contextual changes related to commercialization in the academic realm as well as a range of commercialization activities that emerging scientists are increasingly apt to be exposed to as they pursue scientific careers. In Section C, I identify two "exclusionary encounters" that emerging scientists are likely to have with commercialization laws, policies, and practices. These encounters pertain to 1) inventorship of patentable discoveries, and 2) intellectual property ownership. By way of brief conclusion in Section D, I set out one hypothesis for future empirical inquiry.

RÉSUMÉ (FR): Les laboratoires universitaires sont de plus en plus des sites de commercialisation. Bien que la preuve empirique au sujet de l'impact de l'accent placé sur la commercialisation par les gouvernements, les agences de financement de la recherche, et les institutions de recherche, de même

459

que la preuve concernant la croissance corrélative des activités de commercialisation dans le monde universitaire s'accumulent graduellement, elles se rapportent surtout aux scientifiques universitaires établis. Peu de recherches empiriques se sont concentrées sur les scientifiques universitaires émergents. L'objet de ce chapitre est donc d'identifier une série de préoccupations découlant de l'application aux scientifiques universitaires émergents des lois, des politiques et des pratiques de commercialisation. Ce chapitre est divisé en trois parties. Dans la Partie A, l'auteur décrit les changements contextuels relatifs à la commercialisation dans le milieu universitaire, ainsi qu'une gamme d'activités de commercialisation auxquelles les scientifiques émergents sont de plus en plus susceptibles d'être confrontés dans le cadre de leur carrière scientifique. Dans la Partie B, l'auteur identifie deux « situations d'exclusion » que les scientifiques émergents auront probablement à vivre en raison des lois, politiques et pratiques de commercialisation. Ces situations surviennent lors de 1) l'identification de l'inventeur de découvertes brevetables, et 2) la détermination du titulaire de la propriété intellectuelle. En guise de brève conclusion, la Partie C formule une hypothèse pour une enquête empirique future.

A. INTRODUCTION

Academic laboratories are sites of not only great scientific but also social inquiry. Following Robert Merton's seminal work in the 1950s,[1] sociologists, anthropologists, historians, economists, and other scholars have set upon studying the internal dynamics of academic laboratories and the structures, institutions, and outside actors infiltrating, influencing, and complicating laboratory environments. While important to situate commercially-oriented research practices such as patenting within this broader range of influences that have and will continue to influence academic science,[2] the

1 See, for example, Robert K Merton, "Priorities in Scientific Discovery: A Chapter in the Sociology of Science" (1957) 22 Am Soc Rev 635.

2 A standard response to those who express concerns about the commercialization of academic science is to ask whether the concerns in question are, in fact, more attributable to long-standing norms of competition and secrecy within academic science. Part of the empirical challenge, then, is to disentangle the various influences upon the behaviours and choices of academic scientists. See, for example, Wei Hong & John P Walsh "For Money or Glory? Commercialization, Competition, and Secrecy in the Entrepreneurial University" (2009) 50:1 Sociological Quarterly 145.

university's increasing embrace of the marketplace over the last forty or so years[3] has motivated many investigations of the academic lab.[4]

Today, commercializing academic science ranks high amongst government and institutional priorities.[5] There is an enduring optimism that the commercial potential of university research has yet to be tapped.[6] Others meanwhile contest this policy capture, charging that commercialization threatens free academic inquiry, appropriates public goods, and limits knowledge generation, sharing, and dissemination.[7]

Evidence about the impact of this emphasis on commercialization and the attendant growth of commercialization activities in the academic sphere has been gradually accumulating, especially in the United States,[8] and to a lesser extent in other countries like Canada. For example, one group of researchers has carried out a series of surveys of academic scientists since the early 1990s, highlighting withholding of data as an increasing

3 While important examples of "academic entrepreneurialism" date back to the early twentieth century, it was not until the 1980s and 1990s that governments, research funding agencies, and academic institutions began promoting the commercialization of research in earnest. See Jocelyn Downie & Matthew Herder, "Reflections on the Commercialization of Research Conducted in Public Institutions in Canada" (2007) 1:1 McGill JL & Health 23; and Charles Weiner, "Patenting and Academic Research: Historical Case Studies" (1987) 12:1 Sci Tech & Human Values 50.

4 For recent summaries of these inquiries, see Frank T Rothaermel, Shanti D Agung, & Lin Jiang, "University Entrepreneurship: A Taxonomy of the Literature" (2007) 16:4 Indust & Corp Change 691; see also Maria Theresa Larsen, "The Implications of Academic Enterprise for Public Science: An Overview of the Empirical Evidence" (2011) 40:1 Research Policy 6.

5 See Industry Canada, *Mobilizing Science and Technology to Canada's Advantage: Progress Report 2009* (Ottawa: Public Works and Government Services Canada, 2009), online: www.ic.gc.ca/eic/site/ic1.nsf/eng/04715.html; Association of Universities and Colleges of Canada, *Partners in the Business of Innovation* (Ottawa: AUCC, 2011); and Canadian Institutes of Health Research, *CIHR's Commercialization and Innovation Strategy* (Ottawa: Public Works and Government Services Canada, November 2005), online: www.cihr-irsc.gc.ca/e/30162.html.

6 Nova Scotia, *Summary from the Report on the University System in Nova Scotia* (2010), online: www.gov.ns.ca/premier/publications/EducationReport-Summary.pdf.

7 Jennifer Washburn, *University, Inc.: The Corporate Corruption of American Higher Education* (New York: Basic Books, 2005); Risa L Lieberwitz, "Confronting the Privatization and Commercialization of Academic Research: An Analysis of Social Implications at the Local, National, and Global Levels" (2005) 12:1 Ind J Global Legal Stud 109; Sheldon Krimsky, *Science in the Private Interest: Has the Lure of Profits Corrupted Biomedical Research?* (Lanham: Rowman & Littlefield, 2003).

8 See, for example, Rothaermel et al, above note 4.

concern.[9] However, the purpose of this chapter is not to describe the variety of concerns and existing empirical evidence surrounding commercialization laws, policies, and practices. Rather, the purpose is to identify and to begin to characterize a set of concerns flowing from emerging academic scientists' encounters with commercialization laws, policies, and practices. In the United States, Canada, and elsewhere there is a dearth of empirical evidence focused specifically upon this group; this gap in the empirical literature poses a significant concern.

More specifically, in this chapter I argue that "emerging scientists," which I define to include Masters and PhD students, postdoctoral fellows (PDFs), and research associates, merit empirical investigation for three intertwined reasons. The first reason is evidentiary: emerging scientists are increasingly likely to be exposed to commercialization given systematic increases in patenting and other commercialization practices;[10] however, there is little empirical knowledge as to whether and to what extent commercialization practices influence the choices, commitments, and scientific contributions of emerging researchers, or how their participation in such practices, in turn, shapes the commercialization process. Gathering empirical evidence about these relationships is therefore critical. The second reason to focus on emerging scientists is generational. The increasing prevalence of commercialization activity means that which was once exceptional is becoming routine. It is important to ask what is lost if and when the cognitive dissonance previously associated with commercialization disappears. Finally, the third reason stems from the position of emerging researchers generally and women emerging scientists more specifically. Just as exposure to commercialization activities is systematically increasing, gaining a foothold in academia is becoming a more costly, time-consuming, and competitive process than ever before,[11] during which aspiring academic scientists endure an "extended period of limited intellectual autonomy."[12] In

9 David Blumenthal et al, "Withholding Research Results in Academic Life Science: Evidence From a National Survey of Faculty" (1997) 277:15 JAMA 1224; Eric G Campbell et al, "Data Withholding in Academic Genetics: Evidence From a National Survey" (2002) 287:4 JAMA 473; Darren E Zinner et al, "Participation Of Academic Scientists In Relationships With Industry" (2009) 28:6 Health Affairs 1814.

10 Downie & Herder, above note 3.

11 Paula Stephan & Jennifer Ma, "The Increased Frequency and Duration of the Postdoctorate Career Stage" (2005) 95:2 Am Econ Rev 71.

12 Francis Collins, "Scientists Need a Shorter Path to Research Freedom" (2010) 467 Nature 635.

this sense, emerging scientists are generally vulnerable, and it is necessary to gather evidence about how exposure to commercialization figures in this equation. Further, there is already empirical evidence showing that women scientists are marginalized from commercialization activities such as patenting and membership on company advisory boards.[13] Thus, for normative reasons, it is important to decipher whether and in what ways exposures to commercialization disrupt, inspire, or otherwise shape the careers, commitments, and choices of emerging scientists generally and, in particular, emerging scientists who are women.

The chapter proceeds in three parts. In Section B I describe contextual changes related to commercialization in the academic realm as well as a range of commercialization activities — some formal and others less so — that emerging scientists are increasingly apt to be exposed to as they pursue scientific careers. In the process I survey the existing empirical evidence about emerging scientists and their predecessors, the current elites and established of academic science. In Section C I identify two "exclusionary encounters" that emerging scientists are likely to have with commercialization laws, policies, and practices. These encounters pertain to 1) inventorship of patentable discoveries, and 2) intellectual property ownership. By way of brief conclusion in Section D I set out one hypothesis (motivated by the two exclusionary encounters described in Section C) for future empirical inquiry.

The subtext of this chapter is to motivate further empirical inquiry into commercialization at Canadian academic institutions for few empirical studies of commercialization have been carried out in Canada to date. In the meantime I draw heavily from studies performed elsewhere, especially the United States (US). My analysis moreover aspires to interdisciplinarity insofar as it is constructed from literatures beyond the law, including economics, management, and social studies of science and technology, and the research hypothesis set out in the final part calls for approaches and research techniques outside traditional legal scholarship.

---

13 Waverly W Ding, Fiona Murray, & Toby E Stuart, "An Empirical Study of Gender Differences in Patenting among Academic Life Scientists" (2006) 313 Science 665; Waverly W Ding, Fiona Murray, & Toby E Stuart, "From Bench to Board: Gender Differences in University Scientists' Participation in Commercial Science" *Harvard Business School* (2010), online: Harvard Business School http://hbswk.hbs.edu/item/6483.html; and Waverly Ding & Emily Choi, "Divergent Paths to Commercial Science: A Comparison of Scientists' Founding and Advising Activities" (2011) 40 Research Policy 69.

B. THE COMMERCIALIZATION OF ACADEMIC SCIENCE

1) Commercialization Infrastructure, Activity, and Governance

Since the 1970s there has been a marked growth in commercialization infrastructure and activity amongst academic institutions as well as government and institutional policies pertaining to commercialization.[14] In terms of infrastructure, the "technology transfer offices" (TTOs) now populating academia provide visible evidence of this larger trend. Located on or near university campuses, TTOs serve as "brokers on the boundary" between academic researchers and the private sector.[15] TTO personnel make regular visits to researcher labs, encouraging scientists to communicate interesting findings to their office, cautioning against wider disclosure in order to preserve patenting opportunities,[16] and drumming up university-industry partnering possibilities.[17] While select academic institutions such as Stanford University, the Massachusetts Institute of Technology (MIT), and the University of Wisconsin created TTOs in the early twentieth century, a grand total of twenty-seven TTOs existed in the US before 1980.[18] But between 1983 and 1999 well over a hundred offices were created in the US.[19] In Canada, the first three TTOs were established during the 1970s at McGill University, L'École polytechnique, and Cape Breton University. Eleven

---

14 Downie & Herder, above note 3; see also Janet Atkinson-Grosjean, *Public Science, Private Interests: Culture and Commerce in Canada's Networks of Centres of Excellence* (Toronto: University of Toronto Press, 2006).

15 See Donald Fisher & Janet Atkinson-Grosjean, "Brokers on the Boundary: Academic-Industry Liaison in Canadian Universities" (2002) 44 Higher Education 449.

16 This point in particular is stressed in *A Guide to Protecting Intellectual Property* prepared by the Canadian University Intellectual Property Group (CUIPG), which comprises the Directors of Intellectual Property/Industrial Licensing offices at the following Canadian universities: British Columbia, Alberta, Waterloo, Western, McMaster, Toronto, Queen's, Montreal, McGill, and Laval. See Dalhousie University, Innovation and Industry Liaison, *A Guide to Protecting Intellectual Property*, online: http://innovation.dal.ca/researchers/intellectualproperty.php.

17 The practices and challenges of TTOs are detailed in numerous studies. See, for example, Fisher & Atkinson-Grosjean, above note 15; see also Richard A Jensen, Jerry G Thursby, & Marie C Thursby, "Disclosure and Licensing of University Inventions: 'The Best We Can do With the S**t We Get to Work With'" (2003) 21:9 International Journal of Industrial Organization 1271.

18 Association of University Technology Managers, *AUTM U.S. Licensing Survey: FY 2005, Survey Summary* at 17, online: www.autm.net/FY_2005_Licensing_Survey/8930.htm.

19 *Ibid.*

"key" Canadian universities followed suit during the 1980s,[20] and surveys conducted during the 1990s and early 2000s showed a continuous rise in the number of TTOs, TTO personnel, and financial resources dedicated to commercialization.[21]

Today, essentially every major university engaged in scientific research in the US and Canada has some form of TTO, as do other institutions such as government laboratories, funding councils, private research institutions, and teaching hospitals. TTOs have, in turn, professionalized, forming umbrella organizations such as the Association of University Technology Managers (AUTM)[22] and the Alliance for Commercialization of Canadian Technologies (ACCT).[23] They have also formed networks[24] and feed into public policy debates.[25]

The growth of commercialization infrastructure over the last forty years coincides with increases in a range of commercialization activities.[26] These activities take many forms, but patent applications, patent grants, licensing agreements, research contracts with industry, and university spin-off companies are the most frequently tracked measures of commercialization.[27]

While the overall trends in the US and Canada are in the same direction, the level of commercialization observed at American academic institutions appears to significantly outpace that at their Canadian counterparts. For example, in fiscal year 2010 US-based respondents to the survey conducted by AUTM reported 12,281 total new patent applications whereas the

---

20 Fisher & Atkinson-Grosjean, above note 15.

21 For example, the number of new university-industry intellectual property licences and options executed by TTOs soared from 49 in 1991 to 544 in 2004. This increase (of 1,010.2 percent) is more than four times the increase in number of survey respondents, which rose from ten in 1991 to thirty-four in 2004. See Association of University Technology Managers, *AUTM Canadian Licensing Survey: FY 2004, Survey Summary*, online: www.autm.net/FY_2004_Licensing_Survey/10193.htm; see also Downie & Herder, above note 3, for a discussion of these trends.

22 Association of University Technology Managers, online: www.autm.net/Home.htm.

23 Alliance for Commercialization of Canadian Technologies, online: www.acctcanada.ca/.

24 See, for example, Springboard Atlantic, online: www.springboardatlantic.ca/.

25 See Industry Canada, Advisory Council on Science & Technology, *Public Investments in University Research: Reaping the Benefits* (Ottawa: Industry Canada 1999).

26 David C Mowery et al, "The Growth of Patenting and Licensing by U.S. Universities: An Assessment of the Effects of the Bayh-Dole Act of 1980" (2001) 30:1 Research Policy 99; Downie & Herder, above note 3; and Matthew Herder, *The Rhetoric of Innovation* (LL.M Thesis, Dalhousie University, 2006).

27 *Ibid*.

corresponding figure for Canadian respondents was 928.[28] After accounting for differences in response rate (183 versus 40 in the US and Canada, respectively), US institutions file, on average, four times as many new patent applications per year as Canadian institutions (100:25 new patent applications per institution). However, relative to the amount of money allocated to academic research by federal governments in the US and Canada, these commercialization data points become more comparable. Again, using the most recent AUTM surveys as an example, per $100,000 in federal research expenditures, Canadian institutions file slightly more new patent applications (0.034) compared to those in the US (0.031).[29] In other words, in proportion to the respective public tax dollar investments in academic science, US and Canadian research centres currently appear to engage in roughly equal amounts of commercialization activity such as patenting.

Despite substantially increasing in recent years, commercialization activities may still seem like relatively exceptional events, yet the foregoing measures of commercialization are under-inclusive.[30] To begin, certain commercialization activities are simply not tracked in surveys conducted by AUTM and others.[31] For example, there is no readily available data surrounding agreements signed by students and PDFs to "pre-assign" any intellectual property to their host institutions, "confidentiality agreements" signed by members of research teams, or participation by academic scientists on company advisory boards. There are also a variety of less formal moments in between discrete commercialization events, such as filing a patent application, that are designed to steer researchers toward commercialization. The Internet is littered with "brown bag" lunch sessions put on by universities on the topic of commercialization, ostensibly to "educate" researchers about the importance of vetting a presentation with the university's TTO before attending an academic conference. Otherwise, if the presentation happens to include any new research findings, the researcher

28 Association of University Technology Managers, *U.S. Licensing Activity Survey Highlights: FY2010*, online: www.autm.net/FY_2010_Licensing_Survey/7008.htm.

29 *Ibid*.

30 Aldo Geuna & Alessandro Muscio, "The Governance of University Knowledge Transfer: A Critical Review of the Literature" (2009) 47:1 Minerva 93.

31 Matthew Herder & Josephine Johnston, "Access Concerns and Business Models in Public-Sector Technology Transfer of Genetic Inventions" in E Richard Gold & Bartha M Knoppers, eds, *Biotechnology IP & Ethics* (Markham: LexisNexis Canada, 2009).

risks running afoul of patent law's requirements of "novelty" and "non-obviousness."[32]

Finally, in addition to increases in commercialization infrastructure and activity (both formal and informal), there has been a proliferation of policy instruments tied to commercialization. This is perhaps especially true in Canada where, in distinction from the US, there is no legislation that establishes a uniform set of rules around intellectual property ownership and other commercialization issues for federally funded research.[33] Instead, using an array of policy instruments introduced by the federal government beginning as early as the 1960s and accelerating during the 1980s and 1990s, it can be argued that Canada has embraced patenting as a "policy tool" and technology transfer more generally to an even greater extent than the US.[34] From tax incentives, industry matched funding requirements, to "science to business" programs for budding scientists, the message from governments and funding agencies in Canada and the US is unequivocal: commercializing academic science is expected.[35] Setting out, in concrete terms, commercialization goals, plans, and milestones is in many cases now essential to securing research funding from public sources. Accordingly, research institutions have gradually implemented a slew of policies, which taken together, govern commercialization. These include invention disclosure policies, revenue sharing policies, joint venture policies, intellectual property ownership policies, conflicts of interest policies, and data and materials sharing policies.

The challenge is to discern what impact, if any, these governance mechanisms regarding diverse exposures to, and forces in favour of, commercialization have upon academic science. In the next section, I describe the empirical commercialization literature to date with a narrowing focus on emerging academic scientists.

---

32 See CUIPG, above note 16.

33 Some have recommended that legislation similar to that which is in place in the US be enacted in Canada; however, see Industry Canada, above note 25.

34 Donald Fisher, Janet Atkinson-Grosjean, & Dawn House, "Changes in Academy/Industry/State Relations in Canada: The Creation and Development of the Networks of Centres of Excellence" (2001) 39:3 Minerva 299; and E Richard Gold et al, "The Unexamined Assumptions of Intellectual Property: Adopting an Evaluative Approach to Patenting Biotechnological Innovation" (2004) 18 Pub Affairs Quarterly 299.

35 Downie & Herder, above note 3; Creso M Sa & Jeffrey Litwin, "University-Industry Research Collaborations in Canada: The Role of Federal Policy Instruments" (2011) 38:6 Sci Public Policy 425.

2) Commercialization's Untold Intergenerational Impact?

The empirical literature surrounding the commercialization of academic science has several limitations. First, the literature is still maturing. A recent meta-analysis of the literature suggests the field lacks organization and methodological rigour.[36] Some settings, including Canadian academic institutions, have moreover been the subject of limited study to date.[37] Second, although varying in methodology and object of inquiry, an economic lens dominates empirical studies of commercialization. A robust conceptual framework, capable of assessing the normative implications of conflicting findings is lacking. Consider two investigations into the effects of patenting upon academic science. The first, a survey study, found one in nine researchers abandoned one research project every two years due to concerns about patents.[38] The second, a citation-based analysis, showed that "genetic researchers forego about one in ten research projects . . . through the causal negative impact of a gene patent grant."[39] The two findings are similar but whereas the authors of the survey study inferred that concerns related to academic patenting may be overstated, the authors of the citation analysis used their findings to support the claim that patents inhibited knowledge flows. Finally, there is a significant bias toward studying the formal instruments of commercialization such as patents, presum-

---

36 Rothaermel et al, above note 4 at 699–703.

37 In the period since Downie & Herder, above note 3, was published (when we drew attention to the lack of empirical evidence regarding commercialization in Canada), only ten or so empirical studies have been completed. See, for example, Herder & Johnston, above note 31; Tania M Bubela & Timothy Caulfield, "Role and Reality: Technology Transfer at Canadian Universities" (2010) 28:9 Trends in Biotechnology 447; Fiona A Miller, Carrie B Sanders, & Pascale Lehoux, "Imagining Value, Imagining Users: Academic Technology Transfer for Health Innovation" (2009) 68:8 Social Science & Medicine 1481; CJ Murdoch & Timothy Caulfield, "Commercialization, Patenting and Genomics: Researcher Perspectives" (2009) 1:2 Genome Med 22; Kate Hoye & Fred Pries, "'Repeat Commercializers,' the 'Habitual Entrepreneurs' of University-Industry Technology Transfer" (2009) 29:10 Technovation 682; Kate A Hoye, *University Intellectual Property Policies and University-Industry Technology Transfer in Canada* (PhD Thesis, University of Waterloo, 2006); and E Richard Gold & Julia Carbone, "Myriad Genetics: In the Eye of the Policy Storm" (2010) 12:4 Suppl Genetics in Medicine S39.

38 John P Walsh, Wesley M Cohen, & Charlene Cho, "Where Excludability Matters: Material Versus Intellectual Property in Academic Biomedical Research" (2007) 36 Research Policy 1184.

39 Kenneth G Huang & Fiona E Murray, "Does Patent Strategy Shape the Long-Run Supply of Public Knowledge? Evidence from Human Genetics" (2009) 52:6 Acad Mgmt J 1193 at 1214.

ably because of the relative ease of measurement and, again, the economic orientation of those contributing to the literature. However, unpacking the effects of commercialization requires far greater attention to the "shifting reward structures, changing funding imperatives and normative pressures emerging among scientists themselves."[40] There is a need for greater qualitative study of commercialization laws, policies, and practices.

Despite these limitations, the empirical literature of academic commercialization contains a number of themes that are salient here. To begin, most knowledge exchange between academic institutions and the private sector happens separate from formalized intellectual property transactions. Acquiring information through more traditional means — whether by buying it off the shelf, reading publications, attending conference proceedings, or hiring graduate students — remains the dominant mode of public/private sector knowledge exchange.[41] Historically, this is not surprising given that attitudes toward commercialization have been mixed amongst faculty.[42] But even for the academic scientists on board with that agenda or working in the life sciences where industry relationships are more the norm,[43] the bulk of their forays into that world are nevertheless likely to occur "outside" of negotiations over intellectual property rights.[44] This underscores the importance of paying attention to less formal exposures to commercialization (e.g., brown bag lunch sessions) as discussed above.

Secondly, individuals and the relationships they form appear central to the commercialization process. "Star" academic scientists (and the networks they occupy) have been shown, in hindsight, to substantially explain patterns of technology diffusion and economic growth in a region.[45] Scien-

40 Steven Peter Vallas & Daniel Lee Kleinman, "Contradiction, Convergence and the Knowledge Economy: The Confluence of Academic and Commercial Biotechnology" (2008) 6:2 Socio-Econ Rev 283 at 291.

41 W Cohen et al, "Industry and the Academy: Uneasy Partners in the Cause of Technological Advance" in Roger Noll, ed, *Challenges to the Research University* (Washington DC: Brookings Institution, 1998); Ajay Agrawal & Rebecca Henderson, "Putting Patents in Context: Exploring Knowledge Transfer from MIT" (2002) 48:1 Management Science 44.

42 Henry Etzkowitz, "The Norms of Entrepreneurial Science: Cognitive Effects of the New University-Industry Linkages" (1998) 27:8 Research Policy 823 at 830.

43 Darren E Zinner et al, "Participation of Academic Scientists in Relationships with Industry" (2009) 28:6 Health Affairs 1814.

44 Riccardo Fini, Nicola Lacetera, & Scott Shane, "Inside or Outside the IP System? Business Creation in Academia" (2010) 39:8 Research Policy 1060.

45 Lynne G Zucker & Michael R Darby, "Star Scientists and Institutional Transformation: Patterns of Invention and Innovation in the Formation of the Biotechnology Industry" (1996) 93:23 Proc Natl Acad Sci 12709; Lynne G Zucker, Michael R Darby, & Marilynn B

tists are most likely to identify industry receptors for a given technology, not TTOs,[46] and, without their continued participation, efforts by a university to generate revenues tend to falter.[47] In short, much of academic scientists' value to private sector players — in terms of their tacit knowledge, their prestige, and their networks of potential collaborators — escapes codification. Therefore keeping them engaged, potentially at the expense of their other obligations like teaching, mentoring, and grant writing, not to mention actual research,[48] is key from a commercialization point of view.

Finally, while maintaining an academic scientist's commitment as commercialization haphazardly unfolds is critical, the influence of the institutional and social contexts in which any academic researcher is embedded cannot be discounted. Context can shape an individual's openness to commercialization in the first place. If a researcher was educated at Stanford University, an early mover toward norms of academic entrepreneurialism, she or he is more likely to engage in commercialization.[49] Changes in institutional setting may also undo that very sort of imprinting: academic scientists have been shown to alter their patenting behaviour if it conflicts with the norms of a new institutional home.[50] Further, shaping can occur not just at the institutional level, but also interpersonally. If a postdoctoral fellow's supervisor engages in patenting (or not), then she or he is likely to do so (or not do so) later on.[51]

Brewer, "Intellectual Human Capital and the Birth of U.S. Biotechnology Enterprises" (1998) 88:1 Am Econ Rev 290.

46 Vivek Ramakrishnan, Jiwen Chen, & Krishna Balakrishnan, "Effective Strategies for Marketing Biomedical Inventions: Lessons Learnt from NIH Licence Leads" (2005) 5:4 Journal of Medical Marketing 342; Jerry G Thursby, Richard Jensen, & Marie C Thursby, "Objectives, Characteristics and Outcomes of University Licensing: A Survey of Major U.S. Universities" (2001) 26:1 J Tech Transfer 59; Christina Jansen & Harrison F Dillon, "Where Do the Leads for Licences Come From?: Source Data from Six US Institutions" (2000) 14:3 Industry and Higher Education 150.

47 Ajay Agrawal, "Engaging the Inventor: Exploring Licensing Strategies for University Inventions and the Role of Latent Knowledge" (2006) 27:1 Strategic Management Journal 63; Richard Jensen & Marie Thursby, "Proofs and Prototypes for Sale: The Licensing of University Inventions" (2001) 91:1 Am Econ Rev 240.

48 Fini et al, above note 44: the authors document some of these trade-offs.

49 Janet Bercovitz & Maryann Feldman, "Academic Entrepreneurs: Organizational Change at the Individual Level" (2008) 19:1 Org Sci 69 at 81.

50 *Ibid* at 86.

51 Pierre Azoulay, Christopher Liu, & Toby Stuart, "Social Influence Given (Partially) Deliberate Matching: Career Imprints in the Creation of Academic Entrepreneurs" (2009) 09-136 Harvard Bus Sch Entrepreneurial Mgmt, Working Paper, online: Social Science Research Network http://papers.ssrn.com/sol3/papers.cfm?abstract_id=1410816.

Therein lies part of the impetus for my claim that emerging academic scientists, as a group, merit more empirical attention. While there is a sizeable literature about members of the established academic research community that describes the factors that influence their attitudes about,[52] or willingness to participate in, commercialization,[53] how frequently they do so, and what that engagement tends to entail or result in,[54] comparatively little is known about emerging scientists' experiences of commercialization. Yet, compared to their predecessors, emerging scientists will encounter commercialization far more frequently given the systematic rise in commercialization infrastructure, activity, and governance. It is safe to assume that fewer of today's supervisors were exposed to patenting when they began their academic careers.

The current commonality of commercialization also supports the focus on emerging academic scientists. Once, commercialization was the province of the scientific elite. Although different variables, including gender, research productivity, social networks, and employer influence continue to predict involvement in discrete commercialization activities such as advising versus founding a private firm,[55] participation in commercialization is on the whole now democratized.[56] It is not only the emerging scientists who attend Stanford or MIT who will encounter commercialization. More than that, though, commercialization is also being normalized. There is evidence of established academic scientists foisting commercialization-related tasks such as meeting with TTO representatives upon junior members of their laboratories, not just to avoid the work, but rather to safeguard their more traditional academic selves.[57] Perhaps this strategy mitigates the cognitive dissonance experienced by established academics when participating, dis-

---

52 Pierre Azoulay, Waverly Ding, & Toby Stuart, "The Determinants of Faculty Patenting Behavior: Demographics or Opportunities?" (2007) 63:4 J Econ Beh'r & Org 599 at 603; Etzkowitz, above note 42.

53 Toby E Stuart & Waverly Ding, "When Do Scientists Become Entrepreneurs? The Social Structural Antecedents of Commercial Activity in the Academic Life Sciences" (2006) 112:1 Am J Soc 97.

54 Jensen & Thursby, above note 47; Jason Owen-Smith & Walter W Powell, "To Patent or Not: Faculty Decisions and Institutional Success at Technology Transfer" (2001) 26:1-2 J Tech Transfer 99 at 113.

55 Ding & Choi, above note 13.

56 Stuart & Ding, above note 53 at 124.

57 Sanjay Jain, Gerard George, & Mark Maltarich, "Academics or Entrepreneurs? Investigating Role Identity Modification of University Scientists Involved in Commercialization Activity" (2009) 38:6 Research Policy 922 at 923.

tantly, in the commercialization process. But there is a need to assess how it informs the choices, commitments, and scientific contributions of the emerging scientists left to do the commercialization legwork.

Last, there are normative reasons to examine the situation of emerging scientists vis-à-vis commercialization. Doctoral students, PDF students, and research associates are vulnerable in various ways. The demands of pursuing a career in academic science today are extreme. Due to the sheer volume of knowledge in any given field of inquiry, original insights tend to require many more years of research than in the past.[58] Earning a PhD is necessary for legitimacy and can mean taking on a significant amount of financial debt. The more costly hardship, though, may be that few PhD graduates land a tenure-track position right away.[59] They instead face one, if not two, or three, meagrely paid "postdocs" before they can legitimately entertain going on the academic job market.[60] In the US and elsewhere, there is presently an oversupply of PhD graduates and PDFs.[61] Thus, many highly educated researchers will not secure posts in academic science. Conceivably, commercialization may open up new employment opportunities outside the confines of academe.

Training and job security challenges aside, it is unclear how gratifying the PDF experience usually proves to be. According to one survey, control over the various aspects of a research project is, more often than not, in the hands of the PDF's supervisor or shared between the two.[62] In part, this is the nature of the beast: research increasingly favours teams of scientists over the individual,[63] and junior scientists often are not yet in command of a team. But it is also a function of status and hierarchy dynamics in the lab environment. In some unknown proportion of cases, scientists will come to regard their time as postdocs as transformative learning experiences or, at the very least, as effective bridges to an academic appointment. For the

---

58 Benjamin F Jones, "The Burden of Knowledge and the 'Death of the Renaissance Man': Is Innovation Getting Harder?" (2009) 76:1 Review of Economic Studies 283.

59 Statistics Canada, *Graduates of doctoral programs — who are they and what are their post-degree plans?* (2005), online: www.statcan.gc.ca/pub/81-004-x/2005003/8611-eng.htm.

60 Stephan & Ma, above note 11.

61 David Cyranoski et al, "The PhD Factory" (2011) 472:7343 Nature 276; Mark C Taylor, "Reform the PhD System or Close it Down" (2011) 472:7343 Nature 261.

62 Geoff Davis, "Doctors Without Orders" (2005) 93:3 American Scientist (supplement) online: Sigma XI http://postdoc.sigmaxi.org/results/.

63 Stefan Wuchty, Benjamin F Jones, & Brian Uzzi, "The Increasing Dominance of Teams in Production of Knowledge" (2007) 316:5827 Science 1036.

remainder, the postdoc experience may be remembered as a time when they worked on research problems in which they had only a small personal stake or felt powerless to redefine. Whether and how various exposures to commercialization alter this equation is an open question with normative implications. Perhaps exposure to commercialization and, more specifically, introductions to members of the private sector, will be perceived as a way out of the confusion that an extended time at higher education institutions presently affords.[64] Does commercialization offer emerging scientists opportunities to exercise entrepreneurial autonomy?

Commercialization may also represent a new site of gender- and/or race-based inequality. Although the numbers of women participating in academic science are finally increasing,[65] deep-seated inequalities in academic science remain.[66] Commercialization may be an important contributor to these larger inequalities. Women academic scientists are presently far less likely than their male peers to become patent-holders, be named to private company advisory boards, or found a company of their own.[67] Will commercialization exacerbate or extend the gender gap in academic science for emerging scientists?

In sum, the lack of empirical evidence surrounding emerging academic scientists' commercialization-related experiences, the increasingly prevalent, democratic, and routine nature of those experiences, and the normative implications of commercialization, should motivate further empirical inquiry. In the second part of this chapter, I identify two issues within commercialization law, policy, and practice that are worthy of empirical study.

---

64 Research has shown that PhD students and PDFs view employment in industry versus academia as fundamentally different. Michael Roach & Henry Sauermann, "A Taste for Science? PhD Scientists' Academic Orientation and Self-Selection into Research Careers in Industry" (2010) 39:3 Research Policy 422. As commercialization blurs the boundary between these two employment contexts, there is a need to determine if emerging researchers' assessment of these two career paths has shifted; the extent to which it creates new opportunities or tensions within the laboratory environment; or, more fundamentally still, alters emerging health researchers' understanding of what research projects, collaborations, and interactions are more or less worthwhile.

65 Statistics Canada, *Women in Science and Engineering* (2006), online: www41.statcan.ca/2006/0193/ceb0193_003-eng.htm.

66 Corinne A Moss-Racusin et al, "Science Faculty's Subtle Gender Biases Favor Male Students" *Proceedings of the National Academy of Sciences* (2012), online: Proceedings of the National Academy of Sciences www.pnas.org/content/early/2012/09/14/1211286109.

67 Ding, Murray, & Stuart, above note 13; Ding & Choi, above note 13.

C. EXCLUSIONARY ENCOUNTERS WITH COMMERCIALIZATION

Although emerging academic researchers are increasingly apt to encounter commercialization laws, policies, and practices, I argue below that those encounters are likely to be experienced as moments of exclusion. Relative to more established academics, commercialization laws, policies, and practices are apt to deny emerging researchers' 1) contributions to patented inventions, and 2) ownership interests in intellectual property more generally. I explore each in turn, guided by US and Canadian laws and policies given that they are most likely to govern commercialization efforts emanating from Canadian academic institutions.

1) Patent Inventorship

US and Canadian laws do not pretend that corporations can invent. When a patent application is filed, the human person(s) responsible for the claimed invention must be named.[68] Patent law accommodates multiple inventors, but the standard for "inventorship" and the consequences of misinforming the patent office as to the identity of the inventor(s) are similarly high in the US and Canada. Only those who conceive or contribute to the conception of the invention are proper inventors. Those who engage in verification, perhaps crucial to establishing an invention's utility, are not inventors if they do not contribute to the "inventive concept."[69] Misleading the patent office as to the identity of the inventor(s) can result in the patent being declared invalid. Thus, whether filing in the US or Canada, there is a strong incentive to adhere to the legal standard.

TTOs are often at pains to explain this to academic researchers, yet a disconnect between the legal standard of inventorship and the social practice of science remains. This disconnect derives from the fact that credit for work in the laboratory is allocated not simply based on who did what, but also each researcher's social standing. Empirical research has thus shown that social factors like occupying a position of seniority within a lab or

68 37 CFR § 1.41(a) (2005); 35 USC § 111 (2005).

69 *Apotex v Wellcome Foundation Ltd*, 2002 SCC 77; *Weatherford Canada Ltd v Corlac Inc*, 2011 FCA 228.

enjoying an important reputation within a scientific field influence authorship on scientific publications and, to a lesser extent, patent inventorship.[70]

We can observe the disconnect between the legal standard of inventorship and the social practice of academic science in at least a couple of ways. The first is through "patent-paper pairs," in which the same core knowledge is disclosed in both a patent application and peer-reviewed publication.[71] Several quantitative studies have shown that the listed authors and inventors in a patent-paper pair are unlikely to match, with the former significantly outnumbering the latter.[72] Secondly, litigation reveals how this legal-social disconnect disproportionately affects emerging scientists. Where inventorship over an academic invention is at issue, the absence of graduate students, PDFs, and research associates named as inventors on a patent often animates the dispute.[73]

From an emerging scientist perspective, the outcomes of this litigation have been mixed. The first in this line of cases, *In re Katz*,[74] involved a Harvard University medical school professor whose patent application was rejected, in part, because of an article he had previously published with two graduate student co-authors. The Court of Customs and Patent Appeals overturned the rejection, concluding that "authorship of an article by itself does not raise a presumption of inventorship."[75] Therefore, an affidavit from the students disclaiming inventorship was not necessary; rather, the

---

70 Carolin Häussler & Henry Sauermann, "Credit Where Credit is Due? The Impact of Project Contributions and Social Factors on Authorship and Inventorship" (2012) 42:3 Research Policy 688, online: Social Science Research Network http://ssrn.com/paper=1750240.

71 Fiona Murray, "Innovation as Co-Evolution of Scientific and Technological Networks: Exploring Tissue Engineering" (2002) 31:8–9 Research Policy 1389 at 1392, citing Philippe Ducor, "Intellectual Property: Co-Authorship and -Inventorship" (2000) 289 Science 873.

72 *Ibid*; Francesco Lissoni & Fabio Montobbio, "Inventorship and Authorship in Patent-Publication Pairs: an Enquiry into the Economics of Scientific Credit" (2008) 224 KITeS, online: http://econpapers.repec.org/paper/cricespri/wp224.htm; Martin Meyer & Sujit Bhattacharya, "Commonalities and Differences between Scholarly and Technical Collaboration: An Exploration of Co-Invention and Co-Authorship Analyses" (2004) 61:3 Scientometrics 443.

73 For a review of the jurisprudence prior to 2006, see Sean B Seymore, "My Patent, Your Patent, or Our Patent? Inventorship Disputes Within Academic Research Groups" (2006) 16 Alb LJ Sci & Tech 125; see also *Falana v Kent State University*, 669 F 3d 1349 (Fed Cir 2012); although the focus here is on inventorship, emerging scientists seem prone to not being named as an author as well: see *Johnson v Schmitz*, 119 F Supp 2d 90 (2000); Rochelle Cooper Dreyfuss, "Collaborative Research: Conflicts on Authorship, Ownership, and Accountability" (2000) 53 Vand L Rev 1162 at 1207.

74 687 F 2d 480 (CCPA 1982).

75 *Ibid* at 455.

very fact that they were "working under the direction and supervision"[76] of the professor worked against any inference of joint inventorship.

Chou v University of Chicago[77] was, in contrast to *Katz*, a relative victory for emerging scientists. Chou worked a total of fourteen years for a professor of molecular genetics, first as a graduate student and then as a PDF. The professor, Dr. Roizman, enforced a policy of confidentiality; no laboratory work could be publicly disclosed without his say so, yet he assured Dr. Chou that she would be "fairly treated for the research which she conducted."[78] And, for some time, Chou and Roizman worked collaboratively, generating a number of research articles and patent applications in which they were named as joint inventors. On one occasion, however, without Chou's knowledge, Roizman filed a patent application based upon a series of research papers that listed Chou as the lead author. Roizman also founded a company to exploit the patented technology. Roizman later forced Chou to resign her position, and she sued in return, naming the university, Roizman, and his company as defendants. Overturning a lower court decision, the Federal Circuit ultimately held that one need not own an invention to meet the requirements of standing when inventorship is at issue, and legitimized a variety of tort claims against professors and universities, including fraudulent concealment, breach of contract, and breach of fiduciary duty.

Subsequent decisions in the US emphasize the fact-specific nature of academic inventorship disputes.[79] Relative to universities and established academics, though, emerging scientists are less well positioned to marshal facts and law to their advantage. Presumably, this partially explains why there are no reported decisions involving an academic scientist where inventorship was at issue in Canada.[80] However, there are also obvious risks to an emerging scientist's career in bringing such a suit such as destroying

---

76 *Ibid* at 456.

77 254 F 3d 1347 (Fed Cir 2001).

78 See Seymore, above note 73 at 145, n 142.

79 In *University of West Virginia v VanVoorhies*, 278 F 3d 1288 (Fed Cir 2002), the emerging scientist was, unlike Dr. Chou, knowledgeable of patent law (Dr. VanVoorhies was, in fact, a registered patent agent) and intimately involved in patent-related decision making. His claims against West Virginia University and a professor for, *inter alia*, breach of fiduciary duty thus failed.

80 There have, however, been other cases in Canada where ownership — as opposed to inventorship — and decision making regarding the commercialization of an invention were at issue. See *O'Brien v University of Guelph*, [1996] OJ No 4026; *Balanyk v University of Toronto*, [1999] OJ No 2162; *Corporation de l'École polytechnique de Montréal v Fardad*, 2010 QCCA 992, [2010] QJ No 4729.

the very relationships upon which her or his future career depends. All of the US cases to date involved emerging scientists who had moved on from the supervisors and institutions that allegedly denied them inventorship.

If litigation is rare to non-existent, then, the more important empirical question is how do emerging researchers negotiate these exclusionary encounters, and what impact (if any) do they have upon their everyday experiences, laboratory interactions, and commitments. Before hypothesizing along these lines in Section D of this chapter, consider first one more type of exclusionary encounter.

2) Intellectual Property Ownership

Even if an emerging scientist is included as an inventor, she or he is unlikely to be an owner of the resulting patent or other intellectual property compared to an academic faculty member.[81] Originally, the common law principle was that employees, which captures established and emerging scientists alike, own any inventions made during the course of employment unless they were employed specifically for that purpose.[82] Until recently, US institutions believed that this general rule no longer applied in the context of federally funded research. However, in 2011 the US Supreme Court restored the common law principle, ruling that ownership vests in the inventor(s) absent an agreement otherwise, to be construed as a matter of state law.[83] In Canada, federal legislation is silent with respect to employee inventors, and the common law has fluctuated, favouring employers and employees at different times in different provinces.[84] The main point here remains that emerging scientists appear more likely to be divested of ownership than their more senior colleagues.

---

81 This disassociation between the creator (or inventor) and owner of intellectual property is premised on a centuries old US court decision. See Catherine L Fisk, *Working Knowledge: Employee Innovation and the Rise of Corporate Intellectual Property, 1800–1930* (Chapel Hill: University of North Carolina Press, 2009) at 33, citing *Pennock v Dialogue*, 27 US 1 (1829).

82 *Bloxam v Elsee* (1825), 1 Car & P 558; *United States v Dubilier Condenser Corp*, 289 US 178 (1933); *Comstock Canada v Electec Ltd*, [1991] FCJ No 987.

83 *Board of Trustees of the Leland Stanford Junior University v Roche Molecular Systems Inc*, 131 S Ct 2188 (2011).

84 David Vaver, *Intellectual Property Law: Copyright, Patents, Trade-Marks*, 2d ed (Toronto: Irwin Law, 2011) at 366.

This sort of exclusionary encounter can occur in two principal ways, either by operation of an express agreement such as a university's intellectual property policy or, depending on the circumstances surrounding employment, it can be implied.

Beginning with university policy, in Canada there exists a range of approaches to intellectual property ownership amongst academic institutions.[85] Of the twenty-three universities ranked in the top twenty-five in terms of research funding[86] with intellectual property policies accessible online, the default rule is either the inventor(s) (thirteen) or the institution (seven) owns, with three exceptions of joint ownership. However, at eight of those twenty-three institutions, the ownership interests of emerging scientists are not accounted for or are second class to those of faculty. In the former case, intellectual property ownership is determined by the faculty collective agreement, which does not extend to emerging scientists. In the remaining four institutions, emerging scientists' ownership interests are explicitly differentiated, in one way or another, from those of faculty. The University of Toronto collapses inventorship into ownership: if an emerging scientist arrived at the invention after being directed by a faculty member "specifically with the object of making such an invention," then she or he is not the owner of that invention.[87] The other two institutions take a more blunt approach: whether under the specific direction of a supervisor or not, if any kind of employment relationship between the emerging scientist and the university exists (University of New Brunswick)[88] the emerging scientist has no ownership interest in any resulting patents or, it appears, must "pre-assign" the same to the university (University of Saskatchewan).[89]

---

85 Statistics Canada, *Survey of Intellectual Property Commercialization in the Higher Education Sector* (2010), online: www.statcan.gc.ca/cgi-bin/imdb/p2SV.pl?Function=getSurvey&SDDS=4222&lang=en&db=imdb&adm=8&dis=2.

86 This list of universities is derived from Re$earch Infosource Inc, *Canada's Top 50 Research Universities 2009*, online: www.researchinfosource.com/media/2009Top50List.pdf.

87 University of Toronto, *Inventions Policy* (2007) s 3.3(a), online: www.governingcouncil.utoronto.ca/policies/invent.htm.

88 University of New Brunswick, Office of Research Services, *Guidelines on Intellectual Property Interests for Students Involved in Research at the University of New Brunswick* (7 September 2006), online: www.unb.ca/research/ors/indgovtserv/iptt/guidelines.php.

89 It is unclear whether the University of Saskatchewan requires PDFs to pre-assign any and all inventions to the university. However, a memorandum of understanding with language to that effect is provided as a template on the university's website. See University of Saskatchewan, "APPENDIX IV Memorandum of Agreement — Intellectual Property," online: www.usask.ca/hrd/investigators/appendixes_and_samples.php.

There is no robust data about the prevalence of "pre-assignment" contracts in Canada or the US, but they are reported to be a common component of the PDF hiring process.[90] Thus, even where a university policy suggests otherwise or is silent on the issue, pre-assignment contracts can divest emerging scientists of their ownership interests in any intellectual property that results from their work.

Emerging scientists can also lose ownership by implication by virtue of the "employed to invent" common law exception to employee ownership. This exception has not yet been applied in the context of academic science in Canada,[91] and one notable commentator has suggested that academics are amongst the least likely to fit within this exception given that they are "usually hired to teach and research, not invent and patent."[92] However, others have noted that emerging scientists may be in a different position, "especially where the work in question is clearly directed towards commercial purposes or objectives, as opposed to 'pure' research."[93] The increasing policy emphasis placed upon commercialization highlighted in Section B above thus suggests that emerging scientists are today more apt to be seen as employees hired to invent than their supervisors, especially if they do not have other obligations of the more traditional academic such as teaching.

As with exclusions from patent inventorship, the frequency of emerging scientists' exclusions from intellectual property ownership, by operation of an express or implied arrangement is not presently known. In the final part of this chapter I briefly hypothesize one potential effect that such experiences — however (in)frequent — might have.

D. CONCLUSION: FUTURE RESEARCH QUESTIONS

Emerging scientists' exclusionary encounters with commercialization can ground many hypotheses. I offer one by way of conclusion: that emerging scientists who experience exclusion in some form, paradoxically, learn to prize that which they have been previously denied, i.e., participation in commercialization. This hypothesis derives from previous research in be-

---

90 Seymore, above note 73 at 137, citing Dreyfuss, above note 73.

91 It has, however, been applied to US-based academic scientists in a couple of cases. See *Speck v Northern Carolina Dairy Foundation Inc*, 319 SE 2d 139 (1984) and *Madey v Duke University*, 307 F 3d 1351 (2002).

92 Vaver, above note 84 at 368.

93 Kevin LaRoche, Christine Collard, & Jacqueline Chernys, "Appropriating Innovation: The Enforceability of University Intellectual Property Policies" (2007) 20:2 IPJ 135 at 261.

havioural economics and cognitive psychology, which sheds some light on how individuals value what they own and what they create. Specifically, individuals tend to overvalue that which they already own (an "endowment effect"); and, the process of creating something, rather than simply owning it, heightens that tendency to overvalue (dubbed a "creativity effect").[94] Thus, conceivably, emerging scientists who experience exclusion will prize status as an inventor, or intellectually property ownership, more than someone else who is not similarly excluded from those experiences (a "prizing effect").

The challenge going forward is, of course, to develop an empirical research design capable of probing for this and other possible effects associated with emerging scientists' exclusionary encounters with commercialization. The purpose of this chapter was to argue that the intersection of emerging academic scientists and commercialization laws, policies, and practices provides a rich and important locus of inquiry that has been under-studied and under-theorized to date.

94 Christopher J Buccafusco & Christopher J Sprigman, "The Creativity Effect" (2011) 78:1 U Chicago L Rev 31.

TWENTY-THREE

Copyright's Media Theory and the Internet: The Case of the Chilling Effects Doctrine

JONATHON W PENNEY

ABSTRACT (EN): Despite copyright's expansion into new online spheres and technological contexts, and the increasingly interdisciplinary nature of copyright scholarship, intellectual property scholars, particularly those interested in digital copyright, have offered little exploration of methodology and methodological issues, and scholarship offers even fewer methodological investigations and debates. This area of Internet-related legal research remains, like others, without established "texts, theories, and methodologies." This chapter aims to help fill some of that void, by offering an exploration of the problems that can arise when applying certain legal doctrines to online contexts, through a case study of the "chilling effects doctrine" — a legal doctrine that holds that certain laws and regulatory schemes can "chill" or deter people from engaging in certain kinds of legal (and possibly desirable) activities — and its emergence or "transplantation" into debates about copyright enforcement online. The case study provides a helpful point of entry into a broader methodological discussion about applying legal norms to media. Specifically, the author draws on insights from other disciplines and research fields to unpack and scrutinize the chilling effects doctrine and it methodological, empirical, and normative assumptions.

RÉSUMÉ (FR): Malgré l'expansion du droit d'auteur dans les nouvelles sphères de l'Internet et de la technologie, et de la nature interdisciplinaire de la recherche en droit d'auteur, les spécialistes du droit de la propriété intellectuelle, particulièrement ceux intéressés par le droit d'auteur numérique, n'ont que peu exploré la question de la méthodologie et des problèmes méthodologiques, et les publications savantes révèlent encore moins d'études et de débats méthodologiques. Ce domaine de la recherche juridique reliée à l'Internet, comme d'autres, demeure toujours sans « textes, théories et méthodologies » établies. Ce chapitre essaie de combler partiellement ce vide, en explorant les problèmes qui peuvent survenir lorsqu'on applique certaines doctrines juridiques au contexte de l'Internet, à l'aide d'une étude de cas de la « théorie de l'effet paralysant » — une théorie juridique qui explique que certains régimes législatifs et réglementaires peuvent « paralyser » les gens ou les décourager de prendre part à certaines activités légales (qui pourraient être désirables) — en tant que phénomène émergent ou « transplanté » dans les débats relatifs à la mise en application du droit d'auteur en ligne. Cette étude de cas apporte un point de départ utile à une discussion méthodologique plus large sur l'application des normes légales aux médias. Plus particulièrement, l'auteur tire des enseignements d'autres disciplines et champs de recherche pour analyser et examiner la théorie de l'effet paralysant et ses présupposés méthodologiques, empiriques et normatifs.

A. INTRODUCTION

With the notion that law is an autonomous discipline in decline since the 1960s,[1] legal research has become more "cosmopolitan."[2] That is, legal research has — albeit slowly and certainly not uniformly[3] — become more comparative, interdisciplinary, globally concerned, and, at the same time, more cautious about the limits of legal reasoning and its application to different, including "foreign," contexts.[4]

A good example of this evolution is the continuing debate over "legal transplants" within comparative legal scholarship.[5] Though comparative

1 Richard A Posner, "The Decline of Law as an Autonomous Discipline: 1962–1987" (1987) 100:4 Harv L Rev 761.

2 Michele Graziadei, "Legal Transplants and the Frontiers of Legal Knowledge" (2009) 10:2 Theoretical Inq L 693 at 694.

3 Douglas W Vick, "Interdisciplinarity and the Discipline of Law" (2004) 31:2 JL & Soc'y 163 at 163–64, discussing tensions between those advocating interdisciplinary and doctrinalist approaches in legal research; Brian Bix, "Law as an Autonomous Discipline" in Peter Cane & Mark Tushnet, eds, *The Oxford Handbook of Legal Studies* (Oxford: OUP, 2003) 975 at 981–83, noting differences across different legal jurisdictions, particularly the United States as compared to Europe.

4 *Ibid* at 981–83; see, also, Graziadei, above note 2 at 694.

5 See, generally, Konrad Zweigert & Hein Kotz, *An Introduction to Comparative Law*, 3d ed, translated by Tony Weir (Oxford: Oxford University Press, 1998); Alan Watson, *Legal*

law continues to grow as a branch of legal research, there are countervailing tensions. Once law is understood as a product of "legal culture," including a culture's distinct social and cultural assumptions, lawyers and scholars must not only be cautious when "transplanting" or importing legal norms into different legal cultures and jurisdictions, but also articulate and defend a sound methodology in doing so, particularly in light of the mixed results legal transplants have had in international legal reform efforts.[6]

Legal scholars have arguably not shown the same normative, empirical, and methodological caution when dealing with communications media. Indeed, the notion of a "legal transplant," and the attendant empirical, normative, and methodological risks that legal transplanting raises, provide a useful framework for understanding how similar methodological problems may arise when legal scholars, with little thought or prudence, import, apply, or transplant legal norms and doctrines to online and Internet-related contexts.[7] Yet, while the Internet has spawned a new and still growing body of work — often referred to as "cyberlaw scholarship" — that explores how traditional laws and legal norms like intellectual property should apply to the Internet and its related technologies,[8] the closest thing to a methodological debate within "cyberlaw" is the now tiresome spat over whether it constitutes a distinct field of study or not.[9] And despite copyright's ex-

---

Transplants: An Approach to Comparative Law (Atlanta: University of Georgia Press, 1974); Pierre Legrand, *Le Droit Comparé*, 2d ed (Paris: Presses Universitaires de France, 2005). See also James Q Whitman, "The Neo-Romantic Turn" in Pierre Legrand & Roderick Munday, eds, *Comparative Legal Studies: Traditions and Transitions* (Cambridge: Cambridge University Press, 2003).

6 See Randall Peerenboom, "Toward a Methodology for Successful Transplants" (2012) at 1, online: Social Sciences Research Network http://papers.ssrn.com/sol3/papers.cfm?abstract_id=1981887. See also Graziadei, above note 2 at 697–700, canvassing the substantive and methodological evolution of literature on legal transplants.

7 Indeed, the notion of unpacking the underlying methodological and normative assumptions of copyright law, for example, is not new. See Dan Burk, "Method and Madness in Copyright Law" (2007) 2007:3 Utah L Rev 587.

8 See, e.g., Paul Schiff Berman, "Introduction" in Paul Schiff Berman, ed, *Law and Society Approaches to Cyberspace* (Burlington, VT: Ashgate, 2007) xi at xiii–xix, discussing different "generations" of cyberlaw scholarship; Jack M Balkin, "Virtual Liberty: Freedom to Design and Freedom to Play in Virtual Worlds"(2004) 90 Va L Rev 2043 at 2044, n3. I have elsewhere explored some aspects of this body of scholarship, including its evolution and emerging paradigms. See Jonathon W Penney, "Understanding the New Virtualist Paradigm" (2009) 12 J Internet L 3, discussing the evolution of cyberlaw scholarship and the role of perspective; Jonathon W Penney, "Virtual Inequality: Challenges for the Net's Lost Founding Value" (2012) 10:3 Nw J Tech & IP 209 at 220–21.

9 See Berman, above note 8 at xiv; Frank H Easterbrook, "Cyberspace and the Law of the Horse" (1996) U Chi Legal F 207 at 208, arguing that cyberlaw is simply law involving

pansion into new online spheres and technological contexts,[10] and the increasingly interdisciplinary nature of copyright scholarship,[11] intellectual property scholars, particularly those interested in digital copyright, have offered little more. This of area of Internet-related legal research remains, like others, without established "texts, theories, and methodologies."[12]

This chapter aims to help fill some of that void in the literature, by offering an exploration of the problems that can arise when applying certain legal doctrines to online contexts, without careful consideration for implicit normative and empirical assumptions those legal doctrines may harbour. This exploration will be through a case study of the "chilling effects doctrine" as a "legal transplant" into debates about copyright enforcement online. The chilling effects doctrine (CED), a legal doctrine that holds that certain laws and regulatory schemes can "chill" or deter people from engaging in certain kinds of legal (and possibly desirable) activities,[13] is commonly raised in digital copyright scholarship to criticize the detrimental impact that copyright enforcement in online contexts has on Internet speech, expression, and other legal online activities.[14] Here, the case provides a helpful point of entry into a broader methodological discussion about applying

---

technology, like the Law of the Horse. See also Joseph H Sommer, "Against Cyberlaw" (2000) 15:3 Berkeley Tech LJ 1145 at 1147, arguing that cyberlaw is "nonexistent"; Lawrence Lessig, "The Law of the Horse: What Cyberlaw Might Teach" (1999) 113:2 Harv L Rev 501, responding to both.

10 Neil W Netanel, "Why Has Copyright Expanded? Analysis and Critique" in Fiona MacMillan, ed, *New Directions in Copyright Law*, vol 6 (Cheltenham: Edward Elgar Publishing, 2007) 3 at 3.

11 Eva Hemmungs Wirtén, "'Don't Fence Me In': Travels on the Public Domain" in Fiona MacMillan, ed, *New Directions in Copyright Law*, vol 6 (Cheltenham: Edward Elgar Publishing, 2007) 112 at 112, and 112 n 1.

12 John Monberg, "Science and Technology Studies Approaches to Internet Research" (2005) 21:4 The Information Society 281 at 281.

13 Julie E Cohen, "A Right to Read Anonymously: A Closer Look at 'Copyright Management' in Cyberspace" (1996) 28 Conn L Rev 981 at 1010, 1014, and 1039.

14 See, e.g., Jason Sheets, "Copyright Misused: The Impact of the DMCA Anti-Circumvention Measures on Fair & Innovative Markets"(2000) 23 Hastings Comm & Ent LJ 1; Pamela Samuelson, "Anticircumvention Rules: Threat to Science"(2001) 293 Science 2028 at 2029; Derek J Schaffner, "The Digital Millennium Copyright Act: Overextension of Copyright Protection and the Unintended Chilling Effects on Fair Use, Free Speech, and Innovation" (2005) 14:1 Cornell JL & Pub Pol'y 145; Joseph P Liu, "The DMCA and the Regulation of Scientific Research" (2003) 18:2 Berkeley Tech LJ 501; Jennifer M Urban & Laura Quilter, "Efficient Process or 'Chilling Effects'? Takedown Notices Under Section 512 of the Digital Millennium Copyright Act" (2006) 22:4 Santa Clara Computer & High Tech LJ 621; Wendy Seltzer, "Free Speech Unmoored in Copyright's Safe Harbor: Chilling Effects of the DMCA on the First Amendment" (2010) 24:1 Harvard JL & Tech 171.

legal norms to media. Specifically, I draw on insights from other disciplines and research fields to unpack and scrutinize the CED and its assumptions, to question not necessarily the overall efficacy of the CED itself — there is evidence, for example, of regulatory chilling effects in other contexts like traditional news organizations — but rather its application in online contexts. In the end, I hope to make the broader point that copyright — and laws more generally — embody not only certain cultural assumptions and social theories, but also implicit theories about communications media like the Internet, and how people interact with them. These implicit media theories and assumptions, when not addressed or accounted for, can raise theoretical, normative, empirical, and methodological risks.

In Section B, I briefly draw an analogy between the application of the CED in online contexts and the notion of "legal transplants" in comparative legal studies as a means to think critically about the methodological risks when applying legal doctrines to the Internet. I then provide some background into the CED, including its origins in United States constitutional law, its movement to other contexts, and, briefly, how it has been applied in relation to digital copyright and online contexts. This sets the stage for a broader analysis in Sections C and D, where I unpack the hidden assumptions underlying the CED, and then draw on other fields of research — specifically computer mediated communications, online ethnographic research, and institutional theory — to show how those assumptions are not necessarily sound. In Section E, I conclude with some future directions for research, including suggestions for how lawyers and scholars can minimize these research problems and methodological risks.

B. THE CHILLING EFFECTS DOCTRINE

1) A Different Kind of Legal Transplant

The notion of a "legal transplant," as earlier stated, provides a useful metaphor and framework for understanding the normative, empirical, and methodological issues that arise when legal doctrines are "transplanted" into online and Internet-related contexts. Indeed, just as legal norms — including intellectual property[15] — have been shown to embody or reflect the implicit social and cultural assumptions of the legal jurisdiction in which they

15 Rosemary J Coombe, *The Cultural Life of Intellectual Properties: Authorship, Appropriation, and the Law* (Durham: Duke University Press, 1998).

evolved and developed, legal doctrines also harbour implicit assumptions about communications media. Given that legal doctrines developed in relation to traditional forms of media in offline contexts, it makes sense they would deploy implicit theories and assumptions about communications media, and how people interact with them. The CED, I will argue, is one such example, which has implications for how it might be applied to online contexts where there are unique or differing norms about communications and rule-following — whether these norms make the online communities *culturally distinct* or not — in a way that complicates the doctrine's application.

2) Some Background

The idea of legal or regulatory "chilling effects" gained its earliest (or earliest most prominent) expression in traditional free speech law in the United States. The assertion that a law might "chill" free speech or related activities was first articulated by the US Supreme Court in the 1952 case *Wieman v Updegraff*[16] and a few years later, given its most popular formulation in terms of chilling effects on free expression, by Justice William Brennan in a 1965 case *Dombrowski v Pfister*.[17] At issue was a sweeping "anti-communist" Louisiana state law being used to prosecute civil rights workers in the state. Justice Brennan, writing for the Court, went on to find:

> This overly broad statute also creates a "danger zone" within which protected expression may be inhibited. *Cf. Speiser v. Randall*, 357 U.S. 513, 526 .... So long as the statute remains available to the State the threat of prosecutions of protected expression is a real and substantial one. Even the prospect of ultimate failure of such prosecutions by no means dispels their chilling effect on protected expression.[18]

The Court ultimately found that the law was an unconstitutional abridgement of the civil rights workers' First Amendment rights, the main provision of the US Constitution that protects freedom of speech and the press.[19]

Often referred to by lawyers as the "chilling effects doctrine," the doctrine was a "legal transplant" long before the Internet appeared. Indeed, the

16 *Wieman v Updegraff*, 344 US 183 (1952).

17 *Dombrowski v Pfister*, 380 US 479 (1965).

18 *Ibid* at 494.

19 Frederick Schauer, "Fear, Risk, and the First Amendment: Unraveling the 'Chilling Effect'" (1978) 58:5 BUL Rev 685 at 685.

CED has appeared repeatedly not only in a broad array of US judicial decisions from the 1960s onward, but also has been transplanted and adopted by adventuresome judges around the world, including Canada, Australia, and the United Kingdom.[20] Yet, today, perhaps its most predominant application (or transplant) has been in the context of digital copyright. It is this form of the CED that I will be dealing with here.

3) Chilling Effects Doctrine, Digital Copyright, and the Internet

The notion of legal or regulatory "chilling effects" arises within the global context of increasingly complex Internet regulation and governance.[21] Shifting away from earlier more obvious and direct means of regulating, such as Internet censorship laws or broad-based filtering, many states, including some in the west, have developed more subtle and sophisticated means for Internet regulation — what Ronald Deibert and Rafal Rohozinski call "next generation" regulatory methods like surveillance or intermediary liability — which rely heavily on creating and proliferating regulatory norms to deter targeted activities, like cyber-crime or intellectual property infringement.[22]

This has led to a diverse body of legal scholarship applying the chilling effects doctrine to numerous Internet-related laws and contexts, including laws providing for Internet surveillance and online defamation.[23] But perhaps the most common context in which the CED arises in legal scholarship is in relation to copyright enforcement online. And, within this context, the most popular target for "chilling effects" criticisms is the United States *Digital Millennium Copyright Act* (*DMCA*),[24] which relies on a complex scheme of intermediary liability and third-party content policing to deter illegal online copying and file sharing.

---

20 Andrew T Kenyon, "Investigating Chilling Effects: News Media and Public Speech in Malaysia, Singapore, and Australia" (2010) 4 Int'l J Comm 440 at 442.

21 Mathias Klang, "Virtual Censorship: Controlling the Public Sphere" in Jacques Berleur, Markku I Nurminen, & John Impagliazzo, eds, *Social Informatics: an Information Society For All? In Remembrance of Rob Kling* (New York: Springer, 2006) 185 at 189.

22 Ronald Deibert & Rafal Rohozinski, "Beyond Denial: Introducing Next Generation Information Controls" in Ronald Deibert et al, eds, *Access Controlled: The Shaping of Power, Rights, and Rule in Cyberspace* (Cambridge, Mass.: MIT Press) 3 at 6.

23 Klang, above note 21 at 189.

24 *Digital Millennium Copyright Act*, 112 Stat 2860 (1998) (*DMCA*).

Central to the *DMCA*'s scheme are "take-down" notices. When a copyright holder believes a third-party online service provider (OSP) — like Google or Twitter — is hosting material that infringes her copyright, she sends a *DMCA* take-down notice outlining her legal claim and demanding the OSP take down the offending material or face legal liability. Under the *DMCA*, once OSPs receive such notice, they must remove the infringing material or risk secondary liability for hosting material that directly infringes copyrights. They must also provide notice to the user who originally posted the content that it has been removed. There are two potential kinds of "chilling effects" at work here: one, where content is being removed after-the-fact as a result of targeted *DMCA* take-down notices (think of this as content chill); and, two, the more common concern, that the Internet user is "chilled," or self-censors his or her future speech, as a result of receiving a take-down notice. Though both of these kinds of chill are, arguably, at play, it is the latter form that has received the most attention from critics, who have argued that the *DMCA* regulatory regime, under which take-down notices can be sent to large numbers of online service providers with few costs, has a chilling effect on Internet speech and expression that is entirely legal.[25] In other words, despite the fact that there are very few, if any, systematic or empirical studies that examine how legal norms like the chilling effects doctrine may operate or apply in online contexts,[26] this has not stopped intellectual property lawyers and copyright scholars from applying the chilling effects doctrine to digital copyright issues and debates, most predominantly, mechanisms for copyright enforcement online. In the next section, I provide some reason to believe this may not be a sound practice, substantively or methodologically.

C. UNPACKING AND UNDERSTANDING THE DOCTRINE'S ASSUMPTIONS

Having given some sense of the chilling effects doctrine's background, and its relationship to digital copyright scholarship, I want to unpack its theoretical framework and assumptions. In the most basic sense, the chilling ef-

25 Sheets, above note 14; Samuelson, above note 14; Schaffner, above note 14; Liu, above note 14; Urban & Quilter, above note 14; Seltzer, above note 14.

26 Wyatt Ditzler, Michael Zimmer, & Tomas Lipinski, "DMCA Take-down Notices on Campus: A Case Study" (Paper delivered at the iConference, University of Illinois, October 2010) [unpublished].

fects doctrine describes a form of deterrence. That is, it is concerned about how a law, for whatever reason, deters a kind of activity, in this case, speech or expression. Though it is the person being deterred, it makes sense to speak of their "activity as being chilled."[27] Like most kinds of deterrence, the chilling effect of a law is based on the threat of legal punishment, which in the case of copyright infringement can include fines, statutory damages, and even imprisonment. If you break or transgress the law, it says you will receive the prescribed punishment. People will avoid breaking or transgressing the law in question, so the theory goes, to avoid the punishment. When a law's threat of punishment deters or chills certain kinds of speech or expression, then that is the chilling effects doctrine at work.

Yet, laws rely on more than just formal legal processes and punishment to deter; they also rely on social norms and stigma.[28] That is, because a law is enacted or approved by the broader public or community, then breaking the law — beyond whatever formal punishment follows — will also be met with social disapproval within that broader community. The social stigma attached to legal transgression also deters.[29]

The CED is different from just legal deterrence, however, because it has negative connotations. The central idea underlying CED-based criticisms of a law — like the *DMCA* — is that it is not just deterring an illegal or unwanted activity, but is also deterring or chilling other activities that are both legal and desirable; in the context of chilling effects and digital copyright enforcement, this legal and desirous activity is free and open Internet speech and expression.[30] This chilling effect on legal activity is due to inherent uncertainty and costs within the legal process itself — laws may be too vague or overly broad and hard to define, thus catching legitimate activities within its scope. Or the costs of defending legitimate activities against legal attack may be too great.[31] Whatever the reason, the law's deterrence of legitimate and desirable activities, like speech, is its chilling effect.

Here lies one of the CED's more obvious normative assumptions — that more speech and expression is better than less. And chilling more speech is undesirable. This normative assumption might offer one angle of cri-

27 Schauer, above note 19 at 689.

28 See, generally, Harold G Grasmick & Lynn Appleton "Legal Punishment and Social Stigma: A Comparison of Two Deterrence Models" (1977) 58 Social Science Quarterly 15.

29 *Ibid*.

30 Schauer, above note 19 at 690–92.

31 *Ibid* at 700.

tique — that the CED embodies an American ethos about the value of absolute free speech — but for our purposes, I am more interested in exploring two other assumptions inherent in the CED, which are more theoretical and empirical, apparent from our discussion of the CED and its theoretical framework. These assumptions are related and, as will be seen later, are important to understanding how the CED may or may not be useful in an online context.

The first is that the CED assumes an informed, deliberative, and rational form of speech and expression. By informed, I mean that in order to be chilled or deterred from speaking or expressing something, the person or entity must, at the very least, be informed about the law in question, including its scope and the punishment involved. If the person or entity speaking had no knowledge of the law, they would not be deterred by its potential application to their expression.

The speech or expression must also be deliberative and rational. That is, the CED assumes that the speaker does a cost-benefit analysis before speaking; and taking into account the potential for punishment and social stigma, or the economic costs of defending conduct in a legal process, the person or entity decides that the costs of speaking outweigh the benefits. The CED assumes the speaker undergoes this rational and deliberative process and is deterred or chilled from acting or speaking. The CED assumes a rational and deliberative speaker in another sense too, like a blogger who receives a DMCA "take-down" notice for a post and decides to refrain from posting on that topic or similar topics ever again. The CED thus assumes that the speaker is rational and will act to avoid punishment and social stigma. An irrational, uninhibited, or unthinking speaker likely would not be chilled because they would not necessarily care about, or avoid, punishment or social stigma.

A second central theoretical and empirical assumption of the CED concerns the norm-following behaviour of the speaker. Assuming the speaker is informed, deliberative, and rational, the CED also makes assumptions about what set of norms the speaker will consider. That is, it assumes that the speaker is concerned with the norms of the broader community, and will aim to follow them; the speaker would be concerned about legal norms embodied in the law that might apply to his or her speech or expression, and also with the stigma attached to breaching social norms with his or her community. And these norms would weigh against speaking, leading to a chilling effect.

Of course, neither of these are necessarily unreasonable assumptions, particularly in traditional contexts for speech, expression, and media. In fact, they may, in a sense, disclose a potential *institutional* bias in the CED. Unlike an individual, a media company or publisher may very well undertake a cost-benefit analysis of publishing a story in the face of potential legal claims based in libel. And such an entity might also have access to legal advice and institutional experience, rendering the process to decide to publish (or speak and express) an informed, rational, and deliberative one. In other words, CED harbours, from another angle, an assumption of institutional capacity.

These assumptions suggest a kind of implicit media theory within the CED, that being, people engage in rational and deliberative speech online, pursue norm-following behaviour in ways similar to offline contexts, and, arguably, have the institutional capacity to carry out a cost-benefit analysis of the merits of speaking, publishing, or carrying out some other activity online. In the next section, I explore these assumptions in relation to insights from three fields of research: computer-mediated communications scholarship, online ethnography, and institutional theory.

D. TESTING THE DOCTRINE'S ASSUMPTIONS

Drawing on social science research concerning the Internet, I examine whether the CED's assumptions necessarily hold true in online contexts in relation to speech and expression. The first assumption was that the CED assumes a kind of informed, rational, and deliberative speech or expression, where the speaker considers the cost-benefit analysis of speaking, and, finding costs are too great, elects not to speak. The question, then, is whether this is an accurate reflection or description of online speech, expression, and communication.

1) Online Speech: Informed, Deliberative, and Rational?

Is online speech and expression as informed, deliberative, and rational as the CED assumes? Though there are few, if any, studies measuring the CED in an online context, there has been a growing body of scholarship on computer-mediated communication, which explores the nature and impact of online communication. This research is relevant, since speech and expression on the Internet is a form of computer-mediated communication, as it is mediated by computers, networks, and related technology. The lessons of computer-mediated communication research may tell us something about how the CED works in an online context.

Two positions have dominated computer-mediated communication scholarly debates.[32] The first is that online communications is less social and more impersonal, uninhibited. Early research, which formed the foundation of the "Social Presence" and "Cues Filtered Out" theories, found that compared to face-to-face communication, the lack of facial and other contextual cues in computer-mediated communication led to less personal and effective communication, and more uninhibited behaviour.[33] That is, the "technological features of [computer-mediated communication] trigger psychological states and processes that result in a situation of weak norms and social constraints and more deregulated behavior in the form of uninhibited communication."[34]

The second position, known mainly for the Social Information Processing (SIP) theory, takes a different view. Proponents of this theory argue that social presence theories relied on computer-mediated communication experiments that failed to take into account time pressures. Social information processing theory research suggests that the lack of cues in computer-mediated communication promote uninhibited and deregulated communication only when coupled with short time constraints; and over longer periods, computer-mediated communication is just as personal, deliberative, and regulated as face-to-face communications.[35] With enough time, computer-mediated communication and face-to-face communications show little difference.

So what might all of this tell us about CED and its assumptions concerning speech and expression online? First, at the very least, the CED ought not to be transplanted in an uncritical or blanket and overreaching fashion to online contexts. The computer-mediated communication research based around social presence and cues filtered out theories suggest that online communication — which obviously includes speech and expression — is not necessarily informed, rational, and deliberative. Moreover, SIP theory

---

32 Joseph B Walther, Tracey Loh, & Laura Granka, "Let Me Count the Ways: The Interchange of Verbal and Nonverbal Cues in Computer-Mediated and Face-to-Face Affinity" (2005) 24:1 Journal of Language and Social Psychology 36 at 36–37.

33 Elizabeth V Hobman et al, "The Expression of Conflict in Computer-Mediated and Face-To-Face Groups" (2002) 33:4 Small Group Research 439 at 440–41.

34 *Ibid* at 442 [reference omitted].

35 *Ibid* at 442; Joseph B Walther, "Computer-mediated communication: Impersonal, Interpersonal, and Hypersonal Interaction" (1996) 23 Communication Research 3.

research suggests that time constraints play a central role in promoting this kind of uninhibited and deregulated speech. But instantaneous forms of communication, like instant messaging (IM) or one-to-many forms like Twitter, are becoming more and more popular on the Internet.[36] On SIP theory, such communications are more synchronous allowing for less time for non-verbal communication, thus also promoting the kind of uninhibited and deregulated speech noted in social presence and cues filtered out studies.

In other words, contrary to what the CED assumes, speech, expression, and communication are not necessarily informed, deliberative, and rational in online contexts, particularly where communication is instantaneous. The chilling effects doctrine seems to have less relevance, or application, in these online contexts, given that people are less likely to censor themselves due to rational consideration or fear of legal sanction.

Yet, that is not the end of the story. The chilling effects doctrine would appear to have even greater relevance to *some* forms of online speech and expression, compared to even offline speech and communication. Again, computer-mediated communication research, particularly SIP theory, provides the basis for this insight. Though, as noted, Internet communications, including speech and expression, is moving toward more instantaneous communication (and, with video streaming, computer-mediated communication with more social and non-verbal cues), a great deal of computer-mediated communication on the Internet is far from instantaneous and synchronous. Rather, it is asynchronous allowing much greater periods of time for rational deliberation and cost-benefit analysis before speaking, or, as on the web and certain web forums, posting. This type of asynchronous computer-mediated communication is precisely the kind that SIP theory contemplates providing more effective and less deregulated communication.[37]

Speech and expression on the world wide web is an excellent example of this kind of asynchronous computer-mediated communication. In web discussion forums, participants can take whatever time they wish before posting to a discussion thread, or responding to arguments from other posters. Blogs are another example of this. Before posting an item, a blogger

---

36 Mark Tremayne et al, "Perceived Authority and Communication Channel: Experiments with Instant Messaging" (2008) 28 Social Science Computer Review 178 at 178; Antonio Marturano, "The Ethics of Online Social Networks — an Introduction" (2011) 16 International Review of Information Ethics 3 at 3.

37 *Ibid*; Walther, above note 35 at 26.

can take a lengthy amount of time to decide whether the item might attract social disapproval or might infringe on some law, such as the *DMCA*.

Social media often involve platforms for mixed kinds of computer-mediated communications. For example, Twitter — where links to copyrighted material can easily be propagated to large numbers of followers — is arguably a kind of micro-blogging, though potentially instantaneous and fast moving, and also allows for a measure of asynchronous communication as a Twitter user has time to contemplate before writing a tweet (though this, arguably, could be exaggerated, as the rapid-style of Twitter's "tweet stream" means that a Twitter user has a limited period of time to offer a timely response to a topic or Twitter discussion). Facebook too offers both asynchronous communications (Facebook messaging) but more instantaneous communication possibilities (live chat and status updates). YouTube, arguably, is more asynchronous, as a YouTube user has plenty of time to consider the implications of creating, uploading, and distributing a video via YouTube channels.

With speech and expression in these online contexts, chilling effects may be greater or magnified not only compared to other online contests. In some instances, it may even be so as compared to offline contexts as well. In short, the CED must not be applied in a blanket or uncritical fashion to "the Internet" or all online contexts, as attention to details about the specific online context will have implications for how relevant the notion of legal or regulatory chilling effects will be.

2) Online Communications and Norm Following Behaviour

A second assumption of the CED concerned the norm following behaviour of the speaker. Assuming the speaker is informed, deliberative, and rational, it was also earlier noted that the CED likewise implicitly assumes that speakers are concerned with the norms of the broader community, and will aim to follow them. That is, a speaker would be concerned about legal norms embodied in the law that might apply to his or her speech or expression, and also with the stigma attached to breaching social norms with his or her community. And these norms would weight against speaking, leading to a chilling effect.

Online environments, and how people interact with them, also complicate this assumption. Ethnographic research on virtual worlds, as well as insights offered by computer-mediated communication studies, show that the emergence of norms within online and virtual communities complicates the norm following behaviour of people in these contexts. Several virtual world ethnographic studies, for example, show that while people often follow "real world" conventions in online contexts — as the CED would have to assume — they often do so inconsistently.[38]

One way of explaining this inconsistency might be drawn from the insights of computer-mediated communication research: social individuation/deindividuation or SIDE theory. This theory aims to explain norm following behaviour in online contexts; it holds that because computer-mediated communication, particularly on the Internet, lacks non-verbal social and environmental communication cues, people seek out norms in order to ensure acceptance among their peers.[39] The idea underlying the theory is that there is a tension between our personal and social identities, with the latter often driving us to adopt the behaviour of our peers in online contexts to fit in.[40] In one study, students were more likely to seek acceptance among peers and thus express opinions deemed "unacceptable" to faculty when using computer-mediated communication.[41]

Of course, this is not an exhaustive look at research on point. Rather, the purpose was to show how research in these areas complicate the CED's assumptions about the norms that people will follow when speaking, communicating, or expressing themselves. The CED assumed that people are primarily concerned with the norms of the "real world" community, and the laws that may deter the person from speaking. But these studies indicate that the development of norms in online contexts provides an additional layer, or in some contexts multiple layers, of norms that the speaker may consider before speaking or expressing him or herself. People may consider both online and offline norms when deciding whether to speak or express themselves; and in some cases, as the SIDE model suggests, there may be cases where people online will conform more to online group norms and discount real world ones, to seek peer approval. Indeed, there is even the broader normative question, that goes beyond the scope of this article,

---

38 Ralph Schroeder, *Being There Together: Social Interaction in Shared Virtual Environments* (Oxford: Oxford University Press, 2011) at 213–14, discussing how people may not adhere to typical norms like religious ones in online contexts in the same way they do in other contexts.

39 See, generally, Andrew F Wood & Matthew J Smith, *Online Communication: Linking Technology, Identity, & Culture*, 2d ed (Mahwah, NJ: Lawrence Erlbaum Associates, 2005).

40 *Ibid*.

41 *Ibid* at 86.

about the legitimacy of legal norms and assumptions of doctrines like the CED (and their application) when the norms of online communities differ so much. Again, the relevance and applicability of the CED depends on the nature and context of the online activity.

3) Institutional Theory and the Private Enforcement of Legal Norms

A final point concerns the relationship between institutions and the CED — the doctrine's assumption that online actors engage in cost-benefit assessments to decide whether to speak or act in the face of a potential legal threat means that institutions — be they public institutions, commercial enterprises or organizations — may be less likely "chilled" or deterred by legal threats. This is because they would have access to legal advice, institutional experience, and other mitigating resources, rendering any decision to speak, publish, or act, much more informed, rational, and deliberative. I call this an implicit institutional bias in CED, but, in truth, this bias is applicable to offline contexts as much as the Internet (and may not always hold true in either context, as individuals and institutions have many different motivations for speaking or Internet posting, which may or may not include a concern about legal liabilities or threats).

There is another way that institutional concerns affect the application of the CED to the Internet and online contexts. Earlier, I noted how state governments are increasingly relying on more sophisticated "next generation" regulatory methods, which often involve complex statutory schemes that deploy regulatory norms like intermediary liability — that is, a regime that imposes legal duties and responsibilities on third parties or intermediaries as a means to enforce legal rights or interests.[42] The *DMCA* is a great example of such an intermediary liability regime, since it relies on private actors — online hosts and service providers — to enforce intellectual property claims (received via *DMCA* take-down notices).

However, the inclusion of private institutional actors in the enforcement equation raises a whole host of potential complications, most notably the inconsistent application and enforcement of laws and legal norms. First, institutional and organizational theory and research has convincingly shown that organizations and institutions tend towards path dependency,

---

42 Deibert & Rohozinski, above note 22, at 6.

that is, self-reinforcing behaviour that resists change while "dramatically" narrowing the scope of the organization or institution's action over time.[43] Second, organizational research suggests that national cultures (including, presumably, national legal cultures) plays a minimal role in constraining organizational culture, leaving organizations and institutions with more discretion and freedom to determine what organizational cultural conventions and practices should be entrenched or standardized.[44]

Following the insights of institutional and organizational theory and research, if the *DMCA*, and similar Internet intellectual property-based intermediary liability regimes can have a chilling effect on entirely legal online speech and other behaviour, then the scope, magnitude, and consistency of those chilling effects may turn, in many cases, on what private entity, company, or organization is involved, and their accompanying organizational culture, and the many self-reinforcing processes that preserve and entrench organizational norms. Indeed, the *DMCA*, and other intermediary liability regimes, operate based on what Graham Dinwoodie calls a "private ordering" framework, whereby actors in the private sphere make important decisions about how and when to enforce legal norms and other public goods and values.[45] Some companies, to take one example, may take intellectual property rights more seriously than another; while others will assume the importance of battling cyber-crime, with little interest in policing intellectual property.[46] The regulatory response, and any potential chilling effects, could be under-enforced or over-enforced depending on the specific private institution or organization. In other words, the CED's application to Internet-related contexts is much more complicated and problematic than lawyers and legal scholars have previously let on.

---

43 Georg Schreyögg & Jörg Sydow, "Organizational Path Dependence: A Process View" (2011) 32:3 Organization Studies 321 at 323. See also W Richard Scott, "Institutional Theory: Contributing to a Theoretical Research Program" in Ken G Smith & Michael A Hitt, eds, *Great Minds in Management: The Process of Theory Development* (Oxford: Oxford University Press, 2005).

44 Barry Gerhart, "How Much Does National Culture Constrain Organizational Culture?" (2008) 5:2 Management and Organization Review 241 at 255.

45 See, generally, Graeme B Dinwoodie, "Private Ordering and the Creation of International Copyright Norms: The Role of Public Structuring" (2004) 160:1 Journal of Institutional and Theoretical Economics 161.

46 The idea is not far-fetched. Google, for example, has a unique corporate culture in its approach to copyright, both in terms of its business ventures, as well as its legal responsibilities to enforce such rights. See generally Aurelio Lopez-Tarruella, ed, *Google and the Law: Empirical Approaches to Legal Aspects of Knowledge-Economy Business Models* (The Hague: Asser Press, 2012).

E. DIRECTIONS FORWARD

It is generally assumed that law and legal doctrines, as a product of a specific legal culture, include or incorporate certain implicit social, political, and cultural assumptions. This essay has attempted to illustrate, through a case study of the chilling effects doctrine as applied to Internet contexts, how such legal doctrines, specifically one common to digital copyright scholarship, also reflect implicit theories about communications media and how people interact with, and communicate through, those media. Those implicit media theories and assumptions are not inherently problematic, and, in fact, offer insights not just about "chilling effects" as a legal idea, but also the nature and development of copyright law itself; for the implicit assumptions about media inherent in the many legal doctrines of copyright law might be said to reflect or embody copyright's own media theory. Of course, a proper exploration of "copyright's media theory" goes beyond the scope of this chapter, but is certainly worth pursuing in future research.

This being said, such hidden or implicit media theories and assumptions can also pose serious substantive and methodological risks if left unaddressed. Here, drawing on insights from several different fields, I have tried to show how the media theory implicit in the chilling effects doctrine either does not necessarily hold true in online contexts or, at the very least, complicates the doctrine's application to activities online. These risks can lead not only to incorrect conclusions, false hypotheses, and overall inaccurate research findings, but also to bad public policy: it is impossible to determine whether regulatory schemes like the *DMCA* achieve an appropriate balance between the rights of copyright holders and other public goods like free expression, if we are not attentive to the assumptions and nuances of applying legal doctrines, like the CED, to online contexts.

Though such normative, empirical, and methodological risks probably cannot be entirely avoided, there are steps that intellectual property and "cyberlaw" scholars involved with Internet-related legal scholarship can take, going forward, to minimize such risks. First, legal scholars must do a better job of examining and unpacking the theoretical, empirical, and normative assumptions of the legal doctrines with which they are working, particularly where they wish to "transplant" those doctrines to online contexts. This includes not only cultural, social, and political assumptions, but also assumptions relating to media and how people interact with such media. Second, they need to spend more time investigating what other disciplines and fields of research have to say about the legal doctrines at stake, including any implicit media theories or assumptions. In this case, several of the CED's implicit assumptions proved shaky in light of insights from computer-mediated communication research, online ethnographic research, and institutional/organizational theory. Of course, the examination of other fields in this chapter was far from an exhaustive review; the point, stated earlier, was simply to illustrate the importance and value in seeking guidance beyond legal research.

Thankfully, these additional efforts have benefits for legal scholarship beyond the purpose of seeking out diverse research fields for multidisciplinary insights and methodological guidance. As Michele Graziadei has pointed out, the study of "legal transplants" and the attendant methodological issues and debates, "broadens our understanding of crucial aspects of the law, including those that raise questions of justice."[47] Such an approach would help send a signal to other fields and disciplines that intellectual property scholarship, and legal research more generally, has freed itself from narrow and idiosyncratic methodological debates of the past, and is embarking on a rich, new, interdisciplinary path.

47 See also Graziadei, above note 2 at 695.

TWENTY-FOUR

Ambush Marketing Legislation to Protect Olympic Sponsors: A Step Too Far in the Name of Brand Protection?

BENOIT SÉGUIN & TERESA SCASSA

ABSTRACT (EN): Ambush marketing and its threat to brand equity have been identified as key concerns for mega sport event organizations and their sponsors. In recent years, international sport federations have sought to leverage the enormous interest in hosting their events in order to make anti-ambush marketing legislation a requirement for a successful bid. While sponsors may applaud such added protection, there are potentially a number of negative impacts that deserve consideration when discussing ambush marketing legislation.

In this chapter, the authors examine the growing trend towards anti-ambush marketing legislation. Using the Olympic Games as a model, the authors provide a brief overview of the Olympic brand, Olympic sponsorship, and the brand management/protection strategies developed by the International Olympic Committee. Particular attention is paid to the Vancouver Olympic Committee (VANOC) for the 2010 Olympic Winter Games and to the legislation enacted by the Canadian government to protect the Olympic and Paralympic brands. The authors examine some of the issues that arose around the Vancouver Games, and discuss the impact of the growing use of anti-ambush legislation as the ultimate weapon to protect sponsors. While more research is needed to assess fully the impact of such legislation on various stakeholders, there are signs that it may do more harm than good.

RÉSUMÉ (FR): Le marketing insidieux (« ambush marketing ») et ses éventuelles menaces pour la valeur d'une marque sont considérés comme une préoccupation majeure pour les organisations de méga événements sportifs et leurs commanditaires. Au cours de la dernière année, les fédérations sportives internationales ont cherché à susciter un intérêt considérable en organisant leurs événements de façon à ce qu'une législation contre le marketing insidieux devienne une condition à l'obtention des Jeux. Bien qu'il soit possible que les commanditaires se réjouissent de cette protection supplémentaire, il existe un certain nombre d'éventuels effets néfastes qui doivent être pris en compte lors de toute discussion entourant une législation contre le marketing insidieux.

Dans ce chapitre, les auteurs examinent la tendance croissante parmi les organisateurs de méga événements sportifs d'insister sur l'adoption d'une législation visant à assurer une protection contre le marketing insidieux. En se servant des Jeux Olympiques comme modèle, les auteurs présentent un bref aperçu de la marque olympique, de la commandite des Jeux Olympiques et des stratégies visant la gestion/la protection élaborées par le Comité International Olympique (CIO). L'étude s'attarde plus particulièrement sur le Comité olympique de Vancouver (VANOC) pour les jeux olympiques d'hiver 2010 et sur la législation adoptée par le gouvernement canadien en vue de protéger les marques olympiques et paralympiques. Les auteurs analysent certaines des questions qui surgissent en relation avec les Jeux de Vancouver et discutent ensuite de l'incidence du recours croissant à la législation contre le marketing insidieux en tant qu'arme de dernier ressort pour protéger les commanditaires. Bien qu'il soit nécessaire de mener des recherches plus approfondies si l'on veut évaluer pleinement l'incidence d'une telle législation sur les diverses parties prenantes, certains signes donnent à penser qu'elle pourrait causer plus de tort que de bien.

A. INTRODUCTION

Ambush marketing is now an expected part of the marketing and sponsorship landscape that surrounds major sport events. This is primarily the result of two developments in the sport marketing field. First, global sport properties (e.g., Olympic Games or FIFA World Cup) and national properties (e.g., Hockey Canada, Curling's Brier) have succeeded in building strong brands that connect emotionally with large numbers of consumers. Second, sponsorship "exclusivity" in predetermined product categories has become a key element of all major sport properties' strategy. While "exclusivity" has contributed to significant growth in revenue for sport properties such as the

Olympics, it has also made them valued commodities for corporations wishing to gain benefits through association. For example, the financial contribution of worldwide Olympic sponsors (TOP sponsors) and domestic sponsors for the 2010 Vancouver Olympic Winter Games reached nearly US $1 billion or 60% of the Organizing Committee's budget of $1.6 billion.[1] In the case of FIFA, marketing revenue for the period 2007–10 was more than $1 billion.[2] Given the desirability of such properties and the hefty price tag to acquire exclusive rights, there has been a growth in companies wishing to reap some of the benefits of sponsorship (e.g., brand associations) without paying for those association rights. This is called ambush marketing.

Ambush marketing can be defined as the practice whereby a company, often a competitor of an event's sponsor, intrudes upon public attention surrounding the event, thereby drawing attention to itself and away from the sponsor.[3] For example, during the 2006 FIFA World Cup in Germany, the nose cones of forty airplanes owned by Lufthansa German Airlines were painted to resemble a football, raising the ire of the FIFA, and the official airline sponsor, Air Emirates.[4] While Lufthansa made no claims about any direct association with the World Cup, corporations who use such strategies do so to connect themselves to the event in consumers' minds. Another example linked to the 2010 Olympic Winter Games in Vancouver is Esso (Imperial Oil) and the promotion of its long-time association with Hockey Canada to direct attention to their brand through creative and effective thematic promotion — "Cheers for Canada." This promotion was executed at all Esso stations across Canada through well-placed signage at the point of purchase (i.e., pumps) using imagery and the well-known Hockey Canada brand. While Esso was careful not to infringe on the trademarks associated with the 2010 Games, its promotional campaign played on Canadians' passion for and strong emotional connection to hockey and indirectly to the Olympic Winter Games.

---

1 Dana Ellis, Marie-Ève Gauthier, & Benoit Séguin, "Ambush Marketing, the Olympic and Paralympic Marks Act and Canadian Sports Organisations: Awareness, Perceptions and Impacts" (2011) 4:3 Journal of Sponsorship 253 at 255; all dollar figures in this paper are in US dollar currency.

2 FIFA, *FIFA Financial Report 2010*, online: www.fifa.com/mm/document/affederation/administration/01/39/20/45/web_fifa_fr2010_eng[1].pdf.

3 Tony Meenaghan, "Ambush Marketing — A Threat to Corporate Sponsorship" (1996) 38:1 Sloan Management Review 103 at 103.

4 Bill Wilson, "Protecting Sport Sponsors from Ambush" *BBC News* (20 February 2006) online: BBC News http://news.bbc.co.uk/2/hi/business/4719368.stm.

Such practice is often a planned effort by non-sponsors to gain at least some of the recognition and benefits that are associated with being an official sponsor.[5] In other words, non-sponsors seek to connect themselves to the event's brand in the consumer's mind. Whether ambush marketing is considered a legitimate business practice really depends on which side of the argument one falls. Nonetheless, the financial stakes are real and consequently the pressures placed on event organizers to protect the investments of corporate partners are immense. Rights holders such as the International Olympic Committee (IOC) have responded forcefully to ambush marketing activities by increasing the demands on cities/countries interested in hosting the Olympic Games to control the marketing activities around the Games, to protect their brands, and ultimately to ensure sponsor exclusivity.[6] For instance, the IOC now requires that host countries enact legislation aimed at protecting its brand(s) against ambush marketing.

In this chapter, the Olympic Games are examined to determine how mega sporting events protect their brands against activities such as ambush marketing. We begin with a brief overview of the Olympic brand, Olympic sponsorship, and the brand management/protection strategies developed by the IOC and the Vancouver Olympic Committee (VANOC) for the 2010 Olympic Winter Games, including special legislation to protect the Olympic and Paralympic brands. We then examine some of the issues that arose in relation to the Vancouver Games and discuss the impact of the growing use of anti-ambush legislation as the ultimate weapon to protect sponsors.

B. OLYMPIC MARKETING

The creation of an innovative marketing program in 1985 marked the beginning of a new era for the IOC. In fact, the IOC's decision to take sole control of the negotiation of television and sponsorship rights for the Olympic Games quickly diversified the organization's revenue base and positioned it as one of the most powerful sport organizations in the world. Since 1992, revenue from Olympic marketing programs (i.e., broadcasting, sponsorship,

5 Dennis M Sandler & David Shani, "Olympic Sponsorship vs. 'Ambush' Marketing: Who Gets the Gold?" (1989) 29:4 Journal of Advertising Research 9 at 9.

6 Holger Preuss, Kai Gemeinder, & Benoit Séguin, "Ambush Marketing in China: Counterbalancing Olympic Sponsorship Efforts" (2008) 7:2 Asian Business & Management 243 at 246–47; Benoit Séguin & Norman J O'Reilly, "The Olympic Brand, Ambush Marketing and Clutter" (2008) 4:1 International Journal of Sport Management & Marketing 62 at 74–75.

ticketing, and licensing) generated more than $23.5 billion for the Olympic Movement.[7] The IOC went from a nearly bankrupt "amateur" run organization to a multi-billion dollar business. It reformed its business model and adopted a "strategic brand management" philosophy to its marketing efforts towards the latter part of the 1990s.[8] Such an approach was believed to be innovative for a sport organization but in line with the beliefs of large corporations (e.g., sponsors) that a business should manage its brand strategically in order to maximize its brand equity.[9]

C. OLYMPIC SPONSORSHIP

Olympic sponsorship consists of a complex set of exclusive worldwide (TOP) and national (Olympic Games and National Olympic Committees) rights. The TOP program grants exclusive rights to specific Olympic intellectual property and Olympic marketing opportunities in exchange for financial support and goods and services contributions. The global marketing rights include partnerships with the IOC, all 205 National Olympic Committees (NOCs) and their Olympic teams, and the two Organizing Committees of Olympic Games (OCOGs) — one winter and one summer. The TOP partners can use these rights globally and can activate marketing initiatives nationally. TOP has been one of the most successful sport sponsorship programs in the world generating more than $3 billion in rights fees (cash and in-kind) since its inception in 1985. The most recent program, TOP VII (2009–12), generated $957 million.[10]

Sponsorship is also an important source of revenue for OCOGs and NOCs. In the case of OCOGs, domestic sponsorship programs contribute to the staging of the Games. While sponsors' marketing rights are restricted to the country of the OCOG, the revenues from these programs are comparable to TOP. For example, the 2008 Beijing Olympic Games raised $1.2 billion in domestic sponsorship compared to $866 million for TOP VI (2005–08). In the case of the 2010 Olympic Winter Games in Vancouver, the Organizing Com-

---

7 IOC, *Olympic Marketing Fact File 2012* (Lausanne: International Olympic Committee, 2012) online: www.olympic.org/Documents/IOC_Marketing/OLYMPIC-MARKETING-FACT-FILE-2012.pdf [IOC].

8 Norman O'Reilly & Benoit Séguin, *Sport Marketing: A Canadian perspective* (Toronto: Nelson Education Ltd, 2009) at 367.

9 See, generally, David A Aaker, *Managing Brand Equity: Capitalizing on the Value of a Brand Name* (New York: The Free Press, 1991).

10 IOC, above note 7.

mittee's (i.e., VANOC) domestic sponsorship program brought in $688 million, a record for a Winter Games. Such successful programs are credited in part to the IOC/OCOGs' efforts to control the marketplace in host countries.

1) Olympic Brand

A brand is a name or symbol that helps differentiate one product from another.[11] In recent years, however, marketers have suggested that a brand is also a promise to deliver a specific set of features, benefits, services, or experiences to consumers on a consistent basis.[12] For the Olympic brand, the ideals, and values (e.g., excellence, friendship, community) that have been central to the Olympic movement for more than 100 years have created an aura that differentiates the Olympic system from other professional sport systems. This has made the Olympic brand an attractive proposition for a multitude of stakeholders, including broadcasters, sponsors, governments, international federations, and professional sport leagues, seeking to transfer these associations to their own brands. By establishing strategic brand alliances, the IOC has built a system that contributes to its brand equity and to that of its stakeholders. For example, by integrating/aligning the Olympic brand within their activation programs, sponsors provide the Olympic brand with billions of dollars in promotional value and with an array of other benefits (brand recognition, access to markets worldwide, competitive advantage, etc.), which in the end greatly contribute to brand equity. On the other hand, the values associated with the Olympic brand provide the kinds of extensions that sponsors look for in the property. In addition, being connected to 205 NOCs provides TOP partners with multiple opportunities to activate at the national level. This is possible because of the "rich imagery" and the "compelling stories" associated with the Olympic brand.

While these brand alliances bring great value to the Olympic brand, it is paramount that a brand governance structure that manages and controls the brand and its many assets be established. Otherwise, the issue of clutter and ambush marketing may dilute the brand. Here, clutter refers to the amount of competing communications messages vying for the attention of fans, spectators, and potential consumers.[13]

---

11 Aaker, above note 9 at 7.

12 Philip Kotler & Kevin Keller, *Marketing Management* (Upper Saddle River, NJ: Pearson Prentice Hall, 2005) at 274.

13 Séguin & O'Reilly, above note 6 at 64.

Clutter and ambush marketing are closely related; previous research suggests that a cluttered environment coupled with the presence of ambush marketing enable non-sponsors "to navigate the cluttered marketplace through association with the Olympic brand, which threatens to dilute its promotional effectiveness and decrease its value,"[14] and impact consumers' ability to distinguish between official and unofficial sponsors which can influence their purchase decisions.[15] Hence, it is believed that sponsor activation programs have become an essential strategy for sponsors in their quest to break through the clutter, engage consumers with their brands, enhance brand reputation, and have positive return on their investments.[16] Since the IOC's TOP partners clearly believe that clutter and ambush marketing pose a threat to the value of their sponsorships[17] generated by the Olympic brand, the IOC expanded its marketing role "beyond just revenue raising into disciplined brand management of the world's most powerful brand."[18] Regardless, an important aspect of brand protection is the ability of the rights holder to protect the brand from a variety of potential threats.

2) Brand Protection

The emergence of brand protection practices beyond straightforward Olympic marks and emblem protection results from the IOC's decision to manage its brand strategically. For the IOC, protecting and controlling the Olympic brand is of utmost importance. Essentially, it consists of protecting both the tangible (words, symbols, the Olympic motto, etc.) and intangible aspects (image, values, reputation, etc.) of the brand. The protection of tangible aspects of the brand is evident as *words*, *phrases*, and *marks* are protected through trademark laws as well as numerous requirements expected

14 *Ibid* at 66.

15 Benoit Séguin et al, "Internationalising Ambush Marketing: A Comparative Study" (2005) 6:4 International Journal of Sports Marketing & Sponsorship 216 at 221 and 227.

16 Séguin & O'Reilly, above note 6; Stefan Wally & Amy Hurley, "The Torch Stops Here: Olympic Sponsorship and Corporate Reputation" (1998) 1:4 Corporate Reputation Review 343 at 353.

17 Benoit Séguin, André Richelieu, & Norm O'Reilly, "Leveraging the Olympic Brand Through the Reconciliation of Corporate and Consumers' Brand Perceptions" (2008) 3:1/2 International Journal of Sport Management & Marketing 3 at 11.

18 *International Olympic Committee, Olympic Marks, and Imagery Usage Handbook* (Lausanne: International Olympic Committee, 1999) at 7, as cited in Séguin & O'Reilly, above note 6 at 65; see also Alain Ferrand, Jean-Loup Chappelet, & Benoit Séguin, *Olympic Marketing* (New York: Routledge, 2012) at 57.

of host and bid cities in this area. However, protecting the intangible characteristics of a brand is much more complicated. To this end, an organization such as the IOC needs to be aware of the actions of not only its own members/employees (including volunteers) but also all those associated with the Movement (athletes, officials, NOCs, OCOGs, sponsors, etc.) as they may impact the integrity and potentially the image and value of the brand. This was the case in 1999 when several IOC members were found guilty of accepting bribes in exchange for their votes for Salt Lake City as the 2002 host city. The media scrutiny that followed brought an unprecedented level of negative publicity worldwide upon the IOC and its members. Some sponsors, publicly and privately, relayed their serious concerns about the impact the scandal was having on the brand image of the Movement, some even going so far as to threaten to withdraw their support. The reaction of the public, media, and most importantly sponsors acted as a "wake-up call" for the IOC in recognizing that a vital part of protecting its brand was the regulation of its own conduct and public image.

The protection against ambush marketing is now synonymous with protecting the Olympic brand. In fact, protecting the brand against ambush marketing is an increasingly sophisticated undertaking. In the next section we examine the issue of ambush marketing, and the efforts to manage it including the use of legislation as the "ultimate weapon" to protect the brand.

3) Managing Ambush Marketing

The literature on ambush marketing proposes numerous strategies for organizers to manage their brand so as to prevent ambush marketing. The first is addressing the clutter that surrounds the environment of sporting events, particularly in respect to major events like the Olympic Games. The relationship between high levels of consumer confusion and a cluttered sponsorship environment is well documented in the literature..

A second strategy consists of strategic activation programs by sponsors. Here, activation refers to "collateral communication of a brand's relationship with a property."[19] In other words, it means that additional investments (cash and/or in-kind) are made to ensure that sponsors take advantage of the numerous intangible brand associations that are linked to the property (i.e.,

---

19 Dimitra Papadimitriou & Artemisia Apostolopoulou, "Olympic Sponsorship Activation and the Creation of Competitive Advantage" (2009) 15:1-2 Journal of Promotion Management 90 at 96.

Olympic Games). Common activation techniques used by sponsors include advertising, sales promotions, and hospitality. The level of investment by sponsors can be as much as five dollars on activation for one dollar spent on acquiring the rights of sponsorship.[20] However, it is believed that activation creates a connection in the consumer's mind between the property and the sponsor thus making it more difficult for ambushers to create confusion in consumers' minds.[21] The management and control of broadcast rights is another important aspect of managing ambush marketing opportunities,[22] as are public relations (PR). Essentially, PR serves two important purposes. First, it allows for the opportunity to educate consumers about the sponsorship.[23] Second, it provides an outlet for property rights holders to make a public example of the ambusher in hopes of offsetting the benefits they have received via the ambush, with bad publicity.[24] This strategy was used by VANOC on numerous occasions prior to the 2010 Olympic Winter Games in Canada. In the Esso example given earlier in this chapter, VANOC quickly engaged key stakeholders (e.g., Olympic gold medallists, media partners, and government) to condemn the promotion. Essentially, a press conference was organized at a hotel located next to Imperial Oil's headquarter and the company was depicted as using unethical/unfair means that were equivalent to cheating for athletes to deceive the public. In fact, the athletes' spokesperson, a high profile Olympic gold medallist, suggested that the company was essentially stealing since it jeopardized future funding for athletes. The CEO of VANOC was reported as saying: "How can we credibly appeal to Canadian companies to support our games and our athletes if their competitors can accidentally or deliberately undermine those

---

20 *Ibid.*

21 Dean Crow & Janet Hoek, "Ambush Marketing: A Critical Review and Some Practical Advice" (2003) 14:1 Marketing Bulletin 1 at 11; Meenaghan, above note 3; Francis Farrelly, Pascale Quester, & Stephen A Greyser, "Defending the Co-Branding Benefits of Sponsorship B2B Partnerships: The Case of Ambush Marketing" (2005) 45:3 Journal of Advertising Research 339 at 345 and 347.

22 Crow & Hoek, *ibid* at 10; see also, Meenaghan, above note 3; Stephen Townley, Dan Harrington, & Nicholas Couchman, "The Legal and Practical Prevention of Ambush Marketing in Sport" (1998) 15:4 Psychology & Marketing 333; Séguin & O'Reilly, above note 6.

23 Crow & Hoek, above note 21 at 14; Séguin & O'Reilly, above note 6 at 75 and 79.

24 Steve McKelvey & John Grady, "Sponsorship Program Protection Strategies for Special Sport Events: Are Event Organizers Outmaneuvering Ambush Marketers?" (2008) 22:5 Journal of Sport Management 550 at 560 and 581; Meenaghan, above note 3 at 110.

investments?"[25] He also implied that governments (and hence, taxpayers) would be left to pay any deficit related to the Vancouver Games if sponsors became unwilling to invest.[26] In the end, Esso dropped this specific promotion. Further, it did not engage in any other significant ambush campaign prior to or during the Games in Vancouver.

Along the same line as public relations, education programs targeted at specific stakeholders offer a further strategy for managing ambush marketing. The evolution and expansion of anti-ambush marketing education programs by organizing committees reflect such an approach. In the lead-up to the 2010 Vancouver Winter Olympic Games, VANOC viewed education as the number one tool in fighting and preventing ambush marketing, even with anti-ambush legislation as part of their arsenal. The use of educational campaigns is also a way for the rights holder (i.e., VANOC) to explain the value of sponsors and their role in supporting the event hence differentiating them from potential ambushers. As such, VANOC worked closely with its sponsors to ensure an in-depth understanding of the rights purchased, how best to use those rights, the ability of VANOC to protect those rights, and the challenges to be expected in this regard. The task of educating other stakeholders, including consumers, potential ambushers, sport organizations, athletes, employees, and volunteers, was more complex. VANOC developed a broad communication strategy that included publicizing a brochure, direct mail campaigns, presentations at conferences (public, private, academic, etc.), one-on-one meetings with business/sport leaders, and a website which sought to outline exactly what would be considered ambush marketing in the eyes of the organizing committee.

VANOC also used education as an opportunity to clarify *who can tell what story*. From a marketing/communication perspective this was viewed as essential because the Olympics represent the potential to influence consumers and, therefore, can be a vehicle to deliver marketing value. Strategic leveraging of *stories* can create strong emotional connection with target audiences and create great value for one's brand. It is this value that property owners such as the IOC/OCOG strive adamantly to enhance and protect. While the subject of the Olympic Games and the right of associ-

25 Heenan Blaikie, "Let the Games Begin? Under Pressure, Esso Replaces its Olympic Trip Prize" (February 2006) *Canadian Marketing and Advertising Law Update*, online: www.heenanblaikie.com/fr/publications/item?id=901.

26 *Ibid.*

ation is a complicated one,[27] tapping into Olympic stories and/or IP without having paid for the right to do so is labelled "ambush marketing" by those negatively impacted (e.g., Olympic sponsors) and "savvy marketing" by those benefitting (e.g., non-sponsors). The challenge lies when primary stakeholders (e.g., NOCs, International Federations (IFs), National Sports Organizations (NSOs), athletes, events) claim ownership over stories that may be linked, directly or indirectly, to the Olympics. Given the increased attention brought by the Games, there is growing pressure from various groups to leverage their stories with their own stakeholders — e.g., NSOs and sponsors, athletes and sponsors, and event owners and sponsors. For example, Canada's fast casual restaurant Tim Hortons (also known for its coffee and doughnuts) hired Sidney Crosby to promote their product and be a spokesperson for its youth hockey program, the Timbits Hockey Program, of which he was a member in the early 1990s. In its television commercial that was played in the lead-up to the Vancouver Games, Tim Hortons used footage of a young Sidney Crosby in his Timbits uniform asking his father if he can stay on the ice for a couple of minutes. It fittingly ends with today's Sidney Crosby playing with children and again asking to stay on the ice a little longer. The "story" is one that makes use of Canada's game (hockey) and one of its most popular players to emotionally connect with consumers while appealing to nationalism and patriotic feelings prior to and during the Games. While not planned, Crosby's overtime goal that gave Canada the gold medal in hockey made Tim Hortons's "story" even more powerful. In this example the commercial rights of various stakeholders were at play — athletes (Crosby), NSOs (Hockey Canada) and Olympic rights (IOC/VANOC). While non-sponsor Tim Hortons may have been successful at connecting with all three, it is for such situations that OCOG's role of clarifying *who can tell what story* is now considered essential from a commercial rights management perspective.

Notwithstanding all the aforementioned strategies, many large sport properties including the IOC expect host country governments to enact special legislation aimed at protecting sponsors from ambush marketing. In fact, cities bidding to host the Olympic Games must provide

27 See, for example, Teresa Scassa, "Ambush Marketing and the Right of Association: Clamping Down on References to that Big Event with All the Athletes in a Couple of Years" (2011) 25:4 Journal of Sport Management 354.

> [g]uarantee(s) confirming that the legislation necessary to effectively reduce and sanction ambush marketing and, during the period beginning two weeks before the Opening Ceremony to the Closing Ceremony of the Olympic Games eliminate street vending and control advertising space and air space will be passed as soon as possible . . . .[28]

For the 2010 Olympic Winter Games, the Canadian Government provided such guarantees and enacted the *Olympic and Paralympic Marks Act* (*OPMA*)[29] in 2007. The *OPMA* was designed to enhance the protection provided by existing legislation such as the *Trade-marks Act*[30] that already protected Olympic words, symbols, and slogans. In addition, the *OPMA* included protection against ambush marketing. In terms of enforcement, the *OPMA* offered the organizing committee a more expedient process. This is believed to be essential by event organizers as major sport events take place over a limited period of time and ambush marketers seek to take advantage of this opportunity.

4) Ambush Marketing and Legislation

The IOC's insistence upon ambush marketing legislation as a condition of a successful Olympic bid has contributed to the expansion of such laws outside of the Olympic context. Other major sporting event sponsors now look for legislative protection against ambush marketing. In 2007 the New Zealand government enacted the *Major Events Management Act*,[31] which provides comprehensive protection against ambush marketing. It will apply to any event designated by the government as a "major event." In this way, the legislation can be made a part of any bid for a major international sporting event. There is no reason to expect that ambush marketing legislation will not become more widespread. Such legislation was in place for the 2010 FIFA World Cup in South Africa,[32] and there are indications that Canada will

---

28 IOC, *2016 Candidature Procedure and Questionnaire: Games of the XXXI Olympiad* (Lausanne: International Olympic Committee, 2008) at 124.

29 SC 2007, c 25.

30 RSC 1985, c T-13.

31 *Major Events Management Act 2007* (NZ), 2007/35.

32 B34-2001, *Trade Practices Amendment Bill* (S Afr) 2005, s 1, amending the *Trade Practices Act, 1976*; *Merchandise Marks Amendment Act*, (S Afr), No 61 of 2002; *Second FIFA World Cup South Africa Special Measures Act*, (S Afr), No 12 of 2006.

extend the protection of the *OPMA* to the Pan Am Games to be held in Toronto in 2015.[33]

As demonstrated above, anti-ambush legislation has become a part of an evolving strategy to protect the Olympic brand. Yet it is important to note that there is no clear evidence that sponsors see concrete benefits from the enactment of such legislation. In fact, for a majority of domestic sponsors interviewed after the 2010 Olympic Winter Games, the inherent nature of ambush marketing, which is all about "grey areas and fine lines," makes it nearly impossible to stop ambushers even with legislation.[34] In cases where "offenders" were identified, the retributions consisted of a "slap on the hand." One sponsor even suggested that to be truly effective, the laws would have to be much more rigid and offenders punished harshly. But given the Canadian marketplace and the environment within which sponsors operate, some reported that such an aggressive stance on ambush marketing could actually work against an organizing committee, provoking a public backlash, and ultimately damaging the Olympic brand: "whoever takes the heavy hand is going down in the marketplace for sure, the media will be all over them."[35] This was the case in the lead up to the London 2012 Olympic Games where organizers used the *London Olympic Games and Paralympic Games Act*[36] to stop individuals and small businesses from engaging with the Games. For example, the Fantastic Sausage Factory in Weymouth was reportedly told to take down a sign showing five sausage rings in the shape of the Olympic logo, with 2012 written underneath. The logo was changed to squares and the 2012 for 2013. Others that were caught up included a "florist that put up Olympic rings made of tissue paper and an 81 year-old woman hoping to sell a £1 doll-wearing a hand-knitted sports kit with a GB 2012 logo and Olympic rings in a fund raising sale."[37]

The overall retrospective feeling noted by sponsors was that the legislation was probably not needed and should not necessarily be a priority for

---

33 Toronto 2015 Pan American and Parapan American Games, *Your Moment Is There* (Toronto: 2009) at 189, online: Pan Am Toronto 2015 www.toronto2015.org/assets/files/pdf/Toronto-2015-Bid-Book-EN.pdf.

34 Benoit Séguin, Norm O'Reilly, & Dana Ellis, *Olympic Sponsorship and Ambush Marketing: Summary of Interviews with Grand National Sponsors of the 2010 Vancouver Olympic Winter Games.* (Report presented to the Canadian Olympic Committee, Toronto, 2011.)

35 *Ibid* at 19.

36 *London Olympic Games and Paralympic Games Act 2006* (UK), c 12 [*London Act*].

37 Vanessa Barford, "London 2012: The Great Olympics Sponsorship Bandwagon" *BBC News Magazine* (13 July 2012), online: BBC News www.bbc.co.uk/news/magazine-18182541.

the future. While domestic sponsors (i.e., Grand National Sponsors) for the 2010 Olympic Games claimed unprecedented successes with their sponsorship programs, this was not necessarily proof that the *OPMA* was effective; as suggested earlier, a well-executed and integrated brand management strategy by event organizers in conjunction with their partners and sponsors is much more likely to be at the root of any such success.[38] Post 2010 Games interviews conducted with the six Grand National Sponsors indicated that the level of sponsorship integration within their businesses was unprecedented. It was found that each sponsor appointed either senior level executives or high-level managers specifically responsible for Olympic affairs. Corporate "Olympic teams" were put in place for coordinating efforts and supporting the main strategic objectives of each sponsor. While the level and sophistication of integration varied from sponsor to sponsor, integration occurred both horizontally across departments/business units and vertically from headquarter to store level. Integration was completed by ensuring that all departments (or business units) were involved in creating objectives and activation strategies for their respective units. For one sponsor, having the CEO as the chair of the "project team" (i.e., corporate Olympic team) ensured complete alignment and was identified as critical to ensure a thorough understanding of what had to be done to integrate the various "banners" of the corporation.[39] In the end, it was believed that activation of sponsorships provided meaningful brand experiences for consumers, employees, and businesses.

Given that there is little evidence that ambush marketing laws contribute in a meaningful way to the success of sponsorship programs, their potential negative impacts deserve consideration. These negative impacts have their root in the very nature of the rights that are created by this legislation and their scope.

Ambush marketing legislation essentially creates a new form of intellectual property right. This right is in the event itself, and it is typically vested with the event organizers. In the case of the *OPMA*, for example, the right could be exercised by VANOC or, outside the designated period, by the Canadian Olympic Committee (COC).[40] The right protects against unauthorized associations with the event. Thus, a property right is recognized in the

38 See, for example, Séguin & O'Reilly, above note 6; Séguin, Richelieu, & O'Reilly, above note 17.

39 Séguin, O'Reilly, & Ellis, above note 34 at 11.

40 See above note 29, s 5(2).

goodwill generated by the event; only the event organizers may authorize others to associate themselves with this goodwill.

The right of association protects something different from what is protected by trademark law or the law of passing off. Trademark infringement or passing off arises where a party has attempted to create customer confusion as to the identity of the trade source of particular wares or services. This is done through the use of marks or other indicia that are confusing with those of a trademark owner. There is an overt use or manipulation of the owner's trademarks. By contrast, the right of association is violated when someone creates, in the minds of consumers, an association between their business, wares, or services and the protected event.[41] There is no need to use the trademarks of the event organizers; the association can be created by oblique reference to the event itself, including references to the host city, the time of year, or the general nature of the activities featured at the event.[42] In addition, it is not consumer *confusion* that is the target, but rather the connection that may be triggered in the consumer's mind. In other words, the consumer does not have to be misled in any way; infringement occurs where consumers think, however fleetingly, of the Olympics at the same time as they are viewing the advertising content of the offending business. It is not even necessary that the consumer be misled into thinking that there is an actual commercial association (i.e., a sponsorship relationship) between the ambusher and the event.

5) Negative Impacts of Anti-Ambush Legislation

At the heart of the difficulties posed by ambush marketing legislation and the new right of association is the broad, elusive, and ultimately subjective nature of an "association." The right of association gives event organizers the ability to control commercial associations with the event. Anyone who creates an unauthorized association is liable to civil sanctions, fines, or even imprisonment depending upon the particular statute and the enacting jurisdiction. Yet, thought works by associations. Conferring the right to authorize such associations on event organizers intrudes dangerously into how we think and experience the world around us. Although most statutes

---

41 See, for example, *ibid*, s 4; *London Act*, above note 36, s 1.

42 See, for example, Scassa, above note 27 at 356–58; Dana Ellis, Teresa Scassa, & Benoit Séguin, "Framing Ambush Marketing as Legal Issue: An Olympic Perspective" (2011) 14:3 Sport Management Review 297 at 300.

will provide a list of ordinary words that are considered suspect in the creation of associations,[43] these are not closed lists, and other words, images, juxtapositions, and even physical presence within certain zones or venues can give rise to an offending association.

Another problem with ambush marketing legislation is its scope. Ambush marketing is by nature opportunistic, and in order to anticipate and capture all possible future manifestations of this practice, legislators have sought to frame the right of association in the broadest possible terms. For example, in the debates leading up to the enactment of the *London Olympic Games and Paralympic Games Act*,[44] the UK Minister for Sport expressly admitted that the "right of association" created to counter ambush marketing was drafted in the broadest possible terms in part because there was no consensus as to what type of conduct it was meant to catch, as ambush marketing was a very fluid concept, and in part because the IOC might make future demands on the Organizing Committee to respond to certain types of conduct.[45] Not only is the right often framed in an open-ended manner, the mechanics of the law give it additional breadth. Thus, for example, in the *London Act*, both the advertiser and the person who consents to or provides the space for the advertisement are liable; the regulations passed pursuant to the legislation make it clear that human and animal bodies are included as prohibited vehicles for ambush marketing content.[46]

There has already been extensive criticism of the over-expansion of intellectual property rights generally.[47] Much of this critique has been focused

---

43 For example, the *OPMA*, above note 29, contained a list of suspect words and expressions in Schedule III (now repealed). These included: Games, 2010, Tenth, 21st, Medals, Winter, Gold, Silver, Bronze, Vancouver, and Whistler. The *London Act*, above note 36, also contains a list of suspect words in section 3 of Schedule 4. In the case of the *London Act*, evidence of an illegal "association" may arise where a combination of words from the first group are used (games, "two thousand and twelve," 2012, "twenty twelve") or where a word from the first group is used in conjunction with a word or words from the second group (gold, silver, bronze, London, medals, sponsor, and summer).

44 *Ibid*.

45 UK, HC "Standing Committee" col 79 (19 October 2005).

46 See UK, *The London Olympic Games and Paralympic Games (Advertising and Trading) (England) Regulations 2011*, SI 2011/2898 at Part 2, Regulation 5(1).

47 See, for example, Rochelle Cooper Dreyfuss, Diane Leenheer Zimmerman, & Harry First, eds, *Expanding the Boundaries of Intellectual Property: Innovation Policy for the Knowledge* (Oxford: Oxford University Press, 2001); Viva R Moffatt, "Mutant Copyrights and Backdoor Patents: The Problem of Overlapping Intellectual Property Protection" (2004) 19:4 Berkeley Tech LJ 1473; Peter Drahos & John Braithwaite, *Information Feudalism: Who Owns the Knowledge Economy* (New York: The New Press, 2003); Michael Heller, *The Grid-*

on situations where existing rights have been amplified or extended, but it is also manifested in the creation of new rights.[48] The creation of intellectual property-type rights in major events is part of this trend, and the degree to which the "right of association" has already spread is a matter for concern.[49] Indeed, the right of association seems to expand in breadth and scope with each legislative iteration. Critics of expanding intellectual property rights raise concerns about a shrinking public domain, and about the associated impact on creativity, human expression, and innovation. [50] The right of association, as will be discussed further below, has similar effects, even though it operates within a marketing context. Most significant, perhaps, is its impact on human expression in commercial and para-commercial contexts. Not only does such legislation have the potential to stifle a community's ability to engage with an event that is taking place in its midst, it may also create serious constraints for athletes and the amateur sporting organizations that support them, creating additional barriers to participation in competitive sports. As noted earlier, the legislation augments a brand protection strategy that seeks to control what "stories" can be told about the event and by whom. The multiplicity of stakeholders in Olympic events gives rise to multiple stories. The legislation thus privileges some stories and excludes others.

The scope and breadth of ambush marketing legislation raises freedom of expression issues. While most such laws are drafted so as to apply only to commercial associations, it is not always easy in an age of rampant consumer capitalism to distinguish between individual and commercial expression. For example, individuals are encouraged to embrace brands as an

---

lock Economy: How Too Much Ownership Wrecks Markets, Stops Innovation and Costs Lives (New York: Basic Books, 2008).

48 The *sui generis* database right that was created in Europe in 1995 to give new rights in compilations of data is one example.

49 As noted earlier, New Zealand has enacted general ambush marketing legislation which can be invoked for any event designated as a major event. South Africa also enacted ambush marketing laws for the FIFA World Cup of Soccer.

50 See, for example, Jessica Litman, "The Public Domain" (1990) 39:4 Emory LJ 965; Lawrence Lessig, *The Future of Ideas: The Fate of the Commons in a Connected World* (New York: Vintage Books, 2002); Jennifer Davis, "Protecting the Common: Delineating a Public Domain in Trade Mark Law" in Graeme B Dinwoodie & Mark D Janis, eds, *Trademark Law and Theory: A Handbook of Contemporary Research* (Cheltenham UK: Edward Elgar, 2008) 345; Lewis Hyde, *Common as Air: Revolution, Art, and Ownership* (New York: Farrar, Strauss & Giroux, 2010); James Boyle, *The Public Domain: Enclosing the Commons of the Mind* (New Haven, CT: Yale University Press, 2008); Eva Hemmungs Wirtén, *Terms of Use: Negotiating the Jungle of the Intellectual Commons* (Toronto: University of Toronto Press, 2008).

extension or articulation of their identities, and the wearing or carrying of sometimes ostentatiously branded items is part of this trend.[51] Charities use trademarks and cross-license them for use by private sector companies.[52] The distinction between commercial expression and personal or non-commercial expression is frequently blurred.

In the small business context, it has long been commonplace for local businesses to sell their wares in a manner that reflects events taking place within the community. Bars and restaurants may display the logos of local sports teams that are competing in playoffs, bakeries may ice cakes or cookies for window displays that reference local events,[53] restaurants have entered the spirit of elections by allowing patrons to "vote" based on the meal they have ordered; the examples are nearly endless. There may be a marketing angle to businesses who engage with such events; but there is a human and communicative dimension as well. At the heart of it is the right of businesses to make reference to events that take place within the public sphere. Legislation that prevents a local business from referencing a massive, international event that happens to be taking place a few blocks away restricts a form of expression that is not simply commercial but that also relates to the role that businesses — particularly small, local businesses — play within a community. Certainly, in the case of the London Games, the broadly worded right of association combined with zealous enforcement led to public concern over the extreme manner in which local businesses were treated. Media reports indicate that local bakeries, butcher shops, pub owners, caterers, and even grandmothers who knit doll clothes for church charities were all targeted by officials for the associations they created between their wares or services and the Games.[54] Public resistance

---

51 See, for example, Naomi Klein, *No Logo: Taking Aim at the Brand Bullies*, 10th anniversary ed (Toronto: Vintage Canada, 2010) at ch 3; Lucas Conley, *OBD: Obsessive Branding Disorder: The Illusion of Business and the Business of Illusion* (New York: Public Affairs, 2008) at ch 3.

52 An example of this is the association of the colour pink with breast cancer charities and the cross-licensing of related "pink" trademarks. For a critical examination, see Ann Bartow, "Trademarks, Commoditization, Gender and the Color Pink" (2008), online: www.chicagoip.com/pinkdraft.pdf.

53 It was reported that LOCOG had to be called off its zealous attempts to stop bakeries and other small businesses in London from joining in the spirit of the Games in this manner.

54 See, for example, Matthew Fisher, "Olympic Brand Enforcers Out in Full Force for London Games" *The Ottawa Citizen* (24 July 2012) A8; Christopher Hope, "Have Your Olympic Cakes, Display Them, Too; Minister Tells Logo Police To Go Easy on Small British Shop Owners" *The Ottawa Citizen* (19 July 2012) C6.

to this level of restriction led the UK's Minister responsible for the Olympics to request that officials ease up on their actions against small business operators.[55]

Many of the stories that can be told about an event and the athletes who participate in it have commercial dimensions. An athlete and/or a national sport organization (i.e., Speed Skating Canada) may have sponsors who support high performance programs in the long lead up to a major event like the Olympics. When the athlete succeeds in securing a spot on the national team, when they compete in the event, and when they earn medals, the sponsor will expect a return on their investment in the athlete by linking their name and logos with the athlete and/or sport. Yet, unless this sponsor is also an Olympic sponsor, associating themselves with the event through the athlete will contravene ambush marketing laws by creating an unauthorized association. This can pose a significant challenge for athletes, teams, amateur sporting organizations, and their sponsors. High profile incidents reveal how challenging these issues may be, and how athletes themselves may be placed in situations where they are publicly censured or even fined.[56] Thus, by making anti-ambush laws a condition for a successful bid to host a major event, the sporting organizations influence governments to enact laws that may infringe on the rights of the public on the one hand[57] and create another form of ambush towards NSOs and athletes on the other.[58] For example, Olympic sponsors are offered certain rights to affiliate themselves with athletes and teams during the Games, which may interfere with NSO in-house marketing programs. Such activities may damage long-term sponsorship efforts of NSOs and potentially hurt their ability to gener-

---

55 Hope, *ibid.*

56 For example, during the EURO 2012 football tournament, a player was penalized for lifting his shirt to the cameras to show the waistband of his underwear which bore the logo of a company that was not a UEFA sponsor. See Telegraph Sport, "EURO 2012: Nicklas Bendtner's £80,000 Fine For Sponsored Underwear Exposes Uefa's Skewed Priorities," *The Telegraph* (18 June 2012), online: The Telegraph www.telegraph.co.uk/sport/football/competitions/euro-2012/9339202/Nicklas-Bendtners-80000-fine-for-sponsored-underwear-exposes-Uefas-skewed-priorities.html. In another example, Jamaican Sprinter Usain Bolt faced criticism when he removed his gold Puma shoes during his victory lap after winning the men's 100-metre sprint at the Beijing Olympics. He kissed his shoes and held them up to the camera. Puma was not an Olympic sponsor. See: Marina Palomba, "Is Ambush Marketing Dead?" *Reacts* (May 2010), online: www.advertisingcompliancelaw.com/uploads/file/10-097%20ReACTS%20-%20Is%20ambush%20marketing%20dead.PDF.

57 Ellis, Scassa, & Séguin, above note 42 at 303–4.

58 Ellis, Gauthier, & Séguin, above note 1 at 263.

ate sponsorship revenue.[59] In addition, important stakeholders, NSOs, and athletes are not consulted when governments decide to enact legislation, giving the process a lack of transparency. Future research should examine the impacts of legislation on other stakeholders and re-examine its use as part of a brand management/protection strategy.

D. CONCLUSION

This chapter examined the need for major events to protect/control their brands against activities such as ambush marketing. Though this paper focused mainly on the Olympic Games, the principles presented herein could be applied to other major events such as the FIFA World Cup, ICC Cricket World Cup, Commonwealth Games, and the like. While it has been common practice to develop contingency plans based on potential risks (security, financial trouble, boycotts, etc.) associated with sporting events, the approach to brand protection is rather novel.

The strategic brand management approach adopted by the IOC towards the end of the 1990s transformed the organization and its relationship with its stakeholders.[60] The careful management of the brand by the IOC has made the five interlaced rings one of the most powerful brands in international sport. Its strong brand equity makes the Olympic brand an attractive proposition for a multitude of stakeholders wishing to benefit from an association with the brand. As a result, the Winter and Summer Olympic Games are among the most appealing sporting events in the world, reaching billion of viewers through television. In addition, the development of a sophisticated marketing program has helped the IOC and its main stakeholders, namely OCOGs and NOCs, raise billions of dollars in revenue. Hence, protecting and controlling the Olympic brand and its high level of equity is of the utmost importance for the IOC and its stakeholders.

The issue of ambush marketing and its possible threat to brand equity has been identified as a key concern for sport organizations and their partners. Many strategies are used by event owners (e.g., IOC/OCOGs) and their partners to manage their brands and to counter ambush marketing. Nevertheless, international sport federations have sought to leverage the enor-

---

59 *Ibid.*

60 Séguin, Richelieu, & O'Reilly, above note 17 at 4.

mous interest from cities/countries for hosting major events and to make anti-ambush marketing legislation a requirement for hosting these events.

While major sponsors applaud such added protection, there are potentially a number of negative impacts that deserve consideration when discussing ambush marketing legislation. For example, such legislation creates a new form of intellectual property right referred to in this chapter as the right of association. Given the subjective nature of an "association" and given the multiplicity of stakeholders for any major event, each with their own interests, awarding such rights to event organizers creates a dangerous precedent. The scope and breadth of ambush marketing legislation raises serious issues including freedom of expression. Ambush legislation is framed in the broadest possible terms as a way to encompass all forms — current and new — of associations. There are indications that it can and has been used to prevent small businesses from engaging with major international events that take place within their community. Further, the impact of legislation on athletes and sport organizations has yet to be fully understood. Preventing athletes and sport organizations from sharing compelling stories with the public may impact their ability to raise the necessary funds to finance their training programs through corporate sponsorship. Early research on the subject suggests that the need to protect the interests of sponsors through anti-ambush legislation may actually be creating problems for other sponsors.[61] In a system where value is being co-created by all stakeholders,[62] such actions could be problematic in the future. Since application of anti-ambush marketing legislation rests in large part with organizing committees, the way in which they manage this sensitive issue in the future will dictate whether legislation is the ultimate form of brand protection. The negative media coverage that resulted from FIFA's efforts during the 2010 World Cup, as well as the efforts of LOCOG during the London Games, may point instead to the need to use softer strategies such as education. The strategy adopted by Vancouver 2010 was an aggressive education program targeted at each stakeholder with legislation being used as a deterrent. Future research in this area should examine the impacts of legislation on all stakeholders and define the most advantageous aspects of legislation for each group of stakeholders as their requirements for, and concerns about, such measures may be different.

---

61 Ellis, Scassa, & Séguin, above note 42.

62 Ferrand, Chappelet, & Séguin, above note 18.

TWENTY-FIVE

Copyright as Barrier to Creativity: The Case of User-Generated Content

SAMUEL TROSOW

ABSTRACT (EN): The chapter begins with a definitional overview of user-generated content (UGC) as a growing form of cultural and communicative activity in the digital environment. Its potential economic and cultural value are considered, as well as factors which act as barriers to its further development and distribution. It is argued that overly restrictive copyright policies and the threat of infringement liability unduly constrain the full potential of this emerging practice.

A comparative analysis of UGC's treatment as an exception or limitation to infringement in Canada, the United States, and other jurisdictions is undertaken, and the recently enacted UGC amendment to the Canadian *Copyright Act* is evaluated and critiqued. It is argued that UGC can best flourish as part of a broad fair-dealing right where its transformative nature is a central criterion.

User-generated content as a category of creative activity remains under-theorized, especially with respect to the relationship between the labour of individual creators in the networked environment and copyright policy. This chapter explores how changes in the digital environment necessitate the rethinking of certain aspects of copyright law in order to avoid undue barriers to the further development of digital content.

RÉSUMÉ (FR): Ce chapitre débute avec la présentation d'une vue d'ensemble du contenu généré par l'utilisateur (CGU) en tant que forme grandissante d'activité culturelle et communicative dans le contexte numérique. Ses valeurs économiques et culturelles potentielles, ainsi que les facteurs agissant comme barrières à son développement et à sa distribution future, sont considérées. L'auteur soutient que les politiques trop restrictives du droit d'auteur ainsi que les menaces d'actions en violation de droit d'auteur restreignent indûment le plein potentiel de cette pratique émergente.

Le traitement du CGU, comme exception ou limite à la violation de droit d'auteur, fait l'objet d'une analyse comparative au Canada, aux États-Unis et dans d'autres États, et les modifications récemment apportées à la loi canadienne relativement au CGU sont évaluées et critiquées. L'auteur soutient que les pratiques de CGU peuvent mieux s'épanouir comme partie d'un droit à l'utilisation équitable des œuvres étendu, dans lequel la nature transformée de l'œuvre devient un critère central.

Le contenu généré par l'utilisateur, comme catégorie d'activité créative, reste peu analysé sur le plan théorique, surtout sous l'aspect du travail des créateurs individuels dans un environnement de réseaux interconnectés et des politiques de droit d'auteur. Ce chapitre explore comment les changements dans le contexte numérique nécessitent la reconsidération de certains aspects du droit d'auteur afin d'éviter de créer des entraves démesurées au développement futur du contenu numérique.

A. INTRODUCTION

This chapter looks at the creative processes from the point of view of authors who use existing copyrighted content as part of their creation of new works. Borrowing as a component of creative practice is not a new issue as authors have long been faced with questions concerning the scope of permissible borrowing, or use, in the course of generating new cultural objects. A long trajectory of borrowing practices is well documented in music, literature, and the visual arts. But what is new about the practice of borrowing is an increased tension between two processes. On the one hand, more and more individuals are now creatively engaging with cultural objects in an increasingly connected and networked environment. At the same time, though, content owners have become increasingly protective of their property rights, as they resort to the use of technological protection measures, as they issue take-down notices, and as they threaten litigation. This heightened tension results in an increasingly contentious policy environment, as was recently witnessed as Parliament went through the stages of amending the *Copyright Act*,[1] and which continues to play itself out in the press and the blogosphere.

The conceptual frame of reference for this chapter will be "User-Generated Content" (UGC). This usage is emerging as both an indicator of a range of commonly understood creative practices, and a widely used legal term of art, particularly in the area of copyright law. UGC also exemplifies how contemporary forms of cultural and communicational practices shape intellectual property law, rather than simply being shaped by it. This chapter seeks to define and delineate the concept of UGC as it relates to creative practices; to consider the impacts and effects of copyright laws on its production and dissemination; and also to describe and then critically assess recent changes to Canadian copyright law pertinent to UGC.

This chapter will proceed as follows. Building on recent work on UGC,[2] Section B will review the general nature and characteristics of UGC, including definitional and classification issues. Section C will then consider the interrelationships between the creation and dissemination of UGC and copyright law. This section points to a paradox, one that is an increasing source of tension. On the one hand, copyright restrictions threaten to limit and impede the ability of creators to effectively engage with UGC, a constraint especially salient in institutional environments. On the other hand, creative practices have informally evolved in spite of copyright restrictions, and when practices become widespread and accepted, they become an impetus for reform in a user-oriented direction. The recent amendments to the *Copyright Act*, considered in more depth in Section D, evidence this paradox. While the new digital locks provisions have the potential to limit and impede the ability of end-users to make use of copyrighted works that are otherwise lawful, the expansion of the fair dealing categories to include education, parody, and satire, as well as the time shifting exception,

1 *Copyright Act*, RSC 1985, c C-42 [*Copyright Act*]. All references to "Act" in this chapter are to the *Copyright Act*.

2 Samuel E Trosow et al, "Mobilizing User-Generated Content for Canada's Digital Advantage" (Report Prepared for the Social Sciences and Humanities Research Council of Canada, 1 December 2010), online: Western Libraries http://ir.lib.uwo.ca/fimspub/21 [Trosow et al, "Mobilizing UGC"]; Pamela J McKenzie et al, "User-Generated Online Content 1: Overview, Current State and Context" (2012) 17:6 *First Monday*, online: http://firstmonday.org/htbin/cgiwrap/bin/ojs/index.php/fm/article/view/3912/3266 [McKenzie et al, "UGOC Overview"]; Michael McNally et al, "User-generated online content 2: Policy implications" (2012) 17:6 *First Monday*, online: http://firstmonday.org/htbin/cgiwrap/bin/ojs/index.php/fm/article/view/3913/3267 [McNally et al, "UGOC Policy"].

back-up, and user-generated content exceptions bring the *Act* into a closer fit with what had become established practices, or what Edward Lee calls "gap-fillers."[3]

This chapter concludes that Canada has the potential to become a UGC haven, and that these "digital advantages" will have positive economic, social, and cultural effects. But more explicit policy attention needs to be given to UGC, as it is an essential component of a broader innovation policy. However, there are still several barriers which need to be overcome for these benefits to be realized. Despite the changes to the *Copyright Act* along with very positive signals from the Supreme Court in the pentalogy, there remains the danger that users will still be reluctant to fully embrace the full set of their rights. The fear of infringement liability is still very real. These barriers are likely to be especially persistent in institutional settings where overly restrictive copyright policies will only magnify the problem.

B. REVIEW OF THE GENERAL NATURE AND CHARACTERISTICS OF UGC

There have been various attempts to define and characterize UGC. A good starting point is the 2007 OECD definition as content that "reflects a certain amount of creative effort, and . . . which is created outside of professional routines and practices."[4] UGC has more recently been defined "as content that is voluntarily developed by an individual or a consortium and distributed through an online platform,"[5] and a three-part classification scheme for UGC has been proposed as:

1) Individual textual, audio, image, video, and multimedia productions that are distributed online through software platforms such as blogs, podcasting repositories, Flickr, Twitter, YouTube, and citizen journalism sites;

---

3 Edward Lee, "Warming Up to User-Generated Content" (2008) 2008:5 U Ill L Rev 1459 at 1461.

4 Organisation for Economic Cooperation and Development (OECD), *Participative Web and User-Created Content: Web 2.0, Wikis and Social Networking* (28 September 2007) at 9, online: www.sourceoecd.org/scienceIT/9789264037465.

5 Trosow et al, "Mobilizing UGC," above note 2 at 10; see also McKenzie et al, "UGOC Overview," above note 2 in the "Overview and current state of user-generated content" section. In both of these sources, the term "developed" was used as a surrogate for the more precise copyright categories of originality and transformativity. For purposes of this chapter, these terms will be made more explicit.

2) Software modifications or applications that are written by individuals to operate within or augment specific previously existing datasets or hardware or software platforms (e.g., iPhone applications or "apps," utilities that manipulate publicly-available data sets, game or virtual world modifications); and,
3) Formal or informal consortia that collaboratively produce and distribute UGC, including open source software (OSS), such as the Linux or Apache, and wikis, such as Wikipedia.[6]

While software development of modifications and apps as well as the larger scale projects included in the second and third categories are important types of UGC, this chapter will focus on the first category. As Daniel Gervais noted back in 2009, "[h]undreds of millions of Internet users are downloading, altering, mixing, uploading, and/or making available audio, video, and text content on personal web pages, social sites, or using peer-to-peer technology to allow others to access content on their computer."[7]

At the outset, an important distinction should be made between original UGC and transformative UGC. In order for content to qualify as "UGC" in the first instance, it must possess a degree of creativity. Simply reposted existing content is not UGC.[8] In other words, for content to qualify as UGC it must contain some degree of originality or transformativity (or more likely some combination of both).

> Originally authored creative content ranging from blog posts, a Wikipedia article or new open source software program are *prima facie* examples of how users can produce and distribute new, economically and socially valuable works. However, not all UGC is entirely original. One of the most important kinds of UGC is content where the author/creator has drawn on existing works and transformatively repurposed them into a new work. Transformative uses run the gamut from photo mashups that juxtapose two different images to video remixes drawing on hundreds of pieces of content.[9]

---

6 Trosow et al, "Mobilizing UGC," above note 2 at 4–5; McKenzie et al, "UGOC Overview," above note 2 in the "Introduction" section.

7 Daniel Gervais, "The Tangled Web of UGC: Making Copyright Sense of User-Generated Content" (2009) 11:4 Vand J Ent &Tech L 841 at 845–46.

8 While this point may seem self-evident, see the text accompanying notes 44–46 below.

9 McNally et al, "UGOC Policy," above note 2 in the "Originality, transformativity and UGC" section [emphasis in original].

In terms of how an existing copyrighted work is being used, Rebecca Tushnet argues that "[u]sing a work as a building block for an argument, or an expression of the creator's imagination, should be understood as a transformative purpose, in contrast to consuming a work for its entertainment value."[10]

Tushnet's distinction between consumptive and transformative uses is crucial, and it is reflected in the language of section 29.21 itself. While most original works involve some degree of borrowing, and while transformative works necessarily involve some degree of originality, it is useful to separate the concepts of originality and transformativity for analytical purposes because it is the particular case of transformative UGC that poses the more challenging copyright issues.[11]

This chapter will pay particular attention to transformative UGC where the creator is making substantial uses of existing works or sound recordings in which copyright exists. To the extent that such uses are not licensed or otherwise utilized with the permission of the copyright holder, we are essentially assuming what would technically amount to a *prima facie* case of copyright infringement. Since "UGC creates cultural, symbolic, and affective benefit including personal satisfaction, enhanced skill or reputation, improved functionality for existing games or devices, community building or civic engagement,"[12] the working assumption in this chapter is that copyright policy needs to be able to accommodate a robust set of user-oriented rights which will not simply permit or tolerate, but affirmatively encourage and nurture the development and dissemination of transformative UGC.

---

10 Rebecca Tushnet, "User-Generated Discontent: Transformation in Practice," (2008) 31:4 Colum J L & Arts 497 at 506.

11 Where a use is merely consumptive, or where it involves mere copying without any additional element of added originality, then the new UGC exception does not come into play. Such a use might or might not come within the scope of fair dealing or another special limitation or exception in the Act depending on the circumstances.

As Daniel Gervais points out: "The proposed exception is not a license to freely copy anything or to upload it to any social site. It requires transformation. It is a *limited* right to reuse existing works to create new works, in cases where a licensing transaction is not reasonable and there is no demonstrable impact on the market for existing works": Daniel Gervais, "User-Generated Content and Music File-Sharing: A Look at Some of the More Interesting Aspects of Bill C-32" in Michael Geist, ed, *From "Radical Extremism" to "Balanced Copyright": Canadian Copyright and the Digital Agenda* (Toronto: Irwin Law, 2010) 447 at 465 [footnote omitted].

12 McKenzie et al, "UGOC Overview," above note 2 in the "Value Creation" section.

Finally, before turning to a consideration of how copyright can act as a constraint to the creation and dissemination of UGC, it is useful to first contextualize UGC as a historically disruptive force. While UGC offers an important source of innovation, it also tends to destabilize several entrenched dichotomies, thereby posing a challenge to established business models, especially in the cultural, publishing, and entertainment sectors.

The UGC phenomenon disrupts the traditional dichotomies between the creator and the end user, between the producer and the consumer, between the performer and the audience, and between (waged) work time and (unwaged) leisure time. It also challenges the significance of core copyright concepts such as authorship, ownership, and infringement. For Debora Halbert, UGC is not only creative work in its own right, but work that "generally disrupts the commercial paradigm."[13] She observes that "[t]he user-generated world can and does play with the commodified products of the culture industry, appropriating common cultural symbols and remaking them as personally meaningful connections."[14]

Halbert's Manifesto is important because by explaining UGC as a disruptive force, it helps set the stage for why it has generally become such a contested policy issue and why copyright has become the specific locus of the dispute.

> Where once there existed the relatively stable world of the culture industry in which concentrated control over film, music, literature, and art was easy, the technology of modernity has shifted control into the hands of consumers of culture. Stable control over the culture industry was possible because commodity culture de-skills people as creators, in the same way that industrialization de-skilled the artisan and craftsperson while turning them into fodder for the industrial machine.[15]

C. COPYRIGHT: A CONSTRAINING BARRIER TO UGC

Barriers to UGC production and distribution can take several forms:

> First, to produce and share UGC individuals must have the requisite technology and skills as well as access to appropriate tools. Second, private

13 Debora Halbert, "Mass Culture and the Culture of the Masses: A Manifesto for User-Generated Rights" (2009) 11:4 Vandt J Ent & Tech L 921 at 924. [Halbert, "Manifesto"].

14 *Ibid* at 930.

15 *Ibid* [footnote omitted].

> ordering mechanisms such as licenses and technological protection measures (TPMs) provide content owners increased control over their products even beyond the scope of publicly ordered intellectual property law. Finally, copyright and patent laws directly provide powerful legal mechanisms which impede the creation and dissemination of UGC.[16]

Without downplaying the importance of the other factors, this section will focus on the last factor, the effects of copyright policies as a constraining barrier to UGC.

Using evidence gathered from the Chilling Effects Project,[17] Wendy Seltzer argues that US law, "through copyright and the DMCA, is responsible for this restriction on Internet speech . . . even though the DMCA relies upon private enforcement, because of the incentive structure the DMCA creates for online intermediaries."[18]

Seltzer uses several high-profile examples and she acknowledges they may seem extreme. But she asserts that the

> frequency of error and its bias against speech represents a structural problem with secondary liability and the DMCA: the DMCA makes it too easy for inappropriate claims of copyright to produce takedown of speech. It encourages service providers to take down speech on notice even if the notice is factually questionable or flawed.[19]

While Canadian intermediaries are at an advantage in this regard since at least so far the government has resisted calls for the type of "notice and takedown" regime in effect in the US,[20] it is too early to assess whether the

---

16 McNally et al, "UGOC Policy," above note 2 in the "Barriers to user-generated content production and distribution" section; see also Trosow et al, "Mobilizing UGC", above note 2 at 37–41.

17 Chilling Effects is a joint project of the Electronic Frontier Foundation and several legal clinics in the US. The project is intended to draw attention to overreaching attempts by content owners to use their intellectual property rights to impede protected activity on the Internet, noting that "[a]necdotal evidence suggests that some individuals and corporations are using intellectual property and other laws to silence other online users" and they provide a searchable database of cease and desist letters: see http://chillingeffects.org.

18 Wendy Seltzer, "Free Speech Unmoored in Copyright's Safe Harbor: Chilling Effects of the DMCA on the First Amendment" (2010) 24:1 Harv JL & Tech 171at 175.

19 *Ibid* at 177–78.

20 Sections 41.25 et seq. of the Canadian *Copyright Act*, above note 1, added by Bill C-11 provide for a "notice and notice" regime wherein intermediaries are under an obligation to provide notice to the account holder when they receive a notice from a content owner that there is alleged infringement.

"notice and notice" provisions will create similar problems of chilling effects.[21] But the problem of chilling the full utilization of users' rights is still present in Canada. Canadian rights-holders, especially as represented by collectives such as Access Copyright and SOCAN, very aggressively assert their rights, and they have been successful in discouraging the full utilization of users' rights.[22] Access Copyright has the additional advantage that they do not deal directly with end-users. They contract directly with institutions which are often risk-averse and willing to comply with licensing terms that seek compensation for uses that are otherwise non-compensable,[23] especially when the licensing costs can be downloaded on another party.

In contrast to much of the emphasis on chilling, Edward Lee emphasizes warming. He argues that the most significant copyright development did not come from the legislature, courts, or industry, but rather "from the unorganized, informal practices of various, unrelated users of copyrighted works, many of whom probably know next to nothing about copyright law."[24] Lee's thesis is that these informal practices provide "gap-fillers" and that "these unauthorized mass practices of users may have . . . turned out to be the catalyst for subsequent ratification of those practices . . . ."[25] He introduces the concept of warming to explain how uncertainty in copyright law may actually embolden user behaviour, and that user-generated content on the Internet is particularly conducive to such warming.[26] Lee's analysis seems to be especially on point with a range of the new exceptions and limitations added

---

21 For a further discussion of chilling effects in the Canadian context, see Jonathon Penney, "Copyright's Media Theory and the Internet: The Case of the Chilling Effects Doctrine," Chapter 23 in this volume.

22 For a further discussion on the success of copyright collectives, particularly SOCAN in the area of public performances, see Louis D'Alton, "A Gramscian Analysis of the Public Performance Right," Chapter 10 in this volume.

23 An assessment of institutional risk-aversion and its relationship to the notion of copyright chill is beyond the scope of this essay. For further discussion on how Access Copyright has been able to impede the full utilization of users' rights in the educational context, see Samuel E Trosow, "Bill C-32 and the Educational Sector: Overcoming Impediments to Fair Dealing" in Michael Geist, ed, *From "Radical Extremism" to "Balanced Copyright": Canadian Copyright and the Digital Agenda* (Toronto: Irwin Law, 2010) at 519; Samuel Trosow, Scott Armstrong, & Brent Harasym, "Objections to the Proposed Access Copyright Post-Secondary Tariff and its Progeny Licenses: A Working Paper" (14 August 2012), online: Western Libraries ir.lib.uwo.ca/fimspub/24.

24 Lee, above note 3 at 1460.

25 *Ibid* at 1461.

26 *Ibid* at 1463–64.

to the *Copyright Act* through Bill C-11, especially those contained in sections 29.21 through 29.24.

Perhaps the most significant instances of copyright chill have taken place with respect to the remixing and sampling of musical works and sound recordings. Like Seltzer's examples from the US *Digital Millennium Copyright Act*, these problems emanate from the United States, but they do have spill-over effects in Canada.

Even though the fair use doctrine in the United States allows for the creation of transformative works, cases related to sampling from sound recordings have limited practical application and have created a chilling effect against what were the previous sampling practices in the 1980s.[27] While these cases are of questionable precedent value, they have had a significant chilling effect on the willingness of artists to fully utilize their users' rights and engage in sampling practices.

While most of these constraints seem to emanate from the United States, Canada has not been without its problems. While the application of the fair use doctrine is open-ended in the US, in that there is no need to first come within a threshold category, Canadian fair dealing is still limited to certain enumerated categories.[28] In other words, merely engaging in a transformative use will not necessarily trigger fair dealing in Canada. It is still conceivable, even with the addition of education, parody, and satire to section 29, that a particular instance of UGC might not fit into an allowable fair dealing category. Hence the importance of new section 29.21 of the Canadian *Copyright Act*, which was recently added by the enactment of Bill C-11 in June 2012. The next section will look at the new UGC provision in

27 In *Grand Upright Music Ltd v Warner Bros Records*, 780 F Supp 182 (SDNY 1991), rapper Biz Markie was found liable for infringement for sampling Gilbert O'Sullivan's song "Alone Again Naturally," with Judge Duffy going so far as to note that sampling not only violated US copyright law but also the Seventh Commandment. In *Bridgeport Music, Inc v Dimension Films*, 410 F 3d 792 (6th Cir 2005), the 6th Circuit found that the borrowing of three notes constituted infringement. The court also stated "[g]et a license or do not sample" as a general proposition. While these cases are not binding precedent outside of the 6th circuit and the Southern District of NY (much less in Canada), they have had a persistently persuasive and chilling effect on sampling practices.

28 In order to qualify for fair dealing in Canada, the use must come within the enumerated categories of research and private study (s 29), criticism or review (s 29.1), or news reporting (s 29.2): *Copyright Act*, above note 1, ss 29–29.2. Bill C-11 has added the categories of education, parody, and satire to section 29. As well, Canadian courts have been very clear that these categories should be broadly construed because fair dealing is an important user's right. Still, not all instances of UGC come within one of these categories, even if they are broadly construed.

detail, and also consider its relationship to both fair dealing and the digital locks provisions.

D. EVALUATING THE AMENDMENTS TO THE CANADIAN *COPYRIGHT ACT*

1) The New User-Generated Content Exception: Section 29.21

The new provision in the Canadian *Copyright Act*,[29] section 29.21, (formally labelled "Non-commercial User-generated Content" but also frequently referred to as the YouTube exception) provides a broad exception to copyright infringement for making use of copyrighted content in the creation of new content. Subject to five conditions, an individual can use an existing copyrighted work (or other subject matter like a performance or a sound recording) to create a new original work (or other subject matter). Furthermore, the individual (or a member of the individual's household) can then use it or authorize an intermediary to distribute it. The exception is not limited to works, but can also be applied to other subject matter such as performers' performances and sound recordings.[30]

The term "use" is defined very broadly to include not only making reproductions of the copyrighted content, but also publicly performing it, communicating it to the public, translating it, and making adaptations.[31]

According to the official *Legislative Summary* for Bill C-11:

> New section 29.21 of the Act creates a new exception for content generated by non-commercial users (this has been referred to as the "UGC" (user-generated content) or "mash-up exception"). Under this exception, a consum-

---

29 Most of the provisions of Bill C-11 (including the subject UGC provisions) were proclaimed in force on 7 November 2012; Order Fixing Various Dates as the Dates on which Certain Provisions of the Act Come into Force, (2012) 146:23 C Gaz II, 2447 referring to PC 2012-1392, 25 October 2012), online: www.gazette.gc.ca/rp-pr/p2/2012/2012-11-07/pdf/g2-14623.pdf.

30 The first paragraph of s 29.21 of the *Copyright Act*, above note 1, refers to an "existing work or other subject-matter" which would include performers' performances (ss 15, 26), sound recordings (s 18), and communication signals (s 21). The fact that the UGC exception is not limited to just works is significant as it explicitly applies to material from sound recordings.

31 "Use" is broadly defined to include all of the exclusive owners' rights in s 3 of the *Copyright Act* other than the authorization right. Section 29.21(2) provides: "'use' means to do anything that by this Act the owner of the copyright has the sole right to do, other than the right to authorize anything."

> er has the *right* to use, in a non-commercial context, a publicly available work in order to create a new work. This exception is subject to conditions, namely the identification of the source, the legality of the work or the copy used, and the absence of a substantial adverse effect on the exploitation of the original work.[32]

The five conditions are important because they constrain the potential scope of the UGC right. First, the content being used must have been "published or otherwise made available to the public."[33] Second, the use of the newly resulting UGC (and the authorization to distribute it) must be solely for non-commercial purposes.[34] Third, where it is reasonable under the circumstances to do so, the source (name of the author, etc.) of the content used must be given.[35] Fourth, the user must have had a reasonable belief that the source was not infringing.[36]

The fifth condition is a bit more complex; that "the use of, or the authorization to disseminate, the new work or other subject-matter does not have a substantial adverse effect, financial or otherwise, on the exploitation or potential exploitation of the existing work or other subject-matter — or copy of it — or on an existing or potential market for it, including that the new work or other subject-matter is not a substitute for the existing one."[37]

The first, third, and fourth conditions are relatively straightforward and non-problematic. But the second condition that the UGC be "*solely* for non-commercial purposes," and the last condition regarding lack of substantial effect, even on a *potential* exploitation, as they are so broadly drafted require further discussion. The limitation in paragraph 29.21(1)(a) "the use of, or the authorization to disseminate, the new work or other subject-matter is done solely for non-commercial purposes" purports to create a bright-line distinction between commercial and non-commercial purpos-

---

32 Legal and Legislative Affairs Division, Legislative Summary, "Bill C-11: An Act to Amend the *Copyright Act*" (Publication No 41-1-C11-E) by Dara Lithwick and Maxime-Olivier Thibodeau (Ottawa: Library of Parliament, 20 April 2012) at 12, online: www.parl.gc.ca/Content/LOP/LegislativeSummaries/41/1/c11-e.pdf [emphasis added].

33 *Copyright Act*, above note 1, s 29.21(1).

34 *Ibid*, s 29.21(1)(a) ("the use of, or the authorization to disseminate, the new work or other subject-matter is done solely for non-commercial purposes.").

35 *Ibid*, s 29.21(1)(b)("the source — and, if given in the source, the name of the author, performer, maker or broadcaster — of the existing work or other subject-matter or copy of it are mentioned, if it is reasonable in the circumstances to do so.")

36 *Ibid*, s 29.21(1)(c)("the individual had reasonable grounds to believe that the existing work or other subject-matter or copy of it, as the case may be, was not infringing copyright.")

37 *Ibid*, s 29.21(1)(d).

es. This is not only a difficult distinction to make in such absolute terms at the outset, but the commercial/non-commercial nature usage of the UGC might also shift over time. The language would be easier to comprehend and implement if it said "primarily" instead of "solely." Taken literally, any incidental or even insignificant commercial aspect of the use threatens to nullify the exemption. While the degree of commerciality is certainly an important factor, it should not have been drafted as a bright-line requirement. Does posting UGC on a platform that provides potential economic benefits for popular content nullify the exception? Given YouTube's potential monetization incentive, are postings on YouTube likely to be disqualified? On the one hand, a strict reading of the provision would suggest likely disqualification. Daniel Gervais suggests that such a narrow reading of the exception to restrict it to purely non-commercial uses would offer only limited protection as sites like YouTube and many blogs ultimately have commercial aspects.[38]

On the other hand, the term "YouTube exception" was widely utilized during the discussions on Bills C-32 and C-11 so a strong counter-argument can be made that Parliament did not intend YouTube postings to be necessarily commercial and hence disqualifying. In its *Backgrounder* on Bill C-31, the government summarized the provisions as follows:

> Canadians will also be able to incorporate existing copyrighted material in the creation of new works, such as Internet mash-ups, as long as:
> - it is done for non-commercial purposes;
> - the existing material was legitimately acquired; and
> - the work they create is not a substitute for the original material or does not have a substantial negative impact on the markets for the original material, or on the creator's reputation.[39]

And in a posted Q&A on the provision, the government stated "[f]or users, the Bill will allow the creation of user-generated content using copyright materials, such as mash-up videos, for posting on a blog or video-sharing site."[40]

---

38 Gervais, above note 11 at 473, arguing that an expansive definition of commerciality might cover postings to YouTube.

39 Industry Canada, *Copyright Modernization Act — Backgrounder* (2011), online: www.ic.gc.ca/eic/site/crp-prda.nsf/eng/h_rp01237.html.

40 Industry Canada, *Questions and Answers: The Copyright Modernization Act* (2011), online: www.ic.gc.ca/eic/site/crp-prda.nsf/eng/h_rp01153.html.

Most telling, direct references to YouTube were made by the government prior to the passage of Bill C-11 with respect to the proposed exception. A memorandum for use by ministers in responding to questions for legislative committees entitled "Questions and Answers — Bill C-32: For Ministers' Appearance Before the Legislative Committee" contains a heading entitled "Copyright Owner Concerns Around the UGC Exception."[41] It asks the question: "The YouTube/mash-up exception opens another door to piracy. Why did the government create such a broad and undefined exception?" In a separate document providing a clause-by-clause analysis, the government explicitly indicates posting a video to YouTube as an example of activity that could fall under the exception. In explaining the rationale for the new section, the analysis stated: "The individual who creates this 'user-generated content' can also authorize its dissemination by an intermediary (e.g., YouTube)."[42] These documents provide compelling evidence that a posting to YouTube or similar commercial website should not necessarily be a disqualifying act under paragraph 29.21(a).

More problematic is the question of what happens if the UGC begins as a wholly non-commercial project, such as a school project or a hobby-related activity, and subsequently enjoys a measure of commercial success. Would the previously attached UGC exception remain intact, or would it be nullified? Most likely the exception would remain intact because it would be unusual to suggest that what was a non-infringing act at the time of creation has somehow now morphed into an infringing act.

The final condition also creates unwarranted ambiguity about the scope of the exception and the certainty with which it can be utilized. Of particular concern is the vagueness of the wording "potential exploitation of the existing work" and "potential market for it [the existing work]." If interpreted broadly, these potentialities could be quite large and significantly limit UGC production and distribution. In the extreme, it could be argued orig-

---

41 "Questions and Answers — Bill C-32: For Ministers' Appearance Before the Legislative Committee" (2011); the document has been posted to www.scribd.com/doc/65726239/c32ministerqanda; according to a stamp, it was released pursuant to the *Access to Information Act*: see Michael Geist, "Behind the Scenes of Bill C-32: The Complete Ministerial Q & A" (21 September 2011), online: MichaelGeist.ca www.michaelgeist.ca/content/view/6017/125/.

42 See Michael Geist, "Behind the Scenes of Bill C-32: Govt's Clause-By-Clause Analysis Raises Constitutional Questions" (27 September 2011), online: MichaelGeist.ca www.michaelgeist.ca/content/view/6026/125/, embedding a document containing detailed reviews of, rationales underlying, and changes in Bill C-32, at 45.

inal works could be potentially exploited in an unlimited number of ways and that potential markets for such works include a variety of yet unimaginable (but potential) opportunities. It is important to emphasize that while this final condition appears similar to the sixth fair dealing factor, the effect of the dealing on the work,[43] the limitations in paragraph 29.21(1)(d) seem more explicit and potentially broader. In other words, the analysis that is required under paragraph 29.21(1)(d) could be more complex and fraught with uncertainty for the claimant of the UGC exemption than the same person making a fair dealing claim under the very same circumstances. This additional language regarding the *potential* exploitation of the work has not been inserted into section 29 despite the fact that section 29 was itself amended in Bill C-11. This disparity creates the possibility that under the same set of circumstances, a claim under the UGC exception could be weakened even where fair dealing could still be successfully established.

Despite these clear limitations on the scope of the UGC exception, opponents of the proposed section persistently argued that it would apply to simple re-postings of existing works. For example, in their submission on Bill C-32, the Entertainment Software Association of Canada (ESAC) made the claim that the UGC provision "would allow anyone to copy all of the designs, art assets and even programming code from a game and release a 'copycat' game for free on the Internet."[44] Of course simply re-posting an existing work does not constitute user-generated content even under the most liberal of its definitions. Section 29.21 has an explicit threshold requirement that the content be new, and there is no doubt that under the circumstances of ESAC's example the copying would be disqualified for not

---

43 In *CCH Canadian Ltd v Law Society of Upper Canada*, 2004 SCC 13, [2004] 1 SCR 339, the court set forth the six factors to consider when determining whether a dealing is fair. The sixth factor, the effect of the dealing on the work, was explained in paragraph 59: "[T]he effect of the dealing on the work is another factor warranting consideration when courts are determining whether a dealing is fair. If the reproduced work is likely to compete with the market of the original work, this may suggest that the dealing is not fair. Although the effect of the dealing on the market of the copyright owner is an important factor, it is neither the only factor nor the most important factor that a court must consider in deciding if the dealing is fair." Accordingly, it appears that in a fair dealing analysis the effect of the dealing on the work is only one of six factors, and not a determinative one at that. Yet, the language of section 29.21(1)(d) elevates the effect on the work to a determinative factor, which alone could disqualify the exception.

44 Entertainment Software Association of Canada (ESAC), *Submission to the Legislative Committee on Bill C-32* (December 2010) at 11, online: Parliament of Canada www.parl.gc.ca/Content/HOC/Committee/411/CC11/WebDoc/WD5401532/403_C32_Copyright_Briefs/EntertainmentSoftwareAssociationofCanadaE.pdf.

meeting these conditions. ESAC further claimed that the provision would "allow anyone to reverse engineer and extract the underlying technologies and code from a game (such as a game engine) and offer it for free on the Internet."[45] Similarly, counsel for the Canadian Media Production Association (CMPA) told the Legislative Committee on Bill C-32:

> [W]hile we fully appreciate the rationale for the user-generated content exception, our members are deeply concerned that it sets the creative bar way too low for what would constitute such content. What none of us want is a provision that might, for example, inadvertently permit a user to upload full seasons of *Degrassi* or *Corner Gas* to the Internet. In that scenario, the only thing that's being generated is lost revenue to the people who make *Degrassi*.[46]

Given the explicit language in section 29.21, it appears that the UGC exception, while closely related to fair dealing, is not exactly the same. The two defences exist in parallel and a UGC claimant defending against an infringement action could raise either or both the general fair dealing right or the special UGC exception. In a situation where one of the categories of fair dealing is not present,[47] then the defence under section 29.21 is still available assuming all of its conditions can be met. However, in a situation that is otherwise eligible for fair dealing, the fact that a use is commercial (or somewhat commercial) or where a *potential* exploitation has an adverse effect on the work, fair dealing is not necessarily nullified; it would depend on all of the factors. It is anticipated, however, that in most situations, the same result should be reached under both fair dealing and the UGC exception.

2) Interaction between Section 29.21 and the Digital Locks Provisions

Over the past few years, much concern has been expressed about the interaction between the digital locks provisions contained in Bills C-61, C-32, and ultimately C-11 and their relationship to various users' rights in other sec-

---

45 *Ibid*.

46 Legislative Assembly, *Legislative Committee on Bill C-32: Evidence*, 40th Parl, 3rd Sess (1 February 2011) at 1220, Testimony of Reynolds Mastin, online: Parliament of Canada www.parl.gc.ca/HousePublications/Publication.aspx?DocId=4915240&Language=E.

47 That is, the use qualifies neither as research, private study, parody, or satire under s 29; criticism or review under s 29.1; or news reporting under s 29.2: *Copyright Act*, above note 1, ss 29–29.2.

tions of the Act. Insofar as the text of the anti-circumvention rules added in section 41 of the Act do not contain general limitations for activity that is otherwise non-infringing, the concern has been that users' rights (such as fair dealing or other specific statutory exceptions) would be impaired.

Indeed, several of the new special exceptions in Bill C-11 are explicitly so limited. For example, section 29.22, which adds a safe-harbour for certain instances of private copying provides "the individual, in order to make the reproduction, did not circumvent, as defined in section 41, a technological protection measure, as defined in that section, or cause one to be circumvented."[48] Section 29.23, which provides a limited exception for reproduction of parts of broadcasts for later viewing or listening, contains a similar counter-limitation. The safe-harbour from infringement liability in that section applies only if "the individual, in order to record the program, did not circumvent, as defined in section 41, a technological protection measure, as defined in that section, or cause one to be circumvented."[49] Section 29.24, pertaining to back-up copies, contains the same caveat.[50] Finally, section 30.04, which provides educational institutions with a limited exception to make certain uses of materials that are publicly available on the Internet, contains a specific counter-limitation that "[s]ubsection (1) does not apply if the work or other subject-matter — or the Internet site where it is posted — is protected by a technological protection measure that restricts access to the work or other subject-matter or to the Internet site."[51]

As the above paragraph demonstrates, Parliament has expressed a very clear intent to limit certain exceptions. In contrast to the other new exceptions, the UGC exception in section 29.21 does not contain any reference to it being inapplicable where a technological protection measure is circumvented within the meaning of section 41. In other words, Parliament chose NOT to so limit the availability of the UGC exception where there is an act of circumvention. This is not to say that engaging in a proscribed act of circumvention would not otherwise constitute a violation of section 41; however, unlike sections 29.22, 29.23, 29.24, and 30.04, the exception itself

---

48 *Copyright Act*, above note 1, s 29.22(1)(c).

49 *Ibid*, s 29.23(1)(b).

50 *Ibid*, s 29.24(1)(c).

51 *Ibid*, s 30.04(3). Paragraph 30.04(4)(a) contains the further counter-limitation that the exception does not apply where "that work or other subject-matter — or the Internet site where it is posted — is protected by a technological protection measure that restricts the doing of that act."

is not nullified and to suggest otherwise would be to render the referenced language in these other sections as *surplusage*.

This argument might be countered with the assertion that acts of circumvention would also disqualify the UGC exception because paragraph 29.21(c) nullifies the exception where "the individual had reasonable grounds to believe that the existing work or other subject-matter or copy of it, as the case may be, was not infringing copyright." However, there is an important distinction to be made here. An act of circumvention proscribed by section 41 is not an act of copyright infringement. Nowhere does the Act purport to characterize an act of circumvention as a copyright infringement as such. The remedies provision in section 41 makes explicit reference to the remedies for copyright infringement,[52] and this is very different than characterizing the underlying acts of circumvention as infringement themselves.

E. CONCLUSIONS

Despite its shortcomings and limitations, the new UGC exception added to the *Copyright Act* provides an extra level of protection for creators of user-generated content and it could prove to be exceptionally flexible. It is additive to fair dealing in the nature of a statutory safe-harbour so long as its conditions are met. In situations where failure to meet one of the conditions disqualifies the UGC safe-harbour, resort can still be made to fair dealing. The provision is not limited to using works; it applies to all copyrighted subject matter including sound recordings. It is not limited to making copies, as the term "use" applies to all of the owner's exclusive rights other than the authorization rights, so it applies to public performances, translations, adaptations, and communications to the public of works and sound recordings. As well, while under current usage, UGC generally refers to materials that are distributed online, there is no such limitation in the text of the exception. Thus, it could be applicable to CDs and reprographic reproductions.

52 Subsection 41.1(2) provides: "The owner of the copyright in a work, a performer's performance fixed in a sound recording or a sound recording in respect of which paragraph (1)(*a*) has been contravened is, subject to this Act and any regulations made under section 41.21, entitled to all remedies — by way of injunction, damages, accounts, delivery up and otherwise — that are or maybe conferred by law for the infringement of copyright against the person who contravened that paragraph." There is similar language with respect to violations of the device and service prohibitions in subsection 41.1(4). But referencing the remedies for infringement is very different than characterizing the act itself as infringement.

Yet, it remains to be seen how well the new provision will be received and implemented. While the problem of copyright chill is still present as an inhibiting factor, the new provision may well act as a counter to copyright chilling and result in the soft warming as envisioned by Edward Lee. It could also have the effect of furthering the process of decommodification and the democratization of content provision, as envisioned by Debora Halbert, insofar as the production of creative content is being widely distributed among a large number of dispersed creators.

Creating an environment where UGC creators are enabled and encouraged to produce, distribute, and reuse new materials continues to present a challenge to policy-makers. Given the benefits of UGC, it is not enough that they be merely tolerated; they need to be actively encouraged. While the addition of section 29.21 to the *Copyright Act* is a positive step forward, strategies for encouraging the development of UGC need to be more broadly considered as an essential element of Canada's innovation policy, a policy which remains as yet unarticulated.

Contributors

Bita Amani

Bita Amani, BA (York University, *with Distinction*), LLB (Osgoode), SJD (U of T), is Associate Professor at Queen's University, Faculty of Law, and teaches courses in intellectual property, information privacy, and feminist legal studies. She is author of two books: *State Agency and the Patenting of Life in International Law: Merchants and Missionaries in a Global Society* (Aldershott: Ashgate Publishing Company, 2009) and *Trademarks and Unfair Competition Law in Canada: Cases and Commentary* (Toronto: Carswell, 2011, with Carys Craig). She is Adjunct Professor at Osgoode Hall Law School and has been a Co-Director and Lecturer for the LLM Program in Intellectual Property (with Rosemary Coombe). She was a visiting researcher at the Brocher Foundation (Geneva, Switzerland) and visiting scholar and guest lecturer at the Oxford Intellectual Property Research Centre and at the Centre for International Governance, University Of Leeds School of Law. Dr. Amani has served as government consultant on gene patenting for the Ontario Advisory Committee on Predictive Genetic Technologies and on the E-Laws project for the Ministry of the Attorney General, Office of the Legislative Counsel (Ontario), where she was also briefly a legislative drafter (37th Legislature's Session, 2001). She is called to the Bar of Ontario.

Marcus Boon

Marcus Boon is Professor of English Literature at York University. He is the author of *The Road of Excess: A History of Writers on Drugs* (Harvard University Press, 2002) and *In Praise of Copying* (Harvard University Press, 2010). He writes about music for *The Wire* and *Boing Boing*. He is currently at work on a book entitled *The Politics of Vibration*. Website: www.marcusboon.com.

Carys Craig

Carys J Craig is an Associate Professor at Osgoode Hall Law School, York University, where she has been a member of the full-time faculty since 2002 and director of the Professional LLM Program in Intellectual Property since 2009. A recipient of the Osgoode Hall Legal & Literary Society Excellence in Teaching Award, Dr Craig teaches a variety of JD and graduate courses in the field of intellectual property law. She researches and publishes on domestic, comparative, and international copyright and trademark law and policy, with an emphasis on public interest theory and the public domain. Her award-winning work has been cited with approval by the Supreme Court of Canada. Her recently published monograph, *Copyright, Communication, & Culture: Towards a Relational Theory of Copyright law* (Northampton, MA: Edward Elgar Press, 2011), critically examines the theoretical foundations of modern copyright law. Dr Craig holds a First Class Honours Bachelor of Laws (LLB Hons) from the University of Edinburgh in Scotland, a Master of Laws (LLM) from Queen's University in Kingston, Ontario, and a Doctorate in Law (SJD) from the University of Toronto, where she was a graduate fellow of the Centre for Innovation Law and Policy.

Louis D'Alton

A native of Toronto, Ontario, Louis D'Alton's interest in music began in grade school. He joined Orchestra London Canada as a member of the double bass section in 1983 while at the same time freelancing with other orchestras and small ensembles. He has appeared in numerous concert recordings for the CBC as a member of Orchestra London Canada. Concurrent with his classical performances he has played club and festival dates and recorded with a great many folk and celtic ensembles including the Hot Latke's Klezmer band and Uisce Beatha (a London-based band of the early 90s.)

In 1992 he assumed the role of music librarian for Orchestra London. His work in the music library would subsequently lead him to pursue an MLIS at the former Graduate School of Library and Information Science at Western, from which he graduated in 1996. In 1997 he joined the Don Wright Faculty of Music at the University of Western Ontario as concert manager, where he presently remains overseeing approximately 500 performances each academic year. He received his doctorate in Library and Information Science in June 2012 from the Faculty of Information and Media Studies at Western.

Jeremy De Beer

Jeremy de Beer is a law Professor at the University of Ottawa, working on technological innovation, intellectual property, and international trade and development. Many of his refereed publications on intellectual property issues relating to innovation and creativity appear in top-ranked journals recognized across the disciplines of law, business, communications, and political science. He has authored numerous other papers, studies, and commissioned reports, and published four books, including *Access to Knowledge in Africa: The Role of Copyright*. Professor de Beer teaches multidisciplinary seminars on intellectual property policy, the digital music business, and sustainable international development, and an introduction to the fundamentals of property law. With academic qualifications including a graduate degree in law from the University of Oxford and undergraduate degrees in business and in law from the University of Saskatchewan, he is also a practicing lawyer and an experienced strategy consultant to technology companies, creator groups, law firms, think tanks, governments, and international organizations. After working at MacLeod Dixon LLP and clerking at the Federal Court of Appeal, he was legal counsel to the Copyright Board. He has appeared as counsel before the Federal Court of Appeal and, most recently, in landmark copyright cases before the Supreme Court of Canada.

B Courtney Doagoo

B Courtney Doagoo is a PhD Candidate at the University of Ottawa, Faculty of Law. Her interests in the arts and culture have led her to pursue legal issues at the intersection of intellectual property and creativity, innovation, fashion, commerce, the Internet, the arts, and Traditional Knowledge. She is a regular contributor to IP Osgoode's *IPilogue* (iposgoode.ca) and the *Centre for Art Law* (itsartlaw.com), and is in the process of co-creating an online cultural forum *colours on white background* (coloursonwhitebackground.com). Since 2012 she has been a Director on the Board of MASC: Multicultural Arts | Schools | Communities (masconline.ca).

Daniel Downes

Daniel Downes is Associate Professor of Information and Communication Studies at the University of New Brunswick at Saint John and Fellow of the

Royal Society of Arts. An academic, musician, and broadcaster, Downes has published articles on copyright, the structure of the new media economy, and the role of media in the construction of community and personal identity. His research interests include media literacy (particularly new and social media) and the role of intellectual property in the regulation of cultural industries and popular culture. He is the author of *Interactive Realism: the Poetics of Cyberspace* (McGill University Press, 2005) and co-editor of *Post-Colonial Distances: The Study of Popular Music in Canada and Australia* with Bev Diamond and Denis Crowdy (Cambridge Scholars Publishing, 2008).

Mistrale Goudreau

Mistrale Goudreau is Full Professor at the Civil Law Section of the University of Ottawa where she has been teaching since 1982. Her areas of teaching include intellectual property, law and technology, and statutory interpretation. In the past, Mistrale Goudreau has acted as the Assistant Dean for clinical and applied teaching and the Vice Dean of the Civil Law Section of the University of Ottawa. She is a member of the executive committee of the editorial board of *Les cahiers de propriété intellectuelle*. She has published numerous articles on copyright, unfair competition, legislative drafting, and legal theory. She recently authored a book entitled *International Encyclopaedia of Laws: Intellectual Property Law in Canada,* (Alphen aan den Rijn (Netherlands): Kluwer Law International, 2013).

Gregory Hagen

Greg Hagen is an Associate Professor of Law at the University of Calgary. He earned an LLB at Dalhousie Law School. After being called to the Bar of British Columbia, he practiced in the areas of corporate, securities, intellectual property, and technology law. Later he earned an LLM (concentration in technology law) at the University of Ottawa. He has been a Visiting Professor at Duke University's Asia America Institute in Transnational Law at the University of Hong Kong and at the Faculty of Law, University of Ghana. His research focuses on technology and intellectual property law, and his areas of interest also include legal and political philosophy, philosophy of science, and science policy. Prior to entering the field of law, Greg Hagen earned his PhD in the philosophy of science at the University of Western Ontario. Greg is presently doing research on ethical and legal issues concerning synthetic biology as a co-investigator in the PhytoMetaSyn project. He is also a co-investigator on Rethinking Processual Law: Towards a Cyberjustice, which will study and create new procedural models utilizing the Cyberjustice Laboratory at the Université de Montréal's Centre de Recherche en Droit Public.

Blayne Haggart

Blayne Haggart is an Assistant Professor of political science at Brock University in St Catharines, Ontario. A former economist and journalist, Blayne received his PhD in Political Science with a Specialization in Political Economy from Carleton University. His research focuses on regional governance and copyright policy. His forthcoming book, *Copyfight: The Global Politics of Digital Copyright Reform*, which examines the forces shaping copyright policy in the twenty-first century, is to be published by the University of Toronto Press. He can be found on the web at www.blaynehaggart.com.

Matthew Herder

Professor Herder teaches primarily in the Faculty of Medicine, across the undergraduate and postgraduate curricula, on a variety of health law topics, including informed consent, patient-physician confidentiality, and regulation of the medical profession. Prior to joining the faculty at Dalhousie, he taught in the areas of bioethics and intellectual property law at Loyola University Chicago's School of Law. Professor Herder's research interests cluster around biomedical innovation policy, with particular focus on intellectual property law and practices connected to the commercialization of scientific research. As part of a three-year research project funded by the Canadian Institutes of Health Research, Professor Herder (Principal Investigator) and a team of interdisciplinary researchers are currently collecting empirical evidence about the interrelationships between commercialization laws, policies, and practices, and emerging health researchers. Recent works include an article calling for greater transparency in drug regulation published in the Canadian Medical Association Journal, a paper detailing physician-industry relationships in Open Medicine, and an empirical analysis of patenting by academic researchers in IDEA: The Intellectual Property Law Review.

Cameron Hutchison

Dr Cameron Hutchison is an Associate Professor at the Faculty of Law, University of Alberta. His publications and research interests centre around international and Canadian intellectual property law, statutory interpretation, Internet law, and interdisciplinary perspectives on the law of copyright.

Professor Hutchison currently teaches the following courses: intellectual property, musicians and the law, statutory interpretation, and conflict of laws.

Guillaume Laroche

Guillaume Laroche devotes his research time to music, law, and interdisciplinary topics at the intersection of these two fields. In music, his work emphasizes the analysis and modelling of compositional techniques in post-1950 art and vernacular music, most notably video game soundtracks. In law, he researches intellectual property, language rights, and education law. At the intersection of music and law, his work broadly encompasses how copyright conceives of musical creativity. As a recipient of major scholarships from the Social Sciences and Humanities Research Council of Canada and the Fondation Baxter & Alma Ricard, Guillaume earned a Master of Arts in music from McGill University and a Master of Laws from Osgoode Hall Law School. A public school educator by profession, he remains active as a musician by performing as a pianist and singer, conducting ensembles and composing new works.

Michael McNally

Michael McNally is an Assistant Professor at the School of Library and Information Studies within the Faculty of Education at the University of Alberta. His research focuses on intellectual property and its alternatives, with a specific emphasis on how both IP and its alternatives facilitate and impede innovative activity. Other research interests include examining various theories of the information society, radio-spectrum management and competition in the Canadian wireless sector, user-generated content, and the economic and social aspects of innovation. He received his PhD in Library and Information Science from the University of Western Ontario in 2012, and also holds a Masters of Library and Information Science degree from the University of Western Ontario. He is also a Collaborating Network Investigator in the Graphics, Animation and New Media (GRAND) Networks of Centres of Excellence (NCE).

Pierre-Emmanuel Moyse

Pierre-Emmanuel Moyse is an Associate Professor at McGill University, Faculty of Law, and the Director of the Centre for Intellectual Property Policy. He is also responsible for the joint MBA-Law program in partnership with the Desautels Faculty of Management. Professor Moyse wrote his doctoral thesis on the law of distribution in copyright law (University of Montréal, published 2007) under the direction of Professor Ysolde Gendreau. In the same year, he successfully argued the case of *Euro-Excellence v Kraft Canada* before the Supreme Court of Canada.

He is the Director of the *Innovation and Competition* book series published by Les Éditions Thémis, *Quelle performance? De l'efficacité sociale à l'entreprise citoyenne* (Montréal: Thémis, 2013), and Editorial Director for the *JurisClasseur in Intellectual Property* published by LexisNexis (2013).

A research profile of Pierre-Emmanuel Moyse is available at www.youtube.com/watch?v=hvcwP_u5wxc.

Laura J Murray

Laura J Murray is Associate Professor of English and Cultural Studies at Queen's University. She is co-author with Samuel E Trosow of *Canadian Copyright: A Citizen's Guide* (Between the Lines, 2007; second edition forthcoming 2013), and, with Tina S Piper and Kirsty M Robertson, of *Putting Intellectual Property in Its Place: Rights Discourses, Creative Labour, and the Everyday* (forthcoming, Oxford, 2013). She has published in Indigenous studies and American literature; current research interests include history of reading, the nature of the newspaper, creative economies, and cultural policy.

Meera Nair

Meera Nair completed her PhD at the School of Communication at Simon Fraser University in 2009. Her interest in intellectual property law stems from a BSc in mathematics and ten years' experience in the area of technology transfer between academia and industry. For the 2012–13 academic year she was an Azrieli International Postdoctoral Fellow at Hebrew University in Jerusalem. A list of her publications can be found at her blog, *Fair Duty* (fairduty.wordpress.com), together with an eclectic mix of commentary on copyright, creativity, and culture.

Chidi Oguamanam

Chidi Oguamanam (LLM, PhD) is an Associate Professor in the Faculty of Law, University of Ottawa, (Common Law Section) and he is a faculty member of the Centre for Law, Technology and Society and the Environmental Law Group. Professor Oguamanam's practice and research interests focus on various legal and policy issue-linkages to intellectual property law. He writes, teaches, and consults in the areas of law and technology (including biotechnologies), agricultural knowledge systems, biodiversity and food security; public health law and policy; indigenous peoples, indigenous knowledge; human rights and the global governance of knowledge in development contexts. His most recent book is *Intellectual Property in Global Governance: A Development Question* (Routledge, 2012).

Jonathon Penney

Mr Penney has taught at Dalhousie University's Schulich School of Law since 2012. He is currently a Berkman Fellow at the Berkman Center for Internet & Society at Harvard University, a Research Fellow at the Citizen Lab, Munk School of Global Affairs, University of Toronto, and a doctoral candidate at the Oxford Internet Institute, University of Oxford.

In 2011, he was a Google Policy Fellow at the Citizen Lab, where he helped lead the OpenNet Initiative's new Transparency Project, a research collaboration founded to encourage corporate transparency about government data requests. He was also Project Coordinator for the Privacy Value Networks Project, a large scale, multi-university, multi-million dollar EPSRC (UK) funded project on data privacy, led by the Oxford Internet Institute.

A native Nova Scotian and Dalhousie graduate, he previously studied at Columbia Law School as a Fulbright Scholar and at Oxford as a Mackenzie King Scholar, where he was Associate Editor of the *Oxford University Commonwealth Law Journal*. He previously taught law at Victoria University in Wellington (NZ) and spent time practising civil litigation as a federal lawyer in Toronto.

His research concerns constitutional/human rights, intellectual property, and digital media law & policy, particularly censorship, privacy, and information security.

Graham J Reynolds

Graham J Reynolds is an Assistant Professor at the University of British Columbia, Faculty of Law. He teaches and researches in the areas of copyright law, intellectual property law, property law, and intellectual property and human rights. Prior to joining the UBC Faculty of Law in 2013, Graham was an Assistant Professor at the Schulich School of Law at Dalhousie University, where he was the Co-Editor in Chief of the *Canadian Journal of Law and Technology* and a member of Dalhousie University's Law and Technology Institute. The recipient of an award for excellence in teaching, Graham has completed graduate studies at the University of Oxford, where he studied on a Rhodes Scholarship, and has served as the judicial law clerk to the Honourable Chief Justice Finch of the British Columbia Court of Appeal. Graham is currently completing doctoral studies in law at the University of Oxford. The Social Sciences and Humanities Research Council of Canada and the Pierre Elliott Trudeau Foundation supported his doctoral work, which focuses on the intersection of freedom of expression and copyright in Canada.

Kirsty Robertson

Kirsty Robertson is an Associate Professor of Contemporary Art and Museum Studies at Western University, Canada. Her research focuses on activism, visual culture, and changing economies. She has published widely on the topic and is currently finishing her book *Tear Gas Epiphanies: New Economies of Protest, Vision, and Culture in Canada*. More recently, she has turned her attention to the study of wearable technologies, immersive environments, and the potential overlap(s) between textiles and technologies. She considers these issues within the framework of globalization, activism, and creative economies. Her co-edited volume, *Imagining Resistance: Visual Culture, and Activism in Canada*, was released in 2011.

Madelaine Saginur

Madelaine Saginur is the Executive Director of University of Ottawa's Centre for Law, Technology, and Society. She is also a member of Canadian Blood Services' Research Ethics Board. Previously, she practiced intellectual property law, and also worked as a Research Associate at University of Montreal's Centre de recherche en droit public. She has published in the area of bioethics and health law. She holds a BSc from University of Toronto, as well as BCL & LLB degrees from McGill University.

Teresa Scassa

Teresa Scassa is the Canada Research Chair in Information Law at the University of Ottawa, where she is also a Professor at the Faculty of Law (Common Law Section). She holds degrees in civil and common law from McGill University and an LLM and a doctoral degree in law from the University of Michigan. She is a co-founder and former co-editor of the *Canadian Journal of Law and Technology*, author of the book *Canadian Trademark Law* (LexisNexis, 2010) and co-author of *Electronic Commerce and Internet Law in Canada*, 2d ed (CCH Canadian Ltd, 2012). She is a member of the External

Advisory Committee of the Office of the Privacy Commissioner of Canada and of the Canadian Government Advisory Committee on Open Government. Dr. Scassa has written widely in the areas of intellectual property law, law and technology, and privacy. She is also the author or co-author of a number of articles on ambush marketing legislation.

Norman Siebrasse

Norman Siebrasse is a Professor of Law at the University of New Brunswick. He received his BSc in Engineering Physics and his LLB from Queen's University, before clerking at the Supreme Court of Canada for the Honourable Madam Justice McLachlin during the 1991–92 term. After receiving an LLM from the University of Chicago, he joined the University of New Brunswick Faculty of Law in 1993. Professor Siebrasse teaches in the areas of intellectual property law, commercial law, and remedies. His research focuses on patent law, and his blog www.SufficientDescription.com comments on recent Canadian patent cases.

Andrea Slane

Andrea Slane is Associate Professor and Director of the Legal Studies program at the University of Ontario Institute of Technology. Her research interests follow three general themes: privacy rights, online interpersonal wrongdoing, and intellectual property (trademark, copyright, and personality rights). Her published work on intellectual property includes "Guarding a Cultural Icon: Concurrent Intellectual Property Regimes and the Perpetual Protection of *Anne of Green Gables* in Canada," which appeared in the *McGill Law Journal* in 2011. She holds a PhD in Comparative Literature from the University of California, San Diego, and a JD from the University of Toronto Faculty of Law.

Benoît Séguin

Benoît Séguin is a professor of sport management (School of Human Kinetics) at the University of Ottawa. He specializes in sport marketing. His doctoral research examined the issue of ambush marketing and its impact on the Olympic brand. Dr. Séguin's research on sponsorship, ambush marketing, and Olympic Marketing has been published in a variety of international journals including the *International Journal of Sport Management and Marketing*, the *International Journal of Sport Marketing and Sponsorship*, *Sport Marketing Quarterly*, and *Journal of Sport Management*. He recently co-authored a book titled *Olympic Marketing* with Professors Alain Ferrand (France) and Jean-Loup Chappelet (Switzerland).

Dr Séguin is a regular speaker at international conferences and workshops. He is a regular supervising Professor at the International Olympic Academy (Olympic marketing and sponsoring), at the Russian International Olympic University (Business of Sport and the Olympics), and with the Executive Masters in Sport Organizations Management (MEMOS), an international program supported by Olympic Solidarity.

Matthew Stahl

Matt Stahl (PhD in Communication, University of California, San Diego, 2006) is Associate Professor of Information and Media Studies at the University of Western Ontario, where he is also a member of the Digital Labour Research Group and participant in that group's SSHRC-supported research collaboration with Canadian entertainment and media guilds. Stahl's monograph, *Unfree Masters: Recording Artists and the Politics of Work* (Duke University Press, 2013) examines the representation and regulation of recording artists' labour, professionalization, employment contracts, and intellectual property. Other peer-reviewed publications include examinations of the social relations of a San Francisco indie rock scene, film and television representations of musical labour, divisions of creative labour in film and television animation, changes to recording contracts under digitalization of the entertainment industry, contrasting conceptions of creative cultural labour, and cartoon and boy bands.

Samuel Trosow

Samuel Trosow is an Associate Professor at Western University with a joint appointment in the Faculty of Information and Media Studies (FIMS) and the Faculty of Law. Prior to joining the UWO Faculty, he was a law librarian at University of California Berkeley's Boalt Hall Law School, and his doctorate at UCLA in Library Science focused on information policy issues. Professor Trosow is currently a Principal Network Investigator and Theme Leader in the Graphics, Animation and New Media (GRAND) NCE. He is the co-author of *Canadian Copyright: A Citizen's Guide* (with Laura Murray, Between the Lines, 2007), and maintains a blog at samtrosow.wordpress.com. He is currently a member of the Librarians Committee of the Canadian Association of University Teachers (CAUT) and is a frequent speaker on copyright and other information policy issues.

Joao Velloso

Joao Velloso is a PhD candidate and part-time Professor at the Department of Criminology of the University of Ottawa (Canada). He is specialized in socio-legal studies and conflict resolution in comparative perspectives, combining approaches from Legal Anthropology, Criminology, and Sociology of Law. His research deals with Administrative Law-based forms of punishment and their relationships with Criminal Law. Recent articles include: "Beyond criminocentric dogmatism: Mapping institutional forms of punishment in contemporary societies," *Punishment and Society* (2013, 2); and «Au-delà de la criminalisation: L'immigration et les enjeux pour la criminologie », *Criminologie* (2013, 1).

Margaret Ann Wilkinson

Currently Professor of Law at Western University, Dr Margaret Ann Wilkinson is qualified as both a lawyer and librarian. After practising law in Toronto and then completing a doctorate focused on personal data protection, she was initially appointed to a unique joint professorship in the Faculties of Law and Information & Media Studies at Western. She has held visiting or adjunct positions at Western's Richard Ivey School of Business, Dalhousie University, Osgoode Hall Law School, the University of Toronto, and Newcastle University (UK). Funded variously, including through the Law Foundation of Ontario and Social Sciences and Humanities Research Council of Canada, and awarded Faculty Scholar recognition at Western and the Ontario Library Association's Les Fowlie Intellectual Freedom Award, Professor Wilkinson has taught, spoken, and published widely on copyright, moral rights, patents, confidential information, personal data protection, and privacy, both in the Canadian and international contexts, on pharmaceutical and health regulation, and about professional ethics. Author of *Genealogy and the Law in Canada* (Dundurn Press, 2010) and a co-author of the new *Canadian Intellectual Property: Cases and Materials* (Emond Montgomery, 2013), Professor Wilkinson continues to be involved in graduate education in law, business, library & information science, and health information science.

Index

Printed and bound by CPI Group (UK) Ltd, Croydon, CR0 4YY

16/09/2026

14963279-0001